ADVANTAGE

S E R I E S

MICROSOFT®

# ACCESS 2000

## COMPLETE EDITION

## ADVANTAGE
### S E R I E S

# MICROSOFT®
# ACCESS 2000
## COMPLETE EDITION

Sarah E. Hutchinson

Glen J. Coulthard

Information Technology

McGraw-Hill
Irwin

Boston   Burr Ridge, IL   Dubuque, IA   Madison, WI   New York   San Francisco   St. Louis
Bangkok   Bogotá   Caracas   Lisbon   London   Madrid
Mexico City   Milan   New Delhi   Seoul   Singapore   Sydney   Taipei   Toronto

*McGraw-Hill Higher Education* 🪐

*A Division of The McGraw-Hill Companies*

## MICROSOFT® ACCESS 2000 COMPLETE EDITION

This book is printed on acid-free paper.

1 2 3 4 5 6 7 8 9 0 WEB/WEB 9 0 9 8 7 6 5 4 3 2 1 0 9

ISBN 0-07-234801-1

Vice president/Editor in chief: *Michael W. Junior*

Publisher: *David Kendric Brake*

Executive editor: *Jodi McPherson*

Sponsoring editor: *Trisha O'Shea*

Associate editor: *Steve Schuetz*

Developmental editor: *Erin Riley*

Senior marketing manager: *Jeff Parr*

Project manager: *Christina Thornton-Villagomez*

Production supervisor: *Debra R. Sylvester*

Freelance design coordinator: *Laurie J. Entringer*

Interior designer: *AM Design*

Cover Image: © *Schlowsky/Workbook Co/Op Stock*

Senior supplement coordinator: *Carol Loreth*

New media project manager: *David Barrick*

Compositor: *GTS Graphics*

Typeface: *11/13 Stone Serif*

Printer: *Webcrafters, Inc.*

**Library of Congress Cataloging-in-Publication Data**

Hutchinson, Sarah E.
    Microsoft Access 2000 / Sarah E. Hutchinson, Glen J. Coulthard.—Complete ed.
      p. cm. — (Advantage series)
    ISBN 0-07-234801-1 (softcover : alk. paper)
    1. Microsoft Access.  2. Database management.  I. Title: Access 2000.  II. Coulthard,
Glen J. III. Title.  IV. Series.

QA76.9.D3 H8788 2001
005.75′65—dc21                                            00-033543

http://www.mhhe.com

# InformationTechnology

At McGraw-Hill Higher-Education, we publish instructional materials targeted at the higher-education market. In an effort to expand the tools of higher learning, we publish texts, lab manuals, study guides, testing materials, software and multimedia products.

At Irwin/McGraw-Hill (a division of McGraw-Hill Higher Education), we realize that technology will continue to create new mediums for professors and students to manage resources and communicate information with one another. We strive to provide the most flexible and complete teaching and learning tools available and offer solutions to the changing world of teaching and learning.

**Irwin/McGraw-Hill is dedicated to providing the tools for today's instructors and students to successfully navigate the world of Information Technology.**

- **Seminar Series**—Irwin/McGraw-Hill's Technology Connection seminar series offered across the country every year, demonstrate the latest technology products and encourage collaboration among teaching professionals.

- **Osborne/McGraw-Hill**—A division of The McGraw-Hill Companies known for its best selling Internet titles *Harley Hahn's Internet & Web Yellow Pages* and the *Internet Complete Reference*, offers an additional resource for certification and has strategic publishing relationships with corporations such as Corel Corporation and America Online. For more information visit Osborne at www.osborne.com.

- **Digital Solutions**—Irwin/McGraw-Hill is committed to publishing Digital Solutions. Taking your course online doesn't have to be a solitary venture, nor does it have to be a difficult one. We offer several solutions, which will let you enjoy all the benefits of having course material online. For more information visit www.mhhe.com/solutions/index.mhtml.

- **Packaging Options**—For more information about our discount options, contact your local Irwin/McGraw-Hill Sales representative at 1-800-338-3987 or visit our Website at www.mhhe.com/it.

# Preface
# The Advantage Series

## Goals/Philosophy

*The Advantage Series* presents the **What, Why, and How** of computer application skills to today's students. Each lab manual is built upon an efficient learning model that provides students and faculty with complete coverage of the most powerful software packages available today.

### Approach

*The Advantage Series* builds upon an efficient learning model that provides students and faculty with complete coverage and enhances critical thinking skills. This case-based, "problem-solving" approach teaches the What, Why, and How of computer application skills.

*The Advantage Series* introduces the **"Feature-Method-Practice"** layered approach. The **Feature** describes the command and tells the importance of that command. The **Method** shows students how to perform the feature. The **Practice** allows students to apply the feature in a keystroke exercise.

### About the Series

*The Advantage Series* offers *three levels* of instruction. Each level builds upon the previous level. The following are the three levels of instructions:

**Brief:** Covers the basics of the application, contains two to four chapters, and is typically 120–190 pages long.

**Introductory:** Includes the material in the Brief Lab manual plus two to three additional chapters. The Introductory lab manuals are approximately 300 pages long and prepare students for the *Microsoft Office User Specialist Proficient Exam (MOUS Certification)*.

**Complete:** Includes the Introductory lab manual plus an additional five chapters of advanced level content. The Complete lab manuals are approximately 600 pages in length and prepare students to take the *Microsoft Office User Specialist Expert Exam (MOUS Certification)*.

APPROVED COURSEWARE

### Approved Microsoft Courseware

Use of the Microsoft Office User Specialist Approved Courseware Logo on this product signifies that it has been independently reviewed and approved in complying with the following standards: Acceptable coverage of all content related to the Microsoft Office Exam entitled *Microsoft Access 2000* and sufficient performance-based exercises that relate closely to all required content, based on sampling of text. For further information on Microsoft's MOUS certification program please visit Microsoft's Web site at http://www.microsoft.com/office/traincert/.

# About the Book

*Each lab manual features the following:*

- **Learning Objectives:** At the beginning of each chapter, a list of action-oriented objectives is presented detailing what is expected of the students.

- **Chapters:** Each lab manual is divided into chapters.

- **Modules:** Each chapter contains three to five independent modules, requiring approximately 30–45 minutes each to complete. Although we recommend you complete an entire chapter before proceeding, you may skip or rearrange the order of these modules to best suit your learning needs.

**Case Study**

- **Case Studies:** Each chapter begins with a Case Study. The student is introduced to a fictitious person or company and their immediate problem or opportunity. Throughout the chapter, students obtain the knowledge and skills necessary to meet the challenges presented in the Case Study. At the end of each chapter, students are asked to solve problems directly related to the Case Study.

- **Feature-Method-Practice:** Each chapter highlights our unique "Feature-Method-Practice" layered approach. The **Feature** layer describes the command or technique and persuades you of its importance and relevance. The **Method** layer shows you how to perform the procedure, while the **Practice** layer lets you apply the feature in a hands-on step-by-step exercise.

- **Instructions:** The numbered step-by-step progression for all hands-on examples and exercises are clearly identified. Students will find it surprisingly easy to follow the logical sequence of keystrokes and mouse clicks and no longer worry about missing a step.

**In Addition**

- **In Addition Boxes:** These content boxes are placed strategically throughout the chapter and provide information on advanced topics that are beyond the scope of the current discussion.

- **Self-Check Boxes:** At the end of each module, a brief self-check question appears for students to test their comprehension of the material. Answers to these questions appear in the Appendix.

- **Chapter Review:** The *Command Summary* and *Key Terms* provide an excellent review of the chapter content and prepare students for the short-answer, true-false and multiple-choice questions at the end of each chapter.

Easy ●
Moderate ■
Difficult ◆

- **Hands-On Projects:** Each chapter concludes with six hands-on projects rated according to their difficulty level. The *easy* and *moderate* projects use a running-case approach, whereby the same person or company appears at the end of each chapter in a particular tutorial. The two *difficult* or *on your own* projects provide greater latitude in applying the software to a variety of creative problem-solving situations.

- **Appendix: Microsoft Windows Quick Reference:** Each lab manual contains a Microsoft Windows Quick Reference. This Quick reference teaches students the fundamentals of using a mouse and a keyboard, illustrates how to interact with a dialog box, and describes the fundamentals of how to use the Office 2000 Help System.

# Features of This Lab Manual

**Instructions:** The numbered step-by-step progression for all hands-on examples and exercises are clearly identified. Students will find it surprisingly easy to follow the logical sequence of keystrokes and mouse clicks, and no longer worry about missing a step.

**In Addition Boxes:** These content boxes are placed strategically throughout the chapter and provide information on topics that are beyond the scope of the current discussion.

**Self-Check Boxes:** At the end of each module, a brief self-check question appears for students to test their comprehension of the material. Answers to these questions appear in the Appendix.

**Feature-Method-Practice:** Each chapter highlights our unique "Feature-Method-Practice" layered approach. The *Feature* layer describes the command or technique and persuades you of its importance and relevance. The *Method* layer shows you how to perform the procedure, while the *Practice* layer lets you apply the feature in a hands-on step-by-step exercise.

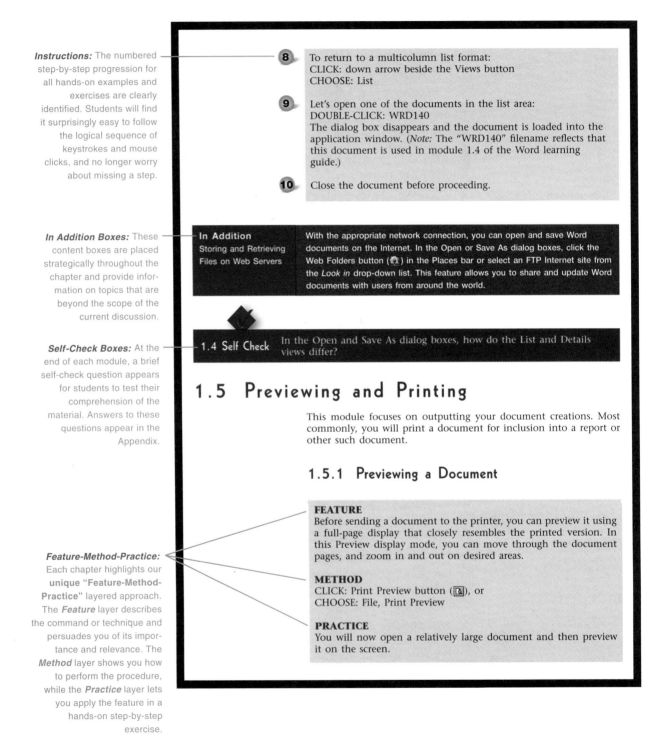

**8** To return to a multicolumn list format:
CLICK: down arrow beside the Views button
CHOOSE: List

**9** Let's open one of the documents in the list area:
DOUBLE-CLICK: WRD140
The dialog box disappears and the document is loaded into the application window. (*Note:* The "WRD140" filename reflects that this document is used in module 1.4 of the Word learning guide.)

**10** Close the document before proceeding.

**In Addition**
Storing and Retrieving Files on Web Servers

With the appropriate network connection, you can open and save Word documents on the Internet. In the Open or Save As dialog boxes, click the Web Folders button (🌐) in the Places bar or select an FTP Internet site from the *Look in* drop-down list. This feature allows you to share and update Word documents with users from around the world.

**1.4 Self Check** In the Open and Save As dialog boxes, how do the List and Details views differ?

## 1.5 Previewing and Printing

This module focuses on outputting your document creations. Most commonly, you will print a document for inclusion into a report or other such document.

### 1.5.1 Previewing a Document

**FEATURE**
Before sending a document to the printer, you can preview it using a full-page display that closely resembles the printed version. In this Preview display mode, you can move through the document pages, and zoom in and out on desired areas.

**METHOD**
CLICK: Print Preview button (🔍), or
CHOOSE: File, Print Preview

**PRACTICE**
You will now open a relatively large document and then preview it on the screen.

## Case Study    1-on-1 Tutoring Services

Dean Shearwater is helping to pay his university tuition by tutoring other university and high school students. Over the last two years, he has developed an excellent reputation for making complex topics simple and easy to remember. While he is an excellent tutor, last year he didn't earn as much as he had expected.

Dean thinks his lackluster earnings can be attributed to poor advertising and inadequate record keeping. This year, he has decided to operate his tutoring services more like a real business. His first priority is to learn how to use Microsoft Word so that he can prepare advertising materials, send faxes and memos, and organize his student notes.

In this chapter, you and Dean learn how to create simple documents from scratch, use built-in document templates, edit documents, and use the Undo command. You also learn how to preview and print your work.

# 1.1  Getting Started with Word

Microsoft Word 2000 is a **word processing** program that enables you to create, edit, format, and print many types of documents including résumés and cover letters, reports and proposals, World Wide Web pages, and more. By the time you complete this learning guide, you will be skilled in creating all types of documents and in getting them to look the way you want. In this module, you load Microsoft Word and proceed through a guided tour of its primary components.

## 1.1.1  Loading and Exiting Word

**FEATURE**
You load Word from the Windows Start menu, accessed by clicking the Start button (Start) on the taskbar. Because Word requires a significant amount of memory, you should always exit the application when you are finished doing your work. Most Windows applications allow you to close their windows by clicking the Close button ([x]) appearing in the top right-hand corner.

# Teaching Resources

The following is a list of supplemental material that can be used to teach this course.

## Skills Assessment

Irwin/McGraw-Hill offers two innovative systems that can be used with the Advantage Series, ATLAS and **SimNet,** which take skills assessment testing beyond the basics with pre- and post-assessment capability.

- **ATLAS—(Active Testing and Learning Assessment Software)**—ATLAS is our **live** in the application skills assessment tool. ATLAS allows Students to perform tasks while working *live* within the office applications environment. ATLAS is web-enabled and customizable to meet the needs of your course. ATLAS is available for Office 2000.

- **SimNet—(Simulated Network Assessment Product)**—SimNet permits you to test the actual software skills students learn about the Microsoft Office Applications in a **simulated** environment. SimNet is web-enabled and is available for Office 97 and Office 2000.

## Instructor's Resource Kits

The Instructor's Resource Kit provides professors with all of the ancillary material needed to teach a course. Irwin/McGraw-Hill is committed to providing instructors with the most effective instructional resources available. Many of these resources are available at our **Information Technology Supersite** at www.mhhe.com/it. Our Instructor's Resource Kits are available on CD-ROM and contain the following:

- **Diploma by Brownstone**—is the most flexible, powerful, and easy-to-use computerized testing system available in higher education. The diploma system allows professors to create an exam as a printed version, as a LAN-based online version and as an Internet version. Diploma includes grade book features, which automate the entire testing process.

- **Instructor's Manual**—This resource includes:
  —Solutions to all lessons and end-of-chapter material
  —Teaching Tips
  —Teaching Strategies
  —Additional Exercises

- **Student Data Files**—To use the Advantage Series, students must have data files to complete practice and test lessons. The instructor and students using this text in classes are granted the right to post the student files on any network or stand-alone computer, or to distribute the files on individual diskettes. The student files may be downloaded from our IT Supersite at www.mhhe.com/it.

- **Series Web Site**—Available at www.mhhe.com/cit/apps/adv/.

## Digital Solutions

**PageOut Lite**—Allows instructors to create their own basic Web sites hosted by McGraw-Hill. PageOut Lite includes three basic templates that automatically convert typed material into HTML Web Pages. Using PageOut Lite an instructor can set up a Home page, Web links, and a basic course syllabus and lecture notes.

**PageOut**—Irwin/McGraw-Hill's Course Webster Development Center. PageOut allows an instructor to create a more complex course Webster with an interactive syllabus and some course management features. Like PageOut Lite, PageOut converts typed material to HTML. For more information, please visit the PageOut Web site at www.mhla.net/pageout.

**OLC/Series Web Sites**—Online Learning Centers (OLCs)/Series Sites are accessible through our Supersite at www.mhhe.com/it. Our OLC/Series Sites provide pedagogical features and supplements for our titles online. Students can point and click their way to key terms, learning objectives, chapter overviews, PowerPoint slides, exercises, and Web links.

**The McGraw-Hill Learning Architecture (MHLA)**—A complete course delivery system. MHLA gives professors ownership in the way digital content is presented to the class through online quizzing, student collaboration, course administration, and content management. For a walkthrough of MHLA, visit the MHLA Web site at www.mhla.net.

## Packaging Options

For more information about our discount options, contact your local Irwin/McGraw-Hill Sales representative at 1-800-338-3987 or visit our Web site at www.mhhe.com/it.

# Acknowledgments

This series of tutorials is the direct result of the teamwork and heart of many people. We sincerely thank the reviewers, instructors, and students who have shared their comments and suggestions with us over the past few years. We do read them! With their valuable feedback, our tutorials have evolved into the product you see before you.

Many thanks go to Trisha O'Shea and Erin Riley from Irwin/McGraw-Hill whose management helped to get this book produced in a timely and efficient manner. Special recognition goes to all of the individuals mentioned in the credits at the beginning of this tutorial. And finally, to the many others who weren't directly involved in this project but who have stood by us the whole way, we appreciate your encouragement and support.

**The Advantage Team**
Special thanks go out to our contributing members on the Advantage team.

> Verlaine Murphy
> Walt Musekamp
> Ingrid Neumann
> Catherine Schuler

An additional thanks to the following Northern Illinois University students who helped to review the manuscript:

> Randall Jackson
> Karen Frett

**Write to Us**
We welcome your response to this tutorial, for we are trying to make it as useful a learning tool as possible. Please contact us at

*Sarah E. Hutchinson*—sarah-hutchinson@home.com
*Glen J. Coulthard*—glen@coulthard.com

Visit www.mhhe.com/it
THE ONLY SITE WITH ALL YOUR CIT AND MIS NEEDS.

# Contents

## DESIGNING FORMS AND REPORTS          CHAPTER 7

## CREATING ADVANCED QUERIES          CHAPTER 8

## BUILDING FORMS, REPORTS, AND DATA ACCESS PAGES          CHAPTER 9

CHAPTER 10

# AUTOMATING AND EXTENDING ACCESS

APPENDIX

# INTRODUCING VISUAL BASIC FOR APPLICATIONS

# ADVANTAGE
# S E R I E S

# MICROSOFT®
# ACCESS 2000

## BRIEF EDITION

# MICROSOFT ACCESS 2000
*Working with Access*

# CHAPTER
## ONE

# Chapter Outline

# Learning Objectives

After reading this chapter, you will be able to:

- Understand basic database terminology

- Describe the different components of the Access application window and the Database window

- Select commands and perform actions using the keyboard and mouse

- Open various database objects, including tables, queries, forms, and reports, for display

- View, edit, and print data in a datasheet

- Insert and delete records in a datasheet

- Open and close a database

| Case Study | **On-Track Seminars** |

Joanna Walsh just started a new job with On-Track Seminars, a company that specializes in career and life skills training. As an administrative assistant, Joanna knows that she is expected to answer phones, write and edit letters, and organize meetings. However, on her first day, Karen Chase, the office director, informs her of some additional expectations: "You will also be using Microsoft Access to manage our basic seminar information. Our instructors will call you if they have a problem or need to modify the database for any reason. Mostly you are required to look up student phone numbers to inform them when a seminar is cancelled." Fortunately, Joanna knows there is a course in Microsoft Access starting next week at the local community college, so she is not overly concerned by this new job requirement.

In this chapter, you and Joanna learn about managing information in desktop databases, how to use the different components and features of Microsoft Access, and how to display and edit the information stored in a database.

# 1.1 Getting Started with Access

Microsoft Access is a desktop database program that enables you to enter, store, analyze, and present data. For end users, power users, and software developers alike, Access provides easy-to-use yet powerful tools most often associated with higher-end **database management systems (DBMS)**. In fact, Access 2000 offers scalability never seen before in desktop database software. At the local or desktop level, Access can help you manage your personal information or collect data for a research study. At the corporate and enterprise level, Access can retrieve and summarize data stored on servers located throughout the world. Access also enables you to create and publish dynamic Web-based forms and reports for intranet and Internet delivery.

While this is not a database theory course, a familiarity with some basic terms will help you become more productive using Microsoft Access 2000. The word **database**, for example, refers to a collection of related information, such as a company's accounting data. The primary object in a database for collecting and storing data is called a **table**. As shown in Figure 1.1, tables are organized into rows and columns similar to an electronic spreadsheet. An individual entry in a table (for example, a person's name and address) is called a **record** and is stored as a horizontal row. Each record in a table is composed of one or more fields. A **field** holds a single piece of data. For example, the table in Figure 1.1 divides each person's record into vertical columns or fields for ID, Surname, Given, Address, City, and State.

ACCESS

**Figure 1.1**

Storing data in an
Access table

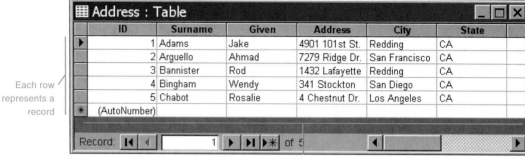

Each row
represents a
record

Each column
represents a field

| | ID | Surname | Given | Address | City | State |
|---|---|---|---|---|---|---|
| ▶ | 1 | Adams | Jake | 4901 101st St. | Redding | CA |
| | 2 | Arguello | Ahmad | 7279 Ridge Dr. | San Francisco | CA |
| | 3 | Bannister | Rod | 1432 Lafayette | Redding | CA |
| | 4 | Bingham | Wendy | 341 Stockton | San Diego | CA |
| | 5 | Chabot | Rosalie | 4 Chestnut Dr. | Los Angeles | CA |
| * | (AutoNumber) | | | | | |

# 1.1.1  Loading and Exiting Access

**FEATURE**

You load Access from the Windows Start menu, accessed by clicking the Start button (Start) on the taskbar. Because Access requires
a significant amount of memory, you should always exit the application when you are finished doing your work. Most Windows
applications allow you to close their windows by clicking on the
Close button (x) appearing in the top right-hand corner. You may
also choose the File, Exit command.

**METHOD**

* To load Access:
  CLICK: Start button (Start)
  CHOOSE: Programs, Microsoft Access
* To exit Access:
  CHOOSE: File, Exit from the Access Menu bar

**PRACTICE**

After loading Microsoft Access using the Windows Start menu, you
open an existing database file in this lesson.

*Setup:* Ensure that you have turned on your computer and that the
Windows desktop appears.

**1** Position the mouse pointer over the Start button (|Start|) appearing in the bottom left-hand corner of the Windows taskbar and then click the left mouse button once. The Start pop-up menu appears as shown here.

**2** Position the mouse pointer over the Programs menu option. Notice that you do not need to click the left mouse button to display the list of programs in the fly-out or cascading menu.

**3** Move the mouse pointer horizontally to the right until it highlights an option in the Programs menu. You can now move the mouse pointer vertically within the menu to select an option.

**4** Position the mouse pointer over the Microsoft Access menu option and then click the left mouse button once. After a few seconds, the Access application window and startup dialog box appear (Figure 1.2). Notice that a new button also appears on the taskbar at the bottom of your screen.

**5** Leave the startup dialog box displayed and proceed to the next lesson.

**Figure 1.2**

Access application window and startup dialog box

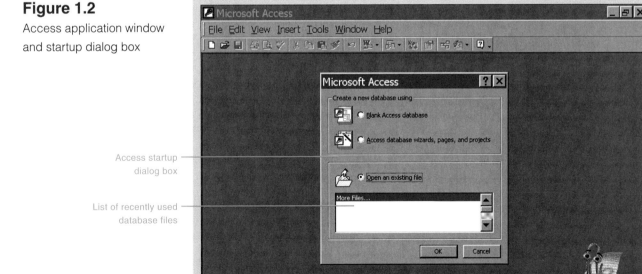

Access startup dialog box

List of recently used database files

Office Assistant

ACCESS

**In Addition**
Switching Among
Applications

Each application that you are currently working with is represented by a button on the taskbar. Switching between open applications on your desktop is as easy as clicking the appropriate taskbar button, like switching channels on a television set.

## 1.1.2  Opening a Database File at Startup

**FEATURE**
You use the Open dialog box to search for and retrieve existing database files that are stored on your local hard disk, a floppy diskette, a network server, or on the Web. If you want to load Access and an existing database at the same time, you can use the Open Office Document command on the Start menu. Or, if you have recently opened a database, you can launch Access and then double-click its file name in the startup dialog box.

**METHOD**
To display the Open dialog box at startup:
1.  CLICK: *Open an existing file* option button in the startup dialog box
2.  SELECT: More Files... in the list box area
3.  CLICK: OK command button

To retrieve a database file using the Open dialog box:
1.  SELECT: *the desired folder* from the Places bar or the *Look in* drop-down list box
2.  DOUBLE-CLICK: *the desired file* from the list area

**PRACTICE**
Using the startup dialog box, you practice opening a database file.

*Setup:* Ensure that you have completed the previous lesson and that you have identified the location of your Advantage student data files.

To open an existing database using the startup dialog box:
CLICK: *Open an existing file* option button
SELECT: More Files... in the list box area
CLICK: OK command button
The Open dialog box appears, as shown in Figure 1.3.

**Figure 1.3**

Open dialog box

Lists the files that you have most recently worked with

The default working folder

Lists common desktop shortcuts

Lists shortcuts to your favorite files and folders

Lists files and folders stored on your intranet or Internet Web Server

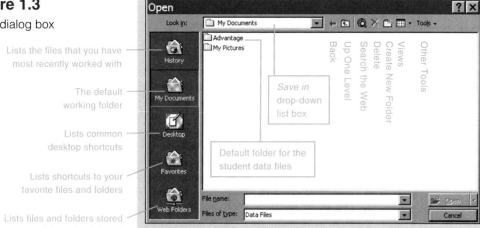

***Important****: In this guide, we refer to the files that have been created for you as the **student data files**. Depending on your computer or lab setup, these files may be located on a floppy diskette, in a folder on your hard disk, or on a network server. If necessary, ask your instructor or lab assistant where to find these data files. To download the Advantage Series' student data files from the Internet, visit McGraw-Hill's Information Technology Web site at:*

**http://www.mhhe.com/it**

**2**   The **Places bar,** located along the left border of the dialog box, provides convenient access to commonly used storage locations. To illustrate, let's view the contents of some folders:
CLICK: History folder button (⌂)
A list of recently opened Office documents appears.

**3**   To view the contents of the My Documents folder:
CLICK: My Documents button (⌂)

**4**   Let's browse the local hard disk:
CLICK: down arrow attached to the Look in drop-down list box
SELECT: Hard Disk C:
The list area displays the folders and files stored in the root directory of your local hard disk.

**5**   To change how the files are displayed in the list area:
CLICK: down arrow beside the Views button (▦·)
CHOOSE: Details
Each folder and file is presented on a single line with additional file information, such as its size, type, and last date modified.
(*Hint:* You can sort the folders and files in the list area by clicking on one of the column heading buttons.)

**6**  To select a multicolumn list format:
CLICK: down arrow beside the Views button (⊞▾)
CHOOSE: List

**7**  Now, using either the Places bar or the *Look in* drop-down list box:
SELECT: *the location of your Advantage student data files*
(*Note:* In this guide, we retrieve and save files to a folder named "Advantage" in the My Documents folder.)

**8**  Let's open one of the Access databases in this folder:
DOUBLE-CLICK: ACC100 in the list area
The Open dialog box disappears and the ACC100 database is loaded into the application window.

## 1.1.3 Touring Access

**FEATURE**
The **application window** (Figure 1.4) acts as a container for the *Database window* and for displaying the database objects that you will create and use in Access. It also contains several key interface components, including the *Windows icons*, *Menu bar*, *Toolbar*, and *Status bar*.

**PRACTICE**
In a guided tour, you now explore some of the interface features of the Access application window.

*Setup:* Ensure that you have completed the previous lessons and that the ACC100 Database window is displayed in the application window.

**1**  The Database window is best displayed as a floating window, although it may be maximized to cover the entire work area. You control the display of the application and Database windows by clicking their Title bar or Windows icons—Minimize (▭), Maximize (▢), Restore (▤), and Close (☒). Familiarize yourself with the components labeled in Figure 1.4.

**Figure 1.4**

Access application window

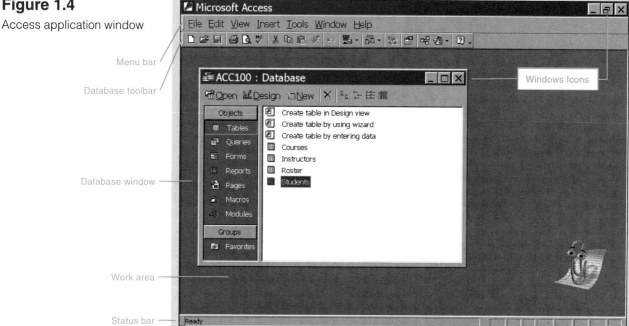

Menu bar

Database toolbar

Database window

Work area

Status bar

Windows Icons

**2** The Menu bar contains the Access menu commands. To execute a command, click once on the desired Menu bar option and then click again on the command. Commands that appear dimmed are not available for selection. Commands that are followed by an ellipsis (...) display a dialog box when selected. To practice using the menu:
CHOOSE: Help
(*Note:* This instruction directs you to click the left mouse button once on the Help option appearing in the Menu bar. All menu commands that you execute in this guide begin with the instruction "CHOOSE.")

**3** To display other pull-down menus, move the mouse pointer to the left over other options in the Menu bar. As each option is highlighted, a pull-down menu appears with its associated commands.

**4** To leave the Menu bar without making a command selection:
CLICK: in a blank portion of the Access work area

**5** Access provides context-sensitive *right-click menus* for quick access to menu commands. Rather than searching for a command in the Menu bar, position the mouse pointer on a database object and right-click to display a list of commands applicable for that object.

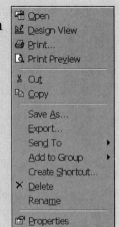

To display the right-click menu for a table:
RIGHT-CLICK: Students in the list area of the Database window
The pop-up menu at the right should appear.

**6** To remove the right-click menu without making a selection:
PRESS: `ESC`

**7** If the Office Assistant currently appears on your screen, do the following to temporarily hide it from view:
RIGHT-CLICK: *the character*
CHOOSE: Hide from the right-click menu
(*Note:* The character's name may also appear in the Hide command.)

## 1.1.4 Selecting Database Objects

**FEATURE**
The Access **Database window** is your command control center; it provides the interface to your database. The **Objects bar**, located along the left border, organizes the available database objects into seven categories named *Tables*, *Queries*, *Forms*, *Reports*, *Pages*, *Macros*, and *Modules*. Most of your time in this guide will be spent working with these objects in the Database window.

**METHOD**
To peruse the objects in a database:
CLICK: *category buttons* in the Objects bar

**PRACTICE**
In the Database window, you practice selecting objects for display.

*Setup:* Ensure that the ACC100 Database window is displayed, as shown in Figure 1.5.

**1** Table objects are the primary element of a database and are used to store and manipulate data. A single database file may contain several tables. To display the contents of a table object, ensure that the *Tables* button in the Objects bar is selected and then do the following:
DOUBLE-CLICK: Students in the list area
The Students table appears in a row and column layout called a *datasheet.* You will learn how to navigate and manipulate the contents of a datasheet in the next module.

**Figure 1.5**
Access Database window

Objects Bar

Category Button

Groups Bar

Database Window Toolbar

New Object Shortcuts

Object List

List Area

**2** To close the Students datasheet:
CLICK: its Close button ([x])

**3** A **query** is a question you ask of your database. The answer, which may draw data from more than one table in the database, typically displays a datasheet of records. To see a list of the stored queries:
CLICK: *Queries* button

**4** The stored query in this database links and extracts data from the Courses and Instructors tables. To display the results of the query:
DOUBLE-CLICK: Courses Query in the list area

**5** After reviewing the query, close the displayed datasheet:
CLICK: its Close button ([x])

**6** Unlike a table's column and row layout, a **form** generally displays one record at a time. To see a list of the stored forms:
CLICK: *Forms* button

**7** To display a form:
DOUBLE-CLICK: Student Input Form in the list area
Your screen should now appear similar to Figure 1.6.

**Figure 1.6**

Displaying a form object

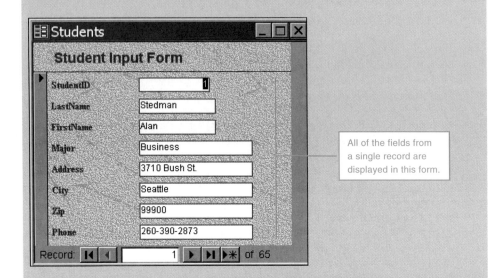

All of the fields from a single record are displayed in this form.

**8** To close the Student Input Form:
CLICK: its Close button (☒)

**9** While datasheets and forms are used to input and modify data, you create **reports** to present, summarize, and print data. To see a list of the stored reports in the database:
CLICK: *Reports* button

**10** To view a report as it will appear when printed:
DOUBLE-CLICK: Students by Major in the list area
The report appears in the Print Preview window.

**11** To close the Print Preview window:
CLICK: its Close button (☒)

**12** To return to displaying the table objects:
CLICK: *Tables* button
(*Note:* If you are proceeding to the next module, keep the database open for use in the next lesson.)

**In Addition**
Additional Database
Objects

The Objects bar lets you access a variety of database objects. Besides *Tables, Queries, Forms,* and *Reports,* the *Pages* category links to external Internet-ready database objects called *data access pages.* The *Macro* category stores objects that you use to automate frequently performed procedures. And for greater control, you can write code *modules* using Visual Basic for Applications (VBA), a subset of the Microsoft Visual Basic programming language.

**1.1 Self Check**    How do you close a window that appears in the Access work area?

# 1.2  Viewing and Printing Your Data

Much like an electronic worksheet, the data stored in a table object appears in rows and columns called a **datasheet**. Each row represents an individual record and each column represents a field. The intersection of a row and column is called a **cell**. This mode, called **Datasheet view**, lets you display and work with many records at once. In this module, you learn how to navigate, customize, and print datasheets.

## 1.2.1  Moving Around a Datasheet

**FEATURE**
To properly manage the data stored in a table object, you must know how to efficiently move the selection cursor to view all parts of a table. As with most Access features, there are mouse methods and there are keyboard methods for moving the cursor. You should try both methods and then select the one that appeals to you most.

**METHOD**

| Keystroke | Task Description |
|---|---|
| ⬆, ⬇ | Moves to the previous or next record |
| ⬅, ➡ | Moves cursor to the left or to the right |
| CTRL + ⬇ | Moves to the bottom of a field column |
| CTRL + ⬆ | Moves to the top of a field column |
| PgUp, PgDn | Moves up or down one screen |
| HOME | Moves to the first (leftmost) field in a record |
| END | Moves to the last (rightmost) field in a record |
| CTRL + HOME | Moves to the top (first record and first field) |
| CTRL + END | Moves to the bottom (last record and last field) |

ACCESS

**PRACTICE**
Using the Students table, you practice moving the cursor around a datasheet.

*Setup:* Ensure that the ACC100 Database window is displayed. If not, open the ACC100 database from your student data files location.

**1** Ensure that the *Tables* button in the Objects bar is selected. To display the Students datasheet, do the following:
DOUBLE-CLICK: Students in the list area
The Students data table is loaded into the computer's memory and displayed in Datasheet view. Depending on your screen size, you may see more or fewer records than shown in Figure 1.7.

**Figure 1.7**
Students table displayed in Datasheet view

This triangular symbol appears in the current or active record.

Cursor

Navigation area for moving the cursor using a mouse

**2** A flashing cursor appears in the leftmost field of the first record. To move to the last field in the current record:
PRESS: ⟨END⟩
The cursor is positioned in the "Phone" column.

**3** To move one field to the left and down to the fourth record:
PRESS: ◄ once
PRESS: ▼ three times
(*CAUTION:* If pressing a cursor movement key does not yield the expected result, you may have activated Edit mode accidentally. To begin navigating between records and fields again, press ⟨F2⟩ or ⟨ENTER⟩ to end Edit mode.)

**4** To move the cursor down by one screen at a time:
PRESS: [PgDn] twice

**5** To move to the top of the datasheet:
PRESS: [CTRL]+[HOME]

**6** Position the mouse pointer over the scroll box on the vertical scroll bar and then drag the scroll box downward. Notice that a yellow Scroll Tip appears identifying the current record number. When you see "Record: 25 of 65" in the Scroll Tip, release the mouse button. (*Note:* Although the window pans downward, this method does not move the cursor.)

**7** For quick mouse selection, Access provides navigation buttons in the bottom left-hand corner of the Datasheet window. To demonstrate:
CLICK: Last Record button ([▶|]) to move to the bottom of the datasheet
CLICK: First Record button ([|◀]) to move to the top of the datasheet

**8** Access allows you to open a number of Datasheet windows at the same time. To display another table, first make the Database window active:
CHOOSE: Window, ACC100 : Database

**9** To display the Roster table:
DOUBLE-CLICK: Roster in the list area
The Roster Datasheet window appears overlapping the other two windows. Similar to the Students table, the Roster table contains a field named StudentID. This common field enables a link to be established between the two tables.

**10** To display the Students datasheet once again:
CHOOSE: Window, Students : Table

**11** Within the Students Datasheet window, you can display course and grade information from the Roster table using subdatasheets. A **subdatasheet** allows you to browse hierarchical and related data for a particular record. In a sense, a subdatasheet provides a picture-in-picture view of your data. To demonstrate, let's drill down and display the courses and grades for Rosa Fernandez:
CLICK: Expand button ([⊞]) in the left-hand column of StudentID 7
Your screen should now appear similar to Figure 1.8.

ACCESS

**Figure 1.8**

Displaying a subdatasheet

Displaying related
records from the Roster
table in a subdatasheet

| StudentID | LastName | FirstName | Major | Address | City | Zip |
|---|---|---|---|---|---|---|
| 1 | Stedman | Alan | Business | 3710 Bush St. | Seattle | 99900 |
| 2 | Hernandez | Pete | Business | 1485 Sonama V | Redmond | 99780 |
| 3 | Mohr | Judy | Arts | 100 Bosley Lan | Redmond | 99780 |
| 4 | Buggey | Diana | Science | 20 Cactus Lane | Redmond | 99804 |
| 5 | Seinfeld | Casey | Arts | 17 Windy Way | Bellevue | 98180 |
| 6 | Alomar | Sandra | Business | PO Box 1465 | Kirkland | 97080 |
| 7 | Fernandez | Rosa | Science | 151 Greer Rd. | Seattle | 99890 |

| EntryID | CourseID | Grade |
|---|---|---|
| 55 | COM200 | 86.00 |
| 66 | COM210 | 74.00 |
| (AutoNumber) | | 0.00 |

| StudentID | LastName | FirstName | Major | Address | City | Zip |
|---|---|---|---|---|---|---|
| 8 | Peters | Bob | Arts | 200 Union St. | Seattle | 99850 |
| 9 | Rinaldo | Sandy | Arts | 1871 Orrinton R | Redmond | 99704 |
| 10 | Finklestein | Sue | Business | 888 Burrard St. | Seattle | 99904 |
| 11 | Mortimer | Bruce | Science | 235 Johnston S | Redmond | 99704 |
| 12 | Jung | Chris | Science | 1005 West 9th | Redmond | 99780 |
| 13 | Abu-Alba | Benji | Arts | 122 Cordova Av | Bellevue | 98200 |
| 14 | Stockton | Gretta | Arts | 4210 Bush St. | Seattle | 99900 |
| 15 | Sakic | Eric | Arts | 875 Cordova Av | Bellevue | 98180 |

Record: 1 of 65

**12** Using the mouse, do the following:
CLICK: a cell in the first row of the subdatasheet
Notice that the record navigation area in the Datasheet window
shows Record 1 of 2. Clicking the First Record (◄◄) or Last
Record (►►) buttons will move the cursor in this subdatasheet
only.

**13** To collapse the subdatasheet:
CLICK: Collapse button (−) for StudentID 7
The record navigation area shows Record 1 of 65 once again.

**14** On your own, expand the subdatasheets for three records in the
Students Datasheet window. When finished, collapse all of the
subdatasheets and then return to the top of the Students
datasheet.

**15** To close the Roster Datasheet window:
CHOOSE: Window, Roster : Table
CLICK: its Close button (✕)

**16** Keep the Students Datasheet window open for use in the next
lesson.

**In Addition**
Moving to a Specific
Record Number

Access displays the current record number alongside the navigation buttons
in the bottom left-hand corner of a Datasheet window. To move to a specific
record in the datasheet or subdatasheet, click the mouse pointer once in this
text box, type a record number, and then press **ENTER**. The cursor immediately moves to the desired record.

## 1.2.2 Adjusting Column Widths and Row Heights

**FEATURE**

By adjusting the column widths and row heights in a datasheet, you can enhance its appearance for both viewing and printing—similarly to how a document uses double-spacing to make text easier to read. To change the width of a column in Datasheet view, you drag its border line in the **field header area**. You can also have Access scan the contents of the column and recommend the best width. Rows behave somewhat differently. When you adjust a single row's height in the *record selection area*, Access updates all of the rows in a datasheet. Figure 1.9 labels the field header and record selection areas for a datasheet.

**METHOD**

- To change a column's width using the mouse:
  DRAG: its right border line in the field header area
- To change a column's width using the menu:
  SELECT: a cell in the column that you want to format
  CHOOSE: Format, Column Width
  TYPE: *the desired width*
- To change the default row height using the mouse:
  DRAG: its bottom border line in the record selection area
- To change the default row height using the menu:
  CHOOSE: Format, Row Height
  TYPE: *the desired height*

**PRACTICE**

In this lesson, you adjust column widths and row heights in a datasheet.

*Setup:* Ensure that the Students datasheet is displayed.

**1** To select a cell in the Zip column:
PRESS: END
PRESS: ⬅

**2** To begin, let's reduce the width of the Zip column using the menu:
CHOOSE: Format, Column Width
The Column Width dialog box appears, as shown here.

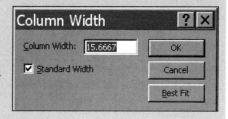

ACCESS

**3** Although you can type the desired width, let's have Access calculate the best width for the column:
CLICK: Best Fit command button
The column's width is decreased automatically.

**4** Now let's adjust the width of the Address column. In the field header area, position the mouse pointer over the border line between the Address and City fields. The mouse pointer changes shape when positioned correctly, as shown below.

Field Header Area
and mouse pointer

| Address ↔ | City |
|-----------|------|
| 3710 Bush St. | Seattle |
| 1485 Sonama V | Redmond |

**5** CLICK: the border line and hold down the mouse button
DRAG: the mouse pointer to the right to increase the width (to approximately the beginning of the word "City")

**6** You can also set the best-fit width for a column using the mouse. To adjust the width of the Major column:
DOUBLE-CLICK: the border line between Major and Address

**7** To reposition the cursor:
PRESS: CTRL + HOME

**8** To change the row height setting in the Datasheet window:
CHOOSE: Format, Row Height
TYPE: 18
CLICK: OK
All of the rows in the datasheet are updated to reflect the formatting change. Your worksheet should now appear similar to Figure 1.9.

**9** Keep the datasheet open for use in the next lesson.

**Figure 1.9**

Formatting the
Datasheet window

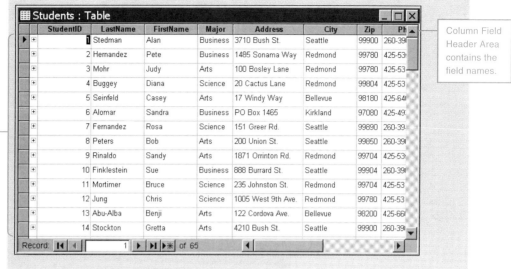

The Record Selection Area
contains row selector buttons.

Column Field
Header Area
contains the
field names.

## 1.2.3 Previewing and Printing

**FEATURE**
Before sending a datasheet to the printer, you can preview it using a full-page display that resembles the printed output. In Preview mode, you can move back and forth through the pages, zoom in and out on desired areas, and modify page layout options such as print margins and page orientation. Once you are satisfied with its appearance, send it to the printer with a single mouse click.

**METHOD**
- To preview the current Datasheet window:
  CLICK: Print Preview button (🔍), or
  CHOOSE: File, Print Preview
- To print the current Datasheet window:
  CLICK: Print button (🖨), or
  CHOOSE: File, Print

**PRACTICE**
You now use the Print Preview mode to display the Students datasheet.

*Setup:* Ensure that you have completed the previous lesson and that the Students datasheet is displayed.

 To preview how the datasheet will appear when printed:
CLICK: Print Preview button (🔍) on the toolbar
The Datasheet window becomes the Print Preview window.

ACCESS

**2** To preview the pages to print, click the navigation buttons at the bottom of the window. Let's practice:
CLICK: Next Page button (▶)
CLICK: Last Page button (▶|)
CLICK: First Page button (|◀)

**3** To zoom in or magnify the Print Preview window, move the magnifying glass mouse pointer over the column headings, centered between the margins, and then click once. Your screen should now appear similar to Figure 1.10.

**Figure 1.10**

Previewing the Students table for printing

Print Preview toolbar replaces the Database toolbar.

Navigation buttons for moving among the preview pages

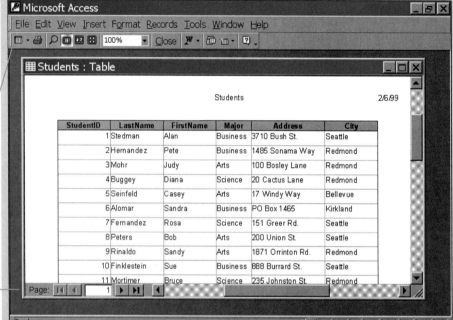

**4** To zoom back out on the page:
CLICK: anywhere on the page in the Print Preview window

**5** You can change the page setup to landscape orientation in order to print more columns of data on each page. Do the following:
CHOOSE: File, Page Setup
CLICK: *Page* tab
The Page Setup dialog box appears as shown in Figure 1.11.

**Figure 1.11**

Page Setup dialog
box: *Page* tab

Select this tab to
specify margin
settings.

Select an option
button to specify
page orientation.

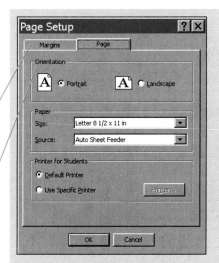

**6** To change the page orientation:
SELECT: *Landscape* option button
CLICK: OK command button
Notice that the Print Preview window is dynamically updated.

**7** On your own, zoom in and out on the Print Preview window
using the magnifying glass mouse pointer.

**8** There are two ways to close the Print Preview window. First, you
can click the Close button (☒), which closes both the Print Preview window and the Students Datasheet window. Second, you
can click the Close command button in the Print Preview toolbar, which returns you to the Datasheet window. To return to
the Students datasheet:
CLICK: Close command button in the toolbar

**9** Now let's close the Students Datasheet window:
CLICK: its Close button (☒)

**10** Since you have made changes to the layout of the Datasheet
window, Access asks you to either save or discard the formatting
changes. Let's discard the changes for now:
CLICK: No command button
You should now see the Database window.

ACCESS

You can also preview and print database objects from the Database window. Do the following:
RIGHT-CLICK: Courses in the list area
CHOOSE: Print Preview
The Courses table object is displayed in a Print Preview window. (*Note:* To send the datasheet to the printer directly, choose the Print command from the right-click menu. It is a good idea, however, to preview a page first to ensure that it will print as expected.)

 To close the Print Preview window:
CLICK: its Close button ([X])

**1.2 Self Check**    Describe two methods to quickly move the cursor to the last record in a large datasheet

# 1.3  Manipulating Table Data

Maintaining a database is difficult work. Updating the contents of a table, adding and deleting records, and fixing mistakes can take a tremendous amount of time. Fortunately, Access provides some tools and features that can help you manipulate data productively. In this module, you learn to enter, edit, and delete data in Datasheet view.

## 1.3.1  Selecting and Editing Data

**FEATURE**
You can edit information either as you type or after you have entered data into a table. In Datasheet view, editing changes are made by selecting the data or cell and then issuing a command or typing. The editing changes are saved automatically when you move the cursor to another record.

**METHOD**

Some points to keep in mind when editing in Datasheet view:

- You can press [F2] to enter and end Edit mode for the current cell.
- If you start typing while data is selected, what you type replaces the selection.
- If the flashing insertion point is positioned in a cell but no data is selected, what you type will be inserted in the field.
- With the insertion point positioned in a cell, press [BACKSPACE] to remove the character to the left of the insertion point and press [DELETE] to remove the character to the right.

**PRACTICE**

In this lesson, you practice editing table data in the ACC100 database.

*Setup:* Ensure that the ACC100 Database window is displayed. If not, open the ACC100 database from your student data files location.

**1** In the Database window, ensure that the *Tables* button in the Objects bar is selected. Then do the following:
DOUBLE-CLICK: Instructors in the list area
The Instructors Datasheet window is displayed.

**2** To position the cursor in the Office column of the first record:
PRESS: ➡ three times
Notice that the entire cell entry "A220" is selected.

**3** To update the Office number:
TYPE: B113
PRESS: [ENTER]
Notice that the new office number replaces the selection. When you press [ENTER], the cursor moves to the first field of the next record.

**4** Rather than replacing an entire entry, let's edit the contents of InstructorID 4. Position the I-beam mouse pointer to the right of the last name "Kunicki" and then click once. A flashing insertion point appears to the right of the trailing letter "i," which means that you are ready to edit the cell's contents. (*Hint:* You can also position the insertion point by first selecting the cell using the cursor keys and then pressing [F2] to enter Edit mode.)

ACCESS

**5** To replace the final "i" in Kunicki with a "y," do the following:
PRESS: (BACKSPACE)
TYPE: y
Notice that a pencil icon (✏) appears in the row's selector button. This icon indicates that you have not yet saved the editing changes.

**6** To complete the editing process:
PRESS: (ENTER)
The pencil icon remains displayed. (*Hint:* You can also press (F2) to toggle Edit mode on and off.)

**7** To save the changes, you must move the cursor to another record:
PRESS: (⬇)
The pencil icon disappears.

**8** When you move the mouse pointer over a cell, it changes shape to an I-beam so that you may easily position the insertion point between characters. In order to select an entire cell for editing, you position the mouse pointer over the top or left grid line of a cell and click once. You know the mouse pointer is properly positioned when it changes shape to a cross. To select the contents of the LastName field for InstructorID 7, position the mouse pointer as shown below.

| 6 | Souder |
| 7 | Huber ✛ |

Positioning the mouse pointer

**9** To select the cell:
CLICK: left mouse button once
The entire "Huber" cell is highlighted in reverse video.

**10** Let's assume that Tessa got married recently and has decided to change her name. Do the following:
TYPE: Moss
The pencil icon appears in the row's selector button.

**11** To save the changes:
PRESS: (⬇) to move to the next record

**In Addition**
Saving Your Changes

Rather than moving to another row, you can save the changes you make to the current record by pressing (SHIFT) + (ENTER). This keyboard shortcut allows you to write the changes permanently to the disk without having to move to another record.

## 1.3.2   Using the Undo Command

**FEATURE**

The **Undo command** allows you to reverse mistakes during editing. Unlike other Office products, Access does not offer a multiple undo capability. Therefore, you must remember to choose the command immediately after making a mistake.

**METHOD**

To reverse the last action performed:
- CHOOSE: Edit, Undo, or
- CLICK: Undo button (⟲), or
- PRESS: CTRL + z

(*Note:* The command's name changes to reflect the action that may be reversed. For example, on the Edit pull-down menu, the command may read Undo Current Field/Record, Undo Delete, or Undo Saved Record.)

**PRACTICE**

Using the Undo command, you practice reversing common editing procedures.

*Setup:* Ensure that you have completed the previous lesson and that the Instructors datasheet is displayed.

**1** You've just been informed that "Robert Harris" prefers to go by the name of "Bobby." Let's edit the table:
SELECT: the FirstName cell for InstructorID 5
The cell containing "Robert" is highlighted, as shown below.

Click the top or left gridline to select the cell.

| Kenyon | A310 |
|---|---|
| Robert | B103 |
| Manfred | B108 |

**2** TYPE: Bobby
PRESS: ENTER
The cursor moves to the next field in the current record.

**3** To undo the last edit using the Menu bar:
CHOOSE: Edit, Undo Current Field/Record
The contents revert back to "Robert," yet the cursor remains in the Office column.

**4**　To practice deleting a cell entry, let's remove the Office assignment for Anna Cortez:
SELECT: the Office cell for InstructorID 8, as shown below

| Tessa | B104 |
|-------|------|
| Anna  | A316 |
| Simon | A319 |

**5**　To remove the entry:
PRESS: (DELETE)

**6**　To save the changes and move to the next record:
PRESS: ⬇

**7**　Even though this change has been saved and recorded to disk, Access lets you reverse the deletion. Do the following:
CLICK: Undo button (⟲)
(*Note:* In this step, clicking the toolbar button executes the Edit, Undo Saved Record command.)

---

**In Addition**
Using (ESC) to
Undo Changes

Instead of choosing the Undo command from the menu, you can undo changes in the current field by pressing (ESC) once. Pressing (ESC) a second time will undo all of the changes made to the current record.

---

## 1.3.3　Adding Records

**FEATURE**
In Datasheet view, you typically add new records to the blank row appearing at the bottom of a datasheet. If the text "(AutoNumber)" appears in a cell, press (ENTER), (TAB), or ➡ to bypass the cell and move to the next field. Any cell containing an *AutoNumber* field is incremented automatically by Access when a new record is added to the table.

**METHOD**
Use any of the following methods to position the cursor in a blank row at the bottom of the datasheet, ready for inserting a new record:
● CLICK: New Record button (▶*) on the toolbar, or
● CLICK: New Record button (▶*) in the navigation bar, or
● CHOOSE: Insert, New Record from the Menu bar

**PRACTICE**
In this lesson, you insert two records into the Instructors datasheet.

*Setup:* Ensure that the Instructors datasheet is displayed.

**1** To position the cursor at the bottom of the datasheet:
CLICK: New Record button (▶) on the toolbar

**2** Because the InstructorID column contains an AutoNumber entry:
PRESS: TAB to move to the next field
(*Note:* You can also press ENTER to move to the next field. The convention in this guide, however, is to use TAB to move the cursor forward and SHIFT + TAB to move the cursor backward.)

**3** Let's enter the new record information:
TYPE: Joyce
PRESS: TAB
Notice that the AutoNumber entry for the InstructorID column is calculated and entered automatically.

**4** To complete the entry:
TYPE: James
PRESS: TAB
TYPE: C230
Your screen should now appear similar to Figure 1.12. Notice that the pencil icon appears in the current row's selector button and that a new row was added, as denoted with an asterisk in its selector button.

**Figure 1.12**

Adding a new record

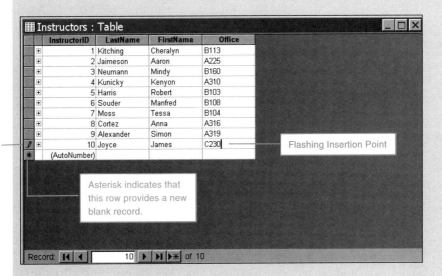

A pencil icon in a row selector button indicates that the current record has not yet been saved.

Asterisk indicates that this row provides a new blank record.

Flashing Insertion Point

**5** To save the record and move to the next row:
PRESS: TAB
(*Note:* Again, you can also press ENTER to move the cursor.)

**6** On your own, add the following two records to the datasheet:

InstructorID: 11               InstructorID: 12
LastName: Melville             LastName: Conrad
FirstName: Herman             FirstName: Joseph
Office: C240                   Office: C220

**7** To return to the top of the datasheet:
PRESS: CTRL + HOME

## 1.3.4  Deleting Records

**FEATURE**
In Datasheet view, Access provides several methods for removing records from a table. To do so efficiently, however, you must learn how to select records. Using the mouse, you click and drag the pointer in the **record selection area**, sometimes called the *row selector buttons*. Refer to the diagram below for clarification on the parts of a Datasheet window.

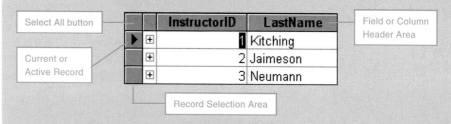

**METHOD**
1. SELECT: a record or group of records
2. CLICK: Delete Record button (⊠), or
   PRESS: DELETE, or
   CHOOSE: Edit, Delete Record

**PRACTICE**
You now practice selecting and removing records from a datasheet.

*Setup:* Ensure that the Instructors datasheet is displayed.

**1** To begin, let's select all the records in the current datasheet:
CLICK: Select All button (☐) in the upper left-hand corner
All of the records should now appear in reverse video (white on black).

**2** To remove the highlighting:
PRESS: HOME

**3** To select record number 3, position the mouse pointer to the left of the desired record in the record selection area. The mouse pointer changes shape to a black horizontal right-pointing arrow (→). When positioned over the row selector button properly, click the left mouse button once to select the entire row.

**4** Let's remove the selected record from the table:
CLICK: Delete Record button (⊠) on the toolbar
A confirmation dialog box appears, as shown in Figure 1.13.
(*CAUTION:* Access displays this dialog box whenever you delete records. Click the Yes command button to permanently remove the record or click No to return the datasheet to its previous state.)

**Figure 1.13**

Removing records from a datasheet

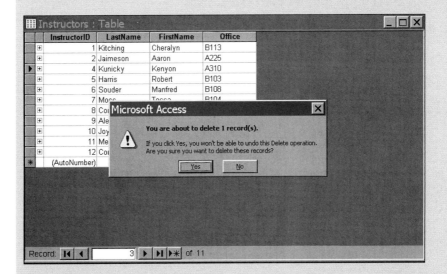

**5** To confirm the deletion:
CLICK: Yes

**6** You can also delete numerous records with a single command. To illustrate, click once in the record selection area for Manfred Souder's entry (InstructorID 6) and hold down the left mouse button. Then drag the mouse pointer downward to Anna Cortez's record (InstructorID 8). Release the mouse button to display the selected records.

**7** To delete the selected records:
PRESS: DELETE
CLICK: Yes to confirm

**8** To close the Instructors datasheet:
CLICK: its Close button (⊠)
You should now see the Database window for the ACC100 database.

**9**  To close the ACC100 database:
CLICK: its Close button (☒)

**10**  To exit Access:
CHOOSE: File, Exit

**1.3 Self Check**  When does Access save the changes that you've made when editing a record?

# 1.4  Chapter Review

Microsoft Access is a full-featured database management application for desktop computers. Database software enables you to store and manipulate large amounts of data such as customer mailing lists. When you first open a database using Access, you are presented with a control center called the Database window. From this one window, you can create and display a variety of objects, including tables, forms, queries, and reports. In this chapter, you learned how to open a database, select database objects, and display and print the contents of a Datasheet window. In addition to navigating a datasheet, you learned to insert, modify, and delete records. You also practiced using the Undo command to reverse your mistakes.

## 1.4.1  Command Summary

Many of the commands and procedures appearing in this chapter are summarized in the following table.

| Skill Set | To Perform This Task . . . | Do the Following . . . |
|---|---|---|
| **Using Access** | Launch Microsoft Access | CLICK: Start button ()<br>CHOOSE: Programs, Microsoft Access |
| | Exit Microsoft Access | CLICK: its Close button (☒), or<br>CHOOSE: File, Exit |
| | Close a database | CLICK: its Close button (☒), or<br>CHOOSE: File, Close |

*Continued*

| Skill Set | To Perform This Task . . . | Do the Following . . . |
|---|---|---|
| **Viewing and Organizing Information** | Expand/collapse subdatasheets in a Datasheet window | CLICK: Expand button (⊞)<br>CLICK: Collapse button (⊟) |
| | Adjust a column's width in in the field header area | DRAG: a column's right border line a datasheet |
| | Adjust the height of all rows in a datasheet | DRAG: a row's bottom border line in the record selection area |
| | Add a new record to a datasheet | CLICK: New Record buttons (▶ or ▶*) |
| | Delete selected record(s) from a datasheet | CLICK: Delete Record button (⋈), or PRESS: DELETE |
| **Working with Access** | Select and open database objects using the Objects bar | CLICK: the desired object category DOUBLE-CLICK: the desired object |
| | Navigate to a specific record | CLICK: in the navigation text box TYPE: the desired record number PRESS: ENTER |
| | Toggle Edit mode on and off for editing a datasheet cell | PRESS: F2 Edit key |
| | Reverse or undo the most recent changes or mistakes | CLICK: Undo button (↺), or CHOOSE: Edit, Undo |
| | Save the editing changes to the current record | PRESS: SHIFT + ENTER |
| | Preview a datasheet for printing | CLICK: Print Preview button (🔍), or CHOOSE: File, Print Preview |
| | Print a datasheet | CLICK: Print button (🖨), or CHOOSE: File, Print |
| | Change the page orientation for a printed document | CHOOSE: File, Page Setup CLICK: *Page* tab SELECT: *Portrait* or *Landscape* |

ACCESS

## 1.4.2  Key Terms

This section specifies page references for the key terms identified in this chapter. For a complete list of definitions, refer to the Glossary at the end of this learning guide.

application window, *p. 10*

cell, *p. 15*

database, *p. 5*

database management system (DBMS), *p. 5*

Database window, *p. 12*

datasheet, *p. 15*

Datasheet view, *p. #15*

field, *p. 5*

field header area, *p. 19*

form, *p. 13*

Objects bar, *p. 12*

Places bar, *p. 9*

query, *p. 13*

record, *p. 5*

record selection area, *p. 30*

report(s), *p. 14*

subdatasheet, *p. 17*

table, *p. 5*

Undo command, *p. 27*

# 1.5 Review Questions

## 1.5.1 Short Answer

1. Provide examples of when you might use a database.
2. Define the following terms: *table, record,* and *field.*
3. What is an *object* in Microsoft Access? Provide examples.
4. Which database object is used to collect and store data?
5. Which database object displays in Preview mode when opened?
6. Why is the Database window referred to as a *control center*?
7. How do you select the contents of a cell in a datasheet?
8. How do you select all of the records displayed in a datasheet?
9. What is the procedure for adding a record in Datasheet view?
10. What is the procedure for deleting records in Datasheet view?

## 1.5.2 True/False

1.  _____ DBMS stands for Database Backup Management System.
2.  _____ When you first launch Access, the startup dialog box appears.
3.  _____ A *form* is a database object that displays multiple records in a column and row layout.
4.  _____ A *query* allows you to ask questions of your data and to combine information from more than one table.
5.  _____ The column widths of a datasheet cannot be adjusted once information has been entered into the cells.
6.  _____ Changing the height of one row in a datasheet affects the height of every row.
7.  _____ If you want to fit more field columns on a single page, you can select landscape orientation for printing.
8.  _____ If you make a mistake while editing a field, you can press ⌈ESC⌉ to undo the error.
9.  _____ In a datasheet, the *record selection area* is the gray area at the top of each column.
10. _____ Access allows you to delete several records at once.

## 1.5.3 Multiple Choice

1.  Which of the following buttons does not appear in the Objects bar?
    a.  Programs
    b.  Modules
    c.  Reports
    d.  Forms

2.  Which database object do you use to display information for one record at a time?
    a.  table
    b.  report
    c.  form
    d.  query

3.  In a datasheet, the intersection of a row and column is called a:
    a.  cell
    b.  cursor
    c.  form
    d.  record

4. In a datasheet, what does each column represent?
   a. database
   b. table
   c. record
   d. field

5. In a datasheet, which mouse pointer do you use to select a cell by clicking on its gridline?
   a. ▹
   b. ✛
   c. ⌛
   d. I

6. In a datasheet, which icon appears at the left side of a record while it is being edited?
   a. Pencil (✎)
   b. Asterisk (✳)
   c. Pointer (▶)
   d. Selector (☐)

7. When editing a record, which keystroke allows you to save the changes without leaving the current record?
   a. CTRL + ENTER
   b. CTRL + ALT
   c. ALT + ENTER
   d. SHIFT + ENTER

8. Which of the following will not reverse the last action performed?
   a. CHOOSE: Edit, Undo *command*
   b. CLICK: Undo button (↺)
   c. PRESS: CTRL + X
   d. PRESS: ESC

9. Any cell containing this type of field is incremented automatically by Access when a new record is added.
   a. AutoElevate
   b. AutoIncrement
   c. AutoNumber
   d. AutoValue

10. The row selector buttons in a datasheet are located in the:
    a. row selection area
    b. record selection area
    c. field selection area
    d. table selection area

# 1.6 Hands-On Projects

 ## 1.6.1 World Wide Imports: Sales Representatives

This exercise lets you practice fundamental database skills, such as opening a database, displaying a table, and navigating a datasheet.

1. Load Microsoft Access using the Windows Start menu.
2. To open an existing database using the startup dialog box:
   SELECT: *Open an existing file* option button
   SELECT: More Files... in the list box area
   CLICK: OK command button
3. Using either the Places bar or the *Look in* drop-down list box:
   SELECT: *the folder location* of your Advantage student data files
   DOUBLE-CLICK: ACC160 in the list area
   The Database window appears.
4. Ensure that the *Tables* button in the Objects bar is selected. Then do the following to display the Sales Reps table:
   DOUBLE-CLICK: 161 Sales Reps in the list area
   A table with 12 records and five field columns is displayed.
5. To move to second field of the third record:
   PRESS: ⬇ two times
   PRESS: ➡ once
   The cursor should now highlight the name "Louis."
6. Now move to the last record using the mouse:
   CLICK: Last Record button (⏭)
7. To quickly move to the top of the datasheet using the keyboard:
   PRESS: CTRL + HOME
8. Each sales rep at World Wide Imports is responsible for servicing specific customer accounts. You can display the customer accounts for each sales rep in a *subdatasheet*. To do so, let's drill down and display the customers assigned to Peter Fink (SalesRep A14):
   CLICK: Expand button (⊞) in the left-hand column of record 5
   Your screen should now appear similar to Figure 1.14.

ACCESS

**Figure 1.14**

Displaying the customers assigned to a sales rep

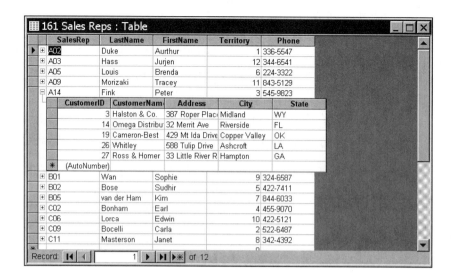

9. On your own, practice opening a few more subdatasheets. When you are finished, hide each subdatasheet by clicking the Collapse button (⊟) in the left-hand column.

10. To close the 161 Sales Reps Datasheet window:
    CLICK: its Close button (☒)

## 1.6.2  CyberWeb: Internet Accounts

In this exercise, you practice adjusting a datasheet's column widths and row heights before previewing it for printing.

1. Ensure that Access is loaded. Then open the data file named ACC160, if its Database window is not already displayed.

2. SELECT: *Tables* button in the Objects bar
   DOUBLE-CLICK: 162 Internet Accounts

3. Let's adjust the width of the Address field column by having Access calculate its best width:
   SELECT: any cell in the Address column
   CHOOSE: Format, Column Width
   CLICK: Best Fit command button

4. Now use the mouse to adjust the width of the Phone column. In the field header area, position the mouse pointer over the border line between the Phone and Amount fields.
   CLICK: the border line and hold down the mouse button
   DRAG: the mouse pointer to the left to decrease the width (to approximately the end of the word "Phone")

5. To set the best-fit width for the Zip column using the mouse:
   DOUBLE-CLICK: the border line between Zip and Phone

6. On your own, adjust the width of the City column so that it is narrower.

7. To change the row height setting for all the rows in the datasheet:
CHOOSE: Format, Row Height
TYPE: **15**
CLICK: OK

8. Now let's see what the datasheet would look like if it was printed:
CLICK: Print Preview button (🔍) on the toolbar

9. On your own, zoom in and out on the Print Preview window using the magnifying glass mouse pointer.

10. If you have a printer connected to your computer, print the datasheet. Otherwise, proceed to step 11.
CLICK: Print button (🖨) on the toolbar

11. To close the Print Preview window so that the 162 Internet Accounts datasheet remains displayed:
CLICK: Close command button in the toolbar

12. To close the datasheet without saving the formatting changes:
CLICK: its Close button (☒)
CLICK: No command button

## 1.6.3  Big Valley Mills: Forest Products

In this exercise, you edit data in an existing datasheet and practice using the Undo command.

*Setup*: Ensure the ACC160 Database window is displayed.

1. SELECT: *Tables* button in the Objects bar
DOUBLE-CLICK: 163 Products

2. To position the cursor in the Species column of the third record:
PRESS: ⊕ two times
PRESS: ⊕ once

3. Let's change this cell value to match the standard abbreviation. With the entry selected, enter the new data:
TYPE: **DFIR**

4. To save the changes, move the cursor to the next record:
PRESS: ⊕
The pencil icon disappears.

5. Now let's edit the product code of record number 4. (*Hint:* Glance at the navigation bar in the Datasheet window to see the current record number.) Position the I-beam mouse pointer to the right of the product code "DF210S" and then click once. A flashing insertion point appears to the right of the letter "S."

6. To delete the final "S" in DF210S and save the change:
PRESS: (BACKSPACE)
PRESS: ⊕

7. SELECT: Grade cell for record 1 using the mouse
   (*Hint:* Position the mouse pointer over the cell's left gridline so that the pointer changes to a cross shape. Then click the left mouse button once to select the entire cell.)
8. Replace the cell's contents with the new Grade code "Utility" and then save the changes.
9. To move the cursor to the last field of the first record:
   PRESS: (CTRL) + (⬆)
   PRESS: (END)
10. To delete the entry and save the change:
    PRESS: (DELETE)
    PRESS: (⬇)
11. To reverse the deletion using the Menu bar:
    CHOOSE: Edit, Undo Saved Record
    (*Note:* Instead of using the menu, you could have clicked the Undo button (🔄) to achieve the same result.)
12. Close the Datasheet window.

## ■ 1.6.4 Silverdale Festival: Contact List

You will now practice adding and deleting records in an existing table.

*Setup*: Ensure the ACC160 Database window is displayed.

1. Display the "164 Contacts" table object in Datasheet view.
2. To position the cursor at the bottom of the datasheet, ready for inserting a new record:
   CLICK: New Record button (⏵*) on the toolbar
3. The first column contains an AutoNumber entry, so we can immediately move to the next field:
   PRESS: (TAB)
4. Let's start entering the new record information:
   TYPE: **Silverdale Search and Rescue**
   PRESS: (TAB)
   Notice that the AutoNumber entry for the ID column is calculated and entered automatically.
5. To continue filling out the record:
   TYPE: **Amy McTell**
   PRESS: (TAB)
   TYPE: **P.O. Box 1359**
   PRESS: (TAB)
   TYPE: **Silverdale**
   PRESS: (TAB)
   TYPE: **474-9636**
   PRESS: (TAB) two times

6. On your own, add the following record to the datasheet:
   Volunteer Group: **Historical Society**
   Contact: **Craig Burns**
   Address: **3528 Pacific Ave.**
   City: **Silverdale**
   Phone 1: **945-6621**

7. To delete a record that was inadvertently entered twice, select ID 61 (which is also record number 61) using the record selection area. (*Hint:* The mouse pointer changes shape to a black horizontal right-pointing arrow (➡) when positioned properly.)

8. Let's remove the selected record from the table:
   CLICK: Delete Record button () on the toolbar

9. To confirm the deletion:
   CLICK: Yes
   Notice that the values in the ID column now jump from 60 to 62. As you can see, an AutoNumber field, such as a record ID number, is just another table value; it does not have to match a record's number.

10. Close the Datasheet window.

## 1.6.5 On Your Own: Office Mart Inventory

To practice navigating and formatting a table's datasheet, open the table object named "165 Inventory" in the ACC160 database. Experiment with the various mouse and keyboard methods for moving the cursor in the datasheet. After you have familiarized yourself with the table, use the keyboard to reposition the cursor to the first field of the first record.

Resize the ProductID, Description, and Suggested Retail columns to their best fit. Adjust the Onhand and Cost columns to 12 characters. Change the height of all the rows to 14 points. Now, use Print Preview to see how the datasheet will look when it's printed. Change the page setup to landscape orientation so that all the columns fit on a single page, as shown in Figure 1.15. If they do not, adjust the widths of the remaining columns until they do. When you are satisfied with the appearance of the page, print a copy of the datasheet and exit Access without saving the changes to the layout.

**Figure 1.15**

Previewing a datasheet with
a landscape print orientation

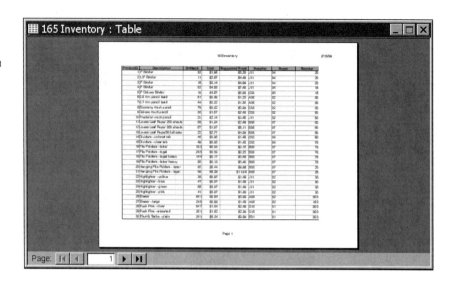

# 1.6.6 On Your Own: Sun Bird Resort

To practice manipulating table data, open the table object named "166 Patrons" in the ACC160 database.

Make the following editing changes:
- Change the spelling of guest ID 2 from "Neely" to "Neally"
- Change the Interest of guest ID 6 from "Tennis" to "Golf"
- Change the Hometown of guest ID 8 from "Clonkurry" to "Mount Isa"
- Change the Best Time of guest ID 22 to "11:30 AM"

Make the following addition:
Guest: **Ric Fernando**
Hometown: **Manila**
State: *(leave blank)*
Co: **PHI**
Interest: **Golf**
Room#: **B311**
#Stay: **1**
Best Time: **1:00 PM**

Finally, delete the record for guest ID 15. Once finished, close the Datasheet window, close the ACC160 database, and exit Microsoft Access.

# 1.7  Case Problems: On-Track Seminars

Joanna has been working at On-Track Seminars for several days now and is starting to become quite comfortable in her new job. In addition to her regular administrative duties, she is responsible for managing an Access database. Having never used database software before, she enrolled in an evening course on Microsoft Access at the local community college. Now she feels ready to open and view the contents of the company's database.

In the following case problems, assume the role of Joanna and perform the same steps that she identifies. You may want to re-read the chapter opening before proceeding.

1.  Midway through the morning, Joanna receives a phone call from an agitated instructor. "Hello Joanna? My name is Mary Sterba and I teach the "Safety in the Workplace" seminars. Due to a family emergency, I can't make my TR145 seminar this Tuesday. Please call the students and ask if they can transfer into TR146 the following week."

    To start, Joanna loads the ACC170 database located in her Advantage student data files folder. From the Database window, she opens the Trainers table and locates Mary Sterba's record. She expands the subdatasheet for Mary's record and verifies that she is indeed scheduled to teach both the TR145 and TR146 seminars. Next she expands the subdatasheet for TR146, as shown in Figure 1.16, to ensure that it does not have more than 10 students registered. After collapsing the subdatasheet, she expands the TR145 subdatasheet in order to list the names and phone numbers of all students registered in the cancelled class. She will use the list to call the students and reschedule them into the next seminar. Having completed her first task using Access, Joanna closes the Trainers table.

ACCESS

**Figure 1.16**

Drilling down into a table's
data using subdatasheets

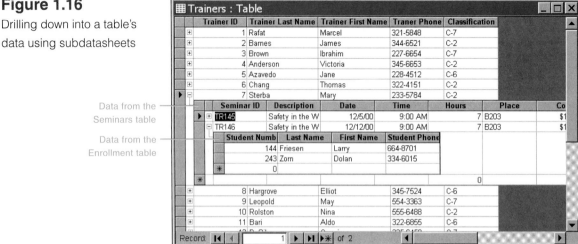

Data from the
Seminars table

Data from the
Enrollment table

2.  Later that day, Karen Chase, the office director, asks Joanna to produce a printout of the currently scheduled seminars. Joanna opens the Seminars table in the ACC170 database and adjusts the column width of the Description field so that the entire title is visible. To provide some additional white space in the printout, she adjusts the height of all the rows to 16 points. Using Print Preview to view the datasheet, Joanna notices that not all columns fit on a single page. To compensate, she changes the page setup to use landscape orientation and adjusts the datasheet's column widths as necessary. When she is satisfied with the appearance of the datasheet, Joanna prints a copy for Karen. Then she closes the Seminars table without saving the formatting changes she has made.

3.  Joanna phones the five students whose phone numbers she wrote down earlier that day and determines that they are all indeed able to switch to the later "Safety in the Workplace" seminar. To update the database, Joanna begins by opening the Enrollment table. She locates the five students' records and changes the Seminar ID for each record from TR145 to TR146. She then switches to the Database window and opens the Seminars table. To finish the task, Joanna deletes the record for Seminar TR145 and closes both datasheets.

4. Toward the end of the day, Joanna receives two phone calls from people wishing to register for seminars. After writing down the information, Joanna is ready to update the database. She opens the Enrollment table and adds two new records:

Student Number: **501**
Last Name: **Haldane**
First Name: **Chris**
Student Phone: **577-9685**
Seminar ID: **TR135**

Student Number: **502**
Last Name: **Zhou**
First Name: **Shih-Chang**
Student Phone: **345-6087**
Seminar ID: **TR146**

She saves the records and closes the datasheet. Then she closes the Database window and exits Microsoft Access.

ACCESS

# NOTES

# NOTES

# NOTES

# MICROSOFT ACCESS 2000
## *Creating a Database*

**CHAPTER**
TWO

# Chapter Outline

# Learning Objectives

After reading this chapter, you will be able to:

- Create a new database using the Database Wizard

- Create a new database from scratch

- Define table objects for storing data

- Specify a primary key and indexes

- Rename, delete, and move fields

- Print a table's structure

## Case Study    Inland Transit

Inland Transit operates a fleet of trucks in the Pacific Northwest. Last week, Inland's management team asked their controller, Mike Lambert, to locate and summarize a variety of information about the business. After spending three days reviewing reports and searching through filing cabinets, Mike came to the realization that he needs a better information management system. He evaluates the leading database software programs and decides to use Microsoft Access to create a company database. Mike starts the process by laying out his design ideas on paper. He wants to ensure that all of the company's relevant business information is collected, stored, and readied for processing.

In this chapter, you and Mike learn about creating databases and tables using Microsoft Access. You also learn how to modify a table's design by adding and removing fields. Lastly, you use a special Access program called the Documenter to produce a printout of a table's structure.

# 2.1 Designing Your First Database

Desktop database software has existed since the first personal computer was introduced by IBM in the early 1980s. Since that time many database programs and applications have been developed for both personal and business use. Whatever your particular data management needs, rarely will you require a truly unique application. Refining or customizing an existing database application is a more common practice. Microsoft Access allows you to take advantage of what others before you have learned and accomplished. Using the Access wizards, you can develop an entire database application in less time than it takes to read this module.

## 2.1.1  Employing the Database Wizard

**FEATURE**
Access provides two main options for creating a new database. First, you can create an empty database structure and then populate it with objects. For example, in an inventory control system, you could create a new database and then add tables for Products, Suppliers, and Customers. Once completed, you would then create the data entry forms, product catalogs, and other reports. The second option is to use the **Database Wizard**. This wizard provides access to professionally designed templates for creating complete database applications. Each template contains tables, queries, forms, reports, and a main menu called a *switchboard* that makes the application's features easier to access.

**METHOD**
From the Access application window:
1.  CLICK: New button (□), or
    CHOOSE: File, New
2.  CLICK: *Databases* tab in the New dialog box
3.  DOUBLE-CLICK: a database wizard (▧)

From the Access startup dialog box:
1.  SELECT: *Access database wizards, pages, and projects* option button
2.  DOUBLE-CLICK: a database wizard (▧) in the New dialog box

**PRACTICE**
Using the Access Database Wizard, you create an inventory control application from scratch.

*Setup:* Ensure that Access is loaded. If you are launching Access and the startup dialog box appears, click the Cancel command button to remove the dialog box from the application window.

**1** To create a new database application:
CLICK: New button (□) on the toolbar

**2** In the New dialog box that appears:
CLICK: *Databases* tab
A list of Database Wizard templates appear in the New dialog box as shown in Figure 2.1. (*Note:* If you haven't installed any database templates, you cannot perform the steps in this lesson.)

**Figure 2.1**

New dialog box:
*Databases* tab

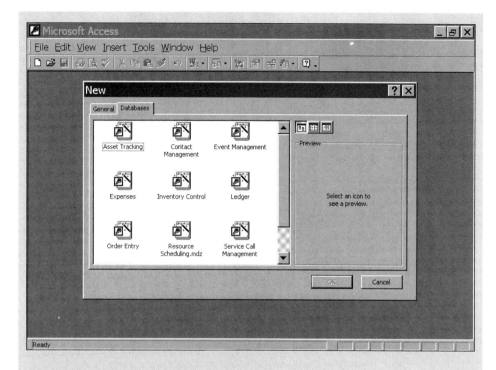

**3** Using the appropriate Database Wizard template, let's create an inventory database application:
DOUBLE-CLICK: Inventory Control wizard (📇)

**4** In the File New Database dialog box that appears, use the Places bar or the *Save in* drop-down list box to select your personal storage location. Then, do the following:
TYPE: **My Inventory** in the *File name* text box
CLICK: Create command button
You should wait patiently as Access displays your new Database window and prepares the Database Wizard dialog box.

**5** The opening screen of the Database Wizard dialog box provides information about the Inventory Control wizard. After reading its contents, proceed to the next step:
CLICK: Next>

**6** Your first task in the Database Wizard, as shown in Figure 2.2, is to select optional fields for inclusion in the database. These fields appear in italic. On your own, click on the names listed in the *Tables in the database* list box. The field names for the selected table then appear in the *Fields in the table* list box.

**Figure 2.2**

Inventory Control
Database Wizard

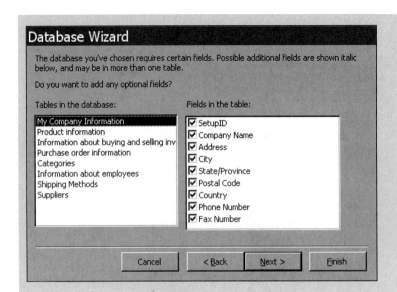

**7** To proceed to the next step:
CLICK: Next >

**8** To select a screen appearance for your forms, click on each option to see a preview and then:
SELECT: SandStone in the list box
CLICK: Next >

**9** To select a page layout for your printed reports, click on each option to see a preview and then:
SELECT: Soft Gray
CLICK: Next >

**10** You can also specify the title of the database and whether to include a logo or picture. To accept the default entries:
CLICK: Next >

**11** At the finish line, you tell Access to create and display the database. Ensure that the *Yes, start the database* check box is selected and then do the following:
CLICK: Finish
The Database Wizard creates the database based on your selections. Depending on your system, this process can take a few minutes.

**12** In this particular wizard, Access displays a dialog box asking you to furnish some company data. Using the TAB key to move forward through the text boxes, type your personal information. When finished:
CLICK: the Close button (⊠) for the dialog box to proceed

The Main Switchboard (Figure 2.3) for the Inventory Control application is displayed. On your own, click on the menu buttons to access and display the forms and reports created by the Database Wizard. Before proceeding, close the form or report Print Preview windows that appear by clicking their Close buttons ([X]).

**Figure 2.3**

Main Switchboard for the
Inventory Control application

Menu buttons on the
Main Switchboard

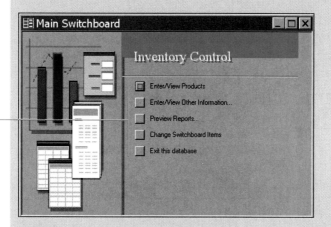

 Let's examine the database objects that were created for this application. From the Menu bar:
CHOOSE: Window, My Inventory : Database

 In the Database window, click on the various buttons in the Objects bar to view the table, query, form, and report objects. You may need to scroll the list area or adjust the size of the Database window to see all of the object names. When you are finished, close the application:
CLICK: its Close button ([X])
(*Note:* You can also choose the File, Close command.)
Notice that the Main Switchboard, which appears as a form object, also disappears when you close the Database window.

## 2.1.2 Planning a Database

**FEATURE**
Many people who have worked with computer databases can attest to the 90/10 rule of database design. Place 90 percent of your effort into designing a database properly in order to spend only 10 percent of your time maintaining it. As you can probably infer from this rule, many problems arising in database management are traceable to a faulty design. In this lesson, you learn some strategies for planning a well-designed database.

**METHOD**
Here are five steps to designing a better database:

1. *Determine your output requirements.* State your expectations in terms of the queries and reports desired from the application. It's often helpful to write out questions, such as "How many customers live in Kansas City?", and to sketch out reports on a blank piece of paper.

2. *Determine your input requirements.* From the output requirements, identify the data that must be collected, stored, and calculated. You should also review any existing paper-based forms used for data collection in order to get a better idea of what data is available.

3. *Determine your table structures.* Divide and group data into separate tables and fields for flexibility in searching, sorting, and manipulating data. Review the following example to see what fields can be separated out of a simple address:

Also ensure that each record can be identified using a unique code or field, such as Order Number or Customer ID. This code need not contain information related to the subject—a numeric field that is automatically incremented works fine.

4. *Determine your table relationships.* Rather than entering or storing the same information repeatedly, strive to separate data into multiple tables and then relate the tables using a common field. For example, in a table containing book information (Books), an AuthorID field would contain a unique code

that could be used to look up the author's personal data in a separate table (Authors). Without such a design, you would need to type an author's name and address each time you added one of their works to the Books table.

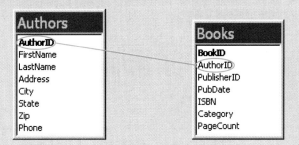

By incorporating common fields into your table structures, you can establish relationships amongst the tables for sharing data. This process, called *normalizing* your data, enhances your efficiency and reduces potential data redundancy and entry errors.

5. *Test your database application*. Add sample records to the table using both datasheets and forms, run queries, and produce reports to test whether the application is robust and accurate. In addition to ensuring the validity and integrity of data, you want the information to be readily accessible.

## 2.1.3 Starting a New Database

**FEATURE**
If you have specific requirements for a database application, you may choose to create a blank structure and then add the appropriate objects. Unlike other Office 2000 applications, such as Word and Excel, Access allows you to work with only one database at a time. Therefore, before starting a new database, you must ensure that there is no active database displayed in the application window's work area.

**METHOD**
1. CLICK: New (⬚), or
   CHOOSE: File, New
2. CLICK: *General* tab in the New dialog box
3. DOUBLE-CLICK: Database template (⬚)

**PRACTICE**
In this lesson, you create a new database file for storing table objects.

ACCESS

*Setup:* Ensure that Access is loaded and that there is no Database window displayed.

**1** To create a new database:
CLICK: New button (🗋) on the toolbar

**2** In the New dialog box that appears:
CLICK: *General* tab
DOUBLE-CLICK: Database template (📳)

**3** You use the File New Database dialog box (Figure 2.4) to select a storage location and file name for permanently saving the database structure. Using the Places bar or the *Save in* drop-down dialog box, select your personal storage location.

**Figure 2.4**

File New Database
dialog box

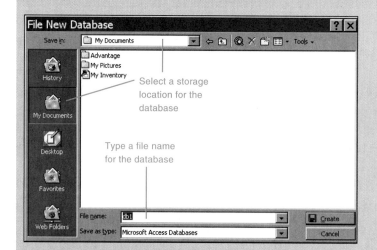

**4** In the *File name* text box:
TYPE: **My Phone Book**
CLICK: Create command button
A new Database window appears in the work area. Notice that the Title bar reads "My Phone Book : Database" and that there are no objects, besides the New Object shortcuts, in the Database window.

**5** To close the Database window:
CLICK: its Close button (🗵)

**2.1 Self Check**    What two objects are most closely associated with the output of a database application?

# 2.2  Creating a Simple Table

An Access database file is simply a container for storing database objects. Your first step in creating an application is to define the table objects for storing data. Each table in your database should be related on some level and contain information about a single topic or subject. In an automobile industry database, for example, one table may contain a list of car dealerships while another table contains a list of manufacturers. Although these tables deal with different subjects, they are related to the automobile industry. In this module, you learn two methods for quickly populating a database structure with table objects. What these methods may lack in power and flexibility, they make up for in ease of use and speed.

## 2.2.1  Creating a Table Using the Table Wizard

**FEATURE**

Access provides the **Table Wizard** to help you create a table structure, much like you created a complete application using the Database Wizard. Rather than defining a new table from scratch, you compile it by picking and choosing fields from existing personal and business tables. This method lets you quickly populate an empty database structure with reliable and usable table objects.

**METHOD**

In the Database window, select the *Tables* button and then:
- DOUBLE-CLICK: Create table by using wizard, or
- CLICK: New button (⬛New) on the Database window toolbar
  DOUBLE-CLICK: Table Wizard in the New Table dialog box

**PRACTICE**

After displaying a new database, you create a table object using the Table Wizard.

*Setup:* Ensure that there is no Database window displayed.

**1** To create a new database:
CLICK: New button (⬛) on the toolbar
CLICK: *General* tab
DOUBLE-CLICK: Database template (⬛)

**2** In the File New Database dialog box:
TYPE: **My Business** into the *File name* text box

**3** Using the Places bar or the *Save in* drop-down dialog box, select your personal storage location. Then, do the following:
CLICK: Create command button
The "My Business" Database window will appear.

**4** Your next step is to add table objects to the empty database structure. To use the Table Wizard, ensure that the *Tables* button is selected in the Objects bar and then do the following:
DOUBLE-CLICK: Create table by using wizard
The Table Wizard dialog box appears, as shown in Figure 2.5.

**Figure 2.5**

Table Wizard dialog box

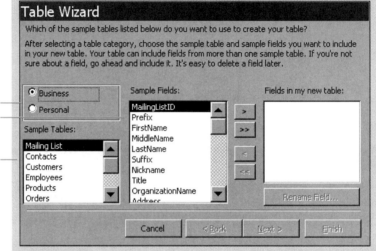

Select a category.
Select fields for a new table object.

Select one of the pre-built tables to display the fields that are available.

**5** By default, the *Business* option button is chosen in the Table Wizard dialog box. And as a result, only business-related table structures appear in the *Sample Tables* list box. To view the Personal tables:
CLICK: *Personal* option button

**6** On your own, scroll the *Sample Tables* list box to view the available table structures.

**7** Let's create a new table to store the company's product information:
CLICK: *Business* option button
SELECT: Products in the *Sample Tables* list box
Notice that the fields for this table structure now appear in the *Sample Fields* list box.

**8** In specifying the fields for a table, select individual fields using ▸ and select all fields by clicking ▸▸. For this step, let's include all of the suggested fields:
CLICK: Include All button (▸▸)

**9** To complete the wizard:
CLICK: [ Finish ]
The new table, called "Products," appears in a Datasheet window ready to accept data.

**10** Close the Products Datasheet window. You should now see the Products table object in the Database window.

## 2.2.2 Creating a Table in Datasheet View

**FEATURE**
Using Datasheet view, you create a table by typing information into a blank datasheet, just as you would when entering data into an Excel worksheet. When you save the table, Access creates the table structure and assigns the proper data types to each field based on the information you've entered. This method lets novice users create tables without an in-depth understanding of table structures and data types.

**METHOD**
In the Database window, select the *Tables* button and then:
- DOUBLE-CLICK: Create table by entering data, or
- CLICK: New button ([ New ]) on the Database window toolbar
  DOUBLE-CLICK: Datasheet View in the New Table dialog box

**PRACTICE**
In this lesson, you create a new table in Datasheet view for storing supplier information.

*Setup:* Ensure that you have completed the previous lesson and that the My Business Database window is displayed.

**1** To create a table using Datasheet view, ensure that the *Tables* button is selected in the Objects bar and then do the following:
DOUBLE-CLICK: Create table by entering data
A blank Datasheet window appears with several field columns and blank records.

ACCESS

**2**  Let's begin by renaming the column headings in the field header area:
DOUBLE-CLICK: Field1
TYPE: `SupplierID`
DOUBLE-CLICK: Field2
TYPE: `Company`
DOUBLE-CLICK: Field3
TYPE: `Contact`
DOUBLE-CLICK: Field4
TYPE: `Phone`
PRESS: · `ENTER`
The cursor should now appear in the first field of the first record.

**3**  On your own, enter the records appearing in Figure 2.6.

**Figure 2.6**

Entering records in
Datasheet view

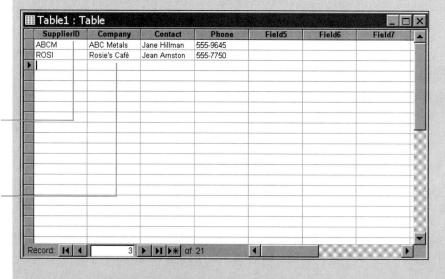

Specify the field names
by double-clicking and
then typing in the field
header area.

Enter sample records
so that Access can
determine the type of
data you want stored.

**4**  To save and name the new table structure:
CLICK: Save button (🖫) on the toolbar
TYPE: `Suppliers`  into the Save As dialog box
PRESS: `ENTER` or CLICK: OK

**5**  In the Alert dialog box that appears, Access offers to define a primary key for the table. A primary key holds a unique value for identifying, locating, and sorting records in a table. To accept the offer:
CLICK: Yes
After a few moments, Access displays the datasheet for the Suppliers table, complete with a new AutoNumber field in the left-hand column.

Close the Suppliers Datasheet window. You should now see the Suppliers table object in the Database window.

 Close the Database window.

**2.2 Self Check**    How do you specify the name of a field when creating a table in Datasheet view?

# 2.3  Using the Table Design View

If all of your database needs are satisfied by the templates found in the Database and Table Wizards, you are already on your way to developing robust desktop database applications. To unlock the real power behind Access, however, you must delve into the inner workings of an Access table structure. Using Design view, you create a table by specifying its properties, characteristics, and behaviors down to the field level. While this method requires the greatest understanding of database design, it is well worth the effort in terms of creating efficient custom table structures.

### 2.3.1  Creating a Table in Design View

**FEATURE**
Table Design view allows you to get down to the nuts and bolts of designing and constructing a table. In Design view, you create the table structure manually, specifying the field names, data types, and indexes. After some practice, you will find that this method affords the greatest power and flexibility in designing and modifying table objects.

**METHOD**
In the Database window, select the *Tables* button and then:
* DOUBLE-CLICK: Create table in Design view, or
* CLICK: New button (New) on the Database window toolbar
  DOUBLE-CLICK: Design View in the New Table dialog box

**PRACTICE**
In Design view, you create a new table structure in this lesson.

*Setup:* Ensure that there is no Database window displayed.

**1** To create a new database:
CLICK: New button (□) on the toolbar
CLICK: *General* tab
DOUBLE-CLICK: Database template (🗐)

**2** In the File New Database dialog box:
TYPE: **My Library** into the *File name* text box

**3** Using the Places bar or the *Save in* drop-down dialog box, select your personal storage location. Then, do the following:
CLICK: Create command button
The "My Library" Database window will appear.

**4** Because tables are the foundation for all your queries, forms, and reports, you need to create at least one table before creating any other database object. To add a new table to the database:
CLICK: New button (🗐New) on the Database window toolbar
The New Table dialog box appears as shown in Figure 2.7.

**Figure 2.7**

New Table dialog box

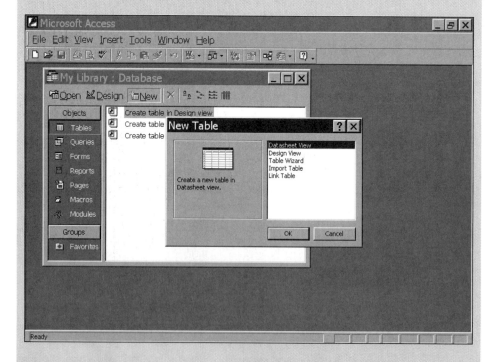

**5** The New Table dialog box offers an alternative to selecting a New Object shortcut in the list area of the Database window. To proceed:
DOUBLE-CLICK: Design View

**6** The table Design window, which is divided into a **Field Grid pane** and a **Field Properties pane**, appears in **Design view**. This window is used to add, delete, and rename fields for the table structure; set a field's data type; specify a field's properties or characteristics; and choose a primary key for organizing and sorting a table. The insertion point should now appear in the *Field Name* column. To define the first field in a table that will store information about the books you own:
TYPE: **BookID**
PRESS: ⎡TAB⎤ to move to the *Data Type* column
(*Note:* As with adding records, you may press ⎡TAB⎤ or ⎡ENTER⎤ to proceed from column to column.)

**7** By default, Access inserts "Text" as the data type for the BookID field. The data type you select determines the kind of values you can enter into the field. To view the other data type options, described further in Table 2.1, do the following:
CLICK: down arrow attached to the field
Your screen should now appear similar to Figure 2.8. (*CAUTION:* Although you can change the data type after you've entered data, you risk losing information if the data types aren't compatible.)

**Figure 2.8**

Displaying the data type options in Design view

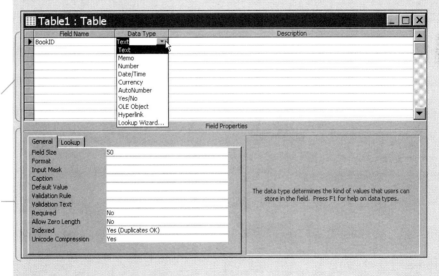

Use the Field Grid pane to define the fields that you want in the table.

Use the Field Properties pane to specify field characteristics, such as size and display format.

**Table 2.1**

Data Types

| Type | Description |
|---|---|
| Text | Alphanumeric data, up to 255 characters. Used for entering text and numbers that are not required for calculation, such as zip codes and phone numbers. |

*Continued*

**Table 2.1**
Data Types
*Continued*

| Type | Description |
| --- | --- |
| Memo | Alphanumeric data, up to 64,000 characters. Used to store notes, comments, or lengthy descriptions. |
| Number | Numeric data that are used to perform mathematical calculations. |
| Date/Time | Dates and times. |
| Currency | Numeric data with a leading dollar sign. Used to store and calculate monetary values. |
| AutoNumber | Numeric value that increments automatically. Used for assigning a unique value to a record, which makes it a fantastic *primary key* field. |
| Yes/No | Logical or Boolean values for toggling (turning on and off) yes/no or true/false results. |
| OLE Object | Object Linking and Embedding (OLE) field for storing objects (Excel worksheets and Word documents), graphics, or other binary data up to one gigabyte (GB) in size. |
| Hyperlink | Text or numbers stored as a hyperlink address. Used to store Web site addresses, also called URLs, such as http://www.mhhe.com/it. |
| Lookup Wizard | A link to another table or to a static list of values for inserting data into the current table. Selecting this option launches a wizard. |

**8** For the BookID field's data type:
SELECT: AutoNumber
PRESS: `TAB`

**9** The *Description* column allows you to store a helpful comment describing the contents of the field. This comment will also appear in the Status bar when you select the field in Datasheet view. To proceed:
TYPE: **Unique code generated by Access**
PRESS: `ENTER` to move to the next row

On you own, complete the Field Grid pane as displayed in Figure 2.9. Notice that the longer field names, such as PageCount, contain mixed case letters to enhance their readability. When finished, keep the table Design window displayed and proceed to the next lesson.

**Figure 2.9**

Completing the
Field Grid pane

Row Selection Area of
the Field Grid pane

| Field Name | Data Type | Description |
|---|---|---|
| BookID | AutoNumber | Unique code generated by Access |
| ISBN | Text | International Standard Book Number |
| Title | Text | Main cover title |
| AuthorSurname | Text | Author's last name |
| AuthorGiven | Text | Author's first name |
| Publisher | Text | Publisher's name |
| PubYear | Number | Year published (i.e., 2000) |
| PageCount | Number | Total number of pages |
| | | |

**In Addition**
**Field Naming Rules**

Access provides specific rules for naming fields in a table. First, names cannot exceed 64 characters in length. Second, names should not contain special symbols or punctuation, such as a period or exclamation point. And lastly, names cannot begin with a space and, in our opinion, should not contain spaces. Descriptive single word names are best.

## 2.3.2 Assigning a Primary Key

**FEATURE**
As you create a table structure, you need to specify a field (or fields) that will uniquely identify each and every record in the table. This field, called the **primary key**, is used by Access in searching for data and in establishing relationships between tables. Once a field is defined as the primary key, its datasheet is automatically indexed, or sorted, into order by that field. Access also prevents you from entering a duplicate or **null value** into a primary key field. An **AutoNumber** data type automatically increments as each new record is added to a table, making this data type one of the best choices for a primary key.

**METHOD**
In table Design view:
1. SELECT: the desired field using the row selection area
2. CLICK: Primary Key button (▧) on the toolbar, or
    CHOOSE: Edit, Primary Key

**PRACTICE**
You now assign a primary key field for the table created in the last lesson.

ACCESS

*Setup:* Ensure that you've completed the previous lesson and that the table Design window is displayed.

**1** To select a field for the primary key:
CLICK: row selector button for BookID
(*Hint:* Position the mouse pointer in the row selection area of the Field Grid pane and click the row selector button next to the BookID field.)

**2** To assign a primary key:
CLICK: Primary Key button (⌐🔑⌐)
Your screen should now appear similar to Figure 2.10.

**Figure 2.10**

Setting the primary key

The primary key icon appears in the field's row selector button.

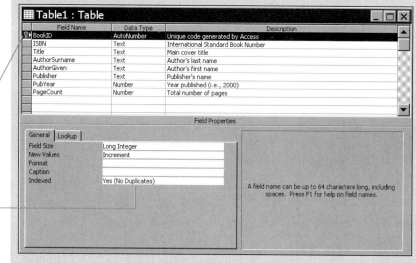

Notice that the field is indexed (sorted) and does not allow duplicate entries.

**3** Now that you've assigned the primary key, you can save the table structure. Do the following:
CLICK: Save button (🖫)

**4** In the Save As dialog box that appears:
TYPE: **Books**
CLICK: OK
Keep the table Design window displayed for use in the next lesson.

## 2.3.3 Defining and Removing Indexes

**FEATURE**
An **index**, like the primary key, is a special mechanism for dynamically organizing and ordering the data stored in a table. By defining indexes, you can speed up the search and sort operations for running queries and reports. However, you do not want to create indexes for all fields as this would slow down the common activities of adding and editing records. As a rule of thumb, just index the fields that you use frequently in searching for and sorting data, such as a Surname or Company Name field.

**METHOD**
To define an index in table Design view:
1.  SELECT: the desired field using the row selection area
2.  SELECT: *Indexed* text box in the Field Properties pane
3.  CLICK: down arrow attached to the *Indexed* text box
4.  SELECT: an indexing option

To remove an index in table Design view:
1.  CLICK: Indexes button (🗹) on the toolbar
2.  RIGHT-CLICK: the desired field's row selection button
3.  CHOOSE: Delete Rows

**PRACTICE**
In this lesson, you create two indexes to complement the primary key and remove an existing index that was created by Access.

*Setup:* Ensure that you've completed the previous lessons and that the Books table Design window is displayed.

**1** In the Books table, you will most likely search for a book based on its title or author. Therefore, let's create indexes for these fields. To begin:
SELECT: Title in the Field Grid pane

**2** Using the I-beam mouse pointer:
SELECT: *Indexed* text box in the Field Properties pane

**3** With the flashing insertion point in the *Indexed* text box, you may select an indexing option from the drop-down list box. To proceed:
CLICK: down arrow attached to the *Indexed* text box
Your screen should now appear similar to Figure 2.11.

ACCESS

**Figure 2.11**

Setting an index

Select a field by clicking its row selector button.

Display the indexing options by clicking the attached arrow.

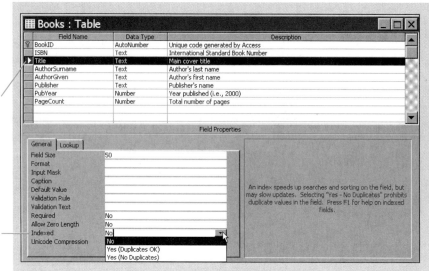

**4** Because you do not want to limit the possibility of duplicate entries (different authors may have written a similarly entitled book):
SELECT: Yes (Duplicates OK)

**5** Let's define another index for the table:
SELECT: AuthorSurname in the Field Grid pane
SELECT: *Indexed* text box in the Field Properties pane

**6** From the drop-down list attached to the *Indexed* text box:
SELECT: Yes (Duplicates OK)

**7** Save the table structure:
CLICK: Save button (🖫)
(*Note:* It's a good habit to save the table after each major change.)

**8** To display the associated indexes for the Books table:
CLICK: Indexes button (📄)
The Indexes window appears as shown in Figure 2.12.

**Figure 2.12**

Indexes window for the
Books table

List of indexes

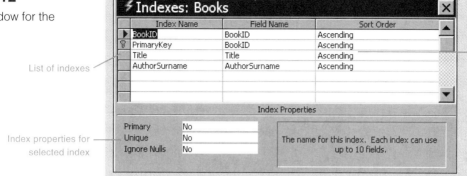

| Index Name | Field Name | Sort Order |
|---|---|---|
| BookID | BookID | Ascending |
| PrimaryKey | BookID | Ascending |
| Title | Title | Ascending |
| AuthorSurname | AuthorSurname | Ascending |

Sort order
(ascending or
descending)

Index Properties

Index properties for
selected index

| Primary | No |
| Unique | No |
| Ignore Nulls | No |

The name for this index. Each index can use
up to 10 fields.

**9** As illustrated in Figure 2.12, Access automatically creates indexes for fields that contain the letters "ID" in their names. The BookID field, for example, is the primary key but also the name of an index. To remove this index:
RIGHT-CLICK: BookID row selector button

**10** In the right-click menu that appears:
CHOOSE: Delete Rows
The BookID index is removed but the BookID primary key remains.

**11** Close the Indexes window.

**12** To clean up the Access work area, save and then close the table Design window. Lastly, close the My Library Database window.

ACCESS

**In Addition**
Setting Field
Properties

Every field in a table has a set of properties. A field property is a specific characteristic of a field or data type that enables you to provide greater control over how your data is entered, stored, displayed, and printed. Some common properties include *Field Size, Format, Decimal Places, Input Mask, Default Value, Required,* and *Indexed.* You set a field's properties using the Field Properties pane in the table Design window.

**2.3 Self Check**   What is an AutoNumber field? Why is it useful as a primary key?

# 2.4 Modifying a Table

A database is a dynamic entity. It isn't uncommon to witness the initial design requirements for a database change once it is set in front of users. Fortunately Access enables you to modify a table's structure quickly and efficiently. Adding, deleting, and changing field specifications in table Design view is similar to editing records in a datasheet. Nonetheless, you should not perform structural changes hastily. When you modify a table's structure, you also affect the forms and reports that are based on the table.

## 2.4.1 Inserting and Deleting Fields

**FEATURE**
After displaying a table structure in Design view, you can easily add and remove fields. Adding a field is as simple as entering a field name and data type on a blank row in the Field Grid pane. Removing a field deletes the field from the Field Grid pane, but also deletes all of the data that is stored in the field.

**METHOD**
To insert a field in table Design view:
1. SELECT: an empty row in the Field Grid pane
2. Type a field name, select a data type, and enter a description.

To delete a field in table Design view:
1. RIGHT-CLICK: row selector of the field you want to remove
2. CHOOSE: Delete Rows

**PRACTICE**
In this lesson, you insert and remove fields in an existing table structure.

*Setup:* Ensure that there is no Database window displayed.

**1** Open the database named ACC240, located in your Advantage student data files location.

**2** This database contains a single table, named Books, that is based on the table structure you created in the last module. To display the table in Datasheet view:
DOUBLE-CLICK: Books

**3** With the Datasheet window displayed:
CLICK: View–Design button (📖▾) on the toolbar
(*Note:* Although the toolbar button is named View, we include the mode name "–Design" for clarity.)

**4** Let's add a new field to the table structure that will store a reviewer's synopsis for each book. In the Field Grid pane:
CLICK: in the *Field Name* column of the next empty row
TYPE: **Synopsis**
PRESS: **TAB**

**5** Since the contents of the field will be entered mostly in paragraph form, select Memo as the field's data type:
CLICK: down arrow attached to the *Data Type* cell
SELECT: Memo
PRESS: **TAB**

**6** In the *Description* column:
TYPE: **Reviewer's synopsis or abstract**
PRESS: **ENTER**

**7** To insert a new field between two existing fields, right-click the desired row selector button and then choose the Insert Rows command. Similarly you can delete an existing field using the right-click menu. To demonstrate, let's remove the PageCount field:
RIGHT-CLICK: row selector button for PageCount
Your screen should now appear similar to Figure 2.13.

**Figure 2.13**
Displaying a field's
right-click menu

Right-click menu for
the PageCount field

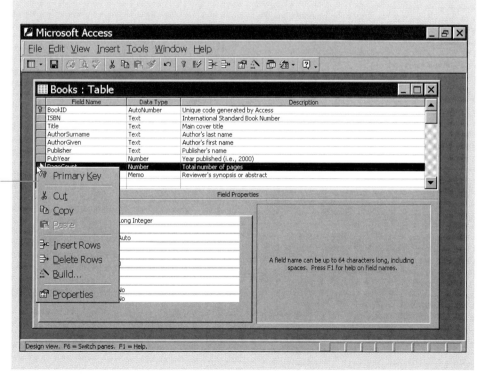

**8** From the right-click menu:
CHOOSE: Delete Rows

**9** To confirm that the deletion will also remove all the data in the field:
CLICK: Yes

**10** Let's save and then view the table:
CLICK: Save button (⊟)
CLICK: View–Datasheet button (▦▾)

**11** To enter a brief synopsis for the first record:
PRESS: `END`
TYPE: `Another thrilling novel about Soviet and American attempts to develop a Strategic Defense Initiative (SDI). A CIA undercover confidant named the Cardinal provides a steady stream of Soviet secrets. Once compromised, however, Jack Ryan and John Clark, an ex-Navy SEAL, are given the task of pulling the Cardinal to safety.`
PRESS: `ENTER`

**12** Close the Datasheet window.

## 2.4.2 Renaming and Moving Fields

**FEATURE**
In addition to modifying a table's structure, renaming and moving fields in Design view affects the display of a datasheet. You may have noticed that the columns in Datasheet view follow the field names and display order appearing in Design view. More importantly, however, you can speed up most database operations by moving frequently used fields (those used as primary keys or in indexes) to the top of a table structure.

**METHOD**
• To rename a field, edit the contents of the *Field Name* column as you would modify a cell entry in a datasheet.
• To move a field, click the field's row selector button and then drag it to the desired target location.

**PRACTICE**
You now practice renaming and moving fields in table Design view.

*Setup:* Ensure that the ACC240 Database window is displayed.

**1** To display the Books table object in Design view:
SELECT: Books in the list area
CLICK: Design button (☒Design) on the Database window toolbar

**2** Let's rename the Author fields. Using the I-beam mouse pointer:
CLICK: to the right of "AuthorSurname" in the *Field Name* column
The flashing insertion point should appear to the right of the name.

**3** To remove the "Surname" portion of the cell entry:
PRESS: **BACKSPACE** seven times

**4** TYPE: **Last**
PRESS: ⬇
The cell entry should now read "AuthorLast."

**5** To remove the "Given" portion of the current entry:
PRESS: **F2** (Edit mode)
PRESS: **BACKSPACE** five times
TYPE: **First**
PRESS: ⬇
The cell entry now reads "AuthorFirst."

**6** Let's move the ISBN field below the AuthorFirst field. To begin:
CLICK: row selector button for ISBN

**7** Using the arrow mouse pointer:
DRAG: row selector button for ISBN downward until a bold gridline appears below the AuthorFirst field

**8** Release the mouse button. Your screen should now appear similar to Figure 2.14.

**Figure 2.14**

Renaming and moving fields in table Design view

| Field Name | Data Type | Description |
|---|---|---|
| BookID | AutoNumber | Unique code generated by Access |
| Title | Text | Main cover title |
| AuthorLast | Text | Author's last name |
| AuthorFirst | Text | Author's first name |
| ISBN | Text | International Standard Book Number |
| Publisher | Text | Publisher's name |
| PubYear | Number | Year published (i.e., 2000) |
| Synopsis | Memo | Reviewer's synopsis or abstract |

**9** To save and then view the changes in Datasheet view:
CLICK: Save button (▣)
CLICK: View–Datasheet button (▦▾)
Notice that the field header area displays the new field names in the modified field order.

**10** Close the Datasheet window.

ACCESS

## 2.4.3 Printing a Table's Design Structure

**FEATURE**
Access provides a special tool called the **Documenter** that allows you to preview and print various design characteristics of your database objects, including a table's structure and field properties. This tool is especially useful when you are planning or revising a table's field specification.

**METHOD**
1. CHOOSE: Tools, Analyze, Documenter
2. CLICK: *Tables* tab
3. SELECT: the desired object or objects
4. CLICK: Options command button
5. SELECT: the desired options
6. CLICK: OK

**PRACTICE**
In this lesson, you prepare a documentation printout of the Books table.

*Setup:* Ensure that the ACC240 Database window is displayed.

**1** To launch the Access Documenter:
CHOOSE: Tools, Analyze, Documenter
The Documenter window appears as shown in Figure 2.15.

**Figure 2.15**

Documenter window

Click the check box to include an object in the Documenter's report

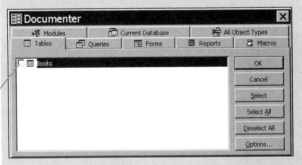

**2** To print the design structure for the Books table object, ensure that the *Tables* tab is selected and then:
SELECT: Books check box so that a "✔" appears

**3** To specify report options:
CLICK: Options command button
The Print Table Definition dialog box appears.

**4** For this example, let's specify that only the table structure is printed. In the *Include for Table* area, remove all of the selections so that no "✔" appears in any of the check boxes.

**5** In the *Include for Fields* area:
SELECT: *Names, Data Types, and Sizes* option button

**6** In the *Include for Indexes* area:
SELECT: *Names and Fields* option button
CLICK: OK

**7** To preview the report printout:
CLICK: OK

**8** On your own, move, size, and scroll the Object Definition window to appear similar to Figure 2.16.

**Figure 2.16**
Object Definition Window

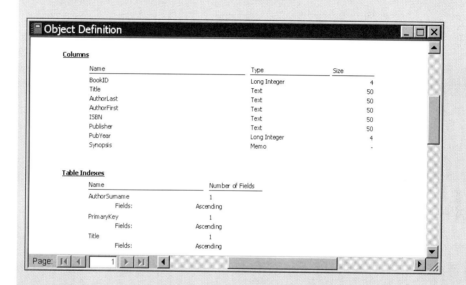

**9** To print the documentation report:
CLICK: Print button () on the toolbar

**10** Close the Object Definition window. Then, close the ACC240 Database window. Lastly, exit Microsoft Access.

**2.4 Self Check**   What happens to your table's data if you delete a field in table Design view?

ACCESS

# 2.5 Chapter Review

Access provides several tools to help novice users create new database applications. The Database Wizard offers a variety of professionally designed template solutions for common database problems. After you proceed through a few simple steps in the wizard, Access creates a comprehensive set of database objects, including tables, forms, and reports, that you can put to use immediately. If you prefer having more control, you can opt to create an empty database and then populate it with standard tables using the Table Wizard. Another straightforward method involves designing a table simply by entering data into a Datasheet window. And lastly, you can use Design view in order to develop a custom table object. In the table Design window, you add, delete, rename, move, and manipulate fields and indexes individually, in addition to specifying each field's properties and characteristics. In this chapter, you learned to design new database applications and to create and modify table objects.

## 2.5.1 Command Summary

Many of the commands and procedures appearing in this chapter are summarized in the following table.

| Skill Set | To Perform This Task . . . | Do the Following . . . |
| --- | --- | --- |
| **Working with Access** | Create a new empty database | CLICK: New button (□) <br> CLICK: *General* tab <br> DOUBLE-CLICK: Database template (▣) |
| | Create a comprehensive application using the Database Wizard | CLICK: New button (□) <br> CLICK: *Databases* tab <br> DOUBLE-CLICK: a database wizard (▣) |
| **Viewing and Organizing Information** | Switch from Datasheet view to Design view | CLICK: View – Design button (▣▾) |
| | Switch from Design view to Datasheet view | CLICK: View – Datasheet button (▣▾) |
| **Building and Modifying Tables** | Create a table using the Table Wizard | SELECT: *Tables* object button <br> DOUBLE-CLICK: Create table by using wizard |

*Continued*

| Skill Set | To Perform This Task . . . | Do the Following . . . |
|---|---|---|
| | Create a table in Datasheet view | SELECT: *Tables* object button<br>DOUBLE-CLICK: Create table by entering data |
| | Create a table in Design view | SELECT: *Tables* object button<br>DOUBLE-CLICK: Create table in Design view |
| | Save the table structure in Design view | CLICK: Save button (⊟) |
| | Assign a primary key in Design view | SELECT: the desired field<br>CLICK: Primary Key button (⬚) |
| | Add a new field in Design view | SELECT: an empty row in the Field Grid pane<br>TYPE: *the field information* |
| | Remove a field in Design view | RIGHT-CLICK: row selector for the desired field<br>CHOOSE: Delete Rows |
| | Move a field in Design view | DRAG: a field's row selector button to its new location |
| **Refining Queries** | Define an index in Design view | SELECT: the desired field<br>SELECT: an indexing option in the *Indexed* property text box |
| | Display the Indexes window | CLICK: Indexes button (⬚) |
| | Remove an index displayed in the Indexes window | RIGHT-CLICK: row selector for the desired Index field<br>CHOOSE: Delete Rows |
| **Using Access Tools** | Launch the Documenter utility | CHOOSE: Tools, Analyze, Documenter |

ACCESS

## 2.5.2 Key Terms

This section specifies page references for the key terms identified in this chapter. For a complete list of definitions, refer to the Glossary at the end of this learning guide.

AutoNumber, *p. 67*

Database Wizard, *p. 52*

Design view, *p. 64*

Documenter, *p. 76*

Field Grid pane, *p. 64*

Field Properties pane, *p. 64*

index, *p. 66*

null value, *p. 67*

primary key, *p. 67*

Table Wizard, *p. 59*

# 2.6  Review Questions

## 2.6.1  Short Answer

1. Name four Database Wizard templates that are available on your computer.
2. What is a switchboard?
3. Name the five steps to designing a better database.
4. Name three methods for creating a table in an Access database.
5. What are the two categories of Table Wizards?
6. What data storage types can be defined in a table structure?
7. What is the difference between the Text and Memo data types?
8. How does a primary key differ from an index?
9. When would you want to insert a row in a table structure?
10. Why must you be careful when changing a field's data type?

## 2.6.2  True/False

1. ____ In creating a new database, you select either the *General* or *Wizards* tab in the New dialog box.
2. ____ In the Database Wizard, the optional fields that you may select for inclusion appear in italic.
3. ____ The process of dividing related data into separate tables in order to reduce data redundancy is called *normalizing* your data.
4. ____ In Word and Excel, you can open multiple Database windows in the Access work area.

5. ＿＿ After selecting a sample table in the Table Wizard, you can specify only the fields that you want included in your new table.
6. ＿＿ In table Design view, you define the names of fields in the Field Grid pane and select data types in the Field Properties pane.
7. ＿＿ Field names cannot exceed 64 characters in length.
8. ＿＿ What you type into the *Description* column of the Field Grid pane appears in the Title bar of a table's Datasheet window.
9. ＿＿ Access prevents you from entering duplicate values into a primary key field.
10. ＿＿ You print a table's structure the same way that you print a table's datasheet.

## 2.6.3 Multiple Choice

1. In an application created using the Database Wizard, the main menu is presented as a ＿＿＿＿＿.
   a. form, called a *switchboard*
   b. report, called a *menu*
   c. table, called a *switchboard*
   d. query, called a *menu*

2. Which of the following is not a step presented in this chapter for designing a better database?
   a. Determine your input requirements.
   b. Test your database application.
   c. Create your tables using wizards.
   d. Determine your table structures.

3. You have the choice of either creating a table structure from scratch or using a(n) ＿＿＿＿＿ to lead you through the process.
   a. assistant
   b. coach
   c. relation
   d. wizard

4. Which data type would you use to store the price of an item within an inventory table?
   a. AutoNumber
   b. Currency
   c. Number
   d. Text

5.  Which data type would you use to store a phone number?
    a.  Currency
    b.  Memo
    c.  Number
    d.  Text

6.  What determines a table's sort order in a datasheet?
    a.  AutoNumber field
    b.  field order
    c.  index field
    d.  primary key

7.  To display a window showing the table's primary key and indexes:
    a.  CLICK: Indexes button (🖫)
    b.  CLICK: Primary Key button (🔑)
    c.  CLICK: View – Datasheet button (🖩)
    d.  CLICK: View – Design button (🗺)

8.  To delete a field in Design view, you right-click the field's selector button and choose the following command:
    a.  Delete Field
    b.  Delete Rows
    c.  Remove Field
    d.  Remove Rows

9.  You use this tool to generate a printout of a table's structure.
    a.  Analyzer
    b.  Designator
    c.  Documenter
    d.  Generator

10.  When printing a table's structure, you use this dialog box to specify the desired options.
     a.  Print Object Definition
     b.  Print Table Definition
     c.  Print Table Setup
     d.  Print Setup Definition

# 2.7  Hands-On Projects

### 2.7.1  World Wide Imports: New Employee Database

This exercise lets you practice creating a new database and adding a table using the Table Wizard.

1. Load Microsoft Access using the Windows Start menu.
2. To create a new database using the startup dialog box:
   CLICK: *Blank Access database* option button
   CLICK: OK command button
3. In the File New Database dialog box:
   TYPE: **World Wide Payroll** into the *File name* text box
4. Using the Places bar or the *Save in* drop-down dialog box, select your personal storage location. Then, do the following:
   CLICK: Create command button
5. To use the Table Wizard, ensure that the *Tables* button is selected in the Objects bar and then do the following:
   DOUBLE-CLICK: Create table by using wizard
6. You will now create a new table to store World Wide Imports' employee records. Do the following:
   SELECT: *Business* option button, if it is not already selected
   SELECT: Employees in the *Sample Tables* list box
7. Let's start by including all of the suggested fields:
   CLICK: Include All button (⏩)
8. Now let's remove an unnecessary field. First scroll to the end of the *Fields in my new table* list. Then do the following:
   SELECT: Photograph
   CLICK: Remove button (◄)
9. On your own, remove the Notes and OfficeLocation fields.
10. To complete the wizard and open the "Employees" table in Datasheet view:
    CLICK: Finish
11. Close the Datasheet window.
12. Close the Database window.

### 2.7.2  CyberWeb: Internet Accounts

In this exercise, you practice creating two new tables in an existing database.

1. Open the database file named ACC270. Ensure that the *Tables* button in the Objects bar is selected.
2. To create a new table in Datasheet view:
   DOUBLE-CLICK: Create table by entering data

ACCESS

3. To start, rename the column headings in the field header area:
   DOUBLE-CLICK: Field1
   TYPE: **City**
   DOUBLE-CLICK: Field2
   TYPE: **AreaCode**
   DOUBLE-CLICK: Field3
   TYPE: **DialUp**
   PRESS: ENTER

4. Now let's enter one record before saving the table:
   TYPE: **Arjuna**
   PRESS: TAB
   TYPE: **555**
   PRESS: TAB
   TYPE: **533-1525**

5. To save and name the new table structure:
   CLICK: Save button (■) on the toolbar
   TYPE: **Cities** into the Save As dialog box
   PRESS: ENTER or CLICK: OK

6. Access warns you that you have not yet defined a primary key. To have Access take care of this for you:
   CLICK: Yes

7. Close the Datasheet window.

8. Now let's create a second table:
   DOUBLE-CLICK: Create table in Design view

9. To define the fields in a table that will store information about CyberWeb's technical support personnel:
   TYPE: **SupportID**
   PRESS: TAB to move to the *Data Type* column
   SELECT: AutoNumber
   PRESS: TAB
   TYPE: **Code to identify Tech Support**
   PRESS: ENTER to move to the next row

10. On your own, add two more fields to the table. First, a "Name" field with a Text data type and the description "First and last name." Then, a "Local" field with a Number data type and the description "4-digit phone local."

11. To save the table structure, do the following:
    CLICK: Save button (■)

12. Enter a name for the new table:
    TYPE: **TechSupport**
    CLICK: OK

13. When Access offers to create a primary key:
    CLICK: Yes

14. Close the Datasheet window.

### ■ 2.7.3 Big Valley Mills: Forest Products

In this exercise, you add a primary key to an existing table and then modify its indexes.

*Setup*: Ensure the ACC270 Database window is displayed.

1. Ensure that the *Tables* button in the Objects bar is selected.
2. To display a table in Datasheet view:
   DOUBLE-CLICK: 273 Orders in the list area
3. To display the table in Design view:
   CLICK: View – Design button (⬚▾)
4. First, let's make the OrderNumber field the primary key of the table:
   CLICK: row selector button for OrderNumber
   CLICK: Primary Key button (⬚)
   Notice that a key icon appears in the row selector button.
5. To speed up search operations for looking up a particular salesperson, let's create an index for this field. To begin:
   SELECT: SalesRep in the Field Grid pane
6. Using the I-beam mouse pointer:
   SELECT: *Indexed* text box in the Field Properties pane
   CLICK: down arrow attached to the *Indexed* text box
7. From the drop-down list attached to the *Indexed* text box:
   SELECT: Yes (Duplicates OK)
8. To display all the indexes for the table:
   CLICK: Indexes button (⬚)
9. Let's remove the OrderDate index:
   RIGHT-CLICK: row selector button for OrderDate
   CHOOSE: Delete Rows
10. Close the Indexes window.
11. To save the table structure:
    CLICK: Save button (⬚)
12. Close the Datasheet window.

### ■ 2.7.4 Silverdale Festival: Contact List

In this exercise, you practice modifying the field structure of an existing table.

*Setup*: Ensure the ACC270 Database window is displayed.

1. To open the 274 Contacts table in Design view:
   SELECT: 274 Contacts in the list area
   CLICK: Design button (⬚Design) on the Database window toolbar

2. First, let's rename one of the fields. Using the I-beam mouse pointer:
   CLICK: to the right of "Contact" in the *Field Name* column

3. TYPE: **Name**
   PRESS: ⬇
   The cell entry should now read "ContactName."

4. You need to add a field to the table structure that stores the contact's email address. In the Field Grid pane:
   CLICK: in the *Field Name* column of the next empty row
   TYPE: **Email**
   PRESS: ⬇
   Notice that the Data Type field accepted the Text data type by default.

5. To delete a field using the right-click menu:
   RIGHT-CLICK: row selector button for Phone 2
   CHOOSE: Delete Rows

6. To confirm that the deletion will remove all of the data in the field:
   CLICK: Yes

7. Let's move the Phone 1 field below the Email field. To begin:
   CLICK: row selector button for Phone 1

8. Using the arrow mouse pointer:
   DRAG: row selector button for Phone 1 downward so that a bold gridline appears below the last field
   (*Note:* Remember to release the mouse button to drop the field.)

9. To save and then view the changes in Datasheet view:
   CLICK: Save button (🖫)
   CLICK: View–Datasheet button (🖳▾)
   Your screen should now appear similar to Figure 2.17.

10. Close the Datasheet window.

**Figure 2.17**

Modifying the structure of a table

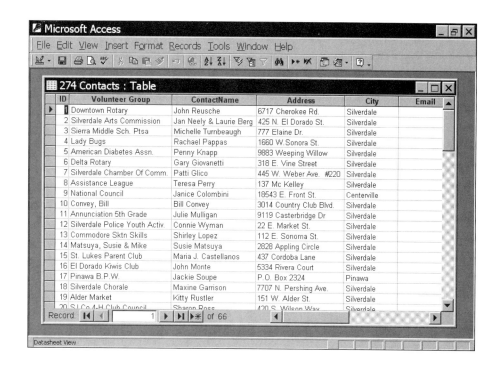

## 2.7.5   On Your Own: Office Mart Inventory

To practice making changes to a table's structure, open the 275 Inventory table in the ACC270 database. After changing to Design view, add a new field named Category between the existing Description and OnHand fields. Assign a data type of Number to the new field. Next, move the Reorder field so that it appears immediately after the OnHand field and then remove the SuggestedRetail field. To speed up your table search and sort operations, create an index for the Buyer field that allows duplicate entries. Finally, in the Indexes window, remove the extraneous index on ProductID that was created by Access. Make sure that you don't remove the primary key for this field. When you are finished, save the table changes and close the table Design window.

## 2.7.6   On Your Own: Sun Bird Resort

In this exercise, you practice creating a new table in the ACC270 database. If this database does not appear in the application window, open it now. Then, using Design view, add a new table named "Sun Packages" to the database. The table should contain the following fields, complete with data types and descriptions.

- *PackageID*: This field, which automatically increments by one each time a new record is added, contains a unique code that identifies each promotional package.
- *Description*: This text field stores the name of each package.
- *Price*: This field stores the suggested price in dollars for each package.
- *Nights*: This field stores the number of nights for accommodation.

Use the Documenter tool to print out the table's design structure. Then, close all windows and exit Microsoft Access.

# 2.8   Case Problems: Inland Transit

Having selected Microsoft Access, Mike Lambert, Inland's controller, focuses his attention on planning and designing a database. In order to reduce data redundancies, Mike splits the company information into three tables. The first table stores operational data for each truck in the fleet. The second table stores personnel data for each driver. The third and final table stores a detailed log of each delivery. Now Mike must launch Access, create a database structure, and initialize these tables.

In the following case problems, assume the role of Mike and perform the same steps that he identifies. You may want to re-read the chapter opening before proceeding.

1. To begin, Mike creates a new database from scratch. He names the database "Inland Transit" and then saves it to his *personal storage location*. Once the Database window appears, he proceeds to create the first table using the Table Wizard. After launching the wizard, Mike ensures that the *Business* option button is selected. He then scrolls the list of sample tables to find a suitable structure. From the list, Mike selects a table named "Assets" and then includes all of the fields for his new table. He then names the new table "Trucks" and lets Access set the primary key. Finally, Mike opens the table in Design view in order to rename three of the fields. In total, he changes "AssetID" to "TruckID," "AssetDescription" to "TruckDescription," and "AssetCategoryID" to "TruckCategoryID." He saves the changes to the table structure and closes the Trucks table.

2. Mike decides to create the second table in Datasheet view. After double-clicking the appropriate New Object shortcut, he renames the column headings in the empty datasheet to create the following fields:

- Name
- Address
- Phone
- Classification

   Mike saves the new table object as "Drivers" and lets Access define a primary key. Then, Mike uses Design view to rename the new ID field, which Access has added to the table structure, to "DriverID." And, lastly, he saves the table structure and then closes the table Design window.

3. For the third table, Mike uses Design view to create the structure shown in Figure 2.18. As shown in the screen graphic, Mike makes the TripID field the primary key. He saves the table as "Trips" and closes the table Design window. Using the Access Documenter tool, he prints out the Trips table structure for later review.

**Figure 2.18**

Creating a table structure in Design view

| Field Name | Data Type | Description |
|---|---|---|
| TripID | AutoNumber | Identifies the delivery |
| TruckID | Number | Identifies the truck |
| Date | Date/Time | Date of the trip |
| Destination | Text | Delivery destination |
| Miles | Number | Round trip mileage |
| DriverID | Number | Identifies the driver |
| LoadWeight | Number | Weight in pounds |

4. Later the same day, Mike realizes he needs to make a few structural changes to some of the tables. He begins by opening the Trips table in Design view and creating an index for the Destination field. Using the Indexes window, he removes the extra index on the TripID field that Access automatically created. After closing the Indexes window, Mike adds a new text field named "Pickup" between the Data and Destination fields. He saves the changes and closes the table Design window.

   For the Trucks table, Mike opens the table in Design view and deletes the DepartmentID and BarcodeNumber fields. He then moves the Make and Model fields to be the third and fourth fields respectively. Satisfied with the progress he has made in setting up Inland Transit's new database, Mike saves his changes and exits Microsoft Access.

# NOTES

# MICROSOFT ACCESS 2000
## *Organizing and Retrieving Data*

# CHAPTER
## THREE

# Chapter Outline

**3.1** Customizing Datasheet View

**3.2** Sorting and Finding Data

**3.3** Using Filters

**3.4** Creating a Simple Query

**3.5** Chapter Review

**3.6** Review Questions

**3.7** Hands-On Projects

**3.8** Case Problems

# Learning Objectives

After completing this chapter, you will be able to:

- Enhance the display and printing of a datasheet using fonts and special effects

- Sort the contents of a datasheet into ascending and descending order

- Find a record by entering search criteria and using wildcard characters

- Filter the records displayed in a datasheet using Filter For Input, Filter By Selection, and Filter By Form

- Create a query using the Simple Query Wizard

## Case Study

## Can-Do Rentals

Ellie Floyd is the office supervisor for Can-Do Rentals, a rental and lease company that specializes in landscaping and gardening equipment. As well as managing the administrative and inside sales staff, Ellie's responsibilities have been extended recently to cover the company's record-keeping. The owner and manager of Can-Do Rentals, Sal Witherspoon, knows that Ellie recently completed a course in Microsoft Access. Because much of the record-keeping data is already stored in a database, Sal asks Ellie to open the company's database using Access and peruse its contents. Sal wants Ellie to become well versed in its operation so that she can eventually take over the day-to-day management of the database.

In this session, you and Ellie learn how to enhance a Datasheet window, organize and sort records in a datasheet, filter information for display, and develop a simple query. All of these techniques enable you to better organize and retrieve information.

# 3.1 Customizing Datasheet View

Access provides numerous options for customizing the appearance, or layout, of a datasheet. Because a datasheet is only an image of the underlying table, you can manipulate the datasheet's column widths, row heights, and field order without affecting the table structure itself. Exceptions to this rule are when you rename or delete a column. These changes flow through to the structural level of the table. Once the table is customized to your satisfaction, save the layout changes by clicking the Save button (🖫) on the toolbar. Otherwise, the modifications are discarded when you close the Datasheet window.

**ACCESS**

### 3.1.1 Formatting a Datasheet

**FEATURE**
You enhance the display and printing of a datasheet by applying fonts and special effects. Any changes that you make affect the entire datasheet but do not affect other database objects such as forms and reports. After formatting the datasheet to suit your needs, remember to save the layout changes for displaying the datasheet thereafter.

**METHOD**
- CHOOSE: Format, Font to select font characteristics
- CHOOSE: Format, Datasheet to apply special visual effects
- CLICK: Save button (▣) to save the layout changes, or CHOOSE: File, Save from the menu

**PRACTICE**
In this lesson, you format and then save an existing datasheet to appear with a custom font, color, and background.

*Setup:* Ensure that Access is loaded. If you are launching Access and the startup dialog box appears, click the Cancel command button to remove the dialog box from the application window.

**1** Open the database file named ACC300, located in the Advantage student data files folder.

**2** To open the Courses table in Datasheet view:
DOUBLE-CLICK: Courses in the list area
The Courses Datasheet window appears in the work area.

**3** You can change the font characteristics of text displayed in a datasheet without affecting any other Datasheet window. To do so:
CHOOSE: Format, Font
The Font dialog box appears, as shown in Figure 3.1. In this one dialog box, you can change the font **typeface**, style, size, and text color.

**Figure 3.1**

Font dialog box

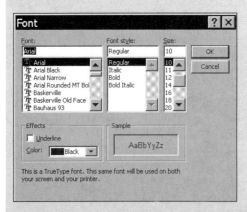

**4** In the Font dialog box, make the following selections:
SELECT: Times New Roman in the *Font* list box
SELECT: Regular in the *Font style* list box
SELECT: 12 in the *Size* list box
SELECT: Navy in the *Color* drop-down list box
Notice that the *Sample* area in the dialog box displays an example of the current selections.

**5** To accept the changes:
CLICK: OK
The Datasheet window is updated to display the font selections.

**6** You can also enhance a datasheet by formatting the window characteristics such as gridlines and its background matting. To do so:
CHOOSE: Format, Datasheet
The Datasheet Formatting dialog box in Figure 3.2 is displayed. Notice that the options selected in the screen graphic are the default settings for a Datasheet window.

**Figure 3.2**

Datasheet Formatting
dialog box

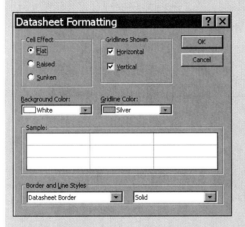

**7** After selecting a few options, you can better appreciate the resulting changes by viewing the *Sample* area of the dialog box. To begin:
SELECT: *Raised* option button in the *Cell Effect* area
Notice that this selection nullifies the other options in the dialog box—they are no longer available for selection.

**8** To specify other formatting enhancements, do the following:
SELECT: *Flat* option button in the *Cell Effect* area
SELECT: *Vertical* check box so that no "✔" appears
SELECT: Teal in the *Gridline Color* drop-down list box

**9** In the *Border and Line Styles* area of the dialog box:
SELECT: Horizontal Gridline in the leftmost drop-down list box
SELECT: Dots in the rightmost drop-down list box
CLICK: OK
The Datasheet window now appears with teal dots separating records in the datasheet as horizontal gridlines.

**10** To save the formatting changes to the datasheet:
CLICK: Save button (🖫) on the toolbar

ACCESS

## 3.1.2  Changing the Field Column Order

**FEATURE**
Access determines the column order displayed in a Datasheet window from the field order in the underlying table structure. You may want to modify the column order in order to display fields side by side or to perform a multiple-field sort operation. One way to change the column order is to modify the field order in table Design view. A less drastic and permanent method is to move fields by dragging their column headings in Datasheet view. This method does not affect the underlying table structure. Once the columns are positioned, you can save the field column order in the datasheet along with other customizing options.

**METHOD**
1.  SELECT: the desired column in the field header area
2.  DRAG: the column heading to its new location

**PRACTICE**
You now practice selecting and moving columns in a datasheet.

*Setup:* Ensure that you've completed the previous lesson and that the Courses Datasheet window is displayed.

**1**  Before moving fields in the datasheet, let's practice selecting columns and changing column widths. Do the following:
CLICK: CourseID in the field header area
Notice that the mouse pointer becomes a downward pointing arrow (↓) when positioned properly on the column heading. The entire column should now appear highlighted.

**2**  Using the horizontal scroll bar, scroll the window so that the last field column is visible:
CLICK: right scroll button (▶) until InstructorID appears

**3**  To change all of the columns in the datasheet at once:
PRESS: SHIFT and hold it down
CLICK: InstructorID in the field header area
All of the columns should now appear highlighted. (*Note:* Although not explicitly stated, you should release the SHIFT key after clicking on the InstructorID column heading.)

**4**  You can now update the columns to their best-fit widths. To do so:
CHOOSE: Format, Column Width
CLICK: Best Fit command button
PRESS: HOME to remove the highlighting

**5** Let's practice moving columns in the datasheet. Using the horizontal scroll bar, scroll the window so that both the Faculty and DeptHead field columns are visible.

**6** CLICK: DeptHead in the field header area

**7** Position the white arrow mouse pointer (⇧) over the field name. Then:
DRAG: DeptHead to the left so that the bold vertical gridline appears between the Faculty and MaxStudents field columns

**8** Release the mouse button to complete the move operation.

**9** To move two fields at the same time:
CLICK: Faculty in the field header area
PRESS: SHIFT and hold it down
CLICK: DeptHead in the field header area
Both columns should now appear highlighted.

**10** You will now reposition the two field columns. Position the mouse pointer on one of the selected column headings. Then:
DRAG: Faculty (or DeptHead) to the left so that the bold vertical gridline appears between Title and StartDate

**11** After releasing the mouse button:
PRESS: HOME to remove the highlighting
Your Datasheet window should now appear similar to Figure 3.3.

**12** Save the layout changes by clicking the Save (▣) button.

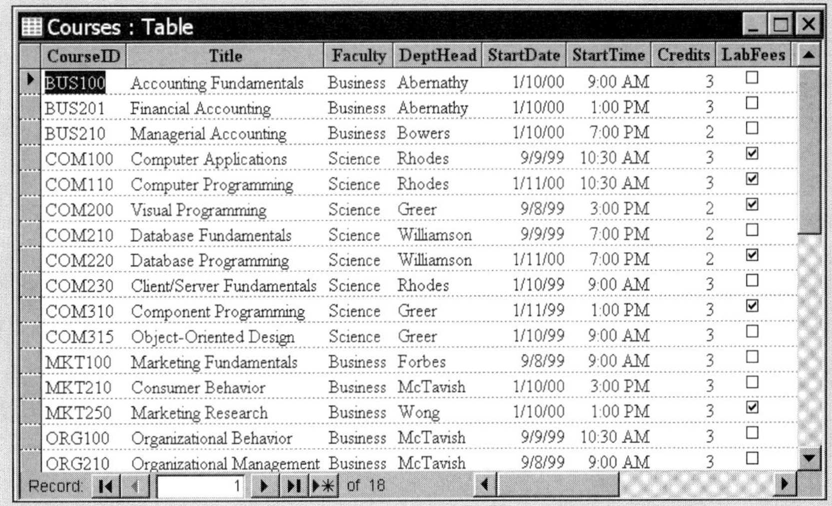

**Figure 3.3**

Changing the field column order

| CourseID | Title | Faculty | DeptHead | StartDate | StartTime | Credits | LabFees |
|---|---|---|---|---|---|---|---|
| BUS100 | Accounting Fundamentals | Business | Abernathy | 1/10/00 | 9:00 AM | 3 | ☐ |
| BUS201 | Financial Accounting | Business | Abernathy | 1/10/00 | 1:00 PM | 3 | ☐ |
| BUS210 | Managerial Accounting | Business | Bowers | 1/10/00 | 7:00 PM | 2 | ☐ |
| COM100 | Computer Applications | Science | Rhodes | 9/9/99 | 10:30 AM | 3 | ☑ |
| COM110 | Computer Programming | Science | Rhodes | 1/11/00 | 10:30 AM | 3 | ☑ |
| COM200 | Visual Programming | Science | Greer | 9/8/99 | 3:00 PM | 2 | ☑ |
| COM210 | Database Fundamentals | Science | Williamson | 9/9/99 | 7:00 PM | 2 | ☐ |
| COM220 | Database Programming | Science | Williamson | 1/11/00 | 7:00 PM | 2 | ☑ |
| COM230 | Client/Server Fundamentals | Science | Rhodes | 1/10/99 | 9:00 AM | 3 | ☐ |
| COM310 | Component Programming | Science | Greer | 1/11/99 | 1:00 PM | 3 | ☑ |
| COM315 | Object-Oriented Design | Science | Greer | 1/10/99 | 9:00 AM | 3 | ☐ |
| MKT100 | Marketing Fundamentals | Business | Forbes | 9/8/99 | 9:00 AM | 3 | ☐ |
| MKT210 | Consumer Behavior | Business | McTavish | 1/10/00 | 3:00 PM | 3 | ☐ |
| MKT250 | Marketing Research | Business | Wong | 1/10/00 | 1:00 PM | 3 | ☑ |
| ORG100 | Organizational Behavior | Business | McTavish | 9/9/99 | 10:30 AM | 3 | ☐ |
| ORG210 | Organizational Management | Business | McTavish | 9/8/99 | 9:00 AM | 3 | ☐ |

Courses : Table

Record: 1 of 18

## 3.1.3  Hiding and Unhiding Columns

**FEATURE**
Hiding columns in a datasheet is useful for temporarily restricting the display of sensitive data, such as salaries or commissions. You can also hide columns that you do not want displayed in a print-out or that you are thinking about deleting permanently. Whatever your reasons, Access makes it very easy to hide and unhide field columns in the Datasheet window.

**METHOD**
To hide a field column:
1.  SELECT: the desired column in the field header area
2.  CHOOSE: Format, Hide Columns

To unhide a field column:
1.  CHOOSE: Format, Unhide Columns
2.  SELECT: the desired columns in the Unhide Columns dialog box
3.  CLICK: Close command button

**PRACTICE**
In this lesson, you hide and unhide columns in the active datasheet.

*Setup:* Ensure that you've completed the previous lessons and that the Courses Datasheet window is displayed.

**1**  Let's assume that you've been asked to print out the Courses datasheet. However, the last three columns in this datasheet are for administrative eyes only and should not be included. Therefore, you must hide the last three field columns before printing. To begin:
PRESS: **END** to move the cursor to the last field column

**2**  Fortunately, the three columns, MaxStudents, MinStudents, and InstructorID, appear next to one another in the datasheet. To select the three columns:
CLICK: MaxStudents in the field header area
PRESS: **SHIFT** and hold it down
CLICK: InstructorID in the field header area
Remember to release the **SHIFT** key after you click InstructorID.

**3.** To hide the selected columns:
CHOOSE: Format, Hide Columns
The columns disappear from displaying in the Datasheet window, although the data remains safe in the table object.

**4.** To specify how the datasheet will now print:
CHOOSE: File, Page Setup
CLICK: *Page* tab
SELECT: *Landscape* option button
CLICK: OK

**5.** To preview the datasheet:
CLICK: Print Preview button (🔍) on the toolbar

**6.** Using the magnifying glass mouse pointer, zoom in and out on the page. Notice that the hidden columns are not displayed in the Print Preview window.

**7.** To return to the Datasheet window:
CLICK: Close on the toolbar

**8.** To unhide the columns:
CHOOSE: Format, Unhide Columns
The dialog box in Figure 3.4 appears.

**Figure 3.4**

Unhide Columns dialog box

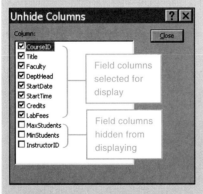

**9.** In the Unhide Columns dialog box:
SELECT: *MaxStudents* check box
SELECT: *MinStudents* check box
SELECT: *InstructorID* check box
CLICK: Close
Notice that the field columns are displayed once again.

**10.** Save the layout changes before proceeding.

## 3.1.4 Freezing and Unfreezing Columns

**FEATURE**

When navigating a large table with many columns, the Datasheet window scrolls automatically to accommodate your cursor movements. The farther right you move the cursor, the more the columns scroll away from view at the left. To more easily identify the current record, Access lets you freeze or lock in place one or more columns, such as a company name or product number, along the left edge of the Datasheet window.

**METHOD**

To freeze a field column:
1. SELECT: the desired column(s) in the field header area
2. CHOOSE: Format, Freeze Columns

To unfreeze columns in a datasheet:
CHOOSE: Format, Unfreeze All Columns

**PRACTICE**

In this lesson, you freeze and unfreeze columns in the active datasheet.

*Setup:* Ensure that you've completed the previous lessons and that the Courses Datasheet window is displayed.

**1** Let's use the right-click menu to freeze the CourseID field column from scrolling off the screen. Do the following:
RIGHT-CLICK: CourseID in the field header
A shortcut menu appears, as displayed to the right.

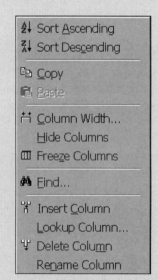

**2** To freeze the column in the Datasheet window:
CHOOSE: Freeze Columns

**3** Now remove the column highlighting:
PRESS: (HOME)
Notice that a vertical gridline appears between the CourseID and Title field columns.

**4** To demonstrate how you use the locked column feature:
PRESS: (END) to move to the last field column
The CourseID column remains displayed at the left side of the
window. This command is especially useful for displaying
datasheets that contain many fields.

**5** To unfreeze the CourseID column:
CHOOSE: Format, Unfreeze All Columns

**6** PRESS: (HOME)

**7** Save the layout changes and then close the Datasheet window.

**8** To prove that the formatting changes were indeed saved:
DOUBLE-CLICK: Courses in the list area
The Datasheet window appears with the same text and window
formatting and field column order.

**9** Close the Datasheet window.

**3.1 Self Check**    Name two reasons for changing the field column order in a datasheet.

ACCESS

# 3.2 Sorting and Finding Data

Information is *processed data*. This processing can take several forms,
from analyzing, organizing, and summarizing data to presenting data
in charts and reports. In this module, you learn how to sort and
arrange records into a precise and logical order. You also learn how
to find and replace data stored in a table.

## 3.2.1 Sorting Records in a Datasheet

**FEATURE**
Records are displayed in the order that they are originally entered
into a table, unless a primary key has been assigned. With a primary key, records are arranged and displayed according to the contents of the primary key field. Even so, Access allows you to
rearrange the records appearing in a datasheet into ascending (0 to
9; A to Z) or descending (Z to A; 9 to 0) order by the contents of
any field. Sorting is often your first step in extracting information
from raw data. It allows you to better organize records and makes
it easier to scan a datasheet for specific information.

**METHOD**
1. SELECT: the desired column(s) in Datasheet view
2. CLICK: Sort Ascending button (⬆) to sort in ascending order
   CLICK: Sort Descending button (⬇) to sort in descending order

**PRACTICE**
You now practice sorting a table into ascending and descending order.

*Setup:* Ensure that the ACC300 Database window is displayed.

**1** To open the Students table in Datasheet view:
DOUBLE-CLICK: Students in the list area
Notice that the datasheet is displayed in order by StudentID, the primary key field.

**2** To sort the records into order by surname:
CLICK: LastName in the field header area
CLICK: Sort Ascending button (⬆) on the toolbar
The datasheet is sorted immediately.

**3** Instead of selecting the entire field column, you can position the cursor in any cell within the desired column for sorting. To illustrate:
CLICK: in any cell within the Zip field column
CLICK: Sort Descending button (⬇)

**4** You can also sort a table by the contents of more than one column, if the columns are adjacent to one another. Access sorts a table starting with the values in the leftmost selected column and then, for identical values, the records are sorted further by the values appearing in the next column. For example, to sort the datasheet into order by Major and then surname, you must move the first or primary **sort key**, Major, to the left of the secondary sort key, LastName. To begin:
CLICK: Major in the field header area
DRAG: Major to the left of LastName
When you release the mouse button, the Major column appears between the StudentID and LastName columns.

**5** Now you must select both columns. Since the Major column is already highlighted, do the following:
PRESS: SHIFT and hold it down
CLICK: LastName in the field header area

**6** To sort the datasheet by the contents of these columns:
CLICK: Sort Ascending button (⬆)
The datasheet should appear similar to Figure 3.5.

**Figure 3.5**

Sorting by multiple
field columns

Primary sort key

Secondary sort key

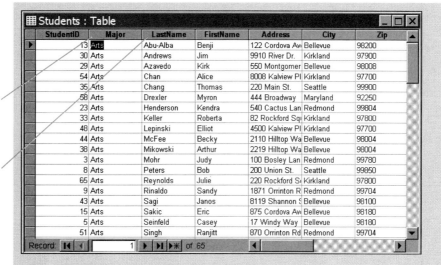

**7** Using the vertical scroll bar, scroll the window down to where
the values in the Major column change from Arts to Business.
Notice that the student records appear sorted by surname within
each major.

**8** Close the Datasheet window without saving the changes.

## 3.2.2 Performing a Simple Search

**FEATURE**
The Find command in Access lets you search an entire table for the
existence of a few characters, a word, or a phrase. With large tables,
this command is especially useful for moving the cursor to a particular record for editing. Most commonly, the Find command is
used to locate a single record. Filters and query objects, discussed
later in this chapter, are best used to locate groups of records meeting a specific criteria.

**METHOD**
1. SELECT: a cell in the field column you want to search
2. CLICK: Find button (🔍) on the toolbar, or
   CHOOSE: Edit, Find
3. SELECT: desired search options

**PRACTICE**
In this lesson, you attempt to find data appearing in a datasheet.

*Setup:* Ensure that the ACC300 Database window is displayed.

ACCESS

**1** Open the Students table in Datasheet view.

**2** Finding data is much easier when the datasheet is sorted by the field in which you want to perform a search. To begin:
PRESS: ➡ to move the cursor to the LastName field column
CLICK: Sort Ascending button (⬇)

**3** Let's find the record for Jimmy Kazo:
CLICK: Find button (🔍) on the toolbar

**4** In the Find and Replace dialog box that appears:
TYPE: **Kazo** in the *Find What* combo box
Notice that the LastName field already appears selected in the *Look In* drop-down list box, as shown in Figure 3.6.

**Figure 3.6**

Find and Replace dialog box:
*Find* tab

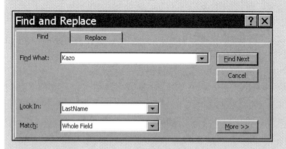

**5** To proceed with the search:
CLICK: Find Next
The cursor moves down the column and stops on the first occurrence of "Kazo." (*Note*: The Find and Replace dialog box does not disappear. Therefore, it may be necessary to drag the dialog window out of the way by its Title bar in order to view the selected record.)

**6** You can continue the search for more entries for Kazo:
CLICK: Find Next
A dialog box appears stating that no more matches were found.

**7** To end the search:
CLICK: OK in the dialog box
CLICK: Cancel in the Find and Replace dialog box

**8** To move the cursor back to the first record:
PRESS: CTRL + HOME

## 3.2.3 Specifying Search Patterns

**FEATURE**
Using the Find command, you can specify several options to control how a search is performed. You can also use **wildcard characters** to help locate words for which you are unsure of the spelling. These wildcards are also useful in defining search criteria for filters and queries.

**METHOD**
- Use the question mark (?) in place of a single character. For example, the search pattern "??S?" matches ROSI and DISC.
- Use the number symbol (#) in place of a single number. For example, the search pattern "##9" matches 349 and 109.
- Use the asterisk (*) to represent a group of characters. For example, the search pattern "Sm*" yields entries beginning with the letters "Sm," such as Smith, Smythe, and Smallwood. You can also use the asterisk in the middle of a search pattern.

**PRACTICE**
You now practice using wildcards in building search criteria.

*Setup:* Ensure that you've completed the previous lesson and that the Students datasheet is displayed.

**1** Your objective in this lesson is to find all the students who live on Bush Street. To begin, select the Address column:
CLICK: Address in the field header area

**2** CLICK: Find button (M)

**3** In the Find and Replace dialog box:
TYPE: **\*Bush\***
Notice that the existing value, Kazo, in the combo box is replaced by the new entry. This search criteria tells Access to find all occurrences of the word Bush anywhere within a cell entry.

**4** To begin the search:
CLICK: Find Next
The cursor moves to record number 47.

**5** To continue the search:
CLICK: Find Next to move the cursor to record number 53
CLICK: Find Next to move the cursor to record number 55
CLICK: Find Next
A dialog box appears stating that the search item was not found.

**6** To accept the dialog box and proceed:
CLICK: OK

**7** To cancel the search and return to the top of the datasheet:
CLICK: Cancel
PRESS: (CTRL) + (HOME)

## 3.2.4 Performing a Find and Replace

**FEATURE**
The Replace command in Access lets you perform a global find and replace operation to update the contents of an entire table. Using the same process as Find, you enter an additional value to replace all occurrences of the successful match. Replace is an excellent tool for correcting spelling mistakes and updating standard fields, such as telephone area codes.

**METHOD**
1.   SELECT: a cell in the field column you want to search
2.   CHOOSE: Edit, Replace
3.   SELECT: desired search and replace options

**PRACTICE**
You now practice using the Find and Replace feature.

*Setup:* Ensure that you've completed the previous lesson and that the Students datasheet is displayed.

**1** In the next few steps, you will replace the word "Science" in the Major field column with the word "CompSci." To begin:
CLICK: Major in the field header area

**2** To proceed with the find and replace operation:
CHOOSE: Edit, Replace

**3** On the *Replace* tab of the Find and Replace dialog box:
TYPE: Science in the *Find What* combo box
PRESS: ⎡TAB⎤
TYPE: CompSci in the *Replace With* combo box
Your dialog box should now appear similar to Figure 3.7

**Figure 3.7**
Find and Replace
dialog box: *Replace* tab

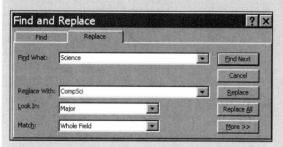

**4** If you want to check the values you are about to replace, click the Replace command button to proceed one change at a time. If, however, you want to change all of the values in a single step, do the following:
CLICK: Replace All

**5** A confirmation dialog box appears:
CLICK: Yes to accept and remove the dialog box
CLICK: Cancel to remove the Find and Replace dialog box

**6** Close the Datasheet window without saving the changes.

ACCESS

**In Addition**
**Finding Spelling**
**Mistakes**
You can check the spelling of entries in a datasheet in the same way that you spell-check a word processing document. With the Datasheet window displayed, click the Spelling button () on the toolbar. A dialog box appears for each word that the Spelling Checker does not recognize or believes to be misspelled. You can correct the spelling, ignore the entry, or add the word to a custom dictionary.

**3.2 Self Check**    How do you perform a sort operation using more than one field column?

# 3.3  Using Filters

A **filter** is a technique that limits the display of records in a table using a simple matching criterion. Similar to a pasta strainer that lets water through but not the pasta, a filter allows only some records to pass through for display. Filtering is an excellent way to find a subset of records to work with that match a particular value or range of values. There are several methods available for filtering records in a table: **Filter For Input, Filter By Selection, Filter Excluding Selection,** and **Filter By Form.** In this module, you learn how to define, apply, and remove filters.

## 3.3.1  Filtering For Input

**FEATURE**

Filtering displays a subset of records from a table. The **Filter For Input** method allows you to specify which records are let through. To apply this filter, you display a field's right-click shortcut menu and then type a value into the Filter For: text box. The datasheet is filtered by finding matches to this value in the current field. You may return to viewing all of the records at any time by clicking the Apply/Remove Filter button ([▽]).

**METHOD**

1. RIGHT-CLICK: any cell in the desired field column
2. CHOOSE: Filter For:
3. TYPE: *filter criteria*

**PRACTICE**

In this lesson, you use the Filter For Input method to apply a filter.

*Setup:* Ensure that the ACC300 Database window is displayed.

**1** Open the Students table in Datasheet view.

**2** Let's apply a filter to the datasheet that displays only those students with a last name beginning with the letter "S." Do the following:
RIGHT-CLICK: Stedman in the LastName field column
Your screen should now appear similar to Figure 3.8.

**Figure 3.8**

Choosing the Filter
For Input command

**3** CHOOSE: Filter For:
A flashing insertion point should appear in the adjacent text box.

**4** In the Filter For: text box:
TYPE: **s***
PRESS: **ENTER**
The datasheet (Figure 3.9) displays eight of the original 65 records.

**Figure 3.9**

A filtered datasheet

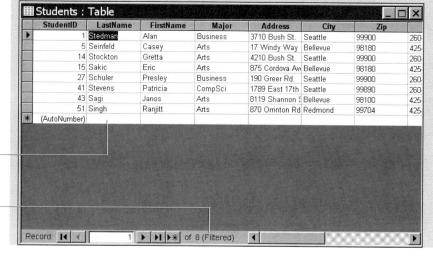

Displays only those students with a last name beginning with "s"

Displays only the filtered results

**5** Once filtered, you can sort the resulting subset of records using the appropriate toolbar buttons. To sort the filtered records:
CLICK: Sort Ascending button (⊞)
The datasheet now appears sorted by surname.

**6** The Apply/Remove Filter button (☒) on the toolbar acts as a toggle to turn on and off the current or active filter. To illustrate:
CLICK: Remove Filter button (☒)

**7** To reapply the last filter:
CLICK: Apply Filter button (☒)
Notice that this toolbar button changes names depending on its toggle status.

**8** Close the Datasheet window without saving the changes.

## 3.3.2 Filtering By Selection

**FEATURE**
Using the **Filter By Selection** method, you apply a filter based on a selected value from the datasheet. The selection may be an entire cell's contents or only a portion of the entry. Likewise, you use the **Filter Excluding Selection** method to display only those records that do not match the selected value.

**METHOD**
To apply a Filter By Selection:
1.  SELECT: all or part of an existing field entry
2.  CLICK: Filter By Selection button (☒), or
    CHOOSE: Records, Filter, Filter By Selection

To apply a Filter Excluding Selection:
1.  SELECT: all or part of an existing field entry
2.  CHOOSE: Records, Filter, Filter Excluding Selection

**PRACTICE**
In this lesson, you use the Filter By Selection method to apply a filter.

*Setup:* Ensure that the ACC300 Database window is displayed.

**1**  Open the Students table in Datasheet view.

**2**  To display only those students living in the city of Redmond:
DOUBLE-CLICK: "Redmond" in any cell of the City field column

**3**  To create a filter based on the selected text:
CLICK: Filter By Selection button (⊠)
A subset of 10 records is displayed in the Datasheet window.

**4**  To remove the filter:
CLICK: Remove Filter button (▽)

**5**  To display only those students who are <u>not</u> taking Arts as their major:
DOUBLE-CLICK: "Arts" in any cell of the Major field column
CHOOSE: Records, Filter, Filter Excluding Selection
A subset of 42 records is displayed in the Datasheet window.

**6**  To remove the filter:
CLICK: Remove Filter button (▽)

**7**  To display only those students living in Seattle and taking Comp-Sci as their major, you apply more than one filter to the datasheet. To begin:
DOUBLE-CLICK: "CompSci" in any cell of the Major field column
CLICK: Filter By Selection button (⊠)
A subset of 20 records is displayed.

**8**  Without removing the filter:
DOUBLE-CLICK: "Seattle" in any cell of the City field column
CLICK: Filter By Selection button (⊠)
Now a subset of 11 records is displayed. These records match the criteria specified in the previous two filter selections.

**9**  To continue, let's filter out those students who live on Greer Road:
DOUBLE-CLICK: "Greer" in any cell of the Address field column
CLICK: Filter By Selection button (⊠)
Four students who live on Greer Road in Seattle are taking CompSci as their major.

**10**  Close the Datasheet window without saving the changes.

ACCESS

### 3.3.3  Filtering By Form

**FEATURE**
For more detailed filtering operations, you use the **Filter By Form** method to set multiple criteria. Unlike Filter For Input or Filter By Selection, a blank datasheet row appears in which you can enter or select the desired criteria. Once you have defined a filter, Access enables you to save it as a query object in the Database window.

**METHOD**
To apply a Filter By Form:
1.  CLICK: Filter By Form button (▤), or
    CHOOSE: Records, Filter, Filter By Form
2.  Enter the desired filtering criteria.
3.  CLICK: Apply/Remove Filter button (▽)

To save a Filter By Form as a Query:
1.  Display the Filter By Form window.
2.  CLICK: Save As Query button (▥)

**PRACTICE**
In this lesson, you use the Filter By Form method to apply a filter.

*Setup:* Ensure that you've completed the previous lesson and that the Students datasheet is displayed.

**1**  Open the Students table in Datasheet view.

**2**  To use the Filter By Form method for filtering a datasheet:
CLICK: Filter By Form button (▤) on the toolbar
Your screen should now appear similar to Figure 3.10.

**Figure 3.10**

Creating a filter
using Filter By Form

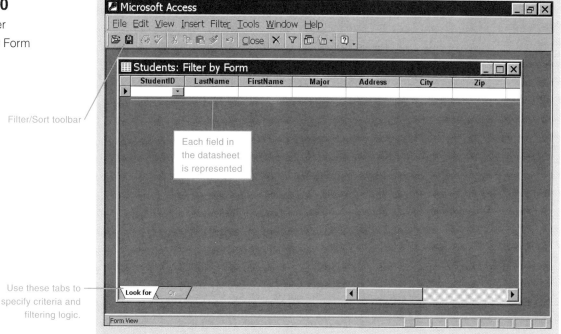

Filter/Sort toolbar

Each field in
the datasheet
is represented

Use these tabs to
specify criteria and
filtering logic.

**3** Let's display only those students living in Kirkland who are taking Arts as their major. To begin:
CLICK: Major cell once, immediately below the field header area
Notice that a down arrow appears next to the cell. You use this arrow to access a drop-down list of unique values taken from the datasheet.

**4** CLICK: down arrow attached to the Major field
SELECT: Arts from the list of three values
The search criteria "Arts" is entered into the cell.

**5** To specify the city criteria:
CLICK: City cell once
CLICK: down arrow attached to the City field
SELECT: Kirkland from the list of five values

**6** To apply the filter and display the results:
CLICK: Apply Filter button (🟰)
A subset of six records is displayed.

**7** To save this filter as a query object:
CLICK: Filter By Form button (🖼)
CLICK: Save As Query button (🖫)
TYPE: **Kirkland Arts Students**
PRESS: ENTER or CLICK: OK

ACCESS

**8** To specify a new filter:
CLICK: Clear Grid button (⊠)
The existing filter criteria are removed from the window.

**9** In addition to selecting values from the drop-down list, you can type values into the Filter By Form window. To illustrate, let's display only those students with a last name starting with the letter "m:"
CLICK: LastName cell once
TYPE: m*
CLICK: Apply Filter button (▽)
A subset of seven records is displayed.

**10** Close the Datasheet window without saving the changes.

**11** In the Database window:
CLICK: *Queries* button in the Objects bar
DOUBLE-CLICK: Kirkland Arts Students in the list area
A datasheet displaying the filtered results appears, as shown in Figure 3.11.

**12** Close the Datasheet window and then:
CLICK: *Tables* button in the Objects bar

**Figure 3.11**

Displaying a query object created using Filter By Form

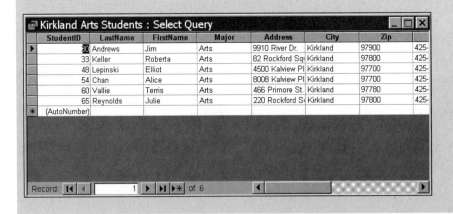

**3.3 Self Check**   In a personnel table, how would you display a subset of those employees working in the Accounting department?

# 3.4  Creating a Simple Query

A query is a question that you ask of your database, such as "How many customers live in Chicago?" or "What is the average age of employees in XYZ Corporation?" Using queries, you can prepare, view, analyze, and summarize your data. The results of a query may also be used when presenting data in forms and reports. And lastly, you can use special queries to perform advanced updating routines in your database.

Although similar to filters, queries differ in several significant areas. While both filters and queries allow you to retrieve and display a subset of records, queries also allow you to display data from multiple tables, control which fields display and in what order they appear, and perform calculations on selected field values. In addition, filters provide a temporary view of a subset of records while queries are saved as independent database objects. Use the following as a guideline—you *find* a record, *filter* a table, and *query* a database.

## 3.4.1  Creating a Query Using the Query Wizard

**FEATURE**

The **Simple Query Wizard** is a step-by-step tool that helps you retrieve data from one or more tables in a database. Unfortunately, the wizard does not allow you to specify search criteria or sort parameters. The type of query object created by the wizard is known as a **select query,** since you use it to select data for display. The results of the query are listed in a Datasheet window, sometimes referred to as a **dynaset.** Other types of queries include action queries for updating, adding, and deleting records in a database and parameter queries for accepting input from users.

**METHOD**

In the Database window, select the *Queries* button and then:
- DOUBLE-CLICK: Create query by using wizard, or
- CLICK: New button (New) on the Database window toolbar
  DOUBLE-CLICK: Simple Query Wizard in the New Query dialog box

**PRACTICE**

You now use the Simple Query Wizard to extract data from two tables for display in a single Datasheet window.

*Setup:* Ensure that the ACC300 Database window is displayed.

ACCESS

**1** The options for creating a new query object are similar to the options for creating a new table object. You can start from scratch in query Design view or get helpful guidance from wizards. In the next few steps, you use the Simple Query Wizard to create a query. To begin:
CLICK: *Queries* button in the Objects bar

**2** To launch the Simple Query Wizard:
DOUBLE-CLICK: Create query by using wizard
The dialog box in Figure 3.12 appears.

**Figure 3.12**

Simple Query Wizard
dialog box

Select a table in
order to specify
fields for display.

Select fields for
display in the query.

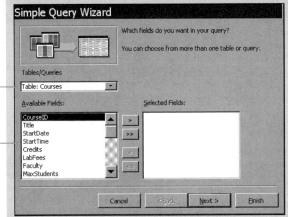

**3** In order to display a listing of courses along with the instructor's name, you must select fields from two tables. To begin, ensure that "Table: Courses" is selected in the *Tables/Queries* drop-down list box.

**4** In the *Available Fields* list box:
SELECT: CourseID
CLICK: Include button ( ▸ )
SELECT: Title
CLICK: Include button ( ▸ )

**5** Now select a new table:
SELECT: Table: Instructors in the *Tables/Queries* drop-down list box
Notice that there are new fields displayed in the associated list box.

**6** In the *Available Fields* list box:
SELECT: LastName
CLICK: Include button ( ▸ )
SELECT: FirstName
CLICK: Include button ( ▸ )

**7** To proceed to the next step in the wizard:
CLICK: Next >

**8** Now let's name the query:
TYPE: **Course Listing Query**
CLICK: Finish
Your screen should appear similar to Figure 3.13. Data in the first two columns is taken from the Courses table and data in the last two columns is taken from the Instructors table.

**9** Close the Datasheet window for the Course Listing Query. Then, close the ACC300 Database window. And, lastly, exit Microsoft Access.

**Figure 3.13**

Creating a query using the Simple Query Wizard

| CourseID | Title | LastName | FirstName |
|---|---|---|---|
| COM200 | Visual Programming | Kitching | Cheralyn |
| ORG100 | Organizational Behavior | Kitching | Cheralyn |
| ORG300 | Executive Decision Making | Kitching | Cheralyn |
| BUS100 | Accounting Fundamentals | Jaimeson | Aaron |
| BUS201 | Financial Accounting | Jaimeson | Aaron |
| COM100 | Computer Applications | Neumann | Mindy |
| BUS210 | Managerial Accounting | Kunicki | Kenyon |
| COM210 | Database Fundamentals | Kunicki | Kenyon |
| ORG210 | Organizational Management | Kunicki | Kenyon |
| ORG220 | Strategic Planning | Kunicki | Kenyon |
| COM110 | Computer Programming | Harris | Robert |
| COM220 | Database Programming | Huber | Tessa |
| COM230 | Client/Server Fundamentals | Cortez | Anna |

Course Listing Query : Select Query

Record: 1 of 18

**ACCESS**

**In Addition**
Specifying Search
Criteria in Queries

Querying a database involves more than limiting its display to specific fields. Using query Design view, you can create and modify queries to extract records from tables that meet a given criterion. You can also adjust the sorting order and perform calculations.

**3.4 Self Check** Name one way that a query's dynaset may differ from a table's datasheet.

# 3.5  Chapter Review

One of the primary advantages of using a computerized database is the ability to manipulate, retrieve, and display information quickly and easily. But making your information pleasing to read requires the ability to format and customize the results. Fortunately, you can spice up your datasheets by applying fonts, styles, and special effects. You can also improve your efficiency in working with a datasheet by moving, hiding, and freezing field columns in Datasheet view.

To help you turn raw data into information, the Sort, Find, and Filter commands enable you to organize, locate, and highlight records in a table. You can also use filters to limit the display of records in a table and queries to ask questions of your database. In addition to being able to draw data from multiple tables, queries enable you to specify complex search criteria and sort parameters. Queries are powerful database objects and the sole subject of more advanced chapters.

## 3.5.1  Command Summary

Many of the commands and procedures appearing in this chapter are summarized in the following table.

| Skill Set | To Perform This Task . . . | Do the Following . . . |
| --- | --- | --- |
| **Viewing and Organizing Information** | Enhance the text displayed in a datasheet using fonts and colors | CHOOSE: Format, Font |
| | Enhance the background and appearance of a Datasheet window | CHOOSE: Format, Datasheet |
| | Change the field column order in a datasheet | SELECT: the desired column<br>DRAG: its column heading into position |
| | Hide a field column in a datasheet | SELECT: the desired column<br>CHOOSE: Format, Hide Columns |
| | Unhide field columns in a datasheet | CHOOSE: Format, Unhide Columns<br>SELECT: the columns to unhide |
| | Freeze or lock a field column into place in a datasheet | SELECT: the desired column<br>CHOOSE: Format, Freeze Columns |

*Continued*

| Skill Set | To Perform This Task . . . | Do the Following . . . |
|---|---|---|
| | Unfreeze all of the locked columns in a datasheet | CHOOSE: Format, Unfreeze All Columns |
| | Save modifications and layout changes made to a datasheet | CLICK: Save button (🖫), or CHOOSE: File, Save |
| | Sort a field column in a datasheet into ascending order | SELECT: the desired column CLICK: Sort Ascending button (🔼) |
| | Sort a field column in a datasheet into descending order | SELECT: the desired column CLICK: Sort Descending button (🔽) |
| | Find or locate a value or record in a datasheet | CLICK: Find button (🔍), or CHOOSE: Edit, Find |
| | Replace an existing value in a datasheet with a new value | CHOOSE: Edit, Replace |
| | Filter a datasheet using the Filter For Input method | RIGHT-CLICK: a cell in the desired column CHOOSE: Filter For: TYPE: *a filter criteria* |
| | Filter a datasheet using the Filter By Selection method | SELECT: a datasheet entry CLICK: Filter By Selection button (▽) |
| | Filter a datasheet using the Filter Excluding Selection method | SELECT: a datasheet entry CHOOSE: Records, Filter, Filter Excluding Selection |
| | Filter a datasheet using the Filter By Form method | CLICK: Filter By Form button (📋) SELECT: the desired criteria |
| | Toggle a filter on or off | CLICK: Apply/Remove Filter button (▽) |
| | Saves the criteria entered using Filter By Form as a query object | CLICK: Save As Query button (📄) |
| | Create a query using the Simple Query Wizard | SELECT: *Queries* object button DOUBLE-CLICK: Create query by using wizard |

ACCESS

### 3.5.2 Key Terms

This section specifies page references for the key terms identified in this chapter. For a complete list of definitions, refer to the Glossary at the end of this learning guide.

dynaset, *p. 115*                         select query, *p. 115*

filter, *p. 108*                          Simple Query Wizard, *p. 115*

Filter By Form, *p. 108*                  sort key, *p. 102*

Filter By Selection, *p. 108*             typeface, *p. 94*

Filter Excluding                          wildcard characters, *p. 105*
Selection, *p. 108*

Filter For Input, *p. 108*

# 3.6   Review Questions

### 3.6.1  Short Answer

1. Name the three *Cell Effect* options for formatting a datasheet.
2. What command allows you to lock one or more columns of a datasheet in place? Name two ways to execute this command.
3. What are the two primary options for sorting a list?
4. What are wildcards? Provide an example of how they are used.
5. Name four methods for filtering records in a table.
6. When would you use the Find command rather than applying a filter?
7. How do the Filter For Input and Filter By Selection methods differ?
8. When would you apply a filter rather than creating a query?
9. What are two limitations of the Simple Query Wizard?
10. What type of query is created by the Simple Query Wizard? What are two additional types of queries?

### 3.6.2  True/False

1. _____ You can change the color of a datasheet's background.
2. _____ In Datasheet view, click Save (▤) to save your editing changes and click Save Layout (▦) to save your formatting changes.
3. _____ To sort a datasheet by more than one column, you must first ensure that the columns are positioned next to one another.

4.  _____ Once you have filtered a datasheet, you can then sort the results using the appropriate toolbar buttons.
5.  ____ The search criteria **\*osf\*** would match "Microsoft."
6.  _____ The search criteria **?crosof?** would match "Microsoft."
7.  _____ You invoke the Filter Excluding Selection method by selecting text in a datasheet and then clicking a toolbar button.
8.  _____ When viewing a table's data in Datasheet view, a filter can be used to limit the display of records in the active datasheet.
9.  _____ When viewing a table's data in Datasheet view, a query can be used to limit the display of records in the active datasheet.
10. _____ You find a record, filter a table, and query a database.

## 3.6.3  Multiple Choice

1.  In the Datasheet Formatting dialog box, which of the following is not an option in the *Border and Line Styles* drop-down list box:
    a.  Datasheet Border
    b.  Datasheet Underline
    c.  Horizontal Gridline
    d.  Vertical Gridline

2.  Which of the following is not an option for customizing a Datasheet window?
    a.  Freeze one column
    b.  Hide one column
    c.  Change one row's height
    d.  Change one column's width

3.  Which of the following is not a command that is selectable from a field column's right-click menu?
    a.  Hide Columns
    b.  Unhide Columns
    c.  Freeze Columns
    d.  Sort Descending

4.  The process of restricting the display of records in a table to those matching a particular criterion is called:
    a.  filtering
    b.  restricting
    c.  sifting
    d.  sorting

5. Which of the following is not a type of filter method described in this chapter?
   a. Filter By Example
   b. Filter By Form
   c. Filter By Selection
   d. Filter For Input

6. What is the name of the Access tool that simplifies the process of creating a query object?
   a. Database Wizard
   b. Simple Filter Wizard
   c. Simple Query Wizard
   d. Table Wizard

7. A collection of records matching the parameters of a query is sometimes called a:
   a. dynaset
   b. field
   c. table
   d. query

8. Which of the following criteria returns only those cities beginning with the letter "B?"
   a. =B
   b. B*
   c. B?
   d. B#

9. Which of the following criteria returns the name "Jones" as a match?
   a. *ne*
   b. J??nes
   c. J#s
   d. ?ne*

10. Which of the following statements is false?
   a. A filter operation limits records displayed in a datasheet.
   b. A query operation returns a Datasheet window of results.
   c. A sort operation modifies the natural order of data in a table.
   d. A find operation that is successful moves the cursor to the record.

# 3.7   Hands-On Projects

 ### 3.7.1   World Wide Imports: Customer Table

In this exercise, you enhance the appearance of a datasheet by applying fonts and specifying background special effects.

*Setup:* Ensure that Access is loaded. If you are launching Access and
the startup dialog box appears, click the Cancel command button to
remove the dialog box from the application window.

1. Open the database file named ACC370. Ensure that the *Tables*
   button in the Objects bar is selected.
2. To open a table in Datasheet view:
   DOUBLE-CLICK: 371 Customers in the list area
3. Let's change the font that is used to display the data. First,
   open the Font dialog box using the menu:
   CHOOSE: Format, Font
4. In the Font dialog box, make the following selections:
   SELECT: Courier New in the *Font* list box
   SELECT: Bold in the *Font style* list box
   SELECT: 11 in the *Size* list box
   SELECT: Maroon in the *Color* drop-down list box
   CLICK: OK
   The Datasheet window is modified to display using the new
   settings.
5. Now let's change the appearance of the datasheet's
   background:
   CHOOSE: Format, Datasheet
6. In the Datasheet Formatting dialog box:
   SELECT: *Raised* option button in the *Cell Effect* area
   CLICK: OK
7. To move the SalesRep column so that it appears beside the
   CustomerID field:
   CLICK: SalesRep in the field header area
8. Position the white arrow mouse pointer (⬉) over the field
   name. Then:
   DRAG: SalesRep to the left so that the bold vertical gridline
   appears between the CustomerID and CustomerName field
   columns
   (*Hint:* Remember to release the mouse button to drop the col-
   umn into place.)
9. Finally, let's adjust some of the column widths:
   CLICK: CustomerName in the field header area
   PRESS: (SHIFT) and hold it down
   CLICK: City in the field header area
   Three columns should now appear selected.

10. To resize the three selected columns to their best-fit widths:
CHOOSE: Format, Column Width
CLICK: Best Fit command button
PRESS: (HOME) to remove the highlighting
Your Datasheet window should now appear similar to Figure 3.14.
11. Save the layout changes by clicking the Save (🖫) button.
12. Close the Datasheet window.

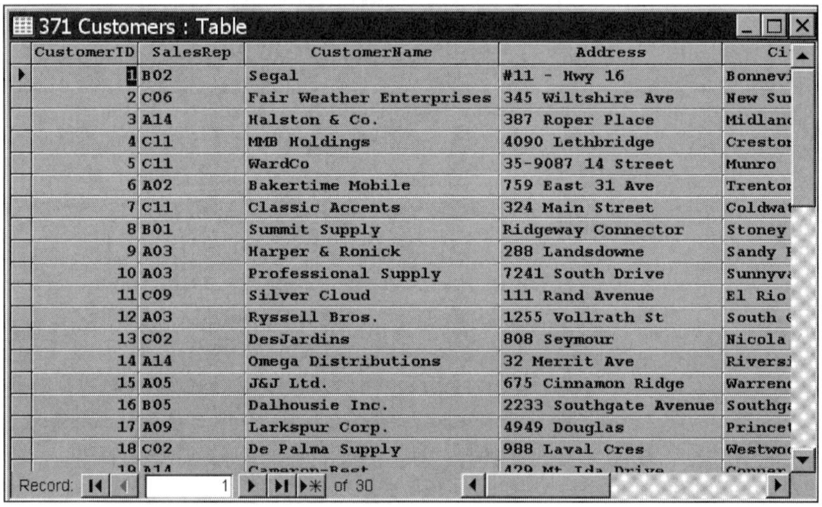

**Figure 3.14**

Applying fonts and background effects to a datasheet

## 3.7.2 CyberWeb: Internet Accounts

You now practice customizing a datasheet using the Freeze, Hide, and Sort commands.

*Setup*: Ensure the ACC370 Database window is displayed.

1. Ensure that the *Tables* button in the Objects bar is selected and then:
DOUBLE-CLICK: 372 Internet Accounts in the list area
2. First, let's freeze a column in the datasheet so that it is always visible when you scroll the window. Do the following:
CLICK: Username in the field header
CHOOSE: Format, Freeze Columns
Notice that the column is moved to the far left of the Datasheet window.
3. To demonstrate the effect of freezing the Username column:
PRESS: (END) to move to the last field column
Notice that the Username column remains visible.
4. To unfreeze the column:
PRESS: (HOME) to move to the first column
CHOOSE: Format, Unfreeze All Columns

5.  PRESS: ⟨END⟩ to move the cursor to the last field column
    Notice that the column is no longer locked into position.
6.  In order to hide the last two columns, you must first select
    them:
    CLICK: Amount in the field header area
    PRESS: ⟨SHIFT⟩ and hold it down
    CLICK: BillingType in the field header area
7.  To hide the selected columns:
    CHOOSE: Format, Hide Columns
    The Amount and BillingType columns are hidden from view
    but are not removed from the table.
8.  To sort the records in the datasheet by city:
    CLICK: City in the field header area
    CLICK: Sort Ascending button (🔼) on the toolbar
    The records are grouped together into sorted order by the
    value appearing in the City field.
9.  To preview what the datasheet looks like when sent to the
    printer:
    CLICK: Print Preview button (🔍) on the toolbar
10. On your own, use the magnifying glass mouse pointer to
    zoom in and out on the Print Preview window.
11. To close the Print Preview window:
    CLICK: Close command button in the toolbar
12. To unhide the columns:
    CHOOSE: Format, Unhide Columns
13. In the Unhide Columns dialog box:
    SELECT: *Amount* check box
    SELECT: *BillingType* check box
    CLICK: Close
14. Save the layout changes by clicking the Save (💾) button.
15. Close the Datasheet window.

### 3.7.3  Big Valley Mills: Forest Products

In this exercise, you sort data using more than one column and practice using the Find and Replace commands.

*Setup*: Ensure the ACC370 Database window is displayed.

1.  Open the 373 Products table for display in Datasheet view.
2.  You now perform a sort operation that orders the table by
    Category and then by ProductCode within each category. To
    begin:
    CLICK: Category in the field header area
    DRAG: Category field column to the left of ProductCode
3.  To sort by category and then by product code:
    SELECT: Category and ProductCode field columns
    CLICK: Sort Ascending button (🔼) on the toolbar

4. Now let's find all of the products made from birch wood:
   PRESS: ➡ two times to move to the Species field column
   CLICK: Find button (🔍) on the toolbar

5. In the Find and Replace dialog box that appears:
   TYPE: **birch** in the *Find What* combo box
   CLICK: Find Next
   (*Note:* By default, the Find command is not case-sensitive.)

6. Use the Find Next button to determine if there are any other products made from birch. When you are finished, close the Find and Replace dialog box.

7. You now use the Replace command to replace all occurrences of the code "Dim." in the Category column with the code "Dimension:"
   PRESS: (CTRL) + (HOME) to move to the first field in the table
   CHOOSE: Edit, Replace

8. On the *Replace* tab of the Find and Replace dialog box:
   TYPE: **Dim.** in the *Find What* combo box
   PRESS: (TAB)
   TYPE: **Dimension** in the *Replace With* combo box
   CLICK: Replace All command button

9. When Access asks you to confirm the replacement:
   CLICK: Yes command button
   CLICK: Cancel to remove the Find and Replace dialog box

10. Close the datasheet without saving your changes.

## 3.7.4 Silverdale Festival: Contact List

You now use the Filter For Input and Filter By Selection methods to display only those records that match a specific criterion.

*Setup*: Ensure the ACC370 Database window is displayed.

1. Open the 374 Contacts table for display in Datasheet view.

2. To begin, you apply a filter so that only the records containing the word "Club" in the VolunteerGroup field column are displayed. Using the I-beam mouse pointer:
   RIGHT-CLICK: the first cell in the VolunteerGroup field column

3. In the right-click or shortcut menu that appears:
   CHOOSE: Filter For:
   TYPE: ***club*** in the Filter For: text box
   PRESS: (ENTER)
   How many groups have "Club" as part of their name?

4. To remove the *club* filter:
   CLICK: Remove Filter button (▽)

5. To display only those groups based in the city of Pinawa:
   DOUBLE-CLICK: "Pinawa" in any cell of the City field column
   CLICK: Filter By Selection button (▿)

6. On your own, remove the current filter and use the Filter By Selection method to display only those groups from the city of Centerville. Then remove the filter so that all records are displayed.

7. Now let's use the Filter Excluding Selection method to view all groups from outside the city of Silverdale. First, select the value to exclude:
   DOUBLE-CLICK: "Silverdale" in any cell of the City field column

8. To exclude all the records containing Silverdale in the city column:
   CHOOSE: Records, Filter, Filter Excluding Selection
   Your screen should now appear similar to Figure 3.15.

**Figure 3.15**

Using the Filter Excluding Selection method

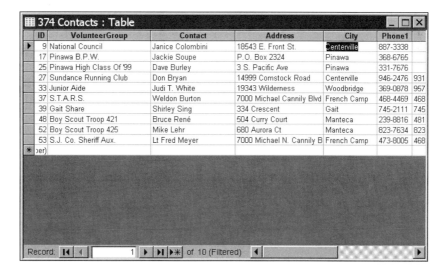

| ID | VolunteerGroup | Contact | Address | City | Phone1 | |
|----|----------------|---------|---------|------|--------|---|
| 9 | National Council | Janice Colombini | 18543 E. Front St. | Centerville | 887-3338 | |
| 17 | Pinawa B.P.W. | Jackie Soupe | P.O. Box 2324 | Pinawa | 368-6765 | |
| 25 | Pinawa High Class Of 99 | Dave Burley | 3 S. Pacific Ave | Pinawa | 331-7676 | |
| 27 | Sundance Running Club | Don Bryan | 14999 Comstock Road | Centerville | 946-2476 | 931 |
| 33 | Junior Aide | Judi T. White | 19343 Wilderness | Woodbridge | 369-0878 | 957 |
| 37 | S.T.A.R.S. | Weldon Burton | 7000 Michael Cannily Blvd | French Camp | 468-4469 | 468 |
| 39 | Gait Share | Shirley Sing | 334 Crescent | Gait | 745-2111 | 745 |
| 48 | Boy Scout Troop 421 | Bruce René | 504 Curry Court | Manteca | 239-8816 | 481 |
| 52 | Boy Scout Troop 425 | Mike Lehr | 680 Aurora Ct | Manteca | 823-7634 | 823 |
| 53 | S.J. Co. Sheriff Aux. | Lt Fred Meyer | 7000 Michael N. Cannily B | French Camp | 473-8005 | 468 |

9. To remove the filter:
   CLICK: Remove Filter button (▽)

10. Close the datasheet without saving your changes.

## 3.7.5  On Your Own: Office Mart Inventory

You now practice organizing, retrieving, and manipulating data in the Datasheet window. Open the 375 Inventory table in the ACC370 database. Perform the following database tasks:

- Using the Find and Replace command, change all records with a Supplier code of "G06" to "J11".
- Use the Filter By Form method to display only those records with a Supplier of "J11" and a Buyer of "02".
- Format the Datasheet window to display using a new and larger font.
- Hide the Reorder column.
- Adjust the widths of the remaining columns so that no data is truncated.
- Move the Supplier column so that it appears as the first field.
- Sort the datasheet by the OnHand amount so that the record with the largest amount is at the top of the datasheet.

When you are finished, preview and then print a copy of the Datasheet window. Lastly, close the datasheet without saving your changes.

## 3.7.6  On Your Own: Sun Bird Resort

You now create a query object using the Simple Query Wizard. The objective of using a query in this exercise is to display data from two tables in the database. To begin, select the *Queries* button in the Objects bar and then launch the Simple Query Wizard. From the 376 Guides table, include the GuideNumber and Guide fields. From the 376 Patrons table, include the Guest, Hometown, and State fields. In the next step of the wizard, save the query as "Guides and Guests Query" and then open the query to view the results (Figure 3.16).

**Figure 3.16**

Displaying the results of a select query

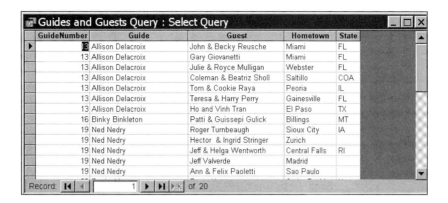

Before printing the dynaset, enhance the datasheet by applying formatting commands and preview the contents of the Datasheet window. Then, save the layout changes and close the datasheet. Lastly, close the Database window and exit Microsoft Access.

# 3.8 Case Problems: Can-Do Rentals

For the past week or so, Ellie Floyd, the office supervisor at Can-Do Rentals, has been familiarizing herself with the table objects in the company's Access database. Feeling confident that she now understands the nature of the table structures, she informs the owner, Sal Witherspoon, that she is ready to begin. Glad for the opportunity to escape the office, Sal provides Ellie with some afternoon work.

In the following case problems, assume the role of Ellie and perform the same steps that she identifies. You may want to re-read the chapter opening before proceeding.

1. To begin, Sal informs Ellie that he needs a formatted printout of Can-Do's equipment inventory. The data is stored in a table object named Equipment in the ACC380 database. While Sal thinks up other tasks for Ellie, she jots down a note to herself that Sal prefers all of his business correspondence and reports to appear using a 12-point Times New Roman font. She plans on opening the table in Datasheet view, applying the new font choice, and then removing the vertical gridlines from the Datasheet window. Just then Sal added to his preferences. In addition to hiding the DataPurchased field column, Sal wants the Cost column to be positioned as the last column in the datasheet. Ellie makes an additional note to preview the datasheet to ensure that the proper fields are hidden and positioned correctly. After printing the datasheet for Sal's review, Ellie closes it without saving the changes.

2. Next on his list, Sal asks Ellie to make some corrections to data stored in the Rentals table. She opens the datasheet and then sorts it into CustomerID sequence. Using the Find command, she locates the record for CustomerID 41. She changes the rental start date to 5/23/00 and the number of rental days to three (3). Then Ellie uses the Filter By Selection method to display and print only the records that have a status of "Active." After removing the filter, she uses the Find and Replace command to change any records that have a value of zero in the Days field to the minimum rental of one day. She closes the Datasheet window without saving the changes.

3. Before he leaves for the afternoon, Sal provides a list of questions for Ellie about Can-Do's customer base. To answer the questions, she must find, filter, and/or query the database. Using these filters, Ellie answers the following questions:

   • Which customers are not eligible for a discount, as determined by a zero value in the Discount field?
   • How many customers living in Pike Mountain have an account?
   • Which customer accounts are eligible for a discount of 10% on their rentals?
   • How many customers are from outside the city of Kelly?

4. Finally, Ellie uses the Simple Query Wizard to create a query that displays data from all three tables. She includes the following fields in the query and then saves it as "Customer Rentals Query."

| Table | Field |
| --- | --- |
| Customers | Name |
| Rentals | StartDate |
| Rentals | Days |
| Rentals | Status |
| Equipment | Description |

When the results are displayed, Ellie applies some formatting options, adjusts the column widths, and prints the Datasheet window. Then she closes all of the open windows, including ACC380, and exits Microsoft Access.

# NOTES

# NOTES

# MICROSOFT ACCESS 2000
## *Presenting and Managing Data*

## CHAPTER
### FOUR

# Chapter Outline

# Learning Objectives

After reading this chapter, you will be able to:

- Create new forms and reports using the AutoForm and AutoReport wizards

- Create new forms and reports using the Form and Report Wizards

- Navigate and edit data using a form

- Preview and print reports from the Database window

- Create a mailing labels report using the Label Wizard

- Rename, copy, and delete database objects

- Compact and repair a database file

## Case Study

# Lagniappe, Inc.

Janice Marchant is the western regional sales representative for Lagniappe, Inc., a New Orleans manufacturer of stylish travel gear. Although she has only worked for the company a short time, she enjoys the job and the challenges it presents. Janice works from her home in San Francisco with a notebook computer and fax machine, but meets once a month with the national sales manager, John Lucci. Like all of the sales representatives at Lagniappe, Janice is responsible for tracking sales to the company's preferred clientele using Microsoft Access. Now that she's getting the hang of entering data in Datasheet view, Janice wants to add a few form objects to facilitate data entry and enable her to focus on one customer at a time. She must also create and submit monthly reports listing the items that were sold and who purchased them. This information helps Lagniappe's management team forecast demand levels and predict next season's sale figures.

In this chapter, you and Janice learn to create forms to help you input data and to use reports to produce professional-looking printouts and Web pages. In addition to creating forms and reports using the Auto-Form and AutoReport Wizards, you employ the Form and Report Wizards for better controlling the layout of information. You also save a report as an HTML document and print out standard mailing labels. Lastly, you learn how to manage the database objects you create and how to compress an Access database file to improve performance and efficiency.

# 4.1 Creating a Simple Form

An alternative to working with numerous records in a datasheet is to focus your attention on a single record at a time using a form. Forms can also be customized to display multiple records and to link with data stored in other tables. Some forms that you may find useful in your database applications include data entry forms that resemble their paper counterparts, switchboard forms that provide menus of choices, and custom dialog boxes that gather input from users. Forms serve many purposes in Access and can enhance the productivity of both novice and expert users. In this module, you learn to create forms using the Access **form wizards.**

## 4.1.1   Creating a Form Using the AutoForm Wizards

**FEATURE**

An **AutoForm Wizard** provides the fastest and easiest way to create a new form. Requiring minimal information from you, the wizard analyzes a table's field structure, designs and builds the form, and then displays it in a **Form window**. There are actually three wizards from which to choose. First, the Columnar AutoForm Wizard displays data from one record in a single column, with each field appearing on a row. The Tabular AutoForm Wizard arranges data in a table format, with field labels as column headings and each row representing a record. Similarly, the Datasheet AutoForm Wizard creates a form of rows and columns resembling a datasheet. If you choose to create an AutoForm by clicking the New Object button ([🗐▾]), Access creates a columnar form based on the open or selected table or query.

**METHOD**

To create a columnar form quickly:
1.   SELECT: a table or query object in the Database window
2.   CLICK: New Object: AutoForm button ([🗐▾])

To create a form using an AutoForm Wizard:
1.   SELECT: *Forms* button in the Objects bar
2.   CLICK: New button ([🗐New]) on the Database window toolbar
3.   SELECT: a table or query from the drop-down list box
4.   DOUBLE-CLICK: an AutoForm Wizard

**PRACTICE**

In this lesson, you create forms using the New Object button and the Tabular AutoForm Wizard.

*Setup:* Ensure that Access is loaded. If you are launching Access and the startup dialog box appears, click the Cancel command button to remove the dialog box from the application window.

**1**   Open the database file named ACC400, located in the Advantage student data files folder.

**2**   To have Access create a form automatically, ensure that the *Tables* button is selected in the Objects bar and then:
SELECT: Books in the table list area
(*Hint:* You do not need to open the Books table. Click once on the table object so that it appears highlighted.)

**3** Once a table (or query) is selected:
CLICK: New Object: AutoForm button (▣▾)
(*Hint:* The New Object button contains a list of wizards used in creating database objects. If the AutoForm image is not currently displayed on the face of the New Object button, click the attached down arrow to show the drop-down list appearing to the right. Then select the AutoForm command.)

| | |
|---|---|
| ▣ | AutoF_o_rm |
| ▣ | AutoR_e_port |
| ▣ | _T_able |
| ▣ | _Q_uery |
| ▣ | _F_orm |
| ▣ | _R_eport |
| ▣ | _P_age |
| ▣ | M_a_cro |
| ▣ | _M_odule |
| ▣ | _C_lass Module |

**4** After a few seconds, Access displays the columnar form shown in Figure 4.1. Notice that each field appears on a separate row in the Form window. You learn how to navigate and manipulate data in a form later in this module.

**Figure 4.1**

A columnar form displays data for a single record

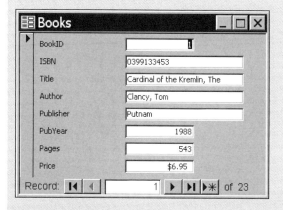

**5** To close the form:
CLICK: its Close button (☒)

**6** Access informs you that the form object has not yet been saved. To proceed with saving and naming the form:
CLICK: Yes command button
TYPE: **Books — Columnar**
PRESS: (ENTER) or CLICK: OK

**7** The new form object is stored in the *Forms* category of the Database window. To view the object:
CLICK: *Forms* button in the Objects bar
DOUBLE-CLICK: Books - Columnar in the list area
The Form window appears as displayed previously.

**8** Close the Form window.

ACCESS

**9** To create a form using a tabular layout:
CLICK: *Tables* button in the Objects bar
SELECT: Books in the list area

**10** To access the other AutoForm wizards:
CLICK: down arrow attached to the New Object button (▣⁞)
CHOOSE: Form
The New Form dialog box appears, as shown in Figure 4.2.

**Figure 4.2**

New Form dialog box

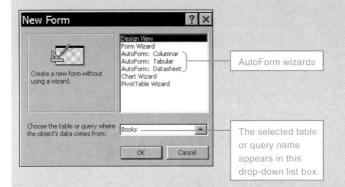

**11** To create a new form using the Tabular AutoForm Wizard:
DOUBLE-CLICK: AutoForm: Tabular

**12** After a few moments, the tabular form in Figure 4.3 is displayed. Close the Form window without saving the changes.

**Figure 4.3**

A tabular form displays numerous records at the same time

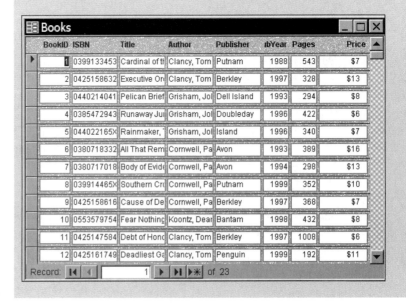

## 4.1.2 Creating a Form Using the Form Wizard

**FEATURE**

The Form Wizard provides a step-by-step approach to creating a form from scratch. Even experienced users find using the Form Wizard a handy way to get started building a new form. Whereas an AutoForm Wizard generates a complete form using a set of default values, the Form Wizard allows you to pick and choose options from a series of dialog boxes. Using the Form Wizard, you specify what fields to display on the form and how you want it to look. The layout options include Columnar, Tabular, Datasheet, and Justified. The columnar and justified layouts are suited to viewing a single record at a time and work especially well for tables with few fields. The tabular and datasheet layouts are best used to display numerous records at a time.

**METHOD**

In the Database window, select the *Forms* button and then:
- DOUBLE-CLICK: Create form by using wizard, or
- CLICK: New button ([New]) on the Database window toolbar
  SELECT: a table or query from the drop-down list box
  DOUBLE-CLICK: Form Wizard

**PRACTICE**

You now use the Form Wizard to create a standard form object.

*Setup:* Ensure that the ACC400 Database window is displayed.

**1** As with other database objects, you may create a form from scratch in Design view or get helpful guidance from the Access wizards. You access the Form Wizard using the New Form dialog box or by double-clicking a shortcut in the Database window. To begin:
CLICK: *Forms* button in the Objects bar

**2** To launch the Form Wizard:
DOUBLE-CLICK: Create form by using wizard
The dialog box in Figure 4.4 appears.

ACCESS

**Figure 4.4**

Form Wizard dialog box

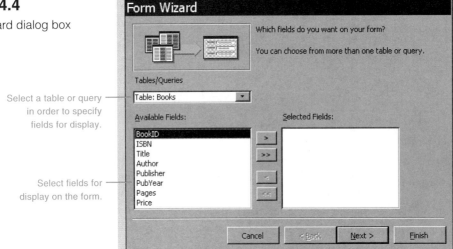

Select a table or query
in order to specify
fields for display.

Select fields for
display on the form.

**3** Let's create a form that displays the data from the Courses table:
SELECT: Table: Courses from the *Tables/Queries* drop-down list box
Notice that the table's fields are displayed in the associated list box.

**4** In the *Available Fields* list box:
SELECT: Title
CLICK: Include button ( > )
Notice that the Title field is no longer displayed in the *Available Fields* list box. (*Hint:* You can double-click a field name to move it between the list boxes.)

**5** Using the same process, add the Faculty, DeptHead, StartDate, and StartTime fields to the *Selected Fields* list box, in the order specified.

**6** To proceed to the next step in the wizard:
CLICK: Next >

**7** In this step, you specify how to arrange the selected fields in the Form window. Notice that three of the four options (Columnar, Tabular, and Datasheet) mirror the AutoForm wizards. On your own, click the layout options one at a time to preview their formats. When you are ready to proceed:
SELECT: *Justified* option button
CLICK: Next >

**8** This step allows you to specify a formatting style for the form. On your own, click the style names appearing in the list box in order to preview their formats. When you are ready to proceed:
SELECT: Sumi Painting
CLICK: Next >
(Note: The next time you use the Form Wizard, the options selected here become the default selections.)

**9** You may now specify the name of the form and whether to open the form for display or editing. Do the following:
TYPE: **Courses – Form Wizard**
CLICK: Finish
The Form window displays only the fields selected in the Form Wizard using a justified (wrapping) layout, as shown in Figure 4.5.

**10** Close the Form window. Notice that the form name appears in the Database window.

**Figure 4.5**

A justified form created using the Form Wizard

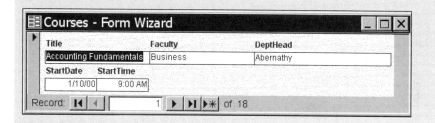

## 4.1.3 Navigating Data Using a Form

**FEATURE**

An Access form provides the same navigational buttons that you find at the bottom of a Datasheet window. Use these buttons, along with the arrow keys (described further below), to move through the records in a table. To move among the fields on a form, press the arrow keys ( ↑ and ↓ ) or use TAB to move forward and SHIFT + TAB to move backward. You can also move quickly to the top of a form using HOME and to the last field on a form using END.

**METHOD**

| Button | Keystroke | Description |
|--------|-----------|-------------|
| ⏮ | CTRL + HOME | Moves to the first field of the first record |
| ◀ | PgUp | Moves to the previous record |
| ▶ | PgDn | Moves to the next record |
| ⏭ | CTRL + END | Moves to the last field of the last record |

**PRACTICE**

In this lesson, you use the AutoForm Wizard to create a form and practice navigating records in the Form window.

*Setup:* Ensure that the ACC400 Database window is displayed.

**1** Let's begin by creating a new columnar form:
CLICK: *Tables* button in the Objects bar
SELECT: Courses in the list area

**2** To launch the AutoForm Wizard:
CLICK: down arrow attached to the New Object button (🔲▾)
CHOOSE: AutoForm
The Courses Form window appears

**3** To save the new form:
CLICK: Save button (💾)
TYPE: **Courses — AutoForm**
PRESS: ENTER or CLICK: OK

**4** Using the form, let's display the last record in the table:
CLICK: Last Record button (⏭) at the bottom of the Form window
Notice that the record navigation area displays Record 18 of 18.

**5** To move to record 15:
PRESS: PgUp three times

**6** To move to the first field in the first record:
PRESS: CTRL + HOME

**7** To move the cursor into the Title field:
PRESS: TAB

**8** Let's use the Find command to locate all courses containing the word "database." Do the following:
CLICK: Find button ()
TYPE: **database** in the *Find What* combo box
SELECT: Any Part of Field in the *Match* drop-down list box
CLICK: Find Next command button

**9** Access moves the cursor to the first matching record. If the Find and Replace dialog box is covering the form, move the windows to appear similar to Figure 4.6.

**Figure 4.6**

Positioning windows
in the work area

Database window

Form window

Record navigation area

Find and Replace
dialog box

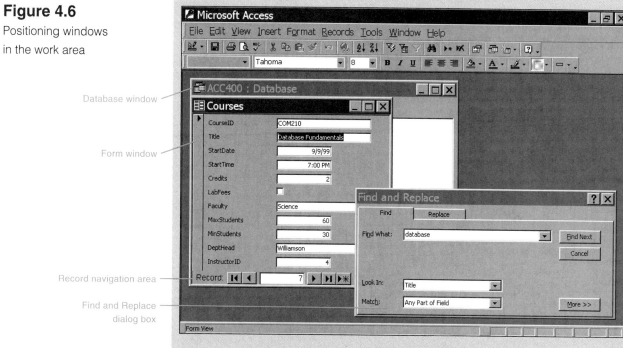

**10** In the Find and Replace dialog box, continue the search:
CLICK: Find Next command button
The next record, Record 8, is displayed.

**11** Close the Find and Replace dialog box.

**12** Close the Form window.

## 4.1.4 Working With a Form

**FEATURE**
The methods for editing data in Form view are nearly identical to editing in Datasheet view. Nevertheless, many people find it easier to edit field data using a form, preferring the less cluttered interface and the ability to focus attention on a single record. After this lesson, you may also find it easier to add, delete, sort, and filter a table's records using a form.

**METHOD**
- CLICK: New Record button (⯈*) to add a new record
- CLICK: Delete Record button (⊠) to remove a record
- CLICK: Sort Ascending button (⏏) to sort into ascending order
- CLICK: Sort Descending button (⏏) to sort into descending order
- CLICK: Print Preview button (🔍) to preview a form
- CLICK: Print button (🖨) to print a form

**PRACTICE**
You now practice sorting, adding, and deleting records, and previewing how a form will appear when printed.

*Setup:* Ensure that you've completed the previous lesson and that the ACC400 Database window is displayed.

**1** Let's start by displaying the form that you created in the last lesson:
CLICK: *Forms* button in the Objects bar
DOUBLE-CLICK: Courses–AutoForm in the list area

**2** Using `PgDn` and `PgUp`, navigate through the records and take notice of the CourseID sort order. Then sort the table's records into ascending order by course title:
PRESS: `CTRL`+`HOME` to move to the first field in the first record
PRESS: `TAB` to position the cursor in the Title field
CLICK: Sort Ascending button (⏏)

**3** Using `PgDn` and `PgUp` once again, you see that the table is now sorted alphabetically by course title.

**4** To add a new record to the table:
CLICK: New Record button (⯈*) on the toolbar

**5.** Enter the data appearing below. Use the `TAB` key to move forward and `SHIFT`+`TAB` to move backward. As you type, notice the pencil icon (🖉) that appears in the record selection area of the form. When you reach the LabFees field, press the Spacebar to toggle the check box. In the last field, InstructorID, enter the value and then press `SHIFT`+`ENTER` to save the record. The pencil icon (🖉) disappears.

CourseID: **ACC351**          Faculty: **Business**
Title: **Equity Management**  MaxStudents: **20**
StartDate: **1/15/00**        MinStudents: **10**
StartTime: **3:30 PM**        DeptHead: **Abernathy**
Credits: **3**               InstructorID: **2**
LabFees: **Yes**

**6.** To delete a record from the table:
PRESS: `PgUp` until you reach record 14, Object-Oriented Design
CLICK: Delete Record button (🗙)
CLICK: Yes command button to confirm

**7.** To preview how a form will print:
CLICK: Print Preview button (🔍)

**8.** On your own, enlarge the Print Preview window and then use the magnifying glass mouse pointer to zoom in on the image. Your screen should appear similar to Figure 4.7.

**Figure 4.7**

Previewing a form

Each page contains as many records as possible, limited by the number of fields and form design.

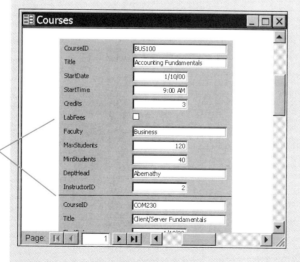

**9.** To return to the Form window:
CLICK: Close command button on the toolbar
Notice that the Form window maintains the same size as the Print Preview window.

**10.** Close the Form window.

ACCESS

**4.1 Self Check**    Name the layout options for designing a form using the Form Wizard.

# 4.2  Creating a Simple Report

A report provides a structured display format for presenting a table's data or a query's results. While most reports are designed for printing, you can also save reports as graphic snapshots or as Web pages. To capture and retain the attention of readers, each report may contain a variety of design elements such as fonts, lines, borders, colors, graphics, and white space. In addition to jazzing up reports, these elements combine with powerful features for summarizing data to present information clearly and concisely. Each day, people make important decisions using reports obtained from database management systems. Some potential uses for reports in a typical business database application include invoices, mailing labels, address books, product catalogs, and inventory listings. In this module, you learn to create reports using the Access **report wizards.**

## 4.2.1  Creating a Report Using the AutoReport Wizards

**FEATURE**
What AutoForm Wizards do for forms, AutoReport Wizards do for reports. Using an **AutoReport Wizard,** you can create a professionally designed report with the click of a button. Access provides two types of AutoReport wizards, Columnar and Tabular. Clicking the New Object button for a report (🗹) generates a relatively unattractive columnar report that presents data down a single column. The Tabular option, selected from the New Report dialog box, prepares a much nicer-looking report.

**METHOD**
To create a columnar report quickly:
1. SELECT: a table or query object in the Database window
2. CLICK: New Object: AutoReport button (📋▾)

To create a report using an AutoReport Wizard:
1. SELECT: *Reports* button in the Objects bar
2. CLICK: New button (🔲New) on the Database window toolbar
3. SELECT: a table or query from the drop-down list box
4. DOUBLE-CLICK: an AutoReport Wizard

**PRACTICE**
In this lesson, you create a columnar report using the AutoReport Wizard.

*Setup:* Ensure that the ACC400 Database window is displayed.

**1** The first step is to select a table or query for which you want to produce a report. To begin:
CLICK: *Tables* button in the Objects bar
SELECT: Instructors in the list area
(*Hint:* You do not need to open the Instructors table. Click once on the table object so that it appears highlighted.)

**2** To generate a report using the AutoReport Wizard:
CLICK: New Object: AutoReport button (📋▾)
(*Hint:* The New Object button contains a list of wizards used in creating database objects. If the AutoReport image is not currently displayed on the face of the New Object button, click the attached down arrow to show the drop-down list appearing to the right. Then select the AutoReport command.)

**3** Access opens a columnar report in the Print Preview window. Each field from the Instructors table appears on a separate row in the report. On your own, use the magnifying glass mouse pointer to zoom in and out on the report (Figure 4.8).

ACCESS

**Figure 4.8**

A columnar report created
using the AutoReport Wizard

**4** To close the report preview:
CLICK: its Close button (⊠)

**5** Access asks if you want to save the report. To proceed:
CLICK: Yes command button
TYPE: **Instructors — Columnar**
PRESS: (ENTER) or CLICK: OK

**6** To view the new object:
CLICK: *Reports* button in the Objects bar
DOUBLE-CLICK: Instructors - Columnar in the list area
The report opens up into the Print Preview window.

**7** Close the Print Preview window.

## 4.2.2 Creating a Report Using the Report Wizard

**FEATURE**
The Report Wizard lets you select options from a series of dialog
boxes in constructing a new report. After selecting the fields to display, you determine grouping and subtotal levels, sorting options,
and presentation styles. The three layout options include Columnar, Tabular, and Justified, similar to the options provided in the
Form Wizard. Once a report has been created and saved, you can
preview and print the report at any time.

**METHOD**

In the Database window, select the *Reports* button and then:
- DOUBLE-CLICK: Create report by using wizard, or
- CLICK: New button (![New]) on the Database window toolbar
  SELECT: a table or query from the drop-down list box
  DOUBLE-CLICK: Report Wizard

**PRACTICE**

You now use the Report Wizard to create a tabular report.

*Setup:* Ensure that the ACC400 Database window is displayed.

**1** To launch the Report Wizard, ensure that the *Reports* button is selected in the Database window and then:
DOUBLE-CLICK: Create report by using wizard
The first dialog box of the Report Wizard appears. Notice the similarity between this dialog box and the Form Wizard in Figure 4.4.

**2** To create a report that displays data from the Students table:
SELECT: Table: Students from the *Tables/Queries* drop-down list box

**3** In the *Available Fields* list box, you select the fields to include:
DOUBLE-CLICK: LastName
DOUBLE-CLICK: FirstName
DOUBLE-CLICK: Major
DOUBLE-CLICK: GradYear
DOUBLE-CLICK: GPA

**4** To proceed to the next step in the wizard:
CLICK: [Next >]

**5** Access now provides the option of grouping records so that you may better organize your data and perform subtotal calculations. To group the student records by their selected major:
DOUBLE-CLICK: Major in the list box
As shown in Figure 4.9, the layout preview area is updated to help you visualize the grouping options selected.

**Figure 4.9**

Report Wizard dialog box:

*Grouping Levels*

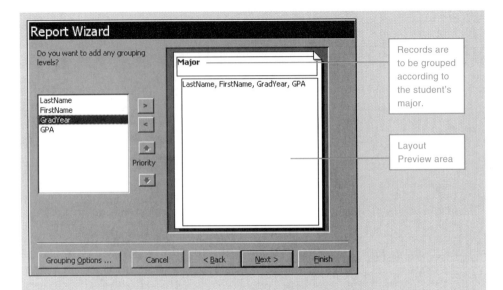

**6** To proceed to the next step:
CLICK: Next >

**7** In this step, you specify sorting options for the report. Since the report is already grouped (and, thus sorted) by major, let's sort the report alphabetically by name:
CLICK: down arrow attached to the first drop-down list box
SELECT: LastName
CLICK: down arrow attached to the second drop-down list box
SELECT: FirstName
(*Hint:* If desired, you can click the Sort Ascending button that appears to the right of each drop-down list box in order to toggle between ascending and descending order.)

**8** If the selected table or query contains numeric or currency fields, you can also include summary calculations in the report. To illustrate:
CLICK: Summary Options command button
The Summary Options dialog box is displayed showing the fields that are eligible for performing calculations.

**9** There are four summary calculations from which to choose. The Sum option totals record values stored in a field, while the Avg option calculates the arithmetic mean or average. The Min and Max options find the minimum and maximum values in a field, respectively. For those fields you sum, you can also calculate each record's percent share of the total value.

In the Students table, these calculations provide no real benefit toward better understanding the GradYear field. However, summarizing the student grade point averages might provide useful information. To proceed, complete the Summary Options dialog box to match the selections shown in Figure 4.10.

**Figure 4.10**

Report Wizard's Summary
Options dialog box

Select primary and
secondary sorting
levels for the report.

Select calculation
options for fields
with the number or
currency data type.

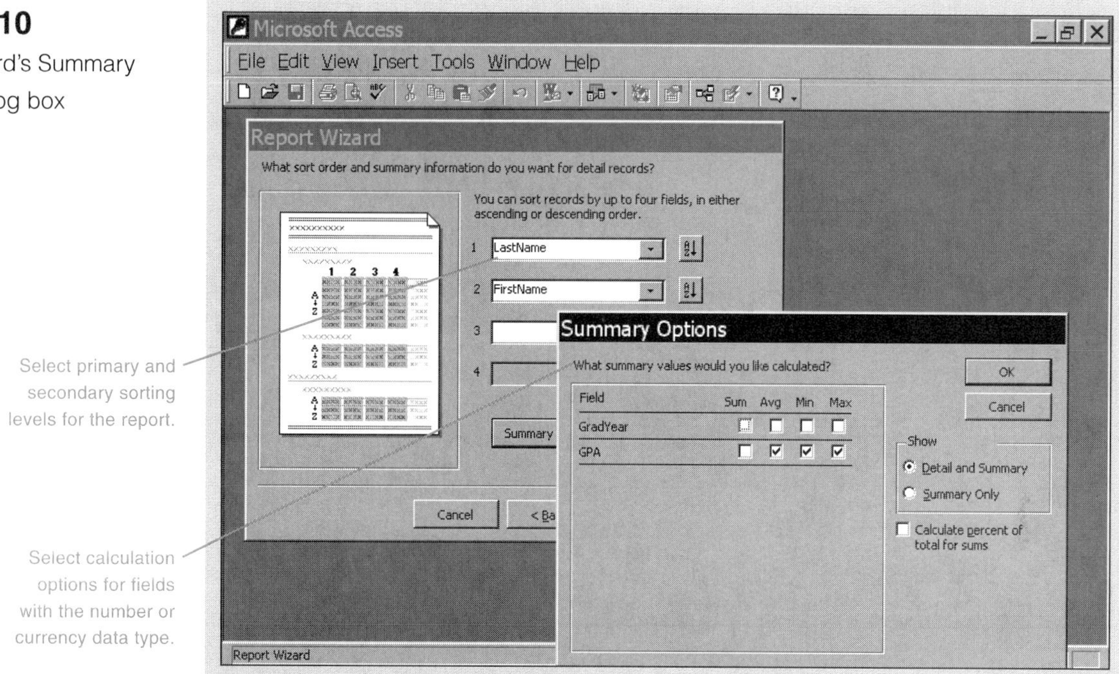

**10** To accept the choices made in the Summary Options dialog box
and proceed to the next step:
CLICK: OK
CLICK: Next>

**11** In this step, you specify the desired layout and page orientation
settings. For grouping data, the Report Wizard provides nice formats for separating and organizing the information. Do the following:
SELECT: *Outline 1* option button in the *Layout* area
SELECT: *Portrait* option button in the *Orientation* area
CLICK: Next>

**12** A style is a formatting template that you can apply to a report.
On your own, click on the style options in the list box to pre-
view their formats. When you are ready to proceed:
SELECT: Corporate
CLICK: Next>

**13** In the final step, you name the report and determine whether to
preview it or perform additional modifications. Do the following:
TYPE: **Students - By Major**
SELECT: *Preview the report* option button
CLICK: Finish
The report is displayed in the Print Preview window.

**14** To close the Print Preview window:
CLICK: its Close button (☒)
The new report object appears in the Database window. In the next lesson, you learn more about previewing and printing the report.

**In Addition**
Using Form and
Report Design Views

Although the form and report wizards let you immediately create usable objects, you may want to create a form or report from scratch or modify an existing object. Although not covered in this chapter, you can further customize forms and reports in Design view.

## 4.2.3  Previewing and Printing a Report

**FEATURE**
Whereas you open tables, queries, and forms, you **preview** reports. Double-clicking a report object in the Database window opens the report for display in a Print Preview window. In this mode, you can navigate pages, zoom in and out, and modify page setup options.

**METHOD**
After selecting the report object in the Database window:
- CLICK: Print Preview button (▨) to preview the report, or
  CHOOSE: File, Print Preview
- CLICK: Print button (▤) to print the report, or
  CHOOSE: File, Print
- CHOOSE: File, Page Setup to specify print options

**PRACTICE**
You now display and print a report using the Print Preview window.

*Setup:* Ensure that you've completed the previous lesson and that the *Reports* button is selected in the ACC400 Database window.

**1** To display a report in Print Preview mode:
DOUBLE-CLICK: Students–By Major

**2** Let's maximize the Print Preview window for a better view:
CLICK: its Maximize button (▢)
Your screen should now appear similar to Figure 4.11.

**Figure 4.11**

Maximized Print
Preview window

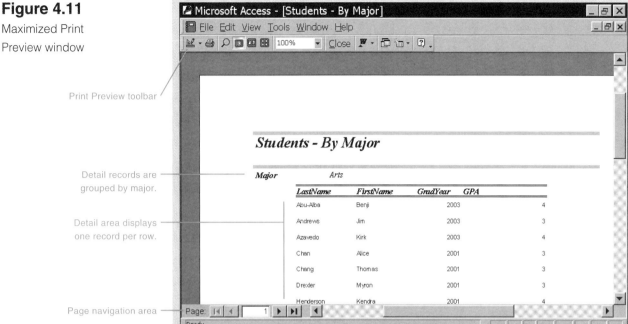

Print Preview toolbar

Detail records are
grouped by major.

Detail area displays
one record per row.

Page navigation area

**3** On your own, move amongst the pages using the navigation buttons appearing at the bottom of the Print Preview window. When you are ready to proceed, return to Page 1 of the report.

**4** To view two pages of the report side by side:
CLICK: Two Pages button (🔲)
(*Hint:* You can also choose the View, Pages command.)

**5** On your own, zoom in and out on different areas of the preview. Take special note of the summary calculations appearing at the end of a category grouping.

**6** To view multiple pages:
CLICK: Multiple Pages button (🔲)
SELECT: 1x3 Pages in the drop-down menu that appears

**7** To return to the view shown in Figure 4.11:
CLICK: One Page button (🔲)
CLICK: down arrow attached to the Zoom button (100% ▾)
SELECT: 100%
(*Hint:* You can also choose the View, Zoom command to change the magnification.)

**8** To stop viewing the report and display the Database window:
CLICK: Database window button (🔲)
Notice that the Print Preview window is restored to a window and is layered behind the Database window.

ACCESS

**9** Close the Print Preview window.

**10** If a printer is attached to your computer, perform this step. Otherwise, proceed to the next lesson.
RIGHT-CLICK: Students–By Major
CHOOSE: Print
The report is sent directly to the printer.

# 4.2.4 Publishing a Report to the Web

**FEATURE**
The **World Wide Web** is an exciting medium for exchanging data. Using **Internet** technologies, the Web provides an easy-to-use multimedia interface for accessing information stored anywhere on the planet. Access makes it easy for you to tap the power of the Web. Once you've created a database object such as a table or report, you can export the object in **HTML** format, the standardized markup language of the Web. While it's true that such a document provides only a static representation or snapshot of a database, Access also provides several advanced tools for creating dynamic real-time Web applications.

**METHOD**
After selecting an object in the Database window:
1. CHOOSE: File, Export
2. TYPE: a file name for the Web document
3. SELECT: HTML documents in the *Save as type* drop-down list box
4. CLICK: Save command button

**PRACTICE**
In this lesson, you export a report object as an HTML document.

*Setup:* Ensure that you've completed the previous lessons and that the *Reports* button is selected in the ACC400 Database window.

**1** To export a report for publishing to the Web:
SELECT: Students–By Major
The object name must appear highlighted in the list area.

**2** CHOOSE: File, Export
The Export Report dialog box appears.

**3** In the *File name* text box:
TYPE: **Students-Web Page**

**4** In the Places bar or the *Save in* drop-down list box:
SELECT: *your personal storage location*

**5** In the *Save as type* drop-down list box
SELECT: HTML documents

**6** To proceed with the export:
CLICK: Save command button

**7** The HTML Output Options dialog box now displays on the screen. You use this dialog box to specify a template file that enhances the report's appearance, navigation, and formatting. To continue without specifying a template:
CLICK: OK

**8** The export process creates one HTML document for each page of the report. You are then returned to the Database window. If you have access to Web browser software, you can open one of the pages for viewing. Click the hyperlinks appearing at the bottom of the page to navigate the report pages. Figure 4.12 provides an example of how the first page of the report is displayed using Internet Explorer.

**Figure 4.12**

Viewing a report page using Internet Explorer

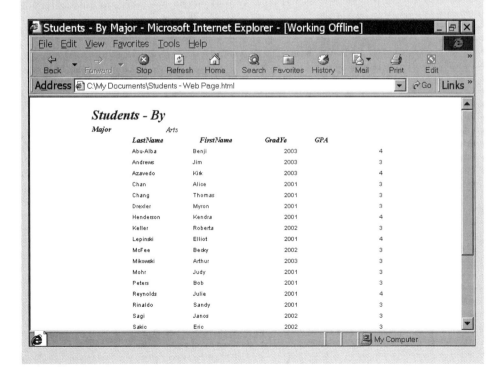

**4.2 Self Check**    What does the term "grouping data" refer to in a report?

# 4.3   Generating a Mailing Labels Report

Using your database to print mailing labels can save you a lot of time in preparing envelopes for greeting cards, birth announcements, or other special mailings. You can even keep track of your computer disks and files in a database and then prepare diskette labels (Avery Product Number 5296) using a report object. In this module, you learn to create and print mailing labels.

## 4.3.1 Creating a Report Using the Label Wizard

**FEATURE**
The Access **Label Wizard** provides an easy way for you to create a mailing labels report and print standard labels that fit on envelopes, packages, and diskettes.

**METHOD**
In the Database window, select the *Reports* button and then:
1.   CLICK: New button () on the Database window toolbar
2.   SELECT: a table or query from the drop-down list box
3.   DOUBLE-CLICK: Label Wizard

**PRACTICE**
You now create a mailing labels report for the Students table.

*Setup:* Ensure that the ACC400 Database window is displayed.

1   Let's generate mailing labels for the Students table. To begin, launch the Label Wizard:
SELECT: *Reports* button in the Objects bar
CLICK: New button () on the Database window toolbar

**2** In the New Report dialog box:
SELECT: Students in the *Choose the table*...drop-down list box
DOUBLE-CLICK: Label Wizard
The first dialog box for the Label Wizard appears, as shown in Figure 4.13. You use this dialog box to specify the label size and format.

**Figure 4.13**

Label Wizard dialog box

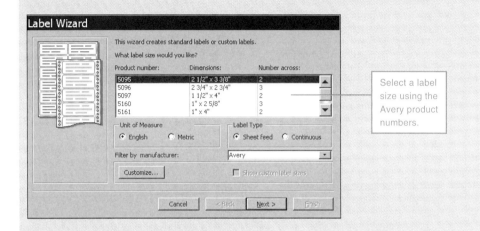

**3** For a standard mailing labels report, ensure that Avery is selected in the *Filter by manufacturer* drop-down list box and then:
SELECT: 5160 in the *Product number* column
CLICK: Next >

**4** In this step, you select the font used for the labels. To accept the default values and proceed:
CLICK: Next >

**5** You now build the appearance of the label by entering text or selecting fields. In the *Available fields* list box:
DOUBLE-CLICK: FirstName
PRESS: Spacebar
DOUBLE-CLICK: LastName
PRESS: ENTER
DOUBLE-CLICK: Address
PRESS: ENTER
DOUBLE-CLICK: City
TYPE: , (a single comma)
PRESS: Spacebar
DOUBLE-CLICK: State
PRESS: Spacebar
DOUBLE-CLICK: Zip
Your label should now appear similar to Figure 4.14.

**Figure 4.14**

Constructing a label

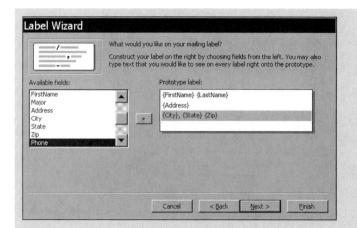

**6** To proceed to the next step:
CLICK: Next >

**7** To sort the mailing labels report by student name:
DOUBLE-CLICK: LastName in the *Available fields* list box
DOUBLE-CLICK: FirstName in the *Available fields* list box
CLICK: Next >

**8** To accept the default selections in the wizard:
CLICK: Finish
After a few moments, the mailing labels report appears in the Print Preview window.

**9** On your own, zoom in and out on pages in the Print Preview window.

**10** Close the Print Preview window.

**4.3 Self Check**    How could you use table and report objects to print diskette labels?

# 4.4 Managing Database Objects

As you continue to use Access, you will create many databases and many database objects, and it is important that you know how to manage them properly. In this module, you learn to rename, copy, and delete database objects and to compress and repair a database file.

## 4.4.1  Renaming, Copying, and Deleting Objects

**FEATURE**
Similar to performing routine file management procedures using Windows Explorer, you can rename, copy, and delete the individual objects stored in a database. In a sense, the Access wizards make it too easy to create database objects. Especially true for novice users, it is common to find Database windows overflowing with trial editions of objects. In other words, users create a form or report using a wizard only to find that they would like to add a few improvements. Because it is often easier to create a new wizard-generated object than to edit the existing one, the Database window can become overpopulated quickly. To avoid capacity and performance issues, these trial objects should be deleted immediately.

**METHOD**
After right-clicking the desired database object:
- CHOOSE: Rename to rename an object
- CHOOSE: Cut to move an object, or CLICK: Cut button (🔲)
- CHOOSE: Copy to copy an object, or CLICK: Copy button (🔲)
- CHOOSE: Paste to paste an object, or CLICK: Paste button (🔲)
- CHOOSE: Delete to remove an object, or CLICK: Delete button (🔲)

**PRACTICE**
You now practice managing objects in the ACC400 database.

*Setup:* Ensure that the ACC400 Database window is displayed.

**1** To begin, let's display the table objects:
CLICK: *Tables* button in the Objects bar

**2** Let's practice adjusting the view options in the list area:
CLICK: Large Icons button (🔲) on the Database window toolbar
CLICK: Details button (🔲) to view additional information
CLICK: List button (🔲) to return to the standard view
(*Hint:* You can also change the order in which the objects are displayed by choosing the View, Arrange Icons command.)

**3** To rename the Books table object to Fiction:
CLICK: the name "Books" once so that it appears highlighted
CLICK: the name "Books" again to enter Edit mode
(*Hint:* You can also select an object and press F2 to enter Edit mode. Notice that you click the name and not the icon to rename an object.)

ACCESS

**4** To rename the table object:
TYPE: **Fiction**
PRESS: [ENTER]

**5** Let's create a copy of the Fiction object and name it Non-Fiction:
SELECT: Fiction
CLICK: Copy button (🗐) on the toolbar
CLICK: Paste button (🗐) on the toolbar
The dialog box in Figure 4.15 appears.

**Figure 4.15**

Paste Table As dialog box

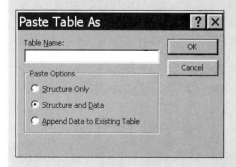

**6** In the *Table Name* text box:
TYPE: **Non-Fiction**
SELECT: *Structure Only* check box
CLICK: OK command button
(*Note:* You copy the structure only since the data stored in the Fiction table is not required for the Non-Fiction table.)

**7** To delete an object using the right-click menu:
RIGHT-CLICK: Non-Fiction
CHOOSE: Delete

**8** In the confirmation dialog box:
CLICK: Yes command button
The table object is removed from the Database window.

## 4.4.2 Compacting and Repairing a Database

**FEATURE**
When you make several changes to a database, such as copying and deleting objects, it may become fragmented. Compacting a database reorganizes and packs the file more closely together, while repairing a database verifies the reliability of objects. An added benefit for those tables that contain AutoNumber fields, and where records have been deleted from the end of the table, is that compacting resets the field to the next sequential value. As a result, the next record added to the table will have an AutoNumber value that is one more than the last record in the table. In addition to saving disk space and resetting AutoNumber fields, compacting a database improves a database's performance.

**METHOD**
CHOOSE: Tools, Database Utilities, Compact and Repair Database

**PRACTICE**
In this lesson, you compact the ACC400 database file.

*Setup:* Ensure that the ACC400 Database window is displayed.

**1** To compact and repair the ACC400 database:
CHOOSE: Tools, Database Utilities, Compact and Repair Database
The automated process begins, processes the database objects, and then ends rather quietly. You can witness its processing status by looking in the Status bar.

**2** Close the ACC400 Database window. Then, exit Microsoft Access. (*Note*: If a warning dialog box appears regarding the Clipboard's contents, accept the dialog box and continue.)

| **In Addition** <br> Backing Up <br> the Database | One of the most important tasks you can perform after creating and adding data to a database is to make a backup copy of it to another storage location. Most people back up a database, along with their other important data files, using "My Computer," Windows Explorer, or a specialized backup program. An Access database is stored in a file ending with the extension MDB or MDE. You can search for this file type using the Find, Files or Folders command on the Start (**Start**) menu. |
| --- | --- |

**4.4 Self Check**  Name two operating system tools that you can use to back up a database.

# 4.5 Chapter Review

The users of a database application are most familiar with its form and report objects. Forms are used in entering and editing data, while reports are used for presenting and displaying information. Besides offering a more attractive interface than datasheets, forms can help you focus your attention on a single record at a time. Reports, which also offer a variety of attractive layouts, are primarily meant for printing. It's uncommon to limit a report to previewing on-screen. Therefore, you must learn to match your printer's capabilities (color versus black-and-white, inkjet versus laser) with the report design and formatting options that are available. In this chapter, you learned to use the Access wizards to create forms, reports, and mailing labels. After experimenting with wizard-generated forms and reports, you also practiced renaming, copying, and deleting objects, and compacting and repairing a database.

## 4.5.1  Command Summary

Many of the commands and procedures appearing in this chapter are summarized in the following table.

| Skill Set | To Perform This Task . . . | Do the Following . . . |
|---|---|---|
| **Building and Modifying Forms** | Create a new form using the AutoForm Wizard | SELECT: the desired table or query<br>CLICK: New Object: AutoForm button ([⚄▾]) |
| | Create a new form using the Form Wizard | CLICK: *Forms* button in the Objects bar<br>DOUBLE-CLICK: Create form by using wizard |
| **Producing Reports** | Create a new report using the AutoReport Wizard | SELECT: the desired table or query<br>CLICK: New Object: AutoForm button ([⚄▾]) |
| | Create a new report using the Report Wizard | CLICK: *Reports* button in the Object bar<br>DOUBLE-CLICK: Create report by using wizard |
| | Create a new mailing labels report using the Label Wizard | CLICK: *Reports* button in the Object bar<br>CLICK: New button ([⚄New])<br>DOUBLE-CLICK: Label Wizard |

*Continued*

| Skill Set | To Perform This Task . . . | Do the Following . . . |
|---|---|---|
| | Preview a report for printing | DOUBLE-CLICK: the report object, or<br>CLICK: Print Preview button (🔲), or<br>CHOOSE: File, Print Preview |
| | Print a report | CLICK: Print button (🖨), or<br>CHOOSE: File, Print |
| **Integrating with Other Applications** | Export a report to HTML format for Web publishing | SELECT: the desired object<br>CHOOSE: File, Export<br>SELECT: HTML documents in the *Save as type* drop-down list box<br>CLICK: Save command button |
| | Export a report as a snapshot file for e-mail and Web distribution | SELECT: the desired object<br>CHOOSE: File, Export<br>SELECT: Snapshot Format in the *Save as type* drop-down list box<br>CLICK: Save command button |
| **Working with Access** | Rename a database object | RIGHT-CLICK: the desired object<br>CHOOSE: Rename |
| | Copy a database object | CLICK: Copy button (📋)<br>CLICK: Paste button (📋)<br>SELECT: a paste option |
| | Delete a database object | RIGHT-CLICK: the desired object<br>CHOOSE: Delete |
| **Using Access Tools** | Compact and repair a database | CHOOSE: Tools, Database Utilities<br>CHOOSE: Compact and Repair Database |
| | Backup and restore a database | Use Windows Explorer or "My Computer" to perform copy, backup, and restore operations for an Access database file (extension .MDB) |

ACCESS

## 4.5.2 Key Terms

This section specifies page references for the key terms identified in this chapter. For a complete list of definitions, refer to the Glossary at the end of this learning guide.

AutoForm Wizard, *p. 136*          Label Wizard, *p. 156*

AutoReport Wizard, *p. 146*          preview, *p. 152*

Form window, *p. 136*          report snapshot, *p. 156*

form wizards, *p. 135*          report wizards, *p. 146*

HTML, *p. 154*          World Wide Web, *p. 154*

Internet, *p. 154*

# 4.6  Review Questions

## 4.6.1  Short Answer

1. Why create forms for use in a database application?
2. Describe the three types of AutoForm Wizards.
3. List the form options available in the New Form dialog box.
4. When would you choose a columnar or justified form layout?
5. When would you choose a tabular or datasheet form layout?
6. Why create reports for use in a database application?
7. Describe the two types of AutoReport Wizards.
8. List the report options available in the New Report dialog box.
9. How would you prepare an Access report for publishing to the Web?
10. Describe two methods for removing objects in the Database window.

## 4.6.2  True/False

1. ____ The default AutoForm Wizard is the Columnar AutoForm Wizard.
2. ____ The Form Wizard allows you to specify a sorting order.
3. ____ You can display data from more than one table in a form.
4. ____ In the Form window, pressing CTRL+END moves the cursor to the last field in the current record.
5. ____ The default AutoReport Wizard is the Tabular AutoReport Wizard.
6. ____ The Report Wizard allows you to specify a sorting order.

7. ＿＿＿ The information that you want summarized in a report can be extracted from either a table or a query.

8. ＿＿＿ A tabular report prints several columns of information, with the field labels appearing down the left margin of the page.

9. ＿＿＿ In the Database window, you can copy a table object without duplicating the data stored in the table.

10. ＿＿＿ You should regularly compact a database using Windows Explorer.

## 4.6.3 Multiple Choice

1. A form is used to display data from which of the following objects:
   a. tables and queries
   b. tables and reports
   c. queries and reports
   d. tables only

2. Which form layout is produced by default when selecting the AutoForm option from the New Object button?
   a. Circular
   b. Columnar
   c. Singular
   d. Tabular

3. Which of the following best describes a tabular form layout?
   a. Data from a single record presented in a single column
   b. Data from numerous records presented in a single column
   c. Data from a single record presented in rows and columns
   d. Data from numerous records presented in rows and columns

4. Which of the following best describes a justified form layout?
   a. Data from a single record presented with stacked fields
   b. Data from numerous records presented with stacked fields
   c. Data from a single record presented in a single column
   d. Data from numerous records presented in rows and columns

5. Which of the following performs the same action as pressing `PgUp` in the Form window?
   a. CLICK: ⏮
   b. CLICK: ◀
   c. CLICK: ▶
   d. CLICK: ⏭

6. The Report Wizard provides the following options that are not available in the Form Wizard.
   a. Grouping and Filtering
   b. Outlining and Sorting
   c. Grouping and Sorting
   d. Outlining and Filtering

7. Which of the following is not a summary calculation available in the Summary Options dialog box of the Report Wizard?
   a. Avg
   b. Count
   c. Max
   d. Sum

8. This chapter discussed which two file format options for exporting a static report page for publishing to the Web?
   a. ASP and HTML
   b. HTML and Java
   c. MDB and MDE
   d. HTML and Snapshot

9. The Label Wizard enables you to create a report format using standard label sizes from this vendor.
   a. Avery
   b. Linux
   c. Microsoft
   d. Sun

10. Which of the following is <u>not</u> a paste option when copying a table object?
    a. Structure Only
    b. Structure and Data
    c. Structure, Forms, and Reports
    d. Append Data to Existing Table

# 4.7  Hands-On Projects

### 4.7.1  World Wide Imports: Forms and Reports

In this exercise, you create two new database objects for World Wide Imports. First, using the AutoForm Wizard, you create a columnar data entry form for the Customers table. Then, you create a tabular report using an AutoReport Wizard.

*Setup:* Ensure that Access is loaded. If you are launching Access and the startup dialog box appears, click the Cancel command button to remove the dialog box from the application window.

1. Open the database file named ACC470. Ensure that the *Tables* button in the Objects bar is selected.
2. To create a data entry form for the Customers table:
   SELECT: 471 Customers in the list area
   (*Hint:* Click once on the name of the table. Do not double-click.)
3. To have Access create a new columnar form:
   CLICK: New Object: AutoForm button (⊞▾)
   (*Hint:* If the AutoForm image is not displayed on the button face, click the attached down arrow and choose the AutoForm command.)
4. Let's save the new form:
   CLICK: Save button (🖫)
   TYPE: **Customer Data Entry Form**
   PRESS: (ENTER) or CLICK: OK
5. To close the new form:
   CLICK: its Close button (☒)
6. Now your objective is to create a tabular report for the Customers table. To begin:
   CLICK: *Reports* button in the Objects bar
   CLICK: New button (▣New) on the Database window toolbar
7. In the New Report dialog box:
   SELECT: 471 Customers from the *Choose the table...*drop-down list box
   DOUBLE-CLICK: AutoReport: Tabular
   A new report is displayed in the Print Preview window.
8. On your own, use the magnifying glass mouse pointer to zoom in and out on the report page.
9. To close the report's Print Preview window:
   CLICK: its Close button (☒)
10. In the confirmation dialog box that appears, save the report:
    CLICK: Yes command button
    TYPE: **Customer AutoReport**
    PRESS: (ENTER) or CLICK: OK
    The new report object should appear in the Database window.

## 4.7.2  CyberWeb: Internet Accounts

CyberWeb's Internet Accounts table contains a listing of current user accounts for an Internet Service Provider. In this exercise, you create a report that groups and summarizes users according to where they live.

*Setup*: Ensure that the ACC470 Database window is displayed.

1. Ensure that the *Reports* button in the Objects bar is selected and then:
   DOUBLE-CLICK: Create report by using wizard

2.  In the first step of the Report Wizard:
    SELECT: Table: 472 Internet Accounts from the *Tables/Queries*
    drop-down list box
3.  Specify the fields that you want included in the report:
    DOUBLE-CLICK: Customer
    DOUBLE-CLICK: Username
    DOUBLE-CLICK: City
    DOUBLE-CLICK: Phone
    DOUBLE-CLICK: Amount
    CLICK: Next >
4.  Specify a grouping level by city:
    DOUBLE-CLICK: City
    CLICK: Next >
5.  Specify an alphabetical sort order by account name:
    SELECT: Username from the first drop-down list box
6.  Now let's select a summary calculation to perform:
    CLICK: Summary Options command button
7.  In the Summary Options dialog box:
    SELECT: *Sum* check box for the Amount field
    CLICK: OK
8.  To specify a report layout and style:
    CLICK: Next >
    SELECT: *Align Left 1* option button in the *Layout* area
    SELECT: *Landscape* option button in the *Orientation* area
    CLICK: Next >
    SELECT: Soft Gray in the *Style* list box
9.  To proceed to the last step in the wizard:
    CLICK: Next >
    TYPE: Internet Accounts By City
    CLICK: Finish
10. Maximize the report's Print Preview window and then:
    SELECT: 75% from the Zoom button (100% ▾)
    Your screen should appear similar to Figure 4.16.

**Figure 4.16**

Previewing a grouped
and sorted report

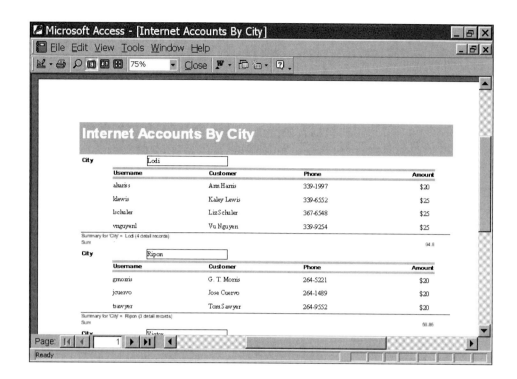

11. To print the report:
    CLICK: Print button (🖨)
12. Restore the Print Preview window by clicking its Restore button (🗗) and then close it by clicking its Close button (☒). (*Hint:* The Print Preview window's Restore button appears on the second row of Windows icons in the upper left-hand corner.)

## 4.7.3 Big Valley Mills: Forest Products

In this exercise, you practice creating and then working with a tabular form using the Form Wizard.

*Setup*: Ensure that the ACC470 Database window is displayed.

1. Display the form objects in the database using the Objects bar.
2. Launch the Form Wizard using the shortcut appearing in the list area.
3. In the Form Wizard dialog box:
   SELECT: Table: 473 Products in the *Tables/Queries* drop-down list box
   CLICK: Include All button (>>) to display all of the fields on the form
4. In the next two steps of the Form Wizard, select a *Tabular* layout and an Expedition style for the form.
5. In the last step of the wizard, enter the name "Products Tabular Form" and then open the form in Form view.

6. Enter the following data after clicking the New Record button
   (▶•):
   ProductCode: **DF99**
   Species: **DFIR**
   Size: **2 X 8**
   Grade: **Ungraded**
   Finish: **RGH**
   Category: **Dim.**
7. Move to the first field in the first record. Then:
   PRESS: ⟨ **TAB** ⟩ to move to the Species field column
8. Using the Sort Descending button (🔠) on the toolbar, sort the
   table into descending order by the Species column.
9. To filter the information displayed in the form:
   DOUBLE-CLICK: SYP in the Species field column
   CLICK: Filter By Selection button (🔽)
   Only records of the SYP species now appear in the new form.
10. Close the form by clicking its Close button (🗙).

### ■ 4.7.4 Silverdale Festival: Contact List

In this exercise, you create a mailing labels report for all the contacts
stored in Silverdale's table object.

*Setup*: Ensure that the ACC470 Database window is displayed.

1. Display the report objects in the database using the Objects bar.
2. To begin creating the mailing labels report:
   CLICK: New button (🔳New) on the Database window toolbar
   SELECT: 474 Contacts in the *Choose the table...*drop-down
   list box
   DOUBLE-CLICK: Label Wizard
   The first step of the wizard is displayed.
3. To use standard mailing labels for printing on a laser printer:
   SELECT: Avery 5160 in the *Product number* column
   SELECT: *Sheet feed* in the *Label Type* area
   CLICK: ⟨ Next › ⟩
4. To adjust the typeface and font style:
   SELECT: Times New Roman in the *Font name* drop-down
   list box
   SELECT: 10 in the *Font size* drop-down list box
   SELECT: Normal in the *Font weight* drop-down list box
   CLICK: ⟨ Next › ⟩

5. You build the label by adding fields from the *Available Fields* list box to the *Prototype label* area and by entering text. Do the following:
   DOUBLE-CLICK: Volunteer Group
   PRESS: (ENTER)
   TYPE: Attn:
   PRESS: Spacebar once
   DOUBLE-CLICK: Contact
   PRESS: (ENTER)
   Notice that you can input text directly onto the label.
6. Finish the label as it appears in Figure 4.17.

**Figure 4.17**

Designing mailing labels

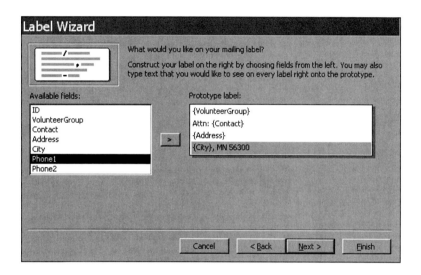

7. To proceed to the next step:
   CLICK: Next >
8. To sort the labels into order by city:
   DOUBLE-CLICK: City in the *Available fields* list box
   CLICK: Next >
9. In the last step of the wizard, enter the name "Volunteer Mailing Labels" and then display the report using the Print Preview window.
10. Print the report and then close the Print Preview window by clicking its Close button ([X]).

## 4.7.5 On Your Own: Office Mart Inventory

The Office Mart 475 Inventory table stores product information, including current stock levels, reorder quantities, costs, and suggested retail prices. Using the Form Wizard, create a justified form named "Inventory Input" to use for entering and editing data. To practice working with the form, enter the following records. (*Hint:* Access automatically adds the dollar signs to the Cost and SuggestedRetail values.) When you are finished, close the Form window.

ProductID: *(Autonumber)*
Description: **Push Pins**
OnHand: **45**
Cost: **$2**
SuggestedRetail: **$4**
Supplier: **E01**
Buyer: **01**
Reorder: **20**

ProductID: *(Autonumber)*
Description: **Project Folders**
OnHand: **112**
Cost: **$9**
SuggestedRetail: **$13**
Supplier: **B05**
Buyer: **07**
Reorder: **40**

Using the Report Wizard, create a report that calculates and displays the minimum and maximum values for the Cost and SuggestedRetail fields as grouped by supplier. Furthermore, sort the report by the product's description. In the last step of the wizard, name the report "Supplier Summary" and then view the report. Before closing the Print Preview window, send a copy of the report to the printer. And lastly, export the report to an HTML document named "Inventory" for posting to the company's internal Web server.

## 4.7.6 On Your Own: Sun Bird Resort

The Sun Bird Resort wants to make life easier for the front-counter clerks. To this end, they've asked you to create two data entry forms. Since the 476 Guides table contains only a few fields, create a tabular form named "Guides Data Entry" using the Tabular AutoForm Wizard. Then, for the 476 Patrons table, use the Form Wizard to create a columnar form named "Patrons Data Entry" and specify the Blends style. To test the usability of the forms, practice selecting records and editing data.

You've also been asked to create a report that includes all of the fields from the Patrons table and then groups the report according to interest. The report is to be sorted in order by the BestTime field. After specifying a layout and style, save the report as "Patrons By Interest." Then preview the report in the Print Preview window before sending it to the printer. When finished, close the ACC470 Database window and then exit Microsoft Access.

# 4.8  Case Problems: Lagniappe, Inc.

Lagniappe, Inc. manufactures and sells a limited line of travel luggage through boutiques in Seattle, San Francisco, Chicago, Boston, and New York. As the western regional sales representative, Janice is primarily responsible for servicing the repeat purchasers in San Francisco and Seattle. To keep in touch with the markets, her boss, John Lucci, has asked that Janice fax him monthly status reports. Since she must create these reports from scratch anyway, Janice decides to take this opportunity to also create form objects for her database.

In the following case problems, assume the role of Janice and perform the same steps that she identifies. You may want to re-read the chapter opening before proceeding.

1.  After launching Access, Janice opens the ACC480 database that is stored in her data files folder. Wanting to get a better feel for the forms Access can create, she uses the AutoForm Wizard to generate a columnar form for the Customers table. She saves the form as "Customers–AutoForm" and then practices moving through the records using the navigation buttons in the Form window. Feeling comfortable with her creation, she closes the Form window.

    Since the AutoForm Wizard did such a nice job with the form, Janice decides to create a new report. She selects the Customers table and launches the AutoReport Wizard using the toolbar. After perusing the report, she closes the window by clicking its Close button (☒) and then saves the report as "Customers–AutoReport." After letting the report sink in for a few moments, Janice concedes that it's not quite what she had hoped for. After displaying the stored report objects, she uses the right-click menu to delete the AutoReport object from the Database window.

2.  Being the adventurous type, Janice wants to create a new form layout for the Products table. To begin, she displays the form objects in the Database window and then double-clicks the "Create form by using wizard" shortcut. In the first step of the wizard, she selects the Products table and includes all of the fields. Then she specifies an International style for the form. Lastly, Janice names the new form "Products–Input Form" and opens it for display. After viewing the new form, she closes it by clicking its Close button (☒).

3.  Janice wants to send out a mailing to all of her preferred customers. Using the Customers table, she prepares a standard Avery 5160 mailing label. The font selected is Times New Roman with a 10-point font size. After specifying that the labels be sorted into ascending order by surname, she saves the report as "Customer Mailing." Figure 4.18 displays the results of the mailing labels report. Janice displays two pages in the Print Preview window and then sends the report to the printer. Lastly, she closes the Print Preview window to return to the Database window.

ACCESS

**Figure 4.18**

Previewing a mailing labels report

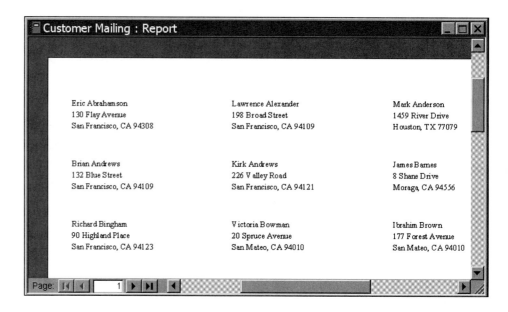

4.  Janice's boss, John, commends her for the new reports, but would like to see her customers grouped by the product that they purchased. Janice knows that the Report Wizard can help her produce this report. After launching the wizard, she selects the Customers table and includes all of its fields for display in the report. Janice selects the ProductID field for grouping the contents of the report and the LastName field for sorting the report. She then selects a layout, page orientation, and style. In the last step of the Report Wizard, Janice names the report "Customers–By ProductID" and then opens it for display in the Print Preview window. Satisfied with the results, Janice prints and then closes the report.

    "Janice, your reports look great!" John exclaims on the answering machine. "I'd like you to show Jose and Wendy how you produced these reports so quickly. They typically spend the last three days of each month compiling their reports." Janice is pleased that the reports have gone over so well. Rather than faxing them to Jose and Wendy, she decides to export the report as an HTML document. In the Database window, Janice selects the "Customers–By ProductID" report object and chooses the File, Export command. After locating her personal storage folder and selecting the "HTML Documents" format, she clicks the Save command button and bypasses the dialog box asking for an HTML template. She will inform her associates that they can preview the report after she finishes uploading it to her personal Web site. Lastly, she closes the ACC480 Database window and exits Microsoft Access.

# NOTES

# NOTES

# MICROSOFT ACCESS 2000
*Working with Tables*

## CHAPTER
### FIVE

# Chapter Outline

# Learning Objectives

After reading this chapter, you will be able to:

- Understand the fundamentals of relational database design, including normalization and referential integrity

- Establish table relationships for the purpose of reducing data redundancy and optimizing data storage

- Customize the appearance and behavior of fields by setting properties in table Design view

- Ensure data integrity by specifying required fields, input masks, validation lists, and lookup tables

- Import data from external sources, export database objects for Web publishing, and copy data to other Office applications

## Case Study

### Just Brew-It

Just Brew-It distributes beer and wine-making supplies in Ottawa, Canada's capital city. Initially established as a warehouse operation serving only retail outlets, the company is now aggressively pursuing its direct channel customers. In fact, the company is looking toward e-commerce on the World Wide Web to sell its kits and market its franchise opportunities.

Just Brew-It recently installed Microsoft Access in its administrative offices. The company's systems analyst, Jack Rowe, was asked to design and implement a relational database system to manage the company's product and sales data. After creating a database and defining a few initial tables, Jack notified management that he required an extended leave for health reasons. Unfortunately, there is still much work to be done before the database system can be used on a daily basis. The office person most familiar with using Access, Janice Winkler, has now assumed responsibility for completing the system.

In this chapter, you and Janice learn how to establish relationships between tables and how to fine-tune a table's structure by setting field properties. You also learn about importing and exporting data, and practice copying records into other Office 2000 applications.

# 5.1  Building a Relational Database

Microsoft Access is a desktop database management system that allows you to create and maintain **relational databases.** The relational database model provides a method for organizing information and limiting the duplication of stored data; thereby reducing your disk space requirements and making the database easier to maintain. A key principle of relational database design is **normalization,** which emphasizes that each data item be stored in a single location. You normalize data by dividing fields into logical groupings of related tables. A database design that does not normalize data is known as a **flat-file database.** Although spreadsheet software provides some data management capabilities, it also exhibits the characteristics and deficiencies of flat-file databases for storing data.

ACCESS

Suppose you've been asked by your school to design a database to store instructor, course, and section data. Each instructor in the school may teach several sections of one or more courses. If you were to design a flat-file database solution, the table structure would appear similar to Figure 5.1. This design requires that you enter the same course and instructor details again and again. Now consider the effort required to update an instructor's phone number or a course description! You would need to locate and update each and every record containing the information to be changed. In addition to being susceptible to data entry errors, the flat-file design is truly inefficient.

**Figure 5.1**

Using a flat-file
database design

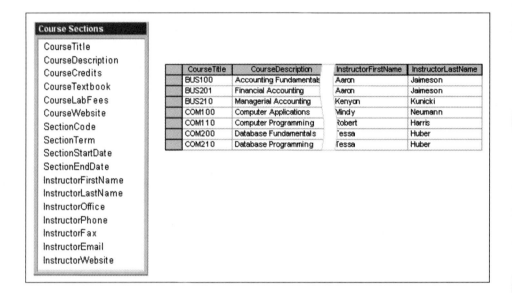

Figure 5.2 shows a relational database solution that divides the data into three tables. Because an instructor's phone number and a course's description appear only once in their respective tables, you need update only those records when a change is required. Not only does this design eliminate the potential for errors, the data consumes far less disk space. Employing proper design strategies is crucial to the validity, integrity, and accuracy of data stored in a database.

**Figure 5.2**

Using a relational
database design

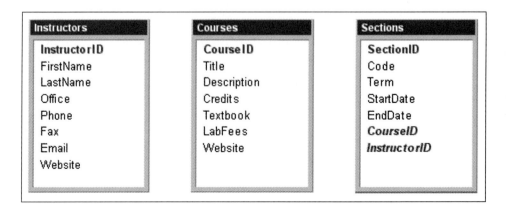

Database designers often speak of the stages of normalization, referred to as "normal forms." For example, data is said to be in the *first normal form* if there are no repeating groups of information in a table. While a discussion of normal forms is an important part of database theory, this guide focuses on the practical application of database designs using Microsoft Access. To this end, strive for the following design goals:

- Each table represents an identifiable subject or topic.
- Each record stores data for one subject or topic item only.
- Each field stores a single piece of data for a record. Do not store multiple items, multiple values, or calculated expressions in a field.
- Assign a primary key field that uniquely identifies each record.
- Relate tables based on common fields and values.

Relational database design using Microsoft Access provides powerful capabilities. After normalizing, you establish relationships between the tables in order to recombine the data for analytical and reporting purposes. To do so requires that you include the primary key from one table as a **foreign key** in another table. In Figure 5.2, the primary key fields are blue and the foreign key fields appear reddish in color. By populating tables with matching key values, related data is easily combined and shared.

Let's examine three types of table relationships: *one-to-one, one-to-many,* and *many-to-many.*

- In a **one-to-one relationship,** a single record in table A relates to a single record in table B, and vice versa. A one-to-one relationship is used when you want to separate data from the main table, perhaps for security reasons. For example, an instructor's compensation data may be stored in a table separate from his or her name and address. Notice that the primary keys in the following tables are identical.

**Instructors**

| | InstID | LastName | FirstName |
|---|---|---|---|
| | 100 | Babych | Dave |
| | 200 | Sundin | Susan |
| | 300 | Griffey | Rose |
| | 400 | Chan | Tom |

**Compensation**

| | InstID | Salary | Benefits |
|---|---|---|---|
| | 100 | 60,000 | Yes |
| | 200 | 45,000 | Yes |
| | 300 | 75,000 | No |
| | 400 | 39,000 | Yes |

- The most common type of relationship is the **one-to-many relationship** (or *many-to-one relationship,* depending on your perspective). In this relationship, a single record in table A can be related to one or more records in table B, *but* a single record in table B is related to only one record in table A. This *parent-child* relationship describes the situation between the Instructors and Sections tables—one instructor may teach one or more sections—and between the Courses and Sections tables in Figure 5.2. Notice that the InstID field in the following diagram is the primary key in the Instructors table and a foreign key in the Sections table.

**Instructors**

| | InstID | LastName | FirstName |
|---|---|---|---|
| | 100 | Babych | Dave |
| | 200 | Sundin | Susan |
| | 300 | Griffey | Rose |
| | 400 | Chan | Tom |

**Sections**

| | SecID | InstID | Term |
|---|---|---|---|
| | C195 | 100 | F-00 |
| | C220 | 300 | F-00 |
| | C295 | 300 | W-00 |
| | F750 | 400 | S-00 |

- In a **many-to-many relationship,** a single record in table A can be related to one or more records in table B, *and* a single record in table B can be related to one or more records in table A. A third **linking table,** sometimes called a *join* or *junction* table, is used to negotiate the connection by storing the primary keys from each table. Figure 5.2 illustrates a many-to-many relationship between the Instructors and Courses tables, with Sections acting as the linking table. For example, instructors may teach one or more courses and, going the other way, courses may be taught by one or more instructors. This is the most complex of the three relationships.

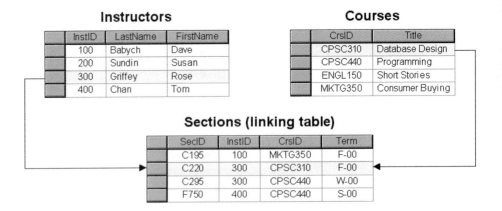

**Instructors**

| | InstID | LastName | FirstName |
|---|---|---|---|
| | 100 | Babych | Dave |
| | 200 | Sundin | Susan |
| | 300 | Griffey | Rose |
| | 400 | Chan | Tom |

**Courses**

| | CrsID | Title |
|---|---|---|
| | CPSC310 | Database Design |
| | CPSC440 | Programming |
| | ENGL150 | Short Stories |
| | MKTG350 | Consumer Buying |

**Sections (linking table)**

| | SecID | InstID | CrsID | Term |
|---|---|---|---|---|
| | C195 | 100 | MKTG350 | F-00 |
| | C220 | 300 | CPSC310 | F-00 |
| | C295 | 300 | CPSC440 | W-00 |
| | F750 | 400 | CPSC440 | S-00 |

Although this discussion of relational database theory is cursory at best, we have attempted to communicate the importance of designing an efficient and easy-to-use database. We recommend further research into relational database design and modeling techniques if you're interested in developing commercial database applications.

## 5.1.1 Defining Table Relationships

**FEATURE**

Creating a relational database in Access requires that you place common fields in each table you want to relate. More specifically, a connection is established when you include the primary key field from one table as a foreign key field in another table. In a one-to-many relationship, the primary key of table A is unique (the "one" side) while the foreign key of table B allows duplicate values (the "many" side). Although you can add a new field into a table structure at any time, it is preferable to identify the potential table relationships early in the database design process.

**METHOD**

1. Close all open tables before establishing a new relationship.
2. CLICK: Relationships button (⊞) in the Database toolbar, or CHOOSE: Tools, Relationships from the menu
3. CLICK: Show Table button (⊞) to select tables, if the Show Table window does not already appear
4. DRAG: a field from one table to the related field in another table
5. Complete the Edit Relationships dialog box.

**PRACTICE**

You now practice inserting foreign key fields and then establishing a one-to-many relationship using the Relationships window.

*Setup:* Ensure that Access is loaded. If you are launching Access and the startup dialog box appears, click the Cancel command button to remove the dialog box from the application window.

**1**   Most database applications begin with a need to store data. After analyzing the input and output needs, you can usually generate a comprehensive list of the *required* and *desired* fields. For example, review the draft planning worksheet in Figure 5.3. This worksheet provides a simple list of fields for storing contact information.

ACCESS

**Figure 5.3**

Listing fields for storing data

# Contact Information

| | |
|---|---|
| First Name | Home Phone |
| Last Name | Home Fax |
| Company Name | Work Phone |
| Home Address | Work Fax |
|   Address1 | Cellular |
|   Address2 | Pager |
|   City | Home E-mail |
|   State | Home Web Page |
|   Zip | Work E-mail |
| Work Address | Work Web Page |
|   Address1 | ICQ Address |
|   Address2 | |
|   City | |
|   State | |
|   Zip | |

**2** Let's evaluate the challenges facing the database designer who is handed this planning worksheet. Since many people may work for the same company, a flat-file design is inefficient—a company's name and address would need to be entered multiple times. Second, while some people may fill in each phone and Internet-related field, many will have only a home phone number. Including all of these field options in one table would result in many blank spaces and, therefore, wasted disk space. Figure 5.4 provides one possible solution for normalizing the data listed in Figure 5.3. (*Note:* The foreign key fields for relating the tables are not yet shown in this diagram.)

**Figure 5.4**

Normalizing data into logical groupings

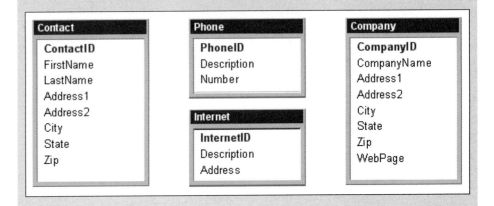

**3** If a unique identifier does not already exist for a set of data, a good design rule to follow in Access is to create an "ID" field using the AutoNumber data type. This unique field is placed at the top of the table structure and becomes the primary key field for the table. Figure 5.4 shows the normalized tables that have been created for you, complete with AutoNumber key fields. Open the database file named ACC510, located in the Advantage student data files folder.

**4** Of the four table structures in this database, only the Company and Contact tables contain data. Furthermore, no relationships have been established between the tables. On your own, display the datasheets for the Company and Contact tables and familiarize yourself with their contents. When ready to proceed, close the datasheets and return to the Database window.

**5** As mentioned previously, one company may employ several people, but a person may work for only one company at a time. In database design terms, Company is the primary or **parent table** and Contact is the subordinate or **child table.** To establish a one-to-many relationship, first create a CompanyID field in the Contact table to hold the foreign key values:
SELECT: Contact in the lists area
CLICK: Design button (⟨Design⟩) on the Database window toolbar

**6** In the table Design window, insert a new row for the foreign key field immediately below the ContactID field:
RIGHT-CLICK: row selector button for FirstName
CHOOSE: Insert Rows
CLICK: in the *Field Name* column of the new row
TYPE: `CompanyID`
PRESS: TAB

**7** The CompanyID field in the Company table is an AutoNumber data type. An important step is to ensure that you select an equivalent data type and field size for the foreign key in the Contact table. On the other hand, you do not need to name the two key fields the same. Do the following to proceed:
CLICK: down arrow attached to the *Data Type* cell
SELECT: Number
PRESS: TAB
(*Hint:* In defining matching key values, an AutoNumber data type is equivalent to a Number data type with a Long Integer field size.)

**8** Let's add a comment in the *Description* column:
TYPE: `Foreign key field for linking to Company table`
The table Design window should now appear similar to Figure 5.5.

ACCESS

**Figure 5.5**

Inserting a foreign key field

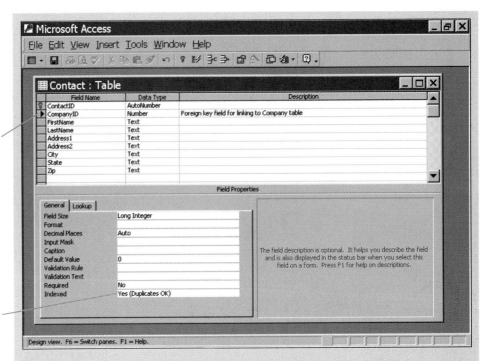

Primary and foreign key fields are placed at the top of a table structure in order to speed operations in larger tables.

Access assigns an index to the "ID" foreign key field automatically.

**9** After analyzing the database, Access selects an *Index* option in the Field Properties pane that allows duplicate values (see Figure 5.5). In essence, Access guesses that you are inserting the CompanyID field in an attempt to establish a table relationship. To continue:
CLICK: Save button (■) in the toolbar
CLICK: Close button (☒) for the table Design window

**10** Both the Phone and Internet tables are capable of storing one or more phone numbers, e-mail addresses, Web page URLs, or ICQ addresses for each person listed in the Contact table. This is another example of a one-to-many relationship. This time, however, Contact is the parent and Phone and Internet are the children. On your own, insert a new foreign key field into each of the Phone and Internet tables that will relate back to the ContactID field of the Contact table. (*Hint:* Name the new field ContactID in both tables and select a Number data type. Provide field descriptions similar to the one entered in step 8.)

**11** Now that the requisite foreign key fields exist, you may relate the tables. Before displaying the Relationships window, ensure that only the Database window appears in the application window. Then, do the following:
CLICK: Relationships button (⊞)
The Show Table window appears, as shown here. (*Hint:* If the Show Table window does not appear automatically, click the Show Table button (⊞) in the toolbar.)

**12**  To select all of the tables for display in the Show Table window:
PRESS: (SHIFT) and hold it down
CLICK: Phone in the table list area
All of the table names should now appear highlighted.

**13**  To add the tables to the Relationship window:
CLICK: Add command button
CLICK: Close command button

**14**  The selected field lists (sometimes called *table objects*) are added to the Relationships window. Notice that the primary key in each field list object appears in boldface. On your own, size each object so that all of its field names are visible. Arrange the objects to appear similar to Figure 5.7 by dragging their title bars.

**15**  To establish a relationship, drag a key field from one field list and drop it on the matching key field in another field list. (*Hint:* If you drag a primary key field over a foreign key field, Access creates a one-to-many table relationship. If you drag a primary key field over another primary key field, Access attempts to create a one-to-one relationship.) To connect the Company and Contact tables in a one-to-many relationship:
SELECT: CompanyID field in the Company field list
DRAG: the selected field and drop it on the CompanyID field in the Contact field list
The Edit Relationship window appears, as shown in Figure 5.6.

**Figure 5.6**

Edit Relationships window

The primary and foreign key fields are displayed from their respective tables.

Select this check box to enforce referential integrity constraints.

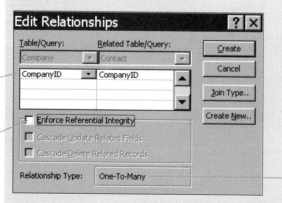

Because only one of the selected fields is a unique primary key, Access assumes a one-to-many relationship.

**16**  To accept the contents of the Edit Relationships window:
CLICK: Create command button
Notice that a relationship line now joins the two field list objects.

**17** To relate the Contact and Phone tables:
SELECT: ContactID field in the Contact field list
DRAG: the selected field and drop it on the ContactID field in the Phone field list
CLICK: Create command button in the Edit Relationships window

**18** To relate the Contact and Internet tables:
SELECT: ContactID field in the Contact field list
DRAG: the selected field and drop it on the ContactID field in the Internet field list
CLICK: Create command button in the Edit Relationships window
Congratulations! You've finished relating all of the tables in the database. Your screen should now appear similar to Figure 5.7.

**Figure 5.7**

Establishing relationships

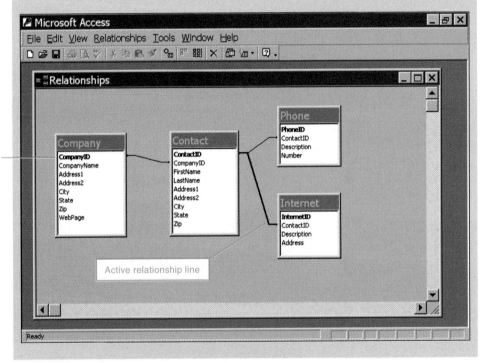

The primary key field in the Company field list object

Active relationship line

## 5.1.2 Working with Related Tables

**FEATURE**
**Referential integrity** refers to a set of rules for maintaining the integrity of data stored in a relational database. The objective of enforcing referential integrity is to promote and ensure the validity, accuracy, and consistency of data and relationships. For example, when referential integrity is enforced, you cannot enter a foreign key value in a related table that does not have a matching value in the primary table. Furthermore, you cannot delete a primary key value that has matching values in related child tables. To modify or delete a primary key value in a parent table, you must first remove all of the related child records.

Access provides two options that allow you to override the standard behavior thus described. By selecting the *Cascade Update Related Fields* check box in the Edit Relationships window, Access modifies the foreign key values in all related child records automatically when you make a change to the primary key value. By selecting the *Cascade Delete Related Records* check box, Access deletes all child records automatically when you delete a record from the primary table. Both of these options maintain referential integrity in your database.

**METHOD**
By default, referential integrity is not enforced. To turn this feature on:

1. CLICK: Relationships button (⊞) in the Database toolbar
2. RIGHT-CLICK: the relationship line that you wish to edit
3. CHOOSE: Edit Relationship
4. SELECT: *Enforce Referential Integrity* check box

**PRACTICE**
You now practice enforcing referential integrity and entering and displaying data in related tables.

*Setup:* Ensure that you've completed the previous lesson and that the Relationships window displayed resembles Figure 5.7.

ACCESS

**1** There are many different scenarios that you must consider when determining referential integrity constraints. When deleting a company record, for example, you don't usually want to wipe out all of the employee contact information. However, when deleting a contact, you should remove all of the contact's related phone and Internet records. To enforce referential integrity, edit the relationship:
RIGHT-CLICK: the relationship line joining the Contact and Phone field list objects

**2** From the right-click menu:
CHOOSE: Edit Relationships
(*Hint:* If a menu appears with the Show Table, Show All, and Save Layout menu commands, reposition the mouse pointer so that the tip of the pointer touches the relationship line before clicking.)

**3** In the Edit Relationships window:
SELECT: *Enforce Referential Integrity* check box
Notice that the other options related to data integrity are now accessible.

**4** To have Access delete all of the child phone records for a deleted parent contact record:
SELECT: *Cascade Delete Related Records*
CLICK: OK command button
New symbols appear on the end points of the relationship line.
(*CAUTION:* The Cascade Delete option is dangerous if used improperly!)

**5** On your own, perform similar steps to enforce the *Cascade Delete Related Records* constraint between the Contact and Internet tables.

**6** To save your work and continue:
CLICK: Save button (▣) in the toolbar
CLICK: Close button (☒) for the Relationships window

**7** To illustrate the relationships established between tables, enter some new information regarding the company where each contact works:
DOUBLE-CLICK: Contact in the list area

**8** Complete the CompanyID field column as shown in Figure 5.8.

**Figure 5.8**

Entering primary key values
from the Company table into
the Contact table

**9** Let's now display the Company table:
CLICK: Close button (☒) for the Contact Datasheet window
DOUBLE-CLICK: Company in the list area

**10** To display the employees who work for Rosie's Cookie Company:
CLICK: Expand button (⊞) in the left-hand column of
CompanyID 2
Notice that a subdatasheet appears (Figure 5.9) showing the
related records from the Contact table.

**Figure 5.9**

Displaying related records

The subdatasheet
displays related
records from the
Contact table.

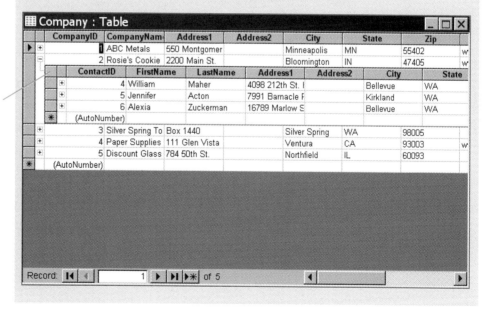

ACCESS

**11** To add a phone number for William Maher:
CLICK: Expand button (⊞) in the left-hand column of ContactID 4
Because more than one table is related to the Contact table, the Insert Subdatasheet dialog box appears requesting that you select one of the tables to display in the subdatasheet. (*Note:* You can nest up to eight levels of subdatasheets in Datasheet view.)

**12** To display related data from the Phone table:
CLICK: Phone in the list area
CLICK: OK command button
A subdatasheet appears under William Maher's record.

**13** To insert two records:
PRESS: ⌶TAB⌶ to bypass the AutoNumber field
TYPE: Work
PRESS: ⌶TAB⌶
TYPE: 425-555-1234
PRESS: ⌶TAB⌶ twice
TYPE: Home
PRESS: ⌶TAB⌶
TYPE: 425-555-5678
PRESS: ⌶SHIFT⌶ + ⌶ENTER⌶ to save the record

**14** To collapse the contents of the Datasheet window:
CLICK: Collapse button (⊟) for ContactID 4
CLICK: Collapse button (⊟) for CompanyID 2

**15** Close the Datasheet window and, if necessary, save the table layout.

## 5.1.3  Printing the Relationships Window

**FEATURE**
Once the table relationships are defined, use the Print Relationships command to print a hardcopy representation of the Relationships window. This command generates an Access report object depicting the tables and relationships that exist in the active database. The report provides an excellent complement to the *Documenter* for printing and documenting table structures and for visualizing the organization of data. As with any report object, you can preview the report before printing.

**METHOD**
1. CLICK: Relationships button (⊞) in the Database toolbar
2. CHOOSE: File, Print Relationships

**PRACTICE**
In this lesson, you generate a report of the table relationships.

*Setup:* Ensure that you've completed the previous lessons and that the ACC510 Database window appears in the application window.

**1** To print the relationships in the ACC510 database:
CLICK: Relationships button (⊞)
The Relationships window appears.

**2** CHOOSE: File, Print Relationships
A report is created to appear similar to the Relationships window. (*Hint:* Using report Design view, you can modify the contents of this report as you would any report object.)

**3** Maximize the Print Preview window for the Relationships report. Your screen should now appear similar to Figure 5.10.

**Figure 5.10**

Previewing the
Relationships report

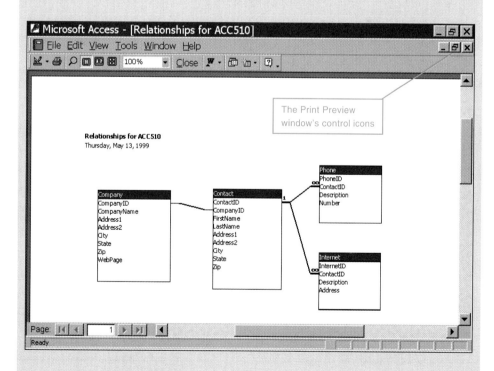

**4** Let's print the report:
CLICK: Print button (⊞)
(*Note:* If you do not have a printer available, proceed to the next step.)

**5**
To save and close the Print Preview window:
CLICK: its Restore button (⊡)
CLICK: its Close button (☒)
CLICK: Yes command button, when asked to save the changes
CLICK: OK command button to accept the default name
A new report object named "Relationships for ACC510" will now appear in the list of stored reports.

**6**
To close the Relationships window:
CLICK: its Close button (☒)

## 5.1.4 Setting Object and Database Properties

**FEATURE**
Generally speaking, a **property** is a characteristic or attribute that may define, describe, empower, or constrain an object. Access enables you to specify properties for numerous objects, including fields, tables, queries, and the entire database. In addition to providing descriptive names, you can input notes and comments about any object in the database. You can also hide an object, such as a table containing sensitive information, from displaying in the Database window. Database properties, such as Title, Author, and Subject, can also be used as search criteria when you need to find a database stored on your computer.

**METHOD**
To set Database properties:
CHOOSE: File, Database Properties

To set an object's properties:

1.  RIGHT-CLICK: the desired object
2.  CHOOSE: Properties

**PRACTICE**
You now practice storing some detailed information about the objects and databases that you've used in this module.

*Setup:* Ensure that the ACC510 Database window is displayed.

**1**
To enter some descriptive information for the database:
CHOOSE: File, Database Properties
CLICK: *Summary* tab, if it is not already selected

**2** On your own, enter the data appearing in Figure 5.11. Replace the *your name, your instructor,* and *your school* entries with your own information. When finished, click the OK command button.

**Figure 5.11**

Database Properties dialog box

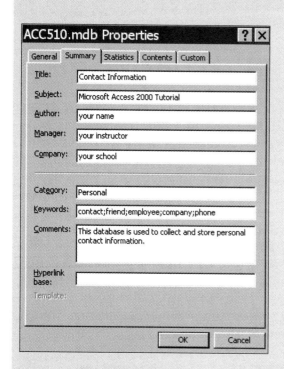

**3** To enter some descriptive information for a table object:
RIGHT-CLICK: Contact in the list area
CHOOSE: Properties
The Contact Properties dialog box appears. Notice the *Hidden* attribute's check box that you may select to hide the object from displaying in the Database window.

**4** In the *Description* text box:
TYPE: **For contacts, friends, and employees.**
(*Hint:* Pressing ⟨ENTER⟩ is the same as clicking the OK command button in most dialog boxes. Therefore, you must use ⟨SHIFT⟩ + ⟨ENTER⟩ if you want to start a new line in the *Description* text box.)

**5** CLICK: OK command button

**6** To view the description in the Database window:
CLICK: Details button (🖾) in the Database window toolbar

**7** To return to a more compact view:
CLICK: List button (🖽) in the Database window toolbar

**8** Close the Database window.

**5.1 Self Check**    Describe the table relationship that might exist between doctors and their patients.

# 5.2 Customizing Fields

One of the most important steps in database design is ensuring that the data that you want to store has been properly described. Some designers engage users in a formal interview process in order to develop specification sheets for each field in the database. Other designers input the required field characteristics directly into the computer. Regardless of the approach, clarifying the features and constraints of each field serves to enhance data integrity. In Access, you describe fields and specify business rules for working with data using *field properties,* such as those listed in Table 5.1. **Business rules** are the guidelines for how a person uses the data in the real world. For example, a commission field may top out at 10 percent or a set of address fields may only allow U.S. addresses to be entered. Enforcing these rules using properties ensures that field-level integrity is maintained in the database.

**Table 5.1**

Common field
properties

| Property | Description |
| --- | --- |
| Field Size | Define the maximum length of a text or numeric field. |
| Format | Specify how text, numbers, dates, and times are displayed and printed. |
| Decimal Places | Specify the number of places to display to the right of the decimal; for numeric and currency fields only. |
| Input Mask | Simplify data entry for fields that have a standard format, such as a phone number. |
| Caption | Define a default field label to appear on forms and reports, instead of using the field name. |
| Default Value | Define a value or expression that is automatically entered for each new record. |
| Validation Rule | Enter an expression that defines the rules for entering data into the specified field. |

| Property | Description |
|---|---|
| **Table 5.1** Common field properties *Continued* | |
| Validation Text | Specify the text to display if you enter invalid data, according to the set rule, into a field. |
| Required | Specify whether a value is required in a field. Access displays an error message if you attempt to skip entering data into the field. |
| Indexed | Specify whether the table should be indexed on this field in order to speed searches. |

To refresh your memory, you modify a field's data type and property settings in table Design view, which is displayed by selecting the desired table object and clicking the Design button (🗹Design). You can also toggle between Design view (🗹▾) and Datasheet view (▦▾) by clicking the View button. (*Note:* The View button changes its appearance depending on whether the active window is a Datasheet or Design window.) In this module, you customize a table by modifying its fields' properties, including captions, sizes, display formats, and data types.

## 5.2.1  Modifying Field Properties

**FEATURE**
Modifying a field's properties entails entering values and specifying characteristics in the Field Properties pane of the table Design window. The number and availability of properties is determined ultimately by the field's data type. For example, a field with the Text data type allows you to limit the number of characters entered, while a Yes/No field does not. Carefully specifying your field's characteristics when designing a table structure can save you and your users a lot of time, effort, and frustration.

**METHOD**
1. Display the table structure in Design view.
2. SELECT: a field in the Field Grid pane
3. SELECT: a property on the *General* tab of the Field Properties pane
4. Modify the field characteristic as desired.

**PRACTICE**
You now practice changing the size and caption properties for fields.

*Setup:* Ensure that no databases appear in the application window.

**1** Open the database file named ACC500, located in the Advantage student data files folder.

**2** To display the table Design window for the Students table:
SELECT: Students in the list area
CLICK: Design button (⩗Design) in the Database window toolbar
Your screen should appear similar to Figure 5.12. With the StudentID field selected in the Field Grid pane, the options displayed in the Field Properties pane are limited by the AutoNumber data type.

**Figure 5.12**

Viewing the Students
table structure

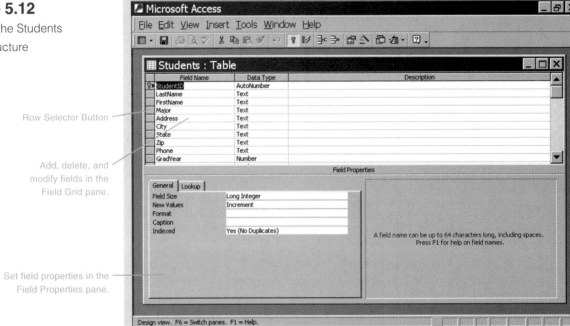

Row Selector Button

Add, delete, and
modify fields in the
Field Grid pane.

Set field properties in the
Field Properties pane.

**3** To make Major the active field in the Field Grid pane:
CLICK: row selector button for Major
(*Note:* You may also click the appropriate cell in the *Field Name* column to make a field active in the Field Grid pane.)

**4** By default, a field of the Text data type is defined with a size of 50 characters. Although you can specify up to 255 characters, smaller sizes enable Access to process the data stored in the field more quickly. In addition, setting a maximum field size lets Access know how much space to set aside for storing data; not to mention letting the user know how much room there is to enter data. For the Major field, 15 characters will provide plenty of space. To modify the field size:
DOUBLE-CLICK: *Field Size* text box in the Field Properties pane

**5** With the default entry (50) highlighted:
TYPE: **15**
The new entry replaces the existing highlighted value.

**6** To modify the State field to accept only a two-character abbreviation:
CLICK: row selector button for State
DOUBLE-CLICK: *Field Size* property text box
TYPE: **2**

**7** Lastly, let's modify the Zip code field to accept only 10 characters:
CLICK: row selector button for Zip
DOUBLE-CLICK: *Field Size* property text box
TYPE: **10**

**8** For the Number data type, the *Field Size* property specifies a value's precision and storage capacity. For example, the Byte option allows a value between 0 and 255 to be entered, while the Decimal option allows a very large and very precise number at the cost of 12 storage bytes. In this exercise, the GradYear field must store four digits (e.g., 2000). To view the field size alternatives:
CLICK: row selector button for GradYear
CLICK: once in the *Field Size* property text box

**9** The default field size for a Number field is "Long Integer." This option enables you to store large values ranging from -2,147,483,648 to 2,147,483,647. An integer takes only half the storage space, while allowing values from –32,768 to 32,767. To save storage space, select an Integer field size for the GradYear field:
CLICK: down arrow attached to the *Field Size* property text box
Your screen should now appear similar to Figure 5.13.

ACCESS

**Figure 5.13**

Selecting a field size for
the Number data type

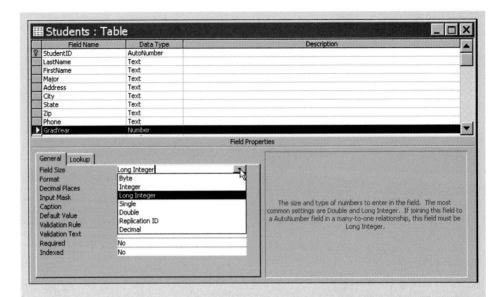

**10** CLICK: Integer option in the drop-down list

**11** Let's set the field size for another Number data type:
CLICK: row selector button for GPA

**12** The GPA field stores decimal numbers ranging from 0.00 to 4.00.
The required decimal precision is far less than the 18 digits cur-
rently specified in the Field Properties pane. To modify the field
size storage precision and display formatting:
DOUBLE-CLICK: *Precision* property text box
TYPE: **3**
DOUBLE-CLICK: *Decimal Places* property text box
TYPE: **2**

**13** A field's *Caption* property enables you to specify the text label to
use in forms and reports. If this property is left blank, the field's
name is used for field labels and column headers. To set field
captions:
CLICK: row selector button for LastName
CLICK: once in the *Caption* property text box
TYPE: `Surname`
CLICK: row selector button for FirstName
CLICK: once in the *Caption* property text box
TYPE: `Given`

**14** To save your modifications:
CLICK: Save button (⊟)
CLICK: Yes command button to confirm that the changes are correct
The dialog box warns you that field sizes have been shortened and that data may be lost. In a real application, you should review the contents of the fields you want to modify prior to setting field sizes. For this exercise, the selections made are correct and no data will be lost.

**15** To view the Students datasheet:
CLICK: View—Datasheet button (▣▾)
Notice that the column headings for the LastName and FirstName fields now use the captions "Surname" and "Given."

**16** On your own, ensure that no data has been lost in the Major, State, Zip, GradYear, and GPA columns. Then, close the Datasheet window.

---

**In Addition**
Optimizing Data
Type Selections

Using the smallest possible field size setting saves storage space and reduces processing time in your database application. The options listed below summarize the field size selections for the Number data type. Select the smallest possible field size that allows you to store an acceptable range of values.

| Field Size | Storage Space | Range of Values |
| --- | --- | --- |
| Byte | 1 byte | 0 to 255 |
| Integer | 2 bytes | −32,768 to 32,767 |
| Long Integer | 4 bytes | −2,147,483,648 to 2,147,483,647 |
| Single | 4 bytes | Numbers with up to 7 decimal places |
| Double | 8 bytes | Numbers with up to 15 decimal places |
| Decimal | 12 bytes | Numbers with up to 28 decimal places |

ACCESS

## 5.2.2  Specifying a Field's Format

**FEATURE**
When defining a new field in the Field Grid pane of the Design window, the selected data type determines how Access stores the data internally. For example, a person's surname may be stored in a Text field, their age in a Number field, and their salary in a Currency field. Using the *Format* property, you can also specify how the data should display and print. You can force letters to display in uppercase, insert spaces between characters, and specify the number of decimal places to include, without changing the data. Depending on the selected data type, Access provides several predefined formats, namely for the Date/Time, Currency, Numbers, and Yes/No data types. If these don't suit your needs, you can create custom formats. (*Note:* To specify the format that data should be entered and stored in the table, refer to the *Input Mask* property described in lesson 5.3.3.)

**METHOD**
1. Display the table structure in Design view.
2. SELECT: a field in the Field Grid pane
3. SELECT: *Format* property in the Field Properties pane
4. SELECT: a predefined format or enter a custom format

**PRACTICE**
In table Design view, you set a field's Format property and then display the table in Datasheet view.

*Setup:* Ensure that the ACC500 Database window is displayed.

**1** To display the Students datasheet:
DOUBLE-CLICK: Students in the list area
Notice that the phone numbers are stored in a Text field without any parentheses or hyphens (e.g., 2603902873).

**2** Let's modify the phone number to display in an easier-to-read format:
CLICK: View—Design button (⬚▾)

**3** To modify the Phone field's display format:
CLICK: row selector button for Phone
CLICK: once in the *Format* property text box

**4** You enter a display format using symbols to represent characters, spaces, and formatting instructions. For example, the @ symbol represents a character or space. The "<" and ">" symbols force all characters to display in lowercase and uppercase, respectively. To enter a phone number display format:
TYPE: (@@@) @@@-@@@@
Notice that you can enter additional characters, such as parentheses, to display along with the data.

**5** To view the new display formatting:
CLICK: Save button (▣)
CLICK: View—Datasheet button (▦▾)
Notice that the phone number column now appears with parentheses, spaces, and hyphens, even though the original data is stored without these characters.

**6** To force the Major field to display using uppercase letters:
CLICK: View—Design button (▧▾)
CLICK: row selector button for Major
CLICK: once in the *Format* property text box
TYPE: >
The existence of a single ">" symbol informs Access to display the field's contents in uppercase letters.

**7** To view the formatting change:
CLICK: Save button (▣)
CLICK: View—Datasheet button (▦▾)
Your screen should now appear similar to Figure 5.14. (*Hint:* Remember that the data stored in the table is unaffected by this formatting change. You've simply described a different method for displaying the data in datasheets, forms, and reports.)

**Figure 5.14**

Formatting the display of field contents

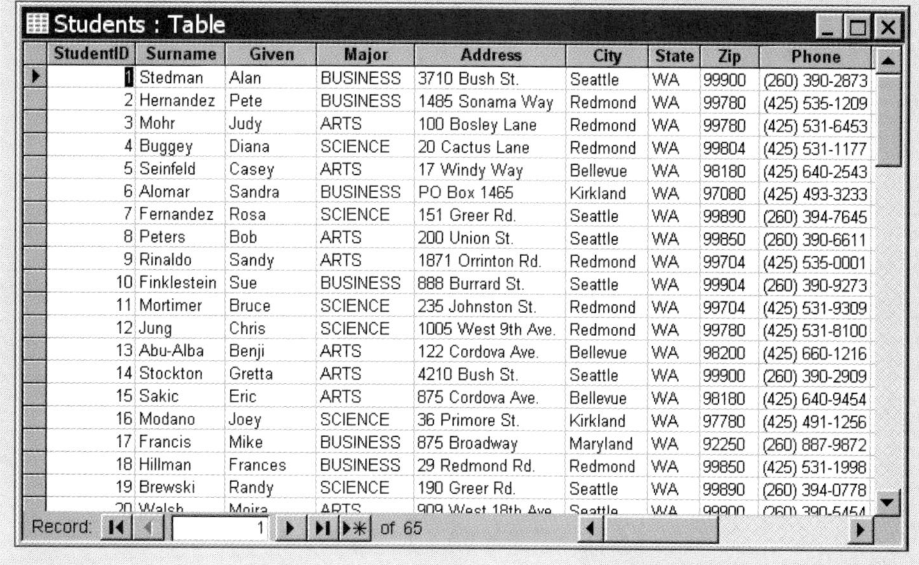

| StudentID | Surname | Given | Major | Address | City | State | Zip | Phone |
|---|---|---|---|---|---|---|---|---|
| 1 | Stedman | Alan | BUSINESS | 3710 Bush St. | Seattle | WA | 99900 | (260) 390-2873 |
| 2 | Hernandez | Pete | BUSINESS | 1485 Sonama Way | Redmond | WA | 99780 | (425) 535-1209 |
| 3 | Mohr | Judy | ARTS | 100 Bosley Lane | Redmond | WA | 99780 | (425) 531-6453 |
| 4 | Buggey | Diana | SCIENCE | 20 Cactus Lane | Redmond | WA | 99804 | (425) 531-1177 |
| 5 | Seinfeld | Casey | ARTS | 17 Windy Way | Bellevue | WA | 98180 | (425) 640-2543 |
| 6 | Alomar | Sandra | BUSINESS | PO Box 1465 | Kirkland | WA | 97080 | (425) 493-3233 |
| 7 | Fernandez | Rosa | SCIENCE | 151 Greer Rd. | Seattle | WA | 99890 | (260) 394-7645 |
| 8 | Peters | Bob | ARTS | 200 Union St. | Seattle | WA | 99850 | (260) 390-6611 |
| 9 | Rinaldo | Sandy | ARTS | 1871 Orrinton Rd. | Redmond | WA | 99704 | (425) 535-0001 |
| 10 | Finklestein | Sue | BUSINESS | 888 Burrard St. | Seattle | WA | 99904 | (260) 390-9273 |
| 11 | Mortimer | Bruce | SCIENCE | 235 Johnston St. | Redmond | WA | 99704 | (425) 531-9309 |
| 12 | Jung | Chris | SCIENCE | 1005 West 9th Ave. | Redmond | WA | 99780 | (425) 531-8100 |
| 13 | Abu-Alba | Benji | ARTS | 122 Cordova Ave. | Bellevue | WA | 98200 | (425) 660-1216 |
| 14 | Stockton | Gretta | ARTS | 4210 Bush St. | Seattle | WA | 99900 | (260) 390-2909 |
| 15 | Sakic | Eric | ARTS | 875 Cordova Ave. | Bellevue | WA | 98180 | (425) 640-9454 |
| 16 | Modano | Joey | SCIENCE | 36 Primore St. | Kirkland | WA | 97780 | (425) 491-1256 |
| 17 | Francis | Mike | BUSINESS | 875 Broadway | Maryland | WA | 92250 | (260) 887-9872 |
| 18 | Hillman | Frances | BUSINESS | 29 Redmond Rd. | Redmond | WA | 99850 | (425) 531-1998 |
| 19 | Brewski | Randy | SCIENCE | 190 Greer Rd. | Seattle | WA | 99890 | (260) 394-0778 |
| 20 | Walsh | Moira | ARTS | 909 West 18th Ave. | Seattle | WA | 99900 | (260) 390-5454 |

Students : Table

Record: ◄ ◄  1  ► ►◄ ►✳  of 65

**8** You can also select from several predefined formats for displaying dates and numbers. To illustrate:
CLICK: View—Design button (🖾▾)
CLICK: row selector button for GPA
CLICK: once in the *Format* property text box

**9** To modify the display format for the GPA field:
CLICK: down arrow attached to the *Format* property text box
CLICK: Standard option in the drop-down list

**10** To save the formatting changes and close the table Design window:
CLICK: Save button (🖫)
CLICK: its Close button (☒)

## 5.2.3  Defining a Hyperlink Field

**FEATURE**
The Hyperlink data type enables you to store an alphanumeric entry of up to 64,000 characters as a **hyperlink.** When you click a hyperlink, you are telling your computer to retrieve an item and display it on your screen. Hyperlink addresses provide an easy way to "drill-down" through layers of information to find what you are looking for. For example, they may be used to quickly launch a Web browser and link to an HTML page stored on the Internet or to send an e-mail message. You can also use hyperlinks to move among your Office documents—click a link to display a worksheet in Microsoft Excel or to open a Microsoft Word document to a specific page.

**METHOD**
To insert a hyperlink field:

1. Display the table structure in Design view.
2. SELECT: an empty row in the Field Grid pane
3. TYPE: *a field name* in the *Field Name* column
4. SELECT: Hyperlink in the *Data Type* column
5. Complete the *Description* column, if desired.

To enter data into a hyperlink field:

1. SELECT: the desired field
2. CLICK: Insert Hyperlink button (🖳)

To remove or edit the contents of a hyperlink field:

1. RIGHT-CLICK: the desired hyperlink address
2. CHOOSE: Hyperlink
3. CHOOSE: Remove Hyperlink to delete the entry, or
   CHOOSE: Display Text to edit the display text, or
   CHOOSE: Edit Hyperlink to modify the hyperlink address

**PRACTICE**
You now insert a new hyperlink field and practice entering data.

*Setup:* Ensure that the ACC500 Database window is displayed.

**1** Let's add a new field that will store a hyperlink to a student's Web page:
SELECT: Students in the list area
CLICK: Design button (📐Design) in the Database window toolbar

**2** To move to an empty row at the end of the table structure:
PRESS: CTRL + ⬇
PRESS: ⬇

**3** To create a new hyperlink field:
TYPE: WebPage in the *Field Name* column
PRESS: TAB
SELECT: Hyperlink in the *Data Type* column
You're done! That's all there is to it.

**4** To save and view the table structure:
CLICK: Save button (🖫)
CLICK: View—Datasheet button (🖩▾)

**5** There are two methods for entering data into a hyperlink field. You can type an address or you can use the Insert Hyperlink dialog box. Let's begin by typing a Web page address:
PRESS: END
TYPE: http://www.mypage.com
PRESS: ⬇
As shown below (when the field is resized), the entry is blue and underlined, as it would appear using Web browser software.

| GPA | WebPage |
|------|---------------------------|
| 3.25 | http://www.mypage.com |
| 3.75 | |

**6** For the next record, use the Insert Hyperlink dialog box:
CLICK: Insert Hyperlink button (🔍)
The dialog box in Figure 5.15 appears. (*Note:* You can also choose the Insert, Hyperlink command to display this dialog box.)

**Figure 5.15**

Insert Hyperlink dialog box

Creates a link to an existing document file or HTML Web page

Creates a link to an object within the active database

Creates a link to a page that has yet to be created

Creates a link for sending an e-mail message

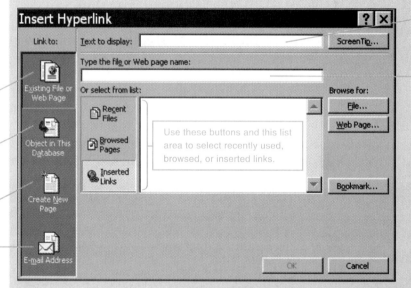

Enter the text to display

Enter the link address

**7** In the Insert Hyperlink dialog box:
TYPE: My Home Page in the *Text to display* text box:
TYPE: http://www.myhome.com in the *Type the file or Web page name* text box
CLICK: OK command button

**8** When you return to the datasheet, notice that the display text is inserted in the field column. In fact, Access stores three pieces of information for each hyperlink entry: the *display text,* the *hyperlink address,* and, if required, the *hyperlink subaddress.* If you type a hyperlink address manually (as in step 5), the display text and the hyperlink address are the same. Move the mouse pointer over the hyperlinks. Notice that the mouse pointer changes shape to a hand. To launch a hyperlink, click the mouse pointer once. Since these hyperlink addresses are fictional, however, proceed to the next step.

**9** To edit the display text of the hyperlink in the first record:
RIGHT-CLICK: http://www.mypage.com in the WebPage column
CHOOSE: Hyperlink
Your screen should now appear similar to Figure 5.16.

**Figure 5.16**

Editing a hyperlink address

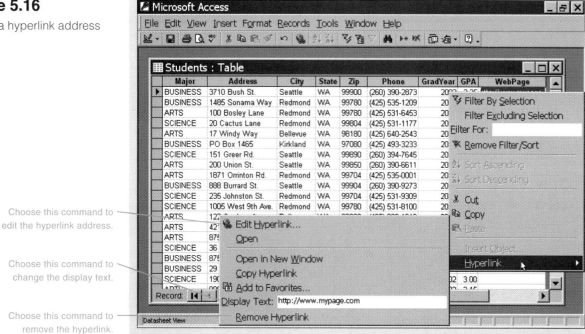

Choose this command to edit the hyperlink address.

Choose this command to change the display text.

Choose this command to remove the hyperlink.

**10** CHOOSE: Display Text
If a flashing insertion point does not appear to the right of the entry in the Display Text command's text box, click once beside the entry.

**11** SELECT: the entry in the Display Text command's text box
TYPE: **My Web Page**
PRESS: [ENTER]
Your typing replaces the selected display text, but does not modify the hyperlink address. The new display text appears in the datasheet.

**12** Close the Students Datasheet window. (*Note:* If you adjusted the column widths in the window, you are asked to save the formatting layout changes to the datasheet.)

## 5.2.4  Changing a Field's Data Type

**FEATURE**

At some point you may need to change a field's data type. Depending on the change you make, Access may not be able to convert the existing data into the new format. Therefore, you should always make a backup copy of your table before converting field data types. Some of the more common examples involve changing a Text field to a Memo field, a Text field to a Hyperlink field, and a Number field to a Currency field. The only change that you should not perform is changing an AutoNumber field.

**METHOD**

1. Display the table structure in Design view.
2. SELECT: row selector of the desired field
3. SELECT: the new data type in the *Data Type* column
4. CLICK: Save button (🖫) to save your changes

**PRACTICE**

In this exercise, you practice changing the data type of a field.

*Setup:* Ensure that you've completed the last lesson and that the ACC500 Database window is displayed.

**1** Let's change the hyperlink field inserted in the last lesson into a text field. Do the following:
SELECT: Students in the list area
CLICK: Design button (⬓Design) in the Database window toolbar

**2** To move to the *Data Type* column of the last field:
PRESS: CTRL + ⬇
PRESS: TAB

**3** SELECT: Text from the drop-down list in the *Data Type* column

**4** To save the table structure:
CLICK: Save button (🖫)
The dialog box in Figure 5.17 warns you that making changes to data types can result in the loss of data.

**Figure 5.17**

A warning is displayed when changing data types

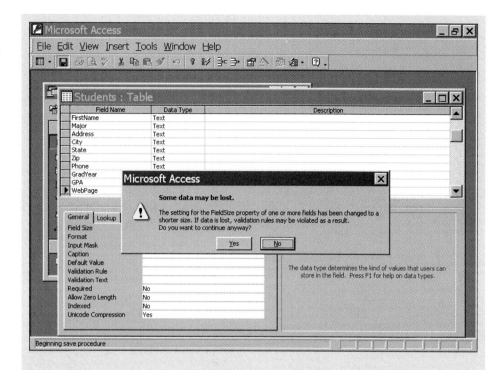

5  To accept the change and continue:
CLICK: Yes command button

6  Let's view the datasheet and see the changes:
CLICK: View—Datasheet button (⊞▾)
PRESS: END to move to the last column

7  Increase the width of the WebPage column by double-clicking its right border in the field header area. Notice that the field values appear in the format *DisplayText#HyperlinkAddress#HyperlinkSubAddress*. As described in the last lesson, this entry illustrates the three portions of a hyperlink that are stored in an Access table.

8  Close the Datasheet window without saving the layout changes.

**5.2 Self Check**  Which field property would you use to ensure that a field's contents always display in uppercase?

# 5.3   Maintaining Your Data's Integrity

In addition to customizing fields and table structures, Access provides several methods related to maintaining your data's field-level integrity. Using field properties, you can impose constraints and restrictions in order to validate data before it is stored in the table. For example, you can force an entry to be made for a field and, if necessary, ensure that the entry falls within a particular range or belongs to a specific list. You can also ensure that data is entered in a particular way using an *input mask*. Lastly, you can define lookup lists and impose field validation rules that limit entries to acceptable values when entering and editing data.

## 5.3.1   Enforcing Required Fields

**FEATURE**
By default, Access requires a value only for the primary key field in a new record. To specify that another field must also contain data, you set its *Required* property to Yes. For each required field, users must enter a value before Access allows them to proceed or save the record. Although activating this property ensures that data is entered, there is no guarantee that the data is valid or even correct.

**METHOD**
1.   Display the table structure in Design view.
2.   SELECT: a field in the Field Grid pane
3.   SELECT: *Required* property in the Field Properties pane
4.   SELECT: Yes from the drop-down list

**PRACTICE**
You now enforce a required field in the Instructors table.

*Setup:* Ensure that the ACC500 Database window is displayed. If not, open the database from the student data files folder.

   To display the field properties for the Instructors table:
SELECT: Instructors in the list area
CLICK: Design button (⧉Design) in the Database window toolbar

**2** The InstructorID AutoNumber field is the table's primary key field. However, a record is meaningless without storing an instructor's surname. To make sure that each new record contains at least a last name entry, do the following:
CLICK: row selector button for LastName
DOUBLE-CLICK: *Required* property text box
(*Hint:* This property text box provides a drop-down list of two choices: Yes and No. Double-clicking the text box toggles the choices.)

**3** Ensure that the *Required* property displays "Yes" and then:
CLICK: Save button (🖫) to save the table structure
CLICK: Yes command button to ensure data integrity

**4** To display the Instructors datasheet:
CLICK: View—Datasheet button (🖩▾)

**5** Let's add a new record to the datasheet:
CLICK: New Record button (▸*) in the toolbar
PRESS: TAB to bypass the AutoNumber field

**6** You will now attempt to save the record after entering the instructor's first name only:
PRESS: TAB
TYPE: Connie
PRESS: SHIFT + ENTER
A dialog box appears informing you that the LastName field requires an entry.

**7** To remove the warning dialog box:
CLICK: OK command button

**8** To complete the new record successfully:
CLICK: in the LastName field
TYPE: Klimek
PRESS: SHIFT + ENTER
The record is saved.

**9** Close the Instructors Datasheet window.

## 5.3.2 Specifying Default Values

**FEATURE**

A field's default value is typically the value most likely to be entered into a field. By setting a field's *Default Value* property, Access inputs the value automatically whenever a new record is added to the table. If 99 percent of your customers live in California, for example, place "CA" in the State field's *Default Value* property text box. Thereafter, each new record contains "CA" in the State field before you even touch the keyboard. It is important to note that a field's default value may be modified or overridden at any time.

**METHOD**

1. Display the table structure in Design view.
2. SELECT: a field in the Field Grid pane
3. SELECT: *Default Value* property in the Field Properties pane
4. TYPE: `desired default value`

**PRACTICE**

You now specify default values for two fields in the Courses table.

*Setup:* Ensure that the ACC500 Database window is displayed.

**1** To display the field properties for the Courses table:
SELECT: Courses in the list area
CLICK: Design button (![Design]) in the Database window toolbar

**2** Let's assume that the majority of entries for this table are 3 credit courses in the Faculty of Business. To begin, specify a default value for the Credits field:
CLICK: row selector button for Credits
DOUBLE-CLICK: *Default Value* property text box
TYPE: `3`

**3** To specify a default value for the Faculty field:
CLICK: row selector button for Faculty
CLICK: *Default Value* property text box
TYPE: `"Business"`
Notice that entering a text value requires quotation marks. (*Hint:* If you type an entry without quotes, Access adds them for you automatically.)

**4** To display the Courses datasheet:
CLICK: Save button (![Save icon])
CLICK: View—Datasheet button (![Datasheet icon])

**5** Scroll to the bottom of the Datasheet window. Notice that the values "3" and "Business" appear in their respective columns of the blank record in the last row. (Remember that you may modify these values when entering a new record.)

**6** Close the Datasheet window.

## 5.3.3 Using an Input Mask

**FEATURE**
To achieve consistency, use an **input mask** to control the way data is entered into a field. For example, phone numbers and international postal codes may be entered in many different ways. With an input mask, the user need only be concerned with typing the correct data. The input mask ensures that the data is formatted correctly prior to being stored. You create an input mask using the Access Input Mask Wizard. (*Note:* To change the display of information in datasheets, forms, and reports, use the *Format* property. Input masks affect how data is entered and stored in a table.)

**METHOD**
1. Display the table structure in Design view.
2. SELECT: a field in the Field Grid pane
3. SELECT: *Input Mask* property in the Field Properties pane
4. CLICK: Build button (⊡) to launch the Input Mask Wizard
5. Specify an input mask to apply.

**PRACTICE**
You now create input masks for two fields in the Instructors table.

*Setup:* Ensure that the ACC500 Database window is displayed.

**1** To display the field properties for the Instructors table:
SELECT: Instructors in the list area
CLICK: Design button (⬚Design) in the Database window toolbar

**2** Each value in the Office field of the Instructors table contains a capitalized building letter followed by a maximum three-digit number (e.g., A40 or B300). Let's create an input mask to ensure that values are entered using this format:
CLICK: row selector button for Office
CLICK: *Input Mask* property text box

ACCESS

**3** An input mask is simply a combination of placeholder characters. For example, a "9" represents an optional numeric digit, a "0" represents a required numeric digit, and an "L" represents a letter. To create an input mask:
TYPE: **>L999**
(*Note:* The ">" symbol ensures that the letter appears in uppercase, but has no affect on the digit placeholders.)

**4** Let's add a new field to the table to store phone numbers:
CLICK: in the *Field Name* column immediately below the Office field
TYPE: **Phone**
PRESS: TAB
SELECT: Text in the *Data Type* column

**5** Rather than entering your own placeholders, you can use the Input Mask Wizard to select an appropriate mask for phone numbers:
CLICK: *Input Mask* property text box
CLICK: Build button (⬚) appearing to the right of the text box
CLICK: Yes command button when asked to save the table
Your screen should now appear similar to Figure 5.18.

**Figure 5.18**

Input Mask Wizard dialog box

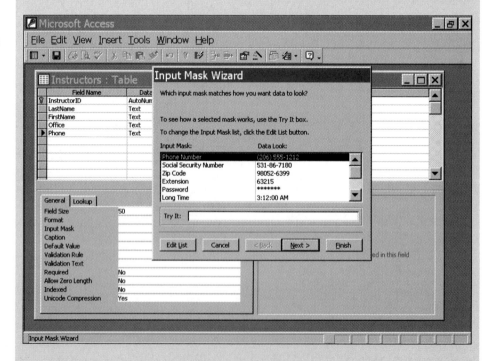

**6** After perusing the list box of input mask options:
SELECT: Phone Number
PRESS: TAB
The cursor moves to the *Try It* text box.

**7**    TYPE: **7085551000**
Notice that the entry appears as (708) 555-1000 in the text box.

**8**    To proceed to the next step:
CLICK: Next >

**9**    If desired, you can customize the way the input mask works.
Let's accept the default options and proceed:
CLICK: Next >

**10**    You must now decide whether to store the additional symbols used in the input mask as part of the field contents. If you are working with a large number of records, the extra storage space consumed by these symbols may become significant. Therefore, most people prefer to store the raw data only. To accept the default option and proceed:
CLICK: Next >

**11**    Now that the wizard is finished asking questions, let's save the structure and view the datasheet:
CLICK: Finish to complete the wizard
CLICK: Save button (□)
CLICK: View—Datasheet button (□▾)

**12**    To test the input masks, enter a new record:
CLICK: New Record button (▸▸)
PRESS: TAB to bypass the AutoNumber field
TYPE: **Gomez**
PRESS: TAB
TYPE: **Peter**
PRESS: TAB

**13**    With your cursor in the Office field, try the first input mask:
TYPE: **b** (the letter is capitalized automatically on-screen)
TYPE: **b** (the letter is not accepted)
TYPE: **2** (the digit is accepted)
TYPE: **22** to complete the entry
PRESS: TAB

**14**    Enter a phone number for the instructor and then save the record:
TYPE: **7085556789**
PRESS: SHIFT + ENTER to save the record
The phone number appears as (708) 555-6789 in the datasheet.

**15**    Close the Datasheet window.

## 5.3.4  Defining a Lookup Field

**FEATURE**

A **lookup field** is a list of acceptable values that may be entered into a field. Whereas an input mask focuses on how data is entered, a lookup field emphasizes what data is entered. Defined using the Lookup Wizard, a lookup field may be populated with a simple list (called a *Value List*) or with the contents of another table (called a *Lookup List*). Lookup lists are extremely useful in validating entries for child records, where a related primary key value must be selected from a primary table. To facilitate selecting the proper value, a lookup list can display multiple fields in addition to the primary key (which is typically an AutoNumber field).

**METHOD**

1.  Display the table structure in Design view.
2.  SELECT: Lookup Wizard in the *Data Type* column of the desired field
3.  Complete the prompts in the Lookup Wizard.

**PRACTICE**

You now create a lookup table for inserting the proper instructor ID into the Courses table.

*Setup:* Ensure that the ACC500 Database window is displayed.

**1**  To display the field properties for the Courses table:
SELECT: Courses in the list area
CLICK: Design button (⬛Design) in the Database window toolbar

**2**  At the bottom of the Field Grid pane:
CLICK: once in the *Data Type* column of the InstructorID field
SELECT: Lookup Wizard from the *Data Type* drop-down list box
The Lookup Wizard dialog box appears, as shown in Figure 5.19.

**Figure 5.19**

Lookup Wizard dialog box

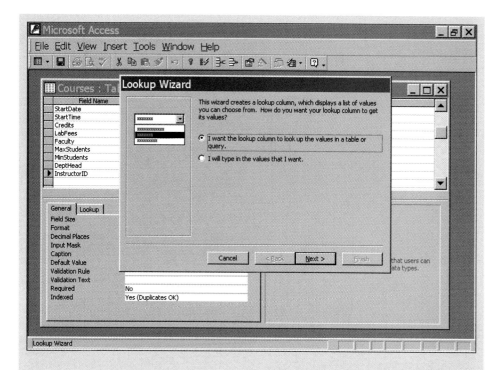

**3** In the first step, ensure that the *...look up the values in a table...* option is selected and then do the following:
CLICK: Next >

**4** You must now specify the table to use for populating records in the lookup's drop-down list box:
SELECT: Instructors
CLICK: Next >

**5** In this step, select the columns that you want to appear in the lookup's drop-down list box. To include the InstructorID, Last-Name, and FirstName fields:
SELECT: InstructorID
CLICK: Include button ( > ) three times
Your screen should now appear similar to Figure 5.20.

**Figure 5.20**

Selecting fields for
the lookup column

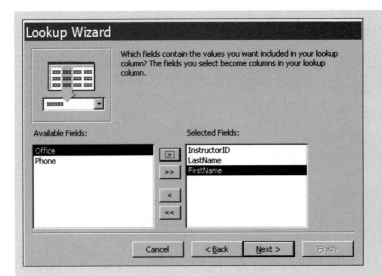

**6** To continue to the next step:
CLICK: Next >

**7** Ensure that the *Hide key column* check box is selected so that the
primary key values do not appear in the list box. Then, change
the width of field columns to their best fit:
DOUBLE-CLICK: the right border of each column heading
CLICK: Next >

**8** In the last step, accept the default label and then continue:
CLICK: Finish to complete the wizard
CLICK: Yes command button, if asked to save the table

**9** To view the Courses datasheet:
CLICK: View—Datasheet button (▦▾)

**10** To use the new lookup field that has been created:
PRESS: END to move to the last field
CLICK: down arrow attached to the field
Your screen should now appear similar to Figure 5.21. Notice
that the datasheet is much more readable with the instructor sur-
names appearing in the field column.

**Figure 5.21**

Displaying the contents
of a lookup field

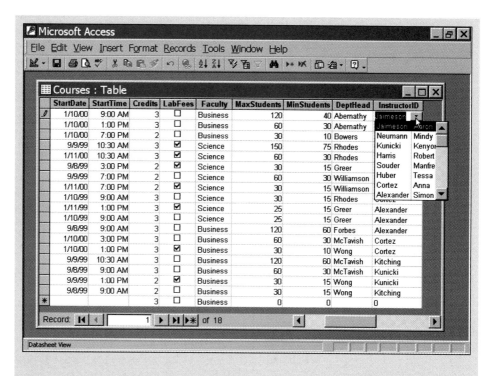

 SELECT: *a new instructor* for the record

 Close the Datasheet window.

## 5.3.5 Inserting a Lookup Column

**FEATURE**
Access allows you to create a new lookup field when viewing a table
in a Datasheet window. Similar to creating a lookup field in table
Design view, the Lookup Wizard helps you create the desired
lookup. Unfortunately, this method cannot be used to edit an existing field in the table.

**METHOD**
1.  Display the table in Datasheet view.
2.  RIGHT-CLICK: a field column to position the new lookup
    field
3.  CHOOSE: Lookup Column
4.  Complete the prompts in the Lookup Wizard.

**PRACTICE**
You now define a lookup value list for a new field in the Instructors table.

*Setup:* Ensure that the ACC500 Database window is displayed.

**1**  Open the Instructors table in Datasheet view.

**2**  RIGHT-CLICK: Phone in the field header area
CHOOSE: Lookup Column
The Lookup Wizard dialog box appears, similar to Figure 5.19.

**3**  Let's create a lookup list containing three static values:
SELECT: *I will type in the values that I want* option button
CLICK: Next >

**4**  In the grid area provided, enter the desired values:
PRESS: TAB to retain the default single column
TYPE: **Home**
PRESS: TAB
TYPE: **Office**
PRESS: TAB
TYPE: **Fax**

**5**  Using the mouse, size the column to appear as
displayed here. When you are ready to proceed:
CLICK: Next >

| Col1 |
|------|
| Home |
| Office |
| Fax |
| |

**6**  Now enter a column heading label:
TYPE: **Type**
CLICK: Finish

**7**  When the datasheet reappears, practice using the lookup drop-down list to first select a phone type and then enter a phone number.

**8**  To confirm that a new field has been created:
CLICK: View—Design button (🔽)

**9**  To display the *Lookup* properties for the new field:
CLICK: row selector button for Type
CLICK: *Lookup* tab in the Field Properties pane
Your screen should now appear similar to Figure 5.22. Notice that the *Display Control* is a Combo Box, the *Row Source* lists the values, and most of the other properties define the appearance of the list box. While you can create a lookup field by entering values from scratch in these text boxes, it is much easier to use the Lookup Wizard!

**10**  Close the table Design window. (*Note:* If you are proceeding to the next module, the ACC500 Database window can remain open.)

**Figure 5.22**

Field properties for a lookup value list

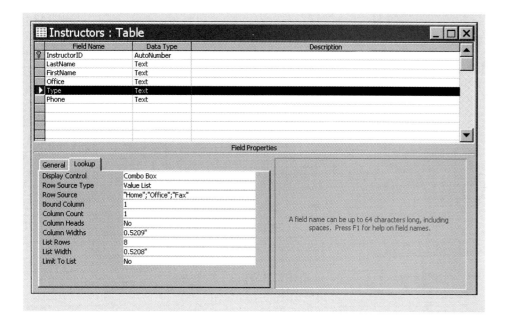

**In Addition**
Setting Validation Rules

A *validation rule* is a range of acceptable values that you specify in a field's property sheet. A validation rule is applied each time data is entered or modified in a field. For example, use a mathematical expression to evaluate whether test scores fall between 0 and 100. You can even customize an error message to display when an illegal entry is made. You can create validation rules manually or by using the Access Expression Builder.

**5.3 Self Check**   Which field property would you use to ensure the proper entry of a Canadian postal code?

# 5.4 Importing, Exporting, and Copying Data

Have you ever started working on a new project only to realize that you've completed something similar in the past? Perhaps the table you created a few months back can be massaged and used again in your current project. At the very least, research the built-in templates and table structures provided by Access for ideas. You can also make use of people's generosity on the Internet. A succinct request for a table structure on a newsgroup may yield many helpful suggestions and shared files. If at all possible, try not to "recreate the wheel!"

ACCESS

Access provides several features to assist you in sharing and exchanging tables and data. In this module, you learn how to import a table and its data, export database objects to the Web, and copy data to external sources, such as spreadsheets and word processing documents.

## 5.4.1  Importing Data into a New Table

**FEATURE**
The more exposure you have to different database files, the more often the opportunity arises to import and export data. For example, a database file containing a table of state abbreviations can be used in most applications. Rather than recreating the table structure and rekeying the data, you can import the table and its data into a new database. In addition to saving a good deal of time, importing reduces the possibility of data entry errors.

**METHOD**
1. Open the database in which you want the data stored.
2. CLICK: *Tables* button in the Objects bar
3. CHOOSE: File, Get External Data, Import
4. SELECT: the database from which to import data
5. SELECT: the desired objects to import
6. CLICK: OK command button

**PRACTICE**
In this lesson, you import a table from one database file into another.

*Setup:* Ensure that the ACC500 Database window is displayed. If not, open the database from the student data files folder.

**1** To demonstrate importing data, let's import a single table from the ACC510 database file into ACC500. To begin:
CHOOSE: File, Get External Data, Import
The Import dialog box appears.

**2** Using the Places bar or the *Look in* drop-down list box, select your personal storage location. Then, do the following:
DOUBLE-CLICK: ACC510 database
The Import Objects dialog box appears, as shown in Figure 5.23. Notice that you can import tables, queries, forms, reports, pages, macros, and modules.

**Figure 5.23**

Importing a table object

Table objects stored in the
ACC510 database file

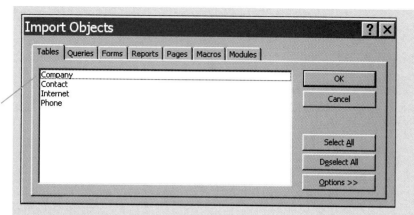

**3** To import the Company table:
SELECT: Company in the list area

**4** The Import Objects dialog box provides a few alternatives for customizing how a table or query is imported. To illustrate:
CLICK: Options command button
The dialog box expands to display some additional options.

**5** In the *Import Tables* area, you can choose to limit an import procedure to a table's structure. For this exercise, ensure that both the structure and data are included:
SELECT: *Definition and data* option button
CLICK: OK command button

**6** While a Company table object now appears in the ACC500 Database window, remember that the original table remains intact in the ACC510 database. Any additions, deletions, or changes you make to this new table's structure or data are not reflected in ACC510. This table object is completely independent of the original Company table object. To display the contents of the table:
DOUBLE-CLICK: Company in the list area

**7** Close the Datasheet window before proceeding.

ACCESS

## 5.4.2  Exporting Data to the Web

**FEATURE**
In Chapter 4, you exported a report object in HTML format for display on the World Wide Web. Using the same process, you may also export table, form, and query objects for Web publishing. It is important to note that the HTML pages created by exporting provide only static representations of the data. In other words, the data may only be viewed (and not manipulated) by a person using Web browser software and the data is reliable and accurate only as of the time of export. However, you can also use Access to generate dynamic data access solutions for the Web. Unfortunately, these features are beyond the scope of this lesson.

**METHOD**
1. SELECT: an object in the Database window
2. CHOOSE: File, Export
3. TYPE: *a file name* for the Web document
4. SELECT: HTML documents in the *Save as type* drop-down list box
5. CLICK: Save command button

**PRACTICE**
You now export table, query, and form objects to HTML pages.

*Setup:* Ensure that the ACC500 Database window is displayed.

**1** To export a table's datasheet for publishing to the Web:
SELECT: Courses in the list area
The object name must appear highlighted in the list area.

**2** CHOOSE: File, Export

**3** In the Export dialog box:
TYPE: **Courses to Web** in the *File name* text box
SELECT: *your personal storage location* using the Places bar or the *Save in* drop-down list box
SELECT: HTML Documents in the *Save as type* drop-down list box
CLICK: Save command button
When Access is finished saving the HTML document, you are returned to the Database window.

**4** To export a query to an HTML document:
CLICK: *Queries* button in the Objects bar
RIGHT-CLICK: Students in Business Faculty
CHOOSE: Export

**5** In the Export dialog box:
TYPE: **Business Students to Web** in the *File name* text box
SELECT: *your personal storage location*
SELECT: HTML Documents in the *Save as type* drop-down list box
CLICK: Save command button

**6** On your own, export the form object named "Instructors Auto-Form" to an HTML document named "Instructors to Web." When the HTML Output Options dialog box appears, click the OK command button.

**7** When you return to the Database window:
CLICK: *Tables* button in the Objects bar

**8** If you have access to Web browser software, you can open the pages created in this lesson for viewing. Figure 5.24 provides an example of how the three pages might appear using Internet Explorer. (*Note:* If necessary, close your Web browser software before proceeding.)

**Figure 5.24**

Viewing HTML pages exported from Access

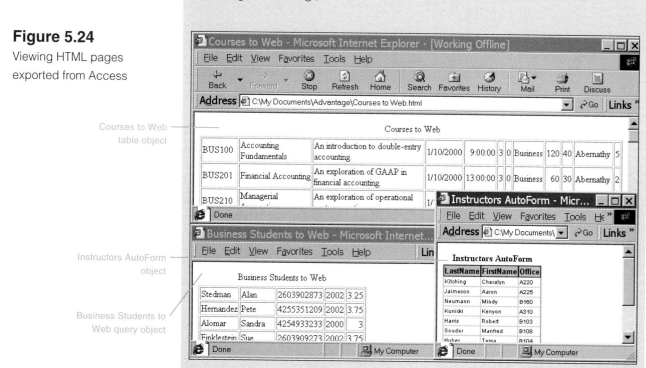

## 5.4.3 Copying Data Using the Office Clipboard

**FEATURE**

Like word processing and spreadsheet software, Access provides tools for copying, moving, and pasting data. The **Windows Clipboard** is used to copy and store a single item of data for quick paste operations. The new **Office Clipboard** is used to collect and store multiple data items that can then be pasted singularly or as a group. For instance, you can use the Office Clipboard to select up to 12 records for pasting into any other Office 2000 application.

**METHOD**

1. CHOOSE: View, Toolbars, Clipboard
2. CLICK: Clear Clipboard button (⊠) to clear the contents
   CLICK: Copy button (🗎) to copy data
   CLICK: Paste button (📋) or Paste All (📋Paste All) to paste data

**PRACTICE**

In this lesson, you copy selected records from a table and paste them into a Word document and into an Excel worksheet.

*Setup:* Ensure that the ACC500 Database window is displayed. This exercise requires that you have Microsoft Word 2000 and Microsoft Excel 2000 available.

**1** Open the Courses table in Datasheet view.

**2** The objective in the next two steps is to copy all of the 100-level courses to other Office 2000 applications. To begin, display the Office Clipboard:
CHOOSE: View, Toolbars, Clipboard
The Office Clipboard toolbar appears, as shown at the right.

**3** If the Clipboard already contains data, do the following:
CLICK: Clear Clipboard button (⊠) on the Clipboard toolbar

**4** To select the first 100-level course:
CLICK: row selector button for BUS100
The entire first row should appear highlighted.

**5** To copy this record to the Office Clipboard:
CLICK: Copy button (🗎) on the Clipboard toolbar
Notice that an Access data icon (📄) appears in the Clipboard.

**6** To add more records to the Clipboard:
CLICK: row selector button for COM100
CLICK: Copy button (🗐)
CLICK: row selector button for MKT100
CLICK: Copy button (🗐)
CLICK: row selector button for ORG100
CLICK: Copy button (🗐)
Depending on your screen resolution, the Office Clipboard may expand to display an additional row of placeholders.

**7** Position the mouse pointer over one of the data icons (📄) in the toolbar. A ToolTip appears displaying the fields stored in the slot, as shown in Figure 5.25.

**Figure 5.25**

Using the Office Clipboard

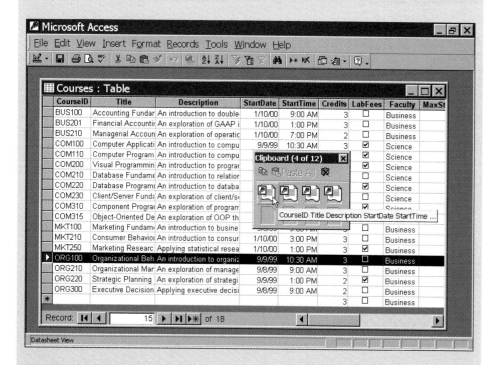

**8** Launch Microsoft Word 2000 and display a blank document.

**9** To paste the records into the new document:
CLICK: Paste All button (🗐Paste All) in the Clipboard toolbar
The field header names and record data are inserted into a table within the document. (*Note:* You may need to apply additional formatting to enhance the appearance of the table in Word.)

**10** Close Word and do not save the changes.

**11** On your own, launch Microsoft Excel 2000. Select cell A1 and then paste the Clipboard data. Notice that each field is assigned a column in the worksheet and each record is stored in a row.

**12**   Close Excel and do not save the changes.

**13**   Let's clear and close the Office Clipboard:
CLICK: Clear Clipboard button ()
CLICK: its Close button (☒)

**14**   Close the Datasheet window and the ACC500 Database Window. Then, exit Microsoft Access.

**5.4 Self Check**   In describing the results of an HTML export, what is meant by static data?

# 5.5   Chapter Review

This chapter emphasizes planning and design in the development of usable, efficient, and accurate database applications. With the relational database model as its theoretical basis, Access provides several features geared toward helping you normalize data, establish table relationships, and enforce referential integrity. You begin this chapter learning about database design elements and how to establish table relationships. You then practice changing the appearance and behavior of fields by setting properties. Field properties can also help you validate data and ensure the integrity of your tables and relationships. Lastly, you import data from an external table into the current database, export table, query, and form objects in HTML format, and copy records to Microsoft Word 2000 and Microsoft Excel 2000.

## 5.5.1   Command Summary

Many of the commands and procedures appearing in this chapter are summarized in the following table.

| Skill Set | To Perform This Task . . . | Do the Following . . . |
|---|---|---|
| **Planning and Designing Databases** | Establish table relationships after normalizing data | CLICK: Relationships button (⊞) <br> CLICK: Show Table button (⊞) <br> DRAG: a key field from one field list object and drop it onto the related field in another field list object |

*Continued*

| Skill Set | To Perform This Task . . . | Do the Following . . . |
|-----------|----------------------------|------------------------|
| **Defining Relationships** | Enforce referential integrity and specify Cascade Update and Cascade Delete options | CLICK: Relationships button (⊞)<br>RIGHT-CLICK: a relationship line<br>CHOOSE: Edit Relationship<br>SELECT: *Enforce Referential Integrity* check box |
| **Using Access Tools** | Print the Relationships window | CLICK: Relationships button (⊞)<br>CHOOSE: File, Print Relationships |
| | Add descriptive information to a database object by setting properties | RIGHT-CLICK: an object<br>CHOOSE: Properties<br>TYPE: *the desired text* |
| | Add descriptive information to a database file by setting properties | CHOOSE: File, Database Properties<br>TYPE: *the desired text* |
| **Building and Modifying Tables** | Modify field properties | SELECT: a table object<br>CLICK: Design button (☒ Design )<br>SELECT: the desired field<br>SELECT: a property text box in the Field Properties pane |
| | In table Design view, specify a field's default size and storage capacity | SELECT: a field in the Field Grid pane<br>TYPE: *a value* into the *Field Size* property text box (or select a numeric option from the drop-down list box) |
| | In table Design view, specify a field's caption for use in forms and reports | SELECT: a field in the Field Grid pane<br>TYPE: *a caption* into the *Caption* property text box |
| | In table Design view, specify a field's display format | SELECT: a field in the Field Grid pane<br>TYPE: *a format* into the *Format* property text box (or select a numeric option from the drop-down list box) |
| | In table Design view, specify that a field must contain data before proceeding or saving a record | SELECT: a field in the Field Grid pane<br>SELECT: Yes in the *Required* property text box |
| | In table Design view, specify a default value for a field | SELECT: a field in the Field Grid pane<br>TYPE: *a default value* into the *Default Value* property text box |

*Continued*

| Skill Set | To Perform This Task . . . | Do the Following . . . |
| --- | --- | --- |
| **Building and Modifying Tables** *Continued* | In table Design view, specify an input mask to force data to be stored in a particular format | SELECT: a field in the Field Grid pane<br>TYPE: *an input mask* into the *Input Mask* property text box (or select the Build button ([...]) to launch the Input Mask Wizard) |
| | In table Design view, launch the Lookup Wizard | SELECT: a field in the Field Grid pane<br>SELECT: Lookup Wizard in the *Data Type* column |
| | While viewing a datasheet, insert a lookup column for validating data | RIGHT-CLICK: a field column<br>CHOOSE: Lookup Column |
| **Utilizing Web Capabilities** | Define a hyperlink field | SELECT: a table object<br>CLICK: Design button ([Design])<br>TYPE: *a new field name*<br>SELECT: Hyperlink in the *Data Type* column of the Field Grid pane |
| **Integrating with Other Applications** | Add a hyperlink address | SELECT: the hyperlink field<br>CLICK: Insert Hyperlink button ([icon])<br>TYPE: *the display text*<br>TYPE: *the file or Web page name* |
| | Modify a hyperlink address | RIGHT-CLICK: the hyperlink address<br>CHOOSE: Hyperlink, Edit Hyperlink |
| | Save a table, query, and form in HTML format for Web publishing | SELECT: the database object to export<br>CHOOSE: File, Export<br>TYPE: *a file name*<br>SELECT: HTML Document in the *Save as type* drop-down list box<br>CLICK: Save command button |
| | Import a table structure and its data from one database into another | CHOOSE: File, Get External Data, Import<br>SELECT: the source database file<br>SELECT: the table objects to import<br>CLICK: OK command button |
| **Viewing and Organizing Information** | Display the Office Clipboard for use in copying and exporting data | CHOOSE: View, Toolbars, Clipboard |

## 5.5.2 Key Terms

This section specifies page references for the key terms identified in this session. For a complete list of definitions, refer to the Glossary provided at the end of this learning guide.

business rules, *p. 196*

child table, *p. 185*

flat-file database, *p. 179*

foreign key, *p. 181*

hyperlink, *p. 204*

input mask, *p. 213*

linking table, *p. 182*

lookup field, *p. 216*

many-to-many
relationship, *p. 182*

normalization, *p. 179*

Office Clipboard, *p. 226*

one-to-many
relationship, *p. 181*

one-to-one relationship, *p. 181*

parent table, *p. 185*

property, *p. 194*

referential integrity, *p. 189*

relational database, *p. 179*

Windows Clipboard, *p. 226*

# 5.6 Review Questions

## 5.6.1 Short Answer

1. What is the primary difference between a relational and a flat-file database?
2. How does a one-to-many relationship differ from a many-to-many relationship?
3. When establishing a relationship between two tables, what happens when you drag a primary key from one field list and drop it onto an identical primary key in another field list?
4. What is a good design rule to follow when creating new tables in Access that require a primary key?
5. When editing a table relationship, how might you ensure that deleting a record in the primary table removes all related records in subsidiary tables?
6. Name two field properties or features that can affect how data is displayed.
7. Name two field properties or features that can save you time entering data.
8. Name two field properties or features that can assist you in validating data that is entered.

9.  How do you edit the contents of a hyperlink field?
10. How do you make the contents of a datasheet readable in Web browser software?

## 5.6.2  True/False

1.  _____ You normalize data by dividing fields into logical groupings of related tables.
2.  _____ For all intents and purposes, a one-to-many table relationship is identical to a many-to-one relationship.
3.  _____ A foreign key is an index that has been imported from another database.
4.  _____ When you choose to print the Relationships window, Access creates and stores a new report object in the database.
5.  _____ You use the *Field Size* property to specify the precision and storage capacity of a field with the Number data type.
6.  _____ You use the *Caption* property to add a ToolTip message to a field for display.
7.  _____ The *Required* property has only two settings: *Yes* and *No*.
8.  _____ Hyperlinks can be used to navigate your Office documents.
9.  _____ You use the Input Mask Wizard to specify the values that you want displayed in a lookup.
10. _____ The Office Clipboard can store up to 12 items for pasting.

## 5.6.3  Multiple Choice

1.  Data is said to be in the *first normal form* when:
    a.  There are no repeating groups of information in a table.
    b.  A primary key field has been identified and created.
    c.  A parent table has been related to its child tables.
    d.  Referential integrity constraints have been applied.

2.  A primary key field that is included in another table is called a(n):
    a.  child key
    b.  parent key
    c.  foreign key
    d.  index

3.  Which of the following table relationships is *not* described in this chapter?
    a.  one-to-one
    b.  one-to-many
    c.  one-to-infinity
    d.  many-to-many

4. In a many-to-many relationship, a third _____ table is used to negotiate the connection by storing primary keys from each table.
   a. child
   b. parent
   c. primary
   d. linking

5. A *property* is best described as:
   a. A characteristic or attribute.
   b. A method or procedure.
   c. A function or expression.
   d. A macro or module.

6. A *business rule* is best described as:
   a. A constraint for limiting how data is entered into a table.
   b. A guideline for how people use data in the real world.
   c. A restriction on how data is deleted from a table.
   d. A restriction on how data is updated in a table.

7. The _____ property lets you change how a Canadian postal code is *displayed* in a datasheet, regardless of how the data is stored.
   a. Caption
   b. Field Size
   c. Format
   d. Input Mask

8. The _____ property lets you change how a Canadian postal code is *entered* in a datasheet, regardless of how the data is stored.
   a. Caption
   b. Field Size
   c. Format
   d. Input Mask

9. The _____ property lets you optimize how numeric entries are stored in a table.
   a. Expression
   b. Field Size
   c. Input Mask
   d. Validate

10. A table, query, form, or report that is exported for publishing to the Web is stored in this format:
    a. ASP
    b. DHTML
    c. HTML
    d. Java

ACCESS

# 5.7    Hands-On Projects

### ●    5.7.1    World Wide Imports: Assigning Sales Reps to Customers

For practice relating tables, you now establish a one-to-many relationship between the Customers and Sales Reps tables.

*Setup:* Ensure that Access is loaded. If you are launching Access and the startup dialog box appears, click the Cancel command button to remove the dialog box from the application window.

1. Open the database file named ACC570. Ensure that the *Tables* button in the Objects bar is selected.
2. Each sales rep at World Wide Imports must service a number of customers. Each customer, on the other hand, is given the name of a single sales rep that is accountable for their business. In this scenario, the Sales Reps table is the primary or parent table and the Customers table is the child table. Open the Sales Reps table in table Design view and make note of the primary key field. What is the primary key's name, data type, and field size?
3. Close the Sales Reps Design window.
4. Open the Customers table in table Design view. Does a foreign key exist that may be used to relate the two tables? If so, ensure that its name, data type, and field size are identical to the primary key field in the Sales Reps table.
5. Close the Customers Design window.
6. To display the Relationships window:
   CLICK: Relationships button (⊞)
   Notice that the Relationships window appears, but the Show Tables dialog box is not displayed automatically.
7. To select tables for display in the Relationships window:
   CLICK: Show Table button (⊞)
8. To relate the Sales Reps and Customers tables:
   SELECT: 571 Customers
   CLICK: Add command button
   SELECT: 571 Sales Reps
   CLICK: Add command button
   CLICK: Close command button
9. On your own, size and arrange the two field list objects so that all the field names are visible.
10. To establish a one-to-many relationship:
    DRAG: SalesRep primary key field in the 571 Sales Reps object and drop it onto SalesRep foreign key field in the 571 Customers object
11. When the Edit Relationships window appears:
    CLICK: Create command button

12. To print the Relationship window:
    CHOOSE: File, Print Relationships
    An Access report object is generated and displayed in Print Preview mode.

13. To print (or not print) the Relationships report:
    CLICK: Print button (🖨) on the toolbar (if a printer is available)
    CLICK: Close button (☒) for the Preview window

14. Close the Relationships window by clicking its Close button (☒).

## 5.7.2 CyberWeb: Helping to Enter Data

In this exercise, you specify a default value for a field and then edit an input mask.

*Setup:* Ensure that the ACC570 Database window is displayed.

1. Let's edit the field properties in the Internet Accounts table. To begin:
   SELECT: 572 Internet Accounts
   CLICK: Design button (🔧Design) on the Database window toolbar

2. The majority of CyberWeb's Internet account registrants opt for the $19.95 per month plan. Therefore, let's specify this value as the default in the Amount field of the table structure. To do so:
   CLICK: row selector button for Amount

3. SELECT: *Default Value* property text box
   (*Hint:* Click the mouse pointer once in the text box.)

4. To set the default value:
   TYPE: **19.95**
   Notice that you don't need to enter a dollar sign or any other formatting characters.

5. To specify an input mask for the Phone field:
   CLICK: row selector button for Phone
   SELECT: *Input Mask* property text box

6. To launch the Input Mask Wizard:
   CLICK: Build button (⋯) attached to the text box
   (*Hint:* If asked, save the table structure to continue.)

7. Because there are no area codes stored in this table, you will modify an existing input mask:
   SELECT: Phone Number
   CLICK: Next >

8. With the current input mask "!(999) 000-0000" highlighted in the *Input Mask* text box, do the following:
   TYPE: **000-0000**

9. To try the input mask:
CLICK: once in the *Try It* text box
PRESS: (HOME) to move to the first character position
TYPE: **5551212**

10. Satisfied with the results:
CLICK: [ Finish ]

11. Save the table and continue:
CLICK: Save button ([🖫])
CLICK: View—Datasheet button ([▦▾])

12. To enter a new record:
CLICK: New Record button ([▸*])
Notice that the default value, $19.95, appears in the Amount column.

13. Enter your own name and address information into the new record. Notice the input mask that appears for the Phone field.

14. When you are ready to proceed, close the Datasheet window.

## 5.7.3 Big Valley Mills: Using Lookup Fields

You now practice creating lookup lists for static values.

*Setup:* Ensure that the ACC570 Database window is displayed.

1. Open the 573 Products datasheet for display.

2. Notice that the Category field currently contains three options: Board, Dim., and Plywood. Assuming that these categories are static, let's convert this field into a validated lookup list. To begin:
CLICK: View—Design button ([🗹▾])

3. CLICK: once in the *Data Type* column for the Category field
SELECT: Lookup Wizard from the drop-down list

4. In the first step of the wizard, choose to type in the values that you want displayed in the lookup list. Then, proceed to the next step.

5. In the lookup grid area, specify one column with the values: Board, Dim., and Plywood. After adjusting the size of the column (Figure 5.26), proceed to the next step.

**Figure 5.26**

Defining a Category
lookup field

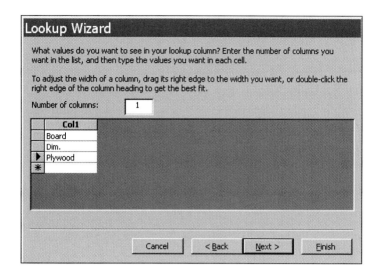

6. Use Category as the lookup column label and then:
   CLICK: Finish
7. Save the table structure and then display the datasheet.
8. On your own, click once in a field in the Category column and then use the drop-down list to select a new category option.
9. Using the same steps, create a lookup list for the Species column. Use the values: BIRCH, DFIR, ROAK, SPF, SYP, WALL, and WPINR. Once completed, test the results of the lookup list in Datasheet view.
10. Close the Datasheet window.

## 5.7.4 Silverdale Festival: Exporting Data

In this exercise, you practice setting field properties. Then, you copy several records to an Excel worksheet and export the Contacts datasheet for publishing to the Web.

*Setup:* Ensure that the ACC570 Database window is displayed.

1. Open the 574 Contacts datasheet for display.
2. This table requires that each record contain a volunteer group entry. To specify that this field is required, switch to Design view and then set its Required property to Yes.
3. With the table structure still displayed, change the captions for the Phone1 and Phone2 fields to read Phone and Fax, respectively. Also, change the VolunteerGroup caption to read Group.
4. Change the field sizes for each text field to 50, except for the two phone fields which should contain 10 characters.
5. Save the table structure and then display the datasheet. Notice that the names in the column header area have changed.
6. Display the Office Clipboard toolbar and clear its contents.

7.  For each record that contains a City value other than "Silverdale," copy the record to the Office Clipboard. When finished, you should have copied 10 records.
8.  Launch Microsoft Excel 2000.
9.  Paste the copied records into a blank worksheet and then save the workbook as "Non-Silverdale Groups." After moving the cell pointer to cell A1, your screen should appear similar to Figure 5.27.

**Figure 5.27**

Copying records to Microsoft Excel

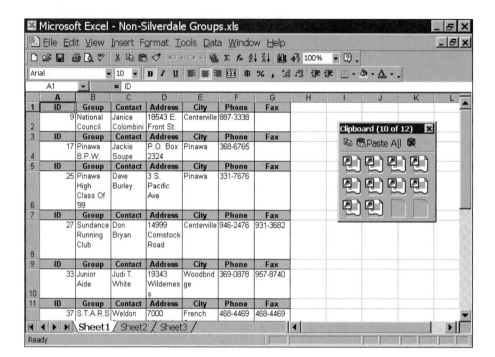

10. Exit Microsoft Excel to return to Access.
11. Close the Office Clipboard and the datasheet window.
12. Export the 574 Contacts datasheet as an HTML document named "Silverdale" to your personal storage location.

### 5.7.5  On Your Own: Office Mart Inventory

To practice working with field properties, you now customize a product inventory table. From the ACC570 Database window, open the 575 Inventory table in Design view. Make the following property settings.

- Specify that the Description field requires an entry.
- Modify the *Field Size* property for the OnHand and Reorder fields from Long Integer to Integer.
- Modify the *Caption* property for the SuggestedRetail field to read **Retail**.
- Enter an input mask of **>L00** for the Supplier field without using the Input Mask Wizard.
- Establish a lookup list for the Buyer field that displays a drop-down list box of the following values: 01, 02, 03, 04, 05, 06, 07, 08, and 09.

When you are finished, save the table structure and close the Design window. Then, practice entering and editing records in Datasheet view. Lastly, close the datasheet.

### 5.7.6  On Your Own: Sun Bird Resorts

Sun Bird Resorts has provided you with two tables: 576 Guides and 576 Patrons. After displaying the tables in Datasheet view, you notice that a third table needs to be created called 576 Interests. You place a single field called "Interest" into this new table and select a Text data type of 15 characters. You also specify that this field is the primary key and then display the table in Datasheet view. Lastly, you populate the table with the following values: Beach, Fishing, Golf, Shopping, Sightseeing, and Tennis. Before proceeding, close the Interests Datasheet window.

Having completed the previous steps, modify the Interest fields in the Guides and Patrons tables to use the new table as a lookup. Ensure that the foreign key fields are the same data type and length as the primary key field in the Interests table. To make sure that the fields work properly, test the Guides and Patrons tables by selecting new interests for existing records. Then, add a new interest called "Boating" to the Interests table. Does the new value appear in the drop-down Interest list for Guides or Patrons? Once you are satisfied with the results, close any open Datasheet windows and exit Microsoft Access.

# 5.8   Case Problems: Just Brew-It

Just Brew-It is in the process of designing and implementing an Access database system to manage its product and sales data. Janice Winkler is responsible for completing the work started by the company's systems analyst, Jack Rowe. Before taking his sick leave, Jack created a database containing five tables, named "Products," "Suppliers," "Customers," "Orders," and "Order Details." Having reviewed Jack's initial design notes, Janice has formulated her plan of attack for completing the system.

In the following case problems, assume the role of Janice and perform the same steps that she identifies. You may want to re-read the chapter opening before proceeding.

1.   Janice needs to relate the normalized tables initially created by Jack. To begin, she loads the ACC580 database and then familiarizes herself with the table structures and data. Knowing that she needs to insert foreign keys before establishing relationships, Janice makes note of the primary key from each table. Specifically, she identifies the following tasks:

   •   A logical relationship exists between the Products and Suppliers tables. Each supplier provides Just Brew-It with one or more products, but each product is purchased from a single supplier. In order to establish this one-to-many relationship using Access, Janice inserts a SupplierID foreign key field into the Products table. She makes sure to use the same field name and assigns a Number data type with a long integer field size. To document the field's purpose, she enters a description in the appropriate column of the Field Grid pane. Lastly, she saves the table structure and closes the Design window.
   •   Janice identifies a relationship between the Customers and Orders tables. While a specific order is related to a single customer, a customer may make many purchases. To relate these tables, Janice needs to insert the primary key field from the Customers table into the Orders table. She notes that the CustomerID field is a text field with a field size of eight characters. Therefore, she knows that she must add an identical field to the Orders table. After doing so, she saves and closes the table structure.

- Another relationship exists between the Orders table and the Order Details table. Fortunately, the Order Details table structure already contains a foreign key field for linking to Orders. However, Janice notices that the Description field in the Order Details table should actually be replaced by a foreign key field from the Products table. After ensuring that there is no data in the Order Details table, Janice displays the Design window and deletes the Description field. She then inserts a foreign key field named SKU for linking to the Products table. Lastly, she saves and closes the table structure.

With all of the foreign key fields in place, Janice displays the Relationships window and uses the Show Table dialog box to display the field list objects for all of the tables. She sizes and arranges the field list objects so that the field names are visible. Then, Janice establishes the following relationships, as shown in Figure 5.28:

- Relate the Suppliers and Products tables using the SupplierID field, but do not enforce referential integrity.
- Relate the Customers and Orders tables using the CustomerID field, but do not enforce referential integrity.
- Relate the Orders and Order Details tables using the Order-Number field, and enforce referential integrity with Cascade Delete.
- Relate the Products and Order Details tables using the SKU field, and enforce referential integrity.

Finally, Janice prints the Relationships window in order to include a hard-copy in the weekly progress report. She saves the new Relationships report object and then closes the Relationships window.

**Figure 5.28**

Relating tables using
common fields

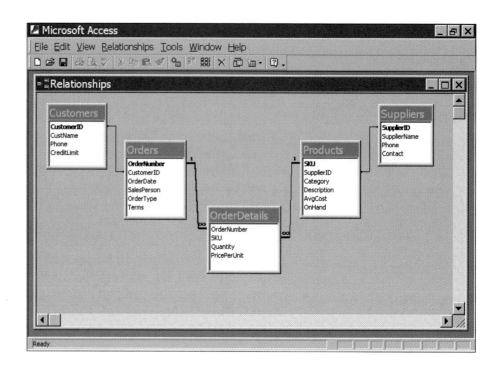

2. After lunch, Janice finds more time to work on the database project. With the ACC580 Database window displayed, she opens the Products and Customer tables for review. Janice realizes that some of the fields need to be changed. First, she opens the Products table in Design view. The Description field is still set at the default field size of 50. Janice selects the field and changes the size to 30 characters. Next, she changes the field size of the OnHand field from long integer to integer to conserve disk space. For reporting purposes, Janice changes the caption property of the AvgCost field to "Our Cost." She saves her changes and then closes the Products table.

Janice turns her attention to the Customers table. After displaying the table in Design view, Janice changes the field size of Phone from 7 to 10 characters so that an area code may be stored. She then selects an input mask to facilitate entering phone numbers and a display format for presenting phone numbers in datasheets, queries, forms, and reports. Lastly, she changes the display format of the CustomerID field so that it displays in uppercase letters. She saves her changes and closes the table Design window.

3. Janice now concerns herself with field-level data integrity issues. Like selecting an input mask for the Customers phone number in the last exercise, Janice evaluates the database for opportunities to ensure the accuracy and consistency of data. Specifically, Janice decides to make the following changes to the database:

   - In the Orders table, the OrderDate and CustomerID fields are designated as required fields. Then, Janice enters **NET 30** as the default value for the Terms field. She saves her changes and closes the Orders table.
   - In the Customers table, the CustName field is designated as a required field. Janice also sets the default value on the CreditLimit to $500. She saves her changes and closes the Customers table.
   - In the Products table, Janice uses the Lookup Wizard to create a lookup table for inserting the SupplierID into the Products table. After adding the SupplierID and Supplier-Name fields to the lookup, she chooses to hide the key column so that only the Supplier name is displayed in the lookup. Janice names the lookup "Supplier" and then tests the lookup by adding Suppliers to the first few Product records. She then closes the Products table.

4. Janice wants to add an employee table to the database to provide information about the company's sales people. Since there is already an employee table in the Human Resources database, Janice decides to import the table. With the ACC580 Database window displayed, Janice imports both the Employees table structure and data from the ACC580A database. Janice then modifies the SalesPerson field in the Orders table to become a foreign key field for linking to the Employees table. In particular, she renames the field "EmpNumber" and selects a Number data type with a field size specification of Double. Using the Relationships window, Janice adds the Employees table using the Show Table button (⊞) and then relates the table to Orders. Once completed, she closes the Relationships window.

5. Janice has just received a call from the Marketing department. They've asked her to export some Product information to an Excel spreadsheet for a planning meeting next week. In the meantime, Janice decides to practice copying records from Access to Excel. She opens the Products table in Datasheet view. She then displays the Office Clipboard and clears its contents. Next, she scrolls to the end of the datasheet and selects the six "Malt" products using the record selection area, and copies them to the Office Clipboard. Janice then selects the seven records for the "Extract" products and copies them. Janice launches Microsoft Excel to display a new worksheet. She selects cell A1 and pastes all the copied records using the Office Clipboard. She saves the workbook as "Beer Supplies" in her personal storage location and then exits both Excel and Access.

# MICROSOFT ACCESS 2000
## *Creating Queries*

**CHAPTER**

**SIX**

# Chapter Outline

# Learning Objectives

After reading this chapter, you will be able to:

- Create a select query from scratch using query Design view

- Modify a query by adding and deleting tables and fields

- Specify search criteria using conditional statements and logical operators

- Create, modify, and print a multitable query

- Enhance a query by sorting, filtering, and hiding results

- Analyze and summarize your data using calculated fields and summary queries

## Case Study    Aspen Grove Veterinary Clinic

Located in a thriving agricultural township, the Aspen Grove Veterinary Clinic serves the needs of both pet owners and farmers with its staff of veterinarians. Unlike most pet owners, who can carry or lead their animals into the clinic, farmers require the doctors to make house calls to treat the less mobile and larger number of animals. As the community continues to grow, the clinic faces mounting pressures to keep up with the demands of its clients. To maintain an acceptable level of service, the clinic must ensure that it is making the most efficient use of its current staff and facility resources. To accomplish this without hiring new doctors, the clinic must accommodate a greater number of visits per day. A further challenge for the staff has to do with the makeup of its patients. While cats, dogs, cows, and horses remain the bread and butter of the clinic, the doctors are being asked to treat exotic animals more frequently.

For over three years now, Michelle Green has enjoyed her position as office manager for the Aspen Grove clinic. Michelle's duties include maintaining client information and accounting records in addition to handling all appointment bookings and staff scheduling. Michelle has recently started using Microsoft Access to track the flow of activities and information at the clinic. She has already constructed a database of four related tables to collect and store customer details and other important data. With three months of data now entered into the system, Michelle can turn her attention to analyzing the data in order to get a better picture of the clinic's operations.

In this chapter, you and Michelle learn how to create and customize query objects using query Design view. You apply queries to extract, sort, and display specific data from the database. Then, you retrieve and summarize data using multitable criteria, calculated fields, and summary queries.

# 6.1 Using the Query Design View

Access provides several tools, features, and methods for organizing and retrieving information from a database. Besides reordering columns in a datasheet, you can sort records into order by clicking the Sort Ascending (🔼) and Sort Descending (🔽) toolbar buttons. For locating data, the Edit, Find command and Find button (🔍) enable you to search an entire table for records containing a few characters or words. Access also provides four filtering methods (*Filter For Input, Filter By Selection, Filter Excluding Selection*, and *Filter By Form*) for limiting the display of records in a datasheet. Understanding the strengths and weaknesses of these features (covered in earlier chapters) is especially important when learning to design, modify, and apply queries in Access.

Queries perform retrieval and analytical operations that are more complex than tables and filters alone can provide. You use queries to ask questions of your database, to construct views of the data, and to update table contents. Queries may also serve as the basis for forms and reports. The most common type of query, called a *select query*, is used to answer the following types of questions:

- How many students live in Chicago? What are their names?
- What is the average age of employees in XYZ Corporation?
- Which customers are overdue on their payments this month?

In addition to select queries, Access provides *action*, *parameter*, and *crosstab* queries. An **action query** performs mass changes to the data it retrieves. The four types of action queries include (1) *update query*, which modifies the data in a table, (2) *append query*, which adds data from one or more tables to another table, (3) *delete query*, which deletes records from one or more tables, and (4) *make table query*, which creates a new table from a query's results. Moreover, a **parameter query** displays a dialog box and accepts input from the user before proceeding. Mainly used for analysis, a **crosstab query** summarizes numerical results in a spreadsheet-like table. Action, parameter, and crosstab queries are beyond the scope of this chapter. Instead, we will focus on creating and customizing select queries using query Design view.

## 6.1.1  Creating a Query in Design View

**FEATURE**

While the Simple Query Wizard makes it easy to get started, the query Design window provides much more power for creating query objects. And, like any other database object, you can create, modify, save, delete, and print query objects. Using a graphical **query-by-example (QBE)** approach, the query Design window lets you select field columns for display, enter criteria statements, specify sort orders, and perform calculations. For more advanced users, Access provides the ability to view and enter SQL (pronounced "sequel") language statements directly. **SQL,** which stands for Structured Query Language, is a powerful database query language supported by many popular database applications. This module discusses the QBE facilities provided in the query Design window.

**METHOD**
To create a new query, select the *Queries* button in the Objects bar and then:

- DOUBLE-CLICK: Create query in Design view, or
- CLICK: New button (⟨🗗New⟩) on the Database window toolbar
  DOUBLE-CLICK: Design View in the New Query dialog box

**PRACTICE**
In query Design view, you practice creating a query that retrieves student information.

*Setup:* Ensure that Access is loaded. If you are launching Access and the startup dialog box appears, click the Cancel command button to remove the dialog box from the application window.

**1** Open the database file named ACC600, located in the Advantage student data files folder. This database contains four tables: Courses, Instructors, Roster, and Students.

**2** To create a new query object:
CLICK: *Queries* button in the Objects bar
DOUBLE-CLICK: Create query in Design view
The Show Table dialog box appears.

**3** The first step in creating a query from scratch is to identify the table or tables required for specifying criteria and extracting data for display. In this exercise, you create a single table query. Do the following:
SELECT: Students
CLICK: Add command button
CLICK: Close command button

**4** On your own, move and size the query Design window by dragging its Title bar and borders so that it appears similar to Figure 6.1. Take a few minutes to familiarize yourself with the various parts of the query Design window. Notice that the window is divided into a **Table pane,** which identifies the source data tables, and the **query Design grid,** which contains the fields for display, filter criteria, and sort order selections.

**Figure 6.1**

Query Design window

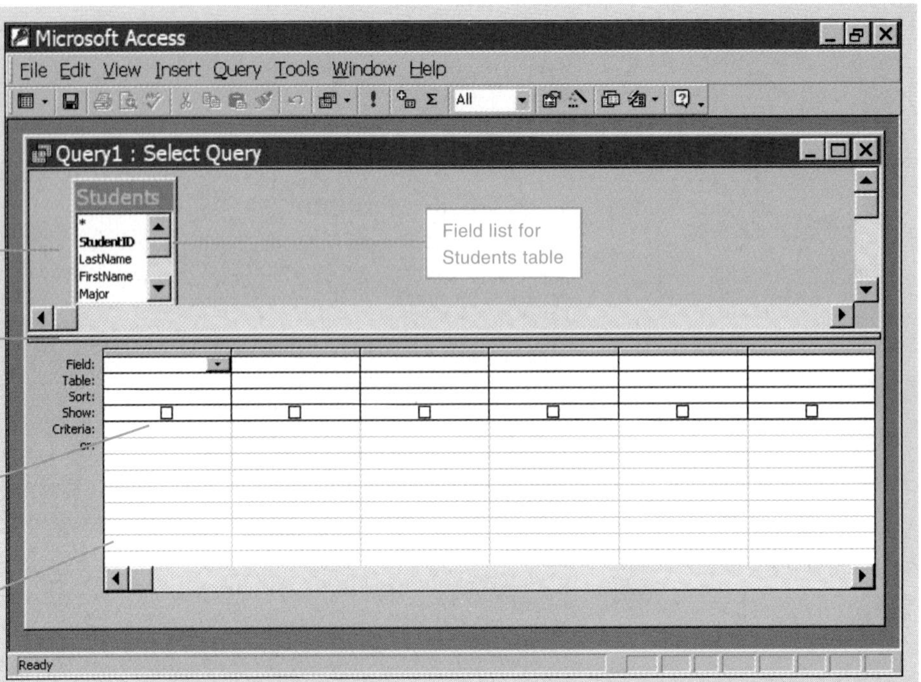

Table pane

Field list for
Students table

Split bar for sizing the
shared space between the
Table pane and query
Design grid

The intersection of a
column and row is
sometimes called a cell.

Query Design grid

**5** Position the mouse pointer over the Split bar separating the Table pane and query Design grid. When the pointer changes shape (✛), drag the Split bar downward to increase the Table pane area and equalize the shared space. Then, if necessary, increase the size of the Students field list object.

**6** At this point, the query does not perform any function. To select data for display or to use a field in specifying criteria, you must add the field to the *Field* row in the query Design grid by dragging or double-clicking its name in the Table pane. To illustrate:
DOUBLE-CLICK: LastName in the Students field list
The LastName field is placed in the first column of the grid.
(*Hint:* Refer to lesson 6.2.2 for more on adding and removing fields.)

**7** To add the FirstName field to the grid by dragging:
DRAG: FirstName from the Students field list and drop it on the next available column in the *Field* row of the grid
Your screen should appear similar to Figure 6.2 as you perform the step. Remember to release the mouse button to drop the field.

**Figure 6.2**

Adding a field to the
query Design grid

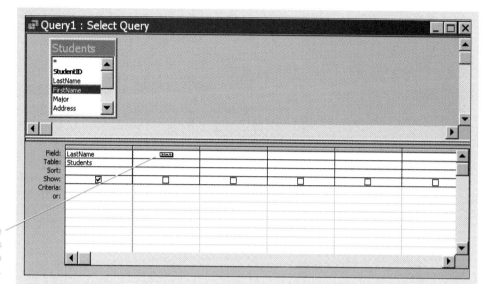

Drag the Firstname
field from the Students
field list and drop it into
this cell of the grid.

**8** There is a third method for placing a field in the query Design grid. Using the I-beam mouse pointer (I), do the following:
CLICK: in the next available column in the *Field* row of the grid
CLICK: down arrow attached to the *Field* text box
SELECT: Phone from the drop-down list box

**9** You have now identified the desired fields for display. To save the query object:
CLICK: Save button (🖫)
TYPE: **Student Phone List** in the Save As dialog box
CLICK: OK command button

**10** You view the query results in a special Datasheet window called a *dynaset*. To proceed:
CLICK: View—Datasheet button (🖩⋅)
(*Hint:* You can also click the Run Query button (❗) in the Query Design toolbar.)

**11** On your own, practice navigating the datasheet as you would a table Datasheet window. The methods, keystrokes, and mouse actions for navigating a dynaset are identical to those used for moving around a datasheet. It is important to note that if you edit the field data in this dynaset, the underlying Students table is changed also!

**12** Close the Datasheet window. The Student Phone List query object should now appear in the Database window.

ACCESS

## 6.1.2  Modifying a Query Object

**FEATURE**
Access provides two views or operating modes for queries: *dynaset Datasheet view* and *query Design view*. You create and modify a query in a Design window. The results of the query, called a dynaset, are displayed in a Datasheet window. Identical to working with tables, the View button is used to toggle between Datasheet view (▥▾) and Design view (▨▾). Some ways that you can modify a query include inserting and removing tables, adding and deleting fields, widening and reordering columns, and specifying sort orders and search criteria. Once satisfied with the result, remember to save the query object.

**METHOD**
After clicking the *Queries* button in the Database window, select one of the following methods to modify a query object:

- SELECT: the query object that you want to modify
  CLICK: Design button (▨Design) on the Database window toolbar
- RIGHT-CLICK: the query object that you want to modify
  CHOOSE: Design View

**PRACTICE**
You now practice modifying the query object created in the last lesson.

*Setup:* Ensure that you've completed the previous lesson and that the ACC600 Database window is displayed.

**1** To modify the query object created in the last lesson:
SELECT: Student Phone List
CLICK: Design button (▨Design)

**2** To change the order in which fields display in the resulting dynaset, select the field that you want to move and then drag it into position. You select a column by clicking the downward pointing mouse arrow (↓) on the narrow header area above the *Field* row. To illustrate:
SELECT: FirstName column by clicking its field header

**3** Now position the white arrow mouse pointer (↳) so that its tip appears over the FirstName header. Then:
DRAG: FirstName column to the left so that the bold vertical gridline appears to the left of the LastName column

**4** Release the mouse button to finish the drag and drop operation.

**Figure 6.3**

Dynaset results for
a modified query

**5** To view the modified query:
CLICK: View—Datasheet button (▥▾)
Notice that the datasheet field columns are displayed in the order they appear in the query Design window (Figure 6.3).

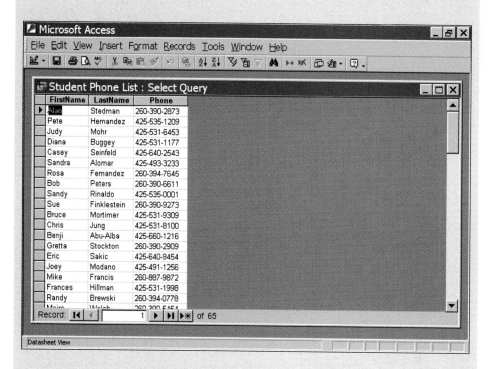

**6** To return to query Design view:
CLICK: View—Design button (▧▾)

**7** To remove the FirstName field from the query:
SELECT: FirstName column by clicking its field header
CHOOSE: Edit, Delete Columns
(*Hint:* Refer to lesson 6.2.2 for more on adding and removing fields.)

**8** To insert the Major field between the LastName and Phone fields:
DRAG: Major from the Students field list and drop it directly on the Phone entry in the *Field* row of the grid
Rather than replacing the existing field, the Major field is inserted into the target column position and the existing entry is moved to the right.

**9** To view the results:
CLICK: View—Datasheet button (▥▾)

**10** Close the Datasheet window and save the changes to the query object.

## 6.1.3  Specifying Search Criteria

**FEATURE**
Querying a table involves more than limiting a datasheet's display to specific fields. Select queries can also extract and organize data meeting a set of conditions. For example, a query can retrieve a customer's purchase history while you are talking to the customer on the phone. A query's results can also be used in generating reports. By basing a report on a query instead of a table, you can print mailing labels for a range of zip codes, monthly statements for customers with overdue accounts, and emergency contact sheets for specific employees.

To limit the records that display in a datasheet, enter a **conditional statement** in the *Criteria* row of the query Design grid. A conditional statement can take one of several forms. First, you can enter an example of the value that you are looking for, such as "Toronto" or "Seattle." Second, you can use the question mark (?) and asterisk (*) wildcard characters to represent one or more alternative characters. Lastly, you can use mathematical operators, such as "<" and ">," to limit records between a given range of values or dates.

**METHOD**
1. Display the query in Design view.
2. SELECT: a *Criteria* text box in the query Design grid
3. TYPE: *a conditional query statement*
4. CLICK: View—Datasheet button (▥▾) to view the results of the query
5. CLICK: View—Design button (▦▾) to return to the Design window

**PRACTICE**
In this lesson, you learn to specify conditional statements for limiting the display of values in a dynaset.

*Setup:* Ensure that you've completed the previous lessons and that the ACC600 Database window is displayed.

**1** To modify the query object created and modified in the last two lessons:
SELECT: Student Phone List
CLICK: Design button (▦ Design)
Three fields should appear in the query Design grid: LastName, Major, and Phone.

**2** To limit the display of values in the dynaset to Business majors only:
CLICK: in the *Criteria* text box in the Major column
TYPE: `Business`
PRESS: `TAB`
Access adds double quotes to the entry automatically. Thankfully, you have a little flexibility when entering expressions into the Criteria field. You can type Business, "Business," =Business, or ="Business." Access correctly evaluates and modifies the entry you make.

**3** CLICK: View—Datasheet button (⊞▾)
Only the Business majors appear in the dynaset.

**4** To return to Design view:
CLICK: View—Design button (▨▾)

**5** To remove the previous criteria, you can select the entry and press `DELETE`. You can also remove all of the criteria entries in the entire row with a single command. To do so, ensure that the cursor (flashing insertion point) appears in the *Criteria* row and then:
CHOOSE: Edit, Delete Rows

**6** Let's add two new fields from the Students field list:
DOUBLE-CLICK: City
DOUBLE-CLICK: Age

**7** To specify a criteria whereby only those students living in a city beginning with the letter "R" are displayed:
CLICK: in the *Criteria* text box in the City column
TYPE: `r*`
PRESS: `TAB`
Notice that Access updates the entry to read `Like "r*"`. Your screen should now appear similar to Figure 6.4.

**Figure 6.4**

Specifying a conditional statement

Field name to evaluate ————

Table that field belongs to ————

Conditional statement for limiting the display of records

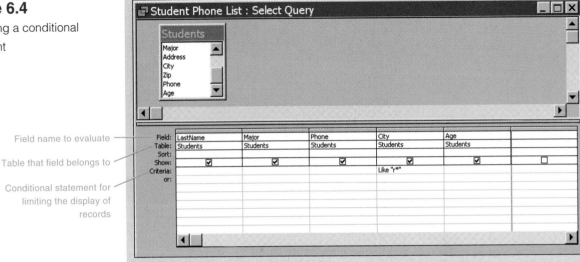

8  CLICK: View—Datasheet button (▦▾)
Only those students from Redmond appear in the dynaset.

9  To return to Design view:
CLICK: View—Design button (▨▾)

10  To remove the existing criteria:
CHOOSE: Edit, Delete Rows
(*Note:* You can also remove criteria by selecting the entry in the *Criteria* text box and then pressing (DELETE).)

11  Let's display only those students over the age of 22:
CLICK: in the *Criteria* text box in the Age column
TYPE: >22
(*Hint:* Table 6.1, at the end of this lesson, summarizes the mathematical query operators and wildcard characters that you can use in specifying criteria.)

12  There may be times when you need to include a field in the Design grid for specifying criteria, but you don't want the field results displayed in the dynaset. To hide a column from displaying:
CLICK: the *Show* check box in the City column so that no "✔" appears
(*Hint:* To delete a column from the grid, click in the column you want to delete and then choose the Edit, Delete Columns command.)

13  View the results of this query and then return to Design view.

**14** To display all students between the ages of 18 and 20:
CLICK: in the *Criteria* text box in the Age column
CHOOSE: Edit, Delete Rows
TYPE: **Between 18 and 20**

**15** View the results of this query. Notice that only those students of ages 18, 19, and 20 are displayed in the dynaset.

**16** Close the Datasheet window and save the changes.

**Table 6.1**

Query Operators

| Operator/Criteria | Description |
| --- | --- |
| > | Greater than; find numbers or dates that are greater than the specified value. For example, >5000 finds all records where the field value is more than 5,000. (*Note:* You don't enter commas in numeric queries.) |
| >= | Greater than or equal to; find numbers or dates that are greater than or equal to the specified value. |
| < | Less than; find numbers or dates that are less than or equal to the specified value. For example, <#05/27/2000# retrieves all records with a date value less than May 27th, 2000. Notice that date values are surrounded by number symbols. |
| <= | Less than or equal to; find numbers or dates that are less than or equal to the specified value. |
| Between X And Y | List those records that contain values between X and Y inclusive. For example, use Between 21 And 65 in an Age field and use Between #01/01/2000# And #12/31/2000# in a Date field. (*Note:* Access adds the number symbols automatically if a date is entered properly.) |
| X Or Y | List those records that contain either X or Y. |
| Not X | List those records not containing X. |

ACCESS

**Table 6.1**

Query Operators

*Continued*

| Operator/Criteria | Description |
|---|---|
| Like "Sm?th" | List those records in which the first letters are "Sm," the next letter is unknown, and the last two letters are "th." Example: Smith, Smyth. |
| Like "Ch*ng" | List those records in which the first letters are "Ch," the middle letters are unknown, and the last letters are "ng." Example: Chang, Chickering. |
| Like "*on*" | List those records in which the field value contains the letter combination "on." Example: Conditional, Conference, Monday. |
| Like "*/*/99" | List those records that end with 99 in the Date field. |

**6.1 Self Check**    Provide a conditional statement that will limit the display of records to those company names starting with the letter "B."

# 6.2  Creating Multitable Queries

Queries, sometimes called *views*, provide an important role in retrieving and displaying data stored in a relational database system. Using table relationships, Access enables you to join tables in your database for the purpose of sharing information and reducing data redundancy. You may recall that the basis for relating tables is the existence of common fields. If relationships have not yet been defined, Access allows you to do so in query Design view. Access can also create relationships between tables automatically, as long as (1) both tables contain a field of the same name and data type and (2) one of the fields is a primary key. Otherwise, you must establish your table relationships manually. This module demonstrates how to work with multiple tables in the query Design window.

## 6.2.1 Adding and Removing Tables

**FEATURE**
Using a query, you can display a dynaset that incorporates data from more than one table. When you begin creating a new query, Access displays the Show Tables dialog box. You use this dialog box to select the tables on which to base the resulting query. When working in query Design view, you redisplay the Show Table dialog box to add a new table. Removing a table from the Table pane is similarly straightforward. Select the table's field list object and then press DELETE.

**METHOD**
To add a table to an existing query:

1. CLICK: Show Table button (🖳)
2. SELECT: the desired table(s) from the *Tables* tab
3. CLICK: Add command button
4. CLICK: Close command button

To remove a table from a query:

1. SELECT: the desired field list object in the Table pane
2. PRESS: DELETE

**PRACTICE**
You now practice adding tables and establishing relationships in the query Design window.

*Setup:* Ensure that the ACC600 Database window is displayed and that the *Queries* button is selected.

**1** Before creating a new multitable query, review the existing table relationships:
CLICK: Relationships button (🔁)
Your screen should now appear similar to Figure 6.5. Notice that several relationships have already been established.

**Figure 6.5**

Viewing the existing
table relationships

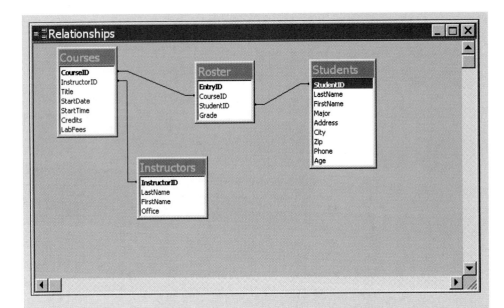

**2** Close the Relationships window by clicking its Close button (☒).

**3** To create a new query based on a single table:
CLICK: New button (New) in the Database window toolbar
SELECT: Design View in the New Query dialog box
CLICK: OK command button

**4** In the Show Table dialog box that appears:
SELECT: Courses
CLICK: Add command button
CLICK: Close command button
The Courses field list object appears in the Table pane of the
query Design window.

**5** To demonstrate how you can add multiple tables at the same time:
CLICK: Show Table button (⌗)
SELECT: Instructors
PRESS: CTRL and hold it down
SELECT: Roster
Both table names should appear highlighted. (*Hint:* Remember to
release the CTRL key when you finish selecting the last item.)

**6** To complete the addition of tables:
CLICK: Add command button
CLICK: Close command button

**7** Increase the Table pane area by dragging the Split bar downward.
Then, using the sizing corners and Title bars, size and move the
query Design window and field list objects to appear similar to
Figure 6.6. Notice that relationship or "join" lines appear
between the field lists.

**Figure 6.6**

Manipulating the appearance
of the query Design window

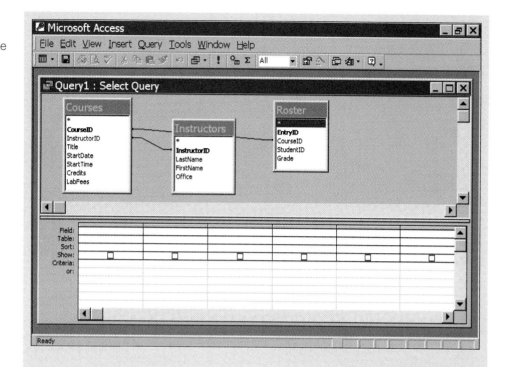

**8** To remove a field list object from the Table pane, select the object
and then press DELETE. Or, using the mouse, do the following:
RIGHT-CLICK: the Roster field list object
CHOOSE: Remove Table

**9** Even though you haven't added fields to the Design grid yet,
let's save and name the new query:
CLICK: Save button (📖)
TYPE: **Course and Instructor List**
CLICK: OK command button

**10** Keep the query Design window open for use in the next lesson.

## 6.2.2 Adding and Removing Fields

**FEATURE**
Once the desired field list objects appear in the Table pane, adding
and removing fields in the query Design grid is easy. Although
there are two or three methods you can use, double-clicking an
item in a field list is the fastest way to add the field to the next
available column in the grid. To remove a field, select its column
in the grid and then choose the Edit, Delete Columns command
or press DELETE. You can also move field columns to rearrange the
field display in a dynaset, as demonstrated earlier in this chapter.

**METHOD**
To add fields to the query Design grid:

- DOUBLE-CLICK: asterisk (*) to add all fields to the grid, or
- DOUBLE-CLICK: a field in the field list object, or
- DRAG: a field from the field list object into the *Field* row, or
- CLICK: in a cell in the *Field* row
  SELECT: a field name from the drop-down list

To remove fields from the query Design grid:

- CHOOSE: Edit, Clear Grid to remove all fields from the grid, or
- SELECT: a field column in the grid area
  CHOOSE: Edit, Delete Columns (or PRESS: [DELETE])

**PRACTICE**
In this lesson, you create a query to display course and instructor information in the same dynaset.

*Setup:* Ensure that the Course and Instructor List query is displayed in the query Design window.

**1** To add fields to the grid from the Courses table:
DOUBLE-CLICK: CourseID in the Courses field list
DOUBLE-CLICK: Title in the Courses field list

**2** To add all of the fields to the grid from the Instructors table:
DRAG: asterisk (*) from the Instructors field list and drop it on the next available column in the *Field* row

**3** CLICK: View—Datasheet button ([▥▾])
Your screen should now appear similar to Figure 6.7.

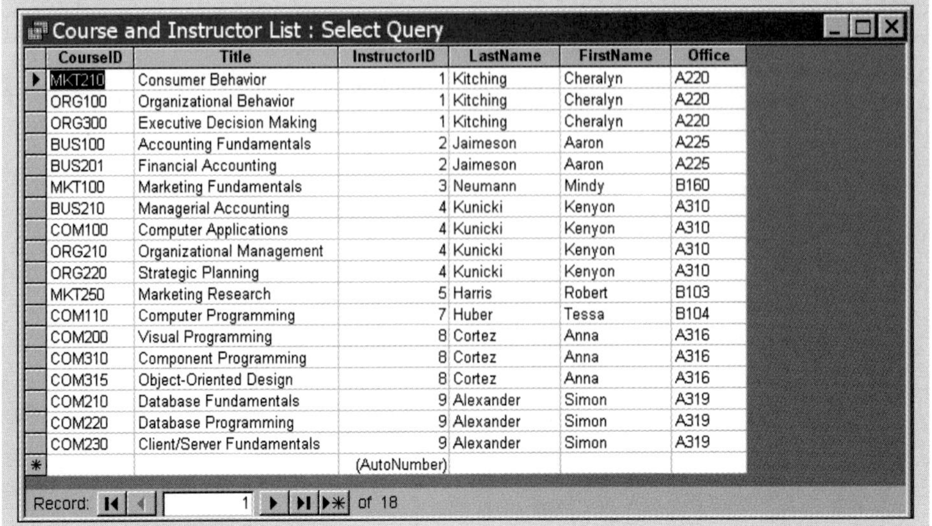

**Figure 6.7**

Viewing a multitable query

| CourseID | Title | InstructorID | LastName | FirstName | Office |
|---|---|---|---|---|---|
| MKT210 | Consumer Behavior | 1 | Kitching | Cheralyn | A220 |
| ORG100 | Organizational Behavior | 1 | Kitching | Cheralyn | A220 |
| ORG300 | Executive Decision Making | 1 | Kitching | Cheralyn | A220 |
| BUS100 | Accounting Fundamentals | 2 | Jaimeson | Aaron | A225 |
| BUS201 | Financial Accounting | 2 | Jaimeson | Aaron | A225 |
| MKT100 | Marketing Fundamentals | 3 | Neumann | Mindy | B160 |
| BUS210 | Managerial Accounting | 4 | Kunicki | Kenyon | A310 |
| COM100 | Computer Applications | 4 | Kunicki | Kenyon | A310 |
| ORG210 | Organizational Management | 4 | Kunicki | Kenyon | A310 |
| ORG220 | Strategic Planning | 4 | Kunicki | Kenyon | A310 |
| MKT250 | Marketing Research | 5 | Harris | Robert | B103 |
| COM110 | Computer Programming | 7 | Huber | Tessa | B104 |
| COM200 | Visual Programming | 8 | Cortez | Anna | A316 |
| COM310 | Component Programming | 8 | Cortez | Anna | A316 |
| COM315 | Object-Oriented Design | 8 | Cortez | Anna | A316 |
| COM210 | Database Fundamentals | 9 | Alexander | Simon | A319 |
| COM220 | Database Programming | 9 | Alexander | Simon | A319 |
| COM230 | Client/Server Fundamentals | 9 | Alexander | Simon | A319 |
| * | | (AutoNumber) | | | |

Course and Instructor List : Select Query

Record: 1 of 18

**4** Let's remove the InstructorID and Office columns from displaying in the dynaset. First, display the query Design window:
CLICK: View—Design button (⬛▾)

**5** Using the downward pointing arrow (↓):
SELECT: Instructors.* column by clicking its field header

**6** You may have noticed that this one column is responsible for displaying all of the Instructors fields in the dynaset. To remove the column:
PRESS: DELETE

**7** To add the desired fields individually:
DOUBLE-CLICK: LastName in the Instructors field list
DOUBLE-CLICK: FirstName in the Instructors field list

**8** CLICK: View—Datasheet button (⬛▾)
Notice that the dynaset provides an integrated view of data from two tables.

**9** Close the Datasheet window and save the design changes.

## 6.2.3 Specifying Multitable Criteria

**FEATURE**
After creating a multitable select query, you can specify criteria for any field that appears in the query Design grid. The second row of the Design grid displays the table name to which the field belongs. If the *Table* row does not appear in the query Design grid, right-click any cell in the grid and choose the Table Names command. Prior to specifying criteria, it is wise to display the query's dynaset in order to check your table relationships. If relationship joins are not defined correctly, Access may display a meaningless combination of records retrieved from the two tables.

**METHOD**
1. Display the query in Design view.
2. Ensure that the table relationships are defined correctly.
3. Ensure that the *Table* row is displayed. If not, choose the Table Names command after right-clicking the grid area.
4. Enter the desired criteria specification.

ACCESS

**PRACTICE**
In this lesson, you enter criteria for a multitable select query.

*Setup:* Ensure that you've completed the previous lessons in this module and that the ACC600 Database window is displayed.

**1** To modify a multitable query:
SELECT: Course and Instructor List
CLICK: Design button (🗹 Design)

**2** To limit the display of the dynaset results to those instructors whose last name begins with the letter K, do the following:
CLICK: in the *Criteria* text box in the LastName column
TYPE: K*
PRESS: TAB

**3** CLICK: View—Datasheet button (🔲▾)
The Datasheet window displays only those courses instructed by Cheralyn Kitching and Kenyon Kunicki.

**4** To return to the query Design window:
CLICK: View—Design button (🗹▾)

**5** To remove the last criteria specification:
CHOOSE: Edit, Delete Rows

**6** To display all courses that include "Behavior" anywhere in their title:
CLICK: in the *Criteria* text box in the Title column
TYPE: *behavior*
PRESS: TAB

**7** CLICK: View—Datasheet button (🔲▾)
Two records are displayed in the dynaset.

**8** To remove the last criteria specification:
CLICK: View—Design button (🗹▾)
CHOOSE: Edit, Delete Rows

**9** To save the query:
CLICK: Save button (🔲)

**10** Close the Design window to return to the Database window.

## 6.2.4 Previewing and Printing the Dynaset

**FEATURE**

In addition to using a query as the basis for a report, you can preview and print a dynaset's Datasheet window. Similar to printing a table (or any other database object), Access lets you preview the output prior to sending it to the printer. Using a query for printing is especially useful for combining data that is stored in multiple tables.

**METHOD**

- To preview a displayed dynaset:
  CLICK: Print Preview button (🔍), or
  CHOOSE: File, Print Preview
- To print a displayed dynaset:
  CLICK: Print button (🖨), or
  CHOOSE: File, Print

**PRACTICE**

You now preview and print the multitable query created in this module.

*Setup:* Ensure that you've completed the previous lessons in this module and that the ACC600 Database window is displayed.

**1** To display the query created in this module:
DOUBLE-CLICK: Course and Instructor List
A Datasheet window appears with columns for CourseID, Title, LastName, and FirstName.

**2** To preview the dynaset for printing:
CLICK: Print Preview button (🔍) in the toolbar

**3** To enlarge the display:
SELECT: 100% from the Zoom button (Fit ▾)
Your screen should now appear similar to Figure 6.8.

**Figure 6.8**

Previewing a dynaset
for printing

Enlarge the display using
the Zoom button.

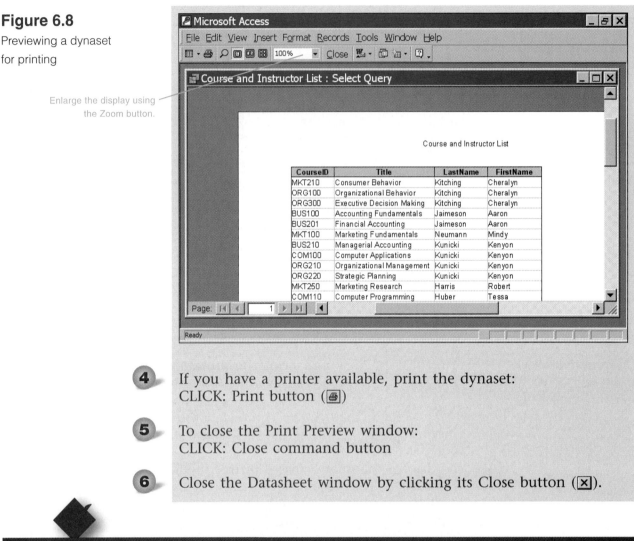

**4** If you have a printer available, print the dynaset:
CLICK: Print button (🖨)

**5** To close the Print Preview window:
CLICK: Close command button

**6** Close the Datasheet window by clicking its Close button (☒).

**6.2 Self Check**    In query Design view, how do you add a new table to the Table pane?

# 6.3   Enhancing a Select Query

So far in this chapter you've used select queries to pick fields for display, limit the display of records to those matching simple criteria statements, and create joined datasheets using data stored in multiple tables. In this module, you enhance select queries by sorting and filtering records and by constructing more elaborate criteria statements.

## 6.3.1 Sorting Query Results

**FEATURE**

The sort order for displaying records in a dynaset is defined using the *Sort* row of the query Design grid. In addition to specifying ascending or descending sort order, you can create multikey sorts by selecting more than one field in the grid. The leftmost field column becomes the primary sort key, while the remaining columns are sorted according to their column order. This feature enables you to perform complex sort operations, such as listing records alphabetically by country, then by state, and lastly by city. In this example, country is the *primary sort key*, state is the *secondary sort key*, and city is a *tertiary sort key*. If you choose not to sort a dynaset, the resulting records display in the same order that governs the underlying table, which may or may not be determined by a primary key field.

**METHOD**

1. Display the query in Design view.
2. CLICK: in the *Sort* text box in the desired field column
3. CLICK: down arrow attached to the *Sort* text box
4. SELECT: Ascending, Descending, or (not sorted)

**PRACTICE**

You now practice creating a new query object and sorting its dynaset.

*Setup:* Ensure that the ACC600 Database window is displayed and that the *Queries* button is selected.

**1** To create a new query:
DOUBLE-CLICK: Create query in Design view

**2** This query uses data stored in the Students table only:
DOUBLE-CLICK: Students
CLICK: Close command button

**3** If necessary, adjust the size and placement of the query Design window. You may also want to adjust the space between the Table pane and the query Design grid.

**4** In the Students field list object:
DOUBLE-CLICK: FirstName
DOUBLE-CLICK: LastName
DOUBLE-CLICK: Major
DOUBLE-CLICK: City

**5**   CLICK: View—Datasheet button (🔲▾)
The dynaset records are displayed in order according to the contents of the underlying primary key field, StudentID.

**6**   To return to query Design view:
CLICK: View—Design button (📐▾)

**7**   To sort the results by last name:
CLICK: in the *Sort* row in the LastName field column
CLICK: down arrow attached to the *Sort* text box
SELECT: Ascending from the drop-down list box

**8**   View the dynaset results in a Datasheet window. Your screen should appear similar to Figure 6.9.

**Figure 6.9**

Sorting a dynaset
by the LastName field

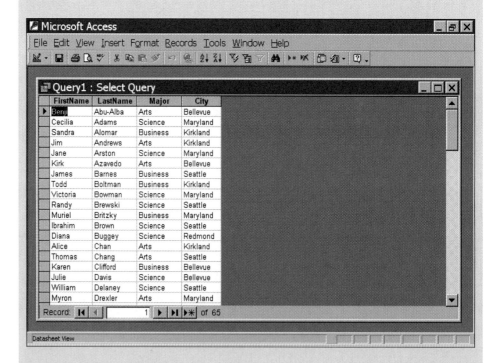

**9**   To return to query Design view:
CLICK: View—Design button (📐▾)

**10**   To sort records into alphabetical order by Major and then, for each Major, by surname, you must move the Major field to appear left of LastName. To begin:
SELECT: Major column by clicking its field header
DRAG: Major column to the left so that a black vertical gridline appears between the FirstName and LastName columns

**11** Release the mouse button to complete the move operation.

**12** SELECT: FirstName column by clicking its field header
DRAG: FirstName column to the right so that a black vertical gridline appears between the LastName and City fields

**13** Release the mouse button.

**14** To specify a sort order for the Major field column:
CLICK: in the *Sort* row in the Major field column
CLICK: down arrow attached to the *Sort* text box
SELECT: Ascending from the drop-down list box

**15** Remove the selection highlighted in the Design grid by clicking once in a blank portion of the Table pane area. Your screen should now appear similar to Figure 6.10.

**Figure 6.10**

Specifying a multikey sort order

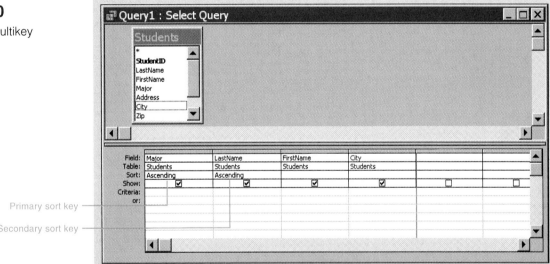

Primary sort key

Secondary sort key

**16** CLICK: View—Datasheet button ()
Notice that the Major entries are sorted alphabetically. Within each major, the records are then sorted using values in the Last-Name field.

**17** Rather than returning to the Design window, you can save the query while viewing the dynaset results:
CLICK: Save button (◻)
TYPE: **Student List By Major**
CLICK: OK command button

**18** Close the Datasheet window.

ACCESS

## 6.3.2  Applying Filters to the Dynaset

**FEATURE**

Filters enable you to temporarily change the view of your data. Rather than including all of your contacts in a datasheet, you can use a filter to limit the display of records to those contacts living in Boston. Because filters are quick and easy to apply, they are an efficient analysis tool. These strengths also apply to filtering the results of a query. When you don't want to modify the criteria specification in a query object, use filters to limit the display of records in a dynaset. If desired, you can save a filter specification as a new query object.

**METHOD**

1. Display the query's dynaset in Datasheet view.
2. Apply a filter using the Filter For Input, Filter By Selection, Filter Excluding Selection, or Filter By Form commands.
3. Remove a filter by clicking the Apply/Remove Filter button (▽).

**PRACTICE**

In this lesson, you apply a filter to the records displayed in a dynaset.

*Setup:* Ensure that you've completed the previous lesson and that the ACC600 Database window is displayed.

**1** To begin, display the query that you created in the last lesson:
DOUBLE-CLICK: Student List By Major

**2** Of the records displayed in the dynaset, let's filter through only those students who live in Bellevue. In the City column, locate a record containing "Bellevue" and then do the following:
DOUBLE-CLICK: Bellevue

**3** With the selection highlighted in the datasheet:
CLICK: Filter By Selection button (▽) in the toolbar
The dynaset is filtered to display only 14 records.

**4** To use the Filter By Form method:
CLICK: Filter By Form button (▣)
A row appears where you can input or select criteria for limiting the display of records in the dynaset.

**5** In addition to filtering the dynaset by City, let's apply an additional filter for displaying only the Business students:
CLICK: in the empty cell in the Major column
CLICK: down arrow attached to the Major text box
SELECT: Business from the drop-down list box
The Filter By Form row should appear as shown below.

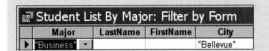

| Major | LastName | FirstName | City |
|---|---|---|---|
| "Business" ▾ | | | "Bellevue" |

Student List By Major: Filter by Form

**6** CLICK: Apply Filter button (▽)
Six records are now displayed in the Datasheet window.

**7** To return to the Filter By Form window:
CLICK: Filter By Form button (▤)

**8** Let's save this dynaset result as a new query object:
CLICK: Save As Query button (▤)
TYPE: **Business Students in Bellevue**
CLICK: OK command button

**9** To return to the Database window:
CLICK: Close command button in the toolbar
CLICK: Close button (✕) for the Datasheet window
CLICK: No command button when asked to save the changes
You should now see an additional query object in the list area.

**10** To display the design specification of the new query:
SELECT: Business Students in Bellevue
CLICK: Design button (⧉ Design)

**11** On your own, adjust the query Design window to appear similar to Figure 6.11. Notice that the query uses the results of the Student List By Major query, as opposed to a table object, as the basis for its data.

**12** Close the Design window without saving the changes.

ACCESS

**Figure 6.11**

Examining a Filter
By Form query

The field list object
displays fields from
another query object.

The Filter By Form
criterion is transferred
into the *Criteria* row.

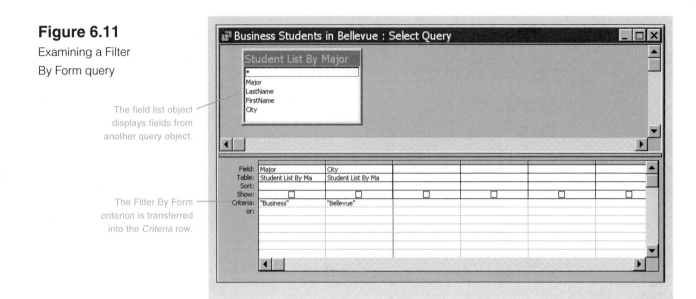

## 6.3.3  Specifying Multiple Criteria in Different Fields

**FEATURE**

Queries enable you to perform simple and complex search and retrieval operations. A simple query involves extracting information based on a single criterion or condition. A complex query, on the other hand, involves more than one criterion and employs conditional logic. **Conditional logic** is the method by which criteria statements are joined and executed in a query. For example, you may want to list all of your Florida customers who deal with a sales agent named Ralph. Namely, the query should display all records where City equals "Florida" AND Agent equals "Ralph." Notice that this query requires that you join the two criteria using a *logical AND* statement. You can also define a *logical OR* query. For example, you can display all records where City equals "Florida" OR Agent equals "Ralph." Using conditional logic to combine criteria statements enables you to ask a variety of questions of your data.

**METHOD**

- Enter criteria on the same *Criteria* row of the query Design grid to join statements using a logical AND. Only records meeting both criteria statements are returned for display in the dynaset.
- Enter criteria on the *Or* rows of the query Design grid in order to join statements using a logical OR. Records meeting any statement are returned for display in the dynaset.

**PRACTICE**

You now practice constructing query statements using conditional logic.

*Setup:* Ensure that the ACC600 Database window is displayed.

**1** To create a new query:
DOUBLE-CLICK: Create query in Design view

**2** This query uses data stored in the Students table only:
DOUBLE-CLICK: Students
CLICK: Close command button

**3** If necessary, adjust the size and placement of the query Design window. You may also want to adjust the space between the Table pane and the query Design grid.

**4** In the Students field list object:
DOUBLE-CLICK: LastName
DOUBLE-CLICK: Major
DOUBLE-CLICK: City
DOUBLE-CLICK: Age

**5** To sort the dynaset results by surname:
CLICK: in the *Sort* row in the LastName field column
CLICK: down arrow attached to the *Sort* text box
SELECT: Ascending from the drop-down list box

**6** Similar to the Filter By Form query that you created in the last lesson, you can enter more than one condition on the *Criteria* row of the Design grid. To demonstrate, let's display all of the Arts students living in Kirkland:
CLICK: in the *Criteria* text box in the Major column
TYPE: **Arts**
PRESS: ⬚TAB⬚
TYPE: **Kirkland**
Only records matching both of these criteria statements will be returned for display.

**7** CLICK: View—Datasheet button (⊞▾)
Six records are displayed in the datasheet.

**8** To return to the query Design window:
CLICK: View—Design button (▨▾)

ACCESS

**9** Adding to this logical AND example, display all of the Arts students living in Kirkland who are over the age of 20. To do so:
CLICK: in the *Criteria* text box in the Age column
TYPE: **>20**
Your screen should appear similar to Figure 6.12.

**Figure 6.12**

Entering multiple
criteria statements

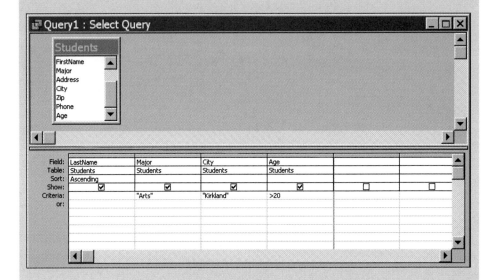

**10** CLICK: View—Datasheet button (▥▾)
Each of the three records displayed meets all of the conditions set forth in the Design grid.

**11** To return to the query Design window:
CLICK: View—Design button (▨▾)

**12** To create a new set of conditions, ensure that the flashing insertion point appears in the *Criteria* row and then do the following:
CHOOSE: Edit, Delete Rows

**13** You will now display all students who are either Science majors living in Redmond or over the age of 24. This query may also be written as a mathematical Boolean expression, *(Major="Science" AND City="Redmond") OR Age>24*. To begin:
CLICK: in the *Criteria* text box in the Major column
TYPE: **Science**
PRESS: (**TAB**)
TYPE: **Redmond**
Notice that "Science" and "Redmond" appear on the same row in the Design grid to represent a logical AND.

**14** To establish a logical OR condition, you enter criteria on the *Or* rows of the Design grid. Do the following:
CLICK: in the *Or* text box in the Age column
TYPE: **>24**

**15** CLICK: View—Datasheet button (▣▾)
Eight records appear in the Datasheet window.

**16** To return to the query Design window:
CLICK: View—Design button (▨▾)

**17** Keep the window open for use in the next lesson.

## 6.3.4   Specifying Multiple Criteria in a Single Field

**FEATURE**
Most of the criteria statements that you've entered thus far identify a particular value or range of values to match in a table. For
example, you enter "Boston" in a City field or ">22" in an Age
field. How would you retrieve records containing either Boston,
Chicago, or New York in the City field? Fortunately, Access allows
you to use the AND and OR operators in a single field column for
constructing conditional logic statements. An AND expression evaluates to true when all conditions are true. An OR expression is true
when any of the conditions are met. To solve the preceding question, for example, enter "Boston" OR "Chicago" OR "New York" in
a single cell in the *Criteria* row. Alternatively, you can enter each
value individually in separate rows of the same field column.

In the following "truth" table, notice that both criteria *a* and criteria *b* must be true when joined by AND to return a true result.
On the other hand, only one criteria must be true when joined
using OR.

| a | b | a AND b | a OR b |
|---|---|---------|--------|
| T | T | T | T |
| T | F | F | T |
| F | T | F | T |
| F | F | F | F |

**METHOD**

- Use a logical AND operator to specify that all conditions must be true for a record to be processed. For example, enter **>20 AND <65** to return values 21 through 64.
- Use a logical OR (or the *Or* row in the grid) to specify that an expression must be true for at least one of the cases. For example, enter **"Personal" OR "Business"** to return records containing either value in the same field.

**PRACTICE**

In this lesson, you enter criteria into a single field using the logical AND and OR operators.

*Setup:* Ensure that you've completed the previous lesson and that the query Design window is displayed.

**1** To reset the *Criteria* and *Or* rows in the Design grid:
CLICK: in any text box in the *Criteria* row
CHOOSE: Edit, Delete Rows
Notice that the condition entered on the *Or* row is moved up to now appear on the *Criteria* row.

**2** CHOOSE: Edit, Delete Rows

**3** You will now enter a criteria statement that displays all students who live in either Redmond or Bellevue. To begin:
CLICK: in the *Criteria* row of the City column
TYPE: **Redmond or Bellevue**

**4** CLICK: View—Datasheet button (▥▾)
You should see 24 records meeting this condition.

**5** To return to the query Design window:
CLICK: View—Design button (☑▾)

**6** Let's add another condition to the Design grid:
CLICK: in the *Criteria* row in the Age column
TYPE: **>20 and <24**
Your screen should appear similar to Figure 6.13.

**Figure 6.13**

Conditional query using the AND and OR operators

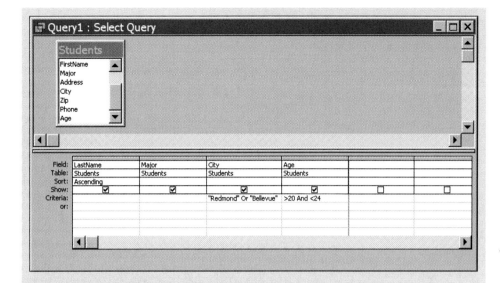

**7** Because the criteria statements are entered on the same row in the grid, the two conditions are joined together with a logical AND. This query displays those students living in Redmond and Bellevue who are between the ages of 20 and 24. To view the five query results:
CLICK: View—Datasheet button ()

**8** To save the query:
CLICK: Save button (🖫)
TYPE: **Student Custom Query**
CLICK: OK command button

**9** Close the Datasheet window.

---

**6.3 Self Check** In an employee database, how would you sort a query by ascending "Department" and then, for each department grouping, by ascending "Surname?"

# 6.4  Performing Calculations

Select queries are often used to perform row-by-row and aggregate calculations for analyzing and summarizing data. A *row-by-row calculation* computes a result for each record returned in a dynaset. An *aggregate calculation* or function computes a single summary result, such as the total and average values, for all records returned in a dynaset. Example calculations include joining a person's first and last name in a single column, calculating the total value of inventory, or determining the average number of vacation days earned by employees. In this module, you learn how to calculate and display computed results using queries.

## 6.4.1 Creating a Calculated Field

**FEATURE**

A **calculated field** enables you to draw data from other field columns and perform a mathematical calculation on a row-by-row basis. Generally, if a value can be calculated for display, you should not store it permanently in the database. For example, you can multiply the contents of a price field by a quantity field to yield a result entitled amount. This field is calculated on the fly and made available for display at any time.

You can perform simple and complex calculations using calculated fields in queries. To create a calculated field, enter an **expression** into the *Field* row of the query Design grid. Expressions may contain table and field names (which are enclosed in square brackets), mathematical operators (+, -, /, and *), comparison operators (< and >), logical operators (AND and OR), and constants (True/False and Null). There are two parts to an expression entered into the query Design grid: the name of the resulting field (e.g. amount) and the expression. You separate the field name and expression using a colon. To further customize a dynaset, you can hide the display of unnecessary fields by removing the "✓" from the check box in the *Show* row of the grid.

**METHOD**
1.  SELECT: an empty field column in the query Design grid
2.  CLICK: in the *Field* text box in the empty column
3.  TYPE: `field name: expression`

**PRACTICE**

In this lesson, you create a calculated field that adjusts the student grades for a particular course.

*Setup:* Ensure that the ACC600 Database window is displayed and that the *Queries* button is selected.

**1** You will now create a multitable query that displays the student grades for the COM200 course. To proceed:
DOUBLE-CLICK: Create query in Design view

**2** In the Show Table dialog box:
DOUBLE-CLICK: Students
DOUBLE-CLICK: Roster
CLICK: Close command button

**3** If necessary, adjust the size and placement of the query Design window. You may also want to adjust the space between the Table pane and the Design grid.

**4** To add fields to the Design grid:
DOUBLE-CLICK: CourseID in the Roster field list
DOUBLE-CLICK: LastName in the Students field list
DOUBLE-CLICK: FirstName in the Students field list
DOUBLE-CLICK: Grade in the Roster field list

**5** To specify a criterion to limit the display of records:
CLICK: in the *Criteria* text box in the CourseID column
TYPE: **COM200**

**6** To sort the list alphabetically by student surname:
CLICK: in the *Sort* text box in the LastName column
CLICK: down arrow attached to the Sort text box
SELECT: Ascending from the drop-down list box

**7** Let's display the new query before adding a calculated field:
CLICK: View—Datasheet button (▦▾)
Your screen should appear similar to Figure 6.14.

**Figure 6.14**

Displaying student
grades for COM200

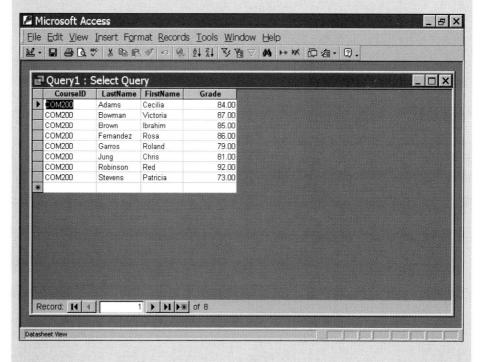

**8** To return to the query Design window:
CLICK: View—Design button (▨▾)

**9** As a teaching assistant for this course, you've been granted the
power to scale the student marks upward by five points. To do so:
CLICK: in the *Field* text box in the next available column
(*Hint:* Ignore the drop-down list box arrow that appears attached
to this text box.)

**10.** To enter an expression that calculates the new grade:
TYPE: `New Grade:[Roster]![Grade]+5`
Notice that you enter a column name for the calculated result, a colon, and then the expression to evaluate. Since this query uses more than one table, we specify the table name [Roster], separated from the [Grade] field using an exclamation point. The expression itself simply adds the value 5 to the existing values in the field. (*Note:* Although Access will add the square brackets for your automatically, it's best to learn now that both table and field names require brackets when used in expressions.)

**11.** CLICK: View—Datasheet button (▦▾)
A new column called "New Grade" appears. Notice that each value is five points greater than the value appearing in the "Grade" column.

**12.** Let's remove the original Grade column from displaying:
CLICK: View—Design button (▨▾)
CLICK: *Show* check box in the Grade column so that no "✔" appears

**13.** To size the calculated field column in the Design grid, position the mouse pointer over the right border line in the field header area. Drag the mouse pointer to the right as you would in sizing a datasheet column. When you release the mouse button, your screen should appear similar to Figure 6.15.

**Figure 6.15**

A calculated field
in the Design grid

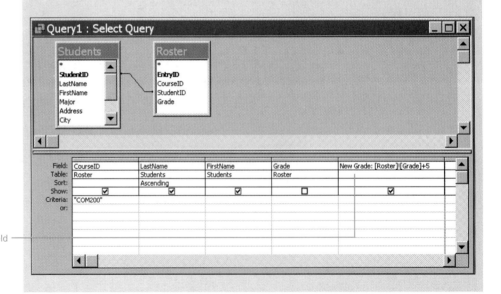

Calculated field

**14** To save the query:
CLICK: Save button (⊟)
TYPE: `New Grades for COM200` in the Save As dialog box
CLICK: OK command button

**15** Close the Design window.

## 6.4.2  Using the Expression Builder

**FEATURE**
Access provides the **Expression Builder** to help you enter expressions for use in defining *calculated fields* and in specifying criteria. This dialog box tool displays lists of tables, field names, operators, constants, and other buttons that you can use in constructing expressions. A large display area, called the *Expression box*, provides immediate feedback as you make your selections.

**METHOD**
1. SELECT: a *Field* text box to create a calculated field, or
   SELECT: a *Criteria* text box to specify a criterion specification
2. CLICK: Build button (⊡) in the toolbar
3. Complete the expression using the Expression Builder dialog box.

**PRACTICE**
You now use the Expression Builder to join two fields together in a query's dynaset.

*Setup:* Ensure that you've completed the previous lesson and that the ACC600 Database window is displayed.

**1** To modify the query created in the last lesson:
SELECT: New Grades for COM200
CLICK: Design button (⊠ Design )

**2** To insert a new field column:
SELECT: LastName column by clicking its field header
CHOOSE: Insert, Columns
A new column appears to the left of the LastName column.

**3** Using the Expression Builder dialog box, you will now create a calculated field that displays a student's surname and given name in the same column. To begin:
CLICK: in the *Field* text box of the new column
CLICK: Build button (⊡) in the toolbar
The dialog box in Figure 6.16 appears.

ACCESS

**Figure 6.16**

Expression Builder
dialog box

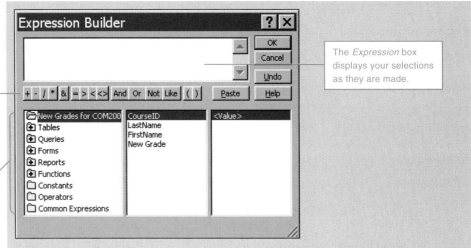

The *Expression* box
displays your selections
as they are made.

Select common operators
by clicking these buttons.

Select a main folder in the
left-hand list box to display
a new set of subcategories
and element values in the
next two list boxes.

**4** You now use the Expression Builder to create an expression that
displays names in the format "Smith, John." To begin:
DOUBLE-CLICK: LastName in the middle list box
The value "[LastName]" appears in the *Expression* box. As you perform the next step, continue to watch the *Expression* box. (*Hint:*
You can access any field by double-clicking the Tables option in
the left-hand list box and then selecting the desired table name.)

**5** You **concatenate** or join values using the ampersand (&) symbol.
In order to display "Surname, Given" for this example, you need
to join the two field values with a comma and space. To do so:
CLICK: ▣ (ampersand) in the row of operator buttons
TYPE: " , "
CLICK: ▣ (ampersand) in the row of operator buttons
DOUBLE-CLICK: FirstName in the middle list box
Notice that the comma and space must be surrounded by quotes
in order to be joined with the field contents.

**6** To complete the expression:
CLICK: OK command button

**7** To name the calculated field:
PRESS: [HOME]
TYPE: Student:
CLICK: *Show* check box in the new column so that a "✔" appears
(*Hint:* Access inserts the name "Expr1" for the calculated field
automatically. You must typically delete this name before typing
your own entry into the text box.)

**8** Now let's hide the individual name columns from displaying:
CLICK: *Show* check box in the LastName column so that no "✔"
appears
CLICK: *Show* check box in the FirstName column so that no "✔"
appears

**9** ▶ CLICK: View—Datasheet button (▥▾)
After adjusting the width of the new column, your screen should appear similar to Figure 6.17. Notice that the dynaset remains sorted by the LastName field.

**10** ▶ To save the query and close the Datasheet window:
CLICK: Save button (▤)
CLICK: its Close button (☒)

**Figure 6.17**

Displaying calculated fields in a dynaset

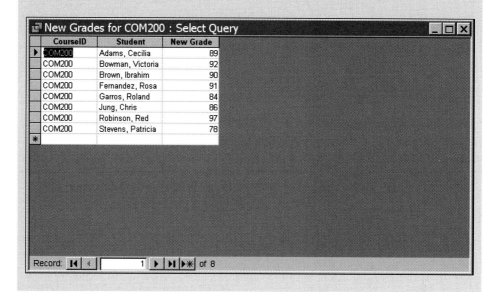

**6.4.3  Creating Summary Queries**

**FEATURE**
A summary query enables you to perform aggregate calculations that summarize groups of data. Often used for statistical analysis, summary queries provide mathematical functions that are used to sum a field's values, find the average, maximum, or minimum values in a field, and calculate the standard deviation or variance for a field. Rather than displaying all the rows in a dynaset, a single row of values or group of row values is returned. To perform more than one summary calculation on a particular field, add the field to the query Design grid for each additional calculation.

**METHOD**
1.  CLICK: Totals button (Σ) in the toolbar, or
    CHOOSE: View, Totals
2.  SELECT: a cell in the *Total* row of the desired column
3.  SELECT: *a calculation option* from the drop-down list box

**PRACTICE**
You now calculate the average age of students using a select query.

*Setup:* Ensure that the ACC600 Database window is displayed and that the *Queries* button is selected.

**1** To create a new query:
DOUBLE-CLICK: Create query in Design view
DOUBLE-CLICK: Students in the Show Table dialog box
CLICK: Close command button

**2** If necessary, adjust the size and placement of the query Design window. You may also want to adjust the space between the Table pane and the Design grid.

**3** You can calculate the average age of all students using a query. To begin, display the *Total* row in the Design grid:
CLICK: Totals button (☐) in the toolbar

**4** Now add the Age field to the grid:
DOUBLE-CLICK: Age in the Students field list

**5** The "Group By" option that appears in the *Total* row is used to group subsets of records in a table. However, we want to perform a calculation using all of the records. To do so, you select a calculation option from the drop-down list attached to a *Total* text box:
CLICK: in the *Total* text box in the Age column
CLICK: down arrow attached to the text box
Your screen should now appear similar to Figure 6.18.

**Figure 6.18**
Creating a summary query

The *Total* drop-down list box displays the calculation options.

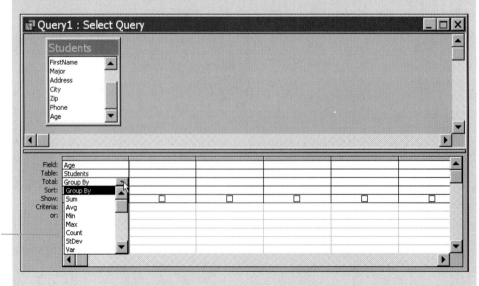

**6** SELECT: Avg in the *Total* drop-down list box

**7** CLICK: View—Datasheet button (⊞▾)
The result, entitled AvgOfAge, appears in a single cell datasheet, as shown below.

| AvgOfAge |
| --- |
| ▶ 20.3230769231 |

**8** You will now calculate the average age of students according to their major. Do the following:
CLICK: View—Design button (◪▾)

**9** To add the Major field to the grid:
DOUBLE-CLICK: Major in the Students field list
SELECT: Major column by clicking its field header
DRAG: Major column to appear left of the Age column
Notice that the Major column has "Group By" in its *Total* row.

**10** CLICK: View—Datasheet button (⊞▾)
The calculation result should appear as shown below. Notice that Access groups together the unique values in the Major column automatically and then performs the calculation.

| Major | AvgOfAge |
| --- | --- |
| ▶ Arts | 20.8260869565 |
| Business | 20.3181818182 |
| Science | 19.75 |

**11** You will now find the maximum and minimum age for students in each major. Do the following:
CLICK: View—Design button (◪▾)

**12** To perform multiple calculations using the same field, you must add additional fields to the Design grid. In the Students field list:
DOUBLE-CLICK: Age twice
You should now have three columns displayed for the Age field.

**13** To complete the Design grid:
CLICK: in the *Total* text box in the middle Age column
SELECT: Min from the *Total* drop-down list box
CLICK: in the *Total* text box in the rightmost Age column
SELECT: Max from the *Total* drop-down list box
Your screen should now appear similar to Figure 6.19.

ACCESS

**Figure 6.19**

Performing multiple calculations in a query

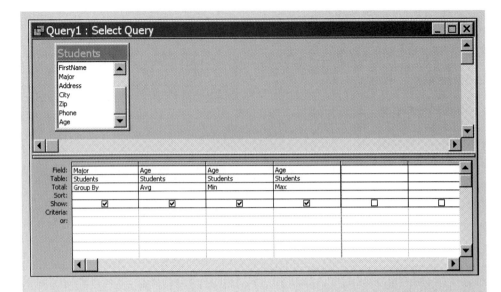

**14** CLICK: View—Datasheet button (⊞▾)
The calculation result should appear as shown below.

| Major | AvgOfAge | MinOfAge | MaxOfAge |
|-------|----------|----------|----------|
| ▶ Arts | 20.8260869565 | 18 | 29 |
| Business | 20.3181818182 | 18 | 25 |
| Science | 19.75 | 18 | 26 |

**15** To save the query:
CLICK: Save button (🖫)
TYPE: **Student Ages by Major** in the Save As dialog box
CLICK: OK command button

**16** Close the Datasheet window and the ACC600 Database Window.
Then, exit Microsoft Access.

**In Addition**
Returning the Top
Values Only

To display the top values from a query, open the query object in query Design view and click the Top Values button (All ▾) on the toolbar. You can then specify a number of rows (for example, the top ten values) or a percentage (for example, the top five percent.) Ensure that only the field that contains the values is selected to display and then view the datasheet to see the results.

**6.4 Self Check**    How would you calculate the average invoice amount from a table that stored only the price and quantity of items sold?

# 6.5   Chapter Review

The importance of learning to create and use queries in Access cannot be understated. In addition to displaying, sorting, filtering, deleting, and updating the records in a database, queries are used to retrieve data for use in forms and reports. Of the several types of queries Access provides, this chapter focuses on designing *select queries* for retrieving data from one or more tables for display. You also learn to use select queries for performing row-by-row and aggregate calculations. From a more global perspective, this chapter attempts to get you comfortable using the query Design window. To this end, you add, delete, and work with field list objects in the Table pane. You also use the query Design grid to select fields for display, sort the query's results, enter conditional criteria statements, create calculated fields, and summarize the numerical data in your database.

## 6.5.1   Command Summary

Many of the commands and procedures appearing in this chapter are summarized in the following table.

| Skill Set | To Perform This Task . . . | Do the Following . . . |
|---|---|---|
| **Viewing and Organizing Information** | Create a new query in Design view | SELECT: *Queries* object button<br>DOUBLE-CLICK: Create query in Design view |
| | Modify an existing query object | SELECT: the desired query<br>CLICK: Design button (⟆Design) |
| | Add a table's field list object to the query Design window | CLICK: Show Table button (⊡)<br>SELECT: the desired tables<br>CLICK: Add command button<br>CLICK: Close command button |
| | Remove a table's field list object from the query Design window | SELECT: the desired field list object<br>PRESS: DELETE |
| | Add a field to the query Design grid | DOUBLE-CLICK: the desired field in a table's field list object |
| | Add all fields from a field list object to the query Design grid | DOUBLE-CLICK: the asterisk (*) option at the top of a table's field list object |

*Continued*

| Skill Set | To Perform This Task . . . | Do the Following . . . |
|---|---|---|
| **Viewing and Organizing Information** *Continued* | Remove a field from the query Design grid | SELECT: a field's column by clicking its header area<br>PRESS: `DELETE` |
| | Enter a criterion specification in query Design view | CLICK: in a *Criteria* text box<br>TYPE: *a conditional query statement* |
| | Delete a *Criteria* row in the query Design grid | SELECT: a cell in the *Criteria* row<br>CHOOSE: Edit, Delete Rows |
| | Move a field in the query Design grid | SELECT: a field's column by clicking its header area<br>DRAG: the field to a new column position |
| | Hide a field from displaying in the dynaset results | CLICK: *Show* check box for a field so that no "✔" appears |
| | Specify a sort order for a dynaset in the query Design grid | CLICK: in a *Sort* text box<br>SELECT: Ascending, Descending, or (not sorted) from the drop-down list box |
| | Create a calculated field | CLICK: in a *Field* text box<br>TYPE: *an expression* |
| **Refining Queries** | Display the Expression Builder | CLICK: in a *Field* or *Criteria* text box<br>CLICK: Build button (⬚) |
| | Create a totals query | CLICK: Totals button (Σ)<br>CLICK: in a *Total* text box<br>SELECT: a calculation option from the drop-down list box |

## 6.5.2 Key Terms

This section specifies page references for the key terms identified in this chapter. For a complete list of definitions, refer to the Glossary provided at the end of this learning guide.

action query, *p. 248*                     Expression Builder, *p. 281*

calculated field, *p. 278*               parameter query, *p. 248*

concatenate, *p. 282*                      query Design grid, *p. 249*

conditional logic, *p. 272*             query-by-example (QBE), *p. 248*

conditional statement, *p. 254*       SQL, *p. 248*

crosstab query, *p. 248*                Table pane, *p. 249*

expression, *p. 278*

# 6.6 Review Questions

## 6.6.1 Short Answer

1. What is the difference between a *select query* and an *action query*?
2. What is meant by the term "query-by-example?"
3. Provide a brief description of the query Design window.
4. Name three methods for adding a field to the query Design grid.
5. Provide two examples of matching surnames for the criteria specification **Like "John*n"**.
6. What two conditions are required for Access to create a table relationship automatically in query Design view?
7. How does Access determine the dynaset sort order when multiple fields are selected for sorting in the query Design grid?
8. Describe the two logical operators used in this chapter for creating conditional statements.
9. Why shouldn't you store the results of a calculated field in a table?
10. List the calculations that you can perform using the *Total* row in the query Design grid.

## 6.6.2 True/False

1. ____ An *update query* is one example of an *action query*.
2. ____ Double-clicking the asterisk in a field list object places an entry in the query Design grid that results in all of the object's fields displaying in the dynaset.
3. ____ You drag the Split bar to adjust the area shared by the Table pane and query Design grid.
4. ____ You click a field's check box in the *Hide* row of the query Design grid in order to hide its display in the dynaset.
5. ____ You use the same methods, keystrokes, and mouse actions for navigating a dynaset as you do to move around a datasheet.
6. ____ In the *Criteria* row of the query Design grid, an entry of `san*` is changed by Access to **"As san*"**.
7. ____ Whether its *Sort* check box is selected or not, the left-most column in the query Design grid provides the primary sort order.
8. ____ Placing criteria on separate rows in the query Design grid evaluates using a logical AND condition.
9. ____ The Expression Builder helps you create expressions for use in calculated fields and for specifying criteria.
10. ____ The ampersand (&) symbol is used to concatenate or join together two text strings for display.

## 6.6.3 Multiple Choice

1. Which of the following is *not* a type of *action query*?
   a.  append query
   b.  delete query
   c.  make table query
   d.  modify query

2. To answer the question "Which employees earn more than $50,000 annually?" you use this type of query:
   a.  crosstab query
   b.  search query
   c.  select query
   d.  update query

3. To answer the question "What is the average salary of employees working in the Marketing department?" you use this type of query:
   a.  compute query
   b.  expression query
   c.  modify query
   d.  select query

4. How do you select an entire column in the query Design grid?
   a. CLICK: the field's name in the *Field* row
   b. CLICK: the field header area for the desired column
   c. CLICK: *Show* check box to ensure that a "‚" appears
   d. CHOOSE: Edit, Select Column

5. To list all of the company names ending with "Inc." type the following into the appropriate *Criteria* text box:
   a. `*inc.`
   b. `"*inc."`
   c. `Like "*inc."`
   d. All of the above

6. To list all of the records entered between January 1ˢᵗ and March 31ˢᵗ, 2000, type the following into the appropriate *Criteria* text box:
   a. `Between #01/01/00# And #03/31/00#`
   b. `From #01/01/00# To #03/31/00#`
   c. `<#01/01/00# And >#03/31/00#`
   d. `>#01/01/00# Or <#03/31/00#`

7. To list all of the records containing either "Active" or "Pending" in a Status field, type the following into the field's *Criteria* text box:
   a. `Active Or Pending`
   b. `Active And Pending`
   c. `(Status="Active") Or (Status="Pending")`
   d. `(Status="Active") And (Status="Pending")`

8. To sort a dynaset first by ZipCode and then by LastName and FirstName, place the field columns in the following order:
   a. FirstName, LastName, ZipCode
   b. ZipCode, LastName, FirstName
   c. ZipCode, FirstName, LastName
   d. You cannot sort by multiple field columns.

9. To launch the Expression Builder dialog box, click the following:
   a. [Σ]
   b. [!]
   c. [⟍]
   d. [⟨?⟩]

10. The expression **[Detail]![Product]*1.30** does the
following:
a. Multiplies the contents of the Detail and Product fields by
1.30
b. Multiplies the result of dividing Detail by Product by 1.30
c. Multiplies the contents of Detail in the Product table by
1.30
d. Multiplies the contents of Product in the Detail table by
1.30

# 6.7  Hands-On Projects

## 6.7.1  World Wide Imports: Creating a Multitable Query

This exercise leads you step-by-step in creating a multitable select
query. Using query Design view, you create a query object that limits the display of data from a table and sorts the dynaset results.

*Setup:* Ensure that Access is loaded. If you are launching Access and
the startup dialog box appears, click the Cancel command button to
remove the dialog box from the application window.

1. Open the database file named ACC670. Ensure that the *Tables*
button in the Objects bar is selected.
2. Management indicates that the current customer listing is
inadequate. Specifically, they cannot seem to remember which
sales representative is assigned to a particular customer. Displaying the sales rep ID number in reports isn't informative
enough. Therefore, you decide to create a multitable query
that displays customer data along with the sales reps' names.
Do the following to create a new query:
CLICK: *Queries* button in the Objects bar
DOUBLE-CLICK: Create query in Design view
3. In the Show Table dialog box:
DOUBLE-CLICK: 671 Customers
DOUBLE-CLICK: 671 Sales Reps
CLICK: Close command button
The two field list objects appear in the Table pane of the
query Design window. Notice that a relationship line joins the
SalesRep fields in the two objects.
4. On your own, adjust the size and placement of the query
Design window. You may also want to adjust the space
between the Table pane and the query Design grid.

5. To add the desired fields to the query Design grid:
   DOUBLE-CLICK: CustomerName in the 671 Customers field list
   DOUBLE-CLICK: City in the 671 Customers field list
   DOUBLE-CLICK: State in the 671 Customers field list
   DOUBLE-CLICK: LastName in the 671 Sales Reps field list
   DOUBLE-CLICK: FirstName in the 671 Sales Reps field list

6. To view the query's result in a dynaset Datasheet window:
   CLICK: View—Datasheet button (⊞▾)
   Data from both table objects are displayed in the same datasheet.

7. To modify the query:
   CLICK: View—Design button (▨▾)

8. To sort the query's results by ascending customer name:
   CLICK: in the *Sort* text box in the CustomerName column
   CLICK: down arrow attached to the *Sort* text box
   SELECT: Ascending

9. Let's limit the display to those customers served by Kim van der Ham:
   SELECT: *Criteria* text box in the LastName column
   TYPE: **van der Ham**

10. To save the query object:
    CLICK: Save button (🖫)
    TYPE: **Kim's Customers** in the Save As dialog box
    CLICK: OK command button

11. CLICK: View—Datasheet button (⊞▾)
    Four records, sorted in ascending order, are displayed for Kim van der Ham in the dynaset Datasheet window.

12. Close the Datasheet window. Notice that the new query object appears in the Database window.

# 6.7.2 CyberWeb: Analyzing Account Information

In this exercise, you analyze a table's data by creating a summary query using the *Total* row in the query Design grid.

*Setup:* Ensure that the ACC670 Database window is displayed and that the *Queries* button is selected in the Objects bar.

1. You will now create a special type of select query, called a summary or totals query, that analyzes the numeric values in a table. To begin, display the query Design window:
   DOUBLE-CLICK: Create query in Design view

2. In the Show Table dialog box:
   DOUBLE-CLICK: 672 Internet Accounts
   CLICK: Close command button

3. On your own, adjust the size and placement of the query Design window. You may also want to adjust the space between the Table pane and the query Design grid.

4. To display the *Total* row in the query Design grid:
   CLICK: Totals button (☰) in the toolbar
5. Let's add a field to the grid area:
   DOUBLE-CLICK: Amount
6. To find the total amount of all monthly billings:
   CLICK: in the *Total* text box in the Amount field column
   CLICK: down arrow attached to the *Total* text box
   SELECT: Sum
7. CLICK: View—Datasheet button (▦▾)
   The answer, $244.45, appears in the dynaset Datasheet window
8. To calculate the total and average values for each billing type:
   CLICK: View—Design button (▱▾)
9. DRAG: BillingType from the field list object and drop it on
   "Amount" in the *Field* text box of the first column
   The Amount field column is moved one column to the right
   and the BillingType field is inserted as the first display
   column.
10. In order to calculate both values, the Amount field must
    appear twice in the query Design grid:
    DOUBLE-CLICK: Amount in the 672 Internet Accounts field list
11. For the newly added Amount field:
    SELECT: Avg in the *Total* drop-down list box
12. To save the new query object:
    CLICK: Save button (▣)
    TYPE: **Billing Analysis** in the Save As dialog box
    CLICK: OK command button
    The query Design window should appear similar to Figure 6.20.
13. CLICK: View—Datasheet button (▦▾)
    Three records appear with summary calculations for CC (credit
    cards), CK (checks), and DD (direct deposit) billing types.
14. Close the Datasheet window.

**Figure 6.20**

Query Design window for the
Billing Analysis Query object

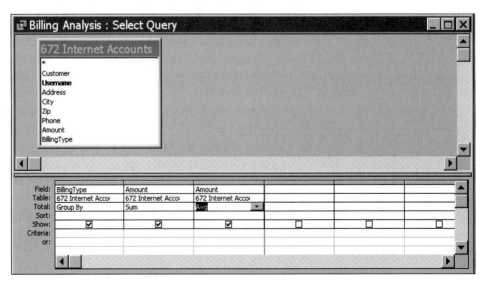

### 6.7.3  Big Valley Mills: Querying Products

You will now practice sorting a dynaset, creating criteria statements, and using AND and OR logic.

*Setup:* Ensure that the ACC670 Database window is displayed and that the *Queries* button is selected in the Objects bar.

1.  Create a new query object using query Design view. Using the Show Table dialog box, add the 673 Products table to the Table pane of the query Design window.
2.  On your own, adjust the size and placement of the query Design window. You may also want to adjust the space between the Table pane and the query Design grid.
3.  Add the following fields to the query Design grid using the double-click or drag method: Species, Grade, Finish, and Category.
4.  Sort the query's dynaset results so that the records are listed in alphabetical order by Category and then by Species.
5.  Display the results in a Datasheet window to check your work. Then, return to Design view.
6.  Now limit the display of records to those of the "Standard" and "Utility" grades only. Check your work in Datasheet view and then return to Design view.
7.  Further limit the display of records to only those "Standard" and "Utility" grade products with an "S4S" finish.
8.  Display the resulting dynaset. How many records are displayed in the Datasheet window?
9.  Save the query as "S4S Standard and Utility Products" and then close the Datasheet window.

### 6.7.4 Silverdale Festival: Presenting Table Data in a Dynaset

This exercise lets you practice creating a select query that uses calculated fields for displaying a table's data.

*Setup:* Ensure that the ACC670 Database window is displayed and that the *Queries* button is selected in the Objects bar.

1. Create a new query object using query Design view. Using the Show Table dialog box, add the 674 Contacts table to the Table pane of the query Design window.
2. On your own, adjust the size and placement of the query Design window. You may also want to adjust the space between the Table pane and the query Design grid.
3. The objective of this query is to concatenate data from multiple fields for display in dynaset. First, you join the Contact and VolunteerGroup fields. Second, you join the Address and City fields. To begin:
   SELECT: *Field* text box in the first column of the query Design grid
4. Launch the Expression Builder dialog box to create the first calculated field.
5. To display the desired fields for use in the calculation:
   DOUBLE-CLICK: Tables in the leftmost list box
   SELECT: 674 Contacts in the tree list
   Notice that the table's fields appear in the middle list box.
6. To build the concatenation expression:
   DOUBLE-CLICK: Contact in the middle list box
   CLICK: 🔲 (ampersand) in the row of operator buttons
   TYPE: " , "
   CLICK: 🔲 (ampersand) in the row of operator buttons
   DOUBLE-CLICK: VolunteerGroup in the middle list box
   CLICK: OK command button
7. To rename the field column header:
   PRESS: (HOME)
   TYPE: **Contact Information:**
8. Let's create the second expression:
   SELECT: *Field* text box in the next column
9. Launch the Expression Builder dialog box.
10. To display the desired fields:
    DOUBLE-CLICK: Tables in the leftmost list box
    SELECT: 674 Contacts in the tree list

11. To build the second concatenation expression:
    DOUBLE-CLICK: Address in the middle list box
    CLICK: 🔲 (ampersand) in the row of operator buttons
    TYPE: " , "
    CLICK: 🔲 (ampersand) in the row of operator buttons
    DOUBLE-CLICK: City in the middle list box
    CLICK: OK command button
12. To rename the field column header:
    PRESS: (HOME)
    TYPE: **Address and City:**
13. To sort the dynaset alphabetically by the Volunteer Group field:
    DRAG: VolunteerGroup from the field list object and drop it on the *Field* text box of the first column
14. Select an ascending sort order for the VolunteerGroup field column and then remove the "✔" from displaying in its *Show* check box.
15. Save the query as "Silverdale Contact List" and then view the dynaset in a Datasheet window. Size the columns in the datasheet by double-clicking their borders in the field header area. Your screen should appear similar to Figure 6.21.
16. Close the Datasheet window.

**Figure 6.21**

Displaying concatenated fields in a dynaset

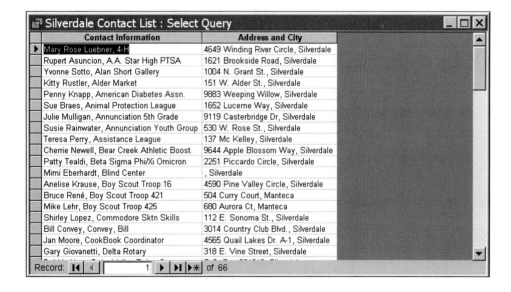

### 6.7.5  On Your Own: Office Mart Inventory

To practice working with the Expression Builder, you will now analyze the on-hand quantity, cost, and retail price data for an inventory listing. From the ACC670 Database window, create a new query object in Design view based on the 675 Inventory table. Ensure that the query Design window is displayed and then perform the following:

- Place the Description field in the first column of the query Design grid.
- To display the inventory value for each product, create a calculated field named "Total Value" that multiplies together the [OnHand] and [Cost] fields.
- To display the potential profit earned, create a second calculated field named "Profit" that subtracts [Cost] from [Retail].
- To display the markup percentage, create a third calculated field named "Markup %" that computes the following expression: (Retail-Cost)/Cost*100.

Save the query as "Inventory Analysis Query" and then print the resulting dynaset Datasheet window. Using this query as the base, remove the Description field column and the Profit calculated field column. Then, calculate the total inventory value and the average markup value for all products in the table. Write down these two values and then close the Datasheet window without saving the changes.

### 6.7.6  On Your Own: Sun Bird Resorts

As operations manager for Sun Bird Resorts, you've been asked to analyze the guest data collected in the 676 Patrons table of the ACC670 database. Using select query objects, you must provide answers to the following questions:

- Which guests live in Iowa (IA)?
- Which guests prefer to play tennis before noon?
- Which guests live in Florida (FL) and list tennis as their main interest?
- How many guests list either beach or shopping as their main interest?
- What is the average stay of US residents?
- What are the average, minimum, and maximum lengths of stay for each interest listed in the table?

Save the queries you create and then close all of the windows, including the ACC670 Database window. Then, exit Microsoft Access.

# 6.8   Case Problems: Aspen Grove Veterinary Clinic

Michelle Green is working on the quarterly operational budget and duty roster for the Aspen Grove Veterinary Clinic. For the past few months, she has entered data into an Access database to record the ongoing activities and flow of information at the clinic. Michelle intends to analyze this data and use the results to help her accomplish her current task. Having studied up on creating select queries and using calculated fields, Michelle is keen to begin extracting and analyzing her data.

In the following case problems, assume the role of Michelle and perform the same steps that she identifies. You may want to re-read the chapter opening before proceeding.

1.   Michelle's first task is to create an address listing of all the clients in the database. To proceed, she launches Microsoft Access and opens the ACC680 database. With the *Tables* button selected in the Objects bar, she opens the Clients table for perusing in Datasheet view. After familiarizing herself with the table data, she closes the datasheet and selects the *Queries* button in the Database window.

To start creating a new query, Michelle double-clicks the "Create query in Design view" option and then selects the Clients table for use in the query Design window. After closing the Show Table dialog box, Michelle sizes the query Design window and then drags the Split bar to adjust the area separating the Table pane and query Design grid. She also widens the Clients field list in order to better see the field names. For an address listing query, Michelle decides to add the following fields to the query Design grid by double-clicking:

- ClientFirstName
- ClientLastName
- ClientAddress
- ClientCity
- ClientPhone

She saves the query as "Client Address List" and then views the results in a dynaset Datasheet window. Immediately noting a few changes that need to be made, Michelle closes the datasheet and confirms that the object appears in the Database window. She opens the Client Address List in query Design view to begin making the modifications. First, she moves the ClientLastName field so that it appears to the left of the ClientFirstName field column. She then deletes the ClientPhone field from the query Design grid. Lastly, she selects an ascending sort order for the ClientLastName column. Michelle saves her changes and then views the dynaset in Datasheet view. Satisfied with the results, she closes the Datasheet window.

2. One of the doctors has been called out to a farm on Potter Drive in Cawston. He asks Michelle to provide him with a list of other clients in the area, in case he has time for an impromptu visit. Michelle realizes that she can use the new Client Address List query to find the necessary information. She opens the query object in Design view. To see how many clients reside in the city of Cawston, she enters the city name in the *Criteria* text box of the ClientCity field column and displays the results. Returning to Design view, Michelle then enters a criterion statement that displays only those clients living on "Potter" Drive in Cawston. After writing down the three names that appear, she closes the Datasheet window and saves the changes to the query object. She hands her notepaper to the doctor as he heads for the door.

3. Michelle has been thinking about next quarter's duty roster. Before approving holidays and assigning office hours, she wants to get a better feel for each doctor's case load. Having already normalized and related tables in the database, Michelle knows that she must create a multitable query to gather the necessary information. To begin, she reviews the existing table relationships in the Relationships window (Figure 6.22). She closes the window before proceeding.

**Figure 6.22**

Viewing table relationships

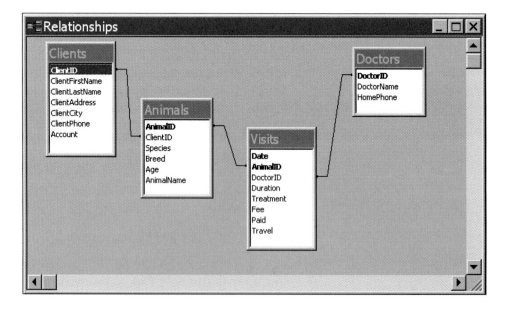

Michelle chooses to create the new query using Design view. Using the Show Table dialog box, she adds the Clients, Animals, and Visits tables to the query's Table pane. She then closes the Show Table dialog box. After sizing and moving the query Design window and the individual field list objects in the Table pane, Michelle adds the following fields to the query Design grid:

- ClientLastName from the Clients table,
- all fields (using the asterisk) from the Animals table, and
- Date and DoctorID from the Visits table.

After viewing the resulting dynaset, Michelle realizes she doesn't really need to see all the fields from the Animals table. In Design view, she removes the Animals.* column from the grid and then selects the Species and Breed fields only. Finally, she saves the query as "Doctor Date Query" and then views the dynaset in Datasheet view.

Michelle decides to further refine the query by replacing the DoctorID column with the Doctors' names. To accomplish this, she first removes the DoctorID column from the query Design grid. Then, she displays the Show Table dialog box and adds the Doctors table to the query Design window. After closing the dialog box, she drags the DoctorName field from the field list object over top of the first column in the query and then drops it into position. Lastly, Michelle selects an ascending sort order for the DoctorName column and saves the query modifications. Her screen appears similar to Figure 6.23. She views and then prints the dynaset. Lastly, she closes the Datasheet window.

**Figure 6.23**

Creating a multitable query

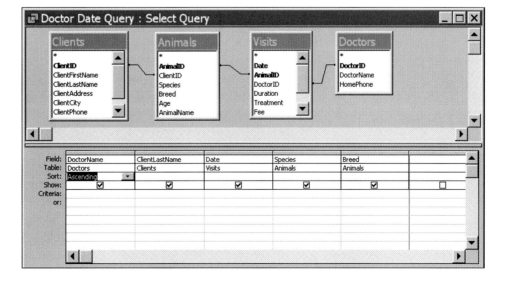

4. In a staff meeting scheduled for later in the week, the Aspen Grove Veterinary Clinic will discuss various planning issues, including upcoming travel requirements and two educational opportunities. Both seminar courses are scheduled on the same date and the doctors must decide which one to attend. While one seminar discusses new equine surgical procedures, the other focuses on treating exotic animals. Michelle offers to analyze the doctors' past workflow in hopes that it will shed some light on where they should spend their time.

Michelle retreats to her computer station and creates a query using Design view. She begins by adding the Doctors, Visits, and Animals tables to the Table pane. After adjusting the appearance of the query Design window to her satisfaction, Michelle selects the following fields for display in the query's dynaset:

- DoctorName from the Doctors table,
- Treatment, Date, and Travel from the Visits table, and
- Species from the Animals table.

Michelle sorts the query into ascending order first by Doctor-Name and then by Treatment. She saves the query as "Doctor Treatment Query" and then opens it in Datasheet view. In order to see how much traveling the doctors have done recently, she uses the Filter by Form method to display only those records that have a check mark in the Travel column. After displaying the results, she returns to the Filter By Form window and then saves the filter as a new query object named "Doctor Travel Query."

Now that Michelle has retrieved the necessary travel information, she turns her attention to the two educational opportunities. She closes the Doctor Travel Query and opens the Doctor Treatment Query in Design view. Using a criterion statement, she displays all visits where the Treatment field contains "Surgery" and the Species field contains "Horse." After writing down the number of records displayed in the resulting dynaset, Michelle returns to Design view. She removes the current criterion and then prepares to enter a new criterion statement that searches for exotic animals. To this end, she uses a logical Or statement to search for Species containing "Llama," "Ostrich," or "Emu." After displaying the results, Michelle makes note of the number of records displayed. She closes the Datasheet window and does not save her changes.

5. Immediately following the staff meeting, Michelle occupies herself with analyzing the clinic's cash flow and fee structure. Specifically, Michelle constructs the following three queries:

   • The first query, named "Outstanding Balances," is based on the Visits table and displays the Date, Fee, and Paid fields. A fourth calculated field, titled Balance, subtracts the Paid value from the Fee value for each record. (*Hint*: The calculated field is entered as **Balance: [Fee]-[Paid]**.)
   • The second query, named "Clients with Accounts," is based on the Clients table and displays the ClientID and Account fields. Instead of displaying the client name fields from the table, Michelle uses the Expression Builder (Figure 6.24.) to create a new field that joins together the client's last name, followed by a comma and a space, and the client's first name. The new field is named "Client" and appears between the ClientID and Account fields.

**Figure 6.24**

Using the Expression Builder

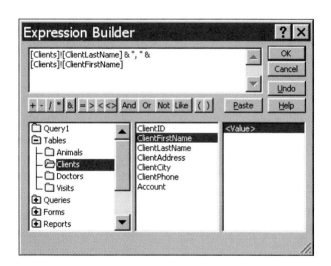

   • The last query, named "Fee Summary," is based on the Visits table and displays the Treatment and Fee fields. To summarize the data, Michelle displays the *Total* row in the query Design grid. She then specifies the Group By option for the Treatment column and the Avg option for the Fee column. After viewing the dynaset, Michelle adds the Fee field to the query Design grid two more times and changes the Total options to show the minimum and maximum fees also. After displaying the dynaset, she saves the query and then exits Microsoft Access.

**MICROSOFT ACCESS 2000**
*Designing Forms and Reports*

**CHAPTER**
SEVEN

# Chapter Outline

# Learning Objectives

After reading this chapter, you will be able to:

- Create and modify a form or report using Design view

- Use the Toolbox to insert bound and unbound controls

- Create a form with an embedded subform

- Move, size, align, and delete controls

- Format controls and set properties

- Use calculated controls in forms and reports

- Apply the AutoFormat command

## Case Study

## Carlton Motors

Carlton Motors is a specialty dealership operating in a large eastern city. While business has been steady and respectable over the last few years, overall growth has been negligible. To remedy this situation, Carlton is planning to build a new facility in the popular Town Center Auto Mall. Undertaking such a large building project will require significant effort and capital. In fact, Carlton's dealer principal, general manager, and lawyers are already talking with several potential investors.

Frank Diaz, the controller for Carlton Motors, is kept very busy with the operational demands of the dealership and with the relocation project. Frank uses Microsoft Access to track the vehicle sales and inventory data for the dealership. In the previous quarter, Frank created forms and reports using the Access wizards, but he now feels that these objects lack some necessary elements. Specifically, Frank wants to tailor the forms and reports to better suit the dealership's needs. For example, he wants to help the sales staff view and enter data for vehicle purchases and sales. In addition, Frank has been asked by Carlton's management team to produce several key reports for distribution to potential investors. These reports must be accurate, well balanced, and visually attractive. Frank knows that Microsoft Access has many features for customizing and formatting forms and reports.

In this chapter, you and Frank use Design view to modify form and report objects. In addition to sizing and moving controls, you enhance the display of objects using formatting commands and the Properties window. You also practice entering expressions into calculated controls and displaying groups and subtotals in reports.

# 7.1 Using the Form Design View

When people sit themselves in front of a database application, forms are the objects they will interact with most often. Forms allow users to insert, modify, delete, and view data stored in tables and returned by queries. In addition to providing an attractive and easy-to-use interface, forms may be printed, distributed via electronic mail, and deployed to Web sites. Reports, which are similar to forms in many ways, are used primarily to format, summarize, and prepare information for printing to paper.

You may recall that Access provides wizards to help you create a variety of form types. For instance, the Form Wizard provides a selection of form layout options. The *columnar* and *justified* form layouts display one record or row of data. The *tabular* and *datasheet* form layouts use columns and rows to display multiple records at a time, similar to Datasheet view. One advantage of choosing a form over displaying a Datasheet window is your ability to customize the objects on a form. Tabular and datasheet forms can also be embedded in other forms, as shown in Figure 7.1. The embedded form, called a **subform,** displays only those records related to the active record on the **main form.** (For more on establishing table relationships, refer to Chapter 5.) Another type of form you can create is called a **switchboard form.** Switchboard forms provide a main menu of command buttons for executing program code or opening other forms or reports. In this module, you learn to open and modify form objects using form Design view.

**Figure 7.1**

A main form and subform

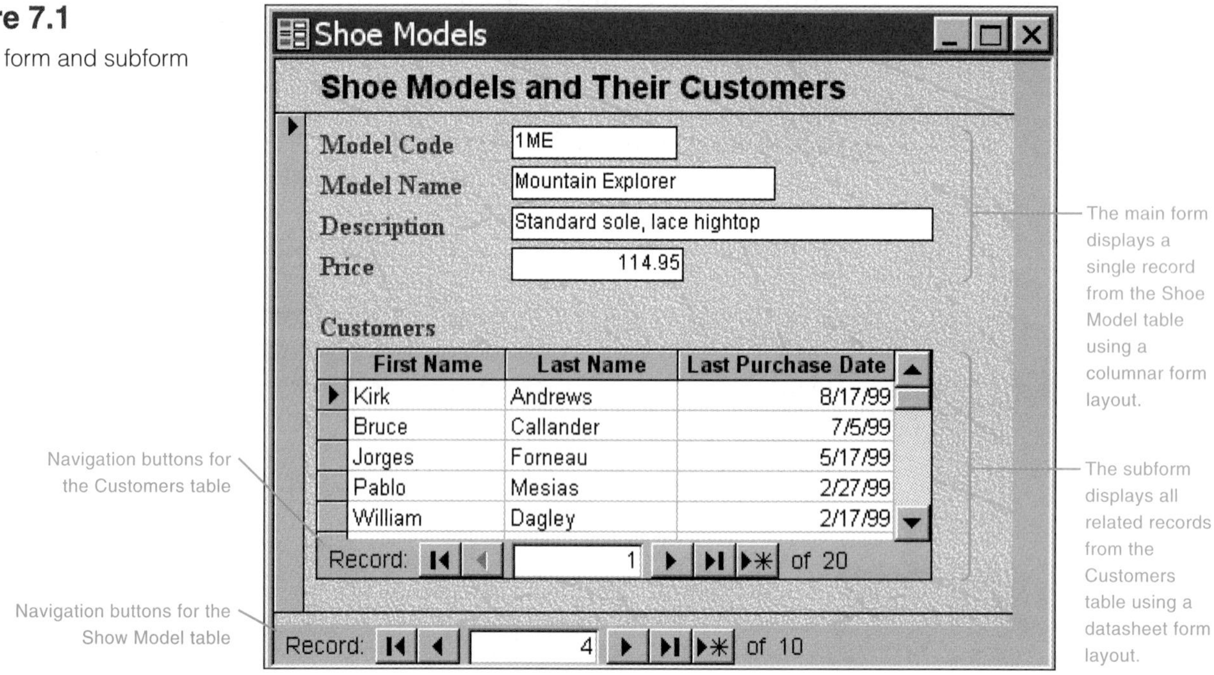

The main form displays a single record from the Shoe Model table using a columnar form layout.

Navigation buttons for the Customers table

Navigation buttons for the Show Model table

The subform displays all related records from the Customers table using a datasheet form layout.

## 7.1.1 Viewing and Modifying a Form

**FEATURE**

Access provides three views for interacting with forms. In Design view, you create new forms from scratch and tinker under the hood of forms that you create using the wizards. Form view allows you to display and interact with forms, while Datasheet view displays records in a Datasheet window. During a form's design, you spend most of the time switching between Design view and Form view.

A form object is typically divided into three sections named *Detail*, *Form Header*, and *Form Footer*. For printing multipage forms, you can also add the *Page Header* and *Page Footer* sections to a form. In truth, the only requirement for a form object is that there exists a **Form Detail** section. Use the Detail section to display the fields, labels, and other items that provide functionality. In addition to viewing and editing field data from a particular record source, you can include graphic objects and calculations in the Detail section. The **Form Header** and **Form Footer** sections hold items that you want to display at the top and bottom of each form, respectively. For instance, add the form's title to the Form Header section and some helpful comments or suggestions in the Form Footer section. The **Page Header** and **Page Footer** sections appear only when a form is printed and are useful for displaying column headings and aggregate or summary calculations.

**METHOD**
In the Database window, click the *Forms* button and then:

1.  SELECT: the form object that you want to view or modify
2.  CLICK: Open button (⬚Open⬚) to view the form in Form view
    CLICK: Design button (⬚Design⬚) to modify the form in Design view

Once a form object is displayed, switch among the views using the View option on the Menu bar or by clicking the following toolbar buttons:

*   CLICK: View—Form button (⬚▾)
*   CLICK: View—Design button (⬚▾)
*   CLICK: View—Datasheet button (⬚▾)

**PRACTICE**
In this lesson, you display a form using all of the available views and then practice selecting and sizing the form sections in Design view.

*Setup:* Ensure that Access is loaded. If you are launching Access and the startup dialog box appears, click the Cancel command button to remove the dialog box from the application window.

**1** Open the database file named ACC700, located in the Advantage student data files folder. This database contains six tables: Authors, Books, Courses, Instructors, Roster, and Students.

**2** As a refresher from Chapter 4, let's use the Form Wizard to create a new form for use in updating the Courses table:
CLICK: *Forms* button in the Objects bar
DOUBLE-CLICK: Create form by using wizard

**3** In the first step of the Form Wizard dialog box:
SELECT: Table: Courses from the *Tables/Queries* drop-down list box

**4** To move all of the fields listed in the *Available Fields* list box to the *Selected Fields* list box:
CLICK: Include All button ( ⟫ )
CLICK: Next › to proceed

**5** The four form layout options appear in the next step of the Form Wizard. For this example:
SELECT: *Columnar* option button
CLICK: Next › to proceed

**6** You now select a formatting style for the form:
SELECT: SandStone
CLICK: Next › to proceed

**7** To name the form and then display it using Form view:
TYPE: Courses Columnar Form in the text box
SELECT: *Open the form to view or enter information* option button
CLICK: Finish
Your screen should now appear similar to Figure 7.2.

**Figure 7.2**

Displaying a form
in Form view

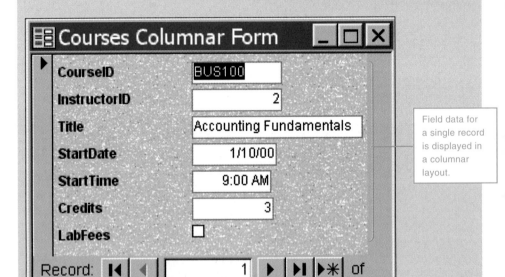

Field data for
a single record
is displayed in
a columnar
layout.

**8** To switch to Datasheet view:
CLICK: down arrow attached to the View button ( ▦⊡ )
CHOOSE: Datasheet View
The table's data is displayed in a Datasheet window.

**9** To switch to form Design view:
CLICK: View—Design button ( ⊠⊡ )

**10** On your own, drag the bottom right-hand sizing corner of the Design window so that it appears similar to Figure 7.3. Notice the horizontal bars separating the Form Header, Form Detail, and Form Footer sections. The Design window also provides horizontal and vertical rulers and gridpoints to help you line up information on a form.

**Figure 7.3**

Display a form in Design view

Form Selector button

Section Selector button

Rulers help you line up the placement of controls on a form.

The Form Header section bar; no Form Header area is shown in this graphic.

The Detail section contains the controls for displaying data.

The Form Footer section bar; no Form Footer area is shown in this graphic.

**Courses Columnar Form : Form**

Form Header
Detail

| CourseID | CourseID |
| InstructorID | InstructorID |
| Title | Title |
| StartDate | StartDate |
| StartTime | StartTime |
| Credits | Credits |
| LabFees | ☑ |

Form Footer

**11** To display the Page Header and Page Footer sections for the form:
CHOOSE: View, Page Header/Footer
Two new sections are added to the form Design window.

**12** To remove the display of these two sections:
CHOOSE: View, Page Header/Footer

**13** You change the size of a form's display area by moving the section bars and dragging the form edges. To illustrate, position the mouse pointer over the right edge of the form, as shown below. Notice that the mouse pointer changes shape when positioned properly.

**14** To enlarge the form's background area:
DRAG: the form's edge to the right for a few gridpoints
When you release the mouse button, the form is resized.

ACCESS

**15** In order to use the Form Header section, you must increase the area displayed between the Form Header and Detail section bars. Position the mouse pointer over the bottom edge of the Form Header section bar, as shown below. Again, the mouse pointer changes shape when positioned properly.

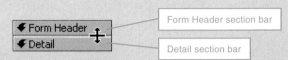

**16** To increase the size of the section:
DRAG: the bar's bottom edge downward so that it appears similar to Figure 7.4

**Figure 7.4**

Displaying the
Form Header area

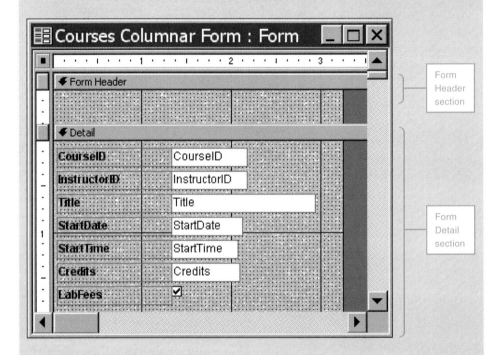

**17** To save and then view the modified form object:
CLICK: Save button (▤)
CLICK: View—Form button (▦▾)
Notice that the form appears larger with more white space around its edges.

**18** To return to form Design view:
CLICK: View—Design button (▨▾)

**19** To practice selecting a section of the form:
CLICK: once on the Detail section bar
The bar appears highlighted when selected. In the Formatting toolbar, you should also notice that the word "Detail" appears in the Object drop-down list box. You can use this list box to select objects and section areas on a form.

**20** To select the entire form:
CLICK: Form Selector button in the top left-hand corner, but below the Form window's Title bar (see Figure 7.3)
When selected, a small black box appears in the middle of the button and the word "Form" appears in the Object drop-down list box.

## 7.1.2   Understanding Bound and Unbound Controls

**FEATURE**
Without controls, a form displays an empty window and a report prints an empty page. **Controls** are the elements on a form or report that provide substance, decoration, and interactivity. Each label, text box, and command button is an independent control with its own set of *properties* and *events*. Properties, such as font size and color, determine a control's appearance, characteristics, and attributes. Events, such as On Click, determine how the control behaves when the user interacts with it. (*Note:* Formatting properties are discussed in later lessons, but events are beyond the scope of this chapter.) Forms and reports are created by placing controls in the various sections of a Form or Report window.

There are three types of controls that determine what displays on a form or report. First, a **bound control** is one whose source of data is an underlying field in a table or query. An example of a bound control is a text box that displays a customer's name. An **unbound control,** on the other hand, is a control that doesn't have a source of data. These controls are used to place descriptive labels, titles, and graphic objects (such as lines and boxes) on a form or report. An easy way to remember the difference is to imagine bound controls as being tied to the data, while unbound controls are free. Lastly, a **calculated control** is similar to a *calculated field* in a query and is used to evaluate and display the results of formula expressions.

**METHOD**
To determine whether a control is bound or unbound:

1.   SELECT: a control (usually a text box) in the Design window
2.   CHOOSE: View, Properties
3.   SELECT: *Data* tab in the Properties window
4.   SELECT: *Control Source* text box

**PRACTICE**
In Design view, you now display the properties associated with controls appearing on a form.

*Setup:* Ensure that you've completed the previous lesson and that the Courses Columnar Form Design window appears.

**1** The Courses Columnar Form object displays bound and unbound controls, as shown in Figure 7.5. Let's view the form in Form view:
CLICK: View—Form button (▦▾)

**Figure 7.5**
Displaying controls
in Form view

Unbound label controls ⎯⎯

Bound text box
controls and one
check box control

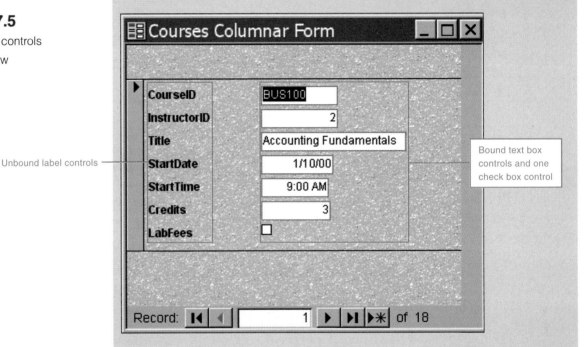

**2** To display the next record in the form:
CLICK: Next Record button (▶)
Notice that unbound label controls display the same information for each record, while the bound text box and check box controls are updated to display data from the underlying Courses table.

**3** To return to Design view:
CLICK: View—Design button (▨▾)

**4** Let's display the form object's Properties window:
CLICK: Form Selector button
CHOOSE: View, Properties
(*Note:* The Properties window displays the name of the currently selected object in its Title bar.)

**5** In the Properties window that appears:
CLICK: *All* tab, if it is not already selected
Your screen should now appear similar to Figure 7.6.

**Figure 7.6**

Form Properties window

The Properties window displays the property settings for the selected objects.

CourseID label control

CourseID text box control

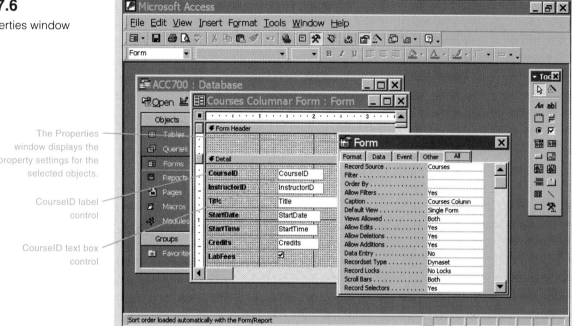

**6** Move the Properties window by dragging its Title bar, so you can see all of the controls in the Design window.

**7** A form can update values in a single table, which is identified in the *Record Source* text box in the Properties window. You can also view the properties for each section and control on a form. To illustrate:
CLICK: CourseID text box control (shown in Figure 7.6)
The Properties window updates immediately to show the property values for the CourseID control. Notice also that the Title bar text changes to reflect the new selection.

**8** To display only the properties related to the control's data source:
CLICK: *Data* tab in the Properties window
Notice that the *Control Source* text box displays the field name that is associated with the control. You can change the data displayed in the form by selecting a new field in the *Control Source* property text box.

**9** To display properties for a label control:
CLICK: CourseID label on the form
Notice that the *Data* tab in the Properties window is blank, since label controls are not bound to data in the underlying table.

To close the Properties window:
CLICK: its Close button ([X])
(*Note:* This chapters discusses relatively few of the multiple properties that you can set in a form.)

## 7.1.3  Inserting, Deleting, Sizing, and Moving Controls

**FEATURE**

Because forms and reports are linked to an underlying table or query, Access knows which fields may be used as bound controls. These fields appear in the **Field List window.** In Design view, you can add these field controls by simply dragging them onto a form. Other controls that you use frequently in creating forms and reports appear in the **Toolbox window** (shown below). In addition to these options, you can purchase a variety of special purpose controls, such as gauge displays and calendars, from third party software vendors. Once a control is placed on a form, you change the appearance and behavior of the control by modifying its properties and events. As a first step, however, you must learn how to insert, move, size, and delete controls in the Form window.

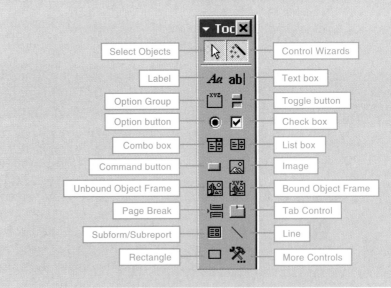

**METHOD**
To toggle the display of the Field List and Toolbox window, use the View option on the Menu bar or click the appropriate toolbar button:

- CLICK: Field List button (⊡) on the Form Design toolbar
- CLICK: Toolbox button (⊠) on the Form Design toolbar

To insert a bound control using the Field List window:

1. DRAG: a field from the Field List window onto the form
2. Release the mouse button to drop the control.

To insert a control using the Toolbox window:

1. CLICK: the desired control button in the Toolbox window
2. CLICK: once on the form to place a default-sized control, or DRAG: the mouse pointer on the form to position and size the control

To manipulate a control, select the desired control and then:

- PRESS: (DELETE) to delete the control
- DRAG: the control's sizing handles to size the control
- DRAG: the control's moving handle or border to move the control

**PRACTICE**
In this lesson, you practice working with controls on a form.

*Setup:* Ensure that you've completed the previous lessons and that the Courses Columnar Form Design window appears.

**1** In addition to using the Object drop-down list box, you can select a control by simply clicking on it. Once selected, a control's sizing and moving handles become visible. On your own, click on each label control in the Design window.

**2** CLICK: InstructorID text box control

**3** When a bound control is placed on a form, Access typically creates a **compound control** that includes both the bound text box and its field label. To move the two controls together, drag the bound control's border using the hand mouse pointer (✋). To move the controls independently, drag one of the large black box moving handles using the pointing hand (☝). To illustrate, position the mouse pointer over the moving handle for the InstructorID text box and do the following:

DRAG: InstructorID text box to the right by a few gridpoints

**4** To move both portions of a compound control, position the mouse pointer over the border of the InstructorID text box. When positioned correctly, the mouse pointer changes shape to a hand (✋). Then:

DRAG: InstructorID text box to the right by a few more gridpoints

Notice that the label and text box controls are moved together.

**5** To undo your last editing action:

CHOOSE: Edit, Undo Move

(*Note:* The Undo command reverses the last editing action only.)

**6** To reduce the size of the InstructorID text box, position the mouse pointer over the sizing handle in the middle of the right-hand vertical border. When positioned properly, the mouse pointer changes shape to a sizing arrow (↔).

**7** DRAG: the text box border to the left until only "Instru" is visible

**8** To adjust the width of all label controls at the same time, you need to select multiple controls on the form:

CLICK: CourseID label control

PRESS: SHIFT and hold it down

**9** With the SHIFT key depressed:

CLICK: each of the remaining label controls

All of the labels should now appear selected in the Form window.

**10** Release the SHIFT key and then position the mouse pointer over the middle right-hand sizing handle for the CourseID label control. When positioned properly, the mouse pointer changes shape to a sizing arrow (↔).

**11** DRAG: the label border to the left until reaching one inch on the ruler, as shown in Figure 7.7 below

**Figure 7.7**

Sizing and moving controls in form Design view

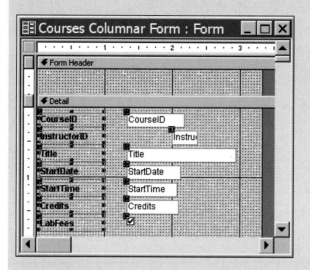

**12** To delete the InstructorID label:
CLICK: Detail section bar to remove the control selection
CLICK: InstructorID label control
PRESS: DELETE
(*Note:* Rather than clicking on a section bar, you can also click an empty part of the form's background to remove the control selection.)

**13** Deleting the InstructorID label control does not affect the associated bound text box control. On your own, move the InstructorID text box control to appear to the right of the CourseID text box.

**14** Deleting a bound control, on the other hand, removes the associated label control in the same step. To illustrate:
CLICK: LabFees check box control
PRESS: DELETE
Notice that both portions of the compound control are deleted.

**15** Rather than using the SHIFT key to select multiple controls, you can drag a rectangular lasso around the desired controls. To do so, position the mouse pointer in the bottom right-hand corner of the form. Then:
DRAG: mouse pointer above and to the left of the Title label control

**16** Release the mouse button to display the control selection. All of the controls should appear selected, except for the CourseID label control and the CourseID and InstructorID text box controls.

**17** Position the hand (✋) mouse pointer over the top border of the Title label control. Then:
DRAG: the selected controls upward to close the gap left from deleting and moving the InstructorID controls

**18** To reinsert the LabFees check box control on the form:
CLICK: Field List button (▣) to display the Field List window (*Note:* You need not perform this step if the Field List window already appears.)

**19** Ensure that both the Field List and Toolbox windows appear in the Access application window. After sizing the Field List window, your screen should appear similar to Figure 7.8.

**Figure 7.8**

Displaying the Field List window and the Toolbox window

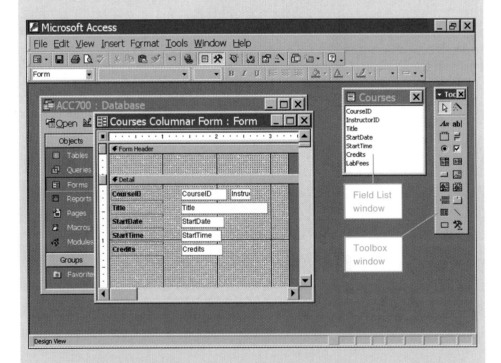

**20** To add the LabFees control (a compound control) to the form:
DRAG: LabFees from the Field List window and drop it below the Credits text box control in the Form window

**21** Now let's add a title to the Form Header section:
CLICK: Label button (▣) in the Toolbox window
CLICK: in the Form Header section, as shown here
(*Hint:* Depending on the type of control selected
and whether the Control Wizards button is
depressed in the Toolbox window, a wizard dialog box may
appear when adding a control. Otherwise, the control simply
appears on the form.)

**22** To enter a title for the form:
TYPE: **Course Details**
CLICK: Form Header section bar to remove the control selection

**23** To view the modified form object:
CLICK: View—Form button (▣▾)
Your screen should now appear similar to Figure 7.9.

**24** Close the Form window and save the changes.

**Figure 7.9**

Displaying the revised
form object in Form view

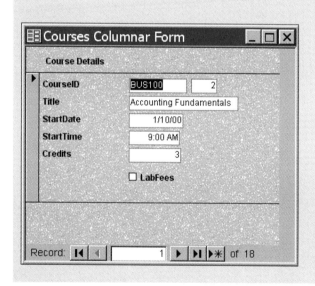

## 7.1.4  Creating a Calculated Control

**FEATURE**

In its simplest form, a *calculated control* is a text box that contains a formula expression. Calculated controls are evaluated at runtime when the form is displayed to the user. Like bound controls, calculated controls can reference field data that is stored in a table. However, calculated controls do not store the results of their calculations permanently.

Similar to creating a calculated field in a query, you define a calculated control by typing an expression directly into a text box control. You can also use the Expression Builder dialog box to help you construct a valid formula. This dialog box allows you to build a formula visually by picking and choosing fields, functions, and operators. For more information, refer to lesson 6.4.2, Using the Expression Builder, in Chapter 6.

**METHOD**

To add a calculated control to a form in Design view:

1. CLICK: Text Box button (⬚) in the Toolbox window
2. CLICK: in the Form window to place the control
3. TYPE: *desired expression*, or
   CLICK: Build button (⬚) to access the Expression Builder

**PRACTICE**

In this lesson, you create a calculated field by typing an expression.

*Setup:* Ensure that the ACC700 Database window is displayed.

**1** Your objective in this lesson is to enhance a form object by inserting a calculated control. To display an existing form, ensure that the *Forms* button is selected in the Objects bar and then: DOUBLE-CLICK: Books Columnar Form in the list area

**2** After perusing the form:
CLICK: View—Design button (⬚)

**3** Ensure that the Field List and Toolbox windows are displayed in the Design window and then increase the size of the Form window.

**4** To compute the profit earned per book, you will now create a calculated control that subtracts the "Cost" value from the "Price" value. To begin, let's add a text box control to the form:
CLICK: Text Box button (abl) in the Toolbox window
CLICK: once beneath the Cost text box control in the Form window
Access inserts a compound control consisting of a label and a text box.

**5** To set the caption or display text for the label control:
RIGHT-CLICK: the new label control
CHOOSE: Properties

**6** In the Properties window:
CLICK: *Format* tab
DOUBLE-CLICK: *Caption* text box to select the existing entry
TYPE: **Profit**

**7** To close the Properties window:
CLICK: its Close button (X)
A Profit label control now appears in the Form window.

**8** Using the techniques learned in the last lesson, move and size the label and text box controls to appear similar to Figure 7.10.

**9** To enter the expression to calculate:
SELECT: Unbound text box control
TYPE: **=[Price]-[Cost]**
Notice that an expression begins with an equal sign (=) and that the field names are placed between square brackets.

**10** You can also use the Properties window to enter or edit an expression. To illustrate:
CHOOSE: View, Properties

**11** CLICK: *Data* tab in the Properties window
Notice that the expression appears in the *Control Source* text box, as shown in Figure 7.10.

**Figure 7.10**

Creating a calculated control

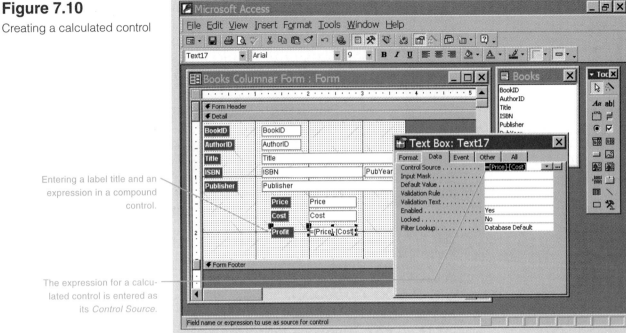

Entering a label title and an expression in a compound control.

The expression for a calculated control is entered as its *Control Source*.

**12** With the Properties window still displayed, you can specify that the result be formatted as currency. Do the following:
CLICK: *Format* tab
SELECT: Currency from the *Format* drop-down list box

**13** To finish the form, let's draw a line under the Cost text box control:
CLICK: Line button (⬚) in the Toolbox window
Notice that you need not close the Properties window.

**14** Position the mouse pointer between the Cost and Profit text box controls. Align the cross-hair mouse pointer with the left edge of the controls.

**15** DRAG: the mouse pointer to the right until reaching the right edge of the text box controls

**16** When you release the mouse button, a dashed line is drawn between the two text boxes. To change the dashed line to a solid line, ensure that the *Format* tab is displayed in the Properties window and then:
SELECT: Solid from the *Border Style* drop-down list box

**17** Close the Properties window.

**18** CLICK: View—Form button (⬚▾)

**19** On your own, navigate the first few records in the table to ensure that the calculated control works as expected.

**20** Close the Form window and save the changes.

## 7.1.5 Creating a Main Form and Subform

**FEATURE**

A main form with an embedded subform is an excellent way to display data from tables associated in a one-to-many relationship. The *main form* displays a single record from the "one" side of the relationship, while the *subform* displays multiple records from the "many" side. For example, on a form that displays an author's name and address, you can embed a subform datasheet showing all of the titles that he or she has written. When you navigate to the next record in the main form, the related titles for the next author appear in the subform. This combined display lets you view related data without having to open additional forms or datasheets.

**METHOD**

To add a subform to an existing form in Design view:

1. CLICK: Subform/Subreport button (▥) in the Toolbox window
2. DRAG: the cross-hair mouse pointer on the form where you want the subform to appear
3. RIGHT-CLICK: Subform control in the Form window
4. CHOOSE: Properties
5. SELECT: the related table in the *Source Object* text box

To create a main form and subform using the Form Wizard:

1. CLICK: *Forms* button in the Database window
2. DOUBLE-CLICK: Create form by using wizard
3. SELECT: the "one" table and add the desired fields
4. SELECT: the "many" table and add the desired fields
5. Complete the wizard steps to specify the form's appearance.

**PRACTICE**

You now practice creating a form and subform combination using the Form Wizard.

*Setup:* Ensure that the ACC700 Database window is displayed.

**1** Let's use the Form Wizard to help embed a subform in a main form. Ensure that the *Forms* button is selected in the Objects bar and then:
DOUBLE-CLICK: Create form by using wizard

**2** In the first step of the Form Wizard dialog box, you specify the table that is the "one" side of the one-to-many relationship:
SELECT: Table: Authors from the *Tables/Queries* drop-down list box

**3** To move all of the fields listed in the *Available Fields* list box to the *Selected Fields* list box:
CLICK: Include All button ( ⟩⟩ )

**4** Now specify the table that is the "many" side of the relationship:
SELECT: Table: Books from the *Tables/Queries* drop-down list box

**5** In the *Available Fields* list box:
DOUBLE-CLICK: Title
DOUBLE-CLICK: ISBN
DOUBLE-CLICK: Publisher
DOUBLE-CLICK: PubYear

**6** To proceed to the next step:
CLICK: Next >

**7** You must now specify that the new form will contain a main form and a subform. Do the following:
SELECT: by Authors in the list box to specify the main form
SELECT: *Form with subform(s)* option button
CLICK: Next > to proceed

**8** Now specify the desired layout and style for the subform:
SELECT: *Datasheet* option button
CLICK: Next > to proceed
SELECT: Expedition in the style list box
CLICK: Next > to proceed

**9** To accept the remaining defaults and view the form:
CLICK: Finish
The completed form is displayed in Form view.

**10** Let's view the design structure of the form:
CLICK: View—Design button ( ⬚· )

**11** To enlarge the subform area:
CLICK: Books label control
PRESS: (DELETE)
CLICK: Subform control
DRAG: the left-hand sizing handle to the left border in order to increase the subform's width

**12** CLICK: View—Form button (⊞ˑ)

**13** On your own, double-click the border lines in the column header area of the subform to adjust the column widths to their best fit. When finished, your screen should appear similar to Figure 7.11.

**14** Close the Form window and save the changes.

**Figure 7.11**

Displaying a form with an embedded subform

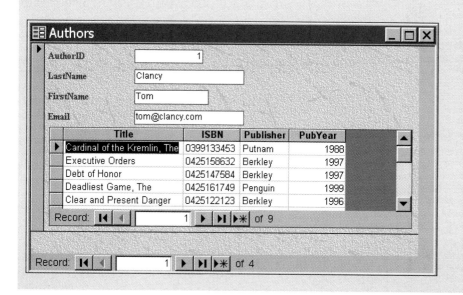

| Title | ISBN | Publisher | PubYear |
|---|---|---|---|
| Cardinal of the Kremlin, The | 0399133453 | Putnam | 1988 |
| Executive Orders | 0425158632 | Berkley | 1997 |
| Debt of Honor | 0425147584 | Berkley | 1997 |
| Deadliest Game, The | 0425161749 | Penguin | 1999 |
| Clear and Present Danger | 0425122123 | Berkley | 1996 |

**7.1 Self Check** How do you move only the label portion of a compound control?

# 7.2  Customizing a Form

Designing forms that are attractive, efficient, and user friendly is challenging. Fortunately, successful software companies have come to realize that adding interface designers and usability engineers to their programming teams yields better products. In fact, an entire research field known as Human-Computer Interaction (HCI) is dedicated to studying how people interact with software and computers. What this means to you is that interface and forms design is an expansive and evolving area. You cannot expect to master the application of each and every design principle right away. However, there are some basic design guidelines that you should keep in mind when learning to create forms.

1. Always involve your users in the design of forms.
2. Create simple and well-balanced forms dedicated to a single task or purpose.
3. Provide descriptive labels, titles, and helpful comments on-screen.
4. Be consistent in selecting controls, labels, and graphical attributes (such as fonts, colors, and icons).
5. Limit the number of fonts, font styles, and colors selected.
6. Limit the number of controls placed on a form.
7. Use emphasis, highlighting, and decorative graphics sparingly.
8. If necessary, provide compatibility with paper forms.

While this list of guidelines is certainly not exhaustive, adhering to these rules will ensure that users find your forms easy-to-learn, easy-to-use, and enjoyable to work with. In this module, you learn how to arrange controls in the Form window, change the tab order, set formatting properties, and use the AutoFormat command.

## 7.2.1  Aligning, Spacing, and Sizing Controls

**FEATURE**
While you can enhance a form or report in many different ways, you should practice restraint and strive for simplicity, unity, and balance. Simplicity means not cluttering the form with unnecessary graphics and controls. To achieve unity, the controls that do appear on a form should not be separated by too much or too little white space. And, lastly, balance and symmetry make your forms visually attractive and enjoyable to read. This lesson introduces several tools and commands that can help you achieve these design goals.

**METHOD**

To modify the form Design window:

- CHOOSE: View, Ruler to display the Ruler
- CHOOSE: View, Grid to display the Grid

To align, space, and size controls in the Design window:

- CHOOSE: Format, Align to align controls with each other
- CHOOSE: Format, Horizontal Spacing to adjust the horizontal spacing between controls
- CHOOSE: Format, Vertical Spacing to adjust the vertical spacing between controls
- CHOOSE: Format, Size to adjust the height and width of controls

**PRACTICE**

In this lesson, you modify a poorly designed form by aligning and spacing controls.

*Setup:* Ensure that the ACC700 Database window is displayed.

**1** Your objective in this module is to take a poorly designed form and enhance its appearance using a variety of customizing features. Ensure that the *Forms* button is selected in the Objects bar and then:
DOUBLE-CLICK: Course Information Form
The form shown in Figure 7.12 is displayed. This form is based on a query object called Courses Query. The query displays data from the Courses and Instructors table and incorporates a calculated control for joining the instructors' first and last names in a single field.

**Figure 7.12**

Course Information Form

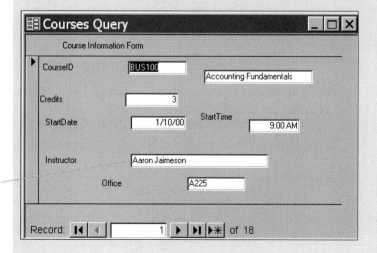

The expression for this concatenation of two field values appears in the underlying query rather than in the form.

**2** As you can see, this form is in great need of some design assistance. To begin, switch to form Design view:
CLICK: View—Design button (📊▾)

**3** On your own, size and move the form Design window so that all sections and controls are visible. Also, ensure that the Field List and Toolbox window appear on-screen.

**4** You can quickly align controls using commands on the Format menu. To illustrate:
CLICK: CourseID text box control
PRESS: (SHIFT) and hold it down
CLICK: Title text box control
Remember to release the (SHIFT) key after all selections have been made.

**5** To align these two controls vertically:
CHOOSE: Format, Align, Top
The two controls are aligned according to the topmost control.

**6** Let's continue the cleanup process. Position the mouse pointer over the moving handle for the CourseID text box control. Then:
DRAG: the control leftward to the one-inch mark on the ruler

**7** Position the mouse pointer over the moving handle for the Title text box control. Then:
DRAG: the control leftward to the two-inch mark on the ruler

**8** To line up several controls with the leftmost control:
CLICK: Detail section bar to remove the control selection
CLICK: CourseID text box control
PRESS: (SHIFT) and hold it down
CLICK: Credits text box control
CLICK: StartDate text box control
CLICK: Instructor text box control
CLICK: Office text box control
(*Note:* Release the (SHIFT) key before proceeding.)

**9** To align the selected controls:
CHOOSE: Format, Align, Left
Notice that the alignment command did not affect the label controls associated with the selected text box controls.

**10** With the five controls still selected:
CHOOSE: Format, Vertical Spacing, Make Equal

**11** CLICK: Detail section bar to remove the control selection

**12** To finish lining up controls on the form:
CLICK: StartTime label control
PRESS: [DELETE]
CLICK: Title text box control
PRESS: [SHIFT] and hold it down
CLICK: StartTime text box control
Release the [SHIFT] key.

**13** CHOOSE: Format, Align, Left
Notice that the two controls are aligned according to the leftmost control.

**14** On your own, select all of the label controls (including the label control in the Form Header section) and then align them to the left.

**15** To select all of the controls appearing in the Detail section, use the rectangular lasso. Position the mouse pointer in the bottom right-hand corner of the Detail section. Then:
DRAG: the mouse pointer to the top left-hand corner of the Detail section

**16** When you release the mouse button, all of the controls are selected. To reduce the space between the controls:
CHOOSE: Format, Vertical Spacing, Decrease
CHOOSE: Format, Vertical Spacing, Decrease (a second time)
CLICK: Detail section bar to remove the control selection

**17** On your own, reduce the size of the form by dragging its rightmost border to the left and the Form Footer section bar upward. Your screen should now appear similar to Figure 7.13.

**18** CLICK: Save button (🖫) to save the form

ACCESS

**Figure 7.13**

Using the Format command to align and space controls

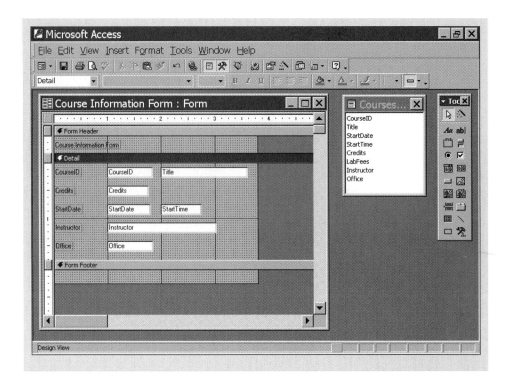

## 7.2.2 Changing the Tab Order

**FEATURE**

A section's **tab order** refers to the movement of the cursor when the user presses ⌈TAB⌉. Typically, a tab order flows from the top left-hand corner to the bottom right-hand corner. When a control is selected, it is referred to as having **focus.** Therefore, pressing ⌈TAB⌉ results in one control losing focus and another control gaining focus. The control that gains focus next is determined by the tab order. You can also press ⌈SHIFT⌉ + ⌈TAB⌉ to move through the tab order in reverse.

**METHOD**

In Design view, select the desired section and then:

1.  CHOOSE: View, Tab Order
2.  CLICK: Auto Order command button to use the default tab order, or
    DRAG: control names appearing in the *Custom Order* list box into the desired order
3.  CLICK: OK command button

**PRACTICE**
You now fix the tab order on the Course Information Form.

*Setup:* Ensure that you've completed the previous lesson and that the Course Information Form is displayed in Design view.

**1** To view the form modified in the previous lesson:
CLICK: View—Form button (⊞▾)
The form looks much better than the initial display in Figure 7.12!

**2** The most commonly used keystroke to advance to the next field in a form is the ⊏ TAB ⊐ key. With the Form window displayed:
PRESS: ⊏ TAB ⊐ to move to the Title text box
PRESS: ⊏ TAB ⊐ once again
You would expect the ⊏ TAB ⊐ key to move you to the next text box on the form. However, this form's tab order is mixed up.

**3** PRESS: ⊏ TAB ⊐ repeatedly to decipher the existing tab order

**4** Let's fix the tab order to more closely match users' expectations:
CLICK: View—Design button (⊠▾)
CHOOSE: View, Tab Order
The dialog box shown in Figure 7.14 appears. Notice that the control order in the list box matches the current tab order.

**Figure 7.14**

Tab Order dialog box

**5** To have Access recalculate the most appropriate tab order:
CLICK: Auto Order command button
CLICK: OK command button
(*Hint:* You can also drag the control names in the list box to specify a custom tab order.)

**6**  To test the new tab order:
CLICK: View—Form button (⊞▾)
PRESS: TAB repeatedly

**7**  Let's return to Design view and save the changes:
CLICK: View—Design button (⚎▾)
CLICK: Save button (🖫)

## 7.2.3  Formatting Controls on a Form

**FEATURE**
After you've made a form "work," it is time to focus your attention on making it aesthetically pleasing. First impressions of a form can stay with a user for a long time. If you contribute to a user's eyestrain, for example, with neon-colored fonts on a lime-green background, you are sure to elicit some negative feedback. Furthermore, ask yourself whether the form's design appears spacious and inviting or cramped and dreary. These are just some of the adjectives that people may use to describe your forms. One of the most important formatting goals is to make on-screen text easy to read. To this end, Access provides several formatting commands and features for enhancing a form.

**METHOD**
Using the Formatting toolbar:

1.  SELECT: a control in the Form window
2.  CLICK: a button on the Formatting toolbar

Using the Properties window:

1.  RIGHT-CLICK: the control to format
2.  CHOOSE: Properties
3.  SELECT: *Format* tab in the Properties window
4.  SELECT: *a property* text box

**PRACTICE**
You now enhance the Course Information Form by applying formatting commands.

*Setup:* Ensure that you've completed the previous lesson and that the Course Information Form is displayed in Design view.

**1** Let's begin formatting the label control in the Form Header section:
CLICK: Course Information Form label control

**2** To change the typeface and font size used in the label:
CLICK: down arrow attached to the Font list box ([Arial ▼])
SELECT: Times New Roman
CLICK: down arrow attached to the Font Size list box ([10 ▼])
SELECT: 14
Don't worry that the label text is no longer visible in the control. We'll fix the label size after a few additional steps.

**3** To apply boldface to the label and make it italic:
CLICK: Bold button (🅱)
CLICK: Italic button (𝐼)

**4** Let's make the label text appear with a bright blue font color:
CLICK: down arrow attached to the Font/Fore Color button (▲▼)
SELECT: a bright blue color

**5** To adjust the size of the label:
CHOOSE: Format, Size, To Fit
The formatted label text now appears in the Form Header section.

**6** To edit the caption of the StartDate label control:
RIGHT-CLICK: StartDate label control
CHOOSE: Properties

**7** In the Properties window:
CLICK: *Format* tab, if it is not already selected
DOUBLE-CLICK: *Caption* text box
TYPE: Date/Time

**8** Close the Properties window.

**9** To size the selected control to its best fit:
CHOOSE: Format, Size, To Fit

**10** You can also access several formatting commands from a control's right-click menu and from the Properties window. To illustrate:
RIGHT-CLICK: label control in the Form Header section
CHOOSE: Properties command

**11** On your own, scroll the list of *Format* properties. Notice that all of the format specifications you just made can be set using the *Font Name, Font Size, Font Weight, Font Italic,* and *Fore Color* properties.

**12** Close the Properties window.

ACCESS

## 7.2.4  Using the AutoFormat Command

**FEATURE**

Rather than spend time selecting formatting options, you can use the **AutoFormat** feature to quickly apply an entire group of formatting commands to a control, a selection of controls, a section, or the entire form. In addition to selecting an AutoFormat style from the list of options used by the Form Wizards, you can customize how the *Font, Color,* and *Border* style attributes are applied. The AutoFormat feature provides an excellent way to ensure consistent formatting across all of your forms.

**METHOD**

1.  SELECT: a control, a section, or the entire form
2.  CLICK: AutoFormat button (🖼️) in the Form Design toolbar, or CHOOSE: Format, AutoFormat
3.  SELECT: an AutoFormat style in the list box
4.  CLICK: OK command button

**PRACTICE**

In this lesson, you apply an AutoFormat style to the Detail section of the Course Information Form.

*Setup:* Ensure that you've completed the previous lesson and that the Course Information Form is displayed in Design view.

**1**  To apply an AutoFormat to a particular section of a form:
CLICK: Detail section bar
CLICK: AutoFormat button (🖼️) in the toolbar

**2**  In the AutoFormat dialog box:
SELECT: Blends in the *Form AutoFormats* list box
CLICK: OK command button
The style options are applied to the controls appearing in the section.

**3**  To view the form:
CLICK: View—Form button (📧▾)

**4**  On your own, size the form so that it appears similar to Figure 7.15.

**5**  Close the form and save the changes.

**Figure 7.15**

Formatted Course
Information Form

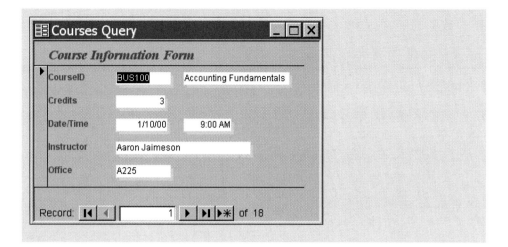

**7.2 Self Check**   Which design guideline or principle does the AutoFormat command help you adhere to?

# 7.3   Using the Report Design View

Many of the concepts and features discussed in the previous two modules also apply to creating and customizing reports in Access. Whereas forms are geared toward display on-screen, reports are designed to be printed. Consequently, reports do not collect data in text boxes or have a tab order. They do, however, make extensive use of calculated controls and aggregate functions. Reports are exceptional for sorting and grouping data and for providing subtotal and summary calculations. In this module, you open a report in Design view and practice adding, creating, and manipulating controls.

ACCESS

# 7.3.1 Viewing and Modifying a Report

**FEATURE**

Access provides three views for interacting with a report object. In Design view, you create new reports and modify existing reports. To view the report as it will appear when printed, select the Print Preview mode. For reports that must access and summarize a large number of records, Print Preview can take a few moments to display. It is for these occasions that Access provides the Layout Preview mode. Use this display mode to provide a quick preview of the report using sample data.

Like a form object, report objects are divided into sections. The **Report Header** section contains information, such as a title page, logo, or abstract, that appears only once at the beginning of a report. The *Page Header* and *Page Footer* bands contain information that you want repeated at the top and bottom of each printed page, such as column headings and page numbers. The **Report Detail** section contains the main body of the report and is used to display the field data from a particular record source. For each record in the underlying table or query, a line is printed in the Detail section. The **Report Footer** appears once at the end of a report and typically displays grand totals and other summary information. In order to group data and calculate subtotals in a report, you display the **Group Header** and **Group Footer** sections and then add the desired controls. As with forms, you create a report by inserting, positioning, and manipulating controls in the different sections of a report object. You select the entire report for formatting by clicking its Report Selector button in the top left-hand corner of the Design window.

**METHOD**

In the Database window, click the *Reports* button and then:

1. SELECT: the form object that you want to view or modify
2. CLICK: Preview button (🔍Preview) to preview the report
   CLICK: Design button (📝Design) to modify the report in Design view

Once a report object is displayed, switch among the views using the View option on the Menu bar or by clicking the following toolbar buttons:

- CLICK: View—Design button (📝▾)
- CLICK: View—Print Preview button (🔍▾)
- CLICK: View—Layout Preview button (🔍▾)

**PRACTICE**
You now practice displaying a report using the available views.

*Setup:* Ensure that the ACC700 Database window is displayed.

**1** To begin, let's create a simple report using the Report Wizard:
CLICK: *Reports* button in the Objects bar
DOUBLE-CLICK: Create report by using wizard

**2** In the first step of the Report Wizard dialog box:
SELECT: Query: Books Query from the *Tables/Queries* drop-down list box
CLICK: Include All button ( » ) to add all of the fields to the report
CLICK: Next> to proceed

**3** When asked how you want to view the data, specify a grouping:
SELECT: by Authors
Notice that the preview area in the dialog box is updated to display the new Author Group Header.

**4** To proceed to the next step:
CLICK: Next>

**5** In addition to the Author Group Header section, Access allows you to specify further grouping options. Do the following:
CLICK: Next> to retain the existing Group Header only

**6** To specify a sort order for records appearing in the Detail section:
SELECT: Title in the first sort drop-down list box
CLICK: Next>

**7** You may now specify layout, orientation, and style options. To do so:
SELECT: *Stepped* option button in the *Layout* area
SELECT: *Portrait* option button in the *Orientation* area
CLICK: Next>
SELECT: Corporate in the list box area
CLICK: Next>

**8** To complete the Report Wizard:
TYPE: **Books Query Report** in the title text box
SELECT: *Preview the report* option button
CLICK: Finish
After adjusting the scroll bars, the report's Preview window should appear similar to Figure 7.16.

**Figure 7.16**

Viewing report sections
in the Preview window

Report Header

Page Header

Author [Group] Header

Report Detail

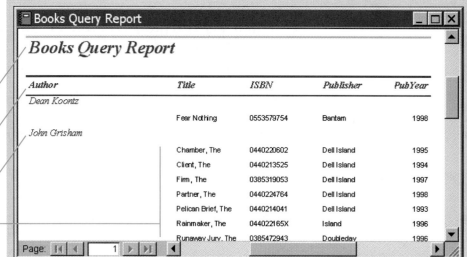

**9** To view this report in Design view:
CLICK: View—Design button ()
Your screen should now appear similar to Figure 7.17. Notice the section bars (Report Header, Page Header, Author [Group] Header, [Report] Detail, Page Footer, and Report Footer) that label the different parts of the report object.

**Figure 7.17**

Report Design window

Report Selector button

Section Selector button

Section bar

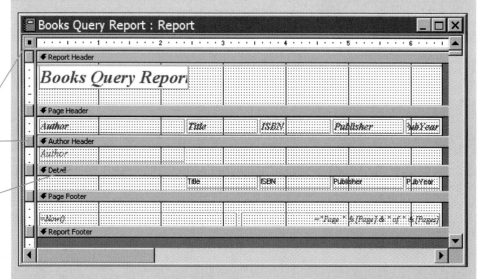

**10** The Layout Preview mode does not lend anything to a report of this size. The Print Preview mode provides a fast and more accurate representation and should be used exclusively for reports under twenty pages. Keep the report Design window displayed for use in the next lesson.

## 7.3.2  Manipulating Controls in a Report

**FEATURE**
Report Design view provides the same tools and features that you used working in form Design view. You can add bound, unbound, and calculated controls to a report using the Field List and Toolbox windows. Once the required controls are inserted in a report, size and move the controls to finalize their placement and appearance.

**METHOD**
To insert a control in report Design view:

- DRAG: a field from the Field List window onto the report, or
- CLICK: the desired control in the Toolbox window
- CLICK: once in the report to place the control

To manipulate a control, select the desired control and then:

- PRESS: DELETE to delete the control
- DRAG: the control's sizing handles to size the control
- DRAG: the control's border to move the control

**PRACTICE**
You now practice moving, sizing, and adding controls to a report.

*Setup:* Ensure that you've completed the previous lesson and that the Books Query Report is displayed in Design view.

**1** In reviewing the Preview window shown in Figure 7.16, there is too much white space between the author's name and the column containing the book titles. To size and move these controls:
CLICK: Author label control in the Page Header section
PRESS: SHIFT and hold it down
CLICK: Author text box control in the Author Header section
(*Hint:* Even though the Author control in the Author Header section does not look the same as the text box controls you placed previously on forms, it is a bound text box control for displaying data.)

**2** With both Author controls selected, position the mouse pointer over one of the control's right-hand sizing handles. When positioned properly, the mouse pointer changes shape to a sizing arrow (↔).

**3** DRAG: the control border to the left until reaching 1.5 inches on the ruler

ACCESS

**4**  Now let's increase the size of the Title controls. Do the following:
CLICK: Title label control in the Page Header section
PRESS: (SHIFT) and hold it down
CLICK: Title text box control in the Detail section

**5**  Position the mouse pointer over one of the control's left-hand sizing handles, until the mouse pointer changes shape to a sizing arrow (↔).

**6**  DRAG: the control border to the left until reaching 1.6 inches on the ruler

**7**  To view the changes and then return:
CLICK: View—Print Preview button (⬛·)
CLICK: View—Design button (⬛·)

**8**  Let's center the label control in the Report Header section:
CLICK: Books Query Report label control

**9**  Position the mouse pointer over the control's border so that the mouse pointer changes shape to a hand (✋).

**10**  DRAG: the label control to the right so that it appears centered between the left and right page margins

**11**  To add a comment to the report:
CLICK: Label button (⬛) in the Toolbox window
(*Hint:* If the Toolbox window isn't displayed, click the Toolbox button (⬛) on the toolbar. You may also want to hide the Field List window from displaying so that you can see more of the Design window.)

**12**  Position the mouse pointer in the top left-hand corner of the Report Header section and then:
DRAG: the mouse pointer down and to the right to create a box similar to the one shown here
TYPE: **Report by** *yourname*

**13**  To view the report and then return:
CLICK: View—Print Preview button (⬛·)
CLICK: View—Design button (⬛·)

**14**  CLICK: Save button (⬛)

| In Addition | As you did with forms, choose the Format, Align command to align controls, |
|---|---|
| Aligning, Spacing, and Sizing Controls in a Report | the Format, Size command to make controls the same size, and the Format, Horizontal/Vertical Spacing commands to increase or decrease the spacing between controls. Refer to lesson 7.2.1 in this chapter for more information. |

## 7.3.3   Creating a Calculated Control

**FEATURE**

A *calculated control* is a text box that performs a calculation using data stored in the underlying table or query. Create a calculated control by typing an expression directly into the control or by using the Expression Builder dialog box. To perform calculations for each record in a report, place calculated controls in the Detail section. When placed in the Group, Page, or Report Footer sections, calculated controls can be used to compute summary totals using the SUM, AVG, and COUNT aggregate functions. For example, you can add together values for subtotals based on date ranges, category groupings, and page breaks. You can also provide grand total summaries for display at the end of the report.

**METHOD**

To add a calculated control to a report in Design view:

1.  CLICK: Text Box button (☒) in the Toolbox window
2.  CLICK: in the Report window to place the control
3.  TYPE: *desired expression*, or
    CLICK: Build button (☒) to access the Expression Builder

**PRACTICE**

You now create a calculated control that counts the number of books listed by author.

*Setup:* Ensure that you've completed the previous lessons and that the Books Query Report is displayed in Design view.

**1**  Unlike the Report and Page sections, the Author Header section does not display an associated Author Footer. In this exercise, you display a new footer section and then add a calculated control. Do the following:
CLICK: Sorting and Grouping button (☒) in the toolbar
The Sorting and Grouping window appears, as shown in Figure 7.18.

**Figure 7.18**

Sorting and Grouping window

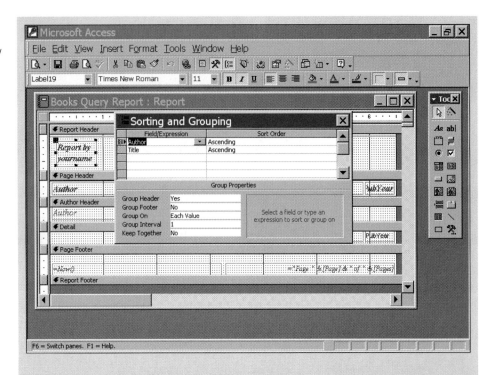

**2** In the *Group Properties* area:
SELECT: Yes in the *Group Footer* text box

**3** To close the Sorting and Grouping window:
CLICK: its Close button (☒)

**4** Now let's add a text box control to the new Author Footer section that appears in the report Design window:
CLICK: Text Box button (abl) in the Toolbox window

**5** Position the mouse pointer in the Author Footer section, lined up with the Title text box control in the Report Detail section. When positioned properly:
CLICK: the mouse pointer once to insert the new text box control

**6** Begin by entering a caption for the label:
RIGHT-CLICK: the new label control
CHOOSE: Properties
CLICK: *Format* tab in the Properties window
DOUBLE-CLICK: *Caption* text box
TYPE: **Total Titles**

**7** Close the Properties window.

**8** To size the label control:
CHOOSE: Format, Size, To Fit

**9** To enter a calculated control:
CLICK: Unbound text box control
TYPE: `=count([Title])`
The COUNT function provides a summary count of the titles (records) printed in the Detail section for each Author. Notice that the field name must be enclosed in square brackets and, since it is a parameter of the function, in parentheses.

**10** To display the report in the Preview window:
CLICK: View—Print Preview button ( )
Your screen should now appear similar to Figure 7.19.

**Figure 7.19**

Displaying the completed report

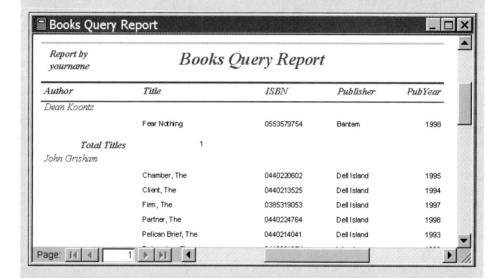

**11** On your own, scroll down the report and view the results of the calculated control.

**12** When finished, close the report Preview window and save the changes.

**7.3 Self Check** What is the primary difference between forms and reports?

# 7.4  Customizing a Report

Customizing a report object involves changing its appearance and structure. A report's appearance is modified by formatting the printed page and the individual controls contained therein. To modify the structure of a report, you manipulate its controls, sections, and sorting options. Additionally, you access the Page Setup dialog box to edit print margins, select a page orientation, and specify the number of columns to use. In this module, you learn to apply several formatting commands, work with report sections, and modify a report's sorting and grouping options.

## 7.4.1  Formatting Controls in a Report

**FEATURE**
Formatting controls in a report is the same as formatting controls on a form. After selecting a control or group of controls, specify the desired formatting options using the Formatting toolbar, the Properties window, or the AutoFormat dialog box. The purpose of enhancing controls is to draw the reader's attention to specific areas of the report. For example, applying boldface to group headings and subtotals separates these report sections from the detail area. Making information legible and easy to read is an important and worthwhile objective.

**METHOD**
1.  SELECT: a control in the Report window
2.  CLICK: a button on the Formatting toolbar

**PRACTICE**
You now practice customizing and formatting controls in an existing report.

*Setup:* Ensure that the ACC700 Database window is displayed.

**1** To open the Student Listing report, ensure that the *Reports* button is selected in the Objects bar and then:
DOUBLE-CLICK: Student Listing

**2** On your own, peruse the report by zooming and scrolling the Preview window.

**3** There are several ways to customize this wizard-designed report. In this lesson, you format several controls in Design view:
CLICK: View—Design button (⊠-)

**4**  To apply an AutoFormat style option to the label controls in the Page Header section:
CLICK: Page Header section bar
CLICK: AutoFormat button (▦) in the toolbar

**5**  In the AutoFormat dialog box:
SELECT: Casual in the *Report AutoFormats* list box
CLICK: OK command button

**6**  Let's emphasize the report's title with a new typeface:
CLICK: Student Listing label control in the Report Header section
CLICK: down arrow attached to the Font list box ([Arial ▾])
SELECT: Arial
CLICK: down arrow attached to the Font Size list box ([10 ▾])
SELECT: 24

**7**  Now let's apply a new font color:
CLICK: down arrow attached to the Font/Fore Color button (▲▾)
SELECT: a teal (greenish blue) color

**8**  To adjust the size of the label:
CHOOSE: Format, Size, To Fit

**9**  Let's increase the font size of the data printed in the Detail section. Using the rectangular lasso or SHIFT +click method:
SELECT: all of the text box controls in the Detail section
CLICK: down arrow attached to the Font Size list box ([10 ▾])
SELECT: 10
CLICK: Detail section bar to remove the control selection

**10**  In order to line up information under their respective column titles, you will now size and align the data displayed in the controls:
CLICK: Age label control in the Page Header section
PRESS: SHIFT and hold it down
CLICK: Age text box control in the Detail section
(*Hint:* Remember to release the SHIFT key before proceeding.)

**11**  CHOOSE: Format, Size, To Widest
CLICK: Center button (▤) in the toolbar

**12**  On your own, increase the width of the GPA label control in the Page Header section to 5.5 inches on the ruler. Then, make the GPA text box control the same width. Lastly, use the Align Right button (▤) to right-align the contents of both controls.

**13**  CLICK: View—Print Preview button (▣▾)
Your screen should appear similar to Figure 7.20.

**Figure 7.20**

Formatting the Student
Listing report

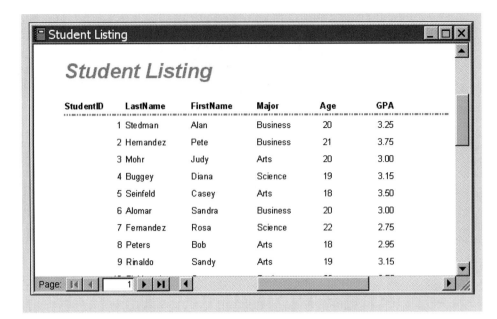

## 7.4.2 Applying Conditional Formatting

**FEATURE**

Using Access' **conditional formatting** feature, you can format controls (in both forms and reports) based on the outcome of a calculated expression. For instance, imagine that you have a calculated control in a report that computes a customer's line of credit. Using the Format, Conditional Formatting command, you can specify that all values greater than the $10,000 limit appear with a bright red font. Now you can easily determine when a customer has exceeded the allowable amount. Conditional formatting is most useful when you need to identify values that stray from a standard result, incorporate visual cues based on performance, categorize or group data, or create your own formatting styles.

**METHOD**

1. SELECT: a control in the Report window
2. CHOOSE: Format, Conditional Formatting
3. Specify up to three conditions, with each having a different set of formatting options to apply.

**PRACTICE**

In this lesson, you apply a red boldface font to those students with a GPA of less than 3.00.

*Setup:* Ensure that you've completed the previous lesson and that the Student Listing report appears in the Preview window.

**1** To apply conditional formatting to the Student Listing report:
CLICK: View—Design button (📷▾)

**2** In this exercise, you specify a condition that evaluates a student's GPA. If less than 3.00, the GPA value is formatted to display in a red boldface font. To begin:
CLICK: Detail section bar to remove the control selection
CLICK: GPA text box control in the Detail section

**3** CHOOSE: Format, Conditional Formatting
The Conditional Formatting dialog box appears. You can specify up to three separate conditions in the dialog box.

**4** In the *Condition1* area of the dialog box:
SELECT: Field Value Is (in the first drop-down list box)
SELECT: less than (in the next drop-down list box)
TYPE: **3.00** in the remaining text box

**5** You now specify the desired formatting attributes to apply when the condition evaluates to true. In the *Condition1* area of the dialog box:
CLICK: Bold button (**B**) in the dialog box
CLICK: down arrow attached to the Font/Fore Color button (A▾)
SELECT: a red color
The dialog box should now appear similar to Figure 7.21. (*CAUTION:* Make sure that you do not click the formatting buttons in the *Default Formatting* area by mistake.)

**Figure 7.21**
Conditional Formatting
dialog box

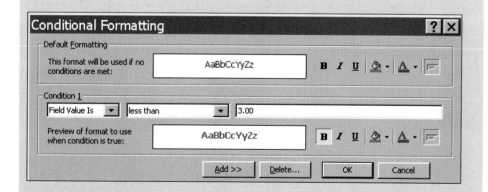

**6** To complete the dialog box:
CLICK: OK command button

**7** CLICK: View—Print Preview button (🔍▾)

**8** On your own, scroll the report so that you can see the conditional formatting results in the GPA column.

# 7.4.3   Sorting and Grouping Data

**FEATURE**

Imagine trying to find a single line item in a report that displays over a thousand unsorted records. This arduous task describes working with data, not information. The distinction between the two is important. One of the primary functions of a report is to process data in order to yield information. But sorting data is only the first step. Access also provides the ability to group and summarize data. For example, you can group textual data by letter (as in this book's index), date values by day, month, or year, and numeric values by range. Once grouped, you can add subtotal calculations to the report. By sorting and grouping data, you can reduce the potential for information overload with a clear, concise, and helpful report.

**METHOD**

After displaying a report object in Design view:

1. CLICK: Sorting and Grouping button (▤) on the toolbar
2. SELECT: a field name in the *Field/Expression* column
3. SELECT: a sort order in the *Sort Order* column
4. Specify the *Group Properties* for the selected field.
5. CLICK: Close button (☒) to close the Sorting and Grouping window

**PRACTICE**

You now establish a new Group Header and apply a sort order to the Student Listing report.

*Setup:* Ensure that you've completed the previous lessons and that the Student Listing report appears in the Preview window.

**1** To create a new header section that groups students by major:
CLICK: View—Design button (▤▾)

**2** CLICK: Sorting and Grouping button (▤) in the toolbar
An empty Sorting and Grouping window appears.

**3** To specify a new Group Header section:
CLICK: down arrow attached to the text box in the *Field/Expression* column
SELECT: Major

**4** In the *Group Properties* area of the window:
SELECT: Yes in the *Group Header* text box

**5** To specify that the records appearing in the Detail section should be sorted by surname:
CLICK: in the next row of the *Field/Expression* column
CLICK: down arrow attached to the text box
SELECT: LastName
Notice that the Ascending option appears automatically in the adjacent *Sort Order* column.

**6** Close the Sorting and Grouping window.

**7** Now move the existing Major controls into the new Group Header section. Using Figure 7.22 as your guide, do the following:
CLICK: Major label control to display the sizing handles
DRAG: Major label control to the far left of the Major Header section
CLICK: Major text box control
DRAG: Major text box control to appear to the right of its label control

**8** On your own, select the six label and text box controls for the StudentID, LastName, and FirstName fields. Then, move the selected controls into position, as shown in Figure 7.22.

**Figure 7.22**

Inserting a Group
Header section

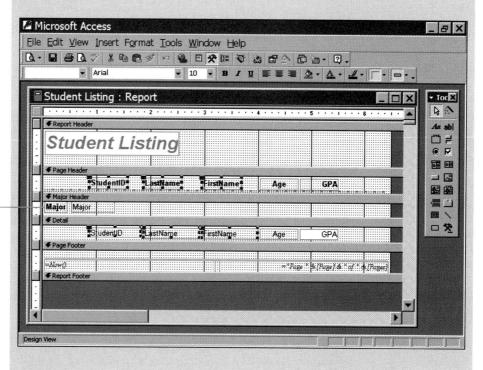

Populating the Major
Group Header section
area with controls.

**9** CLICK: View—Print Preview button (⬛▾)
The report now displays students sorted alphabetically by surname and grouped according to their selected major.

**10** Keep the report Preview window open for use in the next lesson.

# 7.4.4  Adjusting Page and Margin Settings

**FEATURE**
For more control over your printed reports, define page layout settings using the File, Page Setup command. In the Page Setup dialog box, you can specify **margins, orientation,** paper size, and column grid settings. Use the *Margins* tab to select the top, bottom, left, and right page margins and the *Page* tab to specify the paper size and print orientation (for example, portrait or landscape). For printing mailing labels or newspaper-style reports, use the *Columns* tab to specify the number of columns and other related options. With some printers requiring distinct settings, you may need to print a few test reports in order to find the optimal page layout options.

**METHOD**
After displaying or selecting a report object:

1.   CHOOSE: File, Page Setup
2.   CLICK: *Margins, Page,* and *Columns* tabs
3.   SELECT: the desired page layout options

**PRACTICE**
You now finalize the print settings for the Student Listing report.

*Setup:* Ensure that you've completed the previous lessons and that the Student Listing report appears in the Preview window.

**1**  To display the print options for the Student Listing report:
CHOOSE: File, Page Setup

**2**  Let's assume that you want to print this report on your school's letterhead. To do so, you must adjust the print options to allow for a top margin of two inches. To begin:
CLICK: *Margins* tab, if it is not already selected

**3**  To select the existing margin entry:
DOUBLE-CLICK: *Top* text box in the *Margins (inches)* area
TYPE: 2
Notice that the preview in the *Sample* area is updated automatically.

**4**  On your own, select the *Page* and *Columns* tabs to review the print options, but do not change the default settings.

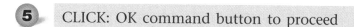

**5** CLICK: OK command button to proceed

**6** Close the Student Listing Preview window and save the changes.

**7** Close the ACC700 Database window. Then, exit Microsoft Access.

**7.4 Self Check** How can you incorporate multiple AutoFormat styles in the same report?

# 7.5 Chapter Review

Forms and reports are the objects that people work with most in a database application. Making these objects easy to use and visually attractive ultimately reflects on your skill as a designer and the effectiveness of the database. One way to ensure user acceptance and satisfaction is by including users in the design process. Collecting user feedback can also be helpful in fine-tuning a form's usability or a report's presentation and for discovering the optimal combination of fonts, sizes, colors, and graphics.

In Design view, Access displays forms and reports divided into sections. To create a form or report, place bound, unbound, and calculated controls in the Form and Report windows and customize their properties. Controls may be moved, sized, aligned, and formatted using a variety of tools and commands. You can also ensure formatting consistency by applying AutoFormat styles to the controls, sections, and objects in a database application. One of the most important design objectives is to keep your form and report objects simple and easy to read.

ACCESS

## 7.5.1 Command Summary

Many of the commands and procedures appearing in this chapter are summarized in the following table.

| Skill Set | To Perform This Task . . . | Do the Following . . . |
| --- | --- | --- |
| **Viewing and Organizing Information** | Switch between the display view modes for a form object | CLICK: View—Form button<br>CLICK: View—Design button<br>CLICK: View—Datasheet button |
| | Switch between the display view modes for a report object | CLICK: View—Design button<br>CLICK: View—Print Preview button<br>CLICK: View, Layout Preview button |
| | Open a form object in Design view | CLICK: *Forms* button in the Objects bar<br>SELECT: the desired form<br>CLICK: Design button |
| | Open a report object in Design view | CLICK: *Reports* button in the Objects bar<br>SELECT: the desired report<br>CLICK: Design button |
| **Building and Modifying Forms** | View a form's sections in the Design window | CHOOSE: View, Page Header/Footer<br>CHOOSE: View, Form Header/Footer |
| | Select the entire form | CLICK: Form Selector button |
| | Change the tab order of controls on a form in Design view | CHOOSE: View, Tab Order<br>CLICK: Auto Order command button<br>CLICK: OK command button |
| **Building Forms and Producing Reports** | Display the Field List window and add controls to a form or report | CLICK: Field List button<br>DRAG: a field control from the Field List window to the form or report |
| | Display the Toolbox window and add controls to a form or report | CLICK: Toolbox button<br>CLICK: a control button<br>CLICK: in the form or report |

*Continued*

| Skill Set | To Perform This Task . . . | Do the Following . . . |
|---|---|---|
| **Building Forms and Producing Reports** | View the Properties window for modifying a control's attributes | SELECT: a control(s) CHOOSE: View, Properties |
| | Delete a control | SELECT: a control PRESS: DELETE |
| | Move a control using the mouse | SELECT: a control DRAG: a control's border or its moving handle |
| | Move, space, and align controls using the menu | SELECT: a group of controls CHOOSE: Format, Align CHOOSE: Format, Horizontal Spacing CHOOSE: Format, Vertical Spacing |
| | Size a control using the mouse | SELECT: a control DRAG: a control's sizing handle |
| | Size controls using the menu | SELECT: a group of controls CHOOSE: Format, Size |
| | Insert a calculated control in a form or report by typing an expression | CLICK: Text Box button (🔤) in the Toolbox window CLICK: in the form or report TYPE: *desired expression* |
| | Insert a calculated control in a form or report using the Expression Builder | CLICK: Text Box button (🔤) in the Toolbox window CLICK: in the form or report CLICK: Build button (🖍) |
| | Format a control on a form or report | SELECT: a control CLICK: the desired button on the Formatting toolbar |
| | Format a control, section, or form/report using the AutoFormat command | SELECT: a control, a section, or the entire form or report object CLICK: AutoFormat button (🔽) SELECT: an AutoFormat style option |
| | Apply conditional formatting to a control on a form or report | SELECT: a control CHOOSE: Format, Conditional Formatting |

*Continued*

| Skill Set | To Perform This Task . . . | Do the Following . . . |
|---|---|---|
| **Building Forms and Producing Reports** *Continued* | Specify print and page setup options, such as margins and orientation | SELECT: a form or report<br>CHOOSE: File, Page Setup |
| **Producing Reports** | View a report's sections in the Design window | CHOOSE: View, Page Header/Footer<br>CHOOSE: View, Report Header/Footer |
| | Display the sorting and grouping options for a report in Design view | CLICK: Sorting and Grouping button (▣) |

## 7.5.2  Key Terms

This section specifies page references for the key terms identified in this chapter. For a complete list of definitions, refer to the Glossary provided at the end of this learning guide.

AutoFormat, *p. 336*

bound control, *p. 313*

calculated control, *p. 313*

compound control, *p. 318*

conditional formatting, *p. 348*

controls, *p. 313*

Field List window, *p. 316*

focus, *p. 332*

Form Detail, *p. 309*

Form Footer, *p. 309*

Form Header, *p. 309*

Group Footer, *p. 338*

Group Header, *p. 338*

main form, *p. 308*

margins , *p. 352*

orientation, *p. 352*

Page Footer, *p. 309*

Page Header, *p. 309*

Report Detail, *p. 338*

Report Footer, *p. 338*

Report Header, *p. 338*

subform, *p. 308*

switchboard form, *p. 308*

tab order, *p. 332*

Toolbox window, *p. 316*

unbound control, *p. 313*

# 7.6  Review Questions

## 7.6.1  Short Answer

1. What controls do you typically find in the Form Detail section?
2. What types of information would you place in the Form Header and Form Footer sections?
3. What is the difference between bound and unbound controls?
4. In a compound control, how do you move a bound text box control separately from its label control?
5. What does it mean to change the tab order on a form?
6. What is the fastest way to make controls the same size?
7. What is the fastest way to align controls on a form or report?
8. In a printed report, where would you find the Report Header, Page Header, and Report Detail sections?
9. Why might you want to apply conditional formatting to a control?
10. How do you create a new Group Header section in a report?

## 7.6.2  True/False

1. _____ Columnar and justified form layouts display one record at a time.
2. _____ Tabular and datasheet form layouts can be used in creating subforms to embed in a main form.
3. _____ A switchboard form is a main form that displays its subform using a variety of different layouts.
4. _____ You use the Expression Formulator dialog box to construct an expression for a calculated control.
5. _____ You can set formatting properties for a control using the Formatting toolbar or the Properties window.
6. _____ To select multiple controls, press and hold down the ⎡ALT⎤ key and then click on the desired controls.
7. _____ When a cursor appears in a text box on a form, the control is said to have *focus*.
8. _____ To calculate a subtotal in a report, insert a calculated control in the desired Group Footer section.
9. _____ You can specify up to three separate conditions for a control in the Conditional Formatting dialog box.
10. _____ To specify margin settings in preparation for printing a report, choose the Format, Page Setup command from the menu.

## 7.6.3  Multiple Choice

1.  Which of the following is *not* a view for interacting with a form object?
    a.   Datasheet view
    b.   Design view
    c.   Form view
    d.   Layout Preview

2.  Which of the following is *not* a legitimate section for form objects?
    a.   Form Detail
    b.   Form Header
    c.   Group Header
    d.   Page Footer

3.  The basic elements of a form or report are called:
    a.   controls
    b.   objects
    c.   properties
    d.   windows

4.  Which of the following control types is most often associated with a bound control?
    a.   command button
    b.   label
    c.   list box
    d.   text box

5.  Which of the following control types do you use to create a calculated control?
    a.   combo box
    b.   command button
    c.   label
    d.   text box

6.  Which of the following is *not* one of the design guidelines mentioned in this chapter?
    a.   Limit the number of controls on a form.
    b.   Limit the number of fonts, font styles, and colors selected.
    c.   Limit the number of calculated controls used in a form.
    d.   Always involve your users in the design of forms.

7.  Which of the following is *not* a view for displaying a report object?
    a.   Datasheet view
    b.   Design view
    c.   Layout Preview
    d.   Print Preview

8. The Report Footer section is most useful for displaying:
   a. column headings
   b. grand totals
   c. subtotals
   d. page numbers

9. Calculated controls can be used to compute aggregate functions in a report, except for the following:
   a. AVG
   b. COUNT
   c. PMT
   d. SUM

10. To print a report using letterhead, you must typically modify this setting:
    a. group
    b. margin
    c. orientation
    d. section

# 7.7  Hands-On Projects

### 7.7.1  World Wide Imports: Listing Customers in a Subform

This exercise leads you step by step through embedding a datasheet subform in a columnar main form. When a record is selected in the Sales Reps main form, the datasheet subform displays all of the rep's customers.

*Setup:* Ensure that Access is loaded. If you are launching Access and the startup dialog box appears, click the Cancel command button to remove the dialog box from the application window.

1. Open the database file named ACC770.
2. To create a new form object:
   CLICK: *Forms* button in the Objects bar
   DOUBLE-CLICK: Create form by using wizard
3. In the first step of the Form Wizard dialog box, you select the tables and queries on which to base the new form. To select the table and fields for the main form:
   SELECT: Table: 771 Sales Reps from the *Tables/Queries* drop-down list box
   CLICK: Include All button ( >> )

4. To select the table for the subform:
   SELECT: Table: 771 Customers from the *Tables/Queries* drop-down list box
5. Now select the fields that you want displayed in the subform datasheet. In the *Available Fields* list box:
   DOUBLE-CLICK: CustomerName
   DOUBLE-CLICK: Address
   DOUBLE-CLICK: City
   DOUBLE-CLICK: State
6. To proceed to the next step:
   CLICK: Next >
7. To specify that you want to embed a subform in a main form:
   SELECT: by 771 Sales Reps in the list box
   SELECT: *Form with subform(s)* option button
   CLICK: Next > to proceed
8. To select a layout and style for the new form:
   SELECT: *Datasheet* option button
   CLICK: Next > to proceed
   SELECT: Industrial from the list box
   CLICK: Next > to proceed
9. To accept the default form names:
   CLICK: Finish
10. When the Form window appears:
    CLICK: View—Design button ([image])
11. On your own, size the Design window to display more of the form.
12. To provide more room for displaying the subform:
    SELECT: 771 Customers label control
    PRESS: DELETE
    CLICK: Subform control
    DRAG: the left-hand sizing handle toward the left edge of the form
13. To view the newly sized subform:
    CLICK: View—Form button ([image])
14. Close the Form window and save the changes.

## 7.7.2 CyberWeb: Listing Accounts By Billing Type

In this exercise, you modify an existing report by adding a Group Header section.

*Setup:* Ensure that the ACC770 Database window is displayed.

1. To begin, display the existing report in Print Preview mode:
   CLICK: *Reports* button in the Objects bar
   DOUBLE-CLICK: 772 Accounts Listing in the list area
   Notice that the report is sorted into alphabetical order by Username.

2. To modify the report:
   CLICK: View—Design button (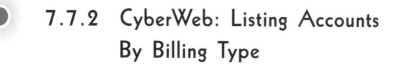)

3. Before creating a new grouping in the report, let's size and indent the Username controls. Do the following:
   CLICK: Username label control in the Page Header section
   PRESS: (SHIFT) and hold it down
   CLICK: Username text box control in the Detail section

4. Position the mouse pointer over the left-hand sizing handle of the Username text box control. When positioned properly, the mouse pointer changes shape (↔).

5. DRAG: the sizing handle to the right until reaching .5 inches on the ruler
   Notice that both of the selected controls are sized accordingly.

6. To insert a new Group Header section:
   CLICK: Sorting and Grouping button (▤) in the toolbar
   The Sorting and Grouping window appears. Notice that the Username field appears in the *Field/Expression* column, indicating that this field is being used to sort the report.

7. To specify that the accounts be grouped according to billing type, let's replace the existing entry. Do the following:
   CLICK: down arrow attached to the Username text box
   SELECT: BillingType

8. In the *Group Properties* area of the window:
   SELECT: Yes in the *Group Header* text box

9. To sort each group of records by customer name:
   CLICK: in the next available row of the *Field/Expression* column
   CLICK: down arrow attached to the text box
   SELECT: Customer

10. Close the Sorting and Grouping window.

11. If the Field List window is not displayed:
    CLICK: Field List button (▣) in the toolbar

12. To add the BillingType field to the BillingType Header section:
DRAG: BillingType from the Field List window to BillingType
Header section and drop the control at the 1-inch mark on
the ruler
13. To view the report in the Preview window:
CLICK: View—Print Preview button ([🔍▾])
Notice that the report is grouped according to CC (credit
card), CK (check), and DD (direct deposit).
14. Close the Preview window and save the changes.

### 7.7.3　Big Valley Mills: Customizing a Product Input Form

You will now practice editing and formatting the appearance of an
existing form.

*Setup:* Ensure that the ACC770 Database window is displayed.

1. Open the 773 Product Input form for display. As you can see,
this form is definitely lacking balance and symmetry.
2. Switch the form to display in Design view. On your own,
enlarge the Design window so that you can see all of the controls and sections in the form.
3. To bring some order to the form:
SELECT: all of the label controls on the form
CHOOSE: Format, Align, Left
4. Now let's manipulate the text box controls:
SELECT: all of the text box controls on the form
CHOOSE: Format, Align, Left
CHOOSE: Format, Vertical Spacing, Make Equal
CHOOSE: Format, Vertical Spacing, Decrease
CHOOSE: Format, Vertical Spacing, Decrease
Notice that a few quick commands have greatly improved the
form.
5. You may have noticed that a field is missing from the form.
Ensure that the Field List window is displayed and then drag
the Grade field control onto the form.
6. Size and move the Grade compound control to appear similar
to the other controls on the form.
7. Select the entire form using the Form Selector button and
then apply the Stone AutoFormat style to the form.
8. Add a "Forest Products" label control to the Form Header
section.
9. Format, size, and reposition the label and text box controls to
appear similar to Figure 7.23. (*Hint:* To move one component
of a compound control, drag the desired control's moving
handle. To move both components, drag the control's border.)

10. To specify the correct tab order in the form:
    CHOOSE: View, Tab Order
    CLICK: Auto Order command button
    CLICK: OK command button
11. View the form in Form view. Then, practice moving through the fields in the form using the (TAB) key.
12. Close the Form window and save the changes.

**Figure 7.23**

Formatting the 773 Product Input form

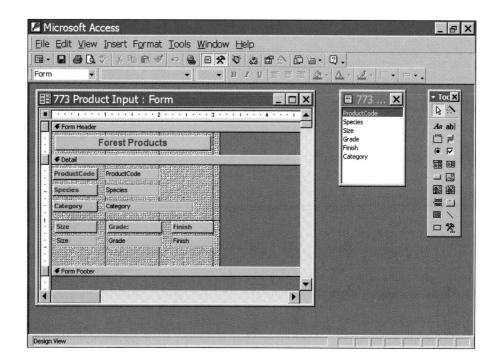

## 7.7.4 Silverdale Festival: Using a Report to Calculate Subtotals

In this exercise, you modify an existing report by defining a new grouping and then adding a calculated control to the Group Footer section.

*Setup:* Ensure that the ACC770 Database window is displayed.

1. Open the 774 Festival Listing for display in Print Preview mode.
2. Your objective is to group and count the volunteer groups from each city. To begin, switch the report to display in Design view.
3. Display the Sorting and Grouping window.
4. In the first row of the *Field/Expression* column, select City from the drop-down list. Then, in the *Group Properties* area, specify a *Group Header* and *Group Footer*.

5. In the second row of the *Field/Expression* column, select VolunteerGroup. This selection ensures that the records are sorted alphabetically within each City grouping.

6. Close the Sorting and Grouping window.

7. Display the Field List window and then drag the City field into the City Header section of the report Design window.

8. Using the Toolbox window, add a text box control to the City Footer section of the report Design window.

9. Specify a caption of **Number** for the new label control and then enter the expression **=count([VolunteerGroup])** into the text box.

10. View the report in Print Preview mode. Then, close the report and save the changes.

## 7.7.5  On Your Own: Office Mart Inventory

To practice working with forms, you are now asked to create the form appearing in Figure 7.24. This form is based on the 775 Inventory table and includes two calculated controls titled "Inventory Value" and "Profit." The Inventory Value expression multiplies the contents of the OnHand text box control by the Cost text box control. The Profit expression subtracts Cost from Retail. In the Detail section, all label controls end with a colon. Notice also that there are label controls in the Form Header and Form Footer sections of the form. (*Hint:* Create an initial columnar form using the Form Wizard and then modify the form in Design view. To apply a fill or background color to a control, use the Fill/Back Color button (⧉) on the Formatting toolbar.) After you've finished formatting the form, save it as "775 Inventory Status" and then close the form.

**Figure 7.24**

Completed Inventory
Status form

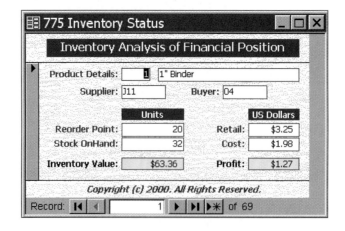

### 7.7.6  On Your Own: Sun Bird Resorts

One of the office clerks at Sun Bird Resorts has created and saved a report entitled "776 Patron Listing" in the ACC770 Database window. After opening and viewing the report in Print Preview mode, you decide to make a few enhancements. Perform the following steps in report Design view:

- Insert a Group Header and Group Footer based on the Interest field.
- Sort the records within each group by guest name.
- Using the Field List window, add the Interest compound control to the Group Header section.
- Using the Toolbox window, add a calculated control to the Group Footer section that counts the total number of guests in each group.
- Apply conditional formatting to the BestTime text box control in the Detail section. If the time value is before 12:00pm (entered as **#12:00  PM#** in the appropriate text box), apply boldface and a green font color to the control. If the time is 12:00pm or later, apply boldface and a blue font color. (*Hint:* Click the Add command button to add another condition in the Conditional Formatting dialog box.)
- Preview the report in Print Preview mode.
- Specify a 2-inch top margin for printing.
- Print the report.

Save the report and then close the Preview window, if it is still displayed. Then, close the ACC770 Database window and exit Microsoft Access.

# 7.8  Case Problems: Carlton Motors

Frank Diaz, the controller at Carlton Motors, is working on two projects that require him to create and customize form and report objects in the company's Access database. First, Frank must create a form that makes it easier for the sales staff to view and update vehicle sales and purchase information. Frank's second project is even more urgent. He must prepare a series of special reports that Carlton's management can distribute to potential investors. If all goes well, Carlton will raise the capital required for its much-needed relocation.

In the following case problems, assume the role of Frank and perform the same steps that he identifies. You may want to re-read the chapter opening before proceeding.

1. While awaiting information on the reports he must design, Frank decides to create a form that will allow the sales staff to view and update Carlton's vehicle inventory. After launching Access, he opens the ACC780 database and selects the *Forms* button in the Objects bar. Rather than starting from scratch, Frank decides to use the Form Wizard to rough out a quick form. After launching the wizard, Frank selects the Vehicles table and then includes the following fields:

   - VehicleID
   - Make
   - Model
   - Category
   - Airbags
   - Color
   - New
   - Asking Price

   In the remaining steps of the Form Wizard dialog box, Frank chooses a Columnar layout and the Expedition formatting style. He saves the form as "Vehicle Information" and opens it for display in the Form window.

   Not completely satisfied with the wizard-created form, Frank switches to Design view to customize several elements. To begin, he focuses on the overall dimensions of the form. He enlarges the Design window and then drags the right edge of the Detail section to the right until it reaches 4 inches on the ruler. In order to add a title, Frank increases the Form Header area by dragging the bottom border of its section bar downward. Using the Label button (![Aa]) in the Toolbox window, Frank adds the title "Vehicle Inventory and Sales" to the Form Header section. He saves the form and views it in Form view.

   Turning his attention to the controls on the form, Frank switches to Design view. Determining that the AskingPrice information is not necessary to display, he deletes the compound control. To conserve space, Frank moves the New compound control to the right of the Airbags check box. Using the Field List window, Frank drags the DealerCost field below the Color text box control. To line up the DealerCost label with the other labels on the form, he moves the DealerCost label to the left by dragging its moving handle. Next, Frank widens the Category text box so that it appears the same width as the Model text box. To finish up the form, Frank formats, sizes, and positions the controls to appear similar to Figure 7.25. He displays the form in Form view and practices navigating through the records. Before proceeding, Frank closes the form and saves the changes.

**Figure 7.25**

Vehicle Information form object

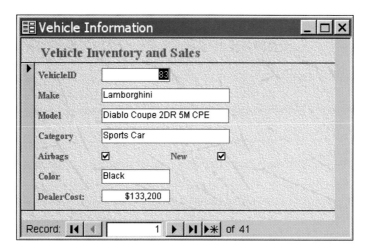

2. The sales staff has asked that Frank provide them with a way to review their recent sales. After some initial contemplation, Frank brainstorms the idea of using the Form Wizard to embed a subform within a main form. Making sure that the *Forms* button is selected in the Objects bar, Frank launches the Form Wizard. The new form will be based on the one-to-many relationship existing between the Salespersons and Vehicles tables. To specify the "main form" table, Frank selects the Salespersons table and then includes the SalesPerson, LastName, and First-Name fields. To specify the "subform" table, he selects the Vehicles table in the same dialog box and includes the Make, Model, SalePrice, SaleDate, and Commission fields.

In the Form Wizard, Frank ensures that the form is created using a main form and subform combination. After selecting a layout and style, he accepts the default names and opens the form for display. Frank notices in the Form window that the information in the subform cannot be viewed without scrolling. To modify the size of the Subform control, he switches to Design view and then deletes the Vehicles label control. Then he widens the Subform control until its left edge appears aligned with the labels on the form. Finally, Frank switches to Form view and adjusts the column widths in the subform datasheet. When finished, Frank closes the form and saves the changes.

3.  For an upcoming meeting with a potential investor, Frank must prepare a report showing the sales transactions for the past 45 days. Having already created a query to gather the necessary information, he must now create a report to present the data. To jump-start the process, Frank clicks the *Reports* button in the Objects bar and then launches the Report Wizard. In the first step of the Report Wizard dialog box, he selects the Sold Vehicles query and includes all of the fields for display in the report. To accept the default settings, he clicks the Finish command button to bypass the remaining Report Wizard options.

    Frank switches the report to Design view for modification. He then performs the following changes:

    *   Apply a "Corporate" AutoFormat style to the entire report.
    *   Edit the report title's label control to read "Vehicle Sales and Profit" in the Report Header section. Then, center the label control between the left and right page margins.
    *   Add a calculated control to the far right-hand side of the Detail section that shows the profit earned for each sale. (*Hint:* Make room in the report by sizing and moving controls. Then insert a text box control in the Detail section. Enter an expression in the text box that subtracts a record's DealerCost, DealerPrep, and Commission values from its SalePrice.)
    *   Using the Properties window, change the *Format* property of the calculated control to "Currency" and the *Decimal Places* property to zero.
    *   Delete the label control attached to the calculated text box control.
    *   Insert a "Profit" label control in the Page Header section that appears directly above the calculated control.
    *   Right-align the SalePrice, DealerCost, DealerPrep, Commission, and Profit label and text box controls.

    Frank saves and then views the report in Print Preview mode. Satisfied with his creation (see Figure 7.26), he sets the top page margin to 2 inches and then sends the report to the printer. Before proceeding, he closes the Preview window and returns to the Database window.

**Figure 7.26**

Vehicle Sales and
Profit report

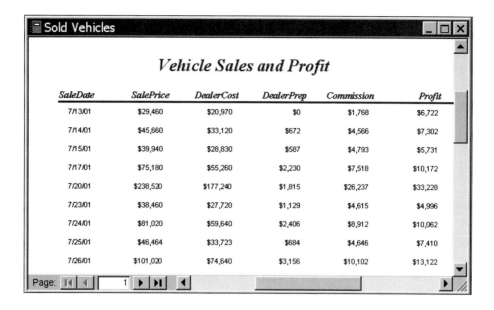

4. The management team appreciated the "Vehicle Sales and Profit" report so much that they've asked Frank to create another. In order to evaluate the effectiveness of the sales staff, Frank must show a breakdown of the vehicle sales by salesperson. Having already used the Report Wizard to create a similar report, Frank need only add some finishing touches. Before proceeding, he opens the existing "Sales Performance" report for display in Print Preview mode. After perusing the report, he switches to Design view to begin making changes.

Frank decides to use some formatting commands to enhance the report's presentation. He applies the "Compact" AutoFormat style to the entire report and then emphasizes the report title by changing its font to Times New Roman and its font to boldface and blue. Frank then uses the Format, Size, To Fit command to ensure that the label is large enough to display the title. He displays the report in Print Preview mode to evaluate how the new formatting style looks.

Returning to Design view, Frank removes the FirstName label and text box controls to reduce the clutter in the report. Using commands on the Format menu, he customizes the appearance of the AskingPrice, SalePrice, and Commission columns. Specifically, Frank makes the labels and their associated controls in the Detail section the same width. After spacing them out, he right-aligns the contents of the selected controls so that the labels appear over their respective amounts. Lastly, Frank applies conditional formatting to the Commission text box control so that any values over $20,000 are displayed using a red boldface font. After previewing the report, Frank sends it to the printer. He then closes any open windows in the application work area, including the ACC780 Database window, and exits Microsoft Access.

ACCESS

# NOTES

# NOTES

# NOTES

# MICROSOFT ACCESS 2000
## *Creating Advanced Queries*

# CHAPTER
## EIGHT

# Chapter Outline

# Learning Objectives

After reading this chapter, you will be able to:

- Set inner and outer join properties for table relationships

- View and edit a query in SQL view mode

- Enter complex expressions in select queries to perform custom searches and sorts

- Use the Find Duplicates, Find Unmatched, and Crosstab Query Wizards

- Create a parameter query for applying dynamic criteria

- Use action queries to update and delete records, make tables, and append records to tables

## Case Study

# Traveling Gadgets, Inc.

Starting out as a home-based business in 1995, Traveling Gadgets, Inc. (TGI) achieved 3 million dollars in catalog sales last year. The company now employs over 20 managerial, clerical, and warehouse staff in a small industrial park. The business of marketing travel accessories nationwide through direct mail is changing significantly with the advent of e-commerce on the World Wide Web. While TGI's marketing plan still favors advertising in travel magazines and attending consumer trade shows, senior management is ramping up for a full-force Web initiative. One of the first steps in their technology plan is to capture and manage customer and order processing data in a Microsoft Access database.

To help achieve their aggressive long-term goals, management has hired Erica Marsden as the company's systems and database administrator. Besides supervising a technical support person and Web developer, Erica is responsible for maintaining the company's local area network and existing Access database. Fortunately, Erica has been given full license to evaluate, modify, and update the database as she deems necessary.

In this chapter, you and Erica explore the use of queries to maintain a database. In addition to establishing joins, designing select queries, and using query wizards, you create special-purpose queries for analyzing data and customizing results. You also learn how to create an archiving system using a sequence of action queries.

# 8.1 Relating Tables and Setting Joins

Before delving into advanced queries, you need a firm grasp on how to establish relationships and set join properties between tables. Previously, in Chapter 5, you learned that a key principle of relational database design is *normalization*, the process of organizing a database in order to eliminate data redundancy. Redundant data wastes disk space, slows data retrieval, and creates maintenance problems. To normalize a database, split larger tables containing redundant data into smaller tables and then link the tables together using common key fields. Normalizing your data improves efficiency and ensures that each subject's record is stored, updated, and maintained in a single location only. Queries are the primary mechanism by which you can rejoin tables for use in forms and reports.

This module reviews the process of identifying foreign key fields and establishing table relationships. You then study the various types of relational joins and practice setting join properties in both the Relationship and query Design windows. Lastly, you use the special SQL view mode to examine the underlying language of a query and to create a new query using programming statements.

## 8.1.1 Creating Table Relationships

**FEATURE**

Relationships are the glue for connecting tables in a relational database application. As you may remember, there are three primary types of relationships—*one-to-one, one-to-many,* and *many-to-many.* In a one-to-one relationship, each record in table A has only one related record in table B, and vice versa. A one-to-many relationship occurs when a record in parent table A is related to one or more records in child table B. A many-to-many relationship means that for each record in table A there can be many related records in table B, and vice versa. This last type of relationship is formed by creating two one-to-many relationships with a third linking table (C). Before establishing a relationship, each table must provide a primary key that uniquely identifies each record. A primary key can be comprised of a single field or multiple fields. You may then insert the primary key values from one table into the linking or foreign key fields in other tables. These common values serve to link the tables together.

Relational database design is largely concerned with the integrity of data. To this end, there are two general integrity rules of which you should be aware. First, the **entity integrity** rule states that a primary key field must contain unique values—there can be no duplicate, null, or empty values in a primary key field. Second, the *referential integrity* rule states that a database must not contain any unmatched foreign keys. This rule requires that a primary key value already exist in the parent table before you can enter it as a foreign key value in a child table. Furthermore, a parent record cannot be deleted if doing so means that orphaned records (unmatched foreign key values) will be left in the child table. Access allows you to specify whether to enforce referential integrity when you define a relationship in the Relationships window.

**METHOD**
To define a table relationship with referential integrity enforced:

1. CLICK: Relationships button (⊞) in the Database toolbar
2. CLICK: Show Table button (⊞) and select the desired tables
3. DRAG: a field from one table to the related field in another table
4. SELECT: *Enforce Referential Integrity* check box to set enforcement
5. CLICK: Create command button

To optimize the process of querying related tables in a database, index the foreign key fields using the following steps:

1. Open the desired table object in Design view.
2. CLICK: row selector button for the foreign key field
3. CLICK: *Indexed* property text box in the Field Properties pane
4. SELECT: Yes (Duplicates OK) from the drop-down list
5. Save your modifications and close the table Design window.

**PRACTICE**
You now use the table Design window to ensure the existence of indexed foreign key fields in child tables. You then use the Relationships window to establish relationships between tables.

*Setup:* Ensure that Access is loaded. If you are launching Access and the startup dialog box appears, click the Cancel command button to remove the dialog box from the application window.

**1** Open the database file named ACC811, located in the Advantage student data files folder. This database, created by a pet store manager, contains three tables: tblFee, tblPuppy, and tblTrick. The manager uses the database to keep track of puppies he hires out to perform at children's birthday parties and other events.

**2** Using the database, the manager wants to identify which puppies perform what tricks. Since several puppies may perform a particular trick and a single puppy may perform several tricks, we need to create a third linking table in order to establish a many-to-many relationship. To begin, create the required table: DOUBLE-CLICK: Create table in Design view

**3** In the table Design window, add a primary key field:
TYPE: `perfID`
PRESS: [ TAB ]
TYPE: `a` (so that "AutoNumber" appears in the *Data Type* column)
PRESS: [ TAB ] twice to move to the next field row

**4** To add the first foreign key field to the table, enter the name of the primary key field from the tblPuppy table:
TYPE: `pupID`
PRESS: [ TAB ]
Notice that the *Indexed* property in the Field Properties pane is set to "Yes (Duplicates OK)." Access has searched the database, identified a common field, and prepared for setting a one-to-many relationship.

**5** To complete the entry:
TYPE: `n` (so that "Number" appears as the Data Type)
PRESS: [ TAB ] twice to move to the next field row
(*Hint:* To facilitate relating tables, ensure that your foreign key field has the same name as the primary key field it relates to. You should also select the same data type, except where an AutoNumber primary key field is used. When this is the case, select a Number data type for the foreign key field and use a Long Integer field size.)

**6** To add the next foreign key field to the table, enter the name of the primary key field from the tblTrick table:
TYPE: `trkID`
PRESS: [ TAB ]
TYPE: `n`
PRESS: [ TAB ]
Again, ensure that the *Indexed* property displays "Yes (Duplicates OK)," as shown in Figure 8.1.

**Figure 8.1**

Creating a linking table for a many-to-many relationship

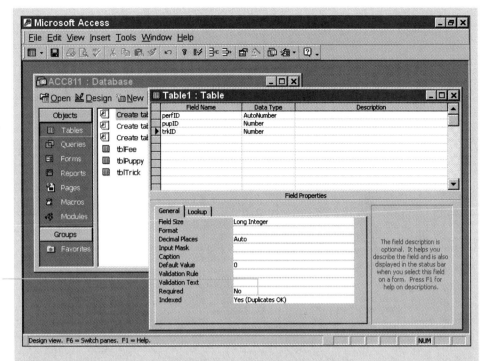

The foreign key field on the many side of a one-to-many relationship should be indexed, allowing duplicate values.

**7** To set the primary key field:
CLICK: perfID row selector button
CLICK: Primary Key button (🔑)
(*Hint:* Rather than introducing a new field (perfID) into the database, you could instead create a multiple-field primary key based upon the two foreign key fields. To do so, you need to select both of the desired row selector buttons before clicking the Primary Key button (🔑).)

**8** To save the new table object:
CLICK: Save button (🖫)
TYPE: `tblPerform`
CLICK: OK command button

**9** Close the table Design window by clicking its Close button (☒).

**10** Now let's establish the relationships between the tables. First, each puppy is assigned an hourly and daily rate that is stored separately in the tblFee table. This table needs to be related to the tblPuppy table using a one-to-one relationship. Second, the tblPuppy and tblTrick tables need to be related to the tblPerform table using a one-to-many relationship. To begin, display the Relationships window:
CLICK: Relationships button (🔗)

ACCESS

**11** To select all of the tables in the Show Table dialog box, ensure that tblFee is highlighted and then do the following:
PRESS: [SHIFT] and hold it down
CLICK: tblTrick at the bottom of the list
All of the tables should now appear highlighted. (*Note:* Remember to release the [SHIFT] key before proceeding.)

**12** To add the selected tables to the Relationships window:
CLICK: Add command button
CLICK: Close command button
Your screen should now appear similar to Figure 8.2.

**Figure 8.2**

Adding tables to the
Relationships window

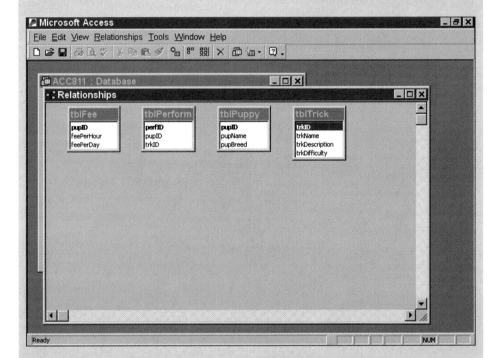

**13** To define a one-to-one relationship between tblFee and tblPuppy:
SELECT: pupID in the tblPuppy field list
DRAG: the selected field and drop it on the pupID field in the tblFee field list

**14** In the Edit Relationships window, notice that the *Relationship Type*, located near the bottom, is shown as "One-to-One."
Because both of these fields are primary keys in their respective tables, Access presupposes the desired relationship. To create the relationship:
CLICK: Create command button

**15** To define a many-to-many relationship between tblPuppy and tblTrick, you need to establish two one-to-many relationships. You will also enforce referential integrity for both of these relationships. To begin:
SELECT: pupID in the tblPuppy field list
DRAG: the selected field and drop it on the pupID field in the tblPerform field list

**16** In the Edit Relationships window:
CLICK: *Enforce Referential Integrity* check box
CLICK: Create command button
Notice that the relationship line displays symbols at its endpoints when referential integrity is enforced. In a one-to-many relationship, the "1" marks the portion of the line attached to the one side of the relationship and the infinity symbol identifies the many side.

**17** To establish the final relationship in the database:
SELECT: trkID in the tblTrick field list
DRAG: the selected field and drop it on the trkID field in the tblPerform field list
CLICK: *Enforce Referential Integrity* check box
CLICK: Create command button

**18** On your own, move the field lists to appear similar to Figure 8.3.

**Figure 8.3**

Relating tables in the Relationships window

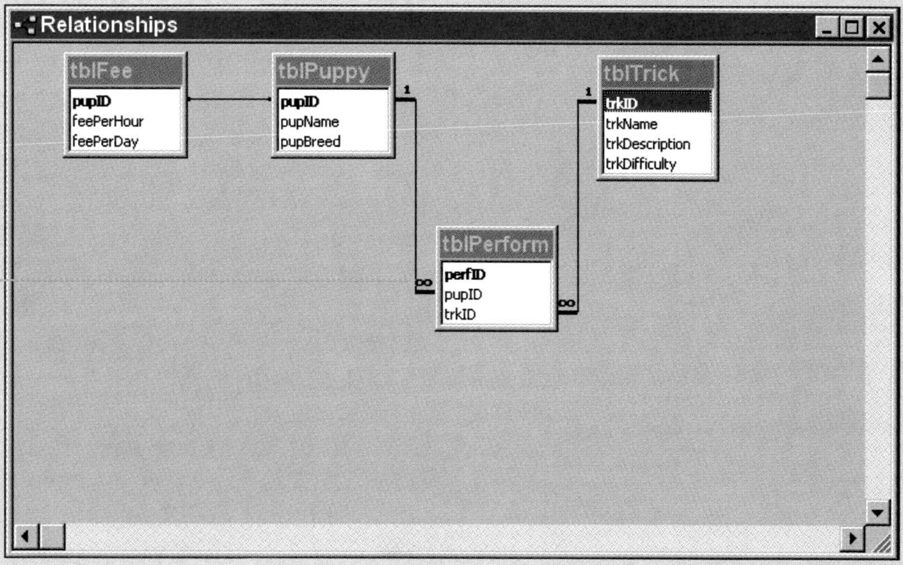

The endpoint symbols inform you that referential integrity is being enforced.

**19** Save and then close the Relationships window.

**20** On your own, open the datasheet windows for the various tables and explore their subdatasheets to view the active relationships. You may also want to enter some data into the tblPerform table in order to see the effects of enforcing referential integrity. When finished, close all open datasheets in the application window.

**21** Close the Database window.

**In Addition**
Indexing Foreign Keys

To speed up the processing of queries, ensure that the foreign key fields stored in related child tables are indexed. An index helps Access sort and find records more quickly. However, indexing every field in a table will actually worsen performance. Therefore, limit indexes to only those fields that are used for retrieving data or establishing relationships.

## 8.1.2  Understanding and Setting Join Properties

**FEATURE**

When establishing a relationship between two tables, you can also specify how Access should process a query that is based upon those tables. By default, the resulting dynaset of an Access query includes only those records whose key or common values appear in both tables. This type of joining method is known as an **inner join**. Alternatively, you can include all of the records from either table by selecting an outer join. In a **left outer join**, a query's dynaset includes all of the records from table A (the parent table), but only those records with matching key values in table B (the child table.) In a **right outer join**, a query's dynaset includes all of the records from table B (the child table), but only those records with matching key values in table A (the parent table.) Be aware that specifying a join type affects only how records are processed in a query—the table is not modified in any way. Furthermore, the left and right labels used in describing an outer join do not refer to the physical location of the field lists in the Relationships or query Design windows. The left table is typically the primary or "one" table in a one-to-many relationship, while the right table is the "many" table.

Access uses the relationship line to indicate the type of join that exists in a relationship. If no arrows appear on the line, an inner join is active. An arrow attached to either endpoint on the relationship line represents an outer join. The arrow points to the table whose values must match in order to be included in the query's dynaset.

**METHOD**
To specify join properties in the Relationships window:

1. DOUBLE-CLICK: the relationship line that you wish to edit
2. CLICK: Join Type command button
3. SELECT: the desired join properties
4. CLICK: OK command button

To specify join properties in the query Design window:

1. DOUBLE-CLICK: the relationship line that you wish to edit
2. SELECT: the desired join properties
3. CLICK: OK command button

**PRACTICE**
You now practice editing relationships and setting join properties. *Setup:* Ensure that there is no Database window displayed.

**1** Open the data file named ACC800, located in the Advantage student data files folder. This database provides several tables for storing data from a continuing education department at a small college.

**2** To view the table relationships that already exist:
CLICK: Relationships button (⊞)
Your screen should now appear similar to Figure 8.4. Notice that most of the relationships enforce referential integrity, as illustrated by the "1s" and infinity symbols at the endpoints of the relationship lines. Since there are no arrows attached to the lines, you can assume that the default inner join property is active for each relationship.

**Figure 8.4**

Displaying table relationships
in the ACC800 database

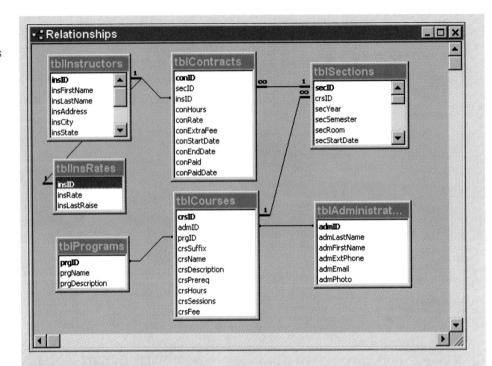

**3** You will now specify a new join property setting for the one-to-manyrelationship between tblPrograms and tblCourses. Specifically, you will choose a right outer join to ensure that all courses (the "many" side) are included in a query, regardless of whether a matching program (the "one" side) exists. To begin:
DOUBLE-CLICK: the relationship line between tblPrograms and tblCourses
The Edit Relationships window appears.

**4** To specify a join property setting:
CLICK: Join Type command button
The dialog box shown in Figure 8.5 appears.

**Figure 8.5**

Join Properties dialog box

Inner join

Left outer join

Right outer join

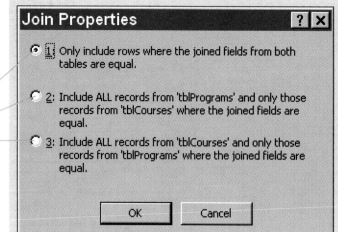

**Join Properties**                              [?] [X]

⦿ 1: Only include rows where the joined fields from both tables are equal.

○ 2: Include ALL records from 'tblPrograms' and only those records from 'tblCourses' where the joined fields are equal.

○ 3: Include ALL records from 'tblCourses' and only those records from 'tblPrograms' where the joined fields are equal.

[ OK ]    [ Cancel ]

**5** Now select the right outer join option:
SELECT: *3: Include All records from 'tblCourses'...* option button
CLICK: OK command button

**6** To complete the Edit Relationships window:
CLICK: OK command button
(*Note:* If you make a change to a relationship's join property using the Relationships window, the modification is saved with the database and will appear as the join type for all queries based on the relationship.)

**7** Close the Relationships window.

**8** To create a new query to demonstrate the right outer join:
CLICK: *Queries* button in the Objects bar
DOUBLE-CLICK: Create query in Design view
The Show Table dialog box appears.

**9** To select the two tables upon which to base the query:
DOUBLE-CLICK: tblPrograms
DOUBLE-CLICK: tblCourses
CLICK: Close command button

**10** To add all of the fields to the query Design grid:
DOUBLE-CLICK: * (asterisk) in the tblPrograms field list
DOUBLE-CLICK: * (asterisk) in the tblCourses field list
Your screen should appear similar to Figure 8.6. Notice that the join arrow on the relationship line points from tblCourses to tblPrograms.

ACCESS

**Figure 8.6**

Using a right outer
join in a query

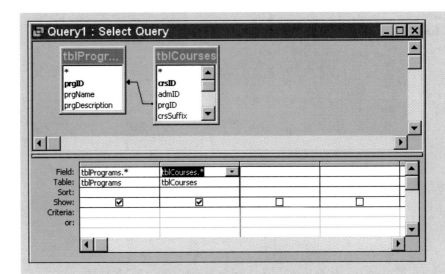

**11** To view the query results:
CLICK: View – Datasheet button (▣▾)

**12** On your own, scroll down the datasheet to search for courses
that do not have an assigned program code. When finished, save
the query as "qryCoursesInPrograms" and then close the
datasheet window.

**13** You will now modify the join property setting of an existing
query object. To begin:
SELECT: qryCoursesByAdmin
CLICK: Design button (⧉Design)
Notice that there is no arrow attached to the relationship line.
Therefore, an inner join exists between tblAdministrators and
tblCourses.

**14** To display the query's dynaset:
CLICK: View—Datasheet button (▣▾)
Notice that 186 records are displayed, with each record contain-
ing both administrator and course data.

**15** Now let's modify the join property setting:
CLICK: View—Design button (⧉▾)
DOUBLE-CLICK: the relationship line between the two tables
(*Hint:* You can also right-click the relationship line and choose
the Join Properties command.) Your screen should now appear
similar to Figure 8.7. This dialog box differs from the one
shown in Figure 8.5 in that you are able to select the tables and
fields to use in the join.

**Figure 8.7**

Displaying the Join Properties dialog box from query Design view

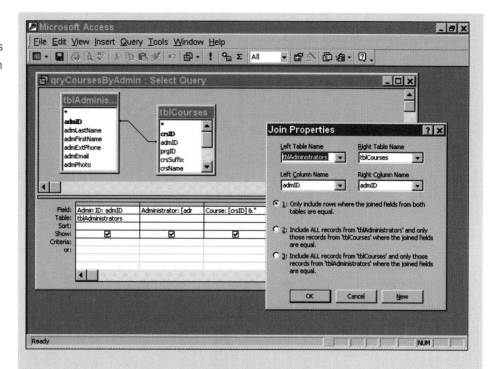

**16** To specify a right outer join property:
SELECT: *3: Include All records from 'tblCourses'...* option button
CLICK: OK command button
(*Note:* The join properties that you specify in query Design view are saved with and limited to the query. The settings do not become part of the database nor are they represented in the Relationships window.)

**17** To display the modified query's dynaset:
CLICK: View—Datasheet button (■▾)
Notice that there are now 198 records displayed in the datasheet. (*Hint:* When no matching record is found in the related table, Access returns a special "null value" in the appropriate field column.)

**18** Save the query and then close the datasheet window.

**In Addition**
Using Naming
Conventions

You may have noticed that the tables and queries in the ACC800 database follow a standard naming format or convention. A **naming convention** is the set of rules that you adhere to when assigning names to your database objects. For the remaining chapters in this book, we use prefixes for table *(tbl)*, query *(qry)*, form *(frm)*, report *(rpt)*, macro *(mcr)*, module *(mod or bas)*, and data access page *(pgs)* objects. Prefixes are also used in naming fields, controls, and variables. Following a naming convention ensures consistency within a database, reduces errors by clarifying the functionality of each object, and makes your programming code much easier to read for other developers.

## 8.1.3  Displaying a Query in SQL View Mode

**FEATURE**
Structured Query Language (SQL), commonly pronounced "sequel," is the programming language that Access uses internally to process queries. When you build a query in query Design view, Access generates the SQL code silently in the background. You can examine the SQL code in a text window by switching from Design view to SQL view. Using standard word processing commands and keystrokes, you can insert, edit, delete, copy, and paste the code that appears. You can even write a query from scratch by typing SQL statements directly into the window. When you switch back to query Design view, the Table pane and Design grid are updated to reflect the commands that you've entered in SQL view.

The basic SQL syntax for retrieving and displaying records is shown below. Each SQL keyword, shown in uppercase, is described further in Table 8.1. Notice that the command spans across multiple lines to enhance its readability. Fortunately, Access knows to treat the separate lines as a single programming statement.

*Syntax*                          *Example*

```
SELECT fields              SELECT crsName, crsHours
FROM tables                FROM tblCourses
WHERE criteria             WHERE crsFee > 500
ORDER BY fields            ORDER BY crsName
```

**Table 8.1**

SQL Keywords

| Keyword | Purpose |
| --- | --- |
| SELECT | Specifies the fields or columns that you want to retrieve for display |
| FROM | Specifies the tables that contain the fields selected for display; defines the join that exists between tables |
| WHERE | Limits the records or rows returned for display using a criteria expression |
| ORDER BY | Sorts the resulting records into ascending (ASC) or descending (DESC) order |

**METHOD**
To display SQL view mode:

1. Display a query in Design view.
2. CHOOSE: View, SQL View, or
   CLICK: View—SQL button (sql)

**PRACTICE**
Using SQL view mode, you examine an existing query object and then program a new query from scratch.

*Setup:* Ensure that you've completed the previous lesson and that the ACC800 database is displayed with the Queries button active.

**1** In order to view a query's SQL programming statements, you must first display the object in query Design view. Do the following:
SELECT: qryCoursesByAdmin
CLICK: Design button (Design)

**2** To view the underlying code:
CHOOSE: View, SQL View
A text window replaces the Design window as the active display.

**3** To remove the text highlighting in the window:
CLICK: anywhere below the selected text
Your screen should now appear similar to Figure 8.8. Notice the words "RIGHT JOIN" in the last line of the screen graphic. You specified this join property setting in the last lesson.

**Figure 8.8**

Displaying a query in
SQL view mode

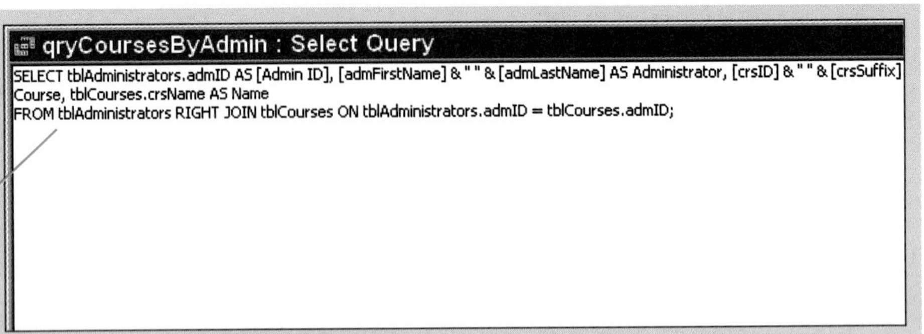

SQL programming state-
ments generated by Access

```
qryCoursesByAdmin : Select Query
SELECT tblAdministrators.admID AS [Admin ID], [admFirstName] & " " & [admLastName] AS Administrator, [crsID] & " " & [crsSuffix]
Course, tblCourses.crsName AS Name
FROM tblAdministrators RIGHT JOIN tblCourses ON tblAdministrators.admID = tblCourses.admID;
```

**4** Although very powerful, the SQL view is often confusing for new users. To return to Design view:
CHOOSE: View, Design View
(*Hint:* You can also click the View—Design button (⬛▾) on the toolbar.)

**5** Close the query Design window.

**6** Let's program a simple query from scratch using SQL statements:
CLICK: New button (⬛New)

**7** In the New Query dialog box:
SELECT: Design View
CLICK: OK command button

**8** When the Show Table dialog box appears:
CLICK: Close command button
An empty query Design window should now appear.

**9** To write a new query in SQL view:
CHOOSE: View, SQL View

**10** Leave the existing text highlighted and then type the following statements:
TYPE: SELECT *
PRESS: ENTER
TYPE: FROM tblAdministrators
PRESS: ENTER
TYPE: ORDER BY admFirstName
(*Note:* In a SELECT statement, use an asterisk (*) in place of a comma-separated field list to retrieve all of the fields for display.)

**11** To view the results:
CLICK: View—Datasheets button (⬛▾)
Notice that all of the fields are displayed and that the records are sorted into ascending order by the admFirstName column.

**12** To edit the query:
CLICK: View—SQL View button (⟦sql·⟧)
(*Hint:* You must first click the down arrow attached to the
View—Design button (⟦⚡·⟧) on the toolbar.)

**13** Let's limit the display of field columns:
SELECT: "*" so that it appears highlighted
TYPE: `admFirstName AS First, admLastName AS Last,`
`admEmail AS EMail`
The new field list replaces the asterisk. (*Note:* The AS keyword
lets you rename the column heading for display in the query's
dynaset.)

**14** To sort the records by descending surname:
DOUBLE-CLICK: admFirstName in the last line
TYPE: `admLastName DESC`
Your screen should now appear similar to Figure 8.9.

**Figure 8.9**

Writing a query in
SQL view mode

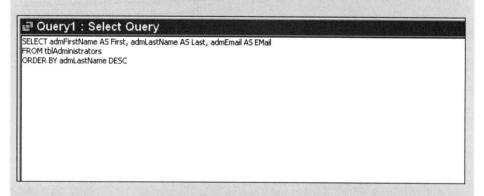

**15** To view the results:
CLICK: View—Datasheets button (⟦▦·⟧)
Notice that there are only three field columns displayed and that
the results are sorted into descending order by last name.

**16** To view the query Design window:
CLICK: View—Design button (⟦⚡·⟧)
When you write SQL statements, Access updates the query
Design window automatically. Therefore, you can easily switch
back and forth between the SQL and Design view modes to make
modifications.

**17** Save the query as "qryMySQLCode" and then close the query
Design window.

**18** Keep the ACC800 Database window open for use in the next
module.

**In Addition**
Creating SQL-Specific
Queries

All of the queries designed in the query Design window are comprised of SQL statements that execute in the background. However, there are certain SQL-specific queries (union, pass-through, and data-definition) that may only be created using the SQL programming language. You can also use SQL statements to define a subquery criterion statement in a standard select query. A *subquery* results when a SELECT statement is nested inside another SELECT statement.

**8.1 Self Check**   What is the difference between an inner join and an outer join?

# 8.2  Working with Select Queries

The select query is an Access developer's best friend. Knowing how to find and retrieve information is critical to the success of any database application. For reasons of security and efficiency, forms and reports are commonly based on select queries rather than their underlying tables. In most cases, you can work with a query's dynaset in the same way that you work with a table. However, unlike a table object, a query's dynaset doesn't exist until you run the query. In this module, you learn some tips and tricks for creating and modifying select queries.

## 8.2.1  Displaying the Highest or Lowest Values

**FEATURE**
A select query can retrieve and sort the highest or lowest values from a table. To display the top values from a query, open the query in Design view and then click the Top Values button ([All ▼]) on the toolbar. You can then specify a number of rows (for example, the top 10 values) or a percentage (for example, the top five percent). By entering or selecting a value from the toolbar, you are in effect setting the Top Values property for the query.

**METHOD**
1.  Display the select query in Design view.
2.  For the desired field, choose an ascending sort order to display the lowest values or a descending order to display the highest values.
3.  SELECT: a value or percentage from the Top Values button ([All ▼])

**PRACTICE**

You will now display the five most expensive courses offered by the continuing education department.

*Setup:* Ensure that the ACC800 Database window is displayed and that the *Queries* button is selected in the Objects bar.

**1** To create a new select query:
DOUBLE-CLICK: Create query in Design view
The Show Table dialog box appears.

**2** To add a table to the Table pane of the query Design window:
DOUBLE-CLICK: tblCourses
CLICK: Close command button

**3** From the tblCourses field list:
DRAG: crsName field to the first column in the Design grid
DRAG: crsFee field to the second column in the Design grid

**4** For Access to accurately apply the Top Values property setting, you must sort the query only by the field that you want evaluated. Therefore, to list the five most expensive courses:
CLICK: in the *Sort* text box in the crsFee column
CLICK: down arrow attached to the *Sort* text box
SELECT: Descending from the drop-down list box
(*Hint:* You must select a descending sort order so that the most expensive courses appear at the top of the list.)

**5** Rather than including all of the records in the dynaset:
CLICK: down arrow attached to the Top Values button ([All ▾])
SELECT: 5 from the drop-down list

**6** To run the query:
CLICK: Run button ([!])
(*Note:* You can also click the View—Datasheet button ([▥▾]).) After adjusting the column widths, your screen should appear similar to Figure 8.10.

ACCESS

**Figure 8.10**

Running a Top Values
select query

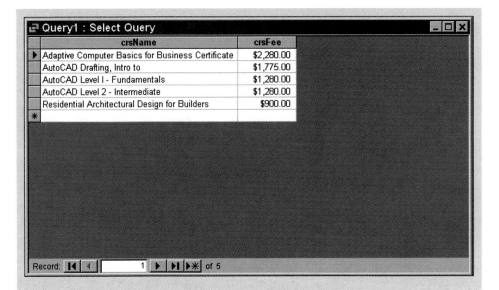

**7** Let's view the property settings for the query:
CLICK: View—Design button (⬚▾)
DOUBLE-CLICK: a blank portion of the Table pane area
The Query Properties dialog box appears. (*Hint:* You can also right-click in the Table pane area and then choose the Properties command.)

**8** To set the Top Values property to display the top ten values:
DOUBLE-CLICK: in the Top Values property text box to select the existing value
TYPE: **10**
PRESS: **DELETE** if another "0" appears due to AutoComplete

**9** Close the Query Properties dialog box by clicking its Close button (⊠). Notice that the Top Values button ([All ▾]) on the toolbar now displays "10."

**10** Run the query to view the top 10 values. Then save the query as "qryTopValues" and close the datasheet window.

## 8.2.2 Testing for Null Values and Zero-Length Strings

**FEATURE**

Let's explain a situation in which nothing may be something and something may be nothing. Although somewhat confusing, null values and zero length strings are important concepts to learn, especially when they are used in queries and for data validation. A *null value* is a value that may exist but is currently unknown. In other words, you just haven't gotten around to inputting the necessary information, such as customer's phone number or address. A **zero length string,** on the other hand, is a value that is known not to exist and is therefore stored as "" in a field. Depending on a field's property settings, the data that is stored in a field is different when you press (ENTER), hit the Spacebar, or type "". For example, if the AllowZeroLength field property is set to Yes, typing "" without a space is a valid entry regardless of the Required property setting. If the AllowZeroLength property is set to no, typing "" is always unacceptable.

**METHOD**

- To display records containing or excluding null values, use the `Null`, `Is Null`, and `Is Not Null` operators in the *Criteria* row of the query Design grid.
- To display records containing a zero-length string, type "" in the Criteria row of the query Design grid. Ensure that there are no spaces between the quotation marks.

**PRACTICE**

You now create a query that tests for the existence of null values in a particular field.

*Setup:* Ensure that the ACC800 Database window is displayed and that the *Queries* button is selected in the Objects bar.

**1** To create a new select query:
DOUBLE-CLICK: Create query in Design view
DOUBLE-CLICK: tblCourses in the Show Table dialog box
CLICK: Close command button

**2** In the tblCourses field list:
DOUBLE-CLICK: crsID
DOUBLE-CLICK: crsName
DOUBLE-CLICK: admID

ACCESS

**3** To display the courses that lack an assigned administrator:
CLICK: in the *Criteria* text box in the admID column
TYPE: `Is Null`
Your screen should now appear similar to Figure 8.11.

**Figure 8.11**

Testing for null values

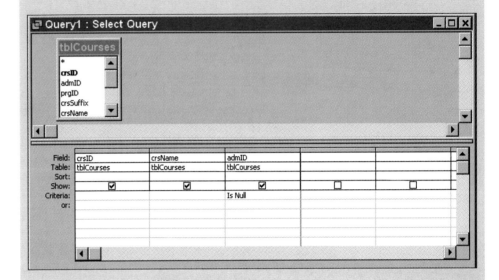

**4** To run the query:
CLICK: Run button (⊡)
The datasheet window displays 12 records. As you can see, this type of query is excellent for finding unfinished entries in a table.

**5** Save the query as "qryIsNull" and then close the datasheet window.

| **In Addition** | What if you need to match zero-length strings and null values in a join? As |
|---|---|
| Using the Nz( ) | mentioned above, these values are not equal. However, you can use the Nz |
| Function | function to convert a null value into a zero-length string, a zero (0), or into |
| | another value that you specify. You can also use the function in the query |
| | Design grid to replace null values with another value. For example, entering |
| | `Nz([admID],0)` into the *Field* row converts null values appearing in the |
| | admID field into 0s (zeros). This function is also useful for ensuring that no |
| | null values appear in reports based on the query. |

## 8.2.3 Entering Complex Expressions

**FEATURE**
To enter complex criteria or perform calculations in a query, you create an expression by combining symbols, values, identifiers, and operators. *Symbols* include quotation marks, colons, and asterisks. *Values* can be literal values ("NY"), constants (True/False and Null), or functions that return values. *Identifiers*, which are typically surrounded by square brackets, refer to the values stored in fields. When dealing with multiple tables in a query, you may need to qualify an identifier by preceding it with a table name and exclamation mark (!, also called the bang operator). *Operators* are the symbols and words that you use to define an expression's logic and to perform an action, such as a calculation or comparison. To build more complex expressions, you may prefer to use the Expression Builder.

**METHOD**
The following operators are commonly used:

- **BETWEEN...And** specifies a range of values
- **IN** specifies a set of acceptable values
- **LIKE** specifies a search pattern for values
- **NOT** reverses or negates the subsequent expression

The following date functions are commonly used:

- **DATE()** returns the current date
- **DATEADD(***interval,number,date***)** adds a value to a date
- **DATEPART(***interval,date***)** extracts a portion of a date
- **MONTH(***date***)** returns the month number
- **YEAR(***date***)** returns the year number

**PRACTICE**
In this lesson, you practice entering complex expressions and date criteria in the query Design window.

*Setup:* Ensure that the ACC800 Database window is displayed and that the *Queries* button is selected in the Objects bar.

**1**

To create a new select query:
DOUBLE-CLICK: Create query in Design view
DOUBLE-CLICK: tblSections in the Show Table dialog box
CLICK: Close command button

ACCESS

**2** In the tblSections field list:
DOUBLE-CLICK: secID
DOUBLE-CLICK: secRoom
DOUBLE-CLICK: secStartDate

**3** Let's start by creating a query to display only those sections in rooms V12 and V14. To begin:
CLICK: in the *Criteria* row in the secRoom column
TYPE: In("V12","V14")
(*Hint:* You can also use the *Or* row to specify a logical condition.)

**4** To run the query:
CLICK: Run button ( [!] )
The datasheet displays 99 records.

**5** To further narrow the list of sections, you will now display only those records with a secStartDate that falls between two dates. To begin:
CLICK: View—Design button ( [▨▾] )
CLICK: in the *Criteria* row in the secStartDate column

**6** Let's open the Zoom window to type this criteria expression:
PRESS: [SHIFT] + [F2] to open the Zoom window
TYPE: Between #1/31/2000# And Date()
Your screen should now appear similar to Figure 8.12.

**Figure 8.12**

Using the Zoom window to enter a criteria expression

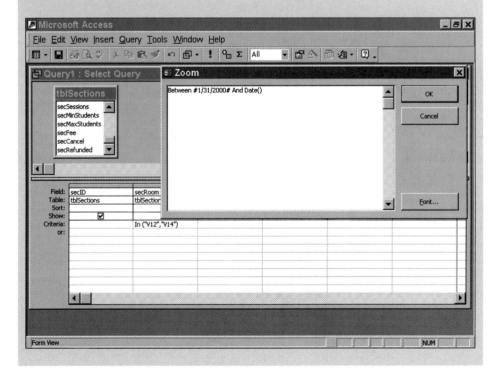

**7** To run the query:
CLICK: OK command button to close the Zoom window
CLICK: Run button (⚡)
Depending on the date you are performing this exercise, up to 34 records will be displayed in the dynaset.

**8** To edit the date criteria:
CLICK: View—Design button (📊▾)
PRESS: SHIFT + F2

**9** With the criteria expression selected:
TYPE: `Between Date() and DateAdd("m",6,Date())`
This criteria returns all records that have a secStartDate between the current date and six months in the future. Notice that the interval argument "m" stands for month.

**10** To run the query:
CLICK: OK command button to close the Zoom window
CLICK: Run button (⚡)
Again, your answer will depend on the current date's value.

**11** On your own, edit the query by placing the NOT operator before BETWEEN in the criteria expression. Then, run the query to display all records other than those containing a secStartDate between the current date and six months in the future.

**12** Save the query as "qryDateExp" and then close the datasheet window.

## 8.2.4 Presenting Data Using a Custom Sort Order

**FEATURE**
There may be times when you want to sort a query's dynaset by a custom or logical sort order, rather than alphabetically or numerically. For example, in a Priority field, you may want to view the "Hot" items first, "Medium" items next, and "Cold" items last. In order to sort a table using these items, you must assign a numeric value to each possible entry (for example, "Hot"=1, "Medium"=2, and "Cold"=3). For a short list of items, use the Switch and IIF functions to assign numeric values. You can also use these functions in calculated controls on forms or reports. For longer lists, insert a new sort field into your table structure or create a related table that contains the desired order.

**METHOD**
- To assign numeric values to specific items and null values to all others, use the Switch function:
  SWITCH(*expr-1, value-1, …expr-n, value-n*)
- To assign numeric values to specific items and another value to all others, use a series of nested IIF functions:
  IIF(*expression, true, false*)

**PRACTICE**
You now practice sorting an address table using a custom sort order.

*Setup:* Ensure that the ACC800 Database window is displayed and that the *Queries* button is selected in the Objects bar.

**1** To create a new select query:
DOUBLE-CLICK: Create query in Design view
DOUBLE-CLICK: tblInstructors in the Show Table dialog box
CLICK: Close command button

**2** In the tblInstructors field list:
DOUBLE-CLICK: insCity
DOUBLE-CLICK: insLastName
DOUBLE-CLICK: insFirstName

**3** You must now add a second insCity field to the far-left column of the Design grid. Do the following:
CLICK: insCity in the tblInstructors field list
DRAG: the insCity field to the *Field* text box in the first column
When you release the mouse button, the field is inserted and the existing fields are pushed one column to the right. There should now be two insCity fields in the Design grid area. You will use the leftmost insCity field to prepare the custom sort order.

**4** To open the Zoom window:
PRESS: (SHIFT) + (F2)

**5** With "insCity" selected in the Zoom window:
TYPE: Switch([insCity]="Seattle",1, [insCity]="Bellevue",2,[insCity]="Lynnwood",3, [insCity]="Edmonds",4,[insCity]="Bothell",5)
Your screen should appear similar to Figure 8.13. (*Note:* You can now appreciate why this method is used only when the custom sort list has relatively few entries!)

**Figure 8.13**

Using an expression to create a custom sort order

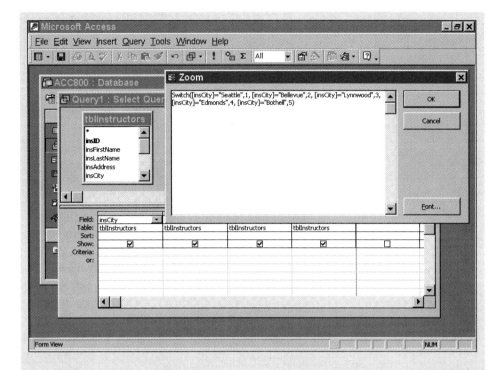

**6** To display the results of this expression:
CLICK: OK command button
CLICK: Run button (⚡)
Notice that numbers now appear in place of the city names in the leftmost column.

**7** To return to query Design view:
CLICK: View—Design button (📈▾)

**8** Now sort the list based on the expression and then hide the column from displaying in the dynaset:
CLICK: in the *Sort* text box in the leftmost "Expr1" column
CLICK: down arrow attached to the *Sort* text box
SELECT: Ascending from the drop-down list box
CLICK: *Show* check box in the leftmost "Expr1" column so that no "✔" appears

**9** To run the query:
CLICK: Run button (⚡)
Notice that the datasheet is sorted into the custom order that you entered into the Zoom window. (*Note:* You do not need to display a field in the Design grid in order to use the column for sorting.)

**10** Save the query as "qryCustomSort" and then close the datasheet window.

## 8.2.5  Setting Field and Query Properties

**FEATURE**

Access enables you to set properties to change the appearance and behavior of various types of objects. For the most part, fields appearing in the query Design grid inherit their properties from their table structure. If desired, you can override several of these property settings for use strictly in the query. For example, you can change the formatting of dates, edit a field's caption, or specify the number of decimal places to display in a query's dynaset. Be aware that these property settings are active only for the query's dynaset; the underlying table structure remains unaffected.

In addition to customizing fields, you can set properties that affect how a query processes records. For example, the Top Values property returns a specified number or percentage of matching records in a dynaset. You can also use query properties to display only the unique values or records in a table. There are also properties for modifying table relationships and for granting access to secure data.

**METHOD**

To display the property settings for a field:

1.  RIGHT-CLICK: a field column in the Design grid
2.  CHOOSE: Properties

To display the property settings for a query:

1.  RIGHT-CLICK: a blank area in the Table pane
2.  CHOOSE: Properties

**PRACTICE**
In this lesson, you use the Field and Query Properties dialog boxes to change the appearance and behavior of a query.

*Setup:* Ensure that the ACC800 Database window is displayed and that the *Queries* button is selected in the Objects bar.

**1** To create a new query:
DOUBLE-CLICK: Create query in Design view
DOUBLE-CLICK: tblSections in the Show Table dialog box
CLICK: Close command button

**2** In the tblSections field list:
DOUBLE-CLICK: secID
DOUBLE-CLICK: secRoom
DOUBLE-CLICK: secStartDate
DOUBLE-CLICK: secFee

**3** CLICK: Run button (▣) to run the query
Make special note of the display formats for the secStartDate and secFee columns.

**4** Now let's modify the field properties in the query:
CLICK: View—Design button (▣▾)
RIGHT-CLICK: in the secStartDate field column
CHOOSE: Properties
The Field Properties dialog box appears.

**5** To enter a description that will appear in the Status bar:
TYPE: **First Day of Class** in the *Description* text box
PRESS: [TAB]

**6** To change the display format of the date:
CLICK: down arrow attached to the *Format* text box
SELECT: Medium Date (19-Jun-94)
PRESS: [TAB]

**7** To change the input format:
CLICK: Build button (▣) attached to the *Input Mask* text box
The Input Mask Wizard appears.

**8** To complete the Input Mask Wizard:
SELECT: Medium Date near the bottom of the list
CLICK: [Finish]
PRESS: [TAB]

ACCESS

**9** To specify a new column heading:
TYPE: `Start Date` in the *Caption* text box
Your screen should now appear similar to Figure 8.14.

**Figure 8.14**

Field Properties dialog box

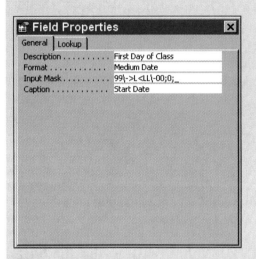

**10** Close the Field Properties dialog box by clicking its Close button ([×]).

**11** CLICK: Run button ([!]) to run the query
CLICK: in the Start Date column
The property settings for the column heading, date format, and Status bar are now displayed in the datasheet window. (*Hint:* In the *Field* text box of the query Design grid, you can also type `Month: Format([secStartDate],"dd-mmm-yy")` to format the display of date values in the dynaset.)

**12** Save the query as "qryFormatDate" and then close the datasheet window.

**13** Now let's assume that you've been asked to print a list of all the rooms used by the Continuing Education department. To begin:
DOUBLE-CLICK: Create query in Design view
DOUBLE-CLICK: tblSections in the Show Table dialog box
CLICK: Close command button

**14** In the tblSections field list:
DOUBLE-CLICK: secRoom

**15** CLICK: Run button ([!]) to run the query
A datasheet window displays over 250 records, with most containing duplicate values.

**16** Although this query correctly displays all the room numbers, it is not a very useful listing. Fortunately, Access lets you adjust the behavior of a query using a property setting. To illustrate:
CLICK: View—Design button (⊠▾)
RIGHT-CLICK: a blank area in the Table pane
CHOOSE: Properties
Your screen should now appear similar to Figure 8.15. (*Note:* The window has been sized so that all the property text boxes are visible.)

**Figure 8.15**

Query Properties dialog box

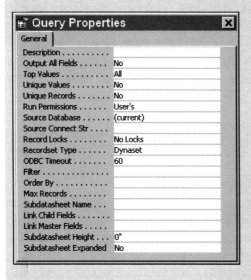

**17** To display only the unique values contained in the secRoom field:
CLICK: in the *Unique Values* property text box
CLICK: down arrow attached to the text box
SELECT: Yes from the drop-down list

**18** Close the Query Properties dialog box by clicking its Close button (⊠).

**19** To run the modified query:
CLICK: Run button (⏺)
Notice that only 22 records appear in the datasheet window.

**20** Save the query as "qryUniqueRooms" and then close the datasheet window. Keep the ACC800 Database window open for use in the next module.

ACCESS

# 8.3    Creating Special-Purpose Queries

Access provides special-purpose queries and wizards to help you answer common questions about your data. Included among these tools are the Find Duplicates, Find Unmatched, and Crosstab query wizards. You can also create dynamic parameter queries that prompt the user for criteria at **run time.** Parameter queries are especially useful in retrieving data for reports. In this module, you learn to create and apply these four types of special-purpose queries.

## 8.3.1    Finding Duplicate Records And Values

**FEATURE**
The **Find Duplicates Query Wizard** allows you to find duplicate records or field values in a table. This wizard is especially useful for checking results after importing data from another table or database. For example, you can check to see whether you have duplicate customer entries listed under different addresses. You can also use the wizard to filter and group values for display, such as all customers who live in a particular city.

**METHOD**
1.   CLICK: *Queries* button in the Objects bar
2.   CLICK: New button (New) on the Database window toolbar
3.   DOUBLE-CLICK: Find Duplicates Query Wizard

**PRACTICE**
You now use the Find Duplicates Query Wizard to locate duplicate values in the ACC800 database.

*Setup:* Ensure that the ACC800 Database window is displayed and that the *Queries* button is selected in the Objects bar.

Let's use the Find Duplicates Query Wizard to locate all of the instructors who have been awarded more than one teaching contract. Ensure that the *Queries* button is selected and then do the following:
CLICK: New button (New) on the Database window toolbar
DOUBLE-CLICK: Find Duplicates Query Wizard
The dialog box in Figure 8.16 appears.

**Figure 8.16**

Find Duplicates Query
Wizard dialog box

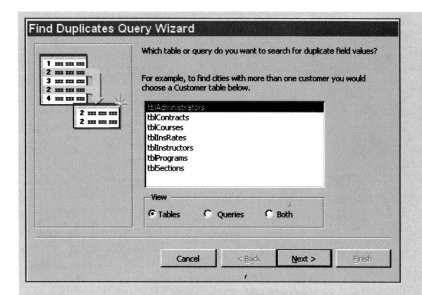

**2** In the first dialog box of the wizard, you select the desired table or query to search for duplicate records or field values:
SELECT: tblContracts
CLICK: Next >

**3** You now specify the field(s) to search for duplicate values:
SELECT: insID in the *Available fields* list box
CLICK: Include button ( > )
CLICK: Next >

**4** In the third dialog box, you select any other fields that you want displayed in the dynaset:
SELECT: conID
CLICK: Include button ( > )
SELECT: secID
CLICK: Include button ( > )
SELECT: conStartDate
CLICK: Include button ( > )
CLICK: Next >

**5** In the last dialog box, name the query and then view the results:
TYPE: qryFindDuplicateInstructors
SELECT: *View the results* option button
CLICK: Finish
A datasheet window appears listing all of the instructors who have more than one contract.

**6** CLICK: View—Design button ( ) to view the Design window

**7** To better view the criteria expression generated by the wizard:
CLICK: in the *Criteria* row of the insID column
PRESS: (SHIFT) + (F2)
Notice that the expression uses both the IN operator and a SQL SELECT statement to retrieve the desired information.

**8** To close the Zoom window:
CLICK: OK command button

**9** Save the query and then close the query Design window.

## 8.3.2  Finding Unmatched Records

**FEATURE**
The **Find Unmatched Query Wizard** displays the records from one table that do not have related records in another table. You can use this wizard to determine which customers do not have sales orders, which puppies do not perform tricks, and which instructors do not have contracts. In effect, you specify the "one" side in a relationship and then let the wizard search the "many" side for related child records.

**METHOD**
1.  CLICK: *Queries* button in the Objects bar
2.  CLICK: New button ([New]) on the Database window toolbar
3.  DOUBLE-CLICK: Find Unmatched Query Wizard

**PRACTICE**
You now use the Find Unmatched Query Wizard to locate unmatched primary key values in the foreign key field of a child table.

*Setup:* Ensure that the ACC800 Database window is displayed and that the *Queries* button is selected in the Objects bar.

**1** Let's use the Find Unmatched Query Wizard to locate all of the programs that do not have courses in the database. Ensure that the *Queries* button is selected and then do the following:
CLICK: New button ([New]) on the Database window toolbar
DOUBLE-CLICK: Find Unmatched Query Wizard
The query wizard's dialog box appears.

**2** In the first dialog box of the wizard, you select the table that contains the primary key values for which you want to search:
SELECT: tblPrograms
CLICK: [Next >]

**3** In the second dialog box, you select the child table containing the related records:
SELECT: tblCourses
CLICK: Next>
The dialog box shown in Figure 8.17 appears.

**Figure 8.17**

Find Unmatched Query
Wizard dialog box

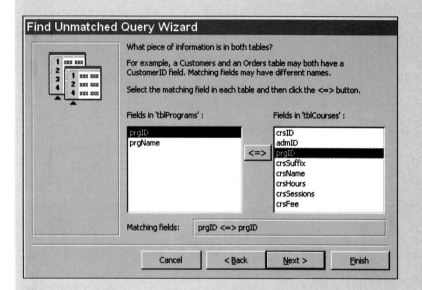

**4** In the third dialog box, you confirm that prgID is the joining field :
CLICK: Next>

**5** You now specify the field(s) to display in the query's dynaset:
CLICK: Include All button (>>)
CLICK: Next>

**6** In the last dialog box, name the query and then view the results:
TYPE: qryFindUnmatchedPrograms
SELECT: *View the results* option button
CLICK: Finish
A datasheet window appears listing the two programs for which there are no courses.

**7** CLICK: View—Design button (□) to view the Design window
Notice the use of a left outer join and the IS NULL operator to test for the existence of prgID in tblCourses.

**8** Save the query and then close the query Design window.

ACCESS

## 8.3.3  Creating a Crosstab Query

**FEATURE**
A crosstab query is a special-purpose query that enables you to display a static table of summarized numerical values. Like a summary or totals query, a crosstab query performs an aggregate calculation. Specifically, the value cells in a crosstab's dynaset are calculated using one of the following total functions: Avg, Count, First, Last, Max, Min, StDev, Sum, or Var. Once executed, you can print a crosstab query's datasheet or export the results to an electronic spreadsheet program.

**METHOD**
1. CLICK: *Queries* button in the Objects bar
2. CLICK: New button ([New]) on the Database window toolbar
3. DOUBLE-CLICK: Crosstab Query Wizard

**PRACTICE**
In this lesson, you use the **Crosstab Query Wizard** to calculate the average student fee generated by each room.

*Setup:* Ensure that the ACC800 Database window is displayed and that the *Queries* button is selected in the Objects bar.

1. You will now use the Crosstab Query Wizard to summarize the data stored in the tblSections table. Ensure that the *Queries* button is selected and then do the following:
CLICK: New button ([New]) on the Database window toolbar
DOUBLE-CLICK: Crosstab Query Wizard
The query wizard's dialog box appears.

2. In the first dialog box, you select the table on which to base the query:
SELECT: tblSections
CLICK: [Next>]
(*Hint:* In order to get all of the desired fields together in one place, you may need to create a temporary query before launching the Crosstab Query Wizard. You can then use this new query as the basis for creating the crosstab query.)

**3** In the second dialog box, you specify the field(s) to use in grouping the data into row headings. Do the following:
SELECT: secYear
CLICK: Include button ( > )
SELECT: secRoom
CLICK: Include button ( > )
CLICK: Next >
(*Note:* The grouping order runs from left to right. Therefore, if you specify more than one row, ensure that the leftmost row is the one that you want to serve as the primary grouping.)

**4** In the third dialog box, you select the field to use in preparing column headings for the crosstab dynaset.
SELECT: secStartDate
CLICK: Next >

**5** Because the previous selection was a date field, you must now specify the interval to use for grouping the information:
SELECT: Quarter
CLICK: Next >

**6** You are now asked to specify the field and function for calculating the data area of the crosstab dynaset. Do the following:
SELECT: secFee (near the bottom of the *Fields* list box)
SELECT: Avg in the *Functions* list box
Your screen should now appear similar to Figure 8.18. Notice that the *Sample* area in the dialog box shows the row and column headings, and the data area calculation.

**Figure 8.18**
Crosstab Query Wizard
dialog box

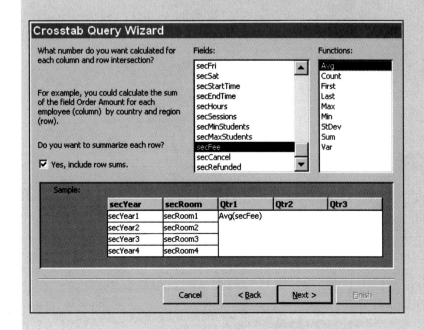

ACCESS

7. To continue to the next step in the wizard:
CLICK: Next >

8. In the last dialog box, name the query and then view the results:
TYPE: **qryCrosstabFee**
SELECT: *View the query* option button
CLICK: Finish
As shown in Figure 8.19, a datasheet window displays the average fee for each room on both a quarterly and annual basis. (*Note:* You cannot change the data appearing in the datasheet, since the results are based on aggregate values.)

**Figure 8.19**
The results of a crosstab query

qryCrosstabFee : Crosstab Query

| secYear | secRoom | Total Of secFee | Qtr 1 | Qtr 2 | Qtr 3 | Qtr 4 |
|---|---|---|---|---|---|---|
| 1999 | A115 | $472.50 | | | $472.50 | |
| 1999 | ARTS3 | $118.67 | | | $105.00 | $120.38 |
| 1999 | C301 | $230.00 | $230.00 | | | |
| 1999 | C302 | $201.67 | | | $199.00 | $202.20 |
| 1999 | D116 | $149.10 | $149.10 | | | |
| 1999 | D221 | $131.25 | | | $131.25 | $131.25 |
| 1999 | D225 | $180.17 | $237.50 | | $151.50 | |
| 1999 | D229 | $95.44 | $105.00 | | $115.00 | $91.29 |
| 1999 | D231 | $131.25 | | $131.25 | | |
| 1999 | D233 | $115.22 | $111.71 | $127.50 | | |
| 1999 | D235 | $182.50 | $199.00 | | $166.00 | |
| 1999 | D344 | $197.63 | $229.50 | $165.75 | | |
| 1999 | D345 | $206.63 | $156.75 | | $256.50 | |
| 1999 | D347 | $341.25 | | | $341.25 | |
| 1999 | D348 | $213.75 | $213.75 | | | $213.75 |
| 1999 | V12 | $170.48 | $167.50 | $179.00 | $129.00 | $196.90 |
| 1999 | V14 | $152.76 | $169.63 | $184.50 | $95.43 | $160.33 |
| 1999 | V15 | $411.08 | $356.00 | $424.33 | $632.50 | $459.17 |
| 2000 | A115 | $195.43 | $196.88 | | $235.50 | $133.88 |

Record: 1 of 36

9. On your own, scroll down the datasheet to view the results for the secYear 2000 grouping. Then open the query in Design view to review the entries made by the wizard in the Design grid.

10. Save the query and then close the query Design window.

## 8.3.4  Creating a Parameter Query

**FEATURE**
A *parameter query* is one of the most useful types of queries and is often used as the basis for printing reports. Rather than retrieving records based on a static criteria expression, a parameter query allows the user to input their own criteria at run time. To create a parameter query, you place prompts, surrounded by square brackets, in the *Criteria* row of the Design grid. These prompts are then displayed in dialog boxes to the user when the query is run. The user's entries are then substituted back into the criteria expression for processing. Although you can specify as many parameters as needed, be careful not to alienate your users by asking for too much information!

**METHOD**
1. Display the select query in Design view.
2. CLICK: in the *Criteria* row in the desired field column
3. Type the criteria expression, substituting the actual criteria values for textual prompts enclosed in square brackets.

**PRACTICE**
You will now create two separate parameter queries for requesting data from the user.

*Setup:* Ensure that the ACC800 Database window is displayed and that the *Queries* button is selected in the Objects bar.

**1** To begin, you will create a parameter query that lets the user specify a range of dates. Do the following:
DOUBLE-CLICK: Create query in Design view

**2** In the Show Table dialog box:
DOUBLE-CLICK: tblSections
DOUBLE-CLICK: tblCourses
CLICK: Close command button
The two field lists are joined by a relationship line in the Table pane.

**3** To add fields to the Design grid:
DOUBLE-CLICK: secID in the tblSections field list
DOUBLE-CLICK: crsName in the tblCourses field list
DOUBLE-CLICK: secStartDate in the tblSections field list

**4** To enter the criteria expression:
CLICK: in the *Criteria* row in the secStartDate field column
PRESS: SHIFT + F2 to open the Zoom window

**5** In the Zoom window:
TYPE: Between [Enter First Date] And
[Enter Last Date]
CLICK: OK command button
(*Note:* Make sure that the prompt text is detailed enough for the user to respond.)

**6** By default, Access saves a parameter as a text value. By changing the default data type, you can ensure that only valid dates are entered into the parameter dialog box. To do so:
CHOOSE: Query, Parameters
The Query Parameters dialog box appears.

**7** In the left column of the Query Parameters dialog box, enter the parameter prompt exactly as it appears in the Design grid (but without the brackets):
TYPE: Enter First Date
PRESS: TAB

**8** In the right column, select the appropriate data type:
CLICK: down arrow attached to the *Data Type* text box
SELECT: Date/Time from the drop-down list
PRESS: TAB

**9** To enter the second parameter:
TYPE: Enter Last Date
PRESS: TAB
CLICK: down arrow attached to the *Data Type* text box
SELECT: Date/Time from the drop-down list
(*Hint:* If you want the entered values to appear in the dynaset, type the parameter names, enclosed in brackets, in the *Field* row of an empty column.) Your screen should now appear similar to Figure 8.20.

**Figure 8.20**

Query Parameters dialog box

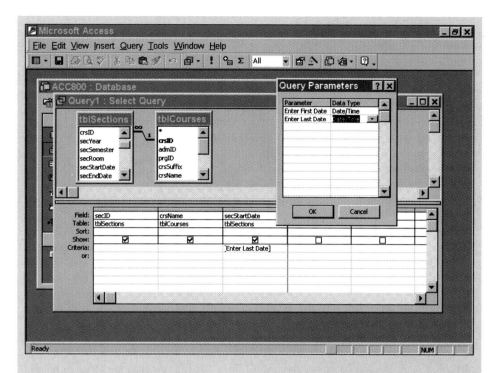

**10** To complete the dialog box and run the query:
CLICK: OK command button
CLICK: Run button ([ ! ])
An Enter Parameter Value dialog box appears as shown below.

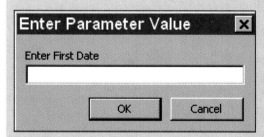

**11** To complete the prompts:
TYPE: 04/01/00
CLICK: OK command button
TYPE: 08/31/00
CLICK: OK command button
The datasheet window displays records matching the date criteria. (*Note:* Your entries are not saved in the query. Therefore, the prompts will appear each time the query is run.)

**12** Save the query as "qryParameter1" and then close the datasheet window.

**13** You will now create a parameter query that returns all of the instructors who live in a particular city. As an added feature, if you don't specify a parameter value, you want Access to return all of the instructors in all of the cities. To create this type of query:
DOUBLE-CLICK: Create query in Design view
DOUBLE-CLICK: tblInstructors in the Show Table dialog box
CLICK: Close button

**14** In the tblInstructors field list:
DOUBLE-CLICK: insFirstName
DOUBLE-CLICK: insLastName
DOUBLE-CLICK: insCity

**15** To enter the criteria expression:
CLICK: in the *Criteria* row in the insCity field column:
TYPE: [Enter a City]

**16** In order to return all of the records when there is no parameter entry, type the prompt followed by "Is Null." If you run the query and click OK without entering a parameter value, all of the records will be returned. To illustrate:
CLICK: in the *Or* row in the insCity field column
TYPE: [Enter a City] Is Null

**17** To run the parameter query for Lynnwood:
CLICK: Run button ([!])
TYPE: Lynnwood
CLICK: OK command button
All of the instructors living in Lynnwood are displayed.

**18** CLICK: View—Design button ([▦▾]) to return to Design view

**19** Now let's run the query without a city entry:
CLICK: Run button ([!])
CLICK: OK command button
All of the instructors are displayed.

**20** Save the query as "qryParameter2" and then close the datasheet window. Keep the ACC800 Database window open for use in the next module.

**8.3 Self Check**  How many calculations can you perform in the data area of a crosstab query?

# 8.4 Creating Action Queries

Unlike special-purpose select queries that retrieve and summarize records in a datasheet window, the four action queries (update, delete, make-table, and append) perform some sort of operation against a table. The **update query,** for example, enables you to perform global changes to your data quickly and easily. The **delete query** lets you delete matching records in a single sweep. The **make-table query** creates a table structure and then populates it with records, while the **append query** is used to add records to another table. Since an action query can modify your data quite drastically, you should always back up a table prior to running the query. Another safeguard is to run the query as a select query first and then convert it to an action query once you are satisfied with the results. These safeguards are important since you cannot reverse an action query once it has been run. You should also note that action queries do not return valid dynasets and, therefore, cannot be used as the basis for a form or report.

## 8.4.1 Creating an Update Query

**FEATURE**

Similar to using the Find and Replace command, an update query allows you to make changes to a specific group of records. For example, you can increase prices in an inventory table by 15 percent or change the area code for everyone living in Bellevue, WA, from 206 to 425. Since an update query is based on a select query, you can specify criteria for limiting the records to update. You can also modify the contents of more than one field in a table. Because there is no undo feature, the safest way to proceed is to create a select query and then convert it to an action query for final processing.

ACCESS

**METHOD**
To create an update query:

1.  If necessary, back up the tables to be changed.
2.  Create and test a select query in Design view.
3.  CLICK: down arrow attached to Query Type button (⊞▾)
4.  SELECT: Update Query
5.  CLICK: in the *Update To* row in the desired field column
6.  Type the update expression for the field.

This lesson also introduces the following two functions for performing a currency calculation and then rounding the result.

- ROUND(*expr1,digits*) rounds a number to the specified decimal places
- CCUR(*expr1*) converts a number to a currency data type when performing calculations that force a result of a floating-point number

**PRACTICE**
You now practice updating selected records in a table using a calculated expression.

*Setup:* Ensure that the ACC800 Database window is displayed and that the *Queries* button is selected in the Objects bar.

**1.** To begin, create a select query that retrieves all of the instructors who have not received a raise in the year 2000. Do the following:
DOUBLE-CLICK: Create query in Design view

**2.** In the Show Table dialog box:
DOUBLE-CLICK: tblInstructors
DOUBLE-CLICK: tblInsRates
CLICK: Close command button
The two field lists are joined by a one-to-one relationship line in the Table pane.

**3.** To add fields to the Design grid:
DOUBLE-CLICK: insID in the tblInsRates field list
DOUBLE-CLICK: insLastName in the tblInstructors field list
DOUBLE-CLICK: insRate in the tblInsRates field list
DOUBLE-CLICK: insLastRaise in the tblInsRates field list

**4** To limit the display of instructors to those who haven't received a raise in the year 2000:
CLICK: in the *Criteria* row in the insLastRaise column
TYPE: <#1/1/2000#

**5** CLICK: Run button (![]) to run the query
Ensure that there are no instructor records displayed with an insLastRaise date greater than 12/31/99.

**6** Now that you've confirmed that the select query retrieves the proper records, let's convert the query to an update query:
CLICK: View—Design button (![]) to return to Design view
CLICK: down arrow attached to the Query Type button (![])
CHOOSE: Update Query
Your screen should now appear similar to Figure 8.21. (*Note:* You can also choose the Query, Update Query command from the menu.)

**Figure 8.21**

Query Design grid
for an update query

Place the update expression in the *Update To* row.

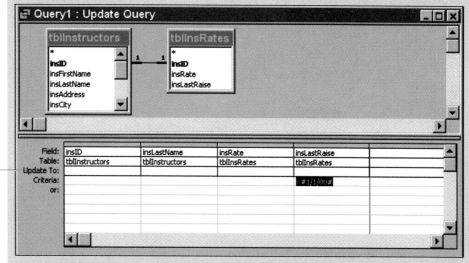

**7** To give a 15 percent raise to the selected instructors and then round the result to the nearest whole dollar value, do the following:
CLICK: in the *Update To* row in the insRate column
PRESS: (SHIFT) + (F2) to display the Zoom window
TYPE: `Round(Ccur([insRate]*1.15),0)`
CLICK: OK command button

**8** In order to enter the current date into the insLastRaise field, do the following:
CLICK: in the *Update To* row in the insLastRaise column
TYPE: Date()

**9** CLICK: Run button (⚡) to run the query
The message box shown below appears.

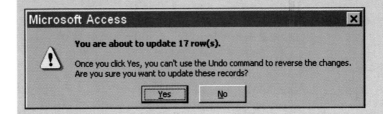

**10** To update the records:
CLICK: Yes command button
(*Hint:* Running the qryUpdInsRate query a second time would produce no changes to the table, since no instructor records would meet the condition of <#1/1/2000#. If you want to specify a date value at run time, you need to convert the criteria into a parameter, as discussed previously in this chapter.)

**11** Save the update query as "qryUpdInsRate" and then close the Design window. (*Note:* When you save the query, all of the field columns that are not used in the update process, such as insID and insLastName, are discarded.)

**12** To view the results of the update query:
CLICK: *Tables* button in the Objects bar
DOUBLE-CLICK: insRates in the list area
Notice that there are no date values in the insLastRaise column that are prior to January 1, 2000. Also, the $25 rate for insID 11 has been updated with a 15 percent increase to $28.75 and then rounded to $29.00.

**13** Close the datasheet window.

**14** CLICK: *Queries* button in the Objects bar
Notice that action queries appear with an exclamation point attached to their icon. This exclamation point indicates that an operation will be executed if you double-click the query object.

## 8.4.2 Creating a Delete Query

**FEATURE**

In the introductory chapters of this text, you deleted single records and contiguous groups of records appearing in a datasheet window. Another method for removing multiple records is the delete query. A delete query can remove records matching a criteria specification from one or more tables. Similar to creating an update query, the best way to proceed is to convert a trusted select query into a delete query. Because the delete query is a destructive operation that cannot be reversed, make a backup of the affected tables prior to running the query. You should also be aware of the effects that deleting records in one table may have on related tables, especially when referential integrity is enforced.

**METHOD**

To create a delete query:

1.  If necessary, back up the tables to be changed.
2.  Create and test a select query in Design view.
3.  CLICK: down arrow attached to Query Type button (⊞▾)
4.  SELECT: Delete Query
5.  CLICK: in the *Delete* row in a column with a criteria specification
6.  SELECT: Where

To back up a table object:

1.  RIGHT-CLICK: the desired table object
2.  CHOOSE: Copy
3.  RIGHT-CLICK: a blank area in the list
4.  CHOOSE: Paste
5.  TYPE: *a table name*
6.  SELECT: *Structure and Data* option button
7.  CLICK: OK command button

**PRACTICE**

You now practice creating and running a delete query to remove instructors who are no longer on the active list.

*Setup:* Ensure that the ACC800 Database window is displayed and that the *Queries* button is selected in the Objects bar.

**1** Let's begin by backing up the tblInstructors table object:
CLICK: *Tables* button in the Objects bar
RIGHT-CLICK: tblInstructors in the list
CHOOSE: Copy
RIGHT-CLICK: a blank area in the list
CHOOSE: Paste
The dialog box shown in Figure 8.22 appears.

**Figure 8.22**

Backing up a table object

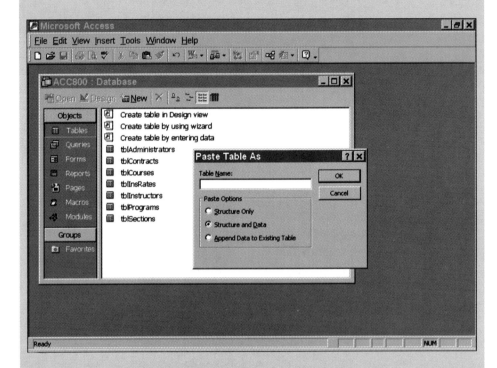

**2** In the Paste Table As dialog box:
TYPE: tblInstructors Backup
SELECT: *Structure and Data* option button
CLICK: OK command button
A new table object appears in the Database window.

**3** Because the tblInstructors and tblInsRates tables are joined in a one-to-one relationship, deleting records in tblInstructors should also have the effect of deleting records in the tblInsRates table. To ensure that this is the case:
CLICK: Relationships button (⊞)
RIGHT-CLICK: relationship line between tblInstructors and tblInsRates
CHOOSE: Edit Relationship

**4**  In the Edit Relationships window, ensure that the *Enforce Referential Integrity* check box is selected and then do the following:
SELECT: *Cascade Delete Related Records* check box
CLICK: OK command button
Notice that the one-to-many relationship with tblContracts does not enforce referential integrity.

**5**  Close the Relationships window.

**6**  To begin creating the delete query:
CLICK: *Queries* button in the Objects bar
DOUBLE-CLICK: Create query in Design view
DOUBLE-CLICK: tblInstructors in the Show Table dialog box
CLICK: Close command button

**7**  Now add fields from the tblInstructors field list to the Design grid:
DOUBLE-CLICK: insFirstName
DOUBLE-CLICK: insLastName
DOUBLE-CLICK: insActive

**8**  To display only those instructors who are not active:
CLICK: in the *Criteria* row in the insActive column
TYPE: `False`

**9**  CLICK: Run button (⊡) to run the query
Three records are displayed in the dynaset.

**10**  You will now convert the select query to a delete query:
CLICK: View—Design button (⊠-) to return to Design view
CLICK: down arrow attached to the Query Type button (⊞-)
CHOOSE: Delete Query
Your screen should now appear similar to Figure 8.23. (*Note:* You can also choose the Query, Delete Query command from the menu.)

**Figure 8.23**

Query Design grid
for a delete query

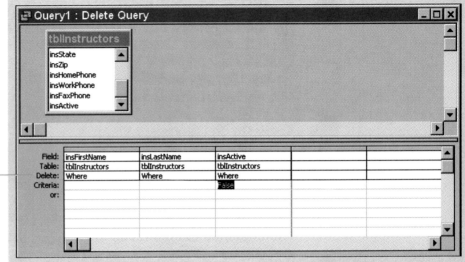

Select "Where" in the
*Delete* row and then
place the criteria in the
*Criteria* row.

 The first two field columns in the Design grid were added only
to ensure that the select query returned the correct records.
These fields are not important to the delete query and will be
removed once the query is saved. Now let's run the query:
CLICK: Run button (⚡) to run the query
The message box shown below appears.

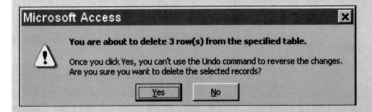

 To delete the records:
CLICK: Yes command button
This query deletes three records from tblInstructors and three
records from tblInsRates.

 Save the delete query as "qryDelInactive" and then close the
Design window. Notice the icon that appears in the *Queries* list
area.

## 8.4.3 Creating a Make-Table Query

**FEATURE**
A make-table query creates a table structure and then copies records into the new table. In addition to controlling the export of data to external applications, a make-table query is an excellent tool for archiving records. After running the query, you can compress the original or source table by deleting the copied records. In fact, simply converting the make-table query to a delete query will remove the desired entries. Be aware that the make-table query does not append records to an existing table. To perform this action, use an append query (discussed in the next lesson.) Make-table queries are also used to create intermediate or temporary tables, sometimes containing aggregate data from a crosstab or totals query, for use in running reports.

**METHOD**
1. Create and test a select query in Design view.
2. CLICK: down arrow attached to Query Type button (⊞▾)
3. SELECT: Make-Table Query
4. TYPE: *a new table name*
5. SELECT: *Current Database* option button
6. CLICK: OK command button

**PRACTICE**
In this lesson, you create an archive table for early 1999 instructor contracts that have already been paid.

*Setup:* Ensure that the ACC800 Database window is displayed and that the *Queries* button is selected in the Objects bar.

**1** To begin, create a select query that retrieves the paid instructor contracts for dates prior to September 1, 1999. Do the following:
DOUBLE-CLICK: Create query in Design view

**2** In the Show Table dialog box:
DOUBLE-CLICK: tblContracts
CLICK: Close command button

**3** To add fields to the Design grid:
DOUBLE-CLICK: asterisk (*)
This ensures that all fields are copied to the new table structure.

**4** To specify the fields for entering criteria:
DOUBLE-CLICK: conStartDate
DOUBLE-CLICK: conPaid

ACCESS

**5** You must now remove the check marks appearing in the *Show* row so that the fields are not repeated in the new table structure. Do the following:
CLICK: *Show* check box in the conStartDate column so that no "✔" appears
CLICK: *Show* check box in the conPaid column so that no "✔" appears

**6** To enter the criteria:
CLICK: in the *Criteria* row in the conStartDate column
TYPE: <#9/1/99#
CLICK: in the *Criteria* row in the conPaid column
TYPE: True

**7** CLICK: Run button (⏺) to run the query
The datasheet window displays 49 records.

**8** You will now convert the select query to a make-table query:
CLICK: View—Design button (▦▾) to return to Design view
CLICK: down arrow attached to the Query Type button (▦▾)
CHOOSE: Make-Table Query
The Make Table dialog box appears, as shown in Figure 8.24. (*Note:* You can also choose the Query, Make-Table Query command from the menu.)

**Figure 8.24**

Make Table dialog box

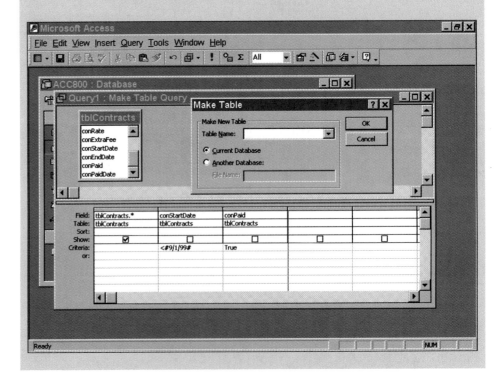

**9** To complete the dialog box:
TYPE: `tblConArchive`
SELECT: *Current Database* option button, if not already selected
CLICK: OK command button

**10** CLICK: Run button ([!]) to run the query
The message box shown below appears.

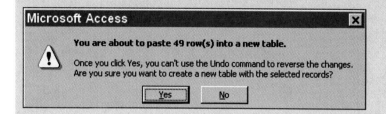

> **Microsoft Access** [×]
>
> ⚠ **You are about to paste 49 row(s) into a new table.**
> Once you click Yes, you can't use the Undo command to reverse the changes.
> Are you sure you want to create a new table with the selected records?
>
> [ Yes ]   [ No ]

**11** To perform the operation:
CLICK: Yes command button

**12** Save the make-table query as "qryMakConArchive" and then close the Design window. (*Hint:* If you were using this query to archive data, you would now delete the records from the source tblContracts table.)

**13** To view the new table:
CLICK: *Tables* button in the Objects bar
DOUBLE-CLICK: tblConArchive
Notice that there are 49 records in the datasheet. (*Note:* The make-table query propagates the new table structure with only the field name and data type. Therefore, you must manually set the desired property settings, such as a check box *Display Control* for the conPaid field.)

**14** Close the datasheet window.

**15** CLICK: *Queries* button in the Objects bar

## 8.4.4   Creating an Append Query

**FEATURE**

An append query copies records from a source table to a target table. Unlike a make-table query, an append query requires that the target table structure already exist, although its structure need not be identical to the source table. To use an append query for archiving data, remember to delete the copied records from the source table after running the append query. For smaller jobs, you might find the Copy and Paste Append commands easier to use for copying records from one table to another.

**METHOD**

1. Create and test a select query in Design view.
2. CLICK: down arrow attached to Query Type button (▣ᐧ)
3. SELECT: Append Query
4. SELECT: the target table from the *Table Name* drop-down list
5. SELECT: *Current Database* option button
6. CLICK: OK command button
7. Match the fields that you want to append or use the asterisk (*).

**PRACTICE**

You now append the paid instructor contracts, with start dates falling between September 1 and December 31, 1999, to the tblConArchive table created in the last lesson.

*Setup:* Ensure that the ACC800 Database window is displayed and that the *Queries* button is selected in the Objects bar. It is important that you complete the previous lesson.

**1** Let's create an append query from scratch:
DOUBLE-CLICK: Create query in Design view

**2** In the Show Table dialog box:
DOUBLE-CLICK: tblContracts
CLICK: Close command button

**3** To add fields to the Design grid:
DOUBLE-CLICK: asterisk (*)
This ensures that all field values are appended to the target table.

**4** To specify the fields for entering criteria:
DOUBLE-CLICK: conStartDate
DOUBLE-CLICK: conPaid

**5**  Now remove the check marks appearing in the *Show* row:
CLICK: *Show* check box in the conStartDate column so that no
"✔" appears
CLICK: *Show* check box in the conPaid column so that no "✔"
appears

**6**  To enter the criteria:
CLICK: in the *Criteria* row in the conStartDate column
TYPE: Between #9/1/99# And #12/31/99#
CLICK: in the *Criteria* row in the conPaid column
TYPE: True

**7**  To convert this query into an append query:
CLICK: down arrow attached to the Query Type button (⊞▾)
CHOOSE: Append Query
The dialog box shown below is displayed.

**8**  In the Append dialog box:
SELECT: tblConArchive from the *Table Name* drop-down list box
SELECT: *Current Database* option button, if not already selected
CLICK: OK command button
Your screen should now appear similar to Figure 8.25. (*Note:* If
field names appear in both tables, Access automatically matches
them.)

**Figure 8.25**

Query Design grid
for an append query

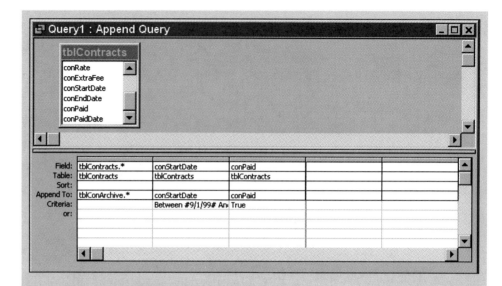

**9** You must stop the two criteria field columns from being appended to the table. Do the following:
DOUBLE-CLICK: in the *Append To* row in the conStartDate column
PRESS: DELETE
DOUBLE-CLICK: in the *Append To* row in the conPaid column
PRESS: DELETE
(*Note:* Appending AutoNumber key fields may also result in conflicts. Therefore, it may be wise to leave out these fields if you are appending data from multiple source tables. If you are always working with the same tables, an AutoNumber field shouldn't produce errors.)

**10** CLICK: Run button (🔲) to run the query
The message box shown below appears.

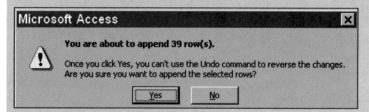

**11** To proceed with the operation:
CLICK: Yes command button

**12** Save the append query as "qryAppConArchive" and then close the Design window. (*Hint:* If you were using this query to archive data, you would now delete the records from the source tblContracts table.)

**13** Close the ACC800 Database window. Then, exit Microsoft Access.

**In Addition**
Troubleshooting
Action Queries

There are four types of errors that Access watches for when you perform an action query: duplicate primary keys, data conversion errors, locked records, and validation rule violations. If you experience one of these errors, follow the directions provided in the message box.

**8.4 Self Check**    Explain how you might use three of the action queries discussed in this module in creating a routine to archive old records in a database.

# 8.5   Chapter Review

Queries are the most powerful objects you can create using Microsoft Access. They are used to retrieve and manipulate data in datasheet windows, electronic forms, and printed reports. A select query, for example, enables you to filter, sort, group, and calculate results for display in a dynaset. You can even use specialized query wizards (Crosstab, Find Duplicates, and Find Unmatched) to help you get started. If you would rather wait to specify the criteria for a query, you can use a parameter query to display a custom dialog box when the query is executed. To change or delete the data retrieved by a query, you simply convert a select query to an action query. By combining the update, delete, make-table, and append action queries, you can produce a full-featured backup routine. As you can see, the ability to use queries for manipulating data is limited only by your creativity. This chapter also introduces the concept of setting joins, indexing foreign keys, and viewing the underlying query code in SQL view mode.

ACCESS

## 8.5.1  Command Summary

Many of the commands and procedures appearing in this chapter are summarized in the following table.

| Skill Set | To Perform This Task . . . | Do the Following . . . |
|---|---|---|
| **Defining Relationships** | Establish a one-to-one relationship | CLICK: Relationships button (⬚) CLICK: Show Table button (⬚) DRAG: the primary key field from one table to the matching primary key field in another table |
| | Establish many-to-many relationships | Create a third linking table that contains the primary key fields from the two "many" tables. Then, establish two one-to-many relationships between the "many" tables and the linking table. |
| **Refining Queries** | Enhance query performance by indexing foreign keys | Display the table object in Design view. SELECT: the desired foreign key field CLICK: *Indexed* property SELECT: Yes (Duplicates OK) |
| | Set join properties in the Relationships window | Display the Relationships window. DOUBLE-CLICK: the relationship line CLICK: Join Type command button SELECT: the desired join property |
| | Set join properties in the query Design window | Display the query Design grid. DOUBLE-CLICK: the relationship line SELECT: the desired join property |
| | View and edit a query in SQL view mode | Display the query Design grid. CHOOSE: View, SQL View, or CLICK: View—SQL button (⬚) |

*Continued*

| Skill Set | To Perform This Task . . . | Do the Following . . . |
|---|---|---|
| **Refining Queries** *Continued* | Test for null values in a query | Use the `Null`, `Is Null`, and `Is Not Null` operators |
| | Test for ranges, patterns, or sets of values in a query | Use the `Between...And`, `In`, `Like`, and `Not` operators |
| | Test for dates and use date functions in a query | Use the `Date`, `DateAdd`, `DatePart`, `Month`, and `Year` functions |
| | Sort data using a custom order based on a limited set of values | Use the `Switch` or `IIf` function |
| | Modify field properties in query Design view | RIGHT-CLICK: a field in the Design grid CHOOSE: Properties |
| | Modify query properties in query Design view | RIGHT-CLICK: a blank area of the table pane CHOOSE: Properties |
| | Display the Zoom window for entering long expressions | PRESS: [SHIFT] + [F2] |
| | Find duplicate records or field values in a table using a wizard | CLICK: New button ([New]) DOUBLE-CLICK: Find Duplicates Query Wizard |
| | Find unmatched child records given a parent table using a wizard | CLICK: New button ([New]) DOUBLE-CLICK: Find Unmatched Query Wizard |
| | Create a crosstab query using a wizard | CLICK: New button ([New]) DOUBLE-CLICK: Crosstab Query Wizard |
| | Create a parameter query | Display a select query in Design view. CLICK: a text box in the *Criteria* row TYPE: `[parameter entry]` |

*Continued*

ACCESS

| Skill Set | To Perform This Task . . . | Do the Following . . . |
|---|---|---|
| **Refining Queries** *Continued* | Create an update action query | Display a select query in Design view.<br>SELECT: Update Query from the Query Type button ([⊞▾])<br>CLICK: a text box in the *Update To* row<br>TYPE: *an update expression* |
| | Create a delete action query | Display a select query in Design view.<br>SELECT: Delete Query from the Query Type button ([⊞▾]) |
| | Create a make-table action query | Display a select query in Design view.<br>SELECT: Make-Table Query from the Query Type button ([⊞▾])<br>TYPE: *a new table name* |
| | Create an append action query | Display a select query in Design view.<br>SELECT: Append Query from the Query Type button ([⊞▾])<br>SELECT: the desired target table<br>Match the fields that you want to append. |

## 8.5.2 Key Terms

This section specifies page references for the key terms identified in this chapter. For a complete list of definitions, refer to the Glossary provided at the end of this learning guide.

append query, *p. 417*

Crosstab Query
Wizard, *p. 410*

delete query, *p. 417*

entity integrity, *p. 376*

Find Duplicates Query
Wizard, *p. 406*

Find Unmatched Query
Wizard, *p. 408*

inner join, *p. 382*

left outer join, *p. 382*

make-table query, *p. 417*

naming convention,
*p. 388*

right outer join, *p. 382*

run time, *p. 406*

update query, *p. 417*

zero-length string, *p. 395*

# 8.6  Review Questions

## 8.6.1  Short Answer

1.  Describe the two general integrity rules mentioned in this chapter.
2.  In defining a foreign key field, what data type should be selected when the primary key that it is based on uses an AutoNumber data type?
3.  Describe the default join setting in a relationship.
4.  Write the SQL code to retrieve all of the data from a table named "tblPuppy," sorted into ascending order by "pupBreed."
5.  Describe the four components that you may use in constructing complex expressions.
6.  How would you display a list of the unique city names represented in a customer or contacts table?
7.  Thinking back to the ACC800 database, how would you determine which instructors did not have teaching contracts?

8. Explain why you shouldn't place too many parameter values in a parameter query.
9. What should you do prior to running an action query?
10. When including all fields in an append query using the asterisk (*), how do you specify a criteria in the Design grid?

## 8.6.2 True/False

1. _____ Use the *Foreign Key* property text box in table Design view to define an index for optimizing query performance.
2. _____ To establish a many-to-many relationship, create a third linking table that contains the primary key fields from the other tables.
3. _____ Specifying a join type affects only how records are processed in a query.
4. _____ If you change a relationship's join property in the query Design window, the modification is saved for use by all queries that are based on the same relationship.
5. _____ While you can view any query in SQL view mode, you can only edit code that you've written from scratch.
6. _____ The *AllowZeroLength* property setting determines whether you can enter zero-length strings in a table.
7. _____ A crosstab query performs an aggregate calculation (Avg, Count, Max, Min, and Sum) in summarizing values for display.
8. _____ A parameter query is often used as the basis for printing reports.
9. _____ Like a select query, an update query returns a dynaset.
10. _____ You can copy records from one table to another using an append query.

## 8.6.3 Multiple Choice

1. In the Relationships window, the appearance of symbols, such as "1" and the infinity symbol, at the endpoints of a relationship line means:
   a. an inner join is set
   b. an outer join is set
   c. referential integrity is enforced
   d. referential integrity is not enforced

2. In the query Design window, the appearance of an arrow at one end of the relationship line means:
   a. an inner join is set
   b. an outer join is set
   c. referential integrity is enforced
   d. referential integrity is not enforced

3. Which of the following are listed in this chapter as the prefixes to use for naming table, query, form, report, macro, and module objects?
   a. tab, que, frm, rpt, mac, mod
   b. tbl, qry, for, rpt, mac, mod
   c. tab, que, frm, rep, mac, bas
   d. tbl, qry, frm, rpt, mac, bas

4. Which of the following statements is the same as entering **"Red" Or "Green" Or "Blue"** in the *Criteria* row of the query Design grid?
   a. **And("Red", "Green", "Blue")**
   b. **Between "Red" And "Green" And "Blue"**
   c. **In("Red", "Green", "Blue")**
   d. **Or("Red", "Green", "Blue")**

5. Which of the following statements replaces the values "Mine," "Yours," and "Theirs" in the Owner field with 1, 2, and 3?
   a. **IIf([Owner]= "Mine",1, "Yours",2, "Theirs",3)**
   b. **IIf([Owner]= "Mine",1,[Owner]= "Yours",2,[Owner]= "Theirs",3)**
   c. **Switch([Owner]= "Mine",1, "Yours",2, "Theirs",3)**
   d. **Switch([Owner]= "Mine",1,[Owner]= "Yours",2,[Owner]= "Theirs",3)**

6. Which of the following is not a query wizard mentioned in this chapter?
   a. Crosstab
   b. Find Duplicates
   c. Find Unmatched
   d. Parameter

7. When creating a parameter query, place the parameter text between the following symbols:
   a. { }
   b. ( )
   c. [ ]
   d. " "

ACCESS

8. Which of the following is not an action query?
   a. Add
   b. Delete
   c. Make-Table
   d. Update

9. Which of the following are not completely copied to the new table structure when you perform a make-table query?
   a. property settings
   b. field names
   c. data types
   d. data

10. Which of the following is not an error that Access watches for when you perform an action query?
    a. duplicate primary keys
    b. duplicate foreign keys
    c. data conversion errors
    d. locked records

# 8.7  Hands-On Projects

### 8.7.1  World Wide Imports: Relating Tables and Setting Joins

This exercise lets you practice establishing relationships between tables and setting join properties.

*Setup:* Ensure that Access is loaded. If you are launching Access and the startup dialog box appears, click the Cancel command button to remove the dialog box from the application window.

1. Open the database file named ACC870. This exercise uses the five tables appearing with the prefix 871 in the Database window.
2. To display the Relationships window:
   CLICK: Relationships button (⬚)
   Notice that the five tables already appear in the Relationships window.
3. First, let's define a one-to-many relationship between the sales representatives and customers. Do the following:
   SELECT: slsID in the tblSalesReps field list
   DRAG: the selected field and drop it on the slsID field in the tblCustomers field list
   The Edit Relationships window appears. Notice that Access assumes the *Relationship Type* is "One-To-Many."

4. To create the relationship:
   CLICK: Create command button
5. You now establish a many-to-many relationship between the carriers and territories. To do so requires you to define two one-to-many relationships using the linking tblCarrierRoute table. Do the following:
   SELECT: carID in the tblCarriers field list
   DRAG: the selected field and drop it on the carID field in the tblCarrierRoutes field list
6. In the Edit Relationships window:
   SELECT: *Enforce Referential Integrity* check box
   CLICK: Create command button
   Notice that the relationship line displays symbols at its endpoints showing the type of relationship.
7. To establish the other side of the many-to-many relationship:
   SELECT: terID in the tblTerritories field list
   DRAG: the selected field and drop it on the terID field in the tblCarrierRoutes field list
   SELECT: *Enforce Referential Integrity* check box
   CLICK: Create command button
8. You must now specify a join property setting for the one-to-many relationship between tblSaleReps and tblCustomers. By changing the default inner join to a right outer join, all customers on the "many" side of the relationship will be included in all query results, regardless of whether or not they have been assigned a sales rep. To begin:
   DOUBLE-CLICK: the relationship line between tblSalesReps and tblCustomers
9. In the Edit Relationships window:
   CLICK: Join Type command button
   SELECT: *3: Include All records from '871 tblCustomers'...* option button
   CLICK: OK command button to close the Join Properties window
   CLICK: OK command button to close the Edit Relationships window
   Your screen should appear similar to Figure 8.26.
10. Save and then close the Relationships window.

ACCESS

**Figure 8.26**

Completing the
Relationships window

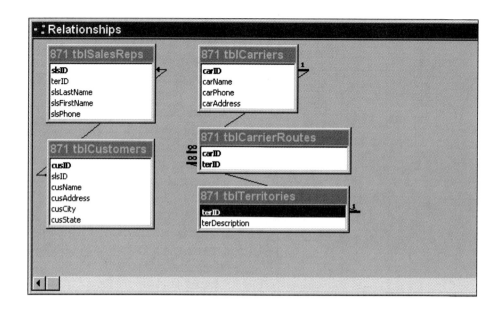

## 8.7.2 CyberWeb: Writing a SQL Account Query

The SQL view mode allows you to work with SQL programming statements in building and modifying queries. Although an advanced feature, this exercise provides an introduction to its capabilities and lets you create a new query from scratch using SQL commands.

*Setup:* Ensure that the ACC870 Database window is displayed.

1. To create a new query from scratch:
   CLICK: *Queries* button in the Objects bar
   DOUBLE-CLICK: Create query in Design view
2. In the Show Table dialog box:
   CLICK: Close command button to display an empty Design window
3. To switch to SQL view mode:
   CHOOSE: View, SQL View
4. Leave the existing text highlighted and then type the following:
   TYPE: **SELECT accCustomer, accUsername**
   PRESS: (ENTER)
   TYPE: **FROM [872 tblAccounts]**
   PRESS: (ENTER)
   TYPE: **ORDER BY accUsername**
   (*Note:* The square brackets surrounding "872 tblAccounts" are necessary because the table name contains a space.)

5. Now, let's view the resulting dynaset:
   CLICK: View—Datasheets button (⊞▾)
   The 11 records that are displayed in the datasheet are sorted into ascending order by the accUsername field.
6. To edit the query:
   CLICK: View—SQL View button (SQL▾)
7. Let's add a criterion statement to limit the rows that are displayed in the datasheet. To add a new line between the FROM and ORDER BY statements, do the following:
   PRESS: HOME to move to the beginning of the ORDER BY line
   PRESS: ENTER to insert a new line
   PRESS: ⬆ to move the insertion point to the new line
8. Now add the following statement:
   TYPE: **WHERE accBillingType = "DD"**
9. To view the results:
   CLICK: View—Datasheets button (⊞▾)
   You should see the following records displayed.

| accCustomer | accUsername |
|---|---|
| Bo Bailey | bbailey |
| Bonnie Mar | bmar |
| G. T. Morris | gmorris |
| Van Nguyen | vnguyen2 |

10. Let's view the query Design window:
    CLICK: View—Design button (▾)
    Notice that the accBillingType field column has an entry in its *Criteria* text box and that its *Show* check box has no "✔" displayed.
11. Save the query as "qrySQLAccounts" and then close the query Design window.

ACCESS

### 8.7.3  Big Valley Mills: Finding Freight Rates

In this exercise, you enter complex expressions and date criteria in a query for the purpose of sourcing freight rates.

*Setup:* Ensure the ACC870 Database window is displayed and that the *Queries* button is selected in the Objects bar.

1.  To begin, create a new select query in Design view. Using the Show Table dialog box, add the "873 tblFreightRates" table to the query Design window.
2.  Now let's add some fields to the query from the "873 tblFreightRates" field list:
    DOUBLE-CLICK: frtCarrier
    DOUBLE-CLICK: frtUnit
    DOUBLE-CLICK: frtRate
    DOUBLE-CLICK: frtRateUnit
    DOUBLE-CLICK: frtStartDate
3.  Your first task is to limit the query's results to only those freight rates that are based on weight, volume, or distance. To begin:
    CLICK: in the *Criteria* row in the frtRateUnit column
    TYPE: In ("CWT","MBF","MI")
4.  Now run the query:
    CLICK: Run button (⏺)
    The datasheet displays 81 records.
5.  To limit the results further, you will display only those records with a frtStartDate value that falls between two dates. To begin:
    CLICK: View—Design button (⬛▾)
    CLICK: in the *Criteria* row in the frtStartDate column
6.  Let's use the Zoom window to enter the criteria statement:
    PRESS: (SHIFT) + (F2)
    TYPE: Between #1/1/00# And Date()
    CLICK: OK command button to close the window
7.  Run the query. The number of records displayed will vary depending on the current date.
8.  Now let's change the date criteria to display only those records with a start date within the next twelve months:
    CLICK: View—Design button (⬛▾)
    PRESS: (SHIFT) + (F2)
9.  With the criteria expression selected:
    TYPE: Between Date() and DateAdd("d",365,Date())
    CLICK: OK command button
10. Run the query. Again, the number of records displayed will vary depending on the current date.
11. On your own, practice making further modifications to the date criteria statement and then run the query.
12. Save the query as "qryDateExp" and then close the window.

## 8.7.4 Silverdale Festival: Creating a Crosstab Query

In this exercise, you create a special-purpose query using the Crosstab Query Wizard. Specifically, you summarize the number of groups performing volunteer functions for the Silverdale festival by city.

*Setup:* Ensure the ACC870 Database window is displayed.

1. Open a datasheet window for the "874 tblContacts" table and familiarize yourself with its contents. When ready to proceed, close the datasheet window.
2. Display the *Queries* list area in the Database window and then:
   CLICK: New button ( New ) on the Database window toolbar
   DOUBLE-CLICK: Crosstab Query Wizard
3. In the first dialog box of the Query Wizard, select the "874 tblContacts" table and then click Next> .
4. In the second dialog box, select the conCity field for the query's row heading and then click Next> .
5. When asked for column headings, select the conFunction field and then click Next> .
6. In the next dialog box, select the "Count" function in the *Functions* list area and then remove the "✔" in the *Yes, include row sums* check box. (*Note:* Since we are counting records in this query, the field name selected in the *Fields* list box is inconsequential.)
7. To proceed to the last dialog box:
   CLICK: Next>
8. You may now name the query and then view the results:
   TYPE: **qryCrosstabFunctions**
   SELECT: *View the query* option button, if not already selected
   CLICK: Finish
9. After adjusting the column widths, your datasheet window should appear similar to Figure 8.27.
10. Close the datasheet window.

**Figure 8.27**

Crosstab query results

| conCity | First Aid | Food | Hospitality | Misc | Publicity | Sanitation | Security |
|---|---|---|---|---|---|---|---|
| Centerville | | 2 | | | | | |
| French Camp | | | | | 1 | 1 | |
| Gait | | 1 | | | | | |
| Manteca | | | | | | 2 | |
| Pinawa | | 1 | 1 | | | | |
| Silverdale | 2 | 13 | 5 | 5 | 4 | 18 | 9 |
| Woodbridge | 1 | | | | | | |

# 8.7.5  On Your Own: Office Mart Inventory

This exercise lets you practice creating a complex query that allows the user to input a criteria statement at run time. Ensure that the ACC870 Database window is displayed and then select the *Queries* button in the Objects bar. To begin, create a new query in Design view based on the "875 tblInventory" table. Add the invProductID, invDescription, and invCost fields to the Design grid. Then, click in the *Field* row in the fourth (empty) column and display the Zoom window. Type the following expression into the Zoom window and then click the OK command button:

**Zoom**

Margin: ([invSuggestedRetail]-[invCost])/[invSuggestedRetail]

To select a display format for the calculated field column, open the Field Properties dialog box for the column and change the *Format* property to Percent. Run the query to view the results and then return to the Design window.

You now convert the select query into a parameter query. In Design view, display the Zoom window for the *Criteria* text box in the invCost column. Enter the following expression and then click the OK command button:

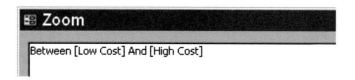

**Zoom**

Between [Low Cost] And [High Cost]

Run the query more than once with different input values for the low and high cost parameters. When you are finished, save the query as "qryCostParameters" and then close the window.

 ## 8.7.6 On Your Own: Sun Bird Resorts

In this exercise, you create an update query that modifies a field based on the contents of another field. You then use a delete query to remove values from the table, after first making a backup copy. To begin, open a datasheet window for the "876 tblGuides" table and familiarize yourself with its contents. When ready to proceed, close the datasheet window.

Your first task is to make inactive all of the guides that list "Shopping" as an interest. After switching to the *Queries* list area, create and run a select query that displays all of the records containing "Shopping" in the gdeInterest field. There are five such records. Now, convert the query to an update query that sets the insActive field to "False" for these records. Save the query as "qryUpdGuides" and then close the Design window. Run the query and then open the table to verify the results. When ready to proceed, close the datasheet window.

Now let's delete all of the guide records that are inactive. Before proceeding, create a backup copy of the "876 tblGuides" table using the Copy and Paste commands. Name the backup "876 tblGuides Backup" and make sure to paste both the table structure and data. Now create and run a select query that shows all of the inactive guides. There should be 13 such records in the table. After switching to Design view, convert the select query to a delete action query. Save the query as "qryDelGuides" and then close the Design window. Run the query to delete the 13 inactive guides. When finished, close the Database window and then exit Microsoft Access.

# 8.8  Case Problems: Traveling Gadgets, Inc.

Erica Marsden, the systems and database administrator for Traveling Gadgets, Inc., has completed her analysis of the company's Access database management system. Her immediate concern is that the volume of data captured is increasing dramatically, resulting in poor overall performance. Furthermore, the time required to perform a daily backup for the database is becoming unacceptable. Erica's first task is to devise a way to improve the database's performance.

Since the database contains a record for each person that has ever requested a catalog from TGI, there are as many records for "hot" customers as there are for "cold" prospects. While all of the data is important for marketing analysis; the majority of data is not required on a daily operational basis. Therefore, Erica decides that the best approach would be to create an archiving system that retains only the most recent requests in the primary tables. The remaining records are extracted from the tables and stored in historical archives.

In the following case problems, assume the role of Erica and perform the same steps that she identifies. You may want to re-read the chapter opening before proceeding.

1.  Erica starts out by opening the ACC880 database, located in the Advantage student data files folder. She notices that there are only two table objects in the entire database: tblCustomers and tblOrders. To better understand the structure of these tables, she opens the Relationships window and takes note of any join or referential integrity options. Satisfied with her preview, Erica closes the Relationships window before proceeding.

    Erica decides to create an archive table to hold the inactive customer records. But instead of moving records to the new table, she wants to copy the table structure only using a make-table action query. To begin, Erica creates a new query in Design view based on the tblCustomers table. She drags the asterisk (*) from the tblCustomers field list into the first column of the Design grid and then runs the query. After ensuring that all 130 customer records are displayed, Erica returns to Design view.

    Next, Erica modifies the query so that no records will be selected. To do so, she adds the cusNumber field to the Design grid and then clicks the *Show* check box so that no "✔" appears. Erica places a 0 in the cusNumber column's *Criteria* text box and then runs the query again. No records appear in the dynaset, but all seven fields are displayed. She returns to Design view.

Erica must now convert the select query to a make-table action query using the menu. When asked for the new table name, she types **tblCusArchive** and then runs the query to create the empty table structure. Lastly, she saves the query as "qryMakCusArchive" and closes the query Design window. Erica switches the Database window to see the new table object appearing in the list area.

2. The next step in creating the archiving system is to create an append action query. Specifically, the query must append records from the tblCustomers table to the new tblCusArchive structure. However, Erica also wants to be able to run this query periodically without having to modify the query parameters each time. She would prefer that the append query simply prompt her for the last date to archive.

   As before, Erica creates a new query in Design view based on the tblCustomers table. She adds all of the table's fields to the query by dragging the asterisk (*) to the Design grid. Next, she adds the cusDateSigned field to the second column in the grid and removes the "✔" in the *Show* text box. To create the required parameter query, Erica clicks in the *Criteria* text box and then displays its Zoom window. She types the criterion: **<[Enter last date to archive]+1** and then clicks the OK command button. To ensure that the user of the query enters a date value, Erica inserts the appropriate entry into the Query Parameters dialog box. At this point, the query Design window appears as shown in Figure 8.28. Erica closes the Query Parameters dialog box before proceeding.

**Figure 8.28**

Parameter query for selecting records to archive

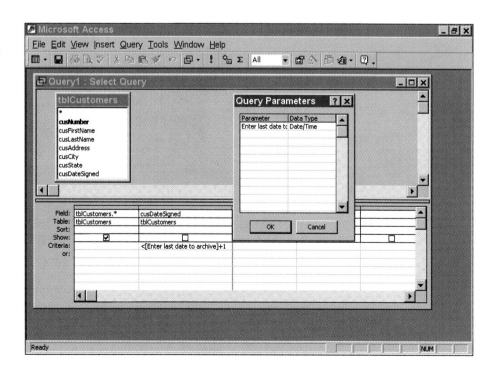

Erica tests the query using a date of "12/31/96" and then returns to Design view after the dynaset displays 22 matching records. Using the menu, she converts the select query into an append action query and selects the tblCusArchive table as the target. She remembers to remove the cusDateSigned field name from the *Append To* row in the Design grid and then saves the query as "qryAppCusArchive." Erica closes the query Design window before proceeding.

To perform the first archive of customer records, Erica double-clicks the qryAppCusArchive query object in the Database window. After confirming her desire to run the query, she enters an archiving date of "12/31/98." Erica confirms the 83 records that are to be appended and is returned to the Database window.

3.  Realizing that the 83 records appended to tblCusArchive still remain in the tblCustomers table, Erica needs to create a delete action query to complete the archiving procedure. Using the Copy and Paste commands, she creates a backup of the tblCustomers structure and data and names the new table "tblCusBackup." Just in case anything goes wrong, Erica wants to make sure that the original data is intact.

    Erica realizes that the append query she just created can serve as a starting point for the new delete query. Using the Copy and Paste commands once again, she copies the qryAppCusArchive query object to a new query named "qryDelCustomers." She then opens the new query in Design view.

    Using the menu, Erica converts the append action query into a delete action query, saves the query, and closes the Design window. Finally, she runs the qryDelCustomers query using the archiving date of "12/31/98." After confirming her intentions, the query displays a warning that 83 rows are to be deleted from the tblCustomers table. Erica clicks the Yes command button to proceed. The table now contains only records with a cusDateSigned value of 1999 or later.

4.  Now that the components for the archiving system are in place, Erica turns her attention to a request from the marketing department. The sales manager wants to send a special mail promotion to people who have received a catalog but have not yet made a purchase from TGI. Erica has been asked to supply a list of these names from the Access database.

To produce the list, Erica launches the Find Unmatched Query Wizard and selects the tblCustomers table in the first step of the dialog box. In the next step, she selects the tblOrders table, which is linked to tblCustomers in a one-to-many relationship. The third step of the wizard correctly identifies the cusNumber as the common linking field, so Erica proceeds to the next step. She specifies that the query results display the following fields: cusFirstName, cusLastName, cusAddress, cusCity, and cusState. Proceeding to the final step, Erica names the query "qryFindUnmatchedCustomers" and selects to view the results. The dynaset displays 22 records. After adjusting the column widths and printing the results, Erica closes the datasheet window (saving the layout changes), closes the Database window, and then exits Microsoft Access.

ACCESS

# MICROSOFT ACCESS 2000
## *Building Forms, Reports, and Data Access Pages*

## CHAPTER
### NINE

# Chapter Outline

9.1  Creating Forms from Scratch

9.2  Building Complex Forms

9.3  Creating Reports from Scratch

9.4  Building Complex Reports

9.5  Creating Data Access Pages

9.6  Chapter Review

9.7  Review Questions

9.8  Hands-On Projects

9.9  Case Problems

# Learning Objectives

After reading this chapter, you will be able to:

- Create and customize forms in form Design view

- Enhance forms using graphics, hyperlinks, tabs, and subforms

- Validate data using field and control properties

- Create and customize reports in report Design view

- Enhance reports using graphics, line numbers, charts, and subreports

- Create data access pages for manipulating data over the Internet using a Web browser

- Design and format grouped data access pages

## Case Study    Joseph Beaner's Fine Coffees

Joseph Beaner's Fine Coffees is a family-owned business that operates a small chain of four coffee shops in the Pacific Northwest. Courtney Hendrickson has taken over the management of Joseph Beaner's since her father, who established the company in 1964, retired last year. Over the years, the company has built and retained a loyal customer base by providing both gourmet coffee and a comfortable ambience. They have also kept up with the latest trends and specialty beverages desired by their clientele.

For the past few months, Courtney has been modernizing the company's information system using Microsoft Access. In fact, she has already completed a sales and purchasing database. While Courtney is well-versed in creating forms and reports using the Access wizards, she is becoming more aware of their limitations each day. To take her application to the next level, Courtney realizes that she must learn to build custom forms and reports.

In this chapter, you and Courtney learn how to build custom forms and reports from scratch. You also learn to enhance forms with graphics, hyperlinks, and other controls. Besides improving a form's visual appearance, you set up validation rules to reduce data-entry errors and improve functionality. Furthermore, you learn to create complex reports and build data access pages to enable users to manipulate data over the Internet.

# 9.1 Creating Forms from Scratch

Access forms are merely windows that contain controls for displaying and interacting with data. From Chapter 7, you may remember that there are three main types of controls. A *bound control*, whose data source is a field in a table or query; an *unbound control*, that has no data source; and a *calculated control*, that displays the results of a formula expression. While a bound control always displays the contents of a field, an unbound control can display a title, a clip art image, or a computed expression such as the concatenation of two fields or the current date. You should also be aware that bound controls inherit properties from their underlying table or query. Therefore, it's a good idea to set field properties in table Design view prior to creating a form. In this module, you learn how to enhance a form using graphics and hyperlinks. You also practice setting properties for the various controls and sections in a form.

## 9.1.1  Creating a Form with a Background Picture

**FEATURE**

Since forms provide the primary interface to a database application, every attempt should be made to ensure that they are attractive, well balanced, and functional. Creating a form from scratch in Design view provides you with maximum control over a form's design. In addition to manipulating controls, you can enhance a form using a variety of tools and techniques. Adding a background picture, for example, can make the information easier to read or can indicate a change in function, purpose, or subject. Sometimes a background picture simply provides a more interesting and captivating display than the typical Windows gray background.

In form Design view, you add and customize a background picture by setting several form properties. After selecting a graphic file from the disk, you can specify whether to align, clip, stretch, zoom, or tile the image. If you want to use the same picture on several forms (or reports), choose to link rather than embed the picture. **Embedding** a picture saves it to the database file. **Linking** a picture simply creates a reference to a graphic file that is stored on the disk. Any changes that you make to the disk-based graphic file are represented automatically in the database application.

**METHOD**

1. Display a form in Design view.
2. DOUBLE-CLICK: Form Selector button (▣)
3. CLICK: *Format* tab in the Form Properties window
4. Use the *Picture* text box to select a picture file.
5. Use the *Picture Type* text box to specify whether the picture is linked or embedded.
6. Use the *Picture Size Mode* text box to clip, stretch, or zoom the picture.
7. Use the *Picture Alignment* text box to align the picture on the page.
8. Specify whether to tile the picture to cover the entire Form window.

**PRACTICE**

In this lesson, you use form Design view to create a new form with a background picture.

*Setup:* Ensure that Access is loaded. If you are launching Access and the startup dialog box appears, click the Cancel command button to remove the dialog box from the application window.

**1** Open the database named ACC900, located in the Advantage student data files folder. This database provides several tables for storing data from a continuing education department at a small college.

**2** To create a new Administrator's form from scratch:
CLICK: *Forms* button in the Objects bar
DOUBLE-CLICK: Create form in Design view

**3** To expand the work area, maximize the Form window by clicking the Maximize button (□) appearing in its Title bar.

**4** At this point in the design process, the form has not been bound to a particular table or query. To define the underlying data source, you must first display the Properties window:
DOUBLE-CLICK: Form Selector button (■)
(*Hint:* You can also click the Properties button (☞) in the toolbar.)

**5** In the Form Properties window:
CLICK: *Data* tab
CLICK: in the *Record Source* text box
CLICK: down arrow attached to the property text box
SELECT: tblAdministrators from the drop-down list
The Field List window appears for the tblAdministrators table, as shown in Figure 9.1. (*Note:* If the Field List window does not appear, click the Field List button (□) on the toolbar.)

**Figure 9.1**

Defining the record
source for a new form

Form Selector button

Specify the *Record Source*
in the Form Properties
window.

The Field List window
displays the fields from the
specified table or query.

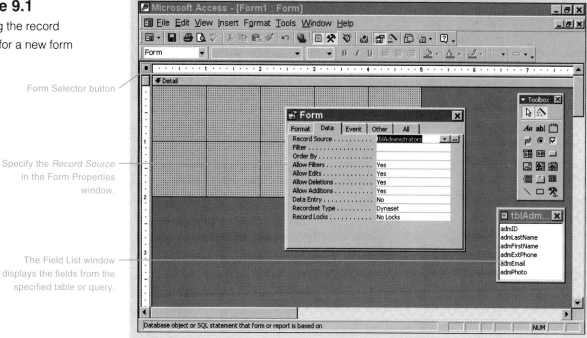

**6** Close the Form Properties window by clicking its Close button (⊠).

**7** To display a Form Header section:
CHOOSE: View, Form Header/Footer
Two new sections are added to the Form window.

**8** Now adjust the size of the Form Footer and Form Header sections:
DRAG: the form's bottom edge upward to meet the Form Footer section bar
DRAG: the bottom edge of the Form Header section downward to the .25-inch mark on the vertical ruler
(*Hint:* If the ruler is not visible, choose the View, Ruler command from the menu.)

**9** To decrease the form's width:
DRAG: the form's right edge leftward to the 4-inch mark on the horizontal ruler

**10** Let's add all of the fields from the Field List window to the Form window, except for the admPhoto field. Do the following:
CLICK: admID in the Field List window
PRESS: SHIFT
CLICK: admEmail in the Field List window
The first five fields should now appear highlighted.

**11** To add these fields to the form:
DRAG: the field selection into the Detail section at approximately the 1-inch mark on the horizontal ruler

**12** With the fields still selected in the Form window, adjust the spacing between the fields:
CHOOSE: Format, Vertical Spacing, Increase

**13** A background picture can sometimes overpower a form's text. For this reason, you may want to increase the font size of labels and apply boldface to improve their readability. Do the following:
CLICK: anywhere in the Form Header section to remove the current selection
CLICK: admID label control
DRAG: the rightmost sizing handle to the right, until the edge of the control touches the admID text box control

Drag the rightmost sizing handle, as shown here

**14** Now select all of the remaining controls:
PRESS: (SHIFT) and hold it down
CLICK: admLastName label control
CLICK: admFirstName label control
CLICK: admExtPhone label control
CLICK: admEmail label control
(*Hint:* Release the (SHIFT) key before proceeding.)

**15** To resize the selected controls and applying formatting:
CHOOSE: Format, Size, To Widest
CLICK: Bold button (B)

**16** To remove the current selection:
CLICK: anywhere in the Form Header section
Your screen should now appear similar to Figure 9.2.

**Figure 9.2**

Adding, resizing, and formatting controls

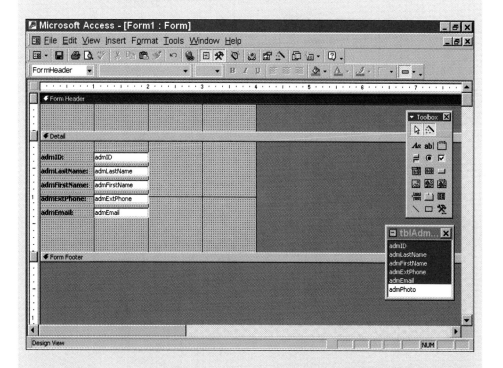

**17** Now let's add a background picture to the form. To display the Form Properties window:
DOUBLE-CLICK: Form Selector button (■)

**18** Your first step is to select a picture from the Advantage student data files folder. In the Form Properties window, do the following:
CLICK: *Format* tab
CLICK: in the *Picture* text box
CLICK: Build button (...) appearing to the right of the text box
The Insert Picture dialog box is displayed.

**19** On your own, locate the Advantage student data files folder and then:
DOUBLE-CLICK: LtBrick in the list area
The filename is placed into the property text box and the graphic shows up immediately on the form. (*Note:* The terms *graphic*, *image*, and *picture* are used interchangeably in this chapter.)

**20** To tile the picture so that it covers the entire form:
SELECT: Yes in the *Picture Tiling* text box

**21** Close the Form Properties window. Then restore the Form window to a window by clicking its Restore button (🗗).

**22** CLICK: View—Form button (📧▾)
Your screen should now appear similar to Figure 9.3.

**23** Save the form as "frmAdmBackground" and then close the Form window.

**Figure 9.3**

Tiling a background picture on a form

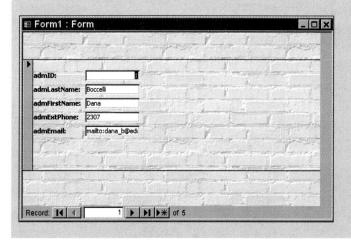

## 9.1.2 Enhancing a Form Using Graphics

**FEATURE**

There are many ways to add graphics, such as lines, rectangles, drawings, photographs, scanned pictures, and company logos, to a form. For simple drawing objects, use the Line (⬛) and Rectangle (⬛) buttons in the Toolbox window. To display a graphic stored in a disk file, you can link or embed the graphic, whether **bitmap** (BMP) or **metafile** (WMF), into an image control or an unbound object frame. Using an image control is the preferred method since it displays graphics faster and uses less memory than an unbound object frame. However, if you want to edit the graphic in the form, you must use an unbound object frame. An unbound object frame can contain any type of OLE Object, including images, sounds, charts, video segments, spreadsheets, and word processing documents. For graphic files stored in an OLE Object field in the database, select a bound object frame to display the field contents (or simply drag the field onto the form from the Field List window). To modify a graphic object, double-click the unbound or bound object frame containing the object.

**METHOD**

To insert a graphic using an image control:

1.  Display a form in Design view.
2.  CLICK: Image button (⬛) in the Toolbox window
3.  CLICK: in the Form window to place the control
4.  Select a graphic file from the Insert Picture dialog box.

To insert a graphic using an unbound object frame:

1.  Display a form in Design view.
2.  CLICK: Unbound Object Frame button (⬛) in the Toolbox window
3.  CLICK: in the Form window to place the control
4.  SELECT: *Create from File* option button in the Insert Object dialog box
5.  CLICK: Browse command button to select a graphic file
6.  Specify whether to link or embed the graphic file and whether to display the object as a picture or an icon.

To insert a graphic using a bound object frame:

1.  Display a form in Design view.
2.  Display the Field List window using the Field List button (⬛).
3.  DRAG: an OLE Object field from the Field List window onto the form

**PRACTICE**

You now modify an existing form to practice inserting graphics.

*Setup:* Ensure that the ACC900 Database window is displayed.

**1** Let's begin by opening an existing form in Design view. Ensure that the *Forms* button is selected in the Objects bar and then:
SELECT: frmAdministrator in the list area
CLICK: Design button (⊾Design)
Your screen should now appear similar to Figure 9.4. (*Hint:* Make sure that the Field List and Toolbox windows are displayed.)

**Figure 9.4**

Displaying the frmAdministrator form in Design view

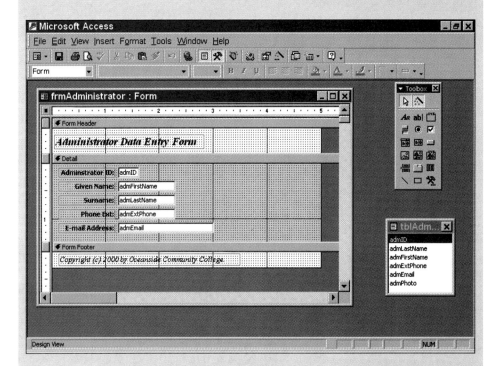

**2** In the next few steps, you will add a bitmap graphic to the Form Header section and a bound object frame to the Detail section. Before proceeding, maximize the Form window to increase your work area.

**3** Let's add an image control to the Form Header section:
CLICK: Image button (🖻) in the Toolbox window

**4** Position the mouse directly beneath the Form Header section bar at 3.5 inches on the horizontal ruler. Now do the following:
CLICK: the left mouse button once
The Insert Picture dialog box should appear.

**5** On your own, locate the Advantage student data files folder and then:
DOUBLE-CLICK: OCCLogo in the list area
The bitmap graphic appears in the Form Header section, affecting both the height of the Form Header section and the width of the form.

**6** To customize the display of the image, use the Properties window:
RIGHT-CLICK: the image control
CHOOSE: Properties
CLICK: *Format* tab in the Properties window
Notice that the name of the graphic file appears in the *Picture* property text box. (*Hint:* Similarly to choosing a background picture, you can specify whether to embed or link the graphic file using the *Picture Type* property. When embedded, Access stores a static copy of the graphic in the form. When linked, Access stores only a pointer to the graphic file's location on the disk.)

**7** To size the graphic logo proportionally to fit in either the height or width of the image control's frame:
CLICK: in the *Size Mode* text box
CLICK: down arrow attached to the property text box
SELECT: Zoom

**8** Close the Properties window to free up some screen real estate.

**9** You can now size the graphic to better fit in the Form Header section. Do the following:
DRAG: the lower right-hand sizing handle of the image control to size it to approximately 1-inch square
(*Hint: Metafile* graphics, which are commonly used for drawing logos, are smaller and scale better than bitmaps. However, *bitmaps* like this logo provide better color and resolution and are the preferred format for storing photographs and background textures.)

**10** Now let's add a bound image to the form:
DRAG: admPhoto from the Field List window to the right of the existing fields in the Detail section of the Form window
A large bound object frame appears in the Detail section.

**11** To start cleaning up the form, remove the object's label:
CLICK: admPhoto label control
PRESS: DELETE

**12** As you did with the image control, size and move the bound object frame and then set its *Size Mode* property to Zoom. Refer to Figure 9.5 for a recommended size and position. Close the Properties window before proceeding to the next step.

ACCESS

**13** Lastly, decrease the form's width and then adjust the height of the Form Header and Detail sections to fit the new controls.

**14** When ready to proceed, restore the form to a window by clicking its Restore button (⬜).

**15** CLICK: View—Form button (⬛▾)
Your screen should now appear similar to Figure 9.5.

**Figure 9.5**

Adding an image control
and a bound object frame
to a form

Image control
containing a
bitmap graphic

Bound object
frame
containing a
bitmap graphic

**16** On your own, navigate through the five records in this table to see the images contained therein. The photographs in the tblAdministrators table were initially linked, rather than embedded, into the table. Therefore, these graphics exist as files in your Advantage student data folders. (*Hint:* To select a different photograph, right-click the object control and choose Insert Object. You can also edit a linked object by choosing the Linked Image Object command.)

**17** To save the form under a different name:
CHOOSE: File, Save As
TYPE: `frmImageAdmin`
CLICK: OK command button

**18** Close the Form window before proceeding.

## 9.1.3 Creating Hyperlinks in a Form

**FEATURE**

The Web might not be so famous if it were not for hyperlinks. They provide an easy way to "drill down" through layers of information to find what you are looking for. With a single mouse click on a hyperlink, you can go from viewing a company's address information to viewing its most recent annual report. Including hyperlinks in a form enables you to send quick e-mail messages related to the current record, access a technical support or e-commerce Web site, or open an external document that is stored on the local computer or on a network. As illustrated in Chapter 5, you can also store hyperlinks as a field data type in a record.

When you click a hyperlink that appears on a form, three different scenarios can result. If the hyperlink contains an URL address for your intranet or an Internet Web site, the default Web browser software is launched and attempts to establish a connection to the site. If the hyperlink contains a valid e-mail address, the default e-mail program launches and the address is inserted automatically into the "To" area of a blank message. Lastly, if the hyperlink contains a reference to an Access object or another document type, the object or document is retrieved from the disk or network and displayed in its source application.

**METHOD**

To create an unbound hyperlink label:

1. Display a form in Design view.
2. CLICK: Insert Hyperlink button (🖳)
3. Complete the Insert Hyperlink dialog box.

To create a bound hyperlink field:

1. Display a form in Design view.
2. Display the Field List window using the Field List button (🖳).
3. DRAG: a Hyperlink field from the Field List window onto the form
4. DOUBLE-CLICK: the field's border using the hand mouse pointer
5. CLICK: *Format* tab in the Field Properties window
6. SELECT: Yes in the *Is Hyperlink* property text box

**PRACTICE**

You now edit an existing form to include unbound and bound hyperlinks.

*Setup:* Ensure that the ACC900 Database window is displayed.

**1** Open the frmAdministrator form in Design view. Your screen should appear similar to Figure 9.4 in the last lesson.

**2** The admEmail text box control displays the contents of a text field, as opposed to a hyperlink. However, you can enable the hyperlink status of a bound control by setting its *Is Hyperlink* property to Yes. To convert a bound control into a hyperlink:
DOUBLE-CLICK: admEmail text box control
CLICK: *Format* tab

**3** Using the vertical scroll bar, move to the bottom of the property list. Then, do the following:
CLICK: in the *Is Hyperlink* text box
CLICK: down arrow attached to the property text box
SELECT: Yes
Your screen should look similar to Figure 9.6. Notice that the contents of the text box control now appear as a blue and underlined hyperlink.

**Figure 9.6**

Enabling the hyperlink status of a bound text box control

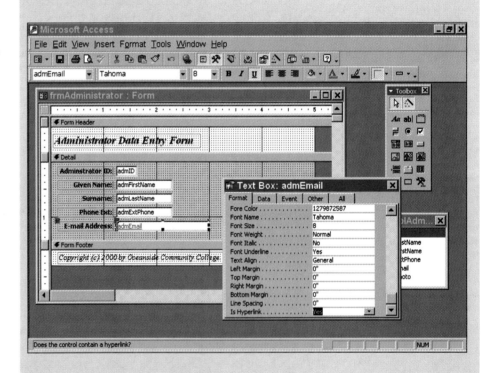

**4** Close the Properties window.

**5** Now let's add a hyperlink label control to the form:
CLICK: Insert Hyperlink button (🔲) on the toolbar
The Insert Hyperlink dialog box appears. (*Hint:* For a description of the elements in this dialog box, refer to Figure 5.15 in this book.)

**6** To define a hyperlink that displays the college's fictional home page:
SELECT: *Text to display* text box
TYPE: OCC Home Page
SELECT: *Type the file or Web page name* text box
TYPE: http://www.oceanside.edu/

**7** You can also specify a ScreenTip to appear when users move their mouse over top of the hyperlink. To do so:
CLICK: ScreenTip command button
TYPE: Open OCC Home Page in Web browser
CLICK: OK command button

**8** To complete the Insert Hyperlink dialog box:
CLICK: OK command button

**9** By default, the hyperlink label control is placed in the top left-hand corner of the Detail section. Let's move the control:
DRAG: OCC Home Page label control to the right-hand side of the Form Header section

**10** CLICK: View—Form button (🔲▾)

**11** Position the mouse pointer over the OCC Home Page hyperlink. A ScreenTip should appear, as shown in Figure 9.7. (*Hint:* To modify the e-mail address hyperlink, you must right-click the contents of the text box control and then choose Hyperlink, Edit Hyperlink.)

**12** Save the form as "frmHyperAdmin" and then close the Form window.

**Figure 9.7**

Adding hyperlinks to a form

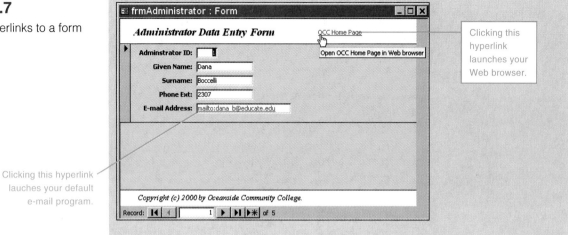

Clicking this hyperlink launches your default e-mail program.

Clicking this hyperlink launches your Web browser.

---

**In Addition**
Using Images and
Command Buttons
as Hyperlinks

You can also make a hyperlink out of an image or button control. To do so, display the Properties window for the desired control and click the *Format* tab. Then specify an e-mail or Web address in the *Hyperlink Address* property text box. You can also use the Build button ( ) to enter an address using the Insert Hyperlink dialog box.

---

# 9.1.4  Setting Control Properties in a Form

**FEATURE**
Setting control properties is a frequent task in building forms and reports from scratch. In the last lesson, for example, you displayed the Properties window to set a bound field's *Is Hyperlink* property to Yes. In Chapter 7, you practiced editing captions and formatting controls using the Properties window. You can also use control properties to specify default values, set validation text, and make a field read-only. This lesson provides some additional practice in selecting and setting control properties.

**METHOD**
- DOUBLE-CLICK: the control's border, or
- RIGHT-CLICK: the desired control
  CHOOSE: Properties

**PRACTICE**
In this lesson, you practice setting additional control properties.

*Setup:* Ensure that the ACC900 Database window is displayed.

**1** Open the frmAdministrator form in Design view.

**2** To assist the user working in a form, you can provide context-sensitive help messages for each field. These messages are displayed in the Status bar when the user enters a field or in a ControlTip. In this step, you create a helpful Status bar message for the admExtPhone field:
RIGHT-CLICK: admExtPhone text box control
CHOOSE: Properties

**3** To define the Status bar message:
CLICK: *Other* tab in the Properties window
CLICK: in the *Status Bar Text* text box
TYPE: `Enter a 4-digit local or extension`

**4** You can also display text in a custom ToolTip that appears when the user places the mouse over top of the control. To illustrate:
CLICK: in the *ControlTip Text* text box
TYPE: `Telephone Extension`

**5** Control properties also allow you to protect the data in your forms. For example, you can modify the *Enabled* and *Locked* text boxes on the *Data* tab of the Properties window. When a field is not enabled, it appears dim (light gray) and is no longer included in the tab order. When a field is locked, the user can access the field but cannot change its value. In the Form window:
SELECT: admEmail text box control

**6** To lock this field as read-only:
CLICK: *Data* tab
CLICK: in the *Locked* text box
CLICK: down arrow attached to the property text box
SELECT: Yes

**7** Close the Properties window.

**8** CLICK: View—Form button (⊞▾)

**9** To view the ControlTip text, position the mouse pointer over the admExtPhone text box. The words "Telephone Extension" should now appear. To view the control's Status bar text:
CLICK: in the admExtPhone text box

**10** Now let's test the *Locked* property:
PRESS: `TAB` to move to the admEmail text box
PRESS: `DELETE`
Notice that nothing happens when you press `DELETE` in the text box.

**11** On your own, attempt to insert and delete characters in the text box. Notice that the admEmail field is effectively locked as read-only.

**12** Save the form as "frmPropAdmin" and then close the Form window.

---

**In Addition**
Changing Property
Settings for Conrols

When you set a property for a bound control, the new setting overrides the field's property appearing in the table structure—but only in that form. If you want to change a field's property setting and have it flow through to all related queries and forms, make the change in the table structure itself.

---

## 9.1.5 Setting Form and Section Properties

**FEATURE**
In addition to specifying a background picture object, there are many properties that you can set to enhance the appearance and functionality of a form. First, you can change the method for displaying records by choosing a form view mode. In Single Form mode, each record appears in its own window. In Continuous Form mode, each record appears in the same window, separated by a single line. You navigate the records by clicking the navigation buttons or by dragging the scroll box on the vertical scroll bar. In Datasheet view mode, records are displayed in a datasheet window. In this lesson, you are introduced to these and other form and section properties.

**METHOD**
To display the Form Properties window:

- DOUBLE-CLICK: Form Selector button (■), or
- CHOOSE: View, Properties

To display a section's Properties window:

- DOUBLE-CLICK: the section bar, or
- RIGHT-CLICK: the section bar
  CHOOSE: Properties

**PRACTICE**
You now practice setting form and section properties.

*Setup:* Ensure that the ACC900 Database window is displayed.

**1** Open the frmAdministrator form in Design view.

**2** To begin, display the Form Properties window:
DOUBLE-CLICK: Form Selector button (■)
CLICK: *Format* tab

**3** To adjust the view setting for the form:
CLICK: in the *Default View* text box
CLICK: down arrow attached to the property text box
SELECT: Continuous Forms

**4** Close the Form Properties window.

**5** To view the new setting, maximize the Form window and then:
CLICK: View—Form button (▦▾)
Your screen should appear similar to Figure 9.8.

**Figure 9.8**

Displaying the Continuous
Forms view mode

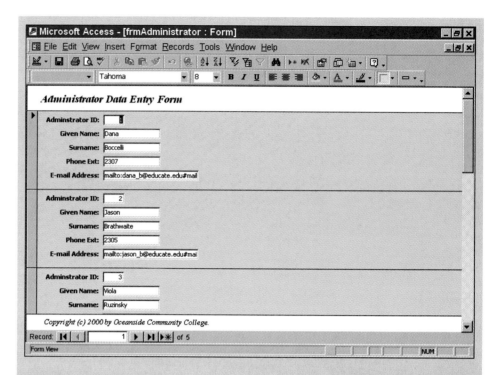

**6** On your own, navigate through the records using the navigation controls and the vertical scroll bar.

**7** Restore the form to a window and then:
CLICK: View—Design button (▨▾) to return to Design view

**8** In the last lesson, you locked a single control to make it read-only. You will now make an entire form read-only:
DOUBLE-CLICK: Form Selector button (▣)
CLICK: *Data* tab
SELECT: No in the *Allow Edits* text box
SELECT: No in the *Allow Deletions* text box
SELECT: No in the *Allow Additions* text box
(*Hint:* You can also specify that a form be used only for data entry by setting its *Data Entry* property.)

**9** You can adjust how various form sections are printed and displayed using property settings. For example, you can hide a particular section until you are ready to print the entire form. To illustrate:
CLICK: Form Footer section bar
The Properties window now shows the section's properties.

**10** To make the Form Footer section invisible:
CLICK: *Format* tab
CLICK: in the *Visible* text box
CLICK: down arrow attached to the property text box
SELECT: No

**11** Now let's change the color of the text in the Form Header section:
CLICK: "Administrator Data Entry Form" label control
CLICK: down arrow attached to the Font/Fore Color button (⬛▾)
SELECT: White

**12** To change the background color of the Form Header section:
CLICK: Form Header section bar
CLICK: in the *Back Color* text box
CLICK: Build button (⬚) appearing beside the text box
SELECT: Black
CLICK: OK command button

**13** Close the Properties window.

**14** CLICK: View—Form button (🖳▾)
Your screen should now appear similar to Figure 9.9. Notice that the Form Footer section is no longer displayed.

**15** Save the form as "frmContAdmin" and then close the Form window.

**Figure 9.9**
Setting form and section properties

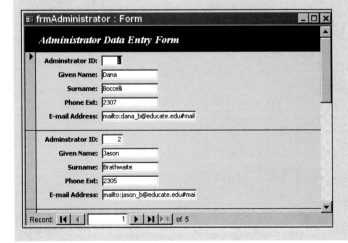

ACCESS

**9.1 Self Check**   How would you create a hyperlink on a form using a company's logo?

# 9.2  Building Complex Forms

For the purpose of this module, a complex form is one that effectively organizes information and possesses some built-in intelligence. Besides the table field properties that are adopted by bound controls, form intelligence involves built-in error-checking and interactivity. Additionally, a complex form incorporates advanced controls for presenting information. This module focuses on building complex forms without programming. Specifically, you are introduced to data validation, automatic lookup queries, list boxes, subforms, and tab controls.

## 9.2.1  Validating Fields and Records

**FEATURE**

To help reduce the number of data entry errors made by users, Access provides several methods for validating data at both the field and record levels. In Chapter 5, you learned to enforce required fields, specify default values, define lookup fields and columns, and use input masks to control the way data is entered. You now learn how to set rules for validating data. A **field validation rule** is an expression that defines the range of legal values for entry in a particular field. You can also define a **record validation rule** that evaluates when the user attempts to leave a record after entering or modifying data. **Validation text** refers to the message that displays in the warning dialog box when an entry violates the rule. Setting field validation rules and message text can be accomplished in either table Design view or form Design view. A record validation rule, on the other hand, is a table property and must be set in table Design view.

**METHOD**
To enforce field-level data validation:

1. Display the table structure in Design view.
2. SELECT: a field in the Field Grid pane
3. SELECT: *Validation Rule* property in the Field Properties pane
4. TYPE: *an expression*
5. SELECT: *Validation Text* property in the Field Properties pane
6. TYPE: *an error message*

To enforce record-level data validation:
1. Display the table structure in Design view.
2. CHOOSE: View, Properties
3. SELECT: *Validation Rule* property text box
4. TYPE: *an expression*
5. SELECT: *Validation Text* property text box
6. TYPE: *an error message*

**PRACTICE**
You now set both field- and record-level validation rules and text.

*Setup:* Ensure that the ACC900 Database window is displayed.

**1** In the next few steps, you will enforce field-level validation in the frmAdministrator form. The validation rule and text that you enter in form Design view applies only to this form. To enforce data validation for all objects that reference a particular field or table, you must set the validation rule and text in table Design view. To begin, open the frmAdministrator form in Design view.

**2** To display the Properties window for the admExtPhone field:
RIGHT-CLICK: admExtPhone text box control
CHOOSE: Properties

**3** Let's restrict the user to entering a phone extension between 2300 and 2399. To enter the validation criterion:
CLICK: *Data* tab in the Properties window
CLICK: in the *Validation Rule* text box
TYPE: `Between 2300 and 2399`
(*Hint:* For entering complex validation criteria, click the Build button (⊡) beside the *Validation Rule* property text box to display the Expression Builder.)

ACCESS

You will now enter some helpful text to assist users in correcting their mistakes. Do the following:
CLICK: in the *Validation Text* text box
TYPE: `Enter an extension between 2300 and 2399`
Figure 9.10 shows the Properties window after clicking the *Data* tab. Notice that you can also specify an *Input Mask* and *Default Value* for use in this particular form.

**Figure 9.10**

Setting a validation criterion and message text

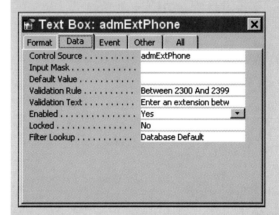

**5** Close the Properties window.

**6** CLICK: View—Form button (🖾▾) to view the form

**7** To test the validation rule:
DOUBLE-CLICK: in the admExtPhone text box
TYPE: `2200`
PRESS: `TAB`
A warning dialog box appears displaying the validation text. (*Note:* You cannot move the insertion point out of the field until you enter a value that does not violate the validation rule.)

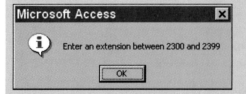

**8** To remove the dialog box:
CLICK: OK command button
PRESS: `ESC` to reverse the previous entry

**9** Save the form as "frmValidate" and then close the Form window.

**10** Now let's set a record-level validation rule using table Design view:
CLICK: *Tables* button in the Objects bar
SELECT: tblSections in the list area
CLICK: Design button (⊾Design)
(*Note:* When creating or modifying a table structure, you set field-level validation rules on the *General* tab of the Field Properties pane.)

**11** To catch data entry mistakes, this next rule checks to ensure that the section's ending date is later than its starting date. Because the rule involves a field comparison, you want to evaluate it after all of the record's data has been entered. Do the following:
CHOOSE: View, Properties
CLICK: in the *Validation Rule* text box
TYPE: `[secStartDate]<=[secEndDate]`
Notice that the field names are contained in square brackets.

**12** To set the validation text:
CLICK: in the *Validation Text* text box
TYPE: `A section's ending date cannot be earlier than its starting date`

**13** Close the Table Properties window.

**14** To test the table's record and field validation rules:
CHOOSE: Edit, Test Validation Rules
The following dialog box appears.

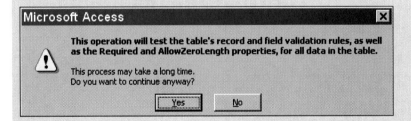

**15** To proceed with the test:
CLICK: Yes command button
CLICK: Yes command button to save the table
(*Note:* Access displays a warning dialog box only if the test fails.)

**16** CLICK: View—Datasheet button (▥▾)

**17** Let's test the record validation rule:
SELECT: 11/2/99 in the secEndDate column of the first record
TYPE: **9/2/99**
PRESS: `TAB`
Notice that Access allows you to enter the invalid date into the field. The criterion for a record validation rule is not evaluated until the cursor leaves the record.

**18** To move to the next record:
PRESS: ⬇
The validation text now appears in a warning dialog box, as shown in Figure 9.11 below.

**Figure 9.11**

Testing a record validation rule

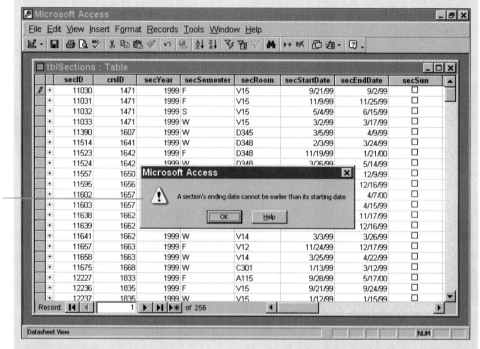

When a value violates the record validation criterion, Access displays the validation text.

**19** To accept the dialog box:
CLICK: OK command button
PRESS: `ESC` to undo the previous change

**20** Close the datasheet window.

**In Addition**
Finding Values that
Violate the Validation
Rule

A validation rule ensures that only legal entries are made in a table. However, if data already exists in the table, you may see a warning dialog box appear when you attempt to create the validation rule. Besides using the Edit, Test Validation Rules command, one way to proceed is to create a filter that displays the records that violate the rule. You may then review, edit, or delete these records as required.

## 9.2.2 Filling In a Form Automatically

**FEATURE**

One reason for basing a form on a query is to gain access to data stored in multiple tables. For example, you can combine tables in a one-to-one relationship in order to update the data in a single Form window. If a one-to-many relationship exists, you can create an **AutoLookup query** that automatically fills in field values from the "one" side of the relationship. In addition to saving time, an AutoLookup query enables you to include information on a form that can be used for data validation. For example, when the user enters a CustomerID, you can display the customer's name and address automatically beside the field. With a quick glance, the user is able to verify that they've entered the correct ID value. If the user changes the ID value, Access automatically looks up and displays the associated values from the related table.

**METHOD**

1. Create a query that combines two tables with a one-to-many relationship.
2. Place the foreign key field (from the "many" side of the relationship) in the query Design grid and then add additional fields as desired.
3. Create a form based on the AutoLookup query.
4. Make the lookup display field(s) read-only.

**PRACTICE**

In this lesson, you create a new form based on an AutoLookup query.

*Setup:* Ensure that the ACC900 Database window is displayed.

**1** Let's define an AutoLookup query to use for creating a new form:
CLICK: *Queries* button in the Objects bar
DOUBLE-CLICK: Create query in Design view
DOUBLE-CLICK: tblAdministrators in the Show Table dialog box
DOUBLE-CLICK: tblCourses in the Show Table dialog box
CLICK: Close command button

**2** In the tblCourses field list:
DOUBLE-CLICK: admID
DOUBLE-CLICK: crsID
DOUBLE-CLICK: crsSuffix
DOUBLE-CLICK: crsName
DOUBLE-CLICK: crsDescription

ACCESS

**3**  In the tblAdministrators field list:
DOUBLE-CLICK: admLastName
DOUBLE-CLICK: admFirstName
Your screen should appear similar to Figure 9.12.

**Figure 9.12**

Creating an
AutoLookup query

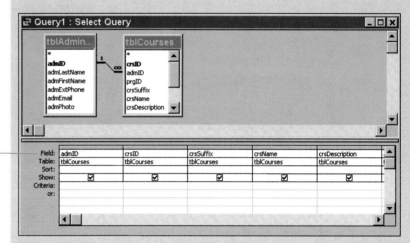

Notice that the foreign key
field appears in the first
column of the grid.

**4**  Save the query as "qryAutoLookup" and then close the query
Design window.

**5**  You now use the query in creating a new form. Do the
following:
CLICK: *Forms* button in the Objects bar
DOUBLE-CLICK: Create form by using wizard

**6**  In the first step of the Form wizard:
SELECT: "Query: qryAutoLookup" in the *Tables/Queries* drop-
down list box, if it isn't already displayed
CLICK: Include All button ( >> )
CLICK: Next >

**7**  In the second step of the wizard:
SELECT: "by tblCourses" in the *How do you want to view your data*
list box
CLICK: Next >

**8**  For the remaining steps:
SELECT: *Columnar* option button
CLICK: Next >
SELECT: Expedition
CLICK: Next >
TYPE: **frmAutoLookup**
SELECT: *Open the form to view or enter information* option button
CLICK: Finish

**9** On your own, browse through the records in the form using the navigation controls. When the value stored in the admID text box changes, notice that the admLastName and admFirstName values also change. When ready to proceed, move to the first record.

**10** To demonstrate the AutoLookup feature, let's change the admID in the first record from "1" to "2." Do the following:
DOUBLE-CLICK: admID text box to select its contents
TYPE: 2
PRESS: ⌨TAB
Notice that the admLastName and admFirstName values are updated automatically to reflect the change. (*Hint:* To keep users from editing an administrator's name, set the *Locked* properties for both the admLastName and admFirstName text box controls to "Yes.")

**11** PRESS: ⌨ESC to return the admID value to 1

**12** Close the Form window.

## 9.2.3 Enhancing a Form Using Combo Boxes

**FEATURE**
The list box, drop-down list box, and combo box controls are especially useful for verifying that the correct data is entered into a form. In Chapter 5, you defined lookup fields and columns to facilitate data entry in a datasheet. In this lesson, you work with combo boxes on a form. A simple example of a combo box that displays a fixed list of name prefixes appears to the right. However, the real benefit of these controls lies in pulling values from related tables. When a value is selected in the list or combo box, Access can either store the displayed value (more likely the key value from its record) or pass the value to another control.

**METHOD**
1. Display a form in Design view.
2. Ensure that the Control Wizards button (🔲) is selected.
3. CLICK: Combo Box button (🔲) or the List Box button (🔲)
4. CLICK: in the Form window to launch the wizard

**PRACTICE**

You now enhance a form by adding a drop-down list box control.

*Setup:* Ensure that the ACC900 Database window is displayed.

**1** Open the frmCourseInfo form in Design view. Your screen should appear similar to Figure 9.13.

**Figure 9.13**

Displaying frmCourseInfo
in Design view

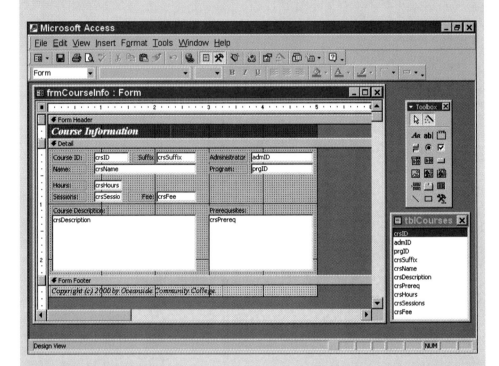

**2** The admID and prgID text box controls appear in the top right-hand corner of the form. You will now change these text box controls to combo boxes. Do the following:
RIGHT-CLICK: admID text box control

**3** From the right-click menu:
CHOOSE: Change To, Combo Box
The control changes shape to include a drop-down arrow, as shown below.

admID

**4** You must now define the contents of the combo box:
RIGHT-CLICK: admID combo box control
CHOOSE: Properties

**5** In the Properties window:
CLICK: *Data* tab
CLICK: in the *Row Source* text box
CLICK: down arrow attached to the property text box
SELECT: tblAdministrators
(*Note:* The *Bound Column* property is set to 1, which is the column location of the admID field in the tblAdministrators table. The combo box stores this column's value when a selection is made.)

**6** The next step is to specify the fields that you want displayed in the combo box control. In order to display the administrator's first and last name, you must specify the first three columns of the tblAdministrators table. Why three columns? Because you cannot extract column data from the middle of the table. You must count from left to right. To begin:
CLICK: *Format* tab
DOUBLE-CLICK: in the *Column Count* text box
TYPE: **3**
(*Hint:* You can specify whether to include column headings in the drop-down list by setting the *Column Heads* property.)

**7** You can now specify the width of each column in the combo box control, separated by semicolons. To make the undesired column, column 1, invisible, set its width to 0. Do the following:
CLICK: in the *Column Widths* text box
TYPE: **0";0.6";0.6"**
(*Hint:* If you leave out the quotation mark or leading zero that appears before a decimal, Access completes the entry for you.)

**8** To test the column widths for the combo box, keep the Properties window open and then display the form:
CLICK: View—Form button (⊞▾)
Notice that the admID combo box displays the administrator's last name rather than his or her ID number.

**9** To display the administrator options that are available:
CLICK: down arrow attached to the admID combo box
Your screen should now appear similar to Figure 9.14. (*Hint:* If the column widths are not sufficient, you can edit the *Column Widths* property that appears in the Properties window.)

ACCESS

**Figure 9.14**

Testing a combo box control

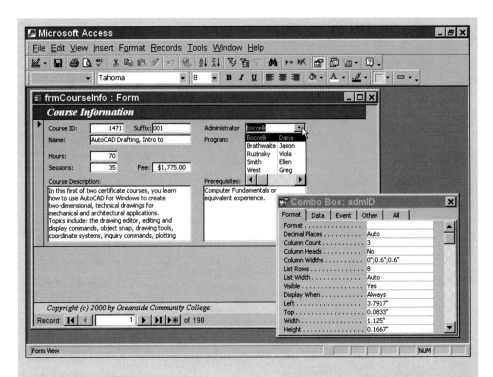

**10** Close the Properties window and then return to Design view.

**11** Let's use the Control Wizards to create a combo box control from scratch. To begin:
SELECT: prgID text box control
PRESS: DELETE

**12** Ensure that the Control Wizards button (⬁) is pressed in and then:
CLICK: Combo Box button (🔠) in the Toolbox window
DRAG: an outline for the new combo box control in the same place that the previous control appeared (as shown below)

**13** When you release the mouse button, the Combo Box Wizard appears. In the first step of the wizard:
SELECT: *I want the combo box to look up the values in a table or query* option button
CLICK: Next >

**14** In the second step of the Combo Box Wizard:
SELECT: tblPrograms
CLICK: Next >

**15** Now select the fields that you want displayed in the combo box:
CLICK: Include All button ([ » ])
CLICK: [ Next > ]

**16** In the fourth step of the Combo Box Wizard, Access presumes that you want to hide the prgID key field and, therefore, selects the *Hide key column* check box automatically. On your own, use the mouse to drag the prgName column's border in the header area in order to adjust its width. Then do the following:
CLICK: [ Next > ]

**17** In the fifth step of the Combo Box Wizard, you assign the selected value to a field in the tblCourses table. Do the following:
SELECT: *Store that value in this field* option button
CLICK: down arrow attached to the drop-down list box
SELECT: prgID
CLICK: [ Next > ]

**18** Lastly, let's rename the control:
TYPE: **cboPrgID**
CLICK: [ Finish ]

**19** On your own, edit the label attached to the combo box control to read "Program:" and then move it into position under the "Administrator:" label. When ready to proceed:
CLICK: View—Form button ([▦▾])

**20** After testing the new combo box control, save the form as "frmCourseCombo" and then close the Form window.

## 9.2.4 Using the Tab and Subform Controls

**FEATURE**

There are many special-purpose **ActiveX controls** that you can use to enhance a form. Two of the more interesting controls, which can be used together quite nicely, are the Tab and Subform controls. In this lesson, you learn how to create and position a subform on a separate tab page in a Form window.

The Access tab control allows you to display multiple pages of information in a single window. This control is especially useful when you need to group fields or when you need to insert a subform of related records. By separating data into pages and not cramming fields together, you are less likely to overwhelm or confuse novice users. As in print-based publishing, the power of using white space in electronic forms should not be underestimated.

As demonstrated in Chapter 7, a subform control allows you to view all of the child records related to any given parent in a one-to-many relationship. When you select a record in the main form, the subform refreshes to display only those records with a matching foreign key. One of the key benefits of incorporating a subform is that data can be entered into two tables using one Form window. Like all relationships, the parent and child tables must share a common field for synchronizing their records.

**METHOD**

To insert a tab control:

1. Display a form in Design view.
2. CLICK: Tab Control button (▱)
3. CLICK: in the Form window to place the control
4. RIGHT-CLICK: Tab Control
5. Choose a menu option to display the control's properties, insert a page, delete a page, reorder the pages, or modify the tab order of controls.

To create a subform:

1. Display a form in Design view.
2. Ensure that the Control Wizards button (▨) is pressed in.
3. CLICK: Subform/Subreport button (▥)
4. CLICK: in the Form window to launch the wizard

**PRACTICE**
You now create a form that incorporates both tab and subform controls.

*Setup:* Ensure that the ACC900 Database window is displayed.

**1** To begin, let's create a new form from scratch:
DOUBLE-CLICK: Create form in Design view

**2** On your own, increase the height of the form by dragging its bottom border to the 3-inch mark on the vertical ruler.

**3** Before proceeding, you must select a parent table as the record source for the form. Do the following:
DOUBLE-CLICK: Form Selector button (□)
CLICK: *Data* tab
CLICK: down arrow attached to the *Record Source* property text box
SELECT: tblCourses

**4** Close the Properties window. Ensure that the Field List window and the Toolbox window appear in the work area before proceeding.

**5** To add a tab control to the form:
CLICK: Tab Control button (□) in the Toolbox window
DRAG: an outline for the tab control so that it matches the image size in Figure 9.15

**Figure 9.15**

Inserting a tab control

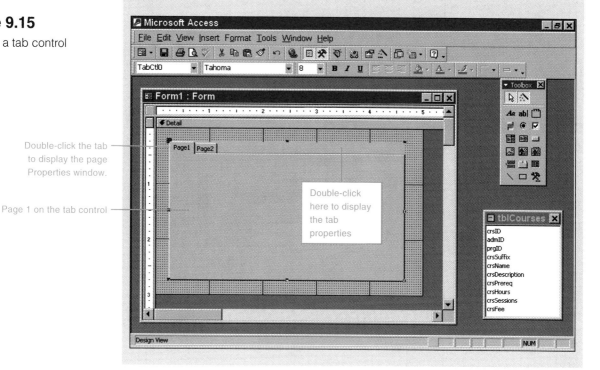

Double-click the tab to display the page Properties window.

Page 1 on the tab control

**6** A tab control provides two windows for setting properties. First, you can display a Properties window for the tab itself by double-clicking the border area outside the page tabs. To display the properties for a specific page, double-click the desired tab. To illustrate:
DOUBLE-CLICK: "Page1" tab
The page's Properties window appears.

**7** To specify a new name for the first tab:
CLICK: *Format* tab in the Properties window
CLICK: in the *Caption* text box
TYPE: `Course Info`
(*Note:* If you do not enter a caption, Access uses the value in the *Name* property text box. You can also attach a picture or icon to a tab using the *Picture* property.)

**8** To edit the second tab's name:
CLICK: "Page2" tab
CLICK: in the *Caption* text box
TYPE: `Sections Available`

**9** Close the Properties window.

**10** Now let's add a few fields to the tab control:
CLICK: "Course Info" tab to make it active
CLICK: crsID in the Field List window
PRESS: SHIFT and hold it down
CLICK: crsName
DRAG: the field selection into the tab control area at approximately the 1.5-inch mark on the horizontal ruler

**11** On your own, adjust the size and position of the controls to appear similar to Figure 9.16.

**Figure 9.16**

Adding fields to a tab control

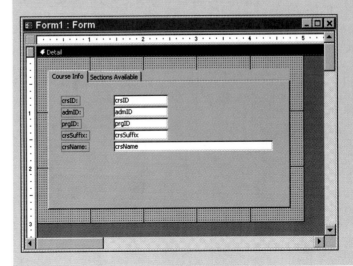

**12.** CLICK: View—Form button (⊞▾) to view the form

**13.** To view the different pages in the Form window:
CLICK: *Sections Available* tab
CLICK: *Course Info* tab

**14.** CLICK: View—Design button (⊠▾) to return to Design view

**15.** Now let's add a subform to the *Sections Available* tab:
CLICK: "Sections Available" tab

**16.** Ensure that the Control Wizards button (⊠) is pressed in and then:
CLICK: Subform/Subreport button (⊞) in the Toolbox window
DRAG: an outline for the tab control so that it matches the image size in Figure 9.17

**17.** When you release the mouse button, the first dialog box of the SubForm Wizard appears. Let's add an existing form to the tab:
SELECT: *Use an existing form* option button
SELECT: frmSubSections in the list box
CLICK: Next >

**18.** In the second step of the wizard, you specify how Access should link the main form and subform control. Since the table relationships are already defined in the Relationships window, Access easily determines the common linking field and suggests an approach. To continue:
SELECT: *Choose from a list* option button, if not already selected
SELECT: "Show tblSections for each record in tblCourses using crsID" in the list box
CLICK: Next >

**19.** To complete the wizard:
CLICK: Finish
The frmSubSections subform appears selected on the *Sections Available* tab.

**20.** On your own, use the sizing handles to adjust the size and position of the new subform to appear similar to Figure 9.17.

ACCESS

**Figure 9.17**

Adding a subform control

Subform label control

Bound subform control

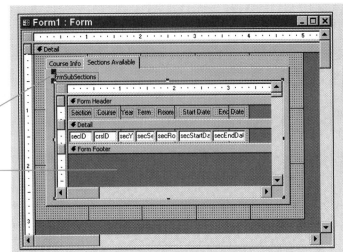

**21** Let's edit the subform label:
CLICK: frmSubSections label control
DOUBLE-CLICK: "frmSubSections" text to select it
TYPE: `Course Sections:`

**22** CLICK: View—Form button (📧▾) to view the form
CLICK: *Sections Available* tab
Only the sections for course 1471 are displayed. (*Note:* This sub-form includes the Course column to illustrate the link between the first page and the second page in the form. For a real-life application, you would place the course number in the Form Header section and then remove it from the subform control.)

**23** On your own, return to the *Course Info* tab and select course 1607. Then move to the *Sections Available* tab to view the results.

**24** When ready to proceed, save the form as "frmCourseControls" and then close the Form window.

---

**In Addition**

Linking and Synchronizing a Subform

One of the most important points in using the subform control is to ensure that it is linked and synchronized with the main form. When you elicit the help of the Form and Subform Wizards, this is a relatively straightforward task. If, however, you create a subform from scratch, you must display the Properties window for the subform and then enter the appropriate linking fields into the *Link Child Fields* and *Link Master Fields* property text boxes on the *Data* tab.

**9.2 Self Check**    Name three methods discussed in this module for verifying that the correct data is entered in a form.

# 9.3 Creating Reports from Scratch

In addition to the report wizards, Access provides many tools and techniques for creating and enhancing reports in report Design view. You can create most any report you can visually imagine. While using the wizards to create a report is quick and easy, consider the impact of a customized report that features an executive summary page, newspaper-style columns, color photographs, and a three-dimensional chart. In report Design view, you possess the power and flexibility required to create such impressive documents. In this module, you learn how to group data into sections, add line numbers to a page, insert bound and unbound graphics, and set report, section, and control properties.

## 9.3.1 Grouping Data in Report Design View

**FEATURE**

The process of sorting and grouping data in reports was first introduced in Chapter 7. Using the Sorting and Grouping window, you can define new sections in a report and sort data into ascending or descending order. This lesson focuses on creating a new report from scratch, specifying a record source, adding grouping levels, and setting basic properties. You also organize and group records for printing.

**METHOD**

1. Display a report in Design view.
2. CLICK: Sorting and Grouping button (▣)
3. SELECT: a field name in the *Field/Expression* column
4. SELECT: a sort order in the *Sort Order* column
5. Use the *Group Header* and *Group Footer* text boxes to specify new header and footer groupings in the report.
6. Use the *Group On* text box to specify how you want the values grouped.
7. Use the *Group Interval* text box to specify the interval for grouping data.
8. Use the *Keep Together* text box to specify how to print groups across multipage reports.

ACCESS

**PRACTICE**
In this lesson, you use report Design view to create a new report with multiple data groupings.

*Setup:* Ensure that the ACC900 Database window is displayed.

**1** To create a new report from scratch:
CLICK: *Reports* button in the Objects bar
DOUBLE-CLICK: Create report in Design view

**2** To expand the work area, maximize the Report window by clicking the Maximize button (⬜) appearing in its Title bar. (*Hint:* You can also double-click a window's Title bar to maximize the window.)

**3** You must now bind the report to a table or query. To define the underlying record source:
DOUBLE-CLICK: Report Selector button (▪)

**4** In the Report Properties window:
CLICK: *Data* tab
CLICK: in the *Record Source* text box
CLICK: down arrow attached to the property text box
SELECT: qryForReport from the drop-down list
The Field List window appears populated with fields from the query. (*Note:* If the Field List window does not appear, click the Field List button (▣) on the toolbar.)

**5** Close the Report Properties window.

**6** To display a Report Header section:
CHOOSE: View, Report Header/Footer

**7** Now let's define a few of the basic features of this report:
CLICK: Sorting and Grouping button (▤)
An empty Sorting and Grouping window appears, as shown in Figure 9.18.

**Figure 9.18**

Displaying the Sorting and
Grouping window

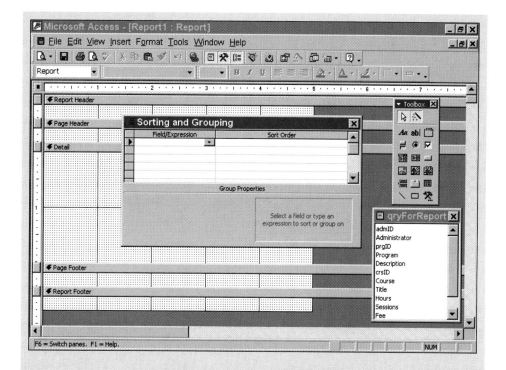

**8** For this report, you will group records by administrator and then
by program. To begin, let's define the administrator grouping:
CLICK: down arrow attached to the first text box in the
*Field/Expression* column
SELECT: admID
CLICK: in the *Group Header* text box
CLICK: down arrow attached to the text box
SELECT: Yes
By default, the *Sort Order* column displays "Ascending" order.
Notice also that a new section band is added to the Report
window.

**9** To define the program grouping:
CLICK: in the next row of the *Field/Expression* column
CLICK: down arrow attached to the text box
SELECT: prgID
CLICK: in the *Group Header* text box
CLICK: down arrow attached to the text box
SELECT: Yes

**10** Lastly, let's ensure that the detail records (courses) are sorted into
ascending order. Do the following:
CLICK: in the next row of the *Field/Expression* column
CLICK: down arrow attached to the text box
SELECT: crsID

**11** Close the Sorting and Grouping window.

**12** Using the Label button (□) in the Toolbox window, add "Course Listing by Administrator" as the report title in the Report Header section. Then select a 14-point, Times New Roman font and make it boldface. You may need to increase the width of the label control and the height of the Report Header section. (*Hint:* For the next few steps, refer to Figure 9.19 to view the final design.)

**13** From the Field List window, drag "Administrator" to the left-hand side of the admID Header section and then adjust its size and position. Apply boldface to both the label and text box controls.

**14** From the Field List window, drag "Program" to the left-hand side of the prgID Header section and then delete its label control. After adjusting the text box control's size and position, make it italic.

**15** Using Figure 9.19 as your guide, drag the "Course" and "Title" fields to the Detail section and then delete their attached label controls. After increasing the height of the prgID Header section, add two new label controls with "Course" and "Title" above the appropriate text boxes in the prgID Header section. Underline these two label controls.

**16** Reduce the height of the Detail section and then adjust the size and position of the controls to appear similar to Figure 9.19. (*Note:* The grid marks have been removed from the screen graphic so that you may view the formatting more clearly.)

**Figure 9.19**

Completing the report design

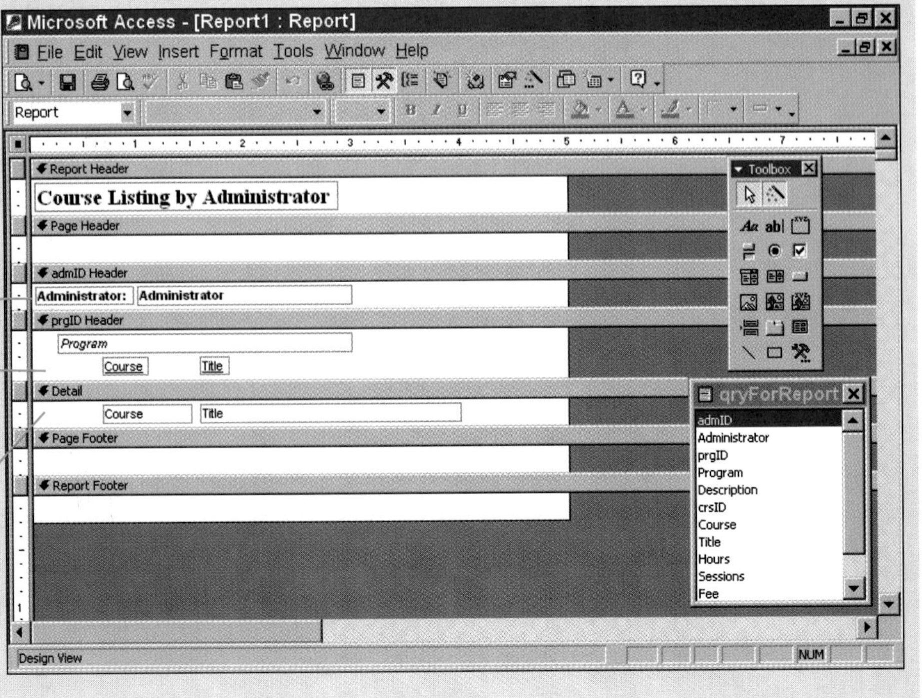

Header section for administrator grouping

Header section for program grouping

Records in the Detail section are sorted into ascending order by crsID.

**17** CLICK: View—Print Preview button (📄▾) to preview the report
The report groups courses according to program area and administrator.

**18** On your own, browse through the pages in the report.

**19** When you are ready to proceed:
CLICK: View—Design button (📄▾) to return to Design view

**20** Save the report as "rptAdmGroup" and keep it open for use in the next lesson.

## 9.3.2 Using a Calculated Control to Add Line Numbers

**FEATURE**

A *calculated control* is a text box that contains an expression. In most cases, these controls are used to perform calculations using data stored in the underlying table or query. However, you can also use Access' built-in functions in calculated controls for a variety of other purposes such as adding the current date to a report's page footer. In this lesson, you add a calculated control to a report in order to print line numbers, similar to those you would find in a legal contract.

**METHOD**

1. Display a report in Design view.
2. Add a text box control to the left side of the Detail section.
3. Delete the label attached to the new text box control.
4. DOUBLE-CLICK: the text box control
5. CLICK: *Data* tab in the Properties window
6. TYPE: =1 in the *Control Source* text box
7. SELECT: Over Group in the *Running Sum* text box

**PRACTICE**

You now add a calculated control to the rptAdmGroup report that you created in the last lesson.

*Setup:* Ensure that you've completed the previous lesson and that the rptAdmGroup report appears in Design view.

**1** To begin, add a text box control to the left of "Course" in the Detail section, as shown below.

Add a text box control to the Detail section.

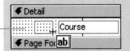

**2** When you release the mouse button, an unbound text box with an attached label control appears. To remove the label control:
SELECT: text box's label control
PRESS: DELETE

**3** To display the Properties window:
RIGHT-CLICK: text box control
CHOOSE: Properties
(*Hint:* You can also double-click the border of the control.)

**4** To set the necessary properties:
CLICK: *Data* tab
CLICK: in the *Control Source* text box
TYPE: =1
CLICK: in the *Running Sum* text box
CLICK: down arrow attached to the property text box
SELECT: Over Group
(*Note:* To number items sequentially throughout the entire report, select the Over All option in the *Running Sum* property text box.)

**5** Close the Properties window.

**6** CLICK: View—Print Preview button (🔍) to preview the report
After adjusting the window, your screen should appear similar to Figure 9.20.

**Figure 9.20**

Adding line numbers
to a report

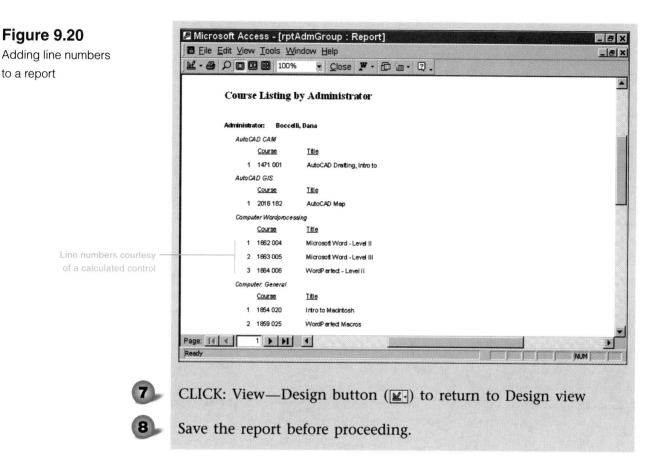

Line numbers courtesy
of a calculated control

**7** CLICK: View—Design button (⊠▾) to return to Design view

**8** Save the report before proceeding.

## 9.3.3 Adding a Background Picture to a Report

**FEATURE**
You can add a *watermark* image to the background of a report by setting a report property. A **watermark** is text, a picture, or a graphic that appears somewhat faded behind existing text. For example, the words DRAFT or CONFIDENTIAL are commonly watermarked on interoffice reports. All of the picture options that are available in setting a form's background are also available for reports.

**METHOD**
1.  Display a report in Design view.
2.  DOUBLE-CLICK: Report Selector button (■)
3.  CLICK: *Format* tab in the Report Properties window
4.  Use the *Picture* text box to select a picture file.
5.  Use the *Picture Type* text box to specify whether the picture is linked or embedded.
6.  Use the *Picture Size Mode* text box to clip, stretch, or zoom the picture.
7.  Use the *Picture Alignment* text box to align the picture on the page.
8.  Specify whether to tile the picture to cover the entire report page.

**PRACTICE**
In this lesson, you add a watermark background picture to the rptAdmGroup report.

*Setup:* Ensure that you've completed the previous lesson and that the rptAdmGroup report appears in Design view.

**1**  The first step is to display the Report Properties window:
DOUBLE-CLICK: Report Selector button (■)
CLICK: *Format* tab

**2**  You must now select a picture to display on the report's background. Do the following:
CLICK: in the *Picture* text box
CLICK: Build button (…) that appears to the right of the text box
The Insert Picture dialog box is displayed.

**3**  On your own, locate the Advantage student data files folder and then:
DOUBLE-CLICK: Draft in the list area
The filename is placed into the property text box. (*Note:* The terms *graphic, image,* and *picture* are used interchangeably in this chapter.)

**4**  To zoom the image to fit the width of the page:
CLICK: in the *Picture Size Mode* text box
CLICK: down arrow attached to the property text box
SELECT: Zoom

**5**  In order for the watermark to show through the text box controls in the report, you must change their *Back Style* property to "Transparent." Do the following:
CLICK: Administrator text box control in the admID Header section
CLICK: in the *Back Style* text box in the Properties window
CLICK: down arrow attached to the property text box
SELECT: Transparent

**6**  On your own, change the *Back Style* property of all text box controls in the report to "Transparent." When ready to proceed, close the Properties window. (*Hint:* You could also use the Select All command and then change the property setting.)

**7**  CLICK: View—Print Preview button (⟨🔍▾⟩) to preview the report

**8**  Scroll the report's Print Preview window to view the new watermark graphic that appears. As you can see, you must create or select a faint graphic for display on a report's background.

**9**  CLICK: View—Design button (⟨📐▾⟩) to return to Design view

**10**  Save the report before proceeding.

## 9.3.4 Enhancing a Report Using Graphics

**FEATURE**
Similar to adding a graphic to a form, you can place drawings, photographs, scanned pictures, and company logos in your reports. You can also use the Toolbox buttons to draw lines and boxes. For most image files, select an image control instead of an unbound object frame. If you need to include a graphic stored in an OLE Object field, select a bound object frame or drag the field from the Field List window. It is important to remember that placing a control in the Detail section will cause a new graphic to appear for each record. As a result, you typically find image controls in the Header and Footer sections and only bound object frames in the Detail section.

**METHOD**
To insert a graphic using an image control:

1.  Display a report in Design view.
2.  CLICK: Image button (⊞) in the Toolbox window
3.  CLICK: in the Report window to place the control
4.  Select a graphic file from the Insert Picture dialog box.

To insert a graphic using a bound object frame:

1.  Display a report in Design view.
2.  Display the Field List window using the Field List button (⊟).
3.  DRAG: an OLE Object field from the Field List window

**PRACTICE**
You now add an image control and a bound object frame to the rptAdmGroup report.

*Setup:* Ensure that you've completed the previous lesson and that the rptAdmGroup report appears in Design view.

**1** To add an image control to the Report Header section:
CLICK: Image button (⊞) in the Toolbox window

**2** Position the mouse directly beneath the Report Header section bar at 3.5 inches on the horizontal ruler. Now, do the following:
CLICK: the left mouse button once
The Insert Picture dialog box should appear.

**3** On your own, locate the Advantage student data files folder and then:
DOUBLE-CLICK: OCCLogo in the list area

**4** To customize the display of the image:
DOUBLE-CLICK: the image control
CLICK: *Format* tab
CLICK: in the *Size Mode* text box
CLICK: down arrow attached to the property text box
SELECT: Zoom

**5** Close the Properties window.

**6** By dragging its lower right-hand sizing handle, size the image control so that it is approximately one-inch square. (*Hint:* When you need to manipulate graphics, metafiles tend to size better than bitmaps.)

**7** To add the administrator's photograph to the admID Header section:
DRAG: admPhoto from the Field List window to the admID Header section at approximately 3.5 inches on the horizontal ruler

**8** On your own, delete the admPhoto label control and then size and position the bound object frame to appear similar to Figure 9.21.

**9** To size the graphic proportionally:
DOUBLE-CLICK: the bound object frame
CLICK: in the *Size Mode* text box
CLICK: down arrow attached to the property text box
SELECT: Zoom

**10** Lastly, adjust the height of the Report Header, Page Header, admID Header, and other sections to appear similar to Figure 9.21.

**11** CLICK: View—Print Preview button (🔍) to preview the report (*Note:* Browse through the report pages to view the latest changes.)

**12** CLICK: View—Design button (📐) to return to Design view

**13** Save the report before proceeding.

**Figure 9.21**

Adding an image control and a bound object frame to a report

Image control

Bound object frame control

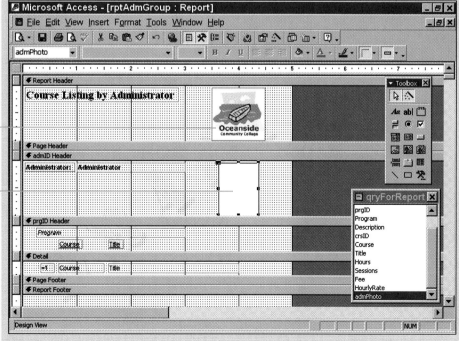

## 9.3.5  Setting Control Properties in a Report

**FEATURE**

As with controls in forms, you can customize the appearance and behavior of most controls appearing in report Design view. The most significant property, the *Control Source* text box on the *Data* tab, contains either the name of an underlying data field or a calculated expression. You can also use the *Format* tab in the Properties window to specify the dimensions, color, font, and alignment of a control. To improve consistency in formatting controls, select several controls at once and then change all of their attributes in a single step.

**METHOD**

- DOUBLE-CLICK: the control's border, or
- RIGHT-CLICK: the desired control
  CHOOSE: Properties

**PRACTICE**

You now set control properties for a new text box control in the rptAdmGroup report.

*Setup:* Ensure that you've completed the previous lesson and that the rptAdmGroup report appears in Design view.

**1** In the next few steps, you will place a new text box control in the prgID Header section. Before doing so, however, remove the Course and Title label controls that appear in this section. (*Hint:* Select the controls and then press DELETE.)

**2** Now decrease the width of the "Program" text box and then add a new text box control to its right, as shown below. Do your best to align the left edge of the new text box control with the left edge of the Title text box in the Detail section.

**3** When you release the mouse button, the text box with its label control appears. To remove the label control:
SELECT: text box's label control
PRESS: DELETE

**4** To display its Properties window:
DOUBLE-CLICK: the text box control

**5** First, set the control's *Control Source* property to the program description field in the query. Do the following:
CLICK: *Data* tab
CLICK: in the *Control Source* text box
CLICK: down arrow attached to the property text box
SELECT: Description

**6** Now let's format the text box control:
CLICK: *Format* tab
CLICK: in the *Back Style* text box
CLICK: down arrow attached to the property text box
SELECT: Transparent

**7** For bound controls that may contain varying amounts of text, you can set the *Can Grow* and *Can Shrink* properties. These properties allow the controls to grow and shrink in height as required by the amount of text. To ensure that all the text in the field is displayed:
CLICK: in the *Can Grow* text box
CLICK: down arrow attached to the property text box
SELECT: Yes

**8** Now scroll down the properties list and then:
CLICK: in the *Font Italic* text box
CLICK: down arrow attached to the property text box
SELECT: Yes

**9** Close the Properties window.

**10** CLICK: View—Print Preview button ([🔍▾]) to preview the report
Your screen should now appear similar to Figure 9.22.

ACCESS

**Figure 9.22**

Displaying a report with
a custom text box control

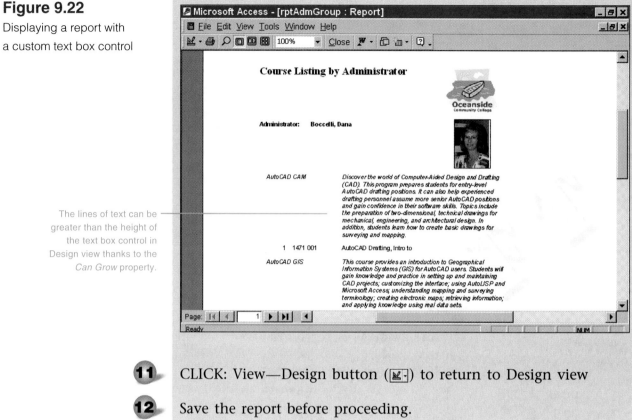

The lines of text can be
greater than the height of
the text box control in
Design view thanks to the
*Can Grow* property.

**11** CLICK: View—Design button (🔲) to return to Design view

**12** Save the report before proceeding.

## 9.3.6 Setting Report and Section Properties

**FEATURE**
Earlier in this module, you used the Report Properties window to specify a record source and background picture for the report. Rest assured that there are several more properties available for customizing a report. In addition, you can set properties to modify the appearance and behavior of the individual header, footer, and detail sections. For example, you can force a new page to begin whenever the value changes in a group header. This lesson explores using properties to fine-tune the individual and combined components that make up a report.

**METHOD**
To display the Report Properties window:

- DOUBLE-CLICK: Report Selector button (▣), or
- CHOOSE: View, Properties

To display a section's Properties window:

- DOUBLE-CLICK: the section bar, or
- RIGHT-CLICK: the section bar
  CHOOSE: Properties

**PRACTICE**
You now practice setting report and section properties.

*Setup:* Ensure that you've completed the previous lesson and that the rptAdmGroup report appears in Design view.

**1** The Report Header section is often used for displaying a title page, logo, or abstract. For these initial pages, you don't normally print the information appearing in the Page Header section. To make this adjustment, you must modify a report property setting as follows:
DOUBLE-CLICK: Report Selector button (▣)

**2** In the Report Properties window, tell Access not to print a Page Header on those pages that contain a Report Header:
CLICK: *Format* tab
CLICK: in the *Page Header* text box
CLICK: down arrow attached to the text box
SELECT: Not with Rpt Hdr

**3** Now tell Access not to print a Page Footer on those pages that contain a Report Footer:
CLICK: in the *Page Footer* text box
CLICK: down arrow attached to the text box
SELECT: Not with Rpt Ftr

**4** You can force a new page before a section to ensure that each group value appears on its own page. To set this section property:
CLICK: admID Header section bar
Notice that the Properties window updates to display the section properties.

**5** To insert a page break:
CLICK: in the *Force New Page* text box
CLICK: down arrow attached to the text box
SELECT: Before Section
(*Hint:* In other words, Access moves to the top of the next page prior to printing the section.)

**6** Close the Properties window.

**7** CLICK: View—Print Preview button (📄▾) to preview the report
Notice that the first page of the report is empty, since Access forces a new page before printing the admID Header section.

**8** On your own, browse through the pages in the report. Notice that each administrator's course listing begins at the top of a new page.

**9** CLICK: View—Design button (📐▾) to return to Design view

**10** Restore the report Design window to a window using the Restore button (🗗).

**11** Save and then close the report Design window.

**In Addition**
Inserting a Page Break
Within a Section

Besides forcing a new page in a group header, you can use the Page Break control to start a new page within any section. For example, in the report header, you can separate the title page from the report's abstract using a page break. To insert a page break, click the Page Break button (🗐) in the Toolbox window and then click in the section where you want the page break to appear. The page break symbol (⸺), which you can move using the mouse, attaches itself to the left-hand border.

**9.3 Self Check** How would you change a report's sort order from ascending to descending order?

# 9.4 Building Complex Reports

For our purposes, a complex report is one that does not follow the typical layout of a wizard-generated report. For example, the first lesson in the module introduces you to a multicolumn parameter report—a very useful report that prints newspaper-style columns of data filtered at run time. You will also learn how to include a chart in a report, insert a *subreport* into a *main report*, and distribute a report to people who do not have Microsoft Access.

## 9.4.1 Creating a Multicolumn Parameter Report

**FEATURE**
As you learned in the last chapter, a parameter query enables you to create a query template and then insert the filtering expression at run time. By basing a new report on a parameter query, you achieve all the same benefits of this very useful query type. For example, you can create a single report template that is used to print several variations of the same report. When you open the report, a parameter dialog box appears to collect the desired filtering expression. The report is then previewed or printed with only those records matching the criteria specification.

**METHOD**
- To create a parameter report, create a new report and select a parameter query for its *Record Source* property.
- To specify multiple columns for printing, enter the number of desired columns in the *Columns* tab of the Page Setup dialog box.

**PRACTICE**
You now create a new multicolumn report in Design view.

*Setup:* Ensure that the ACC900 Database window is displayed.

**1** To create a new report from scratch:
DOUBLE-CLICK: Create report in Design view

**2** To define the underlying record source:
DOUBLE-CLICK: Report Selector button (■)
CLICK: *Data* tab
CLICK: in the *Record Source* text box
CLICK: down arrow attached to the property text box
SELECT: qryInstructorRpt from the drop-down list

**3** Close the Report Properties window.

**4** Using Figure 9.23 as your guide, add the fields shown in the screen graphic. Size, move, and align the fields as necessary. (*Note:* The grid marks have been removed from the screen graphic so that you may view the controls more clearly.)

**5** To enhance the text display, select a 9-point, Arial font for all of the controls. Then apply boldface to the "FullName" text box control and make the "Home," "Work," and "Fax" label controls italic.

**6** Refer to Figure 9.23 to adjust the height of the Detail section and the width of the report.

**7** Lastly, add a horizontal line below the bound data controls using the Line button (◻) in the Toolbox window. Your screen should now appear similar to Figure 9.23, except with grid marks.

**Figure 9.23**

Creating a multicolumn report

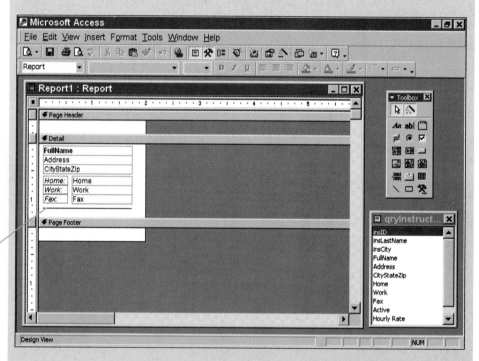

Add a horizontal line to the Detail section.

**8** For the reader's benefit, you should display the expression that is entered into the parameter dialog box at run time in the header or footer area. Let's add a text box control to the Page Header section:
CLICK: Text Box button (◻) in the Toolbox window
DRAG: an outline that covers the majority of the section

**9** To remove the label control that appears attached to the text box:
SELECT: text box's label control
PRESS: DELETE

**10** You will now enter an expression that displays the results of the parameter query. Do the following:
RIGHT-CLICK: the new text box control
CHOOSE: Properties
CLICK: *Data* tab
TYPE: =``"City equals "&[Please enter a city:]``
Notice that the query's parameter name, [Please enter a city:], is referenced by a calculated control inside the report. You must type the parameter name exactly as it appears in the query Design grid.

**11** Close the Properties window.

**12** Now let's specify a newspaper-column format for the report:
CHOOSE: File, Page Setup
CLICK: *Columns* tab
DOUBLE-CLICK: in the *Number of Columns* text box
TYPE: 3
The Page Setup dialog box appears as shown in Figure 9.24.

**Figure 9.24**
Page Setup dialog box

Specify the number and format of columns to display.

Select the *Same as Detail* check box if you've already adjusted the report's width.

Select the order for printing records in the report columns.

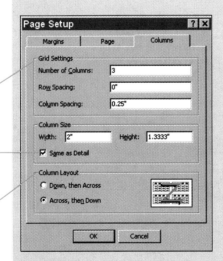

**13** CLICK: OK command button

**14** To view the finished report in the Print Preview window:
CLICK: View—Print Preview button () to preview the report

**15** In the Enter Parameter Value dialog box, enter a criterion to list only those instructors who live in Bellevue. Do the following:
TYPE: `Bellevue`
CLICK: OK command button
You should now see a 3-column report in the Print Preview window with the text "City equals Bellevue" in the page header.

**16** After browsing through the report:
CLICK: View—Design button (🖾▾) to return to Design view

**17** Save the report as "rptParameter" and then close the report Design window.

## 9.4.2 Creating and Displaying a Chart

**FEATURE**
Sporting features similar to Microsoft Excel, Access lets you create, format, and embed a chart in a report (or form) as an OLE object. To plot the data stored in an underlying table or query, you can select among many different chart types, including line charts, column and bar charts, pie charts, and XY scatter plot diagrams. A **line chart** is primarily used to plot trends or show changes over a period of time. When the purpose of a chart is to compare one data element with another, a **column chart** is the appropriate type to select. A **pie chart** shows the proportions of individual components compared to the total. An **XY chart** shows how one or more data elements relate to another data element. Although there are other types of charts, these are the most popular.

**METHOD**
1. Create a query that summarizes the data you want to plot in a chart.
2. CLICK: *Reports* button in the Objects bar
3. CLICK: New button (📄New) in the Database window toolbar
4. SELECT: Chart Wizard in the New Report dialog box
5. SELECT: the desired query from the *Choose...* drop-down list box
6. Proceed using the Chart Wizard.

**PRACTICE**
You now create a report that incorporates a chart in the Detail section.

*Setup:* Ensure that the ACC900 Database window is displayed. (*Note:* You need Microsoft Graph installed in order to use the Chart Wizard.)

**1** You will use the Chart Wizard to create a report. To begin:
CLICK: New button (🗐New) on the Database window toolbar
SELECT: Chart Wizard in the list area

**2** For this lesson, we have prepared a total query that summarizes the financial data stored in the tblSections and tblContracts tables. To select this query:
CLICK: down arrow attached to the *Choose the table or query...* drop-down list box
SELECT: qryForChart
CLICK: OK command button

**3** In the first step of the Chart Wizard dialog box, use the Include button (⟩) to move all of the fields, except for Year, to the *Fields for Chart* list box. When ready to proceed:
CLICK: Next ›
(*Hint:* You can also double-click the field names to move them.)

**4** In this step, you select the type of chart. Do the following:
CLICK: 3-D Column Chart button, shown to the right
CLICK: Next ›
Your screen should now appear similar to Figure 9.25.

**Figure 9.25**

Chart Wizard dialog box: Step 3

Select the data to be plotted in the chart

Specify the data series

Specify the horizontal or X-axis

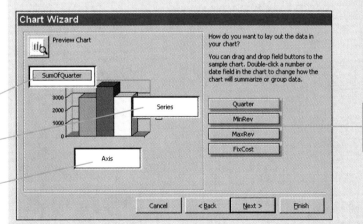

**5** You use the third step in the wizard to create the chart. In order to show the quarters on the horizontal or X-axis:
DRAG: SumOfQuarter button from the Data area to the Axis area
When you drop the button, the button's name changes to "Quarter."

**6** To plot the maximum revenue (MaxRev), minimum revenue (MinRev), and total fixed costs (FixCost) for each quarter:
DRAG: MaxRev field button to the Data area
DOUBLE-CLICK: the SumOfMaxRev field button
SELECT: None in the Summarize dialog box
CLICK: OK command button
(*Note:* Because the total query already summarizes the table values, you do not need the chart to perform a summation.)

**7** Now add the MinRev field button to the Data area:
DRAG: MinRev field button to the Data area, below the MaxRev button
DOUBLE-CLICK: the SumOfMinRev field button
SELECT: None in the Summarize dialog box
CLICK: OK command button

**8** On your own, add the FixCost field button to the Data area and then change its summation value to "None."

**9** To preview the chart:
CLICK: Preview Chart button ( )
The Sample Preview window appears (Figure 9.26.)

**Figure 9.26**

Sample Preview window

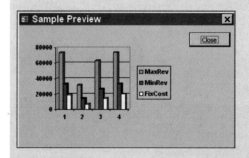

**10** CLICK: Close command button to continue
CLICK: Next >

**11** In the last step of the Chart Wizard dialog box:
TYPE: `Year 2000 Targets`
SELECT: *Yes, display a legend* option button
SELECT: *Open the report with the chart displayed in it* option button
CLICK: Finish
(*Note:* The two option buttons listed above should already appear selected.)

**12** The chart is displayed in the report Print Preview window. You can manipulate the size of the chart object, in addition to customizing each chart element, in report Design view. For this exercise, however, save the chart report as "rptFinanceChart" and then close the Print Preview window by clicking its Close button (⊠). (*Hint:* For more information on creating and editing charts, refer to the Access Help system.)

### 9.4.3 Using the Subreport Control

**FEATURE**
A **subreport** is the name given to a report that is embedded into another report, called the **main report.** A *subreport* is a completely independent and stand-alone report object. The *main report,* whether bound to a table or not, acts as a container for one or more subreports, which may include charts and subforms. For example, a main report can incorporate details from a related table in a multicolumn subreport and then conclude with a column chart summarizing the data in the report's footer. Developers often find it easier to create and manage report objects separately, rather than designing a single large report.

**METHOD**
1. Display a report in Design view.
2. Ensure that the Control Wizards button (◻) is selected.
3. CLICK: Subform/Subreport button (▦)
4. CLICK: in the Report window to launch the wizard

**PRACTICE**
In this lesson, you insert an existing chart report into the Report Footer section of another report.

*Setup:* Ensure that the ACC900 Database window is displayed.

**1** By inserting a subreport into a report header or footer, you can create custom pages for summarizing data. In the following steps, you will add a chart report to the report footer of an existing report. To begin, open the rptMainSection report in Design view. Your screen should appear similar to Figure 9.27.

ACCESS

**Figure 9.27**

Displaying the
rptMainSection report
in Design view

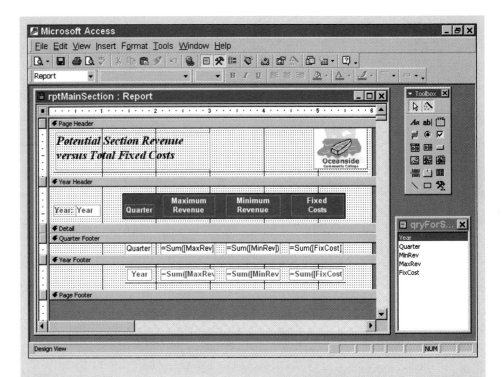

**2** On your own, display the report in the Print Preview window and then return to Design view.

**3** One of the first rules is that you cannot insert a subreport in the Detail section of a main report. You can only use a nonrepeating section, such as the report header or footer. Therefore, do the following:
CHOOSE: View, Report Header/Footer

**4** Close the Report Header section entirely by dragging its bottom border upward. Then:
CLICK: Report Footer section bar

**5** One way of inserting a subreport is to display the Database window and then drag the desired report into the appropriate section. However, we will use the more familiar Control Wizards method. Ensure that the Control Wizards button (⬚) is pressed in and then:
CLICK: Subform/Subreport button (⬚) in the Toolbox window

**6** Move the mouse pointer into the Report Footer section, as shown below, and then click the left mouse button once. The SubReport Wizard dialog box appears.

**7** In the first step of the SubReport Wizard dialog box:
SELECT: *Use an existing report or form* option button
SELECT: rptSubChart in the list area
CLICK: [Finish]
The chart report appears in the Report Footer section.

**8** Move and size the chart to fit in the report. Also, select and then delete the attached label control that appears in the top left-hand corner. (*Hint:* Don't worry if the chart appears as though it is too wide for the report. The borders, rulers, and scroll bars used for displaying the object will be removed when you preview the report.)

**9** To force the chart to print on its own page:
DOUBLE-CLICK: Report Footer section bar
CLICK: *Format* tab
CLICK: in the *Force New Page* text box
CLICK: down arrow attached to the property text box
SELECT: Before Section

**10** Close the Properties window.

**11** CLICK: View—Print Preview button ([🔍▾]) to preview the report

**12** Navigate to page 2 in the report. Your screen should appear similar to Figure 9.28, when viewing the report at 100 percent.

**Figure 9.28**

Displaying a chart in the Report Footer section

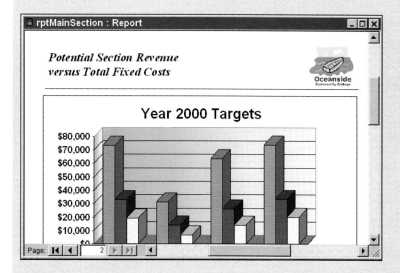

**13** Save the report as "rptSubReport" and then close the Print Preview window.

ACCESS

**14** Let's open another subreport example in Print Preview mode. Do the following:
DOUBLE-CLICK: rptSyncMain
The report shown in Figure 9.29 appears. The main report and subreport are joined and synchronized according to their table relationship. In this particular case, the tblCourses and tblSections tables share the crsID field in common.

**Figure 9.29**

Viewing the Course and Section Listing report

Main report based on the tblCourses table

Subreport based on the tblSections table

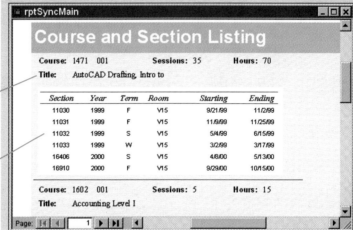

Viewing the Course and Section Listing report

**15** CLICK: View—Design button ( ) to return to Design view

**16** Using the Object drop-down list box ( rptSyncSub ) at the left-hand side of the Formatting toolbar:
SELECT: rptSyncSub
CLICK: Properties button ( ) in the Report Design toolbar

**17** In the Properties window for the subreport:
CLICK: *Data* tab
Notice that both the *Link Child Fields* and *Link Master Fields* contain "crsID," the common key field. This field keeps the records synchronized between the two reports.

**18** Close the Properties window and then close the report Design window.

## 9.4.4 Using the Access Snapshot Viewer

**FEATURE**

If you regularly need to distribute reports to people who do not own or use Microsoft Access, consider sending them a *report snapshot*. A snapshot is a graphic file saved to disk that includes a high-quality representation of each page in a report. You can then e-mail the report snapshot or post the file on a Web site. Microsoft provides a free viewer program for displaying and printing the snapshot files you create in Access.

**METHOD**
1. SELECT: the desired report in the Database window
2. CHOOSE: File, Export
3. TYPE: *a filename*
4. SELECT: Snapshot Format in the *Save as type* drop-down list box
5. CLICK: Save command button

**PRACTICE**

In this lesson, you save a graphic snapshot of the rptSyncMain report.

*Setup:* Ensure that the ACC900 Database window is displayed.

**1** In the *Reports* list area of the Database window:
SELECT: rptSyncMain in the list area
CHOOSE: File, Export

**2** In the Export Report dialog box:
TYPE: Courses in the *File name* text box
SELECT: Snapshot Format in the *Save as type* drop-down list box
(*Note:* A snapshot file ends with the extension .snp.)

**3** Make sure that the *Autostart* check box is selected and then:
CLICK: Save command button
Once you click the Save command button, the Snapshot Viewer program automatically starts and displays a preview of the report.

**4** The Snapshot Viewer offers many of the same features as the Print Preview window in Access. On your own, navigate through the report pages and zoom in and out on the report, as shown in Figure 9.30.

ACCESS

**Figure 9.30**

Snapshot Viewer window

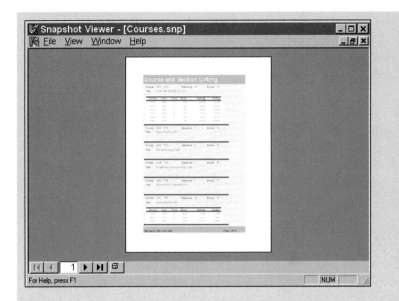

 When ready to proceed, close the Snapshot Viewer by clicking its Close button (⊠).

**9.4 Self Check**    Name two methods for inserting an existing subreport into a main report.

# 9.5  Creating Data Access Pages

New in Access 2000, a **data access page** is a special type of Web page that lets you work with an Access or SQL Server database through a Web browser. Using the data-binding capabilities of dynamic HTML, a data access page connects HTML elements in a Web page with data stored in a server-side database. Besides standard HTML tags, a data access page incorporates several technologies, including Cascading Style Sheets (CSS), Extensible Markup Language (XML), and Vector Markup Language (VML). Data access pages enable users who are attached to an intranet or the Internet to view and work with data, as long as they have Microsoft Internet Explorer 5 installed and own Microsoft Office 2000.

# 9.5.1 Creating a Data Access Page Using a Wizard

**FEATURE**

There are two wizards that you can use to create a data access page. First, the **AutoPage Wizard** works similarly to the AutoForm and AutoReport wizards. The wizard automatically creates a columnar data access page that includes all of the fields and records from the underlying table or query. For more control over the Web page layout, you use the **Page Wizard** in much the same way that you use the Report Wizard to create a report. After selecting the fields that you want included in the page, you then specify the sorting and grouping options. An added benefit to using the Page Wizard is that it enables you to display fields from multiple tables in a single data access page, as demonstrated in the next lesson.

**METHOD**

To create a data access page using the AutoPage Wizard:

1. CLICK: *Pages* button in the Objects bar
2. CLICK: New button (🗐New) on the Database window toolbar
3. SELECT: a table or query from the *Choose* drop-down list box
4. DOUBLE-CLICK: AutoPage: Columnar in the dialog box

**PRACTICE**

In this lesson, you practice creating a data access page using the AutoPage wizard.

*Setup:* Ensure that the ACC900 Database window is displayed.

**1** To create a new data access page using the AutoPage wizard:
CLICK: *Pages* button in the Objects bar
CLICK: New button (🗐New) on the Database window toolbar
SELECT: AutoPage: Columnar in the list area

**2** Let's create a data access page that allows instructors to update their personal and address information over the Web:
CLICK: down arrow attached to the *Choose the table or query...* drop-down list box
SELECT: tblInstructors
CLICK: OK command button
The Access wizard creates a columnar data access page and then opens the Web page in *Page View* mode, as shown in Figure 9.31.

ACCESS

**Figure 9.31**

Viewing a data access
page in Page View mode

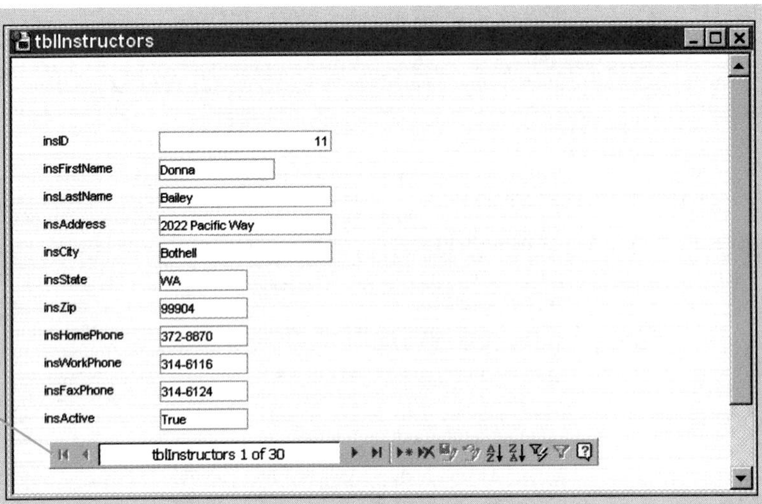

The Record Navigation
control displays the record
source, current record
number, and the total
number of records.

**3** You view data access pages in Access using **Page view** mode, which acts like an interactive Print Preview window. The familiar Record Navigation control allows you to add, delete, sort, and filter the records displayed in a data access page. On your own, use the record navigation buttons to browse through the tblInstructors table.

**4** To navigate the table in ascending order by last name:
CLICK: in the insLastName field text box
CLICK: Sort Ascending button (⊞) on the Record Navigation control
You can now browse the records in alphabetical order.

**5** When you edit the information displayed in a data access page, the modifications are saved to the table when you leave the record. To demonstrate, move to record number 5 for "Garret French" and then:
DOUBLE-CLICK: "Road" in the insAddress field text box
TYPE: **Drive**

**6** To save the record modification to the database:
CLICK: Next Record button (▶) on the Record Navigation control

**7** Data access pages are saved as separate disk files—external to the Access database—to facilitate publishing to a Web server. To save the new data access page to disk:
CLICK: Save button (▣)
TYPE: **pgsAutoPage**
CLICK: Save command button
(*Note:* The data access page is saved with an .HTM file extension to the current folder. You may, however, want to set up a unique folder for storing files that need to be uploaded to a Web server.)

**8** Close the Page View window.

**In Addition**
Viewing a Data Access
Page Using a Web
Browser

Once you've saved a data access page to disk, you can open the page using the Internet Explorer Web browser. However, only users with the appropriate security clearance are allowed to make a connection to the database. As the developer of data access pages, you must ensure that users are granted the required permissions in Access before they attempt to read, update, insert, and delete records in the database. To do so, use the Tools, Security, User and Group Permissions command. For more information, refer to the Access Help system.

## 9.5.2   Creating a Grouped Data Access Page

**FEATURE**
A grouped data access page provides bands of data, similar to grouping records in a report. Unlike a report, however, these bands contain live data and are interactive. You can choose to display only the top-level grouping of data or, by clicking the Expand icon (⊞), you can display additional details. Grouped data access pages are read-only and, therefore, for viewing purposes only.

**METHOD**
To create a data access page using the Page Wizard:

1. CLICK: *Pages* button in the Objects bar
2. DOUBLE-CLICK: Create data access page by using wizard

**PRACTICE**
You now create a grouped data access page using the Page Wizard.

*Setup:* Ensure that the ACC900 Database window is displayed.

**1** To create a grouped data access page using the Page wizard:
CLICK: New button (🗋New)
SELECT: Page Wizard in the list area
SELECT: qryForPage from the *Choose the table or query...* drop-down list box
CLICK: OK command button

**2** The first step in the Page Wizard dialog box asks you to select the fields to include in the data access page. To include all the fields:
CLICK: Include All button (⊡»⊡)
CLICK: Next›

**3** The second step in the Page Wizard dialog box requires you to specify the grouping levels. To proceed:
SELECT: Administrator
CLICK: Include button (▷)
SELECT: Course
CLICK: Include button (▷)
Your screen should now appear similar to Figure 9.32.

**Figure 9.32**

Page Wizard dialog box: Step 2

Access warns you that adding grouping levels to the page results in read-only capabilities.

Click here to specify further grouping options, including setting intervals.

The preview area helps you visualize the final page layout.

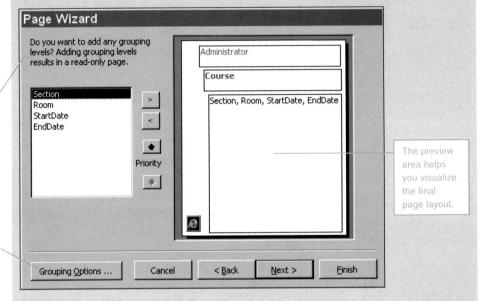

**4** CLICK: Next > to continue

**5** You now specify a sort order for the detail records:
CLICK: down arrow attached to the first *Sort* drop-down list box
SELECT: Section
CLICK: Next >

**6** In the last step of the dialog box, you enter a title that will display at the top of the data access page. Do the following:
TYPE: Course Listing by Administrator
SELECT: *Open the page* option button
CLICK: Finish
After the wizard finishes building the data access page, the Page View window appears.

**7** Maximize the Page View window by clicking its Maximize button (□).

**8** Only the top-level grouping for administrators is displayed in the data access page, as noted in the Record Navigation control. To expand the Administrator level:
CLICK: Expand icon (⊞) for GroupOfqryForPage-Administrator
(*Note:* After displaying the sub-level grouping, the Expand icon (⊞) for the Administrator level changes to a Collapse icon (⊟).)

**9** The Course-level grouping has its own Record Navigation control for browsing only those courses managed by the current administrator. To display the sections that are available for the currently displayed course:
CLICK: Expand icon (⊞) for GroupOfqryForPage-Course
Your screen should now appear similar to Figure 9.33. Notice that each of the three levels is supported by a unique Record Navigation control. Inside the control's text box, you can see that two sections exist for the selected course and that 42 courses are managed by the administrator.

**Figure 9.33**

Displaying a grouped data access page

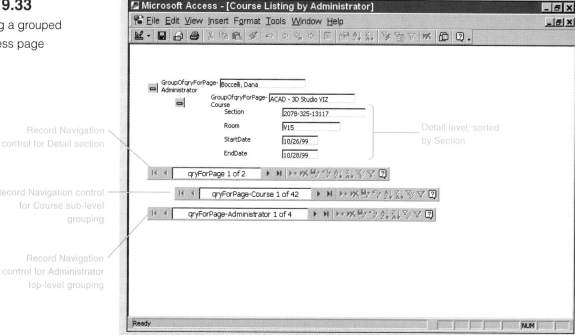

**10** To advance to the next section:
CLICK: Next Record button (▶) on the Detail Record Navigation control

**11** To advance to the next course:
CLICK: Next Record button (▷) on the Course Record Navigation control
Notice that the Detail section is contracted (and the Detail Record Navigation control removed) to speed up your navigation through the Course records. This is the default behavior of the control.

**12** To contract the Course sub-level grouping:
CLICK: Collapse icon (⊟) for GroupOfqryForPage-Administrator

**13** On your own, practice navigating through the records and various levels of the data access page. When ready to proceed, restore the Page View window to a window by clicking its Restore button (⧉).

**14** Save the data access page as "pgsGroupedPage" and then close the Page View window.

## 9.5.3 Customizing a Data Access Page in Design View

**FEATURE**

By now you are quite familiar with manipulating and formatting controls in both the form and report Design views. The page Design view provides similar capabilities. You can add, delete, move, and align controls; apply formatting; and set properties for controls, sections, and the page itself. For example, using the Properties window, you can change a field's *ReadOnly* property to "True" in order to protect it from being modified. You can also autoformat a data access page by applying a preformatted theme, complete with colors, graphics, and HTML heading styles.

A typical data access page consists of a body and two section areas called *Group Header* and *Record Navigation*. The body is comprised of the two section areas, as well as any descriptive text, graphics, or other elements that you might want to add. Content positioned in the body area is relative and adjusts itself to the size of the Web browser window. Controls in the two section areas, on the other hand, remain in an absolute or fixed position. Therefore, the Group Header section is where you most frequently place bound data controls. The Record Navigation section contains the Record Navigation control.

**METHOD**

After clicking the *Pages* button in the Database window, select one of the following methods to open a data access page in Design view:

- SELECT: the data access page that you want to modify
  CLICK: Design button (⬚Design) on the Database window toolbar
- RIGHT-CLICK: the data access page that you want to modify
  CHOOSE: Design View

Use the following commands to format a data access page:

- CHOOSE: Format, Background, Color to change the page color
- CHOOSE: Format, Background, Picture to tile a graphic image
- CHOOSE: Format, Theme to apply a predefined formatting theme

**PRACTICE**

After opening a data access page in Design view, you apply formatting to enhance its appearance.

*Setup:* Ensure that you've completed the previous lesson and that the ACC900 Database window is displayed.

**1** Let's begin by opening the data access page that you created in the last lesson in Design view. Ensure that the *Pages* button is selected in the Objects bar and then:
SELECT: pgsGroupedPage in the list area
CLICK: Design button (⬚Design)

**2** Maximize the window by clicking its Maximize button (⬚) or by double-clicking its Title bar. Then adjust the size and placement of the Toolbox window and the Field List window to appear similar to Figure 9.34. Notice that the Field List window contains a hierarchical listing of all tables and queries in the ACC900 database file.

**Figure 9.34**

Displaying the
pgsGroupedData page in
Design view

Click here in the body
area to add a page title.

Group Header section
for the Detail level.

Record Navigation section
for the Detail level.

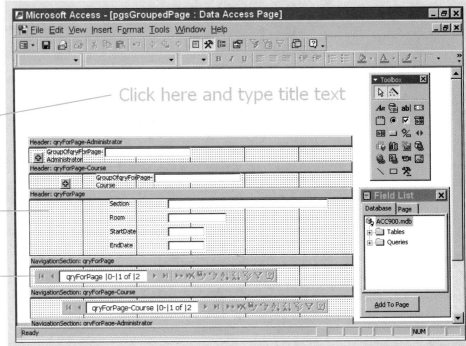

**3**    To add a title to the page:
CLICK: in the body area where it says "Click here and type title text"
TYPE: `Course Listing by Administrator`

**4**    To enhance the appearance of your data access pages, you can apply professionally designed themes. Do the following:
CHOOSE: Format, Theme
The Theme dialog box appears, as shown in Figure 9.35.

**Figure 9.35**

Theme dialog box

**5** To preview and then apply a theme:
SELECT: Expedition in the *Choose a Theme* list box
CLICK: OK command button
(*Note:* You install the assortment of themes from the Office 2000 CDROM. If the Expedition theme is not available on your computer, select an alternative theme.)

**6** Let's replace the existing background with a new tiled image:
CHOOSE: Format, Background Picture
The Insert Picture dialog box should appear.

**7** On your own, locate the Advantage student data files folder and then:
DOUBLE-CLICK: LtMarble in the list area
The background is tiled with the bitmap image.

**8** CLICK: View—Page button (⊞▾) to view the result

**9** CLICK: View—Design button (☒▾) to return to Design view

**10** Now let's adjust the sorting and grouping options in the data access page. If you remember from viewing the page, only one administrator is displayed at a time. To display up to four administrators at a time:
CLICK: Sorting and Grouping button (▤)
The Sorting and Grouping window appears.

**11** With "qryForPage-Administrator" selected in the *Group Record Source* column area:
DOUBLE-CLICK: in the *Data Page Size* text box of the *Group Properties* area
TYPE: 4
Now four administrator records will be displayed at all times.
(*Note:* You can also change the sort order for a particular section using the *Default Sort* property text box.)

**12** Close the Sorting and Grouping window.

**13** CLICK: View—Page button (⊞▾) to view the result
You should now see four records appearing in the Page View window.

**14** CLICK: View—Design button (☒▾) to return to Design view

**15** Restore the Design window to a window using the Restore button (⧉).

**16** Save and then close the data access page.

ACCESS

## 9.5.4    Creating a Data Access Page From Scratch

**FEATURE**
When you create a data access page in Design view, Access displays a blank Web page with an unbound section object. The hierarchical Field List window and the Toolbox window also appear. To begin creating a data access page, you select and then drag fields from the Field List window to the "Section: Unbound" area. The first time that you do this, the unbound section becomes bound to the underlying data source, as noted by the change of title in the header bar. A Record Navigation control is also added to the "NavigationSection" area.

**METHOD**
In the Database window, click the *Pages* button in the Objects bar and then:

- DOUBLE-CLICK: Create data access page in Design view, or
- CLICK: New button ([New]) on the Database window toolbar
  DOUBLE-CLICK: Design View in the New Data Access Page dialog box

You can also limit a new data access page to data entry operations. In this mode, users can enter new records but they cannot view, edit, or remove existing records in the database. To specify a data entry-only page:

1. Display the Properties window.
2. CHOOSE: Edit, Select Page
3. CLICK: *Data* tab
4. CLICK: in the *DataEntry* text box
5. SELECT: True

**PRACTICE**
You now create a data access page in Design view.

*Setup:* Ensure that the ACC900 Database window is displayed.

**1** To create a new data access page from scratch, ensure that the *Pages* button is selected in the Objects bar and then:
DOUBLE-CLICK: Create data access page in Design view

**2** To expand the work area, maximize the Page window by clicking the Maximize button (□) appearing in its Title bar. (*Hint:* You can also double-click a window's Title bar to maximize the window.)

**3** Let's begin by adding a title to the page:
CLICK: in the body area where it says "Click here and type title text"
TYPE: `Program Information`

**4** You will now build a data access page from scratch using the Field List window. This method provides the most flexibility and power for creating complex, hierarchical pages. As long as you have established table relationships, you need not base a data access page on a query simply to join tables.
define the underlying record source:
CLICK: Plus sign (⊞) to expand the Tables list in the Field List window
CLICK: Plus sign (⊞) to expand the tblPrograms table
The Field List window should appear similar to the one shown here.

**5** To position field text box controls in the tblPrograms Group Header section, do the following:
DRAG: prgName into the tblPrograms section and position it at the first gridline from the left border (see Figure 9.36)
DRAG: prgDescription into the tblPrograms section and position it below the prgName control
Notice that a Record Navigation section appears with a control for the tblPrograms table. Your screen should now appear similar to Figure 9.36.

**Figure 9.36**

Positioning controls in the Group Header section

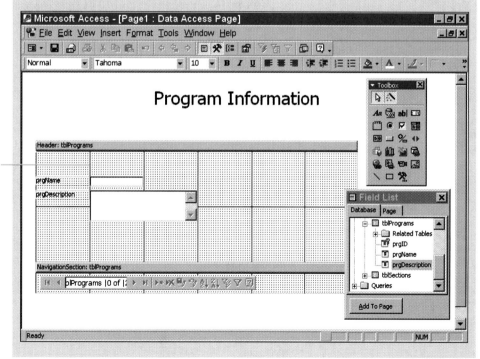

Drag fields to line up with this gridline, but leave a space near the top for another control.

**6** As you may remember from creating forms and reports, moving a field's text box control also moves its label control. However, in data access pages, if you move the label control, the text box does not move. (*Hint:* You can also place bound controls in the body area of the data access page.) On your own, move the text box and label controls so that they are positioned in the tblPrograms Group Header section similar to Figure 9.36.

**7** On your own, edit and apply boldface to the label controls and then size the text box controls to appear similar to Figure 9.37.

**8** For a control that you do not want edited, select the Bound HTML control and then set its *ControlSource* property on the *Data* tab of the object's Properties window. Bound HTML objects display faster than editable text box controls. To illustrate:
CLICK: Bound HTML button (🗔) in the Toolbox window

**9** Position the mouse pointer above the prgName text box control and then click the left mouse button once to place the new control.

**10** To display the Properties window:
RIGHT-CLICK: bound HTML control
CHOOSE: Properties
CLICK: *Data* tab

**11** Let's select the prgID AutoNumber key field:
CLICK: in the *Control Source* text box
CLICK: down arrow attached to the property text box
SELECT: prgID

**12** Close the Properties window.

**13** To apply a theme to the data access page:
CHOOSE: Format, Theme
SELECT: Canvas in the *Choose a Theme* list box
CLICK: OK command button

**14** To sort the results displayed in the data access page:
CLICK: Sorting and Grouping button (▥)

**15** In the Group Properties area:
CLICK: in the *Default Sort* property text box
TYPE: prgName

**16** Close the Sorting and Grouping window.

**17** Restore the Design window to a window using the Restore button (🗗).

**18** CLICK: View – Page button (📄·) to view the result
Your screen should now appear similar to Figure 9.37.

**Figure 9.37**

Page View window for
pgsProgramInfo

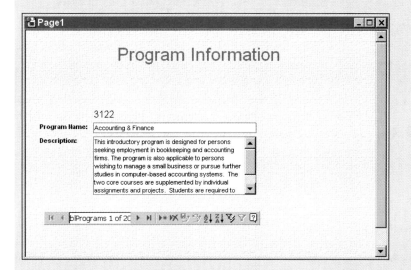

**19** Save the data access page as "pgsProgramInfo" and then close the Page View window.

**20** Close the ACC900 Database window. Then exit Microsoft Access.

ACCESS

---

**In Addition**
Inserting Microsoft
Office Web
Components into a
Data Access Page

You can attach the new **Microsoft Office Web Components** to a data access Web page in order to display dynamic and interactive charts, pivot tables, and spreadsheets. Only users who have installed Microsoft Office 2000 and who are using the Microsoft Internet Explorer Web browser can view and interact with these ActiveX components. For more information, refer to the Microsoft Access Help system.

---

**In Addition**
Sending a Data
Access Page as an
E-mail Message

You can send a data access page in an e-mail message. However, users will not be able to interact with the page unless the database is stored on a shared server and security permissions have been granted. The most secure way to send a data access page is to send only the URL address as a hyperlink. When clicked, the hyperlink launches the default Web browser, loads the data access page, and connects to the database.

---

**9.5 Self Check** Name two reasons why you might choose to display field information using a bound HTML control instead of a text box control.

# 9.6   Chapter Review

One of the essential steps in planning and designing a database application is to document your input and output requirements. Converting these paper-based ideals into an electronic reality, however, can be quite challenging. Fortunately, Access provides many tools, features, and properties that can assist you in building forms (for input) and reports (for output). In this chapter, you incorporate background and foreground graphics to enhance the presentation of both forms and reports. For forms, you access special controls and properties to enforce field- and record-level validation and to incorporate hyperlinks, combo boxes, tabbed pages, and subforms. For reports, you establish data groupings, insert calculated controls, and manipulate properties to yield a variety of effects. You also learn to create and embed charts and subreports and then save these final report objects as graphic snapshots. Lastly, you use the wizards and Design view to create data access pages, which are a special type of Web page that allows you to manipulate and view data stored in an Access database using a Web browser. Data access pages are accessible by users who have installed Microsoft Office 2000 and Microsoft Internet Explorer.

## 9.6.1   Command Summary

Many of the commands and procedures appearing in this chapter are summarized in the following table.

| Skill Set | To Perform This Task . . . | Do the Following . . . |
| --- | --- | --- |
| **Building and Modifying Forms** | Add a background picture to a form in Design view | Display the Form Properties window<br>CLICK: *Format* tab<br>CLICK: Build button (□) for the *Picture* property text box<br>SELECT: a picture from the Insert Picture dialog box |
| | Add an unbound graphic image to a form in Design view | CLICK: Image button (▨) in the Toolbox window<br>CLICK: in the Form window<br>SELECT: a graphic from the Insert Picture dialog box |
| | Add a bound graphic image to a form in Design view | DRAG: an OLE Object field from the Field List window onto the form |

*Continued*

| Skill Set | To Perform This Task . . . | Do the Following . . . |
|---|---|---|
| **Building and Modifying Forms** *Continued* | Place an active hyperlink on a form in Design view | CLICK: Insert Hyperlink button (🔘) |
| | Add combo boxes and list boxes to a form in Design view | CLICK: Combo Box button (▦), or CLICK: List Box button (▦) CLICK: in the Form window |
| | Add a tab control to a form in Design view | CLICK: Tab Control button (▦) CLICK: in the Form window |
| | Embed a subform in a main form in Design view | CLICK: Subform/Subreport button (▦) CLICK: in the Form window |
| | Set control properties in form Design view | RIGHT-CLICK: the desired control CHOOSE: Properties |
| | Set section properties in form Design view | DOUBLE-CLICK: the desired section bar |
| | Set form properties in Design view | DOUBLE-CLICK: Form Selector button (▪) |
| **Building and Modifying Tables** | Enforce field-level validation | Display a field's properties in form Design view or in table Design view SELECT: *Validation Rule* property text box TYPE: *an expression* |
| | Enforce record-level validation | Display a table in Design view CHOOSE: View, Properties SELECT: *Validation Rule* property text box TYPE: *an expression* |
| | Test the existing data against the validation rules | CHOOSE: Edit, Test Validation Rules |
| | Provide text for warning messages when validation rule is violated | Display a field's properties in form Design view or in table Design view SELECT: *Validation Text* property text box TYPE: *an error message* |

ACCESS

*Continued*

| Skill Set | To Perform This Task . . . | Do the Following . . . |
|---|---|---|
| **Producing Reports** | Specify sorting and grouping options in a report | CLICK: Sorting and Grouping button ([≡]) |
| | Add line numbers to a report in Design view | Place a text box in a report<br>Display the Properties window<br>CLICK: *Data* tab<br>TYPE: =1 in the *Control Source* text box<br>SELECT: Over Group in the *Running Sum* text box |
| | Add a background picture or watermark to a report in Design view | Display the Report Properties window<br>CLICK: *Format* tab<br>CLICK: Build button ([…]) for the *Picture* property text box<br>SELECT: a picture from the Insert Picture dialog box |
| | Add an unbound graphic image to a report in Design view | CLICK: Image button ([⊡]) in the Toolbox window<br>CLICK: in the Report window<br>SELECT: a graphic from the Insert Picture dialog box |
| | Add a bound graphic image to a report in Design view | DRAG: an OLE Object field from the Field List window onto the report |
| | Set control properties in report Design view | RIGHT-CLICK: the desired control<br>CHOOSE: Properties |
| | Set section properties in report Design view | DOUBLE-CLICK: the desired section bar |
| | Set report properties in Design view | DOUBLE-CLICK: Report Selector button ([■]) |
| | Set a page break within a section | CLICK: Page Break button ([▤]) in the Toolbox window |
| | Specify a multicolumn report | CHOOSE: File, Page Setup<br>CLICK: *Columns* tab<br>TYPE: *a number* in the *Number of Columns* text box |

*Continued*

| Skill Set | To Perform This Task . . . | Do the Following . . . |
|---|---|---|
| **Producing Reports** *Continued* | Embed a subreport in a main report in Design view | CLICK: Subform/Subreport button (▣) <br> CLICK: in the Report window |
| | Save a report object as a snapshot graphic file | CHOOSE: File, Export <br> TYPE: *a filename* <br> SELECT: Snapshot Format in the *Save as type* drop-down list box <br> CLICK: Save command button |
| **Data Integration** | Present data using a chart | CLICK: New button (⬛New) for reports <br> SELECT: Chart Wizard in the New Report dialog box |
| **Utilizing Web Capabilities** | Create a new data access page using the AutoPage Wizard | CLICK: New button (⬛New) for pages <br> SELECT: AutoPage: Columnar in the New Page dialog box |
| | Create a grouped data access page using the Page Wizard | CLICK: *Pages* button in the Object bar <br> DOUBLE-CLICK: Create data access page by using wizard |
| | Format the background and page elements in a data access page | CHOOSE: Format, Background <br> CHOOSE: Format, Theme |
| | Create a new data access page from scratch | CLICK: *Pages* button in the Object bar <br> DOUBLE-CLICK: Create data access page in Design view |
| | Specify sorting and grouping options in a data access page | CLICK: Sorting and Grouping button (▤) |

ACCESS

### 9.6.2 Key Terms

This section specifies page references for the key terms identified in this chapter. For a complete list of definitions, refer to the Glossary provided at the end of this learning guide.

ActiveX controls, *p. 484*

metafile, *p. 459*

AutoLookup query, *p. 477*

Microsoft Office Web Components, *p. 529*

AutoPage Wizard, *p. 517*

Page view, *p. 518*

bitmap, *p. 459*

Page Wizard, *p. 517*

column chart, *p. 508*

pie chart, *p. 508*

data access page, *p. 516*

record validation rule, *p. 472*

embedding, *p. 454*

subreport, *p. 511*

field validation rule, *p. 472*

validation text, *p. 472*

line chart, *p. 508*

watermark, *p. 495*

linking, *p. 454*

XY chart, *p. 508*

main report, *p. 511*

# 9.7  Review Questions

## 9.7.1  Short Answer

1. Why is it a good idea to set field properties in table Design view prior to creating a form?
2. List some examples of graphics that you might want to add to a form.
3. Describe the difference between metafiles and bitmap graphics.
4. Provide one example in which you might enforce field-level validation in a data entry form.
5. What type of control is created by Access when you drag an OLE Object field from the Field List window onto a report?
6. How do you force a page break to occur before each unique value in a group section?
7. What is the primary reason for creating an Access snapshot file from a report?

8. Name some of the technologies used in building data access pages.
9. What must you keep in mind when placing bound field controls in the body of a data access page?
10. How can you limit a data access page to data entry operations?

## 9.7.2 True/False

1. _____ A calculated control is a text box control that displays the results of a formula expression.
2. _____ To display the Form Properties window, double-click a blank area on the Form window.
3. _____ To display the Properties window for a particular section in a form, double-click its section bar.
4. _____ When you set the *Locked* property for a control, it appears dim (light gray) and is no longer included in the tab order.
5. _____ A record validation rule is not evaluated until you leave the record.
6. _____ One of the benefits of embedding a subform in a main form is that data can be entered into two tables using one Form window.
7. _____ To create a multicolumn report, begin by displaying the Page Setup dialog box and then clicking on the *Columns* tab.
8. _____ You cannot insert a subreport in the Detail section of a main report.
9. _____ Field data that you modify in a data access page is saved when your cursor leaves the field's text box.
10. _____ Depending on the property settings selected, a grouped data access page may be used for both viewing and editing purposes.

## 9.7.3 Multiple Choice

1. The three main types of controls found in forms and reports are:
   a. bound, text box, and list box
   b. bound, unbound, and calculated
   c. text box, label, and combo box
   d. text box, bound, and calculated

2. The three options for sizing a picture in an image control are:
   a. clip, stretch, shrink
   b. crop, shrink, zoom
   c. crop, stretch, zoom
   d. clip, stretch, zoom

3.  The two methods for adding a disk-based graphic file to a form are:
    a.  cutting and pasting
    b.  copying and pasting
    c.  linking and embedding
    d.  bitmap and metafile

4.  The two control properties that you may set to provide visual assistance to users are:
    a.  ControlTip Text and ScreenTip Text
    b.  ControlTip Text and Status Bar Text
    c.  ControlText and ScreenText
    d.  ControlText and Status Bar Text

5.  Which of the following validation rules ensures that the value entered is either "Hot," "Cold," or "Warm"?
    a.  `Between Hot And Cold And Warm`
    b.  `Within("Hot", "Cold", "Warm")`
    c.  `Is("Hot", "Cold", "Warm")`
    d.  `In("Hot", "Cold", "Warm")`

6.  A faint image that you add to the background of a report is called a:
    a.  back style
    b.  border
    c.  gutter
    d.  watermark

7.  The type of chart that shows the proportions of how one or more data elements relate to another data element is called a:
    a.  line chart
    b.  column chart
    c.  pie chart
    d.  XY chart

8.  Which wizard allows you to create a new grouped data access page?
    a.  AutoPage Wizard
    b.  Group Wizard
    c.  Page Wizard
    d.  View Wizard

9.  Which tag is used in this chapter to name data access pages?
    a.  dap
    b.  frm
    c.  pgs
    d.  rpt

10. Which property setting enables you to display more or fewer records in an expanded section of a grouped data access page?
    a.  *Data Group Size*
    b.  *Data Page Size*
    c.  *Group Data Size*
    d.  *Group Page Size*

# 9.8 Hands-On Projects

### 9.8.1  World Wide Imports: Creating a Customer Form

In this exercise, you create a form from scratch and then tile a picture on the form's background.

*Setup:* Ensure that Access is loaded. If you are launching Access and the startup dialog box appears, click the Cancel command button to remove the dialog box from the application window.

1.  Open the database file named ACC980.
2.  You will now create a form to manage the data stored in the 981 tblCustomers table. To create a new form from scratch:
    CLICK: *Forms* button in the Objects bar
    DOUBLE-CLICK: Create form in Design view
3.  To provide more room to work, maximize the Form window by double-clicking its Title bar. Notice that the Toolbox and Field List windows remain displayed on top of the Form window.
4.  The first step is to define the underlying data source. To display the Form Properties window:
    DOUBLE-CLICK: Form Selector button (■)
5.  In the Form Properties window:
    CLICK: *Data* tab
    CLICK: in the *Record Source* text box
    CLICK: down arrow attached to the property text box
    SELECT: 981 tblCustomers from the drop-down list
6.  Close the Form Properties window by clicking its Close button (✕). (*Note:* Ensure that the Field List window appears. If not, click the Field List button (▣) on the toolbar.)
7.  You will now add all of the fields from the Field List window to the Form window. To select all of the fields:
    DOUBLE-CLICK: the Field List window's title bar
    DRAG: the field selection into the Detail section at approximately the 1-inch mark on the horizontal ruler

ACCESS

8.  With the field controls still selected in the Form window, increase the vertical space between the fields to make the form easier to read:
    CHOOSE: Format, Vertical Spacing, Increase
9.  Using Figure 9.38 as your guide, move, size, and format the fields to appear similar to the screen graphic.

**Figure 9.38**

Creating the Customer form from scratch

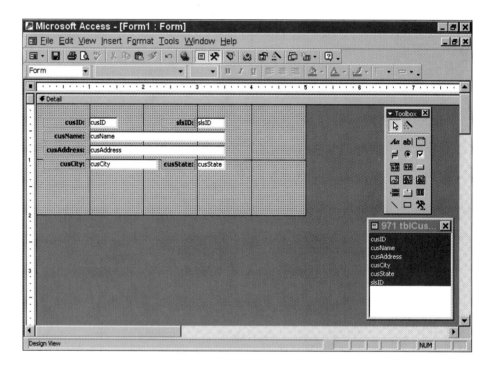

10. Now let's add a background picture to the form. To display the Form Properties window:
    DOUBLE-CLICK: Form Selector button (◾)
11. To select a picture from the Advantage student data files folder:
    CLICK: *Format* tab
    CLICK: in the *Picture* text box
    CLICK: Build button (⋯) appearing to the right of the text box
    The Insert Picture dialog box is displayed.
12. Locate the Advantage student data files folder and then:
    DOUBLE-CLICK: LtMarble in the list area
    The picture appears in the middle of the form.
13. Let's tile the picture so that it covers the entire form:
    SELECT: Yes in the *Picture Tiling* property text box
14. Close the Form Properties window and then restore the Form window to a window by clicking its Restore button (🗗). To view the form:
    CLICK: View—Form button (▣▾)
15. Save the form as "frmCusBackground" and then close the Form window.

## 9.8.2   CyberWeb: Defining Bound and Unbound Hyperlinks

In this exercise, you practice adding bound and unbound hyperlinks to an existing form.

*Setup:* Ensure that the ACC980 Database window is displayed.

1. To modify an existing form, ensure that the *Forms* button is selected in the Objects bar and then do the following:
SELECT: 982 frmAccounts in the list area
CLICK: Design button (⚞Design⚟) on the Database window toolbar
2. Your first step is to change the accEmail text box control from a text field to a hyperlink. To proceed:
RIGHT-CLICK: accEmail text box control
CHOOSE: Properties
CLICK: *Format* tab
3. Using the vertical scroll bar, scroll to the bottom of the property list. Then do the following:
CLICK: in the *Is Hyperlink* text box
CLICK: down arrow attached to the property text box
SELECT: Yes
4. Close the Properties window. Notice that the contents of the text box appear blue and underlined, like a hyperlink in Web browser software.
5. To add a hyperlink label control to the Form Header section:
CLICK: Insert Hyperlink button (🌐) on the toolbar
6. Let's define a hyperlink that displays the company's fictional home page. Do the following:
SELECT: *Text to display* text box
TYPE: `CyberWeb Home Page`
SELECT: *Type the file or Web page name* text box
TYPE: `http://www.cyberweb.com/`
7. To specify a ScreenTip to appear when the mouse pointer is moved over top of the hyperlink:
CLICK: ScreenTip command button
TYPE: `Open CyberWeb Home Page in Web browser`
CLICK: OK command button
8. To proceed:
CLICK: OK command button.
9. You must now move the control from the Detail section to the Form Header section. Do the following:
DRAG: "CyberWeb Home Page" label control to the right-hand side of the Form Header section

ACCESS

10. To enhance the appearance of the hyperlink:
    RIGHT-CLICK: "CyberWeb Home Page" hyperlink
    CHOOSE: Font/Fore Color
    CLICK: a yellow color box
    CLICK: Bold button (B) in the toolbar
11. On your own, increase the width of the label control. Then:
    CLICK: View—Form button (⊞▾)
    Your form should appear similar to figure 9.39.
12. Save the form and then close the Form window.

**Figure 9.39**

Creating a form with hyperlinks

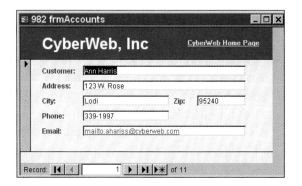

### 9.8.3 Big Valley Mills: Converting Text Boxes to Combo Boxes

You now enhance an existing form by adding combo boxes to facilitate data entry.

*Setup*: Ensure that the ACC980 Database window is displayed and that the *Forms* button is selected in the Objects bar.

1. Open the 983 frmProducts form in Design view.
2. To begin, let's change the spcSpecies text box control to a combo box:
   RIGHT-CLICK: spcSpecies text box control
   CHOOSE: Change To, Combo Box
3. Now display the Properties window for the spcSpecies control:
   RIGHT-CLICK: spcSpecies combo box control
   CHOOSE: Properties
4. On the *Data* tab of the Properties window, set the *Row Source* property to the 983 tblSpecies table.
5. On the *Format* tab, change the *Column Count* to 2 so that the combo box will display both the species code and its name.
6. To specify the width of each column in the combo box control:
   CLICK: in the *Column Widths* property text box
   TYPE: **0.5";1.5"**

7.  To adjust the width of the display area for the combo box:
    DOUBLE-CLICK: in the *List Width* text box
    TYPE: **2"**

8.  Now let's test the combo box. Close the Properties window and then view the form. Click the down arrow attached to the spcSpecies combo box control. The list should appear as shown here.
9.  Return to Design view.
10. On your own, change the finFinish text box to a combo box control. Make sure that the new combo box displays two columns of values from the 983 tblFinish table.
11. Display the form and test the new combo box.
12. When you are finished, save the form and close the Form window.

## 9.8.4  Silverdale Festival: Inserting a Subreport

In this exercise, you practice inserting a subreport into the Report Header section of an existing report. Then you create a report snapshot that can be viewed by people who do not own or use Microsoft Access.

*Setup*: Ensure that the ACC980 Database window is displayed.

1.  To begin, open the report named 984 rptContacts in Design view.
2.  Before inserting the subreport, ensure that the Control Wizards button (⬚) is pressed in and then:
    CLICK: Subform/Subreport button (⬚) in the Toolbox window
3.  Move the mouse pointer into the Report Header section and position it to the right of the title at about the 3-inch mark on the horizontal ruler. Click the left mouse button once to launch the SubReport Wizard.
4.  In the first step of the SubReport Wizard dialog box:
    SELECT: *Use an existing report or form* option button
    SELECT: 984 rptFunctionChart in the list area
    CLICK: Finish
5.  Delete the label control that appears attached to the top left-hand corner of the chart.
6.  Using Figure 3.40 as your guide, move and size the chart to fit in the report Design window.
7.  CLICK: View—Print Preview button (⬚) to preview the report
    Your screen should appear similar to Figure 9.40, when viewing the report at 100%.

**Figure 9.40**

Report with a subreport chart

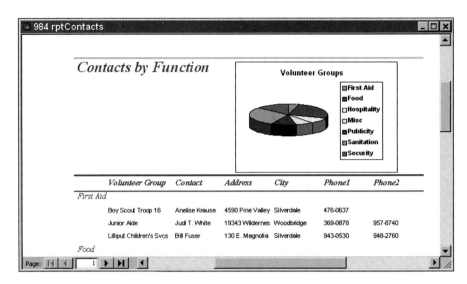

8. Use the File, Save As command to save the report as "rptSubReport" and then close the Print Preview window by clicking its Close button (☒).

9. In the *Reports* list area of the database window, select the rptSubReport report and then export the file as "subSnapshot" using the Snapshot Format file type. Make sure the *Autostart* check box is selected before clicking the Save command button.

10. The Snapshot Viewer program is loaded and the report is displayed. Notice that the subreport is not included in the snapshot. After viewing the report pages, close the Snapshot Viewer window.

## 9.8.5 On Your Own: Office Mart Inventory

This exercise lets you create a report from scratch and then customize the sorting and grouping options. Start by creating a new report in Design view and then maximize the Design window. In the Report Properties window, bind the report to the "985 qryProductBuyer" query by setting its *Record Source* property. Then close the Report Properties window and display the Report Header and Footer sections.

You must now define the sorting and grouping options for the report. Start by displaying the Sorting and Grouping window. Group the data first by Buyer (byrBuyerID) and then by Supplier (invSupplier). Set the *Group Header* property text box to "Yes" for both fields. Lastly, add the invProductID field to the *Field/Expression* column to sort the detail lines in product code sequence. Close the Sorting and Grouping window.

Using the Label button () in the Toolbox window, insert "Product Listing by Buyer" as the report title in the Report Header section. Then select a 16-point, Times New Roman font and make it bold and italic. From the Field List window, drag "byrFirstName" and "byrLastName" to the left-hand side of the byrBuyerID Header section and delete their label controls. Make both text box controls bold. Drag "invSupplier" to the invSupplier Header section and apply italics to both the label and text box controls.

Add the invProductID, invDescription, invOnHand, invCost, and invSuggestedRetail fields to the Detail section. Remove the label controls for each of these fields. Increase the height of the invSupplier Header section and add a column heading for each of the detail fields. Format the column headings to be boldface and underlined. Restore the report Design window to a window and then continue formatting, sizing, and aligning the report controls to appear similar to Figure 9.41. When you are ready, preview the report and make any last changes that are necessary in Design view. Then save the report as "rptProductBuyer" and close the Print Preview window.

**Figure 9.41**

Creating a grouped and sorted report

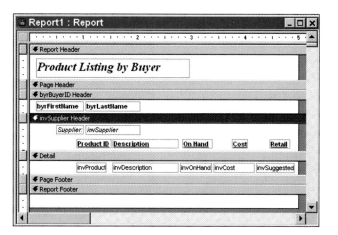

## 9.8.6  On Your Own: Sun Bird Resorts

In this exercise, you create a form from scratch that uses both the Tab and Subform controls. The first page of the new tab control displays guest information for a single record. The second page displays a subform of the charges incurred by each guest.

To begin, create a new form in Design view and increase the form height. Set the *Record Source* property of the form to the "986 tlbGuests" table. Now add a Tab control to the form. Change the caption of the "Page1" tab to "Guests" and the caption of the second tab to "Charges". On the "Guests" tab, add all the fields from the 986 tblGuests table. Arrange and format the text box controls and then modify their field labels, as you deem necessary. On the second tab,

"Charges," add the 986 frmCharges form as a subform using the wizard. (*Hint:* In the second step of the wizard, select the "Show 986 qryCharges for each record in 986 tblGuests using gstGuestID" option in the list box.) Delete the subform's label control and then adjust its size and positioning on the tab.

When ready, test the form by displaying it in a form window and moving between the two tabs. Save the new form as "frmGuestCharges" and then exit Microsoft Access.

# 9.9   Case Problems: Joseph Beaner's Fine Coffees

Courtney Hendrickson is the manager of Joseph Beaner's Fine Coffees. Having recently assumed the leadership role from her father, Courtney wants to impress her new staff by implementing a comprehensive information system based on Microsoft Access. Courtney is especially interested in applying her new Access skills to build custom forms and reports. These skills will be useful in creating attractive and functional objects for the sales and purchasing database. The database must emphasize user friendliness since it will be distributed to less experienced computer users in the other coffee shops.

In the following case problems, assume the role of Courtney and perform the same steps that she identifies. You may want to re-read the chapter opening before proceeding.

1. After launching Microsoft Access, Courtney decides to develop a new data entry form for recording the daily sales information from each store. She opens the ACC990 database and then displays the *Forms* list area in the Database window. To begin designing the new form, Courtney opens and then maximizes a new window in Design view. She sets the form's *Record Source* property to the tblSales table and then closes the Form Properties window. Next, she displays the form's header and footer sections and then reduces the form's width to 3 inches on the horizontal ruler.

Courtney adds all the fields in the tblSales Field List window to the form. She then adds a label control to the left-hand side of the Form Header section to contain the title "Daily Sales." She also places the company's name in the Form Footer section. Using an image control, Courtney adds a bitmap graphic named "Cup," stored in the Advantage student files folder, to the right-hand side of the Form Header section. She reduces the size of the image control slightly and sets its *Size Mode* property to "Zoom." After formatting the controls and sections in the form, her screen appears similar to Figure 9.42. Courtney displays the new form and restores it to a window. She then saves the form as "frmDailySales" and closes the Form window.

**Figure 9.42**

Creating a data entry form

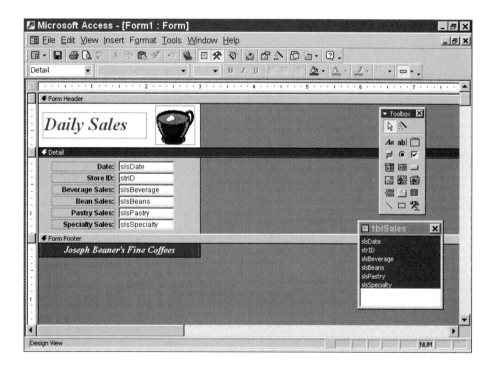

2.  Courtney's next project is to create a custom report. After displaying the *Reports* list area, she opens and maximizes a new report Design window. Her first step is to bind the new report to the "qrySales" query object. She then closes the Report Properties window and opens the Sorting and Grouping window. In the first *Field/Expression* text box, Courtney selects the slsDate field and sets its Group Header to "Yes." She then selects "Week" in the *Group On* property text box. In the next *Field/Expression* text box, she adds the strName field and then assigns both a header and footer. In order to sort the detail section in date order, Courtney adds the slsDate field to the third row of the column. She then closes the Sorting and Grouping window.

Courtney displays the report header section and then adds a label control containing the title "Weekly Sales by Store." She formats the label to appear using a 24-point, Times New Roman font. After making the title bold and italic, she sizes it so that all the text is visible. She then increases the height of the Report Header section and adds a second label control under the title to hold the company's name. Lastly, she adds an image control to the right-hand side of the section for displaying the "Cup" bitmap graphic, and sets its *Size Mode* property to "Zoom." (*Note:* Refer to Figure 9.43 to see the additional formatting that is required in this section.)

Turning her attention to the Group Header sections, Courtney adds the slsDate field to the slsDate Header section and the strName and strManager fields to the strName Header section, as shown in Figure 9.43. After formatting the controls, she adds the slsDate, slsBeverage, slsBeans, slsPastry, and slsSpecialty fields to the Detail section and removes their labels. She then increases the height of the srtName Header section and adds column headings for each of the detail fields.

Using a text box control, Courtney then adds a calculated field to the strName Footer section. She deletes the label control and then moves it directly beneath the slsBeverage field in the Detail section. She places the expression `=Sum([slsBeverage])` in the text box. In the same manner, she adds total fields for the remaining three sales columns. To ensure that the columns line up nicely, she formats the field and text box controls in the Detail and strName Footer sections using a "Currency" format with two decimal places. She then adjusts the height of the different sections to appear similar to Figure 9.43. Finally, Courtney saves the report as "rptWeeklySales" and then displays it in Print Preview mode. When she is ready to proceed, she restores and then closes the Print Preview window.

**Figure 9.43**

Weekly sales report
in Design view

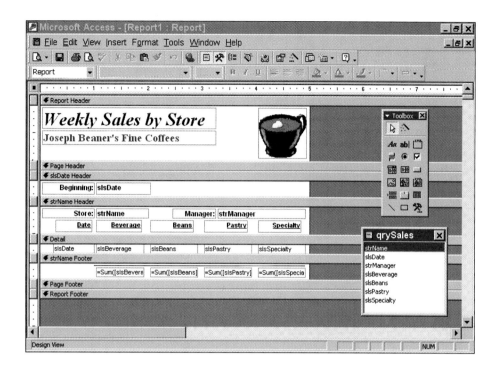

3. To prepare for an upcoming marketing meeting, Courtney has created a query that summarizes sales by category over the last three months. She feels that a chart would better communicate the information than a tabular report. Therefore, she launches the Chart Wizard for the qrySalesSummary query.

   In the first two steps of the Chart Wizard, Courtney selects all the fields in the list to appear in a 3D Column Chart. In the third step, she double-clicks the SumOfTotalBeverage button in the Data area and selects "None" in the Summarize dialog box. She then adds the TotalBeans, TotalPastry, and TotalSpecialty buttons to the Data area and changes their summation values to "None" also. In the last step of the wizard, Courtney enters the title "Sales Summary Chart" and then clicks [ Finish ]. Because she isn't too impressed with the results, Courtney switches to Design view and increases the size of the chart area to approximately 4.5 inches wide by 2.5 inches tall. She then displays the modified chart in a Print Preview window (Figure 9.44). Satisfied with the chart, she closes the Print Preview window and saves the chart as "rptSummaryChart."

**Figure 9.44**

Sales summary chart

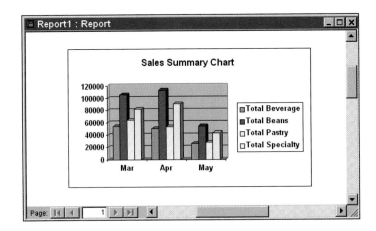

4.  Courtney is pleased with what she has accomplished thus far. But before going home, she decides to tackle one more item on her list. She has been working on a pair of purchasing reports. One report shows a summary of purchases broken down by supplier, while the other report shows a list of all purchases made for each coffee type. Courtney would like to combine these two reports into a single report.

    To begin, Courtney opens the rptSupplierPurchases report in Design view and maximizes the window. She then expands the Report Footer section until it is approximately 1 inch in height. Ensuring that the Control Wizards button ([icon]) is pressed in, she clicks the Subform/Subreport button ([icon]) and then clicks in the top left-hand corner of the Report Footer section. In the first dialog box of the SubReport Wizard, Courtney selects the existing report named "rptCoffeePurchases" from the list area and clicks [Next >]. When asked how the forms are linked, she selects "None" from the list and clicks [Finish]. In the report Design window, Courtney deletes the subreport's label control and then sizes it to fill the section's height and width. She then displays the report in a Print Preview window and navigates between the first and second pages. Satisfied with the report, she saves it as "rptPurchaseSummary" and then closes the Print Preview window. Finished for the day, Courtney closes the Database window and then exits Microsoft Access.

# MICROSOFT ACCESS 2000
## *Automating and Extending Access*

**CHAPTER**

**TEN**

# Chapter Outline

# Learning Objectives

After reading this chapter, you will be able to:

- Create macros to automate common database tasks

- Assign macros to form controls and toolbar buttons

- Create a switchboard form and add menu items to the switchboard

- Publish and merge data with Microsoft Word

- Export and analyze data with Microsoft Excel

- Link table objects to external data files

- Use database utilities such as Table Analyzer, Performance Analyzer, and the Import/Link wizards

- Use replication and the Database Splitter Wizard to design databases for multiuser environments

## Case Study

# Price Laventhol Consulting, Inc.

Price Laventhol is one of the oldest and most established consulting firms in Jackson, Mississippi. The company's reputation is impeccable and its staff is well respected for their professionalism and attention to detail. Recently, Clive Mason was invited to become a partner in Price Laventhol. As a senior manager in their Hospitality division for the past eight years, Clive's specialties included performing valuations and conducting feasibility studies for restaurants and hotels. One of Clive's greatest assets is his desire and willingness to be a hands-on manager. For instance, Clive just finished a course in Microsoft Access 2000 and now wants to automate the billing reports that his division produces using Excel. With only a week until his new partnership appointment, Clive is determined to finish this project as quickly and efficiently as possible.

In this chapter, you and Clive learn how to automate procedures using Access macros. You also create a menu switchboard form, build a custom toolbar, and specify Access startup options. To improve your ability to work with other applications, you also learn to import, export, and link to data stored in external files. Lastly, you practice using several Access utility programs and prepare a database for use in a multiuser environment.

# 10.1  Automating Your Work

In Microsoft Access, a **macro** is a set of one or more actions that is stored as a single object in the Database window. Macros automate the common tasks performed in databases and they allow you to customize responses to user actions. For example, macros are used to open tables, run queries, display forms, validate entries, and print reports. You can even run other macros, code modules, and VBA function procedures from within a macro, or launch external applications like Excel or Word. For more complex requirements, you may include conditional expressions in your macros and combine multiple macros into a single **macro group**.

Macros are most commonly used for carrying out a particular sequence of actions in response to some sort of *event*. An **event** is simply something that happens to an object, such as a window, form, report, or control. For example, when you click a command button, the button's *On Click* event is activated and its attached macro executes. You can also write Visual Basic code in **user defined functions** and **event procedures** and then attach the code to the object's event properties. For more information on writing Visual Basic code, refer to "Introducing Visual Basic for Applications" in the Appendix.

In this module, you learn to create, execute, modify, and print macros. You also create and modify a special user interface form called a *switchboard*. Switchboards provide a menu of choices that allow users to navigate the features of a database application more easily. Lastly, you learn how to customize the Access work environment by assigning macros to toolbar buttons and menu commands and by specifying startup options.

**In Addition**
Using Macros versus
Visual Basic for
Applications

Many people find it difficult to decide whether to create macros or write code using Visual Basic for Applications. The Access Help system recommends that you use macros to carry out simple actions such as opening and closing forms, showing and hiding toolbars, and running reports. Visual Basic is recommended for creating your own functions, providing error-handling routines, and performing maintenance operations such as manipulating data and launching applications. If desired, you can always convert a macro into Visual Basic code later using the Tools, Macro, Convert Macros to Visual Basic command.

## 10.1.1    Creating and Playing Back a Macro

**FEATURE**

The *Macros* list area in the Database window displays the names of stored macros and macro groups that you execute by double-clicking. You can also run a macro by choosing the Tools, Macro, Run Macro command or by attaching a macro to a toolbar button, custom menu command, or form control. Unlike other Office applications, in which macros are recorded, you create a macro in Access by selecting **actions** in the Macro window. These actions are self-contained command instructions that can be joined together to automate frequently performed tasks. Most actions require that you provide additional information, called **arguments**, to describe how to carry out the action. You can also specify conditions in the Macro window that determine when to carry out the action.

**METHOD**
To create a new macro:

1. CLICK: *Macros* button in the Objects bar
2. CLICK: New button ([🗐 New]) on the Database window toolbar
3. SELECT: an action in the *Action* column of the Macro window
4. TYPE: *a description* in the *Comment* column
5. Specify the required details in the *Action Arguments* area.
6. CLICK: Save button ([🖫])

To run a macro from the Database window:

● DOUBLE-CLICK: a macro in the *Macros* list area, or
● SELECT: a macro in the *Macros* list area
  CLICK: Run button ([! Run]) on the Database window toolbar

To run a macro from the Menu bar:

1. CHOOSE: Tools, Macro, Run Macro
2. SELECT: a macro in the *Macro Name* drop-down list box
3. CLICK: OK command button

**PRACTICE**
In this lesson, you create and play back a macro to open and size a read-only form.

*Setup:* Ensure that Access is loaded. If you are launching Access and the startup dialog box appears, click the Cancel command button to remove the dialog box from the application window.

**1** Open the database named ACC1000, located in the Advantage student data files folder. This database provides several tables for storing data from a continuing education department at a small college.

**2** Let's create a macro to open the frmInstructor form. Do the following:
CLICK: *Macros* button in the Objects bar
CLICK: New button ([🗐 New]) on the Database window toolbar
The Macro window appears, as shown in Figure 10.1.

**Figure 10.1**

Macro window

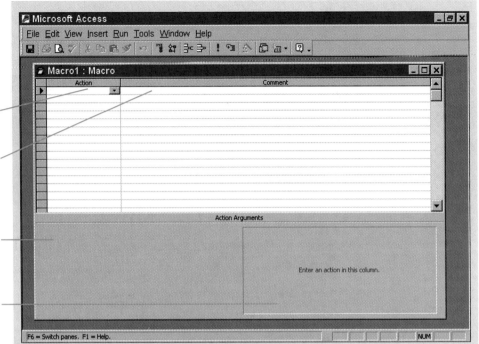

Select macro actions using
the drop-down list box.

Document your macros by
entering comments.

You customize macro
actions by entering
arguments here.

Helpful messages
appear here.

**3** In the Action column, you select the action that you want to perform. To open and display a form:
CLICK: down arrow attached to the *Action* text box
SELECT: OpenForm
Notice that the *Action Arguments* area displays some text boxes for customizing the OpenForm action.

**4** To enter a descriptive comment:
CLICK: in the adjacent *Comment* text box
TYPE: `Display and size the frmInstructor form`

**5** In the *Action Arguments* area, you specify the form that you want to display. Do the following:
CLICK: in the *Form Name* text box
CLICK: down arrow attached to the text box
SELECT: frmInstructor

**6** Now specify the mode in which to open the form:
CLICK: in the *Data Mode* text box
CLICK: down arrow attached to the text box
SELECT: Read Only

**7** To perform another action in the macro:
CLICK: in the next available *Action* text box
CLICK: down arrow attached to the text box
SELECT: MoveSize

**8** In the *Action Arguments* area:
TYPE: **.25"** in the *Right* text box
TYPE: **.25"** in the *Down* text box
TYPE: **5.75"** in the *Width* text box
TYPE: **3"** in the *Height* text box
(*Hint:* You do not need to type the quote mark (") if inches is your default unit of measurement.)

**9** To save the macro:
CLICK: Save button (🖫) in the toolbar
TYPE: `mcrOpen_frmInstructor`
CLICK: OK command button

**10** To run the macro from the Macro window:
CLICK: Run button (🛈)
The frmInstructor is opened and displayed on screen. (*Hint:* To define a macro that opens a table, query, form, or report, you can also drag the desired object from the Database window to a blank action row in the Macro window. Access will automatically enter the necessary arguments for you.)

**11** On your own, try to change a value in one of the field text boxes. Notice that you cannot add a record or edit the contents of a form opened in Read Only mode. When ready to proceed, close the frmInstructor form.

**12** Close the Macro window. Upon returning to the Database window, notice that the "mcrOpen_frmInstructor" macro now appears in the *Macros* list area.

**In Addition**
The AutoExec Macro

When you first open a database, Access looks for a special macro named "AutoExec" and, upon finding it, executes its contents. The **AutoExec macro** is not required, but is very useful for customizing the environment such as hiding toolbars and displaying forms. If you want to bypass the AutoExec macro, hold down the **SHIFT** key as the database opens. (*Note:* You can also perform setup procedures using startup options, discussed later in this chapter.)

ACCESS

## 10.1.2   Automating Objects in a Form or Report

**FEATURE**

While working in Design view, you can create and attach a new macro to a control, section, form, or report. For example, you can place a command button on a form that prints a report when clicked. You can also run a macro in response to any another *event* that occurs on a form or report. An event can be initiated by the user, as in clicking a button, or by some other action, such as closing a window. On the *Event* tab of the Properties window, you can launch the **Macro Builder** tool to help you create macros that respond to events.

**METHOD**

To create a command button:

1.  Make sure that the Control Wizard button (▧) is pressed in.
2.  CLICK: Command button (▣) in the Toolbox window
3.  CLICK: anywhere on the form to place the command button
4.  Respond to the prompts in the wizard's dialog boxes.

To access the Macro Builder tool:

1.  Display the Properties window in Design view.
2.  CLICK: *Event* tab
3.  CLICK: in one of the event property text boxes
4.  CLICK: Build button (▣)
5.  DOUBLE-CLICK: Macro Builder in the list box

**PRACTICE**

You now insert command buttons into forms in order to automate events.

*Setup:* Ensure that the ACC1000 Database window is displayed.

**1**  To place a command button on a form, do the following:
CLICK: *Forms* button in the Objects bar
SELECT: frmCourseInfo
CLICK: Design button (☒Design) on the Database window toolbar

**2**  Ensure that the Control Wizard button (▧) in the Toolbox is pressed in and then do the following:
CLICK: Command Button button (▣) in the Toolbox window

**3** Move the mouse pointer into the form and click a point immediately below the "Program" label control, as shown here. The Command Button Wizard dialog box is displayed (Figure 10.2).

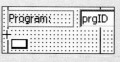

**Figure 10.2**

Command Button
Wizard dialog box

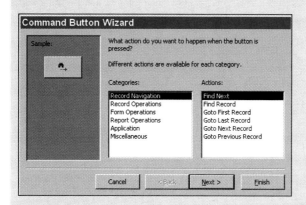

**4** You now create an event procedure that runs a report based on a value appearing in the form. Do the following:
SELECT: Report Operations in the *Categories* list box
SELECT: Preview Report in the *Actions* list box
CLICK: Next >

**5** The only report in the database is displayed in the next dialog box:
CLICK: Next > to proceed

**6** To enter a text label for the command button:
SELECT: *Text* option button
TYPE: `Course Listing` in the adjacent text box, removing the existing text that appears
CLICK: Next >

**7** In the last step, you name the command button control:
TYPE: `cmdRunReport`
CLICK: Finish
You should now see a command button appearing on the form. (*Note:* When you create a command button using the wizard, Access writes VBA code for an event procedure and attaches it to the button. You can view the event procedure code for a form by choosing the View, Code command in the Design view menu.)

**8** To test the new command button:
CLICK: View—Form button (⊞▾)
CLICK: Course Listing command button
Your screen should now appear similar to Figure 10.3.

**Figure 10.3**

Running a report from a form

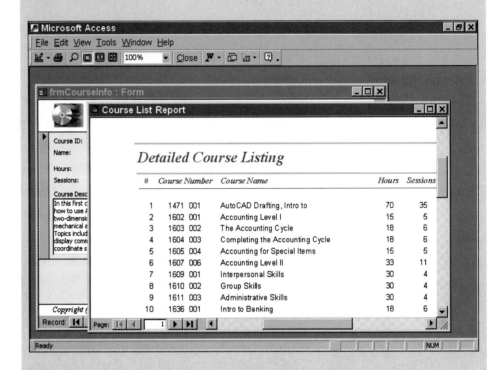

**9** Close the Print Preview window. Then close the frmCourseInfo form and save the changes, if requested to do so.

**10** You now insert a command button onto a form without using the Control Wizard. Do the following:
SELECT: frmAdministrator
CLICK: Design button (⊠Design) on the Database window toolbar

**11** Ensure that the Toolbox window is displayed in Design view. Then insert a command button:
CLICK: Control Wizard button (🖾) so that it is not pressed in
CLICK: Command Button button (⬚) in the Toolbox window
CLICK in the Form Header section at 3 inches on the horizontal ruler
A command button appears next to the form's title. (*Note:* You can move and size the button once it has been placed on the form.)

**12** To set properties for the new command button:
RIGHT-CLICK: the command button control
CHOOSE: Properties
The Properties window appears.

**13** First, let's enter a name and caption for the button:
CLICK: *All* tab
DOUBLE-CLICK: the existing entry in the *Name* property text box
TYPE: `cmdPreviewCourses`
DOUBLE-CLICK: the existing entry in the *Caption* property text box
TYPE: `Preview Courses`

**14** Now let's make the button do something when it is clicked:
CLICK: *Event* tab
CLICK: in the *On Click* property text box
CLICK: Build button (▣) attached to the text box
The Choose Builder dialog box appears, as shown here.

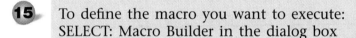

**15** To define the macro you want to execute:
SELECT: Macro Builder in the dialog box
CLICK: OK command button
TYPE: `mcrOpen_rptCourseList` in the *Macro Name* text box
CLICK: OK command button

**16** In the Macro window:
CLICK: down arrow attached to the *Action* text box
SELECT: OpenReport
CLICK: in the adjacent *Comment* text box
TYPE: `Preview the rptCourseList report`

**17** In the *Action Arguments* area:
CLICK: in the *Report Name* text box
CLICK: down arrow attached to the text box
SELECT: rptCourseList
CLICK: in the *View* text box
CLICK: down arrow attached to the text box
SELECT: Print Preview

**18** Now the fun part! You will specify that the report include only those records where the admID field is equal to the administrator record displayed in the frmAdministor form. Do the following:
CLICK: in the *Where Condition* text box
TYPE: `[admID]=[Forms]![frmAdministrator]![admID]`
This expression tells Access to compare the contents of the admID field in each record of the tblCourses table with the current value displayed in the frmAdministrator form.

**19** Save the macro and then close the Macro window to return to the form.

**20** Close the Properties window.

**21** CLICK: View—Form button (⊞▾) to view the form

**22** On your own, navigate to Viola Ruzinsky's record (admID 3.)
Then:
CLICK: Preview Courses command button
Your screen should appear similar to Figure 10.4, after adjusting the Form and Print Preview windows.

**Figure 10.4**

Attaching a macro to a command button

Only the courses with the same admID as the currently displayed record in the form are included in the report.

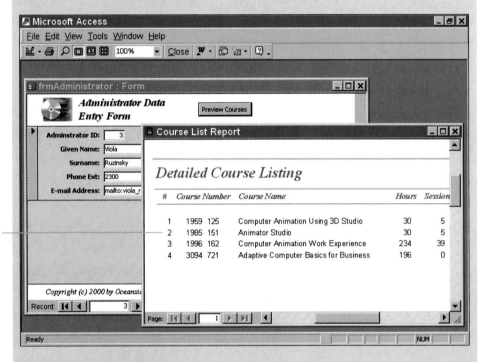

**23** Close the Print Preview window. Then close the Form window and save the changes, if requested to do so.

**24** CLICK: *Macros* button in the Objects bar
Notice that the "mcrOpen_rptCourseList" now appears in the list area.

**In Addition**
Using Macros for
Data Validation

For certain situations, a macro (or an event procedure) offers more flexibility and power than field- and record-level validation rules. Unlike validation rules, you can use a macro to evaluate an entry and then make a decision based upon its value. For example, you can display a warning dialog box when a value contradicts a specified condition. With a macro, the user may override this dialog box and continue the entry. A validation rule, on the other hand, does not offer this flexibility.

## 10.1.3  Using Conditional Expressions in Macros

**FEATURE**
When you run a macro, Access executes each line entry in the *Action* column, starting at the beginning and continuing until it reaches another macro or a blank row. To impose more control over the flow of a macro, you can specify conditional expressions inside the macro. After displaying the *Condition* column, enter an expression that evaluates to true or false. If the condition is true, Access carries out the actions in that row and all of the subsequent rows that contain an ellipsis (...) in the *Condition* column. If the condition is false, Access simply ignores the associated action. Some common actions that you may find next to conditional expressions include "StopMacro," "RunMacro," "CancelEvent," and "MsgBox." You will typically find conditional expressions used inside macro groups.

**METHOD**
To edit a macro:

1.  CLICK: *Macros* button in the Objects bar
2.  SELECT: a macro in the list area
3.  CLICK: Design button ([Design]) on the Database window toolbar

To view additional columns in the Macro window:

*   CLICK: Macro Names ([icon]), or
    CHOOSE: View, Macro Names
*   CLICK: Conditions ([icon]), or
    CHOOSE: View, Conditions

To print a macro:

1.  CLICK: *Macros* button in the Objects bar
2.  SELECT: a macro in the list area
3.  CHOOSE: File, Print

**PRACTICE**

In this example, you practice editing a macro, creating a macro group, and entering conditional expressions.

*Setup:* Ensure that the ACC1000 Database window is displayed.

**1**    To begin, let's review an existing macro. In the *Macros* list area:
DOUBLE-CLICK: mcrMode
The macro opens the Select a Mode dialog box (Figure 10.5), which is actually a form named "frmModeOptions." In this exercise, you will assign a macro to the Proceed command button.

**Figure 10.5**

The "frmModeOptions" form

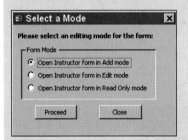

**2**    To close the Select a Mode dialog box:
CLICK: Close command button

**3**    Now let's edit the macro:
SELECT: mcrMode in the *Macros* list area
CLICK: Design button ([Design]) on the Database window toolbar

**4**    For this exercise, you need to display two additional columns in the Macro window. In the Macro Design toolbar:
CLICK: Macro Names ([icon])
CLICK: Conditions ([icon])

**5**    You now convert the mcrMode macro into a macro group containing two separate, but related, macros. To define a new macro inside the group, leave a blank row and then:
CLICK: in the *Macro Name* text box on the third row
TYPE: Options

**6**    This macro will be executed when the user clicks the Proceed command button in the Select a Mode dialog box. In order to open the form in the selected mode, you need to enter conditional expressions into the *Condition* column of the Macro window. Do the following:
CLICK: in the *Condition* text box, adjacent to the "Options" macro name

**7** To specify the action that should occur when the first option button is selected in the Select a Mode dialog box, do the following:
TYPE: `1=[Forms]![frmModeOptions]![frmModes]`
PRESS: [TAB]
CLICK: down arrow attached to the *Action* text box
SELECT: Open Form
(*Note:* This macro action will execute only if the first option button is selected in the frmModeOptions form.)

**8** Now specify the arguments for opening the frmInstructor form in Add mode:
CLICK: in the *Form Name* text box
CLICK: down arrow attached to the text box
SELECT: frmInstructor
CLICK: in the *Data Mode* text box
CLICK: down arrow attached to the text box
SELECT: Add

**9** After displaying the frmInstructor form, you need to stop the macro from processing any further instructions:
CLICK: in the next available row of the *Condition* column
TYPE: . . .
PRESS: [TAB]
CLICK: down arrow attached to the *Action* text box
SELECT: StopMacro
Notice that the ellipsis (...) is required to continue processing commands on the next row of the Macro window.

**10** On your own, size the columns in the Macro window so that you can view the contents of the *Condition* column. Then complete the Macro window as shown in Figure 10.6. (*Note:* The screen graphic shows the argument settings for the first or highlighted action row.) Make sure that you select the Edit mode for the frmInstructor form in option 2 and the Read Only mode for option 3.

ACCESS

**Figure 10.6**

Entering conditional expressions

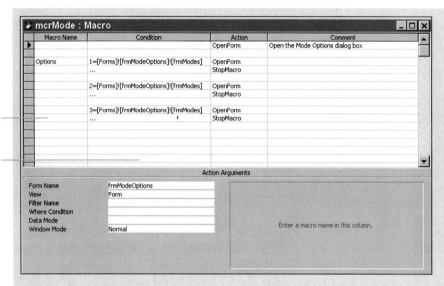

Define a macro group by entering additional macro names in this column.

Define conditional expressions in this column.

**11** Save and then close the Macro window.

**12** To assign the Options macro to the Proceed command button:
CLICK: *Forms* button in the Objects bar
SELECT: frmModeOptions
CLICK: Design button (Design) on the Database window toolbar

**13** To display the appropriate Properties window:
RIGHT-CLICK: Proceed command button
CHOOSE: Properties

**14** Now let's set the desired macro action:
CLICK: *Event* tab
CLICK: in the *On Click* property text box
CLICK: down arrow attached to the text box
SELECT: mcrMode.Options
(*Note:* To refer to a macro within a macro group, use the *macrogroupname.macroname* syntax.)

**15** Close the Properties window.

**16** Save and then close the frmModeOptions Design window.

**17** You may now test the macro. Do the following:
CLICK: *Macros* button in the Objects bar
DOUBLE-CLICK: mcrMode in the list area

**18** In the Select a Mode dialog box:
SELECT: *Open Instructor form in Read Only mode* option button
CLICK: Proceed command button
The frmInstructor form is displayed in Read Only mode.

**19** Close the Form window. Then do the following:
SELECT: *Open Instructor form in Add mode* option button
CLICK: Proceed command button
The form is opened in append mode.

**20** On your own, modify the macro to close the frmModeOptions dialog box before displaying the frmInstructor form. (*Hint:* Use the Insert Rows button (⊟ᴱ) to insert new rows in the Options macro. Before opening the frmInstructor form, use the Close macro action to close the frmModeOptions form. Remember to place an ellipsis (...) in each option's inserted row.)

**21** After testing your macro modifications, close all windows except for the ACC1000 Database window.

| **In Addition**<br>Testing and<br>Debugging Macros | Sometimes macros do not execute as planned. Fortunately, you can find out where errors occur in a macro by opening it in Design view and then stepping through the stored actions one at a time. To step through a macro action by action, click the Single Step button (🔄) on the Macro toolbar or choose the Run, Single Step command. |
| --- | --- |

## 10.1.4  Creating a Switchboard Form

**FEATURE**
Back in Chapter 2 you used the Database Wizard to generate applications based on professionally designed templates. In addition to creating table, form, and report objects, Access supplied a switchboard menu for navigating the application. A switchboard is simply a special-purpose form that is used to access the different features in your application. It is typically the last form you create (or at least polish) before delivering the application to the end user.

You use the **Switchboard Manager** to create, edit, and manage the switchboard menus in an application. To customize a switchboard's display, you modify it as you would any other form. It's important to note that the "Switchboard Items" table in the *Tables* list area of the Database window contains the buttons, text, and commands required for the switchboard to work properly. Without a good understanding of how the switchboard controls are bound to field information, you may risk modifying the form too aggressively and jeopardizing its functionality.

**METHOD**
CHOOSE: Tools, Database Utilities, Switchboard Manager

**PRACTICE**
In this lesson, you create a switchboard menu for automating access to the database objects.

*Setup:* Ensure that you've completed the previous lessons and that the ACC1000 Database window is displayed.

 To create a switchboard menu for the ACC1000 database:
CHOOSE: Tools, Database Utilities, Switchboard Manager
CLICK: Yes command button to create a new switchboard
The Switchboard Manager dialog box appears with the names of the menu pages created by the wizard.

**2** Let's view the results of the wizard:
CLICK: Close command button
CLICK: *Tables* button in the Objects bar
Notice that a new table object named "Switchboard Items" appears in the list area. This table maintains the menu items that are displayed on the switchboard form.

**3** To view the form:
CLICK: *Forms* button in the Objects bar
DOUBLE-CLICK: Switchboard in the list area
An empty switchboard menu page appears, as shown in Figure 10.7. (*Note:* Close the Properties window if it appears.)

**4** Close the Main Switchboard form.

**Figure 10.7**

Displaying a
switchboard form

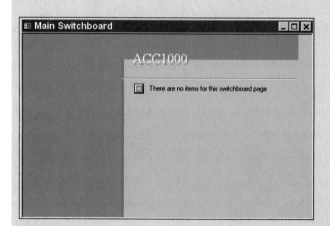

**5** To define menu items for the new switchboard form:
CHOOSE: Tools, Database Utilities, Switchboard Manager

6. Ensure that the Main Switchboard is selected in the list box and then:
CLICK: Edit command button

7. You may now define the items that you want to appear in the switchboard. Do the following:
CLICK: New command button
The Edit Switchboard Item dialog box appears, as shown in Figure 10.8.

**Figure 10.8**

Defining items to appear in the Switchboard

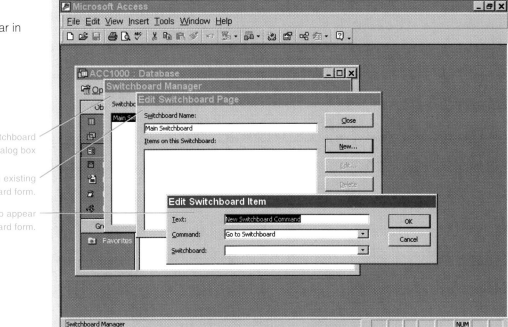

The Switchboard Manager dialog box

Edit an existing switchboard form.

Define the items to appear in the switchboard form.

8. In the Edit Switchboard Item dialog box:
TYPE: **Maintain Administrators** in the *Text* text box
CLICK: down arrow attached to the *Command* drop-down list box
SELECT: Open Form in Edit Mode
CLICK: down arrow attached to the *Form* drop-down list box
SELECT: frmAdministrator
CLICK: OK command button

**9** Now add an item to manage the instructors:
CLICK: New command button
TYPE: `Maintain Instructors` in the *Text* text box
CLICK: down arrow attached to the *Command* drop-down list box
SELECT: Run Macro
CLICK: down arrow attached to the *Macro* drop-down list box
SELECT: mcrMode
CLICK: OK command button

**10** Lastly, let's add an option to run the only report in the database:
CLICK: New command button
TYPE: `Run Course Listing Report` in the *Text* text box
CLICK: down arrow attached to the *Command* drop-down list box
SELECT: Open Report
CLICK: down arrow attached to the *Report* drop-down list box
SELECT: rptCourseList
CLICK: OK command button

**11** To finish editing the Switchboard:
CLICK: Close command button
CLICK: Close command button to close the Switchboard Manager

**12** To view the new switchboard form:
DOUBLE-CLICK: Switchboard in the *Forms* list area

**13** On your own, click each of the menu item buttons and then close the resulting window that appears.

**14** When ready to proceed, close the Main Switchboard form.

## 10.1.5  Customizing the Menu and Toolbars

**FEATURE**
On installing Access, the Menu bar and toolbars are set up in a default configuration. As you gain experience with Access and create macros and modules for automating your work, you may want to customize these features. For example, you can modify menus by adding, arranging, and removing commands. You can also create custom toolbars to display with specific forms or develop global toolbars to use in all your databases. But be prepared; for once your friends and associates see what you can do with Access, they'll be asking you to create personal toolbars for them too!

**METHOD**
To customize a menu or toolbar:

- CHOOSE: Tools, Customize, or
- RIGHT-CLICK: a menu or toolbar
  CHOOSE: Customize

**PRACTICE**
In this lesson, you create a custom toolbar and then add a macro button to the toolbar.

*Setup:* Ensure that you've completed the previous lessons and that the ACC1000 Database window is displayed.

 To customize a toolbar:
CHOOSE: Tools, Customize
CLICK: *Toolbars* tab

**2** Using the vertical scroll bar, scroll to the bottom of the list. You will find two special toolbars, Utility 1 and Utility 2, as shown in Figure 10.9. These two toolbars are initially empty but may be customized for use with all of your databases. In this lesson, however, you will create a new toolbar for restricted use with the ACC1000 database.

**Figure 10.9**

Customize dialog box: *Toolbars* tab

**3** To create a new custom toolbar that is available only in the ACC1000 database, do the following:
CLICK: New command button
TYPE: **My Macros**
CLICK: OK command button
A small empty toolbar appears, as shown here.

**4** Let's add a button to the toolbar:
CLICK: *Commands* tab

**5** Using the vertical scroll bar, scroll to the bottom of the list.
Then:
SELECT: All Macros in the *Categories* list box
SELECT: mcrMode in the *Commands* list box
DRAG: mcrMode selection into the new toolbar,
as shown here

**6** In the Customize dialog box:
CLICK: Modify Selection command button
A pop-up menu appears attached to the command button.

**7** To modify the appearance of the new toolbar button:
CHOOSE: Name ("mcrMode" should appear highlighted)
TYPE: `Select a Mode`
CHOOSE: Change Button Image
CLICK: Book icon (▣)

**8** Now let's add another object to the custom toolbar:
SELECT: All Forms in the *Categories* list box
SELECT: Switchboard in the *Commands* list box
DRAG: Switchboard selection to the right of the "Select a Mode"
button in the new toolbar

**9** To add an existing toolbar button to the custom toolbar:
SELECT: Tools in the *Categories* list box
SELECT: Relationships... in the *Commands* list box
DRAG: Relationships selection to the right of the "Switchboard"
button in the new toolbar

**10** To close the Customize dialog box:
CLICK: Close command button
The My Macros toolbar should now appear as shown below.

**11** On your own, test the toolbar by clicking each button and then
closing the windows that appear.

**12** Now close the My Macros toolbar by clicking its Close button
(☒). (*Hint:* You can use the ShowToolbar macro action to automatically open and close the My Macros toolbar when you enter
or leave a form or report. Using the AutoExec macro, you can
also display and hide custom toolbars when a database is first
opened.)

## 10.1.6  Setting Workplace and Startup Options

**FEATURE**
There are three primary ways that you can customize the Access work environment. First, you can specify workplace options that affect how you view, interact, and work with objects in all databases. For example, you can display and hide components, set print margins, and define default appearances and behaviors for datasheets, forms, and reports. Second, you can specify startup options that affect how a specific database is displayed when it is first opened. And, lastly, you can create custom groups in the Objects bar for better managing a database's objects.

**METHOD**
To set workplace options:
CHOOSE: Tools, Options

To set startup options:
CHOOSE: Tools, Startup

To create custom groups in the Objects bar:

1.  RIGHT-CLICK: in the Objects bar
2.  CHOOSE: New Group

**PRACTICE**
In addition to using the Options and Startup dialog boxes to specify environmental settings, you create a custom group in the Objects bar.

*Setup:* Ensure that you've completed the previous lessons and that the ACC1000 Database window is displayed.

**1** Let's start by reviewing the workplace options:
CHOOSE: Tools, Options
The Options dialog box appears, as shown in Figure 10.10.
Notice the tabs that are displayed: *View, General, Edit/Find, Keyboard, Datasheet, Forms/Reports, Advanced,* and *Tables/Queries.* Each tab contains options that you may set to affect every database you open.

ACCESS

**Figure 10.10**

Options dialog box: *View* tab

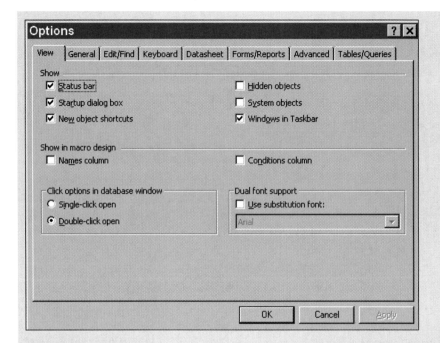

**2**  On your own, click each tab in the Options window and review the options contained therein. Do not make any changes to the settings.

**3**  When ready to proceed:
CLICK: Cancel command button

**4**  To view the specific startup options for the ACC1000 database:
CHOOSE: Tools, Startup
The dialog box shown in Figure 10.11 appears.

**Figure 10.11**

Startup dialog box

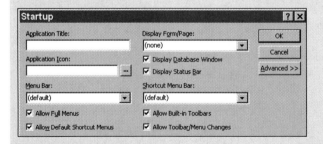

**5**  To display a new title in the Title bar:
TYPE: My School in the *Application Title* text box

**6**  To display the Switchboard form upon startup:
CLICK: down arrow attached to the *Display Form/Page* drop-down list box
SELECT: Switchboard

**7** To complete the configuration:
CLICK: OK command button
Notice that the Application Title bar changes immediately to reflect the new title.

**8** To test the new startup options, close the Database window and then open the ACC1000 database. The Switchboard form is displayed after the Database window is loaded. (*Hint:* You would typically hide the Database window if using a switchboard menu form. To do so, remove the "✔" from the *Display Database Window* check box in the Startup dialog box.)

**9** Close the Main Switchboard window.

**10** There are two major groups in the Objects bar, as shown here. The Objects group contains the standard database objects, while the Groups group contains the default Favorites group and any additional groups that you've defined. In the next few steps, you create a new group to store related database objects for the instructors:
RIGHT-CLICK: anywhere under the Groups bar
CHOOSE: New Group
TYPE: **Instructors**
CLICK: OK command button
A new group folder appears under the Groups bar.

**11** To add tables to the new group:
CLICK: *Tables* button in the Objects bar
DRAG: tblInstructors to the Instructors group
DRAG: tblInsRates to the Instructors group
(*Note:* When you drag an object to the new group, you are not changing or moving the location of the original object in the database. You are simply creating a shortcut to the object.)

**12** Now add the following objects to the group:
CLICK: *Queries* button in the Objects bar
DRAG: qryInsForm to the Instructors group
CLICK: *Forms* button in the Objects bar
DRAG: frmInstructor to the Instructors group
CLICK: *Macros* button in the Objects bar
DRAG: mcrOpen_frmInstructor to the Instructors group
You have now organized the instructor-related objects into a single group to facilitate editing and other maintenance operations.

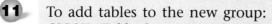

**13** To view the new group's contents:
CLICK: *Instructors* button in the Groups bar
Five objects should now appear in the Database window, as shown in Figure 10.12.

**Figure 10.12**

ACC1000 Database window

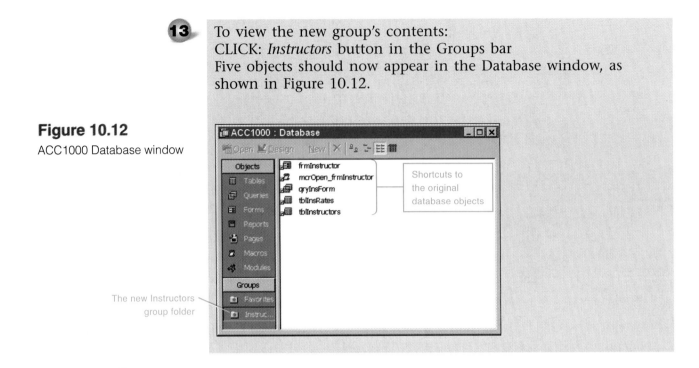

The new Instructors group folder

10.1 Self Check    What macro action is used to open a report in Print Preview mode?

# 10.2  Integrating Access with Word and Excel

Many would say that the essence of Office 2000 is its ability to share data among its suite of applications. For example, you can place an Excel chart in a report written using Word, a document in a PowerPoint presentation, an Access database in an Excel worksheet, and so on. As demonstrated in Chapter 5, Access allows you to export database objects to various file formats using the File, Export command. Additionally, Access provides **OfficeLinks**, which are automation tools for publishing tables, queries, and reports into Word documents and Excel worksheets. Specifically, you can click the Merge It with MS Word (⊞), Publish It with MS Word (⊞), or Analyze It with MS Excel (⊞) buttons on the toolbar or choose the commands from the Tools, OfficeLinks menu. These OfficeLinks enable you to easily share large amounts of information stored in an Access database with the two other primary Office applications.

## 10.2.1 Publishing Data to Word

**FEATURE**

Microsoft Word is a full-featured word processing software program that enables you to create and print documents of varying types, lengths, and styles. Typically you use Word to compile documents such as memos, letters, and reports. Using the Publish It with MS Word (☑️) OfficeLinks feature, you can generate a rich-text (RTF) word processing document containing data from the selected table, query, or report. The document is opened immediately in Word to allow for further editing, formatting, and printing. This feature is a wonderful time-saver when you need to include information from an Access report in a Microsoft Word document. Nearly all of the formatting in the report remains intact thanks to the rich-text format. Whereas the File, Export command simply creates a file, the OfficeLinks feature automates the conversion process and opens the resulting document in Microsoft Word.

**METHOD**

1. SELECT: a table, query, or report in the Database window
2. CLICK: Publish It with MS Word button (☑️) in the toolbar, or CHOOSE: Tools, OfficeLinks, Publish It with MS Word

**PRACTICE**

You now publish an Access report object to Microsoft Word using the Publish It with MS Word (☑️) OfficeLinks feature.

*Setup:* Ensure that the ACC1000 Database window is displayed.

**1**   To publish the rptCourseList report object to Microsoft Word:
CLICK: *Reports* button in the Objects bar
SELECT: rptCourseList in the list area

**2**   To launch the OfficeLinks feature using the menu:
CHOOSE: Tools, OfficeLinks, Publish It with MS Word
A dialog box appears with the current export status. When the process is finished, the new document is opened and displayed in Microsoft Word. Your screen should now appear similar to Figure 10.13.

ACCESS

**Figure 10.13**

Publishing an Access
report to Microsoft Word

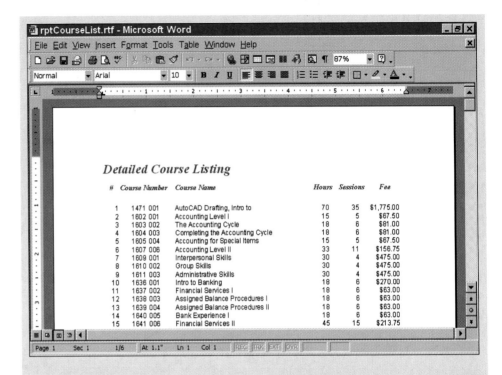

**3** You may have noticed that the document is given the same name as the database object from which it was created. At this point, you can save the document in Word's native format, instead of the rich-text format. Do the following:
CHOOSE: File, Save As from Word's Menu bar

**4** In the Save As dialog box that appears:
SELECT: Word Document from the *Save as type* drop-down list box
CLICK: Save command button

**5** On your own, peruse the document using the vertical scroll bar. Rather than inserting a Word table, the OfficeLinks feature formats the report using tabs to separate columns and paragraph marks to separate rows.

**6** Close Microsoft Word by clicking its Close button (⊠).

## 10.2.2 Merging Data with Word

**FEATURE**

One of the most powerful features of word processing is the ability to merge data into standard document templates for printing. This process, called **mail merge,** can be a huge time-saver because it allows you to use a single document in printing personalized letters to numerous recipients. Although mail merge is used principally for generating form letters, it is also used to print envelopes, mailing labels, invoices, legal contracts, and other documents.

The merge process requires two files: the *main document* and the *data source*. The **main document** (created in Microsoft Word) contains the standard text, graphics, and other objects that will stay the same from document to document. The **data source** (stored in Microsoft Access, in this case) contains the variable data that will be fed into the main document. Although the process of mail merge may sound complicated initially, you can master it quickly, thanks in large part to the helpful prompts of Word's **Mail Merge Wizard.** To launch the wizard from Access, you use the Merge It with MS Word (🖳▾) OfficeLinks feature.

**METHOD**

1. SELECT: a table or query in the Database window
2. CLICK: Merge It with MS Word button (🖳▾) in the toolbar,
   or
   CHOOSE: Tools, OfficeLinks, Merge It with MS Word
3. Respond to the prompts in the Mail Merge Wizard.

**PRACTICE**

In this lesson, you initiate a Microsoft Word mail merge from within Access.

*Setup:* Ensure that the ACC1000 Database window is displayed.

**1** Your objective in this lesson is to merge data from the qryInsForm query into an existing Word document. To begin:
CLICK: *Queries* button in the Database window
SELECT: qryInsForm in the list area
(*Hint:* This query combines data from the tblInstructors and tblInsRates tables.)

**2** To launch the OfficeLinks feature:
CLICK: Merge It with MS Word button (🖳▾) in the toolbar
The Microsoft Word Mail Merge Wizard appears.

**3** In the first step of the wizard:
SELECT: *Link your data to an existing Microsoft Word document*
option button
CLICK: OK command button

**4** In the Select Microsoft Word Document dialog box, ensure that
the Advantage student data files folder is displayed and then:
DOUBLE-CLICK: InsLetter in the list area
Microsoft Word is launched and the document is opened for
display.

**5** Before proceeding, ensure that the Microsoft Word application
window is active and maximized, similar to the screen graphic
shown in Figure 10.14.

**6** On your own, move the flashing insertion point to line 8,
between the current date and the first paragraph. (*Hint:* Look in
the Status bar to see the current line number.)

**7** You insert merge fields into the document using the Mail Merge
toolbar. To begin, do the following:
CLICK: Insert Merge Field button ( Insert Merge Field ▾ )
The field names from the query are listed in the drop-down list.

**8** To create an address:
SELECT: insFirstName
PRESS: Space bar
CLICK: Insert Merge Field button ( Insert Merge Field ▾ )
SELECT: insLastName
PRESS: ENTER

**9** On your own, complete the document in Microsoft Word to
appear similar to Figure 10.14. (*Hint:* You must use the Insert
Merge Field button. Do not type the field identifiers enclosed in
chevrons directly.)

**Figure 10.14**

Inserting merge fields
in a Word document

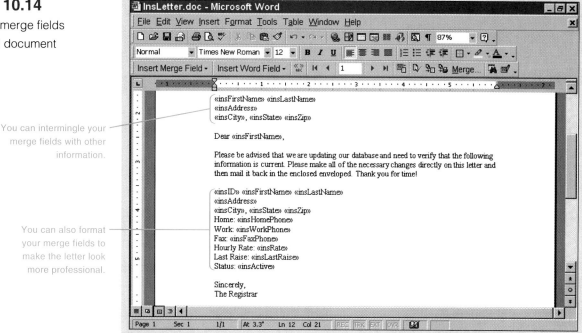

You can intermingle your
merge fields with other
information.

You can also format
your merge fields to
make the letter look
more professional.

**10** CLICK: Save button (🖫) to save the main document

**11** There are two ways to carry out the merge. First, using the Merge to New Document button (🖳), you can merge the results of the query into a new document. Second, using the Merge to Printer button (🖳), you can perform and print the merge results directly. In this step, you create a new document:
CLICK: Merge to New Document button (🖳) in the toolbar
A 30-page document is generated from the merge operation and, depending on your Office configuration, a new application window is opened to display the document.

**12** On your own, peruse the document using the vertical scroll bar. Notice that a different instructor is listed on each page of the new document.

**13** Using the File, Save As command, save the merged document as "Final Merge" to your personal storage location. Then close the new application window by clicking its Close button (☒). The original main document is redisplayed in the first application window.

**14** Save the main document and then close the Word application window by clicking its Close button (☒). You are returned, unharmed, to the Access Database window.

**In Addition**
Importing Access
Data into Word

You can import an Access table or query into Word by clicking the Insert Database button on Word's Database toolbar. The data is inserted into the document as a table, similar in appearance to Datasheet view. Because such a table may extend across several pages, it is wise to use a query to limit the number of imported records.

## 10.2.3 Analyzing Data in Excel

**FEATURE**

Microsoft Excel is an electronic spreadsheet program for storing, manipulating, and charting numeric data. Researchers, statisticians, and businesspeople use Excel to analyze and summarize mathematical, statistical, and financial data. The OfficeLinks feature named Analyze It with MS Excel ([x]) allows you to create an Excel workbook from an Access table, query, or report object. The workbook is then opened in the Excel application window, ready for editing, formatting, and printing.

**METHOD**

1. SELECT: a table, query, or report in the Database window
2. CLICK: Analyze It with MS Excel button ([x]) in the toolbar, or
   CHOOSE: Tools, OfficeLinks, Analyze It with MS Excel

**PRACTICE**

You now create an Excel workbook from a selected table object.

*Setup:* Ensure that the ACC1000 Database window is displayed.

**1** You will now create an Excel workbook using the data stored in the tblSections table. To begin:
CLICK: *Tables* button in the Database window
SELECT: tblSections in the list area

**2** To launch the OfficeLinks feature:
CLICK: down arrow attached to the Merge It with MS Word button ([w])
CLICK: Analyze It with MS Excel ([x])
After a few seconds, a new workbook is opened and displayed in Microsoft Excel. Notice that the workbook is given the same name as its table object. Your screen should appear similar to Figure 10.15.

**Figure 10.15**

Sending data from Access
to Microsoft Excel

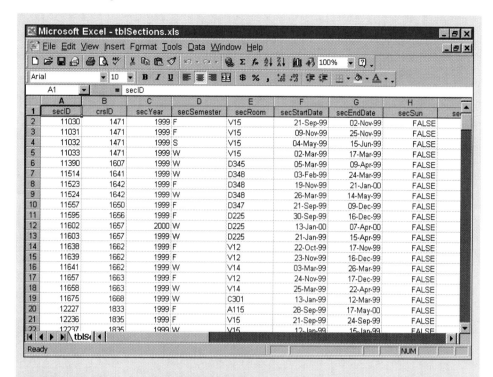

3 On your own, peruse the worksheet using the horizontal and vertical scroll bars.

4 Close Microsoft Excel by clicking its Close button (⊠).

## 10.2.4 Exporting Data to Excel

**FEATURE**

While Access provides better data storage and maintenance capabilities, Excel provides more advanced tools for analyzing data. Therefore, you must frequently transfer data from Access into Excel. One method is to export a table or query object into the Microsoft Excel file format. Another method is to drag and drop a database object into the Excel application window. You can also use the Office Clipboard, discussed in Chapter 5, to copy and paste selected records to a worksheet. In this lesson, you learn how easy it is to share data between these two powerful Office applications.

**METHOD**
To export a database object using the menu:

1. SELECT: an object in the Database window
2. CHOOSE: File, Export
3. TYPE: *a file name* for the new worksheet
4. SELECT: Microsoft Excel 97-2000 in the *Save as type* drop-down list box
5. CLICK: Save command button

To export a database object using drag and drop:

1. Arrange the Access and Excel application windows on the desktop.
2. SELECT: an object in the Access Database window
3. DRAG: the selection to the blank Excel worksheet
4. After dropping the object, save the Excel workbook.

**PRACTICE**
In this lesson, you practice exporting data to Microsoft Excel using the File, Export command and the drag and drop method.

*Setup:* Ensure that the ACC1000 Database window is displayed.

**1** In the next few steps, you export a table object to an Excel workbook file. To begin, ensure that the *Tables* list area is displayed and then:
SELECT: tblContracts in the list area
CHOOSE: File, Export

**2** In the Export dialog box, you provide a name and storage location for the new workbook file:
TYPE: Contracts to Excel in the *File name* text box
SELECT: *your personal storage location* using the Places bar or the *Save in* drop-down list box
SELECT: Microsoft Excel 97-2000 in the *Save as type* drop-down list box
CLICK: Save command button
And that's all there is to exporting database records to an Excel workbook!

**3** Now let's demonstrate the drag and drop method for copying database objects to Excel. On your own, launch Microsoft Excel using the Start button ([Start]). A new workbook should appear with three sheet tabs—*Sheet1*, *Sheet2*, and *Sheet3*—at the bottom of the window.

**4** Ensure that only the Microsoft Access and Microsoft Excel application buttons appear on the taskbar. Then do the following:
RIGHT-CLICK: an empty area on the taskbar
CHOOSE: Tile Windows Vertically
Your screen should appear similar but not identical to Figure 10.16.

**Figure 10.16**

Tiling two open application windows on the desktop

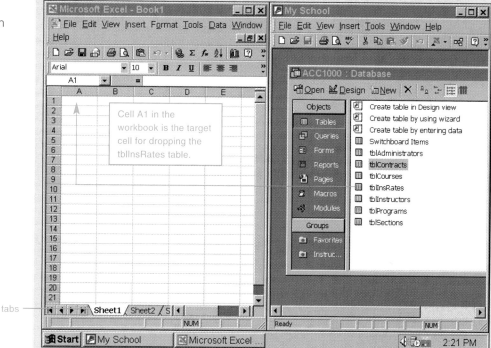

**5** Rather than using the Export command, let's drag the tblInsRates table object into the workbook. Do the following:
SELECT: tblInsRates in the list area of the Database window
DRAG: tblInsRates into cell A1 of the Excel workbook
When you release the mouse button, columns A, B, and C in the worksheet are filled with the contents of the tblInsRates table.

**6** Now let's drag a query object into the same workbook:
CLICK: *Sheet2* tab at the bottom of the window
An empty worksheet appears. (*Hint:* By default, Excel provides three blank worksheets in each new workbook. In addition to adding and removing sheets, you can rename these sheet tabs by double-clicking.)

**7**    To export a query to Excel:
CLICK: *Queries* button in the Access Objects bar
SELECT: qryInsForm in the list area of the Database window
DRAG: qryInsForm into cell A1 of the Excel workbook
When you release the mouse button, the worksheet is filled with data from the query. It is important to note that the data stored in Access is not affected in any way, shape, or form by this process.

**8**    To save the Excel workbook:
CHOOSE: File, Save As from the Excel Menu bar
TYPE: `Export to Excel`
CLICK: Save command button

**9**    Close Microsoft Excel by clicking its Close button (⊠).

**10**    Maximize the Access application window by clicking its Maximize button (▣).

| **In Addition** Importing Access Data into Excel | From within Excel, you can import an Access table or query object using the New Database Query command on the Data, Get External Data menu. The Microsoft Query tool launches and allows you to connect to a variety of database types including Access. |
|---|---|

**10.2 Self Check**    Name the three OfficeLinks features mentioned in this module.

# 10.3 Managing Data in External Databases

Database management on the personal computer cannot be considered a recent development. In fact, dBASE, one of the pioneering desktop software applications, has been around since the early 1980s. Because developing a database application can be a costly and time-consuming venture, businesses tend to stick with a system for several years or until their needs change. As you encounter real-world databases, you will find that many of them are based on older technologies. Often these databases are integral components in larger systems, and you cannot simply extract data from their tables for use in your bright and shiny Access 2000 application. However, there is a way to access this data without causing any disruptions through a process called *linking*. Besides accessing legacy systems, linking enables you to share data among several applications and users. In this module, you learn how to work with data in external Access database files and legacy database systems.

## 10.3.1 Linking to Data in Access Databases

**FEATURE**

In Chapter 5, you copied database objects from one database file into another using the Import command on the File, Get External Data menu. For table objects, the import process copies structural definitions, properties, and data. **Linking** offers an alternative method for accessing data stored in external database files. Through linking, you can establish a connection to a table object that exists in another database file. You can then view and manipulate the data, in most cases, as if it were stored in the local database. When you delete a linked table, you remove the connection in the local database but do not affect the external database in any way.

**METHOD**

1. Open the database file in which you want to create the link.
2. CLICK: *Tables* button in the Objects bar
3. CHOOSE: File, Get External Data, Link Tables
4. SELECT: the database containing the table for linking
5. SELECT: the desired table object to link
6. CLICK: Link command button

**PRACTICE**

In this lesson, you link to a table that is stored in another database file.

*Setup:* Ensure that the ACC1000 Database window is displayed.

**1** The objective of the next few steps is to establish a link to a single table object in an external Access database file. To begin:
CLICK: *Tables* button in the Objects bar
CHOOSE: File, Get External Data, Link Tables
The Link dialog box appears.

**2** Using the Places bar or the *Look in* drop-down list box, select your personal storage location. Then do the following:
DOUBLE-CLICK: ACC1030 database
The Link Tables dialog box appears, as shown in Figure 10.17. The dialog box is similar to the Import Objects dialog box, except you can only select table objects.

**Figure 10.17**

Linking to a table object

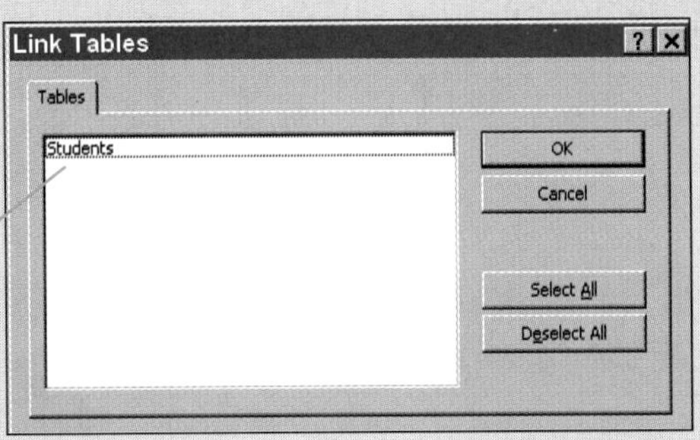

Table object(s) stored in the ACC1030 database file

**3** To link to the only table object in the database:
SELECT: Students in the list area
CLICK: OK command button
The Students table appears in the *Tables* list area. Notice also that a linked table's icon (✦▥) appears with an arrow.

**4** To view the Students table object:
DOUBLE-CLICK: Students in the list area
Access handles the complex task of connecting to the external database and loading the requisite table into a datasheet window. You can now add, edit, delete, and view the table's information as if it were stored locally. Any changes that you make, however, are stored with the table object in the other database file. Pretty cool, huh?

**5** Close the datasheet window before proceeding.

## 10.3.2  Linking to Data in Non-Access Databases

**FEATURE**

In addition to linking to tables in Access database files, you can access data stored in legacy systems built using other database management software. You can also create queries, forms, and reports based on the linked data. Depending on whether specific software programs exist on your computer, you may or may not be able to modify data stored in other database formats. For example, certain versions of dBASE and Paradox files are opened in read-only mode unless you have installed the Borland Database Engine (BDE). Regardless, the ability to link to and view files from other database applications is a very powerful feature.

**METHOD**

1.  Open the database file in which you want to create the link.
2.  CLICK: *Tables* button in the Objects bar
3.  CHOOSE: File, Get External Data, Link Tables
4.  SELECT: the database format in the *Files of type* drop-down list box
5.  SELECT: the desired database file to link
6.  CLICK: Link command button

**PRACTICE**

You now practice linking to dBASE and Paradox database files.

*Setup:* Ensure that the ACC1000 Database window is displayed.

To link to external database files, ensure that the *Tables* list area is displayed and then:
CHOOSE: File, Get External Data, Link Tables

ACCESS

**2** To establish a link to a dBASE file, select the Advantage student data files folder and then:
CLICK: down arrow attached to the *Files of type* drop-down list box
SELECT: dBASE IV
SELECT: DBF1030 in the list area
CLICK: Link command button
A dialog box appears, as shown below, to confirm that the link has been successfully established.

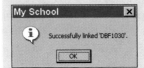

**3** CLICK: OK command button to continue

**4** Now establish a link to a Paradox file:
CLICK: down arrow attached to the *Files of type* drop-down list box
SELECT: Paradox
SELECT: PDX1030 in the list area
CLICK: Link command button
CLICK: OK command button to confirm the link

**5** CLICK: Cancel button to return to the Database window
Notice the dBASE (◆dB) and Paradox (◆Px) linked table icons in the *Tables* list area, as shown in Figure 10.18.

**Figure 10.18**

Linked data files in the ACC1000 Database window

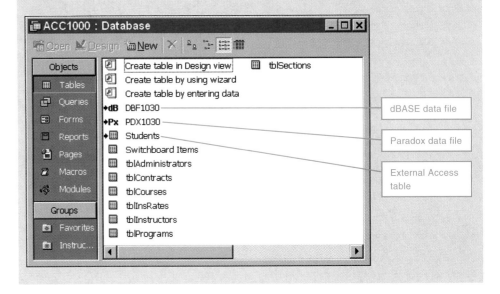

**6** On your own, double-click the linked data files to view their contents. (*Note:* These "old" data files are unrelated to the current school database example, but useful for illustrative purposes.)

**7** When ready to proceed, close all datasheet windows and return to the Database window.

**In Addition**
**Using Open Database**
**Connectivity Drivers**

Access allows you to connect to, open, and work with data files in a variety of different formats, including Microsoft SQL Server, Microsoft FoxPro, Oracle, and DB2, using Open Database Connectivity (ODBC) drivers. The ODBC drivers provide a generic communication layer between Access and these different data formats. For more information, refer to the Access Help system.

## 10.3.3 Using the Linked Table Manager

**FEATURE**
The **Linked Table Manager** is an Access tool that allows you to verify and refresh the storage locations of all linked tables. Use this command to ensure that all linked database files are accessible, especially if you link to files stored on network servers. You also need to perform this command when a linked file is moved to another directory path, disk drive, or computer.

**METHOD**
1.  CHOOSE: Tools, Database Utilities, Linked Table Manager
2.  SELECT: the linked tables that you want to update
3.  CLICK: OK command button

**PRACTICE**
You now practice using the Linked Table Manager.

*Setup:* Ensure that the ACC1000 Database window is displayed.

 To launch the Linked Table Manager:
CHOOSE: Tools, Database Utilities, Linked Table Manager
The dialog box in Figure 10.19 appears. (*Hint:* In previous versions of Access, this command was located on the Tools, Add-ins menu.)

**Figure 10.19**

Linked Table Manager
dialog box

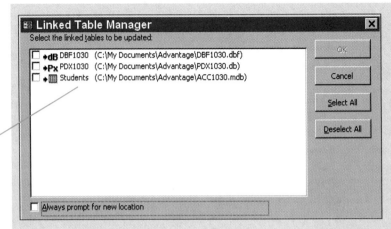

The database files are
stored in the "My
Documents\Advantage"
folder on drive C:.

**2**  Let's update all of the linked tables:
CLICK: Select All command button
CLICK: OK command button
A dialog box appears confirming that the check is complete.

**3**  CLICK: OK command button to proceed

**4**  CLICK: Close command button to return to the Database window

## 10.3.4  Using the Import and Link Wizards

**FEATURE**
Microsoft Access provides two sets of useful wizards for importing
data. To convert data that is stored in an electronic spreadsheet,
you use the **Import Spreadsheet Wizard** or the **Link Spreadsheet
Wizard**, depending on your desired outcome. To convert data that
is stored in an ASCII text file, you use the **Import Text Wizard** or
the **Link Text Wizard**. Regardless of whether you want to import
or link to data, the wizards lead you step-by-step through the
process of converting data into Access database objects.

**METHOD**
To link a text or worksheet file:

1.  CHOOSE: File, Get External Data, Link Tables
2.  SELECT: the file format in the *Files of type* drop-down list box
3.  SELECT: the desired file to link to
4.  CLICK: Link command button
5.  Follow the prompts of the Link wizard.

To import a text or worksheet file:

1.  CHOOSE: File, Get External Data, Import
2.  SELECT: the file format in the *Files of type* drop-down list box
3.  SELECT: the desired file to import
4.  CLICK: Import command button
5.  Follow the prompts of the Import wizard.

**PRACTICE**
In this lesson, you link to an Excel worksheet and then import a text file.

*Setup:* Ensure that the ACC1000 Database window is displayed.

**1** To link to an Excel worksheet file, ensure that the *Tables* list area is displayed and then:
CHOOSE: File, Get External Data, Link Tables

**2** To select the desired worksheet:
CLICK: down arrow attached to the *Files of type* drop-down list box
SELECT: Microsoft Excel
SELECT: ACC1034 in the list area
CLICK: Link command button
The dialog box in Figure 10.20 appears.

**Figure 10.20**
Link Spreadsheet
Wizard dialog box

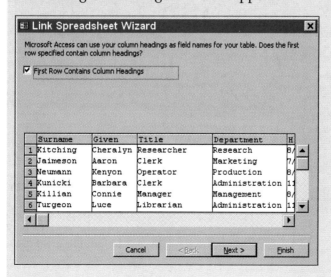

**3** In the first step of the Link Spreadsheet Wizard, specify whether the first row in the worksheet contains column headings or data. In this case, the first row does contain headings. To accept the default:
CLICK: Next >

**4** In the second step of the wizard, specify the name of the linked table object. Do the following:
TYPE: **excHeadOffice**
CLICK: Finish

**5** CLICK: OK command button to accept the confirmation dialog box
Notice the linked table icon (◆📊) for the Microsoft Excel table.

**6** On your own, open and browse through the excHeadOffice linked table object. When ready to proceed, close the datasheet window and return to the Database window.

**7** Most every application program can import and export data using the ASCII text file format. Think of this format as the lowest common denominator for sharing and exchanging data. To import a text file:
CHOOSE: File, Get External Data, Import

**8** To select the desired file:
CLICK: down arrow attached to the *Files of type* drop-down list box
SELECT: Text Files
SELECT: ACC1034 in the list area
CLICK: Import command button
The dialog box in Figure 10.21 appears.

**Figure 10.21**

Import Text Wizard dialog box

Text files exported from other programs typically use commas, quotation marks, and tabs as delimiters between fields.

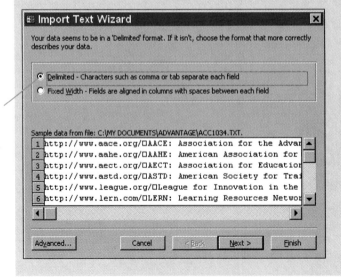

**9** In the first step of the wizard, specify whether the data is delimited (separated by symbols or characters) or fixed width. To accept the default selection:
CLICK: [Next >]

**10** You may now select what type of **delimiter** is used and preview the columns. Ensure that the *Tab* option button is selected and then:
CLICK: [Next >]

**11** In the third step, specify where you would like to store the data. Ensure that the *In a New Table* option button is selected and then:
CLICK: [Next >]

**12** Now specify the field names and data types for the columns. For the first field, ensure that "Hyperlink" is selected in the *Data Type* drop-down list box and then:
TYPE: HomePage in the *Field Name* text box

**13** To set the field properties for the second field:
CLICK: in the horizontal scroll bar of the preview area to move to the next field column
CLICK: Field2 in the column header area, as shown in Figure 10.22

**Figure 10.22**

Specifying field names and types

Set field properties in the *Field Options* area.

Preview area

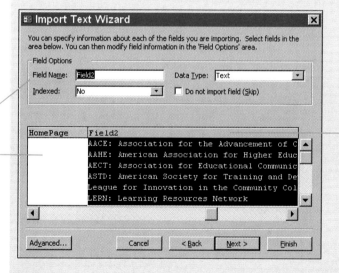

Column header area

**14** Ensure that "Text" is selected in the *Data Type* drop-down list box and that "No" is selected in the *Indexed* drop-down list box. Then:
TYPE: WebResource in the *Field Name* text box
CLICK: [Next >]

**15** In the next step, specify the primary key field. Ensure that the *Let Access add primary key* option button is selected and then:
CLICK: Next >

**16** You may now enter a table name for the new object:
TYPE: `txtWebsites`
CLICK: Finish

**17** CLICK: OK command button to accept the confirmation dialog box
The txtWebsites table now appears in the *Tables* list area.

**18** On your own, open and browse through the txtWebsites linked table object. Adjust the column widths in order to better view the contents of the table. When ready to proceed, save and close the datasheet window and return to the Database window.

## 10.3.5 Converting a Database to a Prior Version

**FEATURE**

Just as there are many different types of databases (Access, dBASE, FoxPro, and Paradox), there are also different versions of Microsoft Access. Unfortunately, the database files created using one version may not be compatible with another version. For example, let's assume that you use Access 2000 at school to create your database files. However, you only have Access 97 loaded on your home computer. Because Microsoft changed the database structure between these two versions, you must first convert the Access 2000 database into an Access 97 file format before you can use it at home. Be aware that not all of the features in Access 2000, such as Data Access Pages, convert to the Access 97 file format.

**METHOD**

CHOOSE: Tools, Database Utilities, Convert Database, To Prior Access Database Version

**PRACTICE**
In this lesson, you convert the ACC1000 database to the Microsoft Access 97 file format.

*Setup:* Ensure that the ACC1000 Database window is displayed.

**1**  To convert the current database into the Access 97 file format:
CHOOSE: Tools, Database Utilities, Convert Database, To Prior Access Database Version
A dialog box appears, allowing you to select a destination and filename for the new database.

**2**  In the Convert Database Into dialog box:
TYPE: 97ACC1000 in the *File name* text box
SELECT: *your personal storage location* using the Places bar or the *Save in* drop-down list box
CLICK: Save command button
The Status bar displays the status of the conversion process.
(*Hint:* You can use the Windows Explorer to check for the existence of the new database file.)

**3**  Before proceeding, close the ACC1000 Database window.

**10.3 Self Check**  Name two general methods for accessing external data from within Microsoft Access. How do they differ?

# 10.4  Developing Database Applications

The key to developing database applications is proper planning. In Chapter 2, you learned the five steps of database design: (1) determine output requirements, (2) determine input requirements, (3) determine your table structures, (4) determine your table relationships, and (5) test your database application. Unfortunately, some applications do not allow for such a structured approach. For instance, you may not be able to gain access to key people or fully comprehend how end users will work with your application in their daily routines. You must also anticipate the need for flexibility in your applications and be able to adapt databases to changing needs and business conditions. To assist you in developing end-user applications, this module introduces Access tools and features for analyzing, enhancing, extending, and securing your databases.

ACCESS

## 10.4.1  Using the Table Analyzer

**FEATURE**
Earlier in this book, you learned that normalizing a database enables you to eliminate redundant information, improve data integrity, and enhance a system's efficiency. To help you develop an efficient relational database, Access provides the **Table Analyzer Wizard**. This wizard normalizes a table by moving fields that contain repeating values into new tables and establishing relationships between them. The wizard is especially useful for analyzing and dissecting data that you import from external sources, such as Excel worksheets.

**METHOD**
CHOOSE: Tools, Analyze, Table, or
CLICK: Analyze Table button (⊞ ▾) on the toolbar

**PRACTICE**
You now analyze an imported worksheet table in an existing database.

*Setup:* Ensure that there is no Database window displayed.

**1** Open the database file named ACC1040, located in the Advantage student data files folder. This database contains two table objects imported from Excel worksheets.

**2** Open the tblPersonnel table in a datasheet window and familiarize yourself with its contents. Close the datasheet window before proceeding.

**3** Let's use the Table Analyzer Wizard to help us normalize the contents of this table object. Do the following:
SELECT: tblPersonnel in the *Tables* list area
CHOOSE: Tools, Analyze, Table
The wizard's dialog box appears, as shown in Figure 10.23.

**Figure 10.23**

Table Analyzer Wizard
dialog box

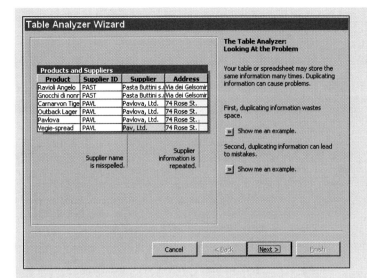

**4** CLICK:  button to proceed

**5** After reading the contents of the next dialog box:
CLICK: Next >

**6** In the third step, you select the table object that you want to
analyze. The tblPersonnel table should already appear highlighted
in the list area. Do the following:
CLICK: Next >

**7** To let the wizard do its thing, ensure that the *Yes, let the wizard
decide* option button is selected and then:
CLICK: Next >
The dialog box should now appear similar to Figure 10.24.

**Figure 10.24**

Using a wizard to split up
a table into related tables

Drag fields and table
objects in this area to
define structures and
relationships in the
database.

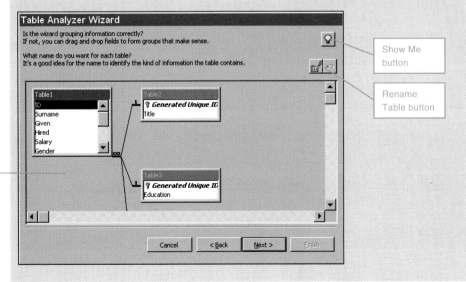

**8** In this step, you confirm and customize the wizard's creation and relation of tables. To display some helpful information:
CLICK: Show Me button (⌷)

**9** After reading the contents of the pop-up Table Analyzer window:
CLICK: its Close button (☒)

**10** To move the "Education" field back to the main table:
SELECT: Education in the Table3 table object
DRAG: Education into the Table1 table object below the Hired field
Notice that the Table3 table object is removed from the dialog box. (*Hint:* Don't worry about the order placement of the Education field in the Table1 table object. You can later modify the field order in table Design view.)

**11** To rename the remaining table objects:
CLICK: Title bar for the Table1 table object
CLICK: Rename Table button (⌷) in the dialog box
TYPE: `newPersonnel`
CLICK: OK command button
(*Note:* You can also double-click a table object's Title bar.)

**12** Using the same process, rename the Table2 object (containing the "Title" field) to `newTitle` and the Table4 object (containing the "Department" field) to `newDept`. When ready to proceed:
CLICK: Next >

**13** In this step of the Table Analyzer Wizard, you select or add a primary key to each table. To read more about the process:
CLICK: Show Me button (⌷)
(*Note:* Normalization requires each table to have a primary key so that every record is uniquely identifiable. Having unique keys helps ensure that the system cannot store duplicate data.)

**14** To proceed, close the window and accept the default selections:
CLICK: Close button (☒) in the pop-up window
CLICK: Next >

**15** The wizard then searches for potential errors in records that contain similar values, as shown here. To confirm that the "Controller" entry is accurate:
CLICK: in the *Correction* text box for the "Controller" title
CLICK: down arrow attached to the text box
SELECT: (Leave as is) near the top of the drop-down list
CLICK: Next >

| Title | | Correction |
|---|---|---|
| ▶ Accountant | | ▾ |
| Analyst | | |
| Foreman | | |
| Librarian | | |
| President | | |
| Controller | --> | Clerk |

**16** In the last step of the wizard, Access offers to create a query that returns a dynaset structured similarly to the original table. This ensures that all forms and reports that were based on the original table will continue to work. (*Note:* The *Record Source* property in the form and report objects is modified to reference the new query object.) To proceed, ensure that the *Yes, create the query* option button is selected and then:
CLICK: *Display Help on working with new tables or query?* check box so that no "✔" appears
CLICK: Finish

**17** To dismiss the dialog box confirming that the query has been built:
CLICK: OK command button
You should now see the tblPersonnel select query displayed. Notice that it appears and works just like the original table object.

**18** Close the Query datasheet window before proceeding. Ensure that the *Tables* list area is displayed in the Database window.

## 10.4.2 Using the Performance Analyzer

**FEATURE**
The **Performance Analyzer Wizard** optimizes the performance (speed) of all objects in a database, including tables, queries, forms, and reports. Whereas the Table Analyzer is used during the database design stage, the Performance Analyzer is best used after the database is populated with its query, form, and report objects. After the wizard finishes performing its analysis, a dialog box containing its recommendations, suggestions, and ideas is presented to the user. Recommendations are the easiest to implement, since the wizard can perform them for you. Suggestions and ideas typically require more work on your part and are often presented with associated warnings and/or potential trade-offs.

**METHOD**
CHOOSE: Tools, Analyze, Performance, or
CLICK: Analyze Performance button (⊞▾) on the toolbar

**PRACTICE**
In this lesson, you use the Performance Analyzer Wizard to analyze the table objects created in the last lesson.

*Setup:* Ensure that the ACC1040 Database window is displayed and that you've completed the previous lesson.

**1.** Before launching the Performance Analyzer Wizard, let's throw a wrench into the database's design. Do the following:
CLICK: Relationships button (⊞) on the toolbar
Three tables appear in the Relationships window, joined together by relationship lines.

**2.** Let's remove the relationship lines and then see if the wizard picks up on the sabotage. Do the following:
CLICK: relationship line appearing between the newDept and newPersonnel table objects
PRESS: DELETE
CLICK: Yes command button to confirm the deletion

**3.** Now remove the second relationship line:
CLICK: relationship line appearing between newTitle and newPersonnel
PRESS: DELETE
CLICK: Yes command button

**4.** Save and then close the Relationships window.

**5.** To launch the Performance Analyzer Wizard:
CHOOSE: Tools, Analyze, Performance
The Performance Analyzer window appears, as shown in Figure 10.25.

**Figure 10.25**

Performance Analyzer dialog box

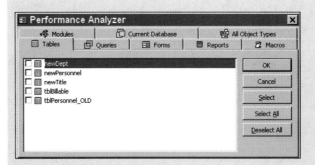

**6.** On the *Tables* tab of the Performance Analyzer Wizard:
SELECT: newDept check box
SELECT: newPersonnel check box
SELECT: newTitle check box

**7.** To analyze the query associated with these tables:
CLICK: *Queries* tab
SELECT: tblPersonnel check box

**8** CLICK: OK command button to begin the analysis
When finished, the dialog box in Figure 10.26 appears. Notice that different graphical icons are used to represent the types of results returned by the wizard.

**Figure 10.26**

Results dialog box in the Performance Analyzer Wizard

Select an option in this list box to display further information in the *Analysis Notes* area.

This area describes the selected option and explains the specific benefits of optimization.

For further information, click the Help command button.

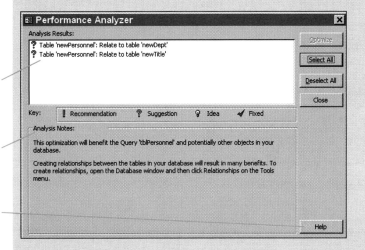

**9** You can ask Access to fix "Recommendations" and "Suggestions" automatically. The "Ideas," on the other hand, must be attended to manually. Do the following:
CLICK: Select All command button
CLICK: Optimize command button
Another dialog box appears, warning you that carrying out the suggested fixes may have side effects.

**10** To proceed with optimization:
CLICK: Yes command button
The "Fixed" check mark now appears next to each suggestion in the list area.

**11** CLICK: Close command button

**12** On your own, open the Relationships window to ensure that the relationships have been reset. Then close the Relationships window when you are ready to proceed.

ACCESS

## 10.4.3   Understanding Replication

**FEATURE**

The power of using database management software is not tied to your desktop computer. With **replication,** you can create multiple copies (**replicas**) of a master database, add and modify data in the copies, and then, at a later time, fold in the changes to update (**synchronize**) the master database. Replication is an especially powerful feature for sales professionals who require local access to databases while they're on the road. Using a notebook computer, these professionals can take key databases with them to a client's site and then, upon returning to the office, connect to the network and exchange any modifications that were made in their absence. Another common use for replication is creating backup copies of a database on a network drive.

The first step in using replication is to convert an existing database into a **Design Master**. This process adds several hidden system tables to your database for tracking design and data changes. The table structures themselves may also be modified to incorporate hidden fields, such as a Replication ID field for uniquely identifying records across a **replica set**. Because this transformation is difficult to undo, you should always make a backup of your database file prior to undertaking replication.

**METHOD**

To create a Design Master and replica from within Access:

1.   Open the database that you want to convert into a Design Master.
2.   CHOOSE: Tools, Replication, Create Replica

To create a Design Master and replica using Briefcase replication:

1.   Locate and select the desired database file using Windows Explorer.
2.   Arrange Windows Explorer on the desktop so that the "My Briefcase" icon is visible. (*Note:* If the "My Briefcase" icon is not present on your desktop, you will need to install this feature using Windows Setup.)
3.   DRAG: the selected database file over the "My Briefcase" icon

**PRACTICE**

You now convert the ACC1040 Database into a Design Master and create a single replica copy.

*Setup:* Ensure that the ACC1040 Database window is displayed and that you've completed the previous lesson.

**1** In a real-world application, you would back up the target database prior to starting replication. For this lesson, however, you perform the backup during the replication process. Do the following:
CHOOSE: Tools, Replication, Create Replica
The following dialog box appears. Take notice of the last sentence, which states that replication typically increases the file size of a database.

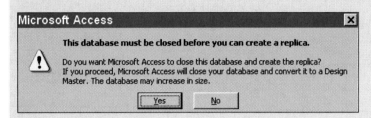

**2** To proceed with the conversion process:
CLICK: Yes command button
The database is closed and the dialog box in Figure 10.27 appears. Notice that Access offers to create a backup copy of your database file.

**Figure 10.27**

Converting a database into a Design Master

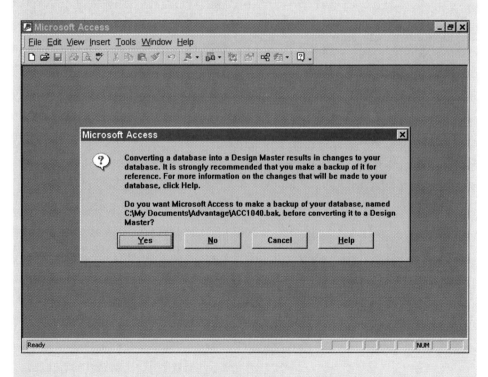

**3** To create a backup copy of the ACC1040 database:
CLICK: Yes command button

In the Location of New Replica dialog box, specify the directory folder location and filename of the first replica to be created from the Design Master. You can also set a priority status for the replica and lock the replica from being able to delete data. For now, ensure that your personal storage location is selected and then:
TYPE: `Replica One`
CLICK: OK command button
The following dialog box appears. Notice that you've not only converted the existing database into a Design Master, you've also created a new replica named "Replica One."

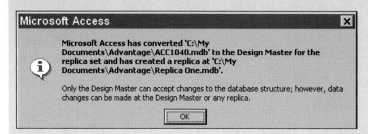

 CLICK: OK command button to proceed
Notice that the Database window now reads "Design Master" and that the table objects appear with new replication icons (🖿▥).

## 10.4.4 Creating and Synchronizing Replicas

**FEATURE**
The Design Master, sometimes called the *master database*, provides the design specifications for all of the database objects in a replica set. To create additional replicas, open the Design Master or another replica and then choose the Create Replica command on the Tools, Replication menu. If you only need a subset of the data stored in the Design Master, launch the **Partial Replica Wizard** to filter the desired data.

If you need to modify the design of a table, query, form, or report object, make your structural changes in the Design Master and then synchronize to the replica set. For specific requirements, you can also create your own local database objects in a replica, but they will not be synchronized with other members in the replica set. After modifying data in a replica, you synchronize its contents with the Design Master or another replica using the Synchronize Now command. If the two replicas contain different "updated" versions of a record, a conflict results and Access makes you choose the correct value.

**METHOD**
To create a new replica:

1. Open the Design Master or a replica.
2. CHOOSE: Tools, Replication, Create Replica

To synchronize replicas:

1. Open the Design Master or a replica.
2. CHOOSE: Tools, Replication, Synchronize Now

To resolve conflicts between replicas:

1. Open the Design Master or a replica.
2. CHOOSE: Tools, Replication, Resolve Conflicts

**PRACTICE**
In this lesson, you practice creating and synchronizing replicas.

*Setup:* Ensure that the ACC1040 Design Master window is displayed and that you've completed the previous lesson.

**1** To create a new replica from the ACC1040 Design Master:
CHOOSE: Tools, Replication, Create Replica
The Location of New Replica dialog box is displayed.

**2** To complete the dialog box:
TYPE: `Replica Two`
CLICK: OK command button
The following dialog box appears.

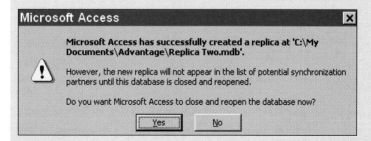

**3** To refresh the Design Master:
CLICK: Yes command button

**4** Although no data changes have been made in the replicas, let's practice synchronizing the Design Master to Replica Two. Do the following:
CHOOSE: Tools, Replication, Synchronize Now
The dialog box in Figure 10.29 appears. (*Note:* You perform synchronization between two replicas or between the Design Master and a replica.)

**Figure 10.28**

Synchronizing the Design
Master to members in a
replica set

Any replica in the set can
take a turn at becoming the
Design Master.

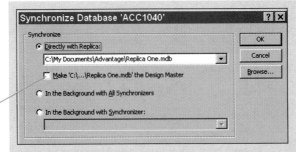

**5** CLICK: down arrow attached to the *Directly with Replica* drop-
down list box
SELECT: the entry for "Replica Two"
CLICK: OK command button

**6** To close the database and proceed with synchronization:
CLICK: Yes command button

**7** CLICK: OK command button when the process is complete
(*Hint:* The Microsoft Office 2000 Developer edition comes with a
special tool called the *Microsoft Replication Manager*. This tool
facilitates creating new replicas, managing replicas, and creating
synchronization schedules.)

**8** Close the ACC1040 Design Master before proceeding.

## 10.4.5 Splitting Up a Database

**FEATURE**
In the module entitled "Linking to Data in Access Databases," you
learned how to establish dynamic links to tables stored in external
database files. One of the greatest benefits of linking is that you
can split up a database application so that the table objects are
stored in one database and the forms, reports, macros, and modules are stored in another database. The splitting up of a database
allows you to place your data in a single, secure, and shared database file on a network server. Multiple people may then access the
shared database using their local database applications. To assist
you in splitting up a database, Access provides the **Database Splitter Wizard**. This wizard exports all of the table objects to a new
database file, deletes the tables from the current database, and then
establishes links to the tables in the new "data only" database.

**METHOD**
CHOOSE: Tools, Database Utilities, Database Splitter

**PRACTICE**
You now split up the objects in a database file for use in a multiuser environment.

*Setup:* Ensure that there is no Database window displayed.

**1** Open the database file named ACC1045. This database contains three tables, one query, one form, and one report. (*Hint:* You should always make backup copies before changing the structure of your database.)

**2** To launch the Database Splitter Wizard:
CHOOSE: Tools, Database Utilities, Database Splitter
The dialog box in Figure 10.29 appears.

**Figure 10.29**
Database Splitter
Wizard dialog box

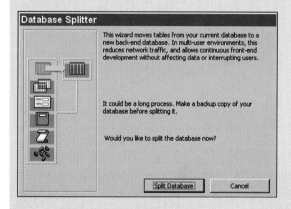

**3** CLICK: Split Database command button to proceed

**4** In the Create Back-end Database window, specify the directory folder location and filename of the new "data only" database. For this step, ensure that your personal storage location is selected and then:
CLICK: Split command button

**5** When the wizard is finished:
CLICK: OK command button to continue
Notice that the table objects in the ACC1045 Database window now appear with link icons (◆▦). All of the objects in the database work exactly as they did before the database was split.

**6** Close the ACC1045 Database window.

**In Addition**
Introducing the
Microsoft Data Engine
and Access Data
Projects

An **Access data project** is a special type of database file that is stored with an .ADP file extension. Access projects allow you to build true client/server applications. Instead of using the JET database engine (.MDB) for data storage and maintenance, you select either the new **Microsoft Data Engine (MSDE)** or a SQL Server back-end. The Microsoft Data Engine is a fully SQL Server-compatible engine that can be distributed royalty free for desktop database applications. While Microsoft does not recommend more than 10 simultaneous users for the new database engine, it enables you to design and create a small-scale version of a SQL Server application. One of the greatest benefits of Access projects is that you can use the front-end features of Microsoft Access 2000 to manage server-based databases. Similar to splitting up a database, the only objects stored in the .ADP file are forms, reports, macros, and modules. All tables, views, and relationships are stored on the database server. Access projects also facilitate migrating your work to larger-scale SQL Server applications when required. For more information, refer to the Help system and Microsoft's Web site.

## 10.4.6 Setting a Password and Encrypting a Database

**FEATURE**

This lesson focuses on two simple methods for keeping your data from prying eyes. First, you can set a database *password* that restricts someone from opening and perusing a database. A **password** is a word or name that is easy for you to remember but difficult for others to guess. The best passwords combine uppercase and lowercase characters with numbers and symbols, such as *Terra4U&4Me*. A second method is to use file encryption to stop someone from viewing the contents of a database using utilities software. **Encrypting** a database makes the contents of the file appear scrambled. **Decrypting** a database simply removes the encryption protection. Access also provides comprehensive user- and group-level security for protecting your work. If security is an important issue for your data, refer to the Help system and Microsoft's Web site for further information.

**METHOD**

To set a database password:

1. Open the database file in Exclusive mode.
2. CHOOSE: Tools, Security, Set Database Password

To encrypt or decrypt a database:

1. Ensure that you are the owner of the database file.
2. CHOOSE: Tools, Security, Encrypt/Decrypt Database

**PRACTICE**

In this lesson, you set a database password.

*Setup:* Ensure that there is no Database window displayed.

**1** In order to set a password for a database, you must first open the file in Exclusive mode. To do so:
CLICK: Open button ([image]) on the toolbar
The Open dialog box is displayed.

**2** Using the Places bar and the *Look in* drop-down list box, select your Advantage student data files folder. Then:
SELECT: ACC1045 in the list area

**3** To specify that the database file should be opened exclusively:
CLICK: down arrow attached to the Open command button
The following pop-up menu appears.

**4** CHOOSE: Open Exclusive

**5** To set a password for the database:
CHOOSE: Tools, Security, Set Database Password
TYPE: Terra4U&4Me in the *Password* text box
PRESS: TAB
TYPE: Terra4U&4Me in the *Verify* text box
CLICK: OK command button
(*Note:* An Access password is case-sensitive.)

**6** To test the password, close the Database window and then re-open the ACC1045 database file in Exclusive mode. Enter the appropriate password in the dialog box that appears. (*Note:* The only reason that you are opening the database in Exclusive mode is in order to remove the password in the next step.)

**7** To remove the password:
CHOOSE: Tools, Security, Unset Database Password
TYPE: `Terra4U&4Me` in the *Password* text box
CLICK: OK command button

**8** Close the ACC1045 Database window. Then exit Microsoft Access.

**10.4 Self Check**   What is the purpose of the Database Splitter Wizard?

# 10.5 Chapter Review

This chapter presents two primary themes: automation and extension. One of the most effective ways to automate Access is to store a set of repetitive actions in a macro object that can be executed at a later time by double-clicking. You can also attach a macro to a control or object so that it executes automatically whenever a particular event occurs. Furthermore, you can assign macros to menu commands, toolbar buttons, and items on a switchboard form—a customizable menu that enhances the usability of an application. The second theme, extension, refers to Access' ability to work with data external to its database and to develop flexible end-user applications. In addition to exchanging data with Microsoft Word and Microsoft Excel, you can establish dynamic links to work with data stored in other database formats. You can also optimize the design, functionality, and adaptability of your databases using the several utilities that Access makes available. Some useful tools introduced in this chapter include Table Analyzer, Performance Analyzer, Linked Table Manager, and Database Splitter. Lastly, this chapter introduces some advanced topics such as replication, multi-user access, and Access data projects.

## 10.5.1 Command Summary

Many of the commands and procedures appearing in this chapter are summarized in the following table.

| Skill Set | To Perform This Task . . . | Do the Following . . . |
|---|---|---|
| **Using Access Tools** | Create a new macro | SELECT: *Macros* object button<br>CLICK: New button ([☑ New]) on the Database window toolbar |
| | Execute a macro from the Database window | SELECT: the desired macro<br>CLICK: Run button ([! Run]) on the Database window toolbar |
| | Execute a macro from the Menu bar | CHOOSE: Tools, Macro, Run Macro |
| | Assign a macro to a control's event procedure in Design view | Display the Properties window<br>CLICK: *Event* tab<br>CLICK: in the desired event property text box<br>CLICK: Build button ([...])<br>DOUBLE-CLICK: Macro Builder |
| | View the Macro Names column in the Macro window | CLICK: Macro Names button ([▤]), or<br>CHOOSE: View, Macro Names |
| | View the Conditions column in the Macro window | CLICK: Conditions button ([☒]), or<br>CHOOSE: View, Conditions |
| | Customize a menu or toolbar | CHOOSE: Tools, Customize |
| | Create custom groups in the Objects bar | RIGHT-CLICK: in the Objects bar<br>CHOOSE: New Group |
| | Set workplace environment options | CHOOSE: Tools, Options |
| | Set startup options | CHOOSE: Tools, Startup |
| | Set and modify a database password | Open the database in Exclusive mode<br>CHOOSE: Tools, Security, Set Database Password |

*Continued*

| Skill Set | To Perform This Task . . . | Do the Following . . . |
|---|---|---|
| **Using Access Tools** *Continued* | Remove a database password | Open the database in Exclusive mode<br>CHOOSE: Tools, Security, Unset Database Password |
| | Encrypt or decrypt a database | CHOOSE: Tools, Security, Encrypt/Decrypt Database |
| | Convert a database to a prior version | CHOOSE: Tools, Database Utilities, Convert Database, To Prior Access Database Version |
| | Launch the Linked Table Manager | CHOOSE: Tools, Database Utilities, Linked Table Manager |
| | Launch the Database Splitter | CHOOSE: Tools, Database Utilities, Database Splitter |
| | Launch the Table Analyzer | CHOOSE: Tools, Analyze, Table, or CLICK: Analyze Table button (⊞▾) |
| | Launch the Performance Analyzer | CHOOSE: Tools, Analyze, Performance, or CLICK: Analyze Performance button (⊞▾) |
| | Create a Design Master for replication | CHOOSE: Tools, Replication, Create Replica |
| | Create a replica from a Design Master or from another replica | CHOOSE: Tools, Replication, Create Replica |
| | Synchronize replicas in a set | CHOOSE: Tools, Replication, Synchronize Now |
| | Resolve conflicts in synchronization | CHOOSE: Tools, Replication, Resolve Conflicts |

*Continued*

| Skill Set | To Perform This Task . . . | Do the Following . . . |
|---|---|---|
| **Building and Modifying Forms** | Create and modify a Switchboard form | CHOOSE: Tools, Database Utilities, Switchboard Manager |
| **Data Integration** | Publish data to Word using the OfficeLinks feature | SELECT: a table, query, or report CLICK: Publish It with MS Word button (![W])|
| | Perform a mail merge with Word using the OfficeLinks feature | SELECT: a table or query CLICK: Merge It with MS Word button (![W])|
| | Export data to Excel using the OfficeLinks feature | SELECT: a table, query, or report CLICK: Analyze It with MS Excel button (![X])|
| | Export data to Excel using the Export command | SELECT: a table or query CHOOSE: File, Export SELECT: Microsoft Excel 97-2000 in the *Save as type* drop-down list box CLICK: Save command button |
| | Export data to Excel using the drag and drop method | Tile the Access and Excel application windows on the Windows desktop SELECT: a table or query in the Access Database window DRAG: the selection to cell A1 in the blank Excel worksheet |
| | Import data from Access and non-Access disk files | CHOOSE: Files, Get External Data, Import |
| | Link to data in Access and non-Access disk files | CHOOSE: Files, Get External Data, Link Tables |

ACCESS

## 10.5.2  Key Terms

This section specifies page references for the key terms identified in this chapter. For a complete list of definitions, refer to the Glossary provided at the end of this learning guide.

Access data project, *p. 608*

actions, *p. 552*

arguments, *p. 552*

AutoExec macro, *p. 555*

data source, *p. 577*

Database Splitter
Wizard, *p. 606*

decrypting, *p. 608*

delimiter, *p. 593*

Design Master, *p. 602*

encrypting, *p. 608*

event, *p. 551*

event procedures, *p. 551*

Import Spreadsheet
Wizard, *p. 590*

Import Text Wizard, *p. 590*

Link Spreadsheet
Wizard, *p. 590*

Link Text Wizard, *p. 590*

Linked Table Manager, *p. 589*

linking, *p. 585*

macro, *p. 551*

Macro Builder, *p. 556*

macro group, *p. 551*

mail merge, *p. 577*

Mail Merge Wizard, *p. 577*

main document, *p. 577*

Microsoft Data Engine
(MSDE), *p. 608*

OfficeLinks, *p. 574*

Partial Replica Wizard, *p. 604*

password, *p. 608*

Performance Analyzer
Wizard, *p. 599*

replica set, *p. 602*

replicas, *p. 602*

replication, *p. 602*

Switchboard Manager, *p. 565*

synchronize, *p. 602*

Table Analyzer Wizard, *p. 596*

user defined functions, *p. 551*

# 10.6 Review Questions

## 10.6.1 Short Answer

1. Name two events associated with a command button.
2. What is the difference between an *event* and an *event procedure*?
3. Name three ways to execute a macro object.
4. At which point in the development process do you typically create a switchboard form? Explain.
5. Why does Access provide the OfficeLinks features?
6. What is one possible limitation of linking to data in non-Access databases?
7. Why might you convert an Access database to a prior version?
8. How do the Table Analyzer and the Performance Analyzer differ?
9. What is a *replica*? Why would you want to create one?
10. When might you use the Microsoft Data Engine (MSDE)?

## 10.6.2 True/False

1. _____ A macro group is a single macro that performs actions on multiple objects at the same time.
2. _____ You can convert a macro object to Visual Basic code.
3. _____ You can drag a table, query, form, or report object into the Macro window in order to define a macro action for opening the object.
4. _____ Switchboard menu items are stored in a query object entitled "Switchboard Items."
5. _____ Custom groups that you add to the Database window appear under the Groups group bar.
6. _____ When using the Publish It with MS Word OfficeLinks feature, Word is launched automatically to display the new document.
7. _____ Deleting a linked table from the Database window removes the link but does not affect the original table in the external data file.
8. _____ You can have Access carry out for you the recommendations, suggestions, and ideas made by the Performance Analyzer Wizard.
9. _____ You can create a replica that contains only a portion of the data stored in the Design Master.
10. _____ You can only use letters and numbers when entering a database password.

ACCESS

## 10.6.3 Multiple Choice

1. After selecting an action in the Macro window, you typically set its:
   a. arguments
   b. constants
   c. parameters
   d. variables

2. When you first open a database, Access looks for a special macro named:
   a. AutoExec
   b. AutoExecute
   c. AutoMacro
   d. AutoRun

3. Which of the following is used to continue processing actions on subsequent lines in a conditional macro?
   a. - - -
   b. _
   c. ...
   d. ContinueMacro

4. To customize a toolbar that may be used with all of your databases, use the following toolbar as a template on which to build:
   a. Custom
   b. Standard
   c. Toolbox
   d. Utility 1

5. Which of the following tabs does not appear in the Options dialog box?
   a. General
   b. Keyboard
   c. Menus
   d. View

6. Which of the following is not an OfficeLinks feature?
   a. Merge It with MS Word
   b. Publish It with MS Word
   c. Analyze It with MS Excel
   d. Publish It with MS Excel

7. Which Access tool helps you verify and refresh a connection with an external database file?
   a. Connect Table Manager
   b. Database Splitter
   c. Linked Table Manager
   d. Table Analyzer

8. Which Access tool do you use to automatically separate out the table objects from a database and then establish links to these tables?
   a. Connect Table Manager
   b. Database Splitter
   c. Linked Table Manager
   d. Table Analyzer

9. Which of the following steps should you take prior to replicating a database?
   a. Back up the database
   b. Rename the database
   c. Open the database in Exclusive mode
   d. Set a password for accessing the database

10. The following process/feature ensures that utility software programs cannot read the contents of a database file:
    a. Decryption
    b. Encryption
    c. Password-Protection
    d. User-Level Security

ACCESS

# 10.7   Hands-On Projects

## 10.7.1   World Wide Imports: Exchanging Data with Word and Excel

Access provides several methods for exchanging data with other applications. In this exercise, you practice using the OfficeLinks feature to publish a query and then create a link to an external Excel worksheet.

*Setup:* Ensure that Access is loaded. If you are launching Access and the startup dialog box appears, click the Cancel command button to remove the dialog box from the application window.

1. Open the database file named ACC1070.
2. Now select the query object that you want to publish:
   CLICK: *Queries* button in the Objects bar
   SELECT: 1071 qryCustomers
3. To launch the OfficeLinks feature:
   CHOOSE: Tools, Office Links, Publish It with MS Word
   Your screen should now appear similar to Figure 10.30. (*Note:* The Word document file is automatically saved as "1071 qryCustomers.rtf" to your personal storage location.)

**Figure 10.30**

Publishing a query to Microsoft Word

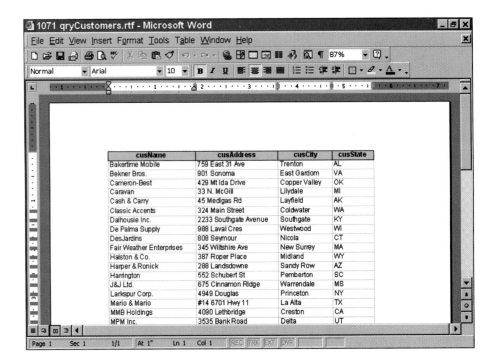

4. Close the Word application window by clicking its Close button ([x]).
5. Now let's create a dynamic link to an Excel worksheet:
   CLICK: *Tables* button in the Objects bar
   CHOOSE: File, Get External Data, Link Tables
   The Link dialog box appears.
6. Using the Places bar or the *Look in* drop-down list box, select your personal storage location. Then do the following:
   CLICK: down arrow attached to the *Files of type* drop-down list box
   SELECT: Microsoft Excel
   DOUBLE-CLICK: ACC1071 in the list area
7. To accept the default selection in the first step of the Link Spreadsheet Wizard dialog box:
   CLICK: Next >
8. In the second step:
   TYPE: `tblOrdersFromExcel`
   CLICK: Finish
9. CLICK: OK command button to proceed
10. On your own, open the tblOrdersFromExcel (◆✖) linked object in a datasheet window and peruse its contents. When ready to proceed, close the datasheet window.

## 10.7.2 CyberWeb: Creating and Executing a Macro from a Form

While working in form Design view, you create a macro using the Macro Builder. In this exercise, you place a command button on a form and then attach a macro that opens a report in Print Preview mode.

*Setup:* Ensure that the ACC1070 Database window is displayed.

1. To begin, let's open a form in Design view:
   CLICK: *Forms* button in the Objects bar
   SELECT: 1072 frmAccounts
   CLICK: Design button ([Design]) on the Database window toolbar
2. Ensure that the Toolbox window is displayed and then:
   CLICK: Control Wizards button ([▨]) so that it is not pressed in

3.  You now place a command button in the Form Header section. When clicked, this button will execute a macro that runs a customer listing report. Do the following:
    CLICK: Command Button button (⬚) in the Toolbox window
    CLICK: in the Form Header section at 3 inches on the horizontal ruler
    A command button should now appear in the section.
4.  To enter a name and caption for the button:
    RIGHT-CLICK: the command button control
    CHOOSE: Properties
    CLICK: *All* tab in the Properties window
    TYPE: **cmdRunMacro** in the *Name* property text box
    PRESS: [TAB]
    TYPE: **Preview Accounts** in the *Caption* property text box
    PRESS: [TAB] to apply the new caption
    Your screen should now appear similar to Figure 10.31.

**Figure 10.31**

Customizing a command button

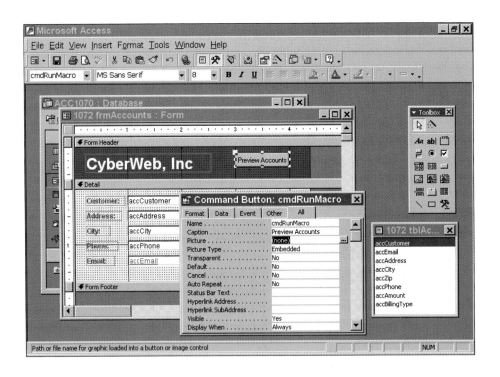

5.  To create a macro that executes when the button is clicked:
    CLICK: *Event* tab
    CLICK: in the *On Click* property text box
    CLICK: Build button (⬚) attached to the text box
6.  To launch the Macro Builder and define a macro:
    SELECT: Macro Builder
    CLICK: OK command button
    TYPE: **mcrRun1072**
    CLICK: OK command button

7. In the Macro window:
   CLICK: down arrow attached to the *Action* text box
   SELECT: OpenReport
8. In the *Action Arguments* area:
   CLICK: in the *Report Name* text box
   CLICK: down arrow attached to the text box
   SELECT: 1072 rptCusListing
   CLICK: in the *View* text box
   CLICK: down arrow attached to the text box
   SELECT: Print Preview
9. Save and then close the Macro window.
10. Close the Properties window. Save and close the form Design window.
11. On your own, open the 1072 frmAccounts form and then click the Preview Report command button. The 1072 rptCusListing report appears in a Print Preview window.
12. When ready to proceed, close the Print Preview window and then close the Form window.

## 10.7.3 Big Valley Mills: Creating a Switchboard Menu

Once you've finished creating the database objects for an application, consider creating a switchboard form to enable quick and easy access to its features. In this exercise, you create a switchboard form for opening a form object in the Big Valley Mills application.

*Setup:* Ensure that the ACC1070 Database window is displayed.

1. To begin, display the *Tables* list area in the Database window.
2. To create a new switchboard:
   CHOOSE: Tools, Database Utilities, Switchboard Manager
   CLICK: Yes command button to create a new switchboard
3. When the Switchboard Manager appears, click the Edit command button to begin editing the contents of the switchboard form.
4. Using the New command button, add two items to the switchboard. The first item, entitled "Open Products Form for Adding Records," should open the 1073 frmProducts form in Add mode. The second item, entitled "Open Products Form for Editing Records," should open the form in Edit mode. When ready to proceed, close the Switchboard Manager.
5. To test the switchboard form:
   CLICK: *Forms* button in the Objects bar
   DOUBLE-CLICK: Switchboard

ACCESS

6. One at a time, click the menu items and close the Form window that appears. Close the Main Switchboard form before proceeding.
7. Display the *Tables* list area and then open the Switchboard Items table in a datasheet window.
8. Close the datasheet window before proceeding.

## 10.7.4 Silverdale Festival: Analyzing a Table

The Table Analyzer Wizard helps you design an efficient database. In this exercise, you use the wizard to analyze a specific table in the database.

*Setup:* Ensure that the ACC1070 Database window is displayed.

1. Open the 1074 tblContacts table in a datasheet window and familiarize yourself with its fields and contents. When ready to proceed, close the datasheet window.
2. To launch the Table Analyzer Wizard:
   CHOOSE: Tools, Analyze, Table
3. To proceed to the meaty section of the wizard, click  twice and then select the 1074 tblContacts table for analysis. Then:
   CLICK: Next >
4. Let the wizard decide which fields go in which tables and then:
   CLICK: Next >
   Your screen should appear similar to Figure 10.32.

**Figure 10.32**

Normalizing a table object

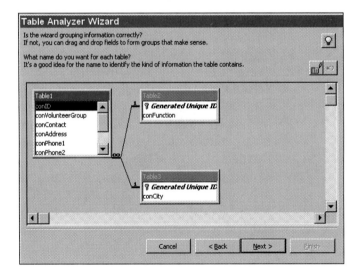

5. On your own, drag the conCity field from the Table3 object back into the primary table (Table1). Position the conCity field underneath conAddress in the Table1 object.
6. Rename the primary table (Table1) to "1074 newContacts" and

the Table2 object to "1074 newFunctions."

7. Proceed to the end of the wizard. In the last step of the dialog box, choose to create a query representing the original table. Then:
CLICK: Finish

8. Close the confirmation dialog box and then close the Query datasheet window.

9. On your own, open the 1074 newFunctions table object to review its contents. Close the datasheet window before proceeding.

# 10.7.5 On Your Own: Office Mart Inventory

The ability to exchange data between applications is one of the most powerful features of Office 2000. Because each application recognizes the other applications' file formats, you can use Access to copy and paste, import and export, and link to data in Word and Excel. In this exercise, you move an Access table object to an Excel worksheet. You also practice importing a text file, since most other applications can strip out their proprietary codes and save data as plain text.

To begin, ensure that the ACC1070 Database window is displayed and then perform the following:

- Launch Microsoft Excel and then tile the Excel and Access application windows side-by-side on the Windows desktop.
- In the Excel application window, ensure that a blank worksheet is displayed and that cell A1 is visible.
- In the Access application window, select the 1075 tblInventory table and then drag it into cell A1 of the Excel worksheet.
- Save the workbook as "1075 tblInventory" and then close Excel.
- Maximize the Access application window.
- Using the File, Get External Data command, import the text file named "ACC1075" into the database. The text file contains a header row and separates fields using a tab delimiter.
- Save the imported data into a table named "1075 txtSupplier."

When you are finished, open the 1075 Supplier table object and peruse its contents. Close the datasheet window before proceeding.

### 10.7.6 On Your Own: Sun Bird Resorts

Preparing a database for use in a multi-user environment can take many directions. One method is to use the Database Splitter to separate a database's table objects from its queries, forms, reports, macros, and modules. Once accomplished, you place the "data only" table on a secure network server and distribute the other database among the users. In this example, you use another approach called replication. This process lets you create and distribute copies of the database. Ensure that the ACC1070 Database window is displayed and then do the following:

- Using the Tools, Replication, Create Replica command, convert the ACC1070 Database into a Design master.
- Make sure that you back up the database before proceeding.
- Name the first new replica "1076 Replica1."
- From the Design Master, create a second replica named "1076 Replica2."

On your own, modify some data in the two replicas and then use the Synchronize Now command to update their contents. When finished, close the Database window and then exit Microsoft Access.

# 10.8 Case Problems: Price Laventhol Consulting, Inc.

Clive Mason, currently a senior manager in the Hospitality division of Price Laventhol Consulting, recently accepted a partnership appointment with the firm. Before leaving his division, Clive wants to complete a small database project in Microsoft Access 2000. Specifically, he wants to transfer the data stored in a billing worksheet into a fully automated database application. Having just finished a course in Access, Clive realizes that there are several tools available to help him get started.

In the following case problems, assume the role of Clive and perform the same steps that he identifies. You may want to re-read the chapter opening before proceeding.

1.  Now that his assistant has provided a worksheet copy of the past two years of billings, Clive can get started building his database. After launching Microsoft Access, Clive creates a new database file in his personal storage location named "ACC1080." He then uses the File, Get External Data command to import the Excel worksheet of the same name into a table called "tblBillings." Clive allows the wizard to add a primary key to the table, so he doesn't have to later.

    Using a similar process, Clive establishes a link to another worksheet file named "ACC1081." He names the new Excel linked table object "tblConsultants." He doesn't want to import this table, since the information is updated and maintained by another division in the company. With the two objects appearing in the *Tables* list area, Clive opens each table and familiarizes himself with their contents. Before proceeding, Clive closes the datasheet windows.

2.  Having imported and linked the necessary tables, Clive can now let Access analyze the design efficiency of the locally stored table object. He lets the Table Analyzer Wizard review the tblBillings table object. Impressed with the results, Clive renames the four tables as shown in Figure 10.33 and then proceeds through the wizard accepting the defaults. In the last step of the wizard, Clive chooses to create a query that represents the original table object. He then closes the query's datasheet window in order to return to the Database window. To check his work, Clive opens the Relationships window and reviews the relationship lines. Satisfied, he closes the window before proceeding.

**Figure 10.33**

Normalizing a table object

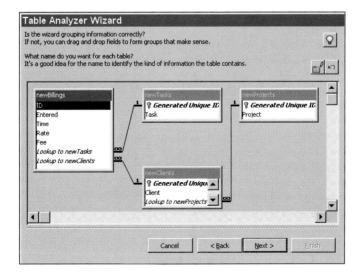

3. To prototype the database application, Clive decides to create a few form and report objects. Not wanting to spend too much time on this step, he uses the AutoForm and AutoReport wizards. First, Clive accesses the AutoForm: Columnar wizard to generate a form for the newBillings table. He saves the form as "frmNewBillings" and then closes the Form window. Next, Clive uses the AutoForm: Tabular wizard to generate a form for the tblConsultants linked table. He saves this form as "frmLnkConsultants." Clive then creates two tabular reports for these same table objects using the AutoReport wizard. He saves the reports as "rptNewBillings" and "rptLnkConsultants" and then returns to the Database window.

Using the Macro window, Clive combines four macros in a single macro object named "mcrFormReport." The first macro, EditBillings, opens the frmNewBillings form in Edit mode. The second macro, AddConsultants, opens the frmLnkConsultants form in Add mode. The third macro, PreviewBillings, opens the rptNewBillings report in Print Preview mode. And, lastly, the PrintConsultants macro prints the rptLnkConsultants report. When Clive finishes entering the last macro, he saves and then closes the Macro window (Figure 10.34).

**Figure 10.34**

Defining macros in a macro group

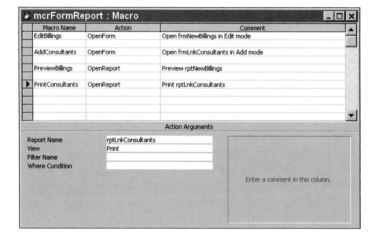

4. To test the macros created in the last step, Clive double-clicks the macro object in the list area to find that it only performs the first macro stored in the macro group. He closes the Form window before proceeding. In order to access the other macros in the group, Clive creates a switchboard form for the database. He attaches each macro in the mcrFormReport group to a separate item in the Main Switchboard. After testing the switchboard form, Clive sets the form to appear when the database is first opened.

Since the new database contains sensitive financial information, Clive decides to password-protect the database file. To do so, he closes and then re-opens the database in Exclusive mode, closing the Main Switchboard when it appears. He defines "ImAPartner" as the password and then closes the database file once again. Wishing to celebrate his new appointment, Clive decides it's time to exit Microsoft Access and call it a day.

ACCESS

# Answers to Self Check Questions

**1.1 Self Check**   How do you close a window that appears in the Access work area? Click on its Close button (⊠).

**1.2 Self Check**   Describe two methods to quickly move the cursor to the last record in a large datasheet. Here are three methods. First, you can use the cursor movement keys **CTRL**+**↓** or **CTRL**+**END** to move the cursor to the last record. Second, you can use the mouse to click the Last Record button (▶❙). And, third, you can scroll the window by dragging the vertical scroll box and then click in a field of the last record. (*Note:* You must click in the record's row in order to move the cursor. Otherwise, you simply scroll the window.)

**1.3 Self Check**   When does Access save the changes that you've made when editing a record? Editing changes to a record are saved permanently to disk when the cursor is moved to another record or when the user presses the **SHIFT**+**ENTER** combination.

**2.1 Self Check**   What two objects are most closely associated with the output of a database application? Query objects (the questions you ask of a database) and Report objects (the structured printed output from a database).

**2.2 Self Check**   How do you specify the name of a field when creating a table in Datasheet view? You double-click the column name in the field header area and then type the desired field name.

**2.3 Self Check**   What is an AutoNumber field? Why is it useful as a primary key? An AutoNumber field is a data type that automatically increments a numeric value each time a new record is added to a table. It is useful as a primary key since it already supplies a unique field value for identifying each record in a table.

**2.4 Self Check**   What happens to your table's data if you delete a field in table Design view? The table data that is stored in the field is removed along with the field definition in Design view.

**3.1 Self Check**   Name two reasons for changing the field column order in a datasheet. Some reasons for changing the field order include customizing a datasheet's appearance for printing, displaying fields side-by-side in a datasheet, and arranging columns for performing multiple-field sort operations.

**3.2 Self Check**   How do you perform a sort operation using more than one field column? You must first ensure that the columns are adjacent to one another. The leftmost column should contain the primary or first sort key. The next column(s) provides the secondary sort level(s). You must then select all of the columns involved in the sort operation and click the appropriate Sort button on the toolbar.

ACCESS

**3.3 Self Check**   In a personnel table, how would you display a subset of those employees working in the Accounting department? Using Filter For Input, you enter "Accounting" as the criterion. Using Filter By Selection, you select "Accounting" from the datasheet. Using Filter By Form, you select "Accounting" from the drop-down list attached to the department field. You then apply and remove the filter by clicking on the Apply/Remove Filter button ( ▽ ) on the toolbar.

**3.4 Self Check**   Name one way that a query's dynaset may differ from a table's datasheet. A query's dynaset may display results from two or more tables in the same Datasheet window.

**4.1 Self Check**   Name the layout options for designing a form using the Form Wizard. Columnar, Tabular, Datasheet, and Justified.

**4.2 Self Check**   What does the term "grouping data" refer to in a report? You can arrange data so that it appears combined into categories in a report. The categories are based on field values and appear sorted into ascending order, by default. Grouping data also enables you to prepare subtotal calculations.

**4.3 Self Check**   How could you use table and report objects to print diskette labels? You store the diskette names, titles, and other information in a table and then use a mailing labels report to print the information using the Avery 5296 diskette label.

**4.4 Self Check**   Name two operating system tools that you can use to back up a database. Windows Explorer and "My Computer."

**5.1 Self Check**   Describe the table relationship that might exist between Doctors and their patients. A single doctor has many patients. However, a patient typically sees only their family doctor. Therefore, a one-to-many table relationship exists. If a patient were to see many specialists, a many-to-many relationship can be argued.

**5.2 Self Check**   Which field property would you use to ensure that a field's contents always display in uppercase? The *Format* property allows you to specify that a text field display in uppercase. Specifically, you use the ">" token to force a field's contents to uppercase.

**5.3 Self Check**   Which field property would you use to ensure the proper entry of a Canadian postal code? The *Input Mask* property affects the entry of data. Specifically, you use the Input Mask Wizard to create a mask that accepts the alphanumeric sequence of the Canadian postal code.

**5.4 Self Check**   In describing the results of an HTML export, what is meant by static data? Exporting a database object in HTML format takes a snapshot of the database at a particular point in time. The HTML document content is not updated in real time. In other words, the content remains the same until the next export process.

**6.1 Self Check**    Provide a conditional statement that will limit the display of records to those company names starting with the letter "B." Like "B*."

**6.2 Self Check**    In query Design view, how do you add a new table to the Table pane? You click the Show Table button (⬚) in the toolbar and then select a table from the Tables tab in the dialog box. Click the Add command button to add the table and then click the Close command button.

**6.3 Self Check**    In an employee database, how would you sort a query by ascending "Department" and then, for each department grouping, by ascending "Surname"? In query Design view, ensure that the Department field appears to the left of the Surname field in the query Design grid. Then, for both field columns, select the Ascending option in the *Sort* row of the grid.

**6.4 Self Check**    How would you calculate the average invoice amount from a table that stored only the price and quantity of items sold? Create a calculated field that multiplied the price and quantity values and then select the "Avg" option from the *Total* drop-down list box for the calculated field.

**7.1 Self Check**    How do you move only the label portion of a compound control? Using the pointing hand mouse pointer, drag the move handle for the label control to the desired position on the form. The label and text box portions of the compound control remain attached.

**7.2 Self Check**    Which design guideline or principle does the AutoFormat command help you adhere to? Consistency. You use the AutoFormat command to apply consistent formatting across all of your forms. As most of the AutoFormat style options have been professionally designed, the AutoFormat command also helps you adhere to additional design guidelines, such as limiting the number of fonts and colors in a form.

**7.3 Self Check**    What is the primary difference between forms and reports? Forms are designed for interaction and to be viewed on-screen. Reports are designed to be printed or faxed.

**7.4 Self Check**    How can you incorporate multiple AutoFormat styles in the same report? Access allows you to select a different AutoFormat style for each section in a report. Especially for those reports using multiple group headers and footers, two or three AutoFormat styles can help make each section more easily identified.

**8.1 Self Check**    What is the difference between an inner join and an outer join? In an inner join, only those records that have matching key values are included in a query's dynaset. In an outer join, every record from one of the tables is included, regardless of whether there is a matching value in the other table.

**8.2 Self Check**    How do you display the Zoom window for entering long expressions? With the insertion point in the *Field* or *Criteria* row of the Design grid, press **SHIFT** + **F2** to open the Zoom window.

**8.3 Self Check**   How many calculations can you perform in the data area of a crosstab query? You can perform only one aggregate calculation.

**8.4 Self Check**   Explain how you might use three of the action queries discussed in this module in creating a routine to archive old records in a database. First, you need to create an archive table using a make-table query. Second, an append query is required to add records to the archive table at the end of each month, year, or other period of time. Lastly, a delete query is used after running a make-table or append query in order to remove all of the records copied from the source table to the archive table.

**9.1 Self Check**   How would you create a hyperlink on a form using a company's logo? Place an image control containing the company logo on the form. Then display the Properties window for the control and click the *Format* tab. Enter the desired URL or e-mail address into the *Hyperlink Address* property text box. If a bookmark exists for the hyperlink, enter the bookmark name into the *Hyperlink Subaddress* text box. To launch the Insert Hyperlink dialog box, click the Build button ( ▪ ) with the insertion point in either property text box.

**9.2 Self Check**   Name three methods discussed in this module for verifying that the correct data is entered in a form. The three methods include:
1.   Specifying acceptable values using a data validation rule.
2.   Displaying related information using an AutoLookup query.
3.   Using list box and combo box controls to pick data from a list.

**9.3 Self Check**   How would you change a report's sort order from ascending to descending order? Display the Sorting and Grouping window and then make the desired selection in the *Sort Order* column. If the report is based on a query, you can also adjust the sort order by modifying the underlying query.

**9.4 Self Check**   Name two methods for inserting an existing subreport into a main report. First, you can drag an existing report object from the Database window and then drop it into the report Design window. Second, you can ensure that the Control Wizards button ( ▨ ) is depressed and then click the Subform/Subreport button ( ▦ ) to launch the SubReport wizard.

**9.5 Self Check**   Name two reasons why you might choose to display field information using a bound HTML control instead of a text box control. First, a bound HTML control enables you to lock a field as read-only, so the user cannot edit its contents. Second, a bound HTML control displays information much faster than a text box control.

**10.1 Self Check**   What macro action is used to open a report in Print Preview mode? You select the OpenReport macro action and then set its View argument to Print Preview.

**10.2 Self Check**   Name the three OfficeLinks features mentioned in this module. The three OfficeLinks are (1) Merge It with MS Word ( ▨ ), (2) Publish It with MS Word ( ▨ ), and Analyze It with MS Excel ( ▨ ).

**10.3 Self Check**   Name two general methods for accessing external data from within Microsoft Access. How do they differ? The two methods for accessing external data are *importing* and *linking*. When you import data, you are copying the data into an Access table object. Any changes that you make to the data in the new table object are saved with the database. There is no longer a connection with the original data file. On the other hand, when you link to external data, you are establishing a connection to the file. Any changes that you make to the data are saved in the original and external data file.

**10.4 Self Check**   What is the purpose of the Database Splitter Wizard? The Database Splitter Wizard splits up a database into two separate database files—one for table objects and the other for queries, forms, reports, macros, and modules. The wizard then creates links to the "data only" database so that the remaining objects continue to work. The reasons for splitting a database are varied. Most commonly, you use the wizard to place the "data only" portion of a database on a shared network server so that multiple users may access the data.

# Glossary

**Access data project**  A special type of Access database file that enables you to work with data stored in a server-side database engine such as the Microsoft Data Engine (MSDE) or SQL Server. An Access project contains the front-end components (including forms, reports, macros, and modules) of a client/server database application.

**action query**  A type of query object that performs mass changes to the data it retrieves from one or more tables. There are four types of action queries: update, delete, make-table, and append.

**actions**  In defining a macro, the command activities that you perform such as opening and closing forms.

**ActiveX controls**  Reusable program components or objects that provide some functionality; for example, calendar applications, Internet connectivity, and interface elements.

**ActiveX Data Objects (ADO) models**  The newest data architecture; provides common objects for accessing data stored in a variety of database engines including JET and SQL Server.

**append query**  A type of query object that adds selected records from one table to another table in the same or a different database.

**application window**  In Windows, each running application appears in its own application window. These windows may be sized and moved anywhere on the Windows desktop.

**arguments**  In the Macro window, the properties or parameters that you enter to control how a macro action executes.

**AutoExec macro**  A special macro object that Access executes automatically when a database is first opened. To stop the AutoExec macro from running, hold down the (SHIFT) key as the database opens.

**AutoForm Wizard**  An Access wizard that creates a form automatically, using all of the fields from the selected table object in the Database window. There are three types of AutoForm Wizards: Columnar, Tabular, and Datasheet.

**AutoFormat**  A software feature that applies professionally designed formatting styles to your documents.

**AutoLookup query**  A type of query object that fetches data automatically from the "one" side of a table relationship for display with data from the "many" side.

**AutoNumber**  A field data type that provides a unique value for each record automatically. The three types of AutoNumber fields include sequential (incremented by 1), random, and replication. You cannot delete or modify the values generated for an AutoNumber field.

**AutoPage Wizard**  An Access wizard that creates a columnar data access page automatically based on the data stored in the selected table or query.

**AutoReport Wizard**  An Access wizard that creates a columnar or tabular report automatically, using all of the fields from the selected table or query object in the Database window. There are two types of AutoReport Wizards: Columnar and Tabular.

**bitmap**  Created by a painting program, a raster graphic file that is created and stored as a series of individual pixels or dots. Raster (bitmap) files are typically larger than vector (metafile) files. Some popular bitmap formats include BMP, GIF, JPG, PCX, and TIF.

**bound controls**  A control whose source of data is a field in a table or query. Bound controls are used to retrieve, store, edit, and display data.

**breakpoint**  In VBA code, a user-defined stopping point that interrupts a procedure's execution and displays the Visual Basic Editor.

**business rules** Guidelines for how data is used by people in the real world. Business rules include the constraints, restrictions, or limitations imposed on a table or field when working with and using data. In Access, these rules are specified and enforced using field properties.

**calculated controls** In a form or report, a control that evaluates an expression and displays a result.

**calculated field** In a query, a field that evaluates an expression and displays a result in a dynaset Datasheet window.

**cell** In a datasheet, the intersection of a column (field) and a row (record).

**child table** In a *one-to-many relationship*, the table containing foreign key values that match the values stored in the primary key field of the *parent table*.

**Code window** In the Visual Basic Editor, the window containing the procedure code; used for *coding* and *debugging* program statements.

**coding** Developing and writing code manually from scratch.

**collection** Object type that acts as a container for a set of similar objects.

**column chart** A chart that compares one data element with another data element and can show variations over a period of time.

**compound control** In a form or report, a bound text box control and its associated label control. These two controls are inserted and manipulated together as a single control.

**concatenate** In Access, joining together data from separate fields using the ampersand "&" operator; combining characters, usually in a calculated field, to form a new string.

**conditional formatting** The ability to format an object automatically based on whether an expression evaluates to true or false.

**conditional logic** The method by which criteria statements are joined and executed in a query statement.

**conditional statement** A query expression or statement that limits the number of records that display in a datasheet.

**constants** *Variables* that do not change; typically used to reference values in your code using English-language terms, such as TAXRATE.

**control structures** Group of program statements that allows you to make decisions and direct the flow of executed instructions; two common control structures are "branching" and "looping."

**controls** Objects or elements of a form or report. Access supplies three types of controls: *bound controls, unbound controls,* and *calculated controls.* Typical controls include labels, text boxes, and command buttons.

**crosstab query** An Access query object that summarizes a field's values and presents the results in a spreadsheet-like table display.

**Crosstab Query Wizard** In Access, a software feature that helps you create a crosstab query that summarizes numeric or currency values using aggregate functions.

**Data Access Object (DAO) model** The first and most established data architecture; provides specific objects for accessing data stored in the Microsoft Access JET database engine.

**data access page** A special type of Web page that is connected to a database and allows you to work with data through the Microsoft Internet Explorer Web browser.

**data source** In a *mail merge,* the variable data that is fed into a *main document* during the merge process.

**database** A collection of related data. In Access, a database includes a collection of objects—tables, queries, reports, forms, and other objects.

**database management system (DBMS)** A software tool that lets you create and maintain an information database.

ACCESS

**Database Splitter Wizard**   In Access, a software feature that separates a database file into two databases—one containing table objects and the other containing everything else. The "data only" database is typically placed on a shared network server. The "interface only" database resides locally and uses linked tables to access data stored on the network server.

**Database window**   The control center for an Access database. Using the *Objects bar,* categorizes and lists the objects stored in a database.

**Database Wizard**   In Access, a software feature for creating a complete database application based on professionally designed database templates.

**datasheet**   A window used for displaying multiple records from a table using an electronic spreadsheet layout of horizontal rows and vertical columns.

**Datasheet view**   The method or mode of displaying table data using a datasheet.

**debugging**   A programming term that means locating errors in your VBA code and correcting those errors.

**decrypting**   The process of deciphering and returning an encrypted database to its original form.

**delete query**   A type of query object that removes selected records from a table.

**delimiter**   A symbol or character, such as a tab or quotation mark, that is used to separate fields or columns of information in a text file.

**Design Master**   In *replication,* the master database file that you use to create new *replicas* and to modify the database objects for a *replica set.*

**Design view**   Each database object in Access may be opened in display mode or Design view mode. You use Design view to define table structures, construct queries, build forms, and design reports.

**Documenter**   In Access, a tool for documenting and printing the design characteristics of a database object.

**dynaset**   In Access, the result of a query. A dynaset is displayed as a table in Datasheet view of the records matching the query parameters.

**embedding**   A way of sharing data and exchanging information; refers to the process of inserting a source object into a destination container object, such as an Access form or report.

**encrypting**   The process of scrambling visually the contents of a database so that other software programs cannot view the data. The database is still accessible to Access, although usually at lesser speeds.

**entity integrity**   A general integrity rule for database design that requires primary key fields to contain unique values. Also, primary key values must not be empty, that is, contain null values or zero-length strings.

**event**   An action or reaction that occurs in Windows programming. You can code unique responses to events such as performing a macro or procedure whenever a button is clicked.

**event procedures**   The macro or procedure code that is executed when a particular *event* occurs.

**event-driven programming**   Coding a program to respond to events that may occur such as clicking a button; uses *objects, properties,* and *methods* to describe elements, attributes, and actions.

**expression**   A combination of field names, mathematical operators, comparison operators, logical operators, and constants that produce a calculated result.

**Expression Builder**   In Access, a software feature that helps you build expressions by providing pick lists of table and field names, operators, and constants.

**field**   A single item, or column, of information in a *record.*

**Field Grid pane**   In table Design view, the top portion of the window where you specify field names, data types, and descriptions.

**field header area**   In an Access Datasheet window, the top frame or border area that contains the field names as column headings.

**Field List window**   In form Design view and report Design view, a window that displays the field names from the underlying table or query. Use the Field List window to drag bound text box controls for placement in a Form or Report window.

**Field Properties pane**   In table Design view, the bottom portion of the window where you specify field properties and characteristics.

**field validation rule**   An expression that evaluates to "True" or "False" when the user inputs or modifies a field value and then attempts to leave the field. If the entry violates the rule (result is "False"), the user is returned to the field and forced to correct the entry or cancel the operation. See also *field validation rule* and *validation text.*

**filter**   The process or method of temporarily restricting the display of records in a table to those that match a particular search criterion or pattern.

**Filter By Form**   In Access, a command that returns a subset of records from a table matching a filter specification.

**Filter By Selection**   In Access, a command that returns a subset of records from a table matching the selected value in a datasheet.

**Filter Excluding Selection**   In Access, a command that returns a subset of records from a table not matching the selected value in a datasheet.

**Filter For Input**   In Access, a command that returns a subset of records from a table matching a filter specification that you enter in a right-click menu's text box.

**Find Duplicates Query Wizard**   In Access, a software feature that helps you create a select query to retrieve duplicate records or field values in a table.

**Find Unmatched Query Wizard**   In Access, a software feature that helps you create a select query to retrieve records that do not have child records in a related table.

**flat-file database**   A database system that is unable to meet the objectives of normalization and to successfully relate tables of records.

**focus**   The state of a control when it is selected. Focus refers to the active control on a form that will accept input or commands from the user.

**foreign-key**   A field that refers to the primary key field in another table.

**form**   A database object used for displaying table data one record at a time.

**Form Detail**   In a form, the section that contains the bound controls for displaying data from a table or query.

**Form Footer**   In a form, the section that contains the items you want to display at the bottom of each form.

**Form Header**   In a form, the section that contains the items you want to display at the top of each form.

**Form window**   In Access, a window that displays a form object.

**form wizards**   Access tools that simplify the process of creating a form.

**Function procedure**   In VBA, a procedure that typically performs a calculation and returns a value to the calling program.

**Group Footer**   In a report, the section that organizes a set of items for display and typically contains subtotals for printing after the group's Detail section.

**Group Header**   In a report, the section that organizes a set of items for display and typically contains column headings for printing before the group's Detail section.

**HTML**   An acronym for Hypertext Markup Language, which is the standardized markup language used in creating documents for display on the *World Wide Web.*

**hyperlink**   In terms of Internet technologies, a text string or graphic that when clicked takes you to another location, either within the same document or to a separate document stored on your computer, an intranet, or onto the Internet.

**Immediate window**   In the *Visual Basic Editor,* the window that you use to enter expressions for immediate calculation; you can also use the debug.print statement to send output from a procedure to the Immediate window.

**Import Spreadsheet Wizard**   A series of dialog boxes that lead you through importing and converting a spreadsheet file to an Access table object.

**Import Text Wizard**   A series of dialog boxes that lead you through importing and converting a text file to an Access table object.

**index**   A feature of a table object that allows you to presort a table based on key values. Indexes speed up searching, sorting, and other database operations. (*Note:* The *primary key* is indexed automatically.)

**inner join**   A type of join for a table relationship that results in a query's dynaset returning only those records with matching key values in both tables.

**input mask**   A combination of characters and symbols that are used to designate formatting placeholders for making data entry easier and less susceptible to error. Selecting or building an input mask is facilitated by the Input Mask Wizard.

**Internet**   A worldwide network of computer networks that are interconnected by standard telephone lines, fiber optics, and satellites.

**keywords**   Reserved words that hold special meaning for the VBA compiler and, therefore, cannot be used as a variable or constant name.

**Label Wizard**   An Access wizard that creates a mailing labels report based on the size, shape, and formatting of standard mailing labels.

**left outer join**   A type of join for a table relationship that results in a query's dynaset returning all of the records from a parent table (A), but only those records with matching key values in the child table (B).

**line chart**   A chart that plots trends or shows changes over a period of time.

**Link Spreadsheet Wizard**   A series of dialog boxes that lead you through defining and linking to an external spreadsheet file.

**Link Text Wizard**   A series of dialog boxes that lead you through defining and linking to an external text file.

**Linked Table Manager**   In Access, a software feature that enables you to verify and refresh the storage locations of linked tables in a database.

**linking**   A way of sharing data and exchanging information; refers to the process of establishing a dynamic link between a source object or database file that is stored on the disk and a destination container object such as an Access table, form, or report.

**linking table**   In a *many-to-many relationship,* the table that contains the primary keys from more than one primary table in order to establish a table relationship.

**lookup field**   A field that displays a drop-down list of acceptable values. A lookup field is populated by data stored in a list (Value List) or in a table (Lookup List). Use the Lookup Wizard to create a lookup field.

**macro**   A set of actions that you store in a database object to automate repetitive procedures.

**Macro Builder**   In Access, a software feature that enables you to define a macro from an object's event procedure property text box.

**macro group**   The combination of two or more macros stored in a single database object.

**mail merge**   In word processing software, the process of combining *main documents* with *data sources* to generate form letters, mailing labels, envelopes, and lists.

**Mail Merge Wizard**   A series of dialog boxes that provide helpful tips for setting up a *mail merge.*

**main document**   In a *mail merge,* the Word document that contains the static information that remains the same for all merged documents.

**main form**   A form that acts as a container for a *subform.* A main form typically displays a single record (the one side in a one-to-many relationship) in a columnar or justified form layout.

**main report**  A report that acts as a container for a *subreport*. A main report typically provides the report header, footer, and summary information, while the subreport provides the details.

**make-table query**  A type of query object that creates a new table structure and then populates the structure with selected records from an existing table.

**many-to-many relationship**  In relational database design, the table relationship that exists when one record in table A is related to multiple records in table B, and vice versa.

**margins**  Space between the edge of the paper and the top, bottom, left, and right edges of the printed document.

**metafile**  Created by a drawing program, a vector or object-oriented graphic file that can be stretched and resized without loss of quality. Some popular metafile formats, which store graphics as dimensions and formulas, include CGM (computer graphics metafile) and WMF (Windows metafile format).

**method**  The actions that can be performed on or by an object, such as activate, open, and close.

**Microsoft Data Engine (MSDE)**  A fully SQL Server-compatible database engine for desktop database applications. The MSDE is primarily used with *Access data projects* in creating small-scale client/server applications.

**Microsoft Office Web Components**  Component objects of executable program code that allow you to view and interact with Microsoft Office 2000 data using the Microsoft Internet Explorer Web browser software.

**naming convention**  The rules that are applied when assigning names to objects, fields, constants, and variables. By following a naming convention, the database is easier to understand for people unfamiliar with your work.

**normalization**  In relational database design, the process of organizing fields and tables to reduce the duplication of data.

**null value**  Represented by an empty field; a value that may exist but is currently unknown.

**object model**  A conceptual map for the hierarchical chain of objects that are exposed by an application.

**Objects bar**  The strip of icon buttons appearing in the Database window that allows you to display a particular category of database objects.

**Office Clipboard**  A program, in Office 2000, that allows you to copy and move information within or among Office 2000 applications. Unlike the Windows Clipboard, the Office Clipboard can store up to twelve items and then paste them all at once.

**OfficeLinks**  In Office 2000, automation tools that facilitate sharing data with other Office 2000 applications.

**one-to-many relationship**  In relational database design, the table relationship that exists when one record in table A is related to multiple records in table B, but one record in table B is related to only one record in table A.

**one-to-one relationship**  In relational database design, the table relationship that exists when one record in table A is related to one record in table B, and vice versa.

**orientation**  Describes how a page is printed. Letter-size paper with a portrait orientation measures 8.5 inches wide by 11 inches high, while a landscape orientation is rotated to measure 11 inches wide by 8.5 inches high.

**Page Footer**  In a form or report, the descriptive information (such as page number and date) that appears at the bottom of each printed page.

**Page Header**  In a form or report, the descriptive information (such as column headings and border lines) that appears at the top of each printed page.

**Page view**  The method or mode of displaying data using a data access page.

**Page Wizard**  An Access wizard that helps you create a data access page by selecting fields and then specifying grouping, sorting, and titling options.

ACCESS

**parameter query**   A type of query object that displays a dialog box and accepts input from a user prior to performing an operation. Parameter queries may be used to accept last-minute or run time criteria entries for retrieving data.

**parent table**   In a *one-to-many relationship*, the table containing the primary key field that is used to establish and control the table relationship.

**Partial Replica Wizard**   In Access, a software feature that you use to create a replica containing only a portion of the complete data set.

**password**   A series of characters that you can use as a lock and key to restrict access to a database file. The best passwords combine letters, numbers, and special symbols, which makes them difficult to guess.

**Performance Analyzer Wizard**   In Access, a software feature that you use to analyze and optimize the performance of database objects.

**pie chart**   A chart that shows the proportions of individual components compared to the whole.

**Places bar**   The strip of icon buttons appearing in the Open and Save As dialog boxes that allow you to display the most common areas for retrieving and storing files using a single mouse click.

**preview**   The act of displaying on-screen a document, worksheet, or report prior to sending it to the printer. An on-screen preview window displays a soft copy of a document while the printer prepares the hard copy.

**primary key**   A field whose values uniquely identify each record in a table. The primary key provides the default sort order for a table and is used to establish connections to and relationships with other tables.

**program statement**   A line of code combining objects, properties, methods, variables, constants, symbols, and/or other elements to perform a task.

**Project Explorer window**   In the *Visual Basic Editor,* the window that displays the open project files, including form, report, and independent modules.

**project file**   In the *Visual Basic Editor,* a project file is a container for storing and organizing related or associated module objects.

**Properties window**   In the *Visual Basic Editor,* the window that displays property settings for the selected object(s); you can change an object's properties at *design time* using this window.

**property**   A characteristic or attribute of an object such as its name or color.

**query**   A database object that you use to ask a question of your data. The results from a query are typically displayed using a *datasheet.*

**Query Design grid**   In query Design view, the bottom portion of the window where you specify the fields to display, enter criteria expressions, and specify sort orders.

**query-by-example (QBE)**   The process of querying a database in a visual mode by selecting field columns, choosing sort orders, and specifying record criteria.

**record**   An individual entry, or row, in a *table.* A record contains one or more *fields.*

**record selection area**   The row frame area located to the left of the first column in a *datasheet.* Used for selecting records.

**record validation rule**   An expression that evaluates to "True" or "False" when the user inputs or modifies field data and then attempts to leave the record. If an entry violates the rule (result is "False"), the user is returned to the record and forced to correct the entries or cancel the operation. See also *field validation rule* and *validation text.*

**referential integrity**   The rules that must be followed to preserve the validity of a table relationship. When enforced, these rules prevent you from entering a foreign key value until a primary key value already exists in the primary table. Furthermore, you may not delete or update a primary key value that has foreign key values in related tables.

**relational database(s)**   A database that is comprised of normalized tables linked via common fields.

**replica** In *replication,* a single copy of the *Design Master* database that can be used independently to add and modify data. A replica can be *synchronized* with other members in the *replica set.*

**replica set** In *replication,* a group of *replicas* that share and synchronize to the same *Design Master.*

**replication** The process of creating copies of a database for the purpose of working independently and to facilitate exchanging and synchronizing updates and database objects with other members in the *replica set.*

**Report Detail** In a report, the section that contains the bound controls for printing data from a table or query.

**Report Footer** In a report, the section that contains the items you want to display at the end of a report.

**Report Header** In a report, the section that contains the items you want to display at the beginning of a report.

**report snapshot** A Windows graphic metafile that stores an accurate representation, including fonts, graphics, and colors, of each page in a report. You do not need Access installed on your computer to view a report snapshot. Instead, you can use the free Microsoft Snapshot Viewer to open, view, and print snapshots.

**report wizards** Access tools that simplify the process of creating a report.

**report(s)** A database object used for viewing, compiling, summarizing, and printing information.

**right outer join** A type of join for a table relationship that results in a query's dynaset returning all of the records from the child table (B), but only those records with matching key values in the parent table (A).

**run time** During execution; when a program or other database object is run.

**scope** The level of visibility in which a procedure or variable operates. A variable's scope or visibility may be at the procedure level (private), module level, or macro level (public).

**select query** A type of query object that lets you ask questions of your database, retrieve data from multiple tables, sort the data, and display the results in a datasheet.

**Simple Query Wizard** In Access, a software feature that simplifies the process of creating a query.

**sort key** The field or column used to sort the contents of a datasheet.

**SQL** Abbreviation for Structured Query Language. A standardized database query language that is popular in client/server database applications. Using SQL, you typically enter language statements instead of making selections from a visual *query-by-example (QBE)* interface.

**Sub procedure** In VBA, the default procedure type that is used to perform a series of instructions and to effect change on its environment.

**subdatasheet** An extension of a datasheet that provides a picture-in-picture display of related or hierarchical data.

**subform** A form that is embedded in a *main form.* A subform typically displays records that are related to the active record in a main form in a tabular or datasheet layout.

**subreport** A report that is embedded in a *main report.* A subreport provides the detail section for a comprehensive report that typically includes report headers, report footers, and other sections.

**switchboard form** A form that acts as a main menu for a database application. A switchboard form displays command buttons that help users navigate among objects, procedures, forms, and reports.

**Switchboard Manager** In Access, a software feature for managing the creation and customization of a *switchboard form.*

**synchronize** In *replication,* the process of exchanging and updating the contents of objects between two members in the *replica set.*

**syntax** In VBA code, the rules that each program statement must follow in order to execute properly.

ACCESS

**tab order**   The order in which text boxes and other bound controls are accessed when the user presses `TAB`. Pressing `SHIFT` + `TAB` reverses the tab order.

**table**   A database object used to collect and store data relating to a particular subject or topic.

**Table Analyzer Wizard**   In Access, a software feature that you use to analyze and normalize table objects in a database.

**Table pane**   In query Design view, the top portion of the window where you display the table objects and field lists that are used in the query.

**Table Wizard**   In Access, a software feature that simplifies the process of creating a table.

**Toolbox window**   In Design view, the window containing controls, such as labels, text boxes, and command buttons, that you can select for use in forms and reports.

**typeface**   The shape and appearance of characters. There are two categories of typefaces: serif and sans serif. Serif type (for example, Times Roman) is more decorative and, some say, easier to read than sans serif type (for example, Arial).

**unbound controls**   A control that doesn't have a source of data. Includes label controls and decorative graphic objects used to enhance a form or report.

**Undo command**   A command that makes it possible to reverse the last command or action performed.

**update query**   A type of query object that performs mass updates to the field values of selected records in a table.

**user defined functions**   In VBA, a function procedure that you code to perform a calculation and return a result.

**validation text**   When a validation rule is violated, the text that displays in the warning dialog box. See also *field validation rule* and *validation text*.

**variable**   A temporary value or storage location in memory for data that can be adjusted and modified.

**variant**   The default data type in VBA that allows you to store any kind of data.

**Visual Basic Editor**   A special utility program for creating, editing, and managing VBA macros and procedures. See *Visual Basic for Applications (VBA)*.

**watermark**   Text or a graphic that appears faded in the background of a form or report.

**wildcard characters**   Special symbols that are used to represent other alphanumeric characters in search, filter, and query operations. You can use the question mark (?) to represent any single character and the asterisk (*) to represent any group of characters.

**Windows Clipboard**   A program, in Windows, that allows you to copy and move information within an application or among applications. The Windows Clipboard temporarily stores the information in memory before you paste the data in a new location.

**World Wide Web**   A visual interface to the Internet based on hyperlinks. Using Web browser software, you click on hyperlinks to navigate resources on the Internet.

**XY chart**   A chart that shows how one or more data elements are related to another data element. Also called scatter plot diagrams.

**zero-length string**   Represented by "" stored in a field; a value that is known not to exist.

# Appendix: Microsoft Windows Quick Reference

## Using the Mouse and Keyboard

Microsoft Windows provides a graphical environment for working in your application, such as Microsoft Word, Excel, Access, or Power-Point. As you work with Windows applications, you will find that there are often three different ways to perform the same command. The most common methods for performing commands include:

- Menu          Choose a command from the Menu bar or from a right-click menu.
- Mouse         Position the mouse pointer over a toolbar button and then click once.
- Keyboard      Press a keyboard shortcut (usually $\boxed{\text{CTRL}}$ + *letter*).

Although you may use a Windows application with only a keyboard, much of a program's basic design relies on using a mouse. Regardless of whether your mouse has two or three buttons, you will use the left or primary mouse button for selecting screen objects and menu commands and the right or secondary mouse button for displaying right-click menus.

The most common mouse actions include:

- Point         Slide the mouse on your desk to position the tip of the mouse pointer over the desired object on the screen.
- Click         Press down and release the left mouse button quickly. Clicking is used to select a screen object, activate a toolbar command, and choose menu commands.
- Right-Click   Press down and release the right mouse button. Right-clicking the mouse pointer on a screen object displays a context-sensitive menu.
- Double-Click  Press down and release the mouse button twice in rapid succession. Double-clicking is used to select screen objects or to activate an embedded object for editing.
- Drag          Press down and hold the mouse button as you move the mouse pointer across the screen. When the mouse pointer reaches the desired location, release the mouse button. Dragging is used to select a group of screen objects and to copy or move data.

You may notice that the mouse pointer changes shape as you move it over different parts of the screen. Each mouse pointer shape has its own purpose and may provide you with important information. There are four primary mouse shapes that appear in Windows applications:

| | | |
|---|---|---|
| ↖ | arrow | Used to choose menu commands and click toolbars buttons. |
| ⧗ | hourglass | Informs you that the application is occupied and requests that you wait. |
| I | I-beam | Used to set the position of the insertion point and to modify and edit text. |
| 🖑 | hand | Used to select hyperlinks in the Windows-based Help systems, in Microsoft Office documents, and on the Web. |

Aside from being the primary input device for entering information, the keyboard offers shortcut methods for performing some common commands and procedures.

## Starting Windows

Because Windows is an operating system, it is loaded into the computer's memory when you first turn on the computer. To start Windows, you must do the following:

1. Turn on the power switches to the computer and monitor. After a few seconds, the Windows desktop will appear. (*Note*: If you are attached to a network, a dialog box may appear asking you to enter your User name and Password. Enter this information now or ask your instructor for further instructions.)

2. A Welcome dialog box may appear providing information about the operating system's major features. If the Welcome dialog box appears on your screen:
   CLICK: Close button (☒) in the top right-hand corner of the Welcome window

3. If additional windows appear open on your desktop:
   CLICK: Close button (☒) in the top right-hand corner of each window

# Parts of a Dialog Box

A dialog box is a common mechanism in Windows applications for collecting information before processing a command. In a dialog box, you indicate the options you want to use and then click the OK button when you're finished. Dialog boxes are also used to display messages or to ask for the confirmation of commands. The following shows an example of the Print dialog box, which is similar across Windows applications.

Print dialog box

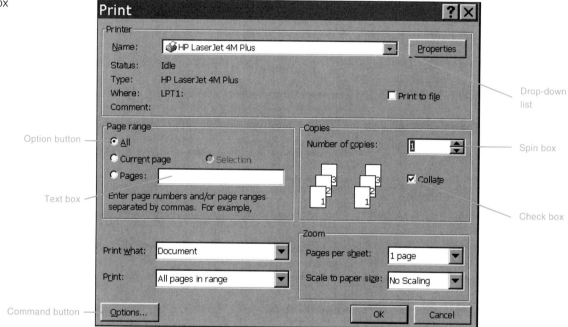

A dialog box uses several types of controls or components for collecting information. We describe the most common components in the following table.

Dialog box components

| Name | Example | Action |
| --- | --- | --- |
| Check box | ☑ Always ☐ Never | Click an option to turn it on or off. The option is turned on when an "✔" appears in the box. |
| Command button | OK / Cancel | Click a command button to execute an action. Click OK to accept your selections or click Cancel to exit the dialog box. |

*Continued*

| Name | Example | Action |
|------|---------|--------|
| Drop-Down list box | Screen Saver / None | Make a choice from the list that appears when you click the down arrow next to the box; only the selected choice is visible. |
| List box | Wallpaper / [None] / Arcade / Argyle | Make a choice from the scrollable list; several choices, if not all, are always visible. |
| Option button | Display: ⊙ Tile ○ Center | Select an option from a group of related options. |
| Slide box | Desktop area / Less — More / 640 by 480 pixels | Drag the slider bar to make a selection, like using a radio's volume control. |
| Spin box | Wait: 6 minutes | Click the up and down arrows to the right of the box until the number you want appears. |
| Tab | Contents Index Find | Click a named tab at the top of the window to access other pages of options in the dialog box. |
| Text box | File name: untitled | Click inside the text box and then type the desired information. |

Most dialog boxes provide a question mark icon ([?]) near the right side of the Title bar. If you have a question about an item in the dialog box, click the question mark and then click the item to display a pop-up help window. To remove the help window, click on it once.

# Getting Help

Windows applications, such as Microsoft Office 2000 applications, provide a comprehensive library of online documentation. This section describes these help features and how to find more detailed information.

# Obtaining Context-Sensitive Help

In Windows applications, you can often retrieve context-sensitive help for menu options, toolbar buttons, and dialog box items. *Context-sensitive help* refers to a program's ability to present helpful information reflecting your current position in the program. The help information is presented concisely in a small pop-up window that you can remove with the click of the mouse. This type of help lets you access information quickly and then continue working without interruption. The following table describes some methods for accessing context-sensitive help while working in Windows applications.

Displaying context-sensitive
Help information

| To display... | Do this... |
| --- | --- |
| A description of a dialog box item | Click the question mark button (⬚) in a dialog box's Title bar and then click an item in the dialog box. Alternatively, you can often right-click a dialog box item and then choose the What's This? command from the shortcut menu. |
| A description of a menu command | Choose the Help, What's This? command from the menu and then choose a command using the question mark mouse pointer. Rather than executing the command, a helpful description of the command appears in a pop-up window. |
| A description of a toolbar button | Point to a toolbar button to display a pop-up label called a ToolTip. |

# Getting Help in Office 2000

## Getting Help from the Office Assistant

In Office 2000 applications, the Office Assistant is your personal computer guru and is available by default when your application is first installed. When you need to perform a task that you're unsure of, simply click the Assistant character and then type a phrase such as "How do I obtain help" in the Assistant balloon. The Assistant analyzes your request and provides a resource list of suggested topics, as shown to the right. Simply click a topic to obtain additional information.

The Assistant also watches your keystrokes and mouse clicks as you work and offers suggestions and shortcuts to make you more productive and efficient. If you find the Office Assistant to be distracting, you can turn it off by choosing "Hide the Office Assistant" from the Help menu. To redisplay it, simply choose "Microsoft *Application* Help" or "Show the Office Assistant" from the Help menu.

## Getting Help from the Help Window

You may prefer to obtain a complete topical listing of your application's Help system. To do this, you must first disable the Office Assistant by clicking the Options button in the Assistant balloon, clearing the *Use the Office Assistant* check box, and then pressing (ENTER). Once the Office Assistant is disabled, simply choose "Microsoft *Application* Help" from the Help menu to display the Help window. If the *Contents*, *Answer Wizard*, and *Index* tabs don't appear, click Show (⏹) in the window's toolbar.

The Help window, shown below, provides three different tools, each on its own tab, to help you find the information you need quickly and easily. You can read the Help information you find onscreen or print it out for later reference by clicking the Print button (🖨) in the window's toolbar. To close the Help window, click its Close button (✖).

Example Help window

The *Contents* tab is currently selected. Use this tab to display the Table of Contents for the entire Help system.

The *Answer Wizard* tab enables you to obtain help information by typing in questions.

The *Index* tab enables you to display topics by selecting keywords or typing in words and phrases.

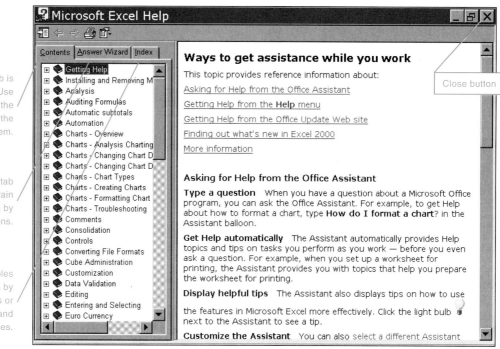

# Getting Help from the Office Update Web Site

Microsoft's Office Update Web site provides additional technical support and product enhancements. You can access this site from any Office application by choosing "Office on the Web" from the Help menu.

# Index

ACCESS

ACCESS

ACCESS

**Microsoft Access 2000**
**Total Objectives: 48**

| Coding Number | Activity | Performance based? | Advantage Lesson |
|---|---|---|---|
| **AC2000.1** | **Planning and designing databases** | | |
| AC2000.1.1 | Determine appropriate data inputs for your database | No | 2.1.2 |
| AC2000.1.2 | Determine appropriate data outputs for your database | No | 2.1.2 |
| AC2000.1.3 | Create table structure | **Yes** | 2.2-3 |
| AC2000.1.4 | Establish table relationships | **Yes** | 5.1/5.1.1 |
| **AC2000.2** | **Working with Access** | | |
| AC2000.2.1 | Use the Office Assistant | No | Appendix |
| AC2000.2.2 | Select an object using the Objects Bar | **Yes** | 1.1.4 |
| AC2000.2.3 | Print database objects (tables, forms, reports, queries) | **Yes** | 1.2.3/throughout |
| AC2000.2.4 | Navigate through records in a table, query, or form | **Yes** | 1.2.1/throughout |
| AC2000.2.5 | Create a database (using a Wizard or in Design View) | **Yes** | 2.1.1/2.1.3 |
| **AC2000.3** | **Building and modifying tables** | | |
| AC2000.3.1 | Create tables by using the Table Wizard | **Yes** | 2.2.1 |
| AC2000.3.2 | Set primary keys | **Yes** | 2.3.2 |
| AC2000.3.3 | Modify field properties | No | 5.2.1 |
| AC2000.3.4 | Use multiple data types | **Yes** | 2.3.1 |
| AC2000.3.5 | Modify tables using Design View | **Yes** | 2.3.1/2.4.1-2 |
| AC2000.3.6 | Use the Lookup Wizard | No | 5.3.4/5.3.5 |
| AC2000.3.7 | Use the input mask wizard | No | 5.3.3 |
| **AC2000.4** | **Building and modifying forms** | | |
| AC2000.4.1 | Create a form with the Form Wizard | **Yes** | 4.1.1-2 |
| AC2000.4.2 | Use the Control Toolbox to add controls | **Yes** | 7.1.3 |
| AC2000.4.3 | Modify format properties (font, style, size, color, caption, etc.) of controls | **Yes** | 7.1.2/7.2.3 |
| AC2000.4.4 | Use form sections (headers, footers, detail) | **Yes** | 7.1.1/7.1-7.2 |
| AC2000.4.5 | Use a Calculated Control on a form | **Yes** | 7.1.4 |
| **AC2000.5** | **Viewing and organizing information** | | |
| AC2000.5.1 | Use the Office Clipboard | No | 5.4.3 |
| AC2000.5.2 | Switch between object Views | **Yes** | 2.4.1-2/throughout |
| AC2000.5.3 | Enter records using a datasheet | No | 1.3.3 |
| AC2000.5.4 | Enter records using a form | **Yes** | 4.1.4 |
| AC2000.5.5 | Delete records from a table | **Yes** | 1.3.4 |
| AC2000.5.6 | Find a record | **Yes** | 3.2.2-4 |
| AC2000.5.7 | Sort records | **Yes** | 3.2.1 |
| AC2000.5.8 | Apply and remove filters (filter by form and filter by selection) | **Yes** | 3.3 |
| AC2000.5.9 | Specify criteria in a query | **Yes** | 6.1.3/6.2.3/6.3.3-4 |
| AC2000.5.10 | Display related records in a subdatasheet | No | 1.2.1 |
| AC2000.5.11 | Create a calculated field | **Yes** | 6.4 |
| AC2000.5.12 | Create and modify a multi-table select query | **Yes** | 6.2 |
| **AC2000.6** | **Defining relationships** | | |
| AC2000.6.1 | Establish relationships | **Yes** | 5.1.1 |
| AC2000.6.2 | Enforce referential integrity | **Yes** | 5.1.2 |

| Standardized Coding Number | Activity | Performance based? | Advantage Lesson |
|---|---|---|---|
| **AC2000.7** | **Producing reports** | | |
| AC2000.7.1 | Create a report with the Report Wizard | Yes | 4.2.1-2/4.3 |
| AC2000.7.2 | Preview and print a report | Yes | 4.2.3 |
| AC2000.7.3 | Move and resize a control | No | 7.3.2 |
| AC2000.7.4 | Modify format properties (font, style, font size, color, capation, etc.) | Yes | 7.4.1 |
| AC2000.7.5 | Use the Control Toolbox to add controls | Yes | 7.3 |
| AC2000.7.6 | Use report sections (headers, footers, detail) | Yes | 7.3-7.4 |
| AC2000.7.7 | Use a Calculated Control in a report | Yes | 7.3.3/7.4.3 |
| **AC2000.8** | **Integrating with other applications** | | |
| AC2000.8.1 | Import data to a new table | Yes | 5.4.1 |
| AC2000.8.2 | Save a table, query, form as a Web page | No | 4.2.4/5.4.2 |
| AC2000.8.3 | Add Hyperlinks | No | 5.2.3 |
| **AC2000.9** | **Using Access Tools** | | |
| AC2000.9.1 | Print Database Relationships | Yes | 5.1.3 |
| AC2000.9.2 | Backup and Restore a database | No | 4.4.1-2 |
| AC2000.9.3 | Compact and Repair a database | No | 4.4.2 |

**Microsoft Access 2000 Expert**
**Total Objectives: 44**

| Coding Number | Activity | Performance based? | Advantage Lesson |
|---|---|---|---|
| **AC2000E.1** | **Building and modifying tables** | | |
| AC2000E.1.1 | Set validation text | Yes | 9.2.1 |
| AC2000E.1.2 | Define data validation criteria | Yes | 9.2.1 |
| AC2000E.1.3 | Modify an input mask | No | 5.3.3 |
| AC2000E.1.4 | Create and modify Lookup Fields | Yes | 5.3.4/5.3.5 |
| AC2000E.1.5 | Optimize data type usage (double, long, int, byte, etc.) | No | 5.2.1 |
| **AC2000E.2** | **Building and modifying forms** | | |
| AC2000E.2.1 | Create a form in Design View | Yes | 7.1/7.2/9.1/9.2 |
| AC2000E.2.2 | Insert a graphic on a form | No | 9.1.1/9.1.2 |
| AC2000E.2.3 | Modify control properties | Yes | 7.1.2/7.2.3/9.1.4 |
| AC2000E.2.4 | Customize form sections (headers, footers, detail) | Yes | 7.1.1/7.2.2/9.1.5 |
| AC2000E.2.5 | Modify form properties | No | 9.1.5 |
| AC2000E.2.6 | Use the Subform Control and synchronize forms | Yes | 7.1.5/9.2.4 |
| AC2000E.2.7 | Create a Switchboard | Yes | 10.1.4 |
| **AC2000E.3** | **Refining queries** | | |
| AC2000E.3.1 | Apply filters (filter by form and filter by selection) in a query's recordset | Yes | 6.3.2 |
| AC2000E.3.2 | Create a totals query | Yes | 6.4.3 |
| AC2000E.3.3 | Create a parameter query | Yes | 8.3.4 |
| AC2000E.3.4 | Specify criteria in multiple fields (AND vs. OR) | Yes | 6.3.3/6.3.4 |
| AC2000E.3.5 | Modify query properties (field formats, caption, input masks, etc.) | Yes | 8.2.1/8.2.5 |
| AC2000E.3.6 | Create an action query (update, delete, insert) | Yes | 8.4 |
| AC2000E.3.7 | Optimize queries using indexes | No | 2.3.3/8.1.1 |
| AC2000E.3.8 | Specify join properties for relationships | Yes | 5.1/8.1.2 |
| **AC2000E.4** | **Producing reports** | | |
| AC2000E.4.1 | Insert a graphic on a report | No | 9.3.3/9.3.4 |
| AC2000E.4.2 | Modify report properties | Yes | 9.3.6 |
| AC2000E.4.3 | Create and modify a report in Design View | Yes | 7.3/9.3/9.4 |
| AC2000E.4.4 | Modify control properties | Yes | 7.3.2/9.3.5 |
| AC2000E.4.5 | Set section properties | No | 9.3.6 |
| AC2000E.4.6 | Use the Subreport Control and synchronize reports | Yes | 9.4.3 |
| **AC2000E.5** | **Defining relationships** | | |
| AC2000E.5.1 | Establish one-to-one relationships | Yes | 5.1.1/8.1.1 |
| AC2000E.5.2 | Establish many-to-many relationships | Yes | 5.1.1/8.1.1 |
| AC2000E.5.3 | Set Cascade Update and Cascade Delete options | No | 5.1.2 |
| **AC2000E.6** | **Utilizing web capabilities** | | |
| AC2000E.6.1 | Create hyperlinks | Yes | 5.2.3/9.1.3 |
| AC2000E.6.2 | Use the group and sort features of data access pages | Yes | 9.5.2-4 |
| AC2000E.6.3 | Create a data access page | Yes | 9.5 |

ACCESS

| Coding Number | Activity | Performance based? | Advantage Lesson |
|---|---|---|---|
| **AC2000E.7** | **Using Access tools** | | |
| AC2000E.7.1 | Set and modify a database password | **Yes** | 10.4.6 |
| AC2000E.7.2 | Set startup options | **Yes** | 10.1.6 |
| AC2000E.7.3 | Use Add-ins (Database Splitter, Analyzer, Link Table Manager) | **Yes** | 2.4.3/10.3.3/10.4 |
| AC2000E.7.4 | Encrypt and Decrypt a database | No | 10.4.6 |
| AC2000E.7.5 | Use simple replication (copy for a mobile user) | No | 10.4.3-4 |
| AC2000E.7.6 | Run macros using controls | No | 10.1.1-3/10.1.5 |
| AC2000E.7.7 | Create a macro using the Macro Builder | **Yes** | 10.1.1-3 |
| AC2000E.7.8 | Convert database to a previous version | No | 10.3.5 |
| **AC2000E.8** | **Data Integration (New Skill Set)** | | |
| AC2000E.8.1 | Export database records to Excel | **Yes** | 10.2.3-4 |
| AC2000E.8.2 | Drag and drop tables and queries to Excel | **Yes** | 10.2.4 |
| AC2000E.8.3 | Present information as a chart (MS Graph) | **Yes** | 9.4.2 |
| AC2000E.8.4 | Link to existing data | No | 10.3.1-4 |